Fundamentals of Logistics Management

THE IRWIN/McGRAW-HILL SERIES IN MARKETING

Alreck & Settle
THE SURVEY RESEARCH HAND-BOOK, 2/E

Anderson, Hair & Bush
PROFESSIONAL SALES MANAGEMENT, 2/E

Arens
CONTEMPORARY ADVERTISING, 6/E

Bearden, Ingram & LaForge
MARKETING: PRINCIPLES & PERSPECTIVES, 2/E

Bearden, Ingram & LaForge
MARKETING INTERACTIVE, 1/E

Belch & Belch
INTRODUCTION TO ADVERTISING AND PROMOTION: AN INTEGRATED MARKETING COMMUNICA-TIONS APPROACH, 4/E

Bernhardt & Kinnear
CASES IN MARKETING MANAGEMENT, 7/E

Berkowitz, Kerin, Hartley & Rudelius
MARKETING, 5/e

Bowersox & Closs
LOGISTICAL MANAGEMENT, 1/E

Bowersox & Cooper
STRATEGIC MARKETING CHANNEL MANAGEMENT, 1/E

Boyd, Walker & Larreche
MARKETING MANAGEMENT: A STRATEGIC APPROACH WITH A GLOBAL ORIENTATION, 3/E

Cateora
INTERNATIONAL MARKETING, 9/E

Churchill, Ford & Walker
SALES FORCE MANAGEMENT, 5/E

Churchill & Peter
MARKETING, 2/E

Cole & Mishler
CONSUMER AND BUSINESS CREDIT MANAGEMENT, 11/E

Cravens
STRATEGIC MARKETING, 5/E

Cravens, Lamb & Crittenden
STRATEGIC MARKETING MANAGEMENT CASES, 5/E

Crawford
NEW PRODUCTS MANAGEMENT, 5/E

Dillon, Madden & Firtle
ESSENTIALS OF MARKETING RESEARCH, 2/E

Dillon, Madden & Firtle
MARKETING RESEARCH IN A MARKETING ENVIRONMENT, 4/E

Dobler, Burt, & Lee
PURCHASING AND MATERIALS MANAGEMENT: TEXT AND CASES, 6/E

Douglas & Craig
GLOBAL MARKETING STRATEGY, 1/E

Etzel, Walker & Stanton
MARKETING, 11/E

Faria, Nulsen & Roussos
COMPETE, 4/E

Futrell
ABC'S OF RELATIONSHIP SELLING, 5/E

Futrell
FUNDAMENTALS OF SELLING, 5/E

Gretz, Drozdeck & Weisenhutter
PROFESSIONAL SELLING: A CONSULTATIVE APPROACH, 1/E

Guiltinan & Paul
CASES IN MARKETING MANAGEMENT, 1/E

Guiltinan, Paul & Madden
MARKETING MANAGEMENT STRATEGIES AND PROGRAMS, 6/E

Hasty & Reardon
RETAIL MANAGEMENT, 1/E

Hawkins, Best & Coney
CONSUMER BEHAVIOR, 7/E

Hayes, Jenster & Aaby
BUSINESS TO BUSINESS MARKETING, 1/E

Johansson
GLOBAL MARKETING, 1/E

Johnson, Kurtz & Scheuing
SALES MANAGEMENT: CONCEPTS, PRACTICES & CASES, 2/E

Kinnear & Taylor
MARKETING RESEARCH: AN APPLIED APPROACH, 5/E

Lambert & Stock
STRATEGIC LOGISTICS MANAGEMENT, 3/E

Lambert, Stock, & Ellram
FUNDAMENTALS OF LOGISTICS MANAGEMENT, 1/E

Lehmann & Winer
ANALYSIS FOR MARKETING PLANNING, 4/E

Lehmann & Winer
PRODUCT MANAGEMENT, 2/E

Levy & Weitz
RETAILING MANAGEMENT, 3/E

Levy & Weitz
ESSENTIALS OF RETAILING, 1/E

Loudon & Della Bitta
CONSUMER BEHAVIOR: CONCEPTS & APPLICATIONS, 4/E

Lovelock & Weinberg
MARKETING CHALLENGES: CASES AND EXERCISES, 3/E

Mason, Mayer & Ezell
RETAILING, 5/E

Mason & Perreault
THE MARKETING GAME!

McDonald
MODERN DIRECT MARKETING, 1/E

Meloan & Graham
INTERNATIONAL AND GLOBAL MARKETING CONCEPTS AND CASES, 2/E

Monroe
PRICING, 2/E

Moore & Pessemier
PRODUCT PLANNING AND MANAGEMENT: DESIGNING AND DELIVERING VALUE, 1/E

Oliver
SATISFACTION: A BEHAVIORAL PERSPECTIVE ON THE CONSUMER, 1/E

Patton
SALES FORCE: A SALES MANAGEMENT SIMULATION GAME, 1/E

Pelton, Strutton & Lumpkin
MARKETING CHANNELS: A RE-LATIONSHIP MANAGEMENT APPROACH, 1/E

Perreault & McCarthy
BASIC MARKETING: A GLOBAL MANAGERIAL APPROACH, 12/E

Perreault & McCarthy
ESSENTIALS OF MARKETING: A GLOBAL MANAGERIAL APPROACH, 7/E

Peter & Donnelly
A PREFACE TO MARKETING MANAGEMENT, 7/E

Peter & Donnelly
MARKETING MANAGEMENT: KNOWLEDGE AND SKILLS, 5/E

Peter & Olson
CONSUMER BEHAVIOR AND MARKETING STRATEGY, 4/E

Peter & Olson
UNDERSTANDING CONSUMER BEHAVIOR, 1/E

Quelch
CASES IN PRODUCT MANAGEMENT, 1/E

Quelch, Dolan & Kosnik
MARKETING MANAGEMENT: TEXT & CASES, 1/E

Quelch & Farris
CASES IN ADVERTISING AND PROMOTION MANAGEMENT, 4/E

Quelch, Kashani & Vandermerwe
EUROPEAN CASES IN MARKET-ING MANAGEMENT, 1/E

Rangan
BUSINESS MARKETING STRATEGY: CASES, CONCEPTS & APPLICATIONS, 1/E

Rangan, Shapiro & Moriarty
BUSINESS MARKETING STRATEGY: CONCEPTS & APPLICATIONS, 1/E

Rossiter & Percy
ADVERTISING AND PROMO-TION MANAGEMENT, 2/E

Stanton, Spiro, & Buskirk
MANAGEMENT OF A SALES FORCE, 10/E

Sudman & Blair
MARKETING RESEARCH: A PROBLEM-SOLVING APPROACH, 1/E

Thompson & Stappenbeck
THE MARKETING STRATEGY GAME, 1/E

Ulrich & Eppinger
PRODUCT DESIGN AND DEVELOPMENT, 1/E

Walker, Boyd & Larreche
MARKETING STRATEGY: PLANNING AND IMPLEMEN-TATION, 2/E

Weitz, Castleberry & Tanner
SELLING: BUILDING PARTNERSHIPS, 3/E

Zeithaml & Bitner
SERVICES MARKETING, 1/E

Fundamentals of Logistics Management

Douglas M. Lambert
The Ohio State University

James R. Stock
University of South Florida

Lisa M. Ellram
Arizona State University

Boston   Burr Ridge, IL   Dubuque, IA   Madison, WI   New York   San Francisco   St. Louis
Bangkok   Bogotá   Caracas   Lisbon   London   Madrid   Mexico City   Milan   New Delhi   Seoul

McGraw-Hill Higher Education

*A Division of The **McGraw-Hill** Companies*

FUNDAMENTALS OF LOGISTICS MANAGEMENT

This book is printed on acid-free paper.

DOMESTIC 5 6 7 8 9 0 DOC/DOC 0 9 8 7 6 5 4 3 2

INTERNATIONAL 4 5 6 7 8 9 0 DOC/DOC 0 9 8 7 6 5 4 3 2 1

ISBN 0-256-14117-7

Vice president and Editorial director: *Michael W. Junior*
Publisher: *Gary Burke*
Executive editor: *Stephen M. Patterson*
Editorial coordinator: *Andrea L. Hlavacek-Rhoads*
Senior marketing manager: *Colleen J. Suljic*
Senior project manager: *Gladys True*
Production supervisor: *Michael R. McCormick*
Compositor: *Shepherd Incorporated*
Typeface: *10/12 Times Roman*
Printer: *R.R. Donnelley & Sons Company*

Library of Congress Cataloging-in-Publication Data

Lambert, Douglas M.
    Fundamentals of logistics management/Douglas M. Lambert, James R. Stock, Lisa M. Ellram.
    p.   cm.
    ISBN 0-256-14117-7
    Includes index.
    1. Business logistics—Management. I. Stock, James R. II. Ellram, Lisa M. III. Title.
HD38.5.L36   1998
658.5—dc21   97-42279

INTERNATIONAL EDITION ISBN 0-07-115752-2

http://www.mhhe.com

To my parents, John and Mary Lambert, who have always been a source of love and encouragement as well as examples of dignity and grace.

—Doug Lambert

To my parents, William and Frances Stock, whose love and support have always been a source of inspiration and encouragement.

—Jim Stock

To my friend, Boodie, who has been a consistent source of inspiration, encouragement, and support, for maintaining a balanced life.

—Lisa Ellram

About the Authors

Douglas M. Lambert is the Raymond E. Mason Professor of Transportation and Logistics and Director of The Global Supply Chain Forum at the Fisher College of Business, The Ohio State University. Prior to joining Ohio State he was The Prime F. Osborn III Eminent Scholar Chair in Transportation, Professor of Marketing and Logistics, and Director of The International Center for Competitive Excellence at the College of Business Administration, University of North Florida. From 1983 to 1985 he was PepsiCo Professor of Marketing at Michigan State University. Dr. Lambert has served as a faculty member for over 400 executive development programs in North and South America, Europe, Asia, Australia, and New Zealand. He is the author of *The Development of an Inventory Costing Methodology, The Distribution Channels Decision, The Product Abandonment Decision,* and co-author of *Management in Marketing Channels, Strategic Logistics Management,* and *Supply Chain Directions for a New North America.* His publications include more than 100 articles and conference proceedings. In 1986 Dr. Lambert received the Council of Logistics Management's Distinguished Service Award, "the highest honor that can be bestowed on an individual for achievement in the physical distribution/logistics industry," for his contributions to logistics management. He holds an honors B.A. and M.B.A. from the University of Western Ontario and a Ph.D. from The Ohio State University. Dr. Lambert is co-editor of *The International Journal of Logistics Management.*

    James R. Stock is Professor of Marketing and Logistics at the College of Business Administration, University of South Florida. Dr. Stock held previous faculty appointments at Michigan State University, the University of Oklahoma, and the University of Notre Dame. From 1986 to 1988 he held the position of Distinguished Visiting Professor of Logistics Management, School of Systems and Logistics, at the Air Force Institute of Technology, Wright-Patterson Air Force Base. Dr. Stock is the author or co-author of over 90 publications including books, monographs, articles, and proceedings papers. He is author of *Reverse Logistics;* co-author of *Distribution Consultants: A Managerial Guide to Their Identification, Selection, and Use;* and co-author of *Strategic Logistics*

Management. He currently serves as editor of the *International Journal of Physical Distribution and Logistics Management.* He received the Armitage Medal (1988) from the Society of Logistics Engineers in recognition of his scholarly contributions to the discipline of logistics. Dr. Stock holds B.S. and M.B.A. degrees from the University of Miami (Florida) and a Ph.D. from The Ohio State University.

Lisa M. Ellram is Associate Professor of Supply Chain Management at Arizona State University. She has lectured in North America, Asia, Europe, and Australia. Her current research interests include total cost of ownership, international and domestic supply chain management, buyer-seller relationships, and purchasing strategy. Dr. Ellram has published over 50 articles and monographs that have appeared in a wide variety of logistics, purchasing, accounting, and marketing journals. She is co-author of *Purchasing for Bottom Line Impact.* Dr. Ellram received her B.S.B. and M.B.A. from the University of Minnesota, and her Ph.D. from The Ohio State University. She is a Certified Purchasing Manager, Certified Public Accountant, and Certified Management Accountant.

Preface

Logistics has moved to center stage as a result of trading agreements such as MERCO-SUR, NAFTA, and Europe 1992, a continued explosion of computer and information technology, the further development of global markets resulting in a larger number of companies with operations worldwide, and a corporate emphasis on quality and customer satisfaction.

The first edition of *Fundamentals of Logistics Management* reflects these and the many other developments that have made logistics critical for corporate success. *Fundamentals of Logistics Management* takes a marketing orientation and views the subject from a customer satisfaction perspective. While emphasizing the marketing aspects of logistics, it integrates all of the functional areas of the business as well as incorporating logistics into corporate strategy.

Logistics is big business. Its consumption of land, labor, capital, and information—coupled with its impact on the world's standard of living—is enormous. Curiously, it has only been within the past 35 years that the business community has taken a real interest in logistics. However, during that period logistics has increased in importance from a function that was perceived as barely necessary to (1) an activity where significant cost savings could be generated; (2) an activity that had enormous potential to impact customer satisfaction and hence increase sales; and (3) a marketing weapon that could be effectively utilized to gain a sustainable competitive advantage. The importance of logistics is being recognized all over the world.

Fundamentals of Logistics Management approaches the topic from a managerial perspective. Each chapter introduces basic logistics concepts in a format that is useful for management decision making. Of course, the basics—terms, concepts, and principles—are covered, but they are examined in light of how they interrelate and interface with other functions for the firm. In each chapter we have included examples of corporate applications of these concepts to illustrate how logistics activities can be managed to properly implement the marketing concept. Each chapter contains examples of how logistics is being implemented globally, how technology is being used to improve logistics efficiency and effectiveness, and how businesses are creatively solving logistics problems.

This book includes a good balance of theory and practical application. All the traditional logistics functions such as customer service, transportation, warehousing, and inventory management, have been included. However, there are several important topics that are approached in a different way than in most texts. For example, the financial control of logistics is discussed in a separate chapter, as well as being interwoven throughout all chapters. We have purposely taken this approach because of the impact of logistics on the firm's profitability. Because logistics ultimately affects marketing's ability to generate and satisfy demand—and thus create customer satisfaction—the customer service activity is emphasized early in the book. Customer service can be considered the output of the logistics function. For this reason, customer service provides a focal point for the entire book and customer service implications are considered in each of the 15 chapters.

A number of important topics not covered in many other logistics text are covered in this book: order processing and management information systems, materials flow, financial control of logistics performance, logistics organizations, global logistics, decision support systems, channels of distribution, and the strategic logistics plan. Other topics covered include partnerships, green marketing, computer technology, globalization of markets, warehouse location, strategic planning, and customer service. Given the importance of globalization, the global issues are not only included in a separate chapter but are incorporated in every chapter of the book. Our goal in covering these topics in addition to the traditional activities is to provide readers with a grasp of the total picture of the logistics process.

We have Suggested Readings at the end of each chapter and margin notes are used throughout the text. Terms included in the Subject Index are bolded in the text so that they can be located more easily. We believe that this book is readable for both the instructor and student. Our aim has been to present instructors and students with the best textbook of this type on the market. We believe we have succeeded.

The pragmatic, applied nature of the book and its managerial orientation make it a useful reference book for present and future logistics professionals. The end-of-the-chapter questions, problems, and cases are structured to challenge readers' managerial skills. They are integrative in nature and examine issues that are important to today's logistics executive.

Douglas M. Lambert
James R. Stock
Lisa M. Ellram

Acknowledgments

Throughout the development of this text, a number of persons from the business and academic sectors provided invaluable input. Many of our academic colleagues were very helpful in suggesting changes and providing input to the text.

Special thanks must go to colleagues at The Ohio State University including Dean Joseph A. Aluto of the Fisher College of Business, and Professor Robert E. Burnkrant, Chairman, Department of Marketing, for providing a supportive and collegial environment. The support of Dean Robert L. Anderson and Professor William B. Locander, Chairman, Department of Marketing, at the University of South Florida are acknowledged and warmly appreciated. The assistance of Steve Patterson, Andrea Hlavacek-Rhoads, and Gladys True at Irwin/McGraw-Hill is very much appreciated, as is the support of photo researcher, Michael J. Hruby and permissions researcher, Tom Mellers.

We are grateful to the following persons and companies for providing us with exhibits, case material, and other assistance: William C. Copacino, Andersen Consulting; Professor Martin G. Christopher, Cranfield School of Management, U.K.; Gary Ridenhower, 3M Company; Donald R. Heide, Target Stores; and Randall Carter, Rohm and Haas Company. Our students at The Ohio State University, University of South Florida, and Arizona State University, and former students at Michigan State University, Air Force Institute of Technology, University of North Florida, and University of Oklahoma, as well as the thousands of business executives with whom we have interacted on executive development programs, have had a strong influence on the contents of this book.

Without the support of our families, the task of writing a text would be impossible. The first author wishes to thank his parents, John and Mary Lambert, who have always been a source of love and encouragement. Their many positive influences have contributed significantly to whatever success he has enjoyed thus far in life. It is to them that he dedicates this book. His wife, Lynne, was a steadfast source of love and friendship. She also provided assistance with preparation of the manuscript and encouragement to get the job done.

The second author wishes to thank his parents, William and Frances Stock, who have been a constant source of inspiration and encouragement over the years. They instilled in him the notion that of the two ways to accomplish a task—the easy way and the right way—it is always best to do it right the first time. Appreciation is also given to Herbert and Bettye Townsend, the parents of his wife, Katheryn, who during their lives, provided testimonies of hard work and a concern for others. Their continual support will be sorely missed, but their daughter will carry on their proud tradition. Katheryn has been a constant companion, providing love and encouragement, as well as moral support and manuscript assistance. Special thanks go to his daughter, Elizabeth, and his son, Matthew, for giving up so many hours of time with their father so that he could write.

The third author would like to thank her life-long friend, Boodie, who has been a consistent source of inspiration, encouragement, and support, for maintaining a balanced life. She would also like to thank her parents, Ergav and Aime Ellram, for the many sacrifices they made on her behalf, and for their love. She would also like to give special thanks to her sister, Ruth Lubansky, who has always been there for her, through good times and bad times.

To all those persons who provided assistance and to the publishers and authors who graciously granted permission to use their material, we are indeed grateful. Of course, responsibility for any errors or omissions rests with the authors.

D.M.L.
J.R.S.
L.M.E.

Contents

6   Managing Materials Flow   181

7   Transportation   215

13   Methods to Control Logistics Performance   467

14   Supply Chain Management   503

The Role of Logistics in the Economy and Organization

Chapter Objectives

- To identify how logistics affects the economy and the profitability of corporations.
- To briefly explore how logistics has developed over time.
- To understand how logistics contributes to value creation.
- To understand the concept of the systems approach as it relates to logistics and marketing, the total cost concept, and profitability.

Introduction

Logistics Has Many Implications for Consumers

Logistics is a broad, far-reaching function which has a major impact on a society's standard of living. In a modern society, we have come to expect excellent logistics services, and tend to notice logistics only when there is a problem. To understand some of the implications to consumers of logistics activity, consider:

- The difficulty in shopping for food, clothing, and other items if logistical systems do not conveniently bring all of those items together in one place, such as a single store or a shopping mall.
- The challenge in locating the proper size or style of an item if logistical systems do not provide for a wide mix of products, colors, sizes, and styles through the assortment process. This was a continual problem in the former Soviet Union.
- The frustration of going to a store to purchase an advertised item, only to find out the store's shipment is late in arriving.

These are only a few of the issues often taken for granted which illustrate how logistics touches many facets of our daily lives. Because of the magnitude of the impact of logistics on society and individuals, a macro approach is taken in this initial chapter.

This chapter focuses on how logistics has developed over time, explains the systems approach as it applies to logistics, explores the role of logistics in the economy and the firm, and examines the key interfaces of logistics with other marketing activities. This chapter also shows the relationship between the systems concept and the total cost of ownership perspective. The discussion closes with a summary of key trends and current issues in logistics management.

Definition of Logistics Management

Because logistics is the topic of this textbook, it is important to establish the meaning of the term. Logistics has been called by many names, including the following:

- Business logistics
- Channel management
- Distribution
- Industrial logistics
- Logistical management
- Materials management
- Physical distribution
- Quick-response systems
- Supply chain management
- Supply management

What these terms have in common is that they deal with the management of the flow of goods or materials from point of origin to point of consumption, and in some cases

The logistics of supplying products to highly populated cities such as Hong Kong is difficult and complex. Highly efficient and effective logistics systems provide consumers with goods and services that improve their standard of living.

even to the point of disposal. The Council of Logistics Management (CLM), one of the leading professional organizations for logistics personnel, uses the term *logistics management* to describe:

Logistics Management Defined

the process of planning, implementing and controlling the efficient, effective flow and storage of goods, services, and related information from point of origin to point of consumption for the purpose of conforming to customer requirements.[1]

Throughout this text, the CLM definition is used. This definition includes the flow of materials and services in both the manufacturing and service sectors. The service sector includes entities such as the government, hospitals, banks, retailers and wholesalers.[2] In addition, the ultimate disposal, recycling, and reuse of the products need to be considered because logistics is becoming increasingly responsible for issues such as removing packaging materials once a product is delivered and removing old equipment.

Logistics Is Relevant to All Types of Organizations

Logistics is not confined to manufacturing operations alone. It is relevant to all enterprises, including government, institutions such as hospitals and schools, and service orga-

---

[1]Definition provided in, *What's It All About?* (Oak Brook, IL: Council of Logistics Management, 1993).

[2]Peter A. Smith et al., *Logistics in Service Industries* (Oak Brook, IL: Council of Logistics Management, 1991), p. xvii.

Moving materials and personnel to space stations orbiting the Earth can be a daunting task. Overcoming the enormous distances challenges the logistics capabilities of NASA, but offers significant opportunities for furthering future space exploration.

nizations such as retailers, banks, and financial service organizations. Examples from these sectors will be used throughout the book to illustrate the relevance of logistics principles to a variety of operations.

Some of the many activities encompassed under the logistics umbrella are given in Figure 1–1, which illustrates that logistics is dependent upon natural, human, financial, and information resources for inputs. Suppliers provide raw materials which logistics manages in the form of raw materials, in-process inventory, and finished goods. Management actions provide the framework for logistics activities through the process of planning, implementation, and control. The outputs of the logistics system are competitive advantage, time and place utility, efficient movement to the customer, and providing a logistics service mix such that logistics becomes a proprietary asset of the organization. These outputs are made possible by the effective and efficient performance of the logistics activities shown at the bottom of Figure 1–1. Each of these activities will be explained in varying depth in this chapter and throughout the book.

FIGURE 1–1

Components of logistics management

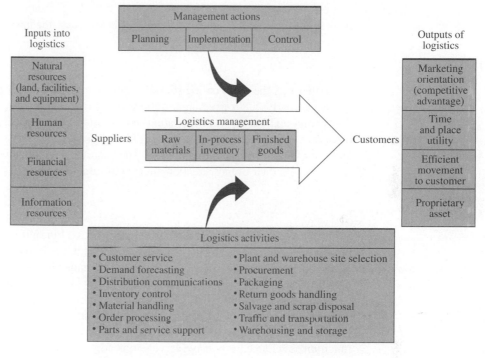

Development of Logistics

Logistics activity is literally thousands of years old, dating back to the earliest forms of organized trade. As an area of study however, it first began to gain attention in the early 1900s in the distribution of farm products,[3] as a way to support the organization's business strategy,[4] and as a way of providing time and place utility.[5]

Military Logistics

Following the clear importance of the contribution of logistics toward the Allied victory in World War II, logistics began to receive increased recognition and emphasis. Just as in the Persian Gulf War in 1990–1991, the ability to efficiently and effectively distribute and store supplies and personnel were key factors in the success of the U.S. Armed Forces.[6]

[3]John F. Crowell, *Report of the Industrial Commission on the Distribution of Farm Products,* vol. 6 (Washington, DC: U.S. Government Printing Office, 1901).

[4]Arch W. Shaw, *An Approach to Business Problems* (Cambridge: Harvard University Press, 1916).

[5]L. D. H. Weld, *The Marketing of Farm Products* (New York: Macmillan, 1916).

[6]William G. Pagonis, *Moving Mountains: Lessons in Leadership and Logistics from the Gulf War* (Boston: Harvard Business School Press, 1992).

The first dedicated logistics texts began to appear in the early 1960s,[7] which also is the time that Peter Drucker, a noted business expert, author, and consultant, stated that logistics was one of the last real frontiers of opportunity for organizations wishing to improve their corporate efficiency.[8] These factors combined to increase the interest in logistics.

Deregulation

Shippers Have More Options

To further fuel the focus on logistics, deregulation of the transportation industry in the late 1970s and early 1980s gave organizations many more options and increased the competition within and between transportation modes. As a result, carriers became more creative, flexible, customer-oriented, and competitive in order to succeed. Shippers are now faced with many more transportation options. They can focus on negotiation of rates, terms, and services, with their overall attention directed toward getting the best transportation buy.

Competitive Pressures

Global Logistics

With rising interest rates and increasing energy costs during the 1970s, logistics received more attention as a major cost driver. In addition, logistics costs became a more critical issue for many organizations because of the globalization of industry. This has affected logistics in two primary ways.

First, the growth of world class competitors from other nations has caused organizations to look for new ways to differentiate their organizations and product offerings. Logistics is a logical place to look because domestic organizations should be able to provide much more reliable, responsive service to nearby markets than overseas competitors.

Second, as organizations increasingly buy and sell offshore, the supply chain between the organization and those it does business with becomes longer, more costly, and more complex. Excellent logistics management is needed to fully leverage global opportunities.

Cost Control

Another factor strongly contributing to the increased emphasis and importance of logistics is a continued and growing emphasis on cost control. A survey of chief executive officers of Fortune 500 manufacturing firms and Fortune 500 service firms indicated that they believed that the most important way to improve company profitability was through cost cutting and cost control.[9] Thus, despite all the talk and emphasis on other issues, such as quality and customer service which CEOs rated as second and third in importance, cost cutting is still seen as the most important factor.

Information Technology

At about this same time, information technology really began to explode. This gave organizations the ability to better monitor transaction intensive activities such as the ordering, movement, and storage of goods and materials. Combined with the availability of comput-

---

[7]See, for example, Edward W. Smykay, Donald J. Bowersox, and Frank H. Mossman, *Physical Distribution Management* (New York: Macmillan, 1961).

[8]Peter F. Drucker, "The Economy's Dark Continent," *Fortune* (Apr. 1962), pp. 103, 265–70.

[9]"CEO's Still Don't Walk the Talk," *Fortune* (Apr. 18, 1994), pp. 14–15.

erized quantitative models, this information increased the ability to manage flows and to optimize inventory levels and movements. Systems such as materials requirements planning (MRP, MRP II), distribution resource planning (DRP, DRP II), and just-in-time (JIT) allow organizations to link many materials management activities, from order processing to inventory management, ordering from the supplier, forecasting and production scheduling.

Other factors contributing to the growing interest in logistics include advances in information systems technology, an increased emphasis on customer service, growing recognition of the systems approach and total cost concept, the profit leverage from logistics, and the realization that logistics can be used as a strategic weapon in competing in the marketplace. These, and other factors, will be discussed throughout this book.

Channel Power

Shifting of Channel Power from Manufacturers to Retailers

The shifting of channel power from manufacturers to retailers, wholesalers, and distributors has also had a profound impact on logistics. When competition rises in major consumer goods industries, there is a shakeout of many suppliers and manufacturers, so that a few leading competitors remain. Those remaining are intensely competitive and offer very high-quality products. In many cases, the consumer sees all of the leading brands as substitutes for each other. Lower brand-name loyalty decreases a manufacturer's power. This increases the retailer's power because sales are determined by what is in stock, not by what particular brands are offered.

Profit Leverage

The profit leverage effect of logistics illustrates that $1.00 saved in logistics costs has a much greater impact on the organization's profitability than a $1.00 increase in sales. In most organizations, sales revenue increases are more difficult to achieve than logistics cost reductions. This is particularly true in mature markets, where price cuts are often met by the competition, and revenue in the whole industry thus declines. The impact of the profit leverage effect is illustrated in Table 1–1.

There are many costs associated with a sale, such as the cost of goods sold and logistics-related costs. Thus, a $1.00 increase in sales does not result in a $1.00 increase in profit. If, for example, an organization's net profit margin (sales revenue less costs) is 2 percent, the firm only receives a before tax profit of $0.02, from each sales dollar. Yet, any dollar saved in logistics does not require sales or other costs to generate the savings. Therefore, a dollar saved in logistics costs is a dollar increase in profit! As a result, logistics cost savings have much more leverage, dollar for dollar, than an increase in sales. Thus, the term, the "profit leverage effect of logistics," is relevant.

The Profit Impact of Logistics Cost Savings

Systems Approach/Integration

The systems approach is a critical concept in logistics. Logistics is, in itself, a system; it is a network of related activities with the purpose of managing the orderly flow of material and personnel within the logistics channel. This is illustrated in Figure 1–2. It shows a

TABLE 1–1   Profit Leverage Provided by Logistics Cost Reduction

If Net Profit on the Sales Dollar is 2.0 Percent, Then. . .

A Saving of	Is Equivalent to a Sales Increase of
$ 0.02	$ 1.00
2.00	100.00
200.00	10,000.00
2,000.00	100,000.00
20,000.00	1,000,000.00

Source: Bernard J. LaLonde, John R. Grabner, and James F. Robeson, "Integrated Distribution Systems: A Management Perspective," *International Journal of Physical Distribution Management,* October 1970, p. 46.

FIGURE 1–2

Distribution channel: Logistics manages to flow through the channel

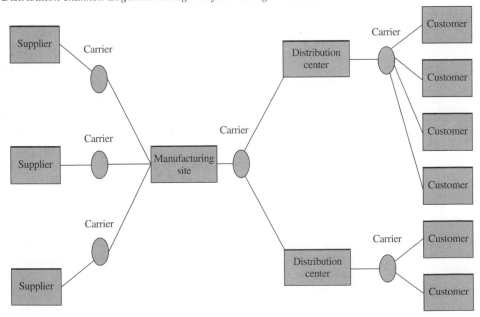

While the flow is primarily left to right, logistics is also responsible for returns, or movements from right to left, hence the term *reverse logistics* has developed.

Global

Hewlett-Packard's Systems Approach to Inventory Management

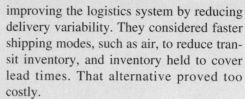

Hewlett-Packard (HP) is a leading global supplier of computer printers, particularly the ink-jet and laser-jet variety. It has over $3 billion invested in inventory worldwide. HP has a division located in Vancouver, Washington, which manufactures and distributes the DeskJet Plus printer worldwide. It has three distribution centers, one each in North America, Europe, and Asia.

HP faced a situation where high inventories of printers, approximately seven weeks' worth, were required to meet their 98 percent service goal in Europe. High inventories were required in part because each country has unique power cord and transformer requirements, and needs the proper language manual. Initially, the "differentiation" of the printers to meet the needs of the local market was done at the Vancouver facility. HP apparently faced the prospect of high inventory costs or reduced customer service levels, neither of which was an acceptable option.

The management at the Vancouver site considered many options for reducing inventory while maintaining customer service. They first worked on improving the logistics system by reducing delivery variability. They considered faster shipping modes, such as air, to reduce transit inventory, and inventory held to cover lead times. That alternative proved too costly.

However, by looking at the entire system as a whole, HP was able to develop a better solution. It could delay the differentiation of printer power sources and manuals until firm orders were received. This allowed HP to reduce inventory to five weeks while maintaining 98 percent service levels. This saved over $30 million annually. In addition, transportation dropped by several million dollars because generic printers can be shipped in larger volumes than printers specific to a particular country. Because HP viewed the system as a whole and understood the interactions, they were able to develop this innovative logistical solution.

Source: Adapted from Tom Davis, "Effective Supply Chain Management," *Sloan Management Review*, 34, no. 4 (Summer 1993), pp. 35–46; and Corey Billington, "Strategic Supply Chain Management," *OR/MIS Today* 21, no. 2 (Mar.–Apr. 1994), pp. 20–27.

simplified example of the network of relationships that logistics has to manage in a channel of distribution.

The Systems Approach Defined

The systems approach is a simplistic yet powerful paradigm for understanding interrelationships. The **systems approach** simply states that all functions or activities need to be understood in terms of how they affect, and are affected by, other elements and activities with which they interact. The idea is that if one looks at actions in isolation, he or she will not understand the big picture or how such actions affect, or are affected by, other activities. In essence, the sum, or outcome of a series of activities, is greater than its individual parts.[10]

[10]For a more thorough discussion of the systems approach, see C. W. Churchman, *The Systems Approach and Its Enemies* (New York: Basic Books, 1979); R. L. Ackoff, "Science in the Systems Age: Beyond IE, OR and MS," *Operations Research* 21, no. 3 (1973), pp. 661–71; Heiner Müller Merback, "A System of Systems Approaches," *Interfaces* 24, no. 4 (July–Aug. 1994), pp. 16–25; and Peter Senge, *The Fifth Discipline* (New York: Doubleday/Currency, 1990).

While it might be desirable to have high inventory levels in order to improve customer order fulfillment, high inventory levels increase storage costs as well as the risk of obsolescence. Those unfavorable factors must be "traded off" with the favorable aspects of a decision before arriving at a decision on inventory levels. Without considering the impact of decisions on the larger system, such as the firm or the distribution channel, suboptimization often occurs. That means while the individual activities in that system appear to be operating well, the net result on the total system is relatively poor performance.

Systems Must Be Viewed as a Whole

To understand the opportunities for improvement, and the implication of those opportunities, the system must be viewed as a whole.

Without understanding the channelwide implications of logistics decisions to improve service levels, excess inventory will begin to build up at the links along the supply chain. This excess inventory will tend to increase costs throughout the channel, but it serves as a buffer to protect against the uncertainty of how other channel members will behave. Thus, the system as a whole is less efficient than it could otherwise be. To get around that issue, organizations like Hewlett-Packard's DeskJet Division have taken a systems approach to managing channel inventories.

The systems approach is at the core of the next several topics discussed. The systems approach is key to understanding the role of logistics in the economy, its role in the organization, including its interface with marketing, the total cost concept, and logistics strategy.

The Role of Logistics in the Economy

Logistics Is an Important Component of GDP

Logistics plays a key role in the economy in two significant ways. First, logistics is one of the major expenditures for businesses, thereby affecting and being affected by other economic activities. In the United States, for example, logistics contributed approximately 10.5 percent of GDP in 1996. U.S. industry spent approximately $451 billion on transportation of freight and about $311 billion on warehousing, storage, and carrying inventory. These and other logistics expenses added up to about $797 billion.[11]

In 1980, logistics expenditures accounted for around 17.2 percent of GDP. If logistics expenditures were still that high by 1996, an additional $510 billion would have been spent on logistics costs in the United States. This would translate into higher prices for consumers, lower profits for businesses, or both. The result could be a lower overall standard of living and/or a smaller tax base. Thus, by improving the efficiency of logistics operations, logistics makes an important contribution to the economy as a whole.

Second, logistics supports the movement and flow of many economic transactions; it is an important activity in facilitating the sale of virtually all goods and services. To understand this role from a systems perspective, consider that if goods do not arrive on time, customers cannot buy them. If goods do not arrive in the proper place, or in the proper condition, no sale can be made. Thus, all economic activity throughout the supply chain will suffer.

---

[11]Robert V. Delaney, "CLI's 8th Annual 'State of Logistics' Report," remarks to the National Press Club, Washington, DC (June 2, 1997), pp. 3–6.

Logistics Adds Value by Creating Time and Place Utility

One of the fundamental ways that logistics adds value is by creating utility. From an economic standpoint, utility represents the value or usefulness that an item or service has in fulfilling a want or need. There are four types of utility: form, possession, time, and place. The later two, time and place utility, are intimately supported by logistics.

Form utility is the process of creating the good or service, or putting it in the proper form for the customer to use. When Honda of America Manufacturing transforms parts and raw materials into a car, form utility is created. This is generally part of the production or operations process.

Possession utility is the value added to a product or service because the customer is able to take actual possession. This is made possible by credit arrangements, loans, and so on. For example, when General Motors Acceptance Corporation extends a loan to a prospective auto purchaser, possession utility becomes possible.

The Five Rights of Logistics

While form and possession utility are not specifically related to logistics, neither would be possible without getting the right items needed for consumption or production to the right place at the right time and in the right condition at the right cost.[12] These "five rights of logistics," credited to E. Grosvenor Plowman, are the essence of the two utilities provided by logistics: time and place utility.

Time utility is the value added by having an item when it is needed. This could occur within the organization, as in having all the materials and parts that are needed for manufacturing, so that the production line does not have to shut down. This occurs when the logistics function at Pillsbury delivers flour from one of its mills to a production facility so that cake mix may be produced on schedule. Or it could occur in the marketplace, as in having an item available for a customer when the customer wants it. The item does the customer no good if it is not available when it is needed.

This is closely related to **place utility,** which means having the item or service available where it is needed. If a product desired by consumers is in transit, in a warehouse, or in another store, it does not create any place utility for them. Without both time and place utility, which logistics directly supports, a customer could not be satisfied.

The Role of Logistics in the Organization

In recent years, effective logistics management has been recognized as a key opportunity to improve both the profitability and competitive performance of firms. By the late 1980s and early 1990s, customer service took center stage in many organizations. Even organizations that had previously adhered to the "marketing concept" were reexamining what it meant to be customer-driven. The trend toward strong customer focus continues today.

Logistics Supports Marketing

The Marketing Concept

The **marketing concept,** as mentioned above, is a "marketing management philosophy which holds that achieving organizational goals depends on determining the needs and

---

[12]George A. Gecowets, "Physical Distribution Management," *Defense Transportation Journal* 35, no. 4 (Aug. 1979), p. 5.

FIGURE 1–3

Marketing/logistics management concept

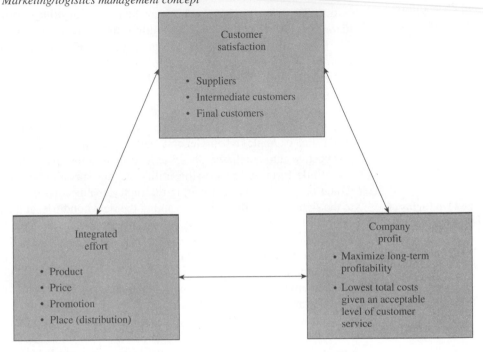

wants of target markets and delivering the desired satisfactions more effectively and efficiently than competitors."[13] Thus, the marketing concept is a "customer-driven" perspective which holds that a business exists to meet customer needs. The relationships between logistics and the three critical elements of the marketing concept (customer satisfaction, integrated effort/systems approach, and adequate corporate profit), are shown in Figure 1–3. Logistics plays a key role in each of these elements in several ways.

The "Four P's" of the Marketing Mix

The "four P's" of the marketing mix require that for a firm to be successful, any marketing effort must integrate the ideas of having the right product, at the right price, publicized with the proper promotion, and available in the right place. Logistics plays a critical role particularly in support of getting the product to the right place. As discussed previously in conjunction with utility, a product or service provides customer satisfaction only if it is available to the customer when and where it is needed. Figure 1–4 summarizes the trade-offs required between and among the major elements of the marketing mix and logistics.

Thus, the organization needs to use the "systems approach" in linking the needs foreseen by marketing with production as well as logistics. Achieving customer satisfaction requires an integrated effort both internally and with suppliers and ultimate customers.

---

[13]Phillip Kotler and Gary Armstrong, *Principles of Marketing,* 5th ed. (Englewood Cliffs, NJ: Prentice Hall, 1993), p. 22.

FIGURE 1–4

Cost trade-offs required in marketing and logistics

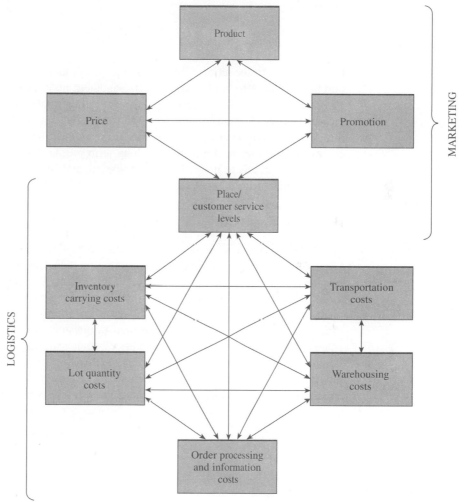

Marketing objective: Allocate resources to the marketing mix to maximize the long-run profitability of the firm.
Logistics objective: Minimize total costs given the customer service objective where Total costs = Transportation costs + Warehousing costs + Order processing and information costs + Lot quantity costs + Inventory carrying costs.

Source: Adapted from Douglas M. Lambert, *The Development of an Inventory Costing Methodology: A Study of the Costs Associated with Holding Inventory* (Chicago: National Council of Physical Distribution Management, 1976), p. 7.

Making Trade-Offs in Logistics Is Important

Also, it is important to understand that a central goal of an organization is to maximize long-term profitability or effective use of assets in the public or nonprofit sectors. One of the key ways to accomplish that, as shown in Figure 1–4 and presented later, is through examining trade-offs among alternatives, thereby reducing the overall total cost of activities within a system.

To better understand Figure 1–4, the sections below explore the manner in which each of the major elements of the marketing mix interact and are affected by logistics operations.

Product

Product refers to the set of utilities/characteristics that a customer receives as a result of a purchase. In an effort to lower price, management may decide to reduce product quality, eliminate product features, reduce the breadth of product offerings, reduce customer service or warranty support, or increase the time between model changes. However, any of these actions may reduce the attraction of the product for consumers, creating a loss of customers and thereby a reduction in long-term profits. To avoid making poor decisions, management needs to understand the trade-off and interrelationships between logistics and other marketing activities.

Price

Price is the amount of money that a customer pays for the product or service offering. Some of the items that should be factored into price include discounts for buying in quantities or for belonging to a certain class of customers, discounts for prompt payment, rebates, whether inventory is offered on consignment, and who pays delivery costs. A supplier may attempt to increase sales by reducing the price of its product, changing the terms or service offering. Unless the item in question is very price sensitive (i.e., sales change dramatically due to changes in price), such a strategy may create higher unit sales, but not enough to offset the lower price, yielding lower profit. This is particularly true in mature industries where customer demand is relatively fixed and the competition may follow the price decrease. The sales and the profitability of the entire industry suffer.

Promotion

Selling Value-Added to Customers

Promotion of a product or service encompasses both personal selling and advertising. Whereas increasing advertising expenditures or the size of the direct sales force can have a positive impact on sales, there is a point of diminishing returns. A point exists where the extra money being spent does not yield sufficiently high increases in sales or profits to justify the added expense. It is important for organizations to understand when they reach that point, so that they can avoid misallocating funds. A more prudent idea may be to try to use those funds more effectively, perhaps training the sales force to provide more value-added services to the customer, or make the customer more aware of the value added it currently provides through superior logistics service.

Place

Place is the key element of the marketing mix with which logistics interfaces directly. Place expenditures support the levels of customer service provided by the organization. This includes on-time delivery, high order fill rates, consistent transit times, and similar issues.

Customer Service Is an Output of the Logistics System

Customer service is an output of the logistics system. On the other hand, when the organization performs well on all the elements of the marketing mix, customer satisfaction occurs.

For many organizations, customer service may be a key way to gain competitive advantage.[14] By adjusting customer service levels to meet what the customer desires and is willing to pay, the organization may simultaneously improve service levels and reduce cost. All of the logistics trade-offs illustrated in the bottom of Figure 1–5 must be considered in terms of their impact on customer service levels. To accomplish this analysis, the total cost concept must be used.

Total Cost Concept

The **total cost concept** is the key to effectively managing logistics processes. The goal of the organization should be to reduce the *total* cost of logistics activities, rather than focusing on each activity in isolation.[15] Reducing costs in one area, such as transportation, may drive up inventory carrying costs as more inventory is required to cover longer transit times, or to balance against greater uncertainty in transit times.[16] National Semiconductor was actually able to reduce costs while improving logistics performance (see the Creative Solutions box at the end of this chapter) by taking a total cost approach.

There Are Six Major Logistics Cost Categories

Management should be concerned with the implications of decision making on all of the costs shown in Figure 1–5. These six major cost categories cover the 14 key logistics activities that will be discussed in this text. Figure 1–5 illustrates how the logistics activities drive the six major logistics cost categories. To provide a better understanding of the total cost concept, each of these activities will be briefly described.

Key Logistics Activities

Outlined below are the key activities required to facilitate the flow of a product from point of origin to point of consumption. All of these activities, listed alphabetically below, may be considered part of the overall logistics process.

Major Logistics Activities

- Customer service
- Demand forecasting/planning
- Inventory management
- Logistics communications
- Material handling

---

[14]Joseph B. Fuller, James O'Conor, and Richard Rawlinson, "Tailored Logistics: The Next Advantage," *Harvard Business Review* 71, no. 3 (May–June 1993), pp. 87–98.

[15]This section draws heavily on work by Douglas M. Lambert, *The Development of an Inventory Costing Methodology: A Study of the Costs Associated with Holding Inventory* (Chicago: National Council of Physical Distribution Management, 1976), pp. 5–15, 59–67.

[16]Joseph Cavinato, "A Total Cost/Value Model for Supply Chain Competitiveness," *Journal of Business Logistics* 13, no. 2 (1992), pp. 285–301.

FIGURE 1–5

How logistics activities drive total logistics costs

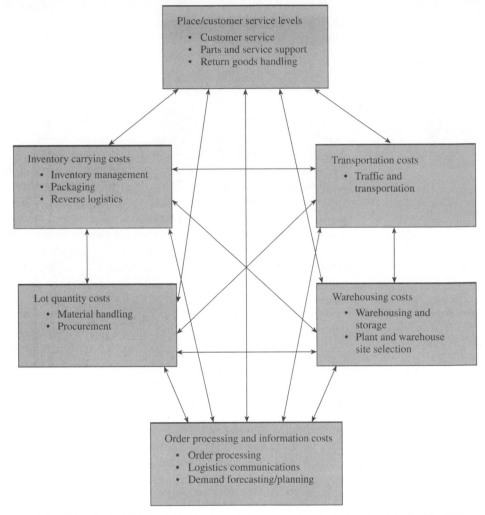

Source: Adapted from Douglas M. Lambert, *The Development of an Inventory Costing Methodology: A Study of the Costs Associated with Holding Inventory* (Chicago: National Council of Physical Distribution Management, 1976), p. 7.

- Order processing
- Packaging
- Parts and service support
- Plant and warehouse site selection
- Procurement
- Return goods handling
- Reverse logistics

- Traffic and transportation
- Warehousing and storage

While all organizations may not explicitly consider these activities to be part of logistics activities, each activity affects the logistics process, as shown in Figure 1–1.

Customer Service

Good Customer Service Supports Customer Satisfaction

Customer service has been defined as "a customer-oriented philosophy which integrates and manages all elements of the customer interface within a predetermined optimum cost-service mix."[17] Customer service is the output of the logistics system. It involves getting the right product to the right customer at the right place, in the right condition and at the right time, at the lowest total cost possible. Good customer service supports customer satisfaction, which is the output of the entire marketing process. Customer service is the topic of the next chapter.

Demand Forecasting/Planning

There Are Many Types of Demand Forecasts

There are many types of demand forecasts. Marketing forecasts customer demand based on promotions, pricing, competition, and so on. Manufacturing forecasts production requirements based on marketing's sales demand forecasts and current inventory levels. Logistics usually becomes involved in forecasting in terms of how much should be ordered from its suppliers (through purchasing), and how much of finished product should be transported or held in each market that the organization serves. In some organizations, logistics may even plan production. Thus, logistics needs to be linked to both marketing and manufacturing forecasting and planning.

Forecasting is a complex issue, with many interactions among functions and forecast variables. This topic will be explored in greater depth in Chapters 5 and 13.

Inventory Management

The Financial Impacts of Inventories

Inventory management involves trading off the level of inventory held to achieve high customer service levels with the cost of holding inventory, including capital tied up in inventory, variable storage costs, and obsolescence. These costs can range from 14 to over 50 percent of the value of inventory on an annual basis![18] With high costs for items such as high-tech merchandise, automobiles, and seasonal items that rapidly become obsolete, many organizations, including Hewlett-Packard, Xerox, and Sears, are giving inventory management much more attention.[19] These issues will be explored in Chapters 4 and 5.

---

[17]Bernard J. La Londe and Paul H. Zinszer, *Customer Service: Meaning and Measurement* (Chicago: National Council of Physical Distribution Management, 1976), p. iv.

[18]Lambert, *The Development of an Inventory Costing Methodology,* pp. 104–24.

[19]Tom Davis, "Effective Supply Chain Management," *Sloan Management Review* 34, no. 4 (Summer 1993), pp. 35–46.

Logistics Communications

Communications are becoming increasingly automated, complex, and rapid. Logistics interfaces with a wide array of functions and organizations in its communication processes. Communication must occur between:

1. The organization and its suppliers and customers.
2. The major functions within the organization, such as logistics, engineering, accounting, marketing, and production.
3. The various logistics activities listed previously.
4. The various aspects of each logistics activity, such as coordinating warehousing of material, work in process, and finished goods.
5. Various members of the supply chain, such as intermediaries and secondary customers or suppliers who may not be directly linked to the firm.

Communication Is Vital

Communication is key to the efficient functioning of any system, whether it be the distribution system of an organization or the wider supply chain. Excellent communications within a system can be a key source of competitive advantage. Part of Wal-Mart's success can be attributed to computerized advance communications systems which link their suppliers to their actual customer sales on a regular basis, so that the suppliers can plan based on up-to-date demand information, and provide timely and adequate replenishment to Wal-Mart stores. This is presented in more depth in Chapter 3, which describes information systems.

Materials Handling

Materials handling is a broad area that encompasses virtually all aspects of all movements of raw materials, work in process, or finished goods within a plant or warehouse. Because an organization incurs costs without adding value each time an item moves or is handled, a primary objective of materials management is to eliminate handling wherever possible. That includes minimizing travel distance, bottlenecks, inventory levels, and loss due to waste, mishandling, pilferage, and damage. Thus, by carefully analyzing material flows, materials management can save the organization significant amounts of money, as illustrated in Chapter 9.

Order Processing

Order processing entails the systems that an organization has for getting orders from customers, checking on the status of orders and communicating to customers about them, and actually filling the order and making it available to the customer. Part of the order processing includes checking inventory status, customer credit, invoicing, and accounts receivable. Thus, order processing is a broad, highly automated area. Because the order processing cycle is a key area of customer interface with the organization, it can have a big impact on a customer's perception of service and, therefore, satisfaction.[20] In-

---

[20]Benson P. Shapiro, V. K. Rangan, and J. J. Sviokla, "Staple Yourself to an Order," *Harvard Business Review* 70, no. 4 (July–Aug. 1992), pp. 113–22.

creasingly, organizations today are turning to advanced order-processing methods such as electronic data interchange (EDI) and electronic funds transfer (EFT) to speed the process and improve accuracy and efficiency. This will be described in greater depth in Chapter 3.

Packaging

Packaging Promotes and Protects

As Chapter 9 will explain, packaging is valuable both as a form of advertising/marketing, and for protection and storage from a logistical perspective. Packaging can convey important information to inform the consumer. Aesthetically pleasing packaging also can attract the consumer's attention. Logistically, packaging provides protection during storage and transport. This is especially important for long distances over multiple transportation modes such as international shipping.

Packaging can ease movement and storage by being properly designed for the warehouse configuration and materials handling equipment.

Parts and Service Support

In addition to supporting production through the movement of materials, work in process, and finished goods, logistics also is responsible for providing after-sale service support. This may include delivery of repair parts to dealers, stocking adequate spares, picking up defective or malfunctioning products from customers, and responding quickly to demands for repairs. Downtime can be extremely costly to industrial customers who may have to stop or delay production while awaiting repairs! This is discussed in conjunction with materials handling in Chapter 9.

Plant and Warehouse Site Selection

Determining the location of the company's plant(s) and warehouse(s) is a strategic decision that affects not only the costs of transporting raw materials inbound and finished goods outbound, but also customer service levels and speed of response. This topic is overviewed in Chapter 8. Issues to consider include the location of customers, suppliers, transportation services, availability and wage rates of qualified employees, governmental cooperation, and so on.

Intel Corporation Locates a Semiconductor Facility

In recent times, there has been a great deal of competition for new manufacturing facilities. An example of this is Intel Corporation's decision regarding where to locate a semiconductor facility. It received bids from a number of major cities, including Portland, Oregon; Austin, Texas; and Chandler, Arizona, a suburb of Phoenix. Ultimately, Intel chose Chandler because it already had a facility there, the Phoenix area was growing and had an attractive labor force, and the company had a good relationship with and was provided attractive incentives by the local government.[21]

---

[21]"Intel Building $1.5 Billion Plant," *Rocky Mountain Construction* 74, no. 24 (Dec. 20, 1993), p. 15; and William Carlisle, "States Are Closing Firms' 'Candy Store,'" *Arizona Republic* (July 24, 1994), pp. 1E–2E.

Procurement

With the increase in outsourcing of goods and services, the procurement function plays a more important role in the organization. Most U.S. industries spend from 40 to 60 percent of their revenues on materials and services from sources outside of the organization.[22]

Procurement Defined **Procurement** is the purchase of materials and services from outside organizations to support the firm's operations from production to marketing, sales, and logistics. Procurement, also referred to as purchasing, supply management, and by a number of other names, includes activities such as supplier selection, negotiation of price, terms and quantities, and supplier quality assessment. As organizations form longer-term relationships with fewer key suppliers, procurement continues to grow in importance and contribution to the organization. This is examined in greater depth in Chapter 10.

Return Goods Handling

Return Goods Handling Is Complex and Costly Returns may take place because of a problem with the performance of the item or simply because the customer changed his or her mind. Return goods handling is complex because it involves moving small quantities of goods back from the customer rather than to the customer as the firm is accustomed. Many logistics systems have a difficult time handling this type of movement. Costs tend to be very high. The cost of moving a product backward through the channel from the consumer to the producer may be as much as nine times as high as moving the same product forward from the producer to the customer.[23] Thus, this significant cost and service area is beginning to receive more attention. The topic is discussed in Chapter 9.

Reverse Logistics

Logistics is also involved in removal and disposal of waste materials left over from the production, distribution, or packaging processes. There could be temporary storage followed by transportation to the disposal, reuse, reprocessing, or recycling location. As the concern for recycling and reusable packaging grows, this issue will increase in importance. This is of particular concern in Europe, which has very strict regulations regarding removal of packaging materials and even obsolete product due in part to limited landfill space.

Traffic and Transportation

A key logistics activity is to actually provide for the movement of materials and goods from point of origin to point of consumption, and perhaps to its ultimate point of disposal as well. Transportation involves selection of the mode (e.g., air, rail, water, truck, or

---

[22]Michiel Leenders and Harold E. Fearon, *Purchasing and Materials Management,* 10th ed. (Burr Ridge, IL: Richard D. Irwin, 1993).

[23]Douglas M. Lambert and James R. Stock, *Strategic Logistics Management,* 3rd ed. (Burr Ridge, IL: Richard D. Irwin, 1993), p. 18.

Growing concerns about the quality of the environment have made materials recycling an important aspect of logistics.

pipeline), the routing of the shipment, assuring of compliance with regulations in the region of the country where shipment is occurring, and selection of the carrier. It is frequently the largest single cost among logistics activities. Transportation issues are covered in Chapter 7.

Warehousing and Storage

Warehousing supports time and place utility by allowing an item to be produced and held for later consumption. It can be held near the location where it will be needed, or transported later. Warehousing and storage activities relate to warehouse layout, design, ownership, automation, training of employees, and related issues. These issues are presented in Chapter 8.

The Relationship of Logistics Activities to Logistics Costs

Logistics costs are driven or created by the activities that support the logistics process. Each of the major cost categories—customer service, transportation, warehousing, order processing and information, lot quantity and inventory carrying—are discussed below.

Customer Service Levels

The key cost trade-off associated with varying levels of customer service is the cost of lost sales. Monies that are spent to support customer service include the costs associated with order fulfillment, parts, and service support. They also include the costs of return goods handling, which has a major impact on a customer's perception of the organization's service as well as the ultimate level of customer satisfaction.

Cost of a Lost Sale

The cost of lost sales includes not only the lost contribution of the current sale, but also potential future sales from the customer and from other customers due to word-of-mouth negative publicity from former customers. A recent estimate indicated that every disgruntled customer tells an average of nine others about his or her dissatisfaction with the product or service.[24] It is no wonder that it is extremely difficult to measure the true cost of customer service!

The Objective Is to Minimize Total Costs Given the Customer Service Objectives

Thus, the best approach is to determine desired levels of customer service based on customer needs, and how those needs are affected by expenditures on other areas of the marketing mix. The idea is to minimize the total cost, given the customer service objectives. Because each of the other five major logistics cost elements work together to support customer service, good data are needed regarding expenditures in each category.

Transportation Costs

The activity of transporting goods drives transportation costs. Expenditures that support transportation can be viewed in many different ways, depending on the unit of analysis. Costs can be categorized by customer, product line, type of channel such as inbound versus outbound, and so on. Costs vary considerably with volume of shipment (cube), weight of shipment, distance, and point of origin and destination. Costs and service also vary considerably with the mode of transportation chosen. These costs will be described in more depth in Chapter 7.

Warehousing Costs

Warehousing costs are created by warehousing and storage activities, and by the plant and warehouse site selection process. Included are all of the costs that vary due to a change in the number or location of warehouses. Warehousing costs are explored in Chapter 8.

Order Processing/Information Systems Costs

This category includes costs related to activities such as order processing, distribution communications, and forecasting demand. Order processing and information costs are an

---

[24]George R. Walther, *Upside-Down Marketing* (New York: McGraw-Hill, 1994), summarized by Audio-Tech Books, no. 2 (Mar. 1994), p. 8.

Examples of Order Processing Costs

extremely important investment to support good customer service levels and control costs. Order processing costs include such costs as order transmittal, order entry, processing the order, and related internal and external costs such as notifying carriers and customers of shipping information and product availability. Shippers and carriers have invested a great deal in improving their information systems, to include technology such as electronic data interchange (EDI), satellite data transmission, and bar coding and scanning shipments and sales. There also has been a growth in more sophisticated information technology, such as decision support systems, artificial intelligence (AI), and expert systems. These are the topics of Chapter 3.

Lot Quantity Costs

The major logistics lot quantity costs are due to procurement and production quantities. **Lot quantity costs** are purchasing- or production-related costs that vary with changes in order size or frequency and include:

The Components of Lot Quantity Costs

1. *Setup costs.*
   a. Time required to set up a line or locate a supplier and place an order.
   b. Scrap due to setting up the production line.
   c. Operating inefficiency as the line begins to run, or as a new supplier is brought on board.
2. *Capacity lost* due to downtime during changeover of line or changeover to a new supplier.
3. *Materials handling,* scheduling, and expediting.
4. *Price differentials* due to buying in different quantities.
5. *Order costs* associated with order placement and handling.

These costs must not be viewed in isolation because they also may affect many other costs. For example, a consumer goods manufacturer that produces large production runs may get good prices from suppliers and have long efficient production runs, but requires more storage space to handle large runs. Customer service levels may suffer as order fulfillment declines because products are produced infrequently, in large batches, and with inventory going to zero and creating stockout situations in between runs. This may increase information and order processing costs, as customers frequently call to check on availability of back-ordered products, and cancel back orders.

Transportation costs also may rise as customers are sent partial or split shipments. Inventory carrying costs will rise as large quantities of inventory are held until depleted, due to large batch sizes. The implication of one cost upon another must be explicitly considered. Transportation issues are further detailed in Chapter 7.

Inventory Carrying Costs

The logistics activities that make up inventory carrying costs include inventory control, packaging, and salvage and scrap disposal. Inventory carrying costs are made up of many elements. For decision-making purposes, the only relevant inventory costs to consider are

The Relevant Inventory Costs Are Those That Vary with the Amount of Inventory

those that vary with the amount of inventory stored. These costs will be explored in detail in Chapter 4. The four major categories of inventory cost are:

1. **Capital cost,** or **opportunity cost,** which is the return that the company could make on the money that it has tied up in inventory.
2. **Inventory service cost,** which includes insurance and taxes on inventory.
3. **Storage space cost,** which includes those warehousing space-related costs which change with the level of inventory.
4. **Inventory risk cost,** including obsolescence, pilferage, relocation within the inventory system, and damage.

Developing Logistics Strategy

Understanding the organization's overall strategy and the key trade-offs in that organization are important to developing logistics strategy. The primary goal of logistics in any organization is to support the organization's customer service goals in an effective and efficient manner. To do that, the logistics function and the organization's management need to know:

Primary Goal of Logistics Is to Provide Customer Service

1. What do customers desire in terms of customer service levels and capabilities?
2. How is the competition performing in terms of customer service?
3. How is the organization performing today compared with the competition and, particularly, on those areas that the customer perceives as important?

Logistics costs also are an important aspect of analyzing alternative logistics service offerings. The next section provides an overview of some of the key issues in developing logistics strategy.

External and Internal Audits Provide Information for Decision Making

Answering questions one and two above can be accomplished through a marketing and logistics audit of the external environment. This is outlined briefly in Chapter 15. Answering the third question can be accomplished by conducting an internal audit in conjunction with customer service, as described in Chapter 2, and in Chapter 15, in conjunction with strategy.

Based on this analysis, an organization can identify its own strengths and weaknesses, and what may be potential opportunities and hazards in the marketplace. Objectives or goals for the logistics function are thus formulated. Based on the objectives, alternative strategies or plans of action need to be developed in support of those objectives. The analysis should include the implications of each alternative on other functions and performance parameters, as well as an analysis of the total cost of each alternative. Thus, a systems approach is required.

Once a decision has been made concerning logistics strategy, the organization must ensure that its current logistics structure is adequate to achieve that strategy, or adjust the channel structure accordingly. Proper channel design is an important concern for logistics professionals. The next section addresses some additional future challenges facing logistics professionals, and highlights some key areas for logistics performance improvement.

Future Challenges and Areas for Logistics Performance Improvement

This section presents some of the key challenges and issues that logistics faces today and will continue to face in the future. These themes will be integrated throughout this text to provide continuity and an understanding of how these issues affect the performance and perceived importance of various logistics activities.

As the role of logistics grows and takes on greater importance in achieving the overall goals of the organization, logistics needs to meet the challenge and improve its performance to support those goals. Some areas of opportunity include:

- Greater participation in setting organizational strategy and the strategic planning process.
- Total quality management (TQM).
- Identification of opportunities for using logistics as a competitive weapon/marketing strength.
- Just-in-time (JIT) logistics.
- The use of quick response (QR) and efficient consumer response (ECR) techniques.
- Improved understanding of and accounting for logistics costs.
- Better understanding of global logistics issues and improved logistics information systems.
- Greater participation of logistics professionals on work teams.
- Appropriate understanding and use of outsourcing, partnerships, and strategic alliances.
- Greater understanding and appropriate application of technology.
- Green marketing.

Each of these issues is explored below.

Strategic Planning and Participation

Strategic Planning at Bergen Brunswig

Table 1–2 shows the increasing participation of the logistics function in competitive strategy. Activities such as logistics budgeting and control, inventory planning and positioning, and customer service have become important parts of the organization's strategic planning process. A study supported by the Council of Logistics Management illustrates that strategic planning is performed by the majority of logistics organizations studied.[25] Bergen Brunswig, a multibillion dollar drug wholesaler, reports that logistics participation in strategic planning is critical, with the vice president of Logistics attending corporate strategy meetings and serving on the task force which thinks strategically about the future.[26]

---

[25]Martha C. Cooper, Daniel E. Innis, and Peter R. Dickson, *Strategic Planning for Logistics* (Oak Brook, IL: Council of Logistics Management, 1992), p. 10.

[26]Ibid., p. 105.

TABLE 1–2   Strategic Planning by Departments

		Planning Level		
	Corporate	Marketing	Manufacturing	Logistics *(Staff)*	Logistics *(Function)*
Is strategic planning done at this level?	97%	93%	86%	82%	70%
Is there a formal written plan at this level?	90%	85%	75%	65%	55%
How many years has this formal system existed?	8	8	5	4	3
How many people are involved?	11	10	10	5	5

Note: Percentage of survey respondents indicating a "Yes" response.

Source: Based on the mail survey; Martha C. Cooper, Daniel E. Innis, and Peter R. Dickson, *Strategic Planning for Logistics* (Oak Brook, IL: Council of Logistics Management, 1992), p. 10.

Total Quality Management

Total quality management (TQM) is a philosophy that should be embedded in all aspects of logistics operations. Going beyond simple "quality control," which monitors for problems in actual performance after the fact, TQM is a philosophy that is integrated in designing logistics systems to achieve desired results, performing logistics activities, and monitoring results. Total quality management involves being proactive in performing the right activity the right way the first time, and continuing to perform it to the required level. In logistics, that could translate into short, predictable transit times, certain levels of in-stock availability, and certain fill rates on customer orders.

Malcolm Baldrige National Quality Award

One reason that logistics has received more attention as a strategic function is the growing recognition given to it in the **Malcolm Baldrige National Quality Award.** This award, administered by the U.S. Department of Commerce, was designed to recognize organizations that have achieved an outstanding level of quality and competitive excellence in the global marketplace. Many organizations are using the award criteria to evaluate and improve their quality procedures, even if they do not intend to apply for the award.[27] The scoring criteria are shown in Table 1–3.

Twenty-five percent of the points used in judging applicants for awards are based on customer satisfaction. The "customer focus and satisfaction" category rates the company's knowledge of the customer, responsiveness, overall customer service systems, and ability to meet requirements and expectations.[28] Thus, an organization must have a good

---

[27]David Greisling, "Quality: How to Make It Pay," *Business Week,* Aug. 8, 1994, pp. 54–59.

[28]Lambert and Stock, *Strategic Logistics Management,* p. 19.

TABLE 1–3   Scoring the Baldrige Award, 1995 Criteria

1.0	Leadership (90 points)
1.1	Senior executive leadership (45)
1.2	Leadership system and organization (25)
1.3	Public responsibility and corporate citizenship (20)
2.0	Information and analysis (75 points)
2.1	Marketing of information and data (20)
2.2	Competitive comparisons and benchmarks (15)
2.3	Analysis and use of company-level data (40)
3.0	Strategic planning (55 points)
3.1	Strategy development (35)
3.2	Strategy deployment (20)
4.0	Human resources development and management (140)
4.1	Human resource planning and evaluation (20)
4.2	High-performance work systems (45)
4.3	Employee education, training, and development (50)
4.4	Employee well-being and satisfaction (25)
5.0	Process management (140)
5.1	Design and introduction of products and services (40)
5.2	Process management: Product and service production and delivery (40)
5.3	Process management: Support services (30)
5.4	Management of supplier performance (30)
6.0	Business results (250)
6.1	Product and service quality results (75)
6.2	Company operational and financial results (130)
6.3	Supplier performance results (45)
7.0	Customer focus and satisfaction (250 points)
7.1	Customer and market knowledge (30)
7.2	Customer relationship management (30)
7.3	Customer satisfaction determination (30)
7.4	Customer satisfaction results (100)
7.5	Customer satisfaction comparison (60)

Total points = 1,000

Source: *Malcolm Baldrige National Quality Award 1995 Criteria* (Milwaukee, WI: ASQC, 1995), p. 20.

logistics system and include logistics in its strategic planning process to score well in this major area.

ISO 9000 Programs   The **ISO 9000** (International Organization for Standardization) series is an internationally recognized certification program whereby the quality processes of firms are audited to verify whether they have well-documented and effective quality processes in place. It was born in Europe in 1987 in an effort to support trade between countries and companies.[29]

---

[29]James R. Evans and William M. Lindsay, *The Management and Control of Quality,* 2nd ed. (St. Paul, MN: West, 1993), pp. 412–15.

Just-in-Time

The Implications of JIT on Logistics

Just-in-time (JIT) is an inventory management philosophy aimed at reducing waste and redundant inventory by delivering products, components, or materials just when an organization needs them. As will be discussed in Chapters 9 and 10, JIT has profound implications on logistics systems. JIT requires close coordination of demand needs among logistics, carriers, suppliers, and manufacturing. JIT also represents a tremendous opportunity for the logistics function to contribute to the organization's success by reducing inventory while simultaneously maintaining or improving customer service levels. Thus, JIT represents an important trend in inventory management that will be discussed throughout this text. Applications of JIT principles to the retail and grocery sectors are discussed below in relation to quick response and efficient consumer response.

Quick Response

Quick response (QR) is a retail sector strategy which combines a number of tactics to improve inventory management and efficiency, while speeding inventory flows. Most QR is between manufacturer and retailer only. When fully implemented, QR applies JIT principles throughout the entire supply chain, from raw material suppliers through ultimate customer demand.

The concept works by combining electronic data interchange (EDI) with bar coding technology, so that the customer sales are tracked immediately. This information can be passed on to the manufacturer, who can then notify its raw material suppliers, and schedule production and deliveries as required to meet replenishment needs. This allows inventory reductions while speeding response time, lowering the number of out-of-stock products, and reducing handling and obsolescence. While QR began in the textile and apparel industry, it is now being applied by many industries in the retail sector. The grocery industry has begun an adaptation of this approach, called efficient consumer response, as discussed in the next section.

Cross-Docking

QR has had a major impact on distribution operations. Rather than "warehousing" product, distribution centers are now charged with "moving" the product through quickly. This frequently entails **cross-docking,** whereby the inbound product is unloaded, sorted by store, and reloaded onto trucks destined for a particular store, without ever being warehoused. As a result of QR, Mercantile Stores has reduced the number of distribution centers it owns from 12 to 8.[30]

Creating Floor-Ready Merchandise with Logistics

To further improve retail efficiency, some suppliers are shipping goods prehung and preticketed. This concept, known as "floor-ready merchandise," is growing in popularity. As noted by Randy Burnette, director of QR for Mercantile, "Our strategy and goal is to maximize the portion of business that is floor ready."[31] One retail executive commented that merchandise routinely spends an additional three days in the distribution center (DC) if it does not have retail price tickets and the proper hangers.[32] Floor-ready merchandise may lead to a reduction in the number of DCs, and processing time can be greatly reduced.

---

[30]Gary Robins, "Less Work, More Speed," *Stores,* Mar. 1994, p. 24.
[31]Ibid., p. 26.
[32]Susan Reda, "Floor-Ready Merchandise," *Stores,* Apr. 1994, p. 41.

Technology

Quick Response, Canadian Style

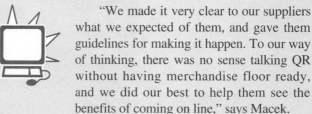

Executives at Toronto-based Hudson's Bay Company left the pioneering spirit to U.S. retailers when it came to developing quick response technology. They sat on the sidelines watching and learning from their U.S. counterparts for years.

Then, in late 1991 the decision was made to implement QR technology. Hudson's Bay executives quickly made up for lost time. Everything from UPC codes to floor-ready processes were set up and put into effect in less than two years. Ironically, as U.S. retailers and manufacturers hammer out guidelines for floor-ready merchandise today, they're looking to their neighbors to the north for tips.

According to Peggy Macek, director of merchandise systems at Hudson's Bay Company, getting suppliers to comply with the various standards, including floor-ready merchandise processing, involves a lot of partnering and understanding, and a bit of clout and coercion as well.

Computer technology allows for easy and accurate inventory control.

"We made it very clear to our suppliers what we expected of them, and gave them guidelines for making it happen. To our way of thinking, there was no sense talking QR without having merchandise floor ready, and we did our best to help them see the benefits of coming on line," says Macek. "There were suppliers who balked initially, but we're the largest retailer in Canada. They quickly came to the conclusion that you can't fight city hall."

No doubt, the fact that The Bay cut off one of its largest suppliers for one month for refusing to comply with standards sent a clear message to Canadian manufacturers.

Currently, the retailer requires suppliers to price merchandise prior to shipping. Hangers have been standardized by merchandise type, and shipping cartons are moving through the DC [distribution center] without being opened.

While the Canadian retail scene is quite different from that in the United States—fewer retailers and manufacturers are more spread out, for example—the benefits realized by The Bay are significant.

"We're saving millions of dollars in distribution functions," reports Macek. "We used to have five distribution centers. Now, because of the technology that's been implemented and the speed with which we can push goods through the pipeline, we were able to shut down three DCs."

In the past, it took as long as two to three weeks for product to get from the DC to the selling floor at The Bay. Today, product bound for stores in Toronto and Montreal is usually on the selling floor within a day or two of arriving at the DC. Stores located in more remote areas of the country can have product on the selling floor five to six days after arrival at the DC.

Hudson's Bay Company, the oldest retailer in North America, had total sales in excess of $5 billion in 1993. The retailer operates 102 full-line department stores called The Bay, and a discount store division known as Zellers.

Source: *Stores,* Apr. 1994, p. 42.

Efficient Consumer Response

Efficient consumer response (ECR) combines several logistics strategies in an effort to improve the competitiveness of the grocery industry by cutting waste in the supply chain. It is the grocery industry's answer to QR.[33] ECR includes the following strategies:[34]

Strategies of Efficient Consumer Response

1. Widespread implementation of electronic data interchange up and down the supply chain, both between suppliers and manufacturers, manufacturers and distributors, and distributors and customers.
2. Greater use of point-of-sale data obtained by greater and more accurate use of bar coding.
3. Cooperative relationships between manufacturers, distributors, suppliers, and customers.
4. Continuous replenishment of inventory and flow through distribution.
5. Improved product management and promotions.

By applying the fourth point, continuous replenishment and flow through distribution, inventory is managed on a just-in-time basis, rather than stockpiled in warehouses and distribution centers. Product is cross-docked, whereby it is unloaded at one dock, broken down into store-sized shipments, and reloaded on trucks to go directly to the stores. Thus, cooperation and coordination are very important to ensure proper sequencing of truck loading and unloading, as well as the proper product mix. The belief is that the potential exists to reduce pipeline inventory by up to 40 percent.[35]

A key feature of ECR that distinguishes it from QR is the emphasis on moving away from the grocery industry's "deal mentality." Cooperation is required among industry participants to move away from the heavy use of promotional strategies. Such strategies encourage grocers to "stockpile" or forward buy product due to promotions such as a temporary low price or "buy two, get one free" deals. This creates excessive inventory in the supply chain, and reduces the number of times inventory turns over each year.

The ECR strategy was developed to offset some of the pressure on the grocery industry by mass merchandisers like Wal-Mart, and Warehouse clubs. It will be referred to throughout the text.

Logistics as a Competitive Weapon

Logistics Can Create a Competitive Advantage

Logistics may be the best source of competitive advantage for a firm because it is less easily duplicated than other elements of the marketing mix: product, price, and promotion. Consider, for example, forming close, ongoing relationships with carriers or logistics service providers can help give the firm a distinct competitive advantage in speed to the customer, reliability, availability, or other customer service factors.[36]

---

[33]For an excellent example of such a program, see Joseph C. Andranski, "Foundations for Successful Continuous Replenishment Programs," *The International Journal of Logistics Management* 5, no. 1 (1994), pp. 1–8.

[34]Carol Casper, "ECR: Waiting to Move Center Stage?" *Industrial Distribution,* Feb. 1994, pp. 83–85.

[35]Ibid.

[36]Donald J. Bowersox, "The Strategic Benefits of Logistics Alliances," *Harvard Business Review* 68, no. 4 (July–Aug. 1990), pp. 36–42.

The power of logistics in achieving an organization's customer service goals and supporting customer satisfaction has received an increased amount of attention in the press.[37] Companies that understand and utilize the potential of logistics as a competitive weapon include logistics as a key component of their strategic planning process. In recognition of the key role of logistics in supporting strategic customer service initiatives, the logistics function of Levi Strauss and Company began reporting to marketing rather than operations in 1990. To support this, logistics began formal strategic planning for 1990.[38]

Accounting for Logistics Costs

Implementation and utilization of the integrated logistics concept requires total cost analysis to be effective. The focus of management should be to minimize total logistics costs for a given customer service level. Thus, it is important to understand the costs associated with the logistics trade-offs in Figure 1–5.

Activity-Based Costing

In general, accounting systems have not changed and adapted to accurately account for the many trade-offs inherent in logistics activity and logistics decision making. The availability of timely, accurate, and meaningful logistics information is relatively rare in practice. However, this is beginning to change as more organizations move into activity-based costing (ABC) systems to allocate costs to activities on a more accurate and meaningful basis.[39] Much work remains to be done in this area. Some of the issues associated with the use of ABC in logistics are presented in greater depth in Chapter 13.

In addition, accounting and management support systems that are flexible in nature are needed. Logistics professionals must be able to get the information required to make decisions as they arise. Not all logistics decisions can be anticipated in advance and prepared for in a regularly scheduled logistics report. Thus, accounting systems that provide easy access to real-time data are needed to support unanticipated decisions.

Logistics as a Boundary-Spanning Activity

Logistics Plays a Key Role throughout the Supply Chain

As we have described extensively in this chapter, the logistics function and the activities performed by logistics do not exist in isolation. Logistics plays a key role in activities throughout the supply chain, both within and outside the organization. Outside the organization, logistics interfaces with customers in the order processing, order fulfillment, and delivery cycles. Logistics also interfaces with carriers, warehousers, suppliers, and other third parties that play a role in the supply chain.

---

[37]See Ulf Casten Carlberg, "Information Systems Must Offer Customized Logistics and Increase Profitability," *Industrial Engineering* 26, no. 6 (June 1994), p. 23–30; Daniel Innis and Bernard J. La Londe, "Customer Service: The Key to Customer Satisfaction, Customer Loyalty and Market Share," *Journal of Business Logistics* 15, no. 1 (1994), pp. 1–28; and "Logistics Mandate Is Customer Satisfaction," *Transportation and Distribution* 34, no. 12 (Dec. 1993), pp. 28–30.

[38]Cooper et. al., *Strategic Planning for Logistics,* pp. 165–78.

[39]Terrance Lynn Pohlen, *The Effect of Activity-Based Cost on Logistics Management,* doctoral dissertation, Ohio State University, 1993; and David A. Chudik, "Activity Based Costing for Distribution Operations," *Annual Conference Proceedings of the Council of Logistics Management,* Washington, DC (Oct. 3–6, 1993), pp. 37–52.

Within the organization, logistics interfaces with virtually every functional area in some capacity. Logistics interfaces with finance in the planning process and in the analysis of capital expenditures on investments in building and equipment to support distribution, transportation, warehousing, information technology, and related issues.

Logistics interfaces with accounting in establishing logistics costs (transportation, distribution, storage) for various products, customers, and distribution channels. Logistics also requires information from accounting regarding budgets and actual expenditures.

As discussed earlier, the interaction of logistics with other marketing activities is extensive. Logistics plays an instrumental role in customer satisfaction by providing high levels of customer service through good product availability, reliable service, and efficient operations that keep prices competitive.

Logistics must work closely with production and operations in a number of capacities. First, logistics often receives order releases for materials from production, and it needs to ensure that the items required are ordered, transported, and received on a timely basis. Storage also may need to be arranged. Logistics often manages the flow of materials or work in process within the organization. Logistics also must work with production in terms of stocking and shipping the finished product as it is available.

Logistics should be involved with research and development, product engineering, packaging engineering, and related functions in the new product development process. This often occurs through logistics participation on a new product team. It is vital for the logistics area to be represented very early in the new product development process.[40] This is critical in terms of designing the proper distribution channel, anticipating needs for inventory buildup, ensuring the availability of materials for production, and properly configuring the packaging for maximum efficiency and production within the distribution channel.

An increasing number of organizations are using the team approach to facilitate communications, create buy-in from multiple functions, and to anticipate problems. Logistics should be an active participant on teams that deal with issues affecting the supply chain.[41]

Global Logistics

Many leading organizations are heavily involved in international markets through purchasing inputs to production, other importing, exporting, joint ventures, alliances, foreign subsidiaries and divisions, and other means. This creates a need for familiarity with global logistics and global logistics networks. This need is likely to continue in the future. The Ohio State University's study of logistics career patterns reported that the top-rated global trends that are expected to have an impact on the careers of logistics professionals are:

The Most Important Global Trends

- The growth of information technology (21 percent)
- Supply chain management (15 percent)
- Globalization (11 percent)

---

[40]Phillip R. Witt, *Cost Competitive Products* (Reston, VA: Reston Publishing, 1986).

[41]See "Brewing Up a Logistics Partnership," *Distribution* 92, no. 9 (Sept. 1993), p. 49; and "How Sears Leverages Its LTL," *Distribution* 91, no. 9 (Sept. 1993), p. 46.

FIGURE 1–6

Logistics responsibilities: Allocation of time and effort

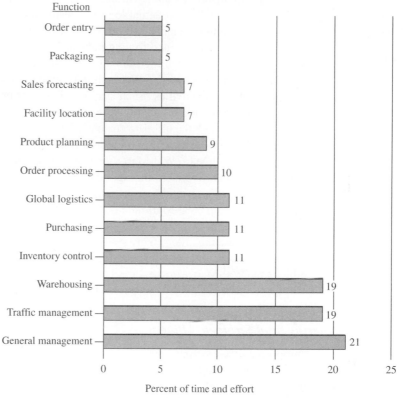

Source: James M. Masters and Bernard J. La Londe, *The 1996 Ohio State University Survey of Career Patterns in Logistics* (Columbus: The Ohio State University, 1996).

Increasing Skill Requirements

As suggested above, the demands on logistics professionals are increasing. As logisticians become increasingly involved in setting corporate strategy and other aspects of the strategic planning process, different skill sets are required in quality issues, global logistics, and improving relationships with third-party providers. One of the best sources of longitudinal data for trends in logistics careers has been the Logistics Career Patterns Study conducted annually by The Ohio State University. As shown in Figure 1–6, this study indicates that the greatest proportion of logistics time and effort is spent on general management issues.

A small percentage of time is spent on very repetitive issues such as order entry and packaging.[42] Information systems also are playing an increasingly important role in logistics, as discussed in the next section.

---

[42]James M. Masters and Bernard J. La Londe, *The 1996 Ohio State University Survey of Career Patterns in Logistics* (Columbus: The Ohio State University, 1996).

Logistics Information Systems

Information Is the Key to Integrated Logistics Management

Part of an organization's ability to use logistics as a competitive weapon is based on its ability to assess and adjust actual logistics performance real time. This means the ability to monitor customer demands and inventory levels as they occur, to act in a timely manner to prevent stockouts, and to communicate potential problems to customers. This requires excellent, integrated logistics information systems. These systems impact all of the logistics activities presented earlier, and must be integrated and take into account marketing and production activities. Such systems also must be integrated with other members of the supply chain, to provide accurate information throughout the channel from the earliest supplier through the ultimate customer.

Logistics information systems may link a variety of information technologies, as is the case with Wal-Mart. Wal-Mart uses EDI to communicate with suppliers, receiving information such as shipment, timing, quantities, and even invoicing. It uses bar coding to scan sales as customers make their purchases. The bar-coded information is thus captured at the point of sale. Wal-Mart then downloads the information to suppliers. Suppliers use these data to determine the orders they need to supply to Wal-Mart, rather than having Wal-Mart create the orders. This system provides suppliers with rapid feedback on sales, so that they can anticipate production requirements based on accurate, near real-time sales data. Wal-Mart also benefits because it no longer has to place orders with many suppliers, and it can keep its inventory levels to a minimum.

Outsourcing, Partnering, and Strategic Alliances

During the 1980s, many organizations began to recognize that they could not effectively and efficiently "do it all" themselves and still remain competitive. They began to look to third-party specialists to perform activities that were not a part of their "core competency." This activity is known as **outsourcing,** in which an organization hires an outside organization to provide a good or service that it traditionally had provided itself, because this third party is an "expert" in efficiently providing this good or service, while the organization itself may not be.

Outsourcing

Recently, outsourcing has been an area of growing interest and activity. Logistics outsourcing often involves third-party warehouses and use of public or contract transportation carriers. Outsourcing offers the opportunity for organizations to use the best logistics providers available to meet their needs.[43] Outsourcing may involve a partnership relationship or be ad hoc, on a transaction to transaction basis. Traditionally, such relationships have been arm's-length, with each party concerned only for its own welfare.[44]

Partnering

Managers in many firms are accepting the concept of partnering or establishing close, long-term working relationships with suppliers of goods or services, customers,

---

[43]Bernard J. La Londe, Martha C. Cooper and Thomas Noodeweir, *Customer Service: A Management Perspective,* (Oak Brook, IL: Council of Logistics Management, 1988), pp. 71–94.

[44]For an excellent discussion of outsourcing issues, see Arnold B. Maltz, "Outsourcing the Warehousing Function: Economics and Strategic Considerations," *Logistics and Transportation Review* 30, no. 2 (1994), pp. 245–66.

and third-party providers. This concept has been embraced by Bose Corporation, in the JIT II program. Bose uses the concept of an "in-plant," where key suppliers or service providers are actually on location at Bose's facility. Bose has such a relationship with Roadway Express, Inc. Bose states that this relationship creates efficiency between it and the carrier, creating improved communications, better service, and shared cost savings.[45]

Strategic Alliances

The most closely integrated partnerships are often referred to as **strategic alliances.** For a partnership to be a strategic alliance, it must be strategic in nature and must directly support one of the organization's distinctive competencies. Strategic alliances are rare in actual practice.

Technology

There has been a proliferation of technological developments in areas that support logistics. As discussed above, there have been major technological developments in the information systems area: EDI, bar coding, point-of-sale data, and satellite data transmissions are only a few examples. In addition, improvements in automated warehousing capabilities should be integrated into logistics plans for upgrading technology. Technology is having a profound effect on the way that logistics personnel interface with other functional areas, creating the ability to access more timely, accurate information. Combining information technology with automated warehousing reduces inherent human variability, creating an opportunity to improve customer service.

Green Marketing

Environmental Issues Are Becoming More Important

Environmental issues have been an area of growing concern and attention for businesses on a global scale. Transportation and disposal of hazardous materials are frequently regulated and controlled. In Europe, organizations are increasingly required to remove and dispose of packaging materials used for their products. These issues complicate the job of logistics, increasing costs and limiting options. Organizations are continually looking at reducing, reusing, and reapplying packaging materials, by-products of production, and obsolete items. Companies are substituting items that are more readily recyclable. Some have even gone so far as to begin designing products with disassembly specifically in mind.[46] These activities are covered in the term **green marketing.**

We have briefly summarized some of the current and future issues facing logistics professionals. These issues are recurring themes that will appear throughout this text.

Summary

In this chapter, we introduced the concept of logistics and described its development and relevance to the organization and economy as a whole. The concept of the systems

---

[45]William J. Warren, "JIT II Puts Bose a Little Ahead of the Cutting Edge," *American Shipper* 33, no. 12 (Dec. 1991), p. 47.

[46]"Manufacturing for Recovery," *Fortune,* Jan. 23, 1995, pp. 63–68ff.

Creative Solutions

Delivering the Goods

National Semiconductor, the world's 13th largest computer chip manufacturer began looking at how to increase logistical efficiency in the early 1990s in an effort to turn its profitability around. It discovered that it delivered 95 percent of its products within 45 days of the time they were ordered. While this was not satisfactory, the other 5 percent required as much as 90 days! Since the customers could not be sure which 5 percent would be late, they required 90 days worth of stock on everything. The system was overloaded with inventory.

After doing a profitability analysis, National cut 45 percent of its product line. To get the remaining

products to market on time, it simplified—going from 20,000 routes on 12 airlines, involving 10 warehouses, to 1 central facility in Singapore. To speed that product to market, it hired Federal Express to handle all of its sorting, shipping, and storage at its Singapore distribution center. This has resulted in major operating improvements. National can move products from factory to customer in four days or less. Distribution costs are down from 2.6 percent of revenues to 1.9 percent.

Source: Ron Henkoff, "Delivering the Goods," *Fortune*, Nov. 28, 1994, pp. 64–78.

approach was introduced and related to the role of logistics and its interface with marketing and other functions. The key role of logistics in customer service was emphasized. The systems approach was also related to the total cost concept and the principle of trade-offs as it relates to both the performance of logistics activity and the costs associated with such activity. The key logistics costs identified were customer service, inventory carrying costs, transportation, warehousing, order processing/information systems costs, and lot quantity costs.

We also examined the issue of logistics strategy, and the role of logistics in corporate strategy. This chapter closed with a summary of future challenges for logistics professionals. These challenges range from playing an active role in the strategic planning process to improving accounting information, information technology, and other types of technology and practices, such as TQM, JIT, QR, and ECR. The changing nature of logistics relationships, from team participation to forming partnering relationships with suppliers, was also explored.

There are many opportunities and challenges that face the logistics function in the future. We will begin to describe these in more depth in Chapter 2, which focuses on customer service.

Suggested Readings

Bowersox, Donald J.; Patricia J. Daugherty; Cornelia I. Dröge; Richard N. Germain; and Dale S.
Rogers. *Logistical Excellence: It's Not Business as Usual.* Burlington, MA: Digital Press, 1992.
Heskett, James L. "Sweeping Changes in Distribution." *Harvard Business Review* 51, no. 2
(Mar.–Apr. 1973), pp. 123–32.

Lambert, Douglas M. *The Development of an Inventory Costing Methodology: A Study of the Costs Associated with Holding Inventory.* Chicago: National Council of Physical Distribution Management, 1976.

Leenders, Michiel, and Harold E. Fearon. *Purchasing and Materials Management,* 11th ed. Burr Ridge, IL: Irwin/McGraw-Hill, 1997.

Mentzer, John T. "Managing Channel Relations in the 21st Century." *Journal of Business Logistics* 14, no. 1 (1993), pp. 27–41.

Smith, Peter A.; Jack Barry; Joseph L. Cavinato; John J. Coyle; Steven J. Dunn; and William Grenoble. *Logistics in Service Industries.* Oak Brook, IL: Council of Logistics Management, 1991.

Stock, James R. "Logistics Thought and Practice: A Perspective." *International Journal of Physical Distribution and Logistics Management* 20, no. 1 (1990), pp. 3–6.

———. *Reverse Logistics.* Oak Brook, IL: Council of Logistics Management, 1992.

Trunick, Perry A. "Logistics: An Agent for Change In the 90's." *Transportation and Distribution* 34, no. 11 (Nov. 1993), pp. 36–41.

Turner, J. R. "Integrated Supply Chain Management: What's Wrong with This Picture?" *Industrial Engineering* 25, no. 12 (Dec. 1993), pp. 52–55.

Questions and Problems

1. How do improvements in logistics productivity affect the economy as a whole, as well as the position of individual consumers?

2. How is logistics related to the marketing effort? Be sure to discuss customer service/customer satisfaction, integration of efforts, and cost and performance outputs.

3. What are the different types of utility? How does logistics directly or indirectly affect each one?

4. Why has logistics recently been receiving more attention as a strategic function of the organization?

5. What is meant by the profit leverage affect of logistics? What are the greatest cost savings opportunities for logistics?

6. Based on the examples shown in the text, what is the profit leverage effect of logistics in a firm with pretax profit of 5%? Of 10%? How could you use this information to get favorable attention for a logistics cost-saving effort?

7. Discuss the key challenges facing logistics today. What do you see as the greatest area of opportunity for logistics? Why?

8. How has the role and performance of logistics been enhanced by the growth of technology, particularly information technology? What do you see as key trends in the future?

9. Of the 14 areas of logistics responsibility, which do you believe will experience the most change in the next five years or so? Why?

THE DISTRIBUTION CHALLENGE!
PROBLEM: TORN IN THE U.S.A.

Call it the American dilemma: a company with long-range ideals that is required to show short-term results.

In order to satisfy the demanding financial community, a client of consultant Ernst & Young must demonstrate ever-improving earnings on a quarterly basis. At the same time, it must boost profitability by rapidly introducing new products. Virtually no lag is permitted, according to Stan Brown and Mike Brown, senior managers of Ernst & Young. Yet this relentless pressure is having a serious impact on the company's supply-chain performance.

One of this company's business units experiences a demand spike in sales during the last few days of each month. Up to half its monthly business might be transacted in that brief period. But the irregular pattern of supply and demand isn't the result of any oddities in the industry. It's purely an artificial situation, caused by the sales force scrambling for business at the end of each reporting period. Often that means artificially pulling demand forward to make sales targets. What's more, the erratic pace of sales leads to periods during which the company might not have enough inventory to fulfill demand.

Two problems result. One is that retailers are conditioned to order product only when promotions are provided, so they wait until then in hope of securing deep discounts. The other is that the seller's warehouse is overwhelmed by orders as it struggles to cope with a 150 percent utilization factor during a 24-hour period. Naturally, the warehouse is viewed by sales "as the bad guy, because it can't deliver," says Stan Brown.

The challenge: In a situation that is driven by the financial community—the demand for short-term profits—where is this company's leverage? What can it do to smooth out the flow of product without seriously compromising its profitability?

What Is Your Solution?

Source: "Distribution: The Challenge." *Distribution* 96, no. 4 (Apr. 1997), p. 76.

Customer Service

Chapter Objectives

- To define customer service.
- To show the central role that customer service plays in an organization's marketing and logistics efforts.
- To show how to calculate cost-revenue trade-offs.
- To illustrate how to conduct a customer service audit.
- To identify opportunities for improving customer service performance.

Introduction

In times of tough competition when many organizations offer similar products in terms of price, features, and quality, customer service differentiation can provide an organization with a distinct advantage over the competition.[1] Customer service represents the output of the logistics system as well as the "place" component of the organization's marketing mix. Customer service performance is a measure of how well the logistics system functions in creating time and place utility, with a focus on external customers.

The level of service provided to functions, such as marketing and production, affects the organization's ability to serve the needs of customers and will determine how well these functions communicate and interact with logistics on a day-to-day basis.[2] The level of customer service provided to customers determines whether the organization will retain existing customers and how many new customers it will attract.[3]

In virtually every industry today, from computers to clothing to cars, customers have a wide variety of choices. A company cannot afford to offend its customers. The customer service level that an organization provides has a direct impact on its market share, its total logistics costs and, ultimately, its overall profitability.

The Importance of Attracting and Retaining Customers

To illustrate, a key to corporate profitability is to successfully attract and retain customers. However, it has been estimated that the average customer turnover is between 10 and 30 percent for all U.S. companies.[4] If customer turnover could be reduced by 5 percent, bottom-line profitability could possibly increase significantly, perhaps by 60–95 percent annually.[5]

For these reasons, it is of the utmost importance that customer service be an integral part of the design and operation of all logistics systems.

Customer Service Defined

The definition of **customer service** varies across organizations. Suppliers and their customers can view the concept of customer service quite differently. In a broad sense, customer service is the measure of how well the logistics system is performing in providing time and place utility for a product or service. This includes activities such as the ease of checking stock, placing an order, and postsale support of the item.

Customer service is often confused with the concept of customer satisfaction. In contrast to customer service, **customer satisfaction** represents the customer's overall assessment of all elements of the marketing mix: product, price, promotion, and place. Thus, cus-

---

[1]"An Energized Process for Improving Customer Service," *NAPM Insights,* Apr. 1992, pp. 9–11; and Graham Sharman, "The Rediscovery of Logistics," *Harvard Business Review* 62, no. 5 (Sept.–Oct. 1984), pp. 71–79.

[2]Peter E. O'Reilly, "Getting to Know Them," *NAPM Insights,* May 1994, p. 8.

[3]Christopher Power, Lisa Driscoll, and Earl Bohn, "Smart Selling: How Companies Are Winning Over Today's Tougher Customer," *Business Week,* Aug. 3, 1992, p. 46.

[4]Toby B. Gooley, "How Logistics Drive Customer Service," *Traffic Management* 35, no. 1 (Jan. 1996), p. 46.

[5]Ibid.

tomer satisfaction is a broader concept that encompasses customer service. A thorough description of customer satisfaction can be found in many introductory marketing textbooks.[6]

Customer Service Can Be Viewed in Three Ways

In most organizations, customer service is defined in one or more ways, including (1) an activity or function to be managed, such as order processing or handling of customer complaints; (2) actual performance on particular parameters, such as the ability to ship complete orders for 98 percent of orders received within a 24-hour period; or (3) part of an overall corporate philosophy, rather than simply an activity or performance measures.[7] If an organization views customer service as a philosophy, it will likely have a formal customer service function and various performance measures.[8]

A Recent View of Customer Service

Customer service can be defined as:

Customer Service Defined

. . . a process which takes place between the buyer, seller, and third party. The process results in a value added to the product or service exchanged. This value added in the exchange process might be short term as in a single transaction or longer term as in a contractual relationship. The value added is also shared, in that each of the parties to the transaction or contract are better off at the completion of the transaction than it was before the transaction took place. Thus, in a process view: Customer service is a process for providing significant value-added benefits to the supply chain in a cost-effective way.[9]

Successful implementation of the marketing concept requires that companies both win and retain customers. Too often, the emphasis is on winning new customers and gaining new accounts. But this is an extremely shortsighted approach for an ongoing business concern. Many business strategy textbooks used to say that "the objective of a firm is to make a profit," but this attitude is shifting. The objective of the firm is still to make a profit, but before that can take place, the firm needs to establish service policies and programs that will satisfy customers' needs and deliver them in a cost-efficient manner; that is, customer service.

Companies like L. L. Bean, Marriott, Procter & Gamble, Motorola, and Saturn Corporation have gained significant advantage in the marketplace by meeting and sometimes exceeding a customer's service expectations. Here are a few examples of how these firms and others have addressed customer service issues:

Customer Service Examples

- Marriott hotels regularly shares customer assessments with employees. Involving customers in the regular, formal evaluation process, allows Marriott to get employees committed to its focus on customer service.

---

[6]See, for example, Philip Kotler and Gary Armstrong, *Principles of Marketing,* 5th ed. (Englewood Cliffs, NJ: Prentice Hall, 1993).

[7]Bernard J. La Londe and Paul H. Zinszer, *Customer Service: Meaning and Measurement* (Chicago: National Council of Physical Distribution Management, 1976), pp. 156–59.

[8]For an overview of how customer service has been viewed during the previous 25 years, see, "A Compendium of Research in Customer Service," *International Journal of Physical Distribution and Logistics Management* 24, no. 4 (1994), pp. 1–68.

[9]Bernard J. La Londe, Martha C. Cooper, and Thomas G. Noordewier, *Customer Service: A Management Perspective* (Chicago: Council of Logistics Management, 1988), p. 5.

A customer service representative of Merck-Medco Managed Care fields a call, quickly accesses the patient's prescription information, and reminds the patient that a refill is due.

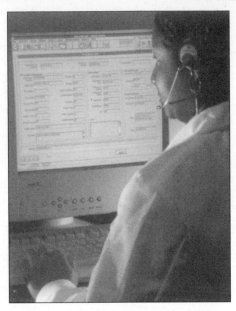

- Home Depot reviews home project tasks with customers to help improve the quality of its efforts.
- Printer Quad/Graphics sponsors a workshop twice a year. Customers meet the CEO, and employees escort them through plant facilities. The goal is to exchange information, so that the company and its employees are trained and oriented with respect to their roles in the service design and production activities.[10]

TQM and Customer Service

Do Customers Always Complain to Firms?

It is very expensive to win customers. Keeping customers should be a paramount concern. Determining what customers need in terms of service levels and delivering upon those needs in a cost-effective and efficient manner should be a key concern of the logistics function. A goal should be to "do it right the first time," to prevent complaints from ever occurring. A recent study indicates that for every customer that complains, as many as 19 simply choose to stop doing business with the organization, and usually tell their associates about their negative experience.[11]

However, the complainers have much to offer in terms of potential learning. They may alert the organization to a widespread problem which, if addressed, could reduce future complaints and help retain those "noncomplaining" customers who otherwise would

---

[10]How Companies Involve Customers," *Executive Report on Customer Satisfaction* 8, no. 9 (May 15, 1995), p. 7.

[11]George R. Walther, "Upside Down Marketing," Audio-Tech Business Book Summary 3, no. 5, section 1 (Mar. 1994), p. 4.

Box 2–1

L. L. Bean: Customer Service Excellence

L. L. Bean is a catalog distributor of high-quality, durable outdoor clothing and sportswear. Located in Freeport, Maine, L. L. Bean has been widely noted as a leading company in providing excellent customer satisfaction and excellent customer service through its logistics/distribution operations.

L. L. Bean receives most of its orders by telephone. It needs to respond quickly and accurately to filling and shipping customer orders for products that vary a great deal in size and shape. As a result, orders are filled manually. One of the secrets to L. L. Bean's success is that, based on worker suggestions, it stocks high sales volume items close to packing stations. This minimizes excessive movement of product, reducing order-filling time and improving efficiency.

L. L. Bean's performance is phenomenal. It boasts of a fill rate that averages 99.9 percent even during the Christmas season when it ships over 134,000 packages a day. As a result of its outstanding performance in distribution, many leading organizations, such as Xerox and Chrysler, have benchmarked L. L. Bean's logistics operations.

Source: Synthesized from Otis Port, John Carey, Kerin Kelly, and Stephanie Anderson, "Special Report: Quality," *Business Week,* Nov. 30, 1992, pp. 66–72; and Otis Port, "Beg, Borrow and Benchmark," *Business Week,* Nov. 30, 1992, pp. 74–75.

---

have simply walked away. In addition, if handled well, complaining customers actually become more loyal, and are nine times more likely to do business with that organization again in the future.[12]

Thus, quality in customer service, from initial dealings with the customer to proper handling of problems, is critical in achieving high levels of customer service. This in turn contributes to high levels of customer satisfaction.

Elements of Customer Service

Customer Service before, during, and after the Sale

The elements of customer service can be classified into three groups: pretransaction, transaction, and posttransaction elements. These groups are linked to the definitions of marketing which incorporate the notion of market transactions—before, during, and after the sale.[13] This conceptualization is depicted in Figure 2–1.

Pretransaction Elements.   The pretransaction elements of customer service tend to be related to the organization's policies regarding customer service, and can have a significant impact on customers' perceptions of the organization and their overall satisfaction. These elements are not all directly related to logistics. They must be formulated and in place before the organization can consistently implement and execute its customer service activities. Pretransaction elements include the following:

A Written Statement of Customer Service Policy Is Vital

1. **A written statement of customer service policy.** This policy would define service standards, which should be tied to customers' needs. It should include metrics for

---

[12]Ibid.

[13]La Londe and Zinszer, *Customer Service,* pp. 272–82.

FIGURE 2–1

Elements of customer service

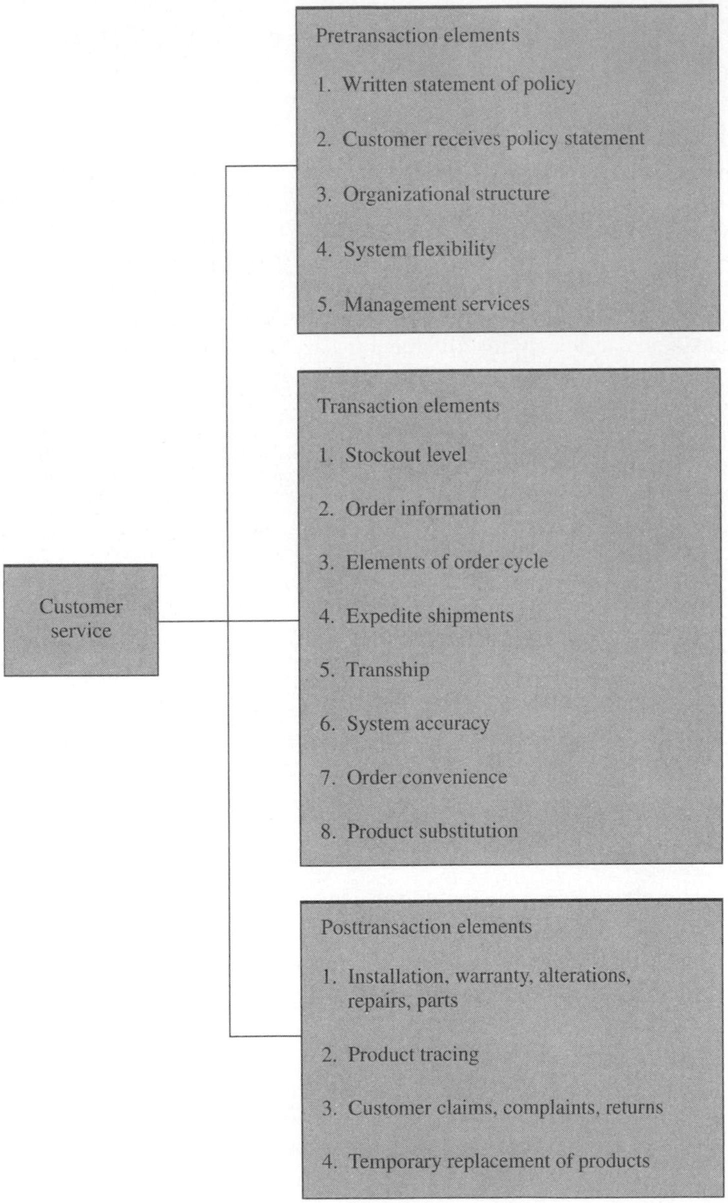

Pretransaction elements
1. Written statement of policy
2. Customer receives policy statement
3. Organizational structure
4. System flexibility
5. Management services

Transaction elements
1. Stockout level
2. Order information
3. Elements of order cycle
4. Expedite shipments
5. Transship
6. System accuracy
7. Order convenience
8. Product substitution

Posttransaction elements
1. Installation, warranty, alterations, repairs, parts
2. Product tracing
3. Customer claims, complaints, returns
4. Temporary replacement of products

Customer service

Source: Bernard J. La Londe and Paul H. Zinszer, *Customer Service: Meaning and Measurement* (Chicago: National Council of Physical Distribution Management, 1976), p. 281.

A ConAgra grocery products sales rep creates a greater market presence with more personal involvement at the store level.

tracking service performance and the frequency of reporting actual performance, and be measurable and actionable.

2. **Customers provided with a written statement of policy.** A written statement lets the customer know what to expect and helps to safeguard against unreasonable expectations. It should provide the customer with information about how to respond if expected service levels are not achieved by the firm.

Organizations Must Be Structured so that They Are Responsive to Customers

3. **Organization structure.** The organization structure best suited to ensure the achievement of customer service goals varies across organizations, but the senior logistics executive should be positioned at a high level and have high visibility within the firm. The structure should facilitate both internal and external communication of policies, performance, and corrective actions as needed. Customers should have easy access to individuals within the organization who can satisfy their needs and answer their questions. Imagine the frustration felt by a customer who has experienced a problem with product delivery or performance, who telephones the selling organization only to be put on hold, and transferred from one representative to another, continually reexplaining his or her entire problem! The customer may never call that organization again for anything.

4. **System flexibility.** Flexibility and contingency plans should be built into the system, which allow the organization to successfully respond to unforeseen events such as labor strikes, material shortages, and natural disasters such as hurricanes or flooding.

5. **Management services.** Providing the customers with help in merchandising, improving inventory management, and ordering are examples of some of the services an organization may provide to its customers. These may be provided in the form of

training manuals, seminars, or one-on-one consultation. The services may be free of charge or fee based.

All of these pretransaction elements may be experienced by the customer outside of the normal order cycle. Decisions relating to the pretransaction elements tend to be relatively stable, long-term decisions that are changed infrequently. This provides some stability for the customer in terms of expectations.

Transaction Elements.   Transaction elements are the elements that are *normally* considered to be associated with customer service, and include the following:

How Much Inventory Should a Firm Have to Satisfy Customer Demand?

1. **Stockout level.** The stockout level measures product availability. Stockouts should be monitored by product and customer in order to better track potential problems. When stockouts occur, the organization should endeavor to maintain customer goodwill by offering a suitable substitute, drop-shipping from another location to the customer if possible, or expediting the shipment once the out-of-stock item arrives.

2. **Order information availability.** Customers' expectations regarding access to all types of information related to their orders have increased dramatically because of the availability of relatively inexpensive computing power. This includes information on inventory status, order status, expected or actual shipping date, and back-order status. Tracking back-order performance is important because customers pay close attention to problems and exceptions to delivery. Back-orders should be tracked by customer and by product type, so that recurring problems become visible and can be addressed in a timely fashion.

3. **System accuracy.** In addition to the ability to rapidly obtain a wide variety of data, customers expect that the information they receive about order status and stock levels will be accurate. Inaccuracies should be noted and corrected as quickly as possible. Continuing problems require major corrective action and a high level of attention. Errors are costly to correct for customers and suppliers in terms of time delays and paperwork created.

Order Cycle Defined

4. **Consistency of order cycle.** The order cycle is the total time from customer initiation of the order through receipt of the product or service by the customer. Thus, if a salesperson obtains an order from a customer and holds it for five days before entering the order, that adds five days to the order cycle time, even though those five days were invisible to the distribution center. Elements of the order cycle include placing the order, order entry if separate from placement, order processing, order picking and packing for shipment, transit time, and the actual delivery process. Customers tend to be more concerned with the consistency of lead times than with absolute lead time, so it is important to monitor actual performance in this regard and take corrective action if needed. However, with the increased emphasis on time-based competition, reducing total cycle time has received greater attention. This topic will be discussed later in this chapter.

5. **Special handling of shipments.** Special handling of shipments relates to any order that cannot be managed through the normal delivery system. This could happen because it needs to be expedited or has unique shipping requirements. The costs of such shipments are considerably higher than standard shipments. However, the cost of a lost customer could be higher still. The company should determine which customers or situations warrant special treatment and which do not.

6. **Transshipment.** Transshipments refer to shipping products between various distribution locations to avoid stockouts. For companies with multiple locations, some sort

Figure 2–2

Impact of product substitution on customer service levels

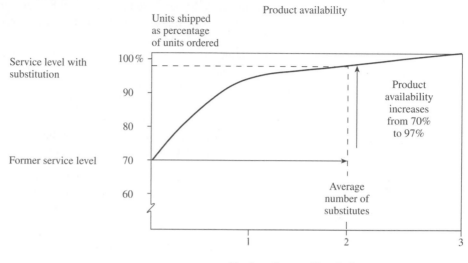

Number of acceptable substitutes

of policy should be in place concerning transshipments as opposed to back-ordering or drop-shipping directly to a customer from more than one location.

7. **Order convenience.** Order convenience refers to how easy it is for a customer to place an order. Customers prefer suppliers that are user-friendly. If forms are confusing, terms are not standardized, or the waiting time on hold on the telephone is long, customers may experience dissatisfaction. Order-related problems should be monitored and identified by talking directly with customers. Problems should be noted and corrected.

When Should Customers Be Offered Substitutes for Items That Are Not Available?

8. **Product substitution.** Product substitution occurs when the product that the customer ordered is not available, but is replaced by a different size of the same item or a different product that will perform just as well or better. Figure 2–2 illustrates that if a product currently has a 70 percent service level and one acceptable substitute that also has a 70 percent service level, a manufacturer can effectively raise its service level for that product to 91 percent. If the product has two acceptable substitutes, the in-stock availability becomes 97 percent! Thus, the ability to provide a customer with acceptable substitutes can significantly improve the firm's service level.

Developing Product Substitution Policies

The manufacturer should work with its customers to develop product substitution policies and should keep its customers informed of those policies. It is always a good idea to check with the customer before substituting one product for another. For example, if a custom furniture manufacturer orders one-gallon cans of lacquer, and the distributor is out of stock, the distributor may offer five-gallon units in their place. This may not be suitable because the furniture manufacturer may use only two gallons for each job and does not want to have partially used five-gallon containers of lacquer. However, if the distributor offers one-half-gallon cans at the same price per gallon, this may be a perfectly acceptable substitute to the customer.

The transaction elements of customer service often receive the most attention, because they are the most immediate and apparent to the customer. For example, in a recent survey of 1,300 companies, Ryder Systems found that 80 percent of respondents believed delivery of the product was as important as the quality of the product itself.[14]

Service after the Sale

Posttransaction Elements. The posttransaction elements of customer service support the product or service after the customer has received it. Historically, this has tended to be the most neglected of the three groups of customer service elements, in part because a relatively small proportion of customers complain about poor service. However, retaining and satisfying current customers can be much more profitable than finding new customers. For example, Ford Motor Company estimated that "the lifetime value of a typical customer [is] $178,000."[15] Posttransaction elements include:

1. **Installation, warranty, repairs, and service parts.** These elements should be an important consideration in almost all purchases, especially purchases of capital equipment where such costs tend to far outweigh the cost of the purchased item itself.[16] These elements should receive the same attention and scrutiny as transaction elements.

2. **Product tracking.** Product tracking, also referred to as product tracing, is an important customer service element. For example, in order to inform consumers of potential problems, firms must be able to recall potentially dangerous products from the market once the potential hazard has been identified.

Reverse Logistics

3. **Customer complaints, claims, and returns.** To resolve customer complaints, an accurate on-line information system is needed to process the data from the customer, monitor trends, and provide the customer with the most current information available. Logistics systems are designed to move products to customers, so the cost of nonroutine handling, particularly of small shipments such as customer returns, tends to be high. Customer returns go through the logistics process in reverse; hence the term **reverse logistics.**[17] Corporate policies should be established to handle these complaints as efficiently and effectively as possible.

4. **Product replacement.** Depending on the item, having backup product temporarily available when the item is being serviced can be critical. For example, some automobile dealerships provide loaner cars to their customers at no charge while their cars are being serviced. This minimizes the inconvenience and may create a more loyal customer.

Importance of Customer Service for Gaining Strategic Advantage

Customer Service Is the Key Interface between Marketing and Logistics

Customer service is the output of the logistics system and is the key interface between the marketing and logistics functions, supporting the "place" element of the marketing

---

[14]"The Future of Transportation," advertisement in _Fortune_, Mar. 21, 1995.

[15]Walther, "Upside Down Marketing," p. 12.

[16]Lisa M. Ellram, _Total Cost Modeling in Purchasing_ (Tempe, AZ: Center for Advanced Purchasing Studies, 1994), p. 10.

[17]Reverse logistics often refers to various environmental aspects such as disposal and recycling. However, the term is more encompassing and includes product recalls and product returns.

Technology

Delivery Speed Keeps Electronic Boutique at the Top of Its Game

"What moves faster than Sonic the Hedgehog?" Probably Electronics Boutique, the video game, computer software and hardware, and accessories retailer. The firm stocks between 2,500 and 3,500 SKUs in each of its 527 stores in the United States, United Kingdom, Canada, and Puerto Rico. Approximately 50 percent of its business occurs during the Christmas selling season. In a highly competitive industry, the firm has become a leader in fast order cycle times, rapid product replenishment, and customer service.

Especially important from a customer service perspective is that the peak sales period of a new video game occurs in the first two weeks after its introduction. This means that if Electronics Boutique

does not have the product in its stores, sales do not occur. "Miss the mark on getting a new release into the stores, and you've disappointed your customers, sending them across the mall to competitors such as Software Etc., Babbage's, or even Toys "Я" Us."

The firm does such a good job in getting new products on its shelves earlier than competitors that Sega selected Electronics Boutique as one of only three retailers to get advance release of the video game called "Saturn," a highly sought-after game during the 1995 Christmas season.

About two years ago, in a new 120,000 square-foot distribution center . . . which handles all replenishment and half of new release distribution, a technological revolution has been taking place. The center now runs on a computerized order management program that structures "putaway" of new receipts . . . Order picking is driven by a paperless pick system Rapistan Demag designed and installed two years ago. An As/400 computer generates pick orders for the stores, creating bar-code labels that are slapped on the three to five boxes each store receives daily, containing 15 to 90 titles each . . . Order pickers scan the bar codes, and LEDs at each pick site light up to indicate the number of pieces of each SKU to pick.

Each box contains the labels store personnel need for the goods in that box . . . When the day's delivery reaches the store, store personnel can rip open the key box with the hottest release and sell right out of the carton, if customers demand it, rather than wasting time unpacking and labeling a whole day's shipment. Store managers can check via computer what's in transit and which carton it's in.

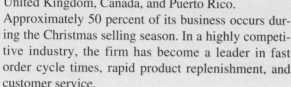

With 2,500 to 3,500 different products in a typical Electonics Boutique retail store, the logistics of providing the right combination of products and services requires the company to be a leader in fast order cycle times, and rapid product replenishment.

Source: Laurie Joan Aron, "Delivery Speed Keeps Electronics Boutique at the Top of Its Game," *Inbound Logistics* 16, no. 1 (Jan. 1996), pp. 30–40.

mix. But even more important, customer service plays a significant role in developing and maintaining customer loyalty and ongoing satisfaction.

The product, pricing, and promotion elements of the marketing mix create value added for customers. However, when the performance of competitors is similar on these attributes, it is customer service that really brings the customer back.

Products and prices are relatively easy for competitors to duplicate. Promotional efforts also can be matched by competitors, with the possible exception of a well-trained and motivated sales force. The satisfactory service encounter, or favorable complaint resolution, is one important way that the organization can really distinguish itself in the eyes of the customer. Thus, logistics can play a key role in contributing to the organization's competitive advantage by providing excellent customer service.

How to Establish a Customer Service Strategy

An organization's entire marketing effort can be neutralized by poorly conceived or executed customer service policies. Yet customer service is often a neglected element of the marketing mix. As a result, customer service standards tend to be based on industry norms, historical practices, or management's judgment of what the customer wants, rather than what the customer really desires. Management often treats all customers the same, not recognizing that different customers want different levels and types of services.[18]

Service Policies Must Be Based on Customer Requirements

It is essential that a firm establish customer service policies based on customer requirements and supportive of the overall marketing strategy. What is the point of manufacturing a great product, pricing it competitively, and promoting it well, if it is not readily available to the consumer? At the same time, customer service policies should be cost efficient, contributing favorably to the firm's overall profitability.

Competitive Benchmarking

One popular method for setting customer service levels is to benchmark competitors' customer service performance. While it may be interesting to see what the competition is doing, this information has limited usefulness. In terms of what the customer requires, how does the firm know if the competition is focusing on the right customer service elements? Therefore, competitive benchmarking alone is insufficient.

Competitive benchmarking should be performed in conjunction with customer surveys that measure the importance of various customer service elements. Opportunities to close the "gaps" between customer requirements and the firm's performance can be identified. The firm can then target the primary customers of specific competitors while protecting its own key accounts from potential competitor inroads.

A number of methods have been suggested for establishing customer service strategies. Four have the greatest value:

1. Determining customer service levels based on customer reactions to stockouts at the retail level.
2. Cost/revenue trade-offs.

---

[18]Joseph Fuller, James O'Conor and Richard Rawlinson, "Tailored Logistics: The Next Advantage," *Harvard Business Review* 94, no. 3 (May–June 1994), pp. 87–94.

3. ABC analysis of customer service.

4. Customer service audits.

Each of these techniques is discussed below.

Customer Reactions to Stockouts

Most manufacturers do not sell exclusively to end users. Instead, they sell to wholesalers or other intermediaries who sell to the final customer. For this reason, it may be difficult for a manufacturer to assess the impact of stockouts on end users. For example, an out-of-stock situation at the manufacturer's warehouse does not necessarily mean an out-of-stock product at the retail level. One way to establish the desirable level of customer service at the retail level is to determine consumers' response to stockouts, which can include substituting another size of the same brand, switching brands, or perhaps going to a different store to buy the items. For most products, consumers will switch stores only if they believe that the product they desire is superior to or considerably less expensive than the available substitutes.

Stockouts Have Different Effects on Channel Members

To see how stockouts have a different effect at various levels of the channel of distribution, we can examine the infant formula industry. Most infant formula manufacturers do not advertise their products on national television, and generally limit the amount they spend on consumer-directed media advertising. They also limit the use of price promotion. Instead, they spend their marketing dollars on sample products to give to doctors and hospitals, who in turn give the product samples to new mothers. New mothers are often told not to switch brands because the baby develops a preference and may not adapt well to another brand. In addition, most mothers assume that their doctor would give them only the recommended products as samples. Thus, when the mother goes to the store to buy infant formula and the product is out of stock, she will go to a different store rather than risk switching products.

Understanding behavior at different levels in the channel is critical in formulating customer service strategies.[19] The penalty for being out of stock at a particular retail store is relatively low for the manufacturer of infant formula because the vast majority of customers will switch stores.

However, the penalty of running out of stock at a particular doctor or hospital is very high if, for example, it causes the doctor to switch from Mead Johnson's brand, Enfamil, to Ross Laboratories' brand, Similac. Mead Johnson will likely lose all the potential future business from mothers who give birth at that hospital and continue to feed their baby with Similac rather than Enfamil. Thus, the customer service implications are clear: Hospitals and doctors require a very high level of customer service, which may mean in-stock availability above 99 percent, and very short lead times of 24 to 48 hours.

The retailer also is likely to lose the sale if it is out of the customer's preferred brand of infant formula. The inventory position on an item such as infant formula, which would actually cause the customer to switch stores in case of a stockout, must be monitored

---

[19]See Larry W. Emmelhainz, Margaret A. Emmelhainz, and James R. Stock, "Logistics Implications of Retail Stockouts," *Journal of Business Logistics* 12, no. 2 (1991), pp. 129–42.

closely by the retailer. Frequent stockouts on such an item can cause customers to switch stores permanently.

When the manufacturer is aware of the implications of stockouts at the retail level, it can make adjustments in order cycle times, fill rates, transportation options, and other strategies that will result in higher levels of product availability in retail stores.

Sears and Whirlpool Establish Strategies to Avoid Stockouts

For some items, customers may be more willing to wait, even expecting to place a special order rather than have the item available in stock. For example, in the 1970s, Sears and Whirlpool conducted a study of customers and discovered that, in general, customers did not expect to take delivery of major appliances the same day they were purchased. Frequently, they were willing to wait five to seven days for the appliance, unless it was an emergency. This knowledge had major implications for the logistics system. Sears was required to have only floor models available for display purposes at the retail level and few if any appliances were required in inventory at their distribution centers (DCs).

Whirlpool used this knowledge to create and refine a new logistics approach. Appliances were manufactured and shipped to a large mixing warehouse in Marion, Ohio. Sears regional DCs were shipped products only when orders were received from Sears customers. Once there, they were cross-docked to a truck for delivery to the consumer. Using this system, Whirlpool was able to provide delivery of appliances to Sears consumers in 48 to 72 hours in most major U.S. markets.

For some products, consumers who face an out-of-stock situation on the particular stockkeeping unit (SKU) they desire will choose to switch brands or sizes. A **stockkeeping unit (SKU)** is an individual product that differs from other products in some way. The difference could be in size, color, scent, flavor, or some other relevant characteristic. If a customer switches to another size of the same product, the customer service level should be measured relative to the desired SKU and all substitutes. If a customer switches brands, then that manufacturer has lost a sale today; in addition, the customer may come to prefer the new brand, so that significant future sales are lost as well. The value of these lost sales is difficult to determine. As long as some sort of acceptable substitute is available to the customer, retailers are less concerned with this type of stockout because they have still made the sale.

If there are unplanned decreases in customer service levels because of labor strikes, materials shortages, or other factors, the company can look at sales "before," "during," and "after" such events to assess the impact of various levels of customer service on retail sales. This assessment is only relevant if the competitor's product was still available during the same period.

Cost/Revenue Trade-Offs

Cost Trade-Offs in Integrated Logistics Management

The total of logistics expenditures such as carrying inventory, transportation, and information/order processing can be viewed as the company's expenditures on customer service. Figure 2–3 illustrates the cost trade-offs and considerations required to implement an integrated logistics management concept. The objective is to provide the organization with the lowest total logistics costs, given a specific customer service level. While Figure 2–3 shows logistics issues as trade-offs, in some cases simultaneous improvement may occur in multiple areas, and the organization reduces its total cost while providing im-

FIGURE 2–3

Cost trade-offs required in a logistics system

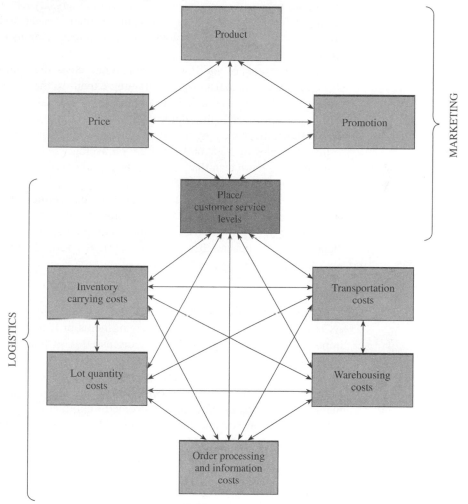

Marketing objective: Allocate resources to the marketing mix to maximize the long-run profitability of the firm.
Logistics objective: Minimize total costs given the customer service objective where: Total costs = Transportation costs + Warehousing costs + Order processing and information costs + Lot quantity costs + Inventory carrying costs.

Source: Adapted from Douglas M. Lambert, *The Development of an Inventory Costing Methodology: A Study of the Costs Associated with Holding Inventory* (Chicago: National Council of Physical Distribution Management, 1976), p. 7.

proved customer service. This is only possible by taking the perspective of the total system in the long run.

An Example of Cost Trade-Offs in Retailing

For example, if a major department store chain wishes to increase its retail in-stock levels to 98 percent, point-of-sale (POS) data that track actual sales by store and by SKU might be used. Thus, it has to invest in information technology such as in-store scanners of bar codes at each cash register and software to compile and analyze the data in addition to generating meaningful management reports. To maximize its leverage, the discount store chain also might want to invest in an **electronic data interchange (EDI)** system to provide rapid, two-way communication with its suppliers. Hypothetically, this could cost the chain roughly $200,000 per store. Thus, management appears to be making a trade-off: By investing in information technology, the store is increasing its costs to improve customer service levels.

If each dollar of additional sales revenue costs the company 60 cents in product costs, plus variable logistics and marketing expenses, the contribution margin is 40 percent. For each additional dollar of sales revenue, what sales need to be generated to break even? We can calculate the additional sales required to offset this investment by dividing the $200,000 investment by the 40 percent contribution margin. Thus, the company needs to increase sales by $500,000 per store, on average, to break even on this investment. If sales increase more than that, they will be ahead on this investment, achieving a positive return, rather than "trading off."

This decision would need to be evaluated considering how likely it is that each store would increase sales by $500,000 over some specified time period.[20] If current sales are $10 million per store per year, it would seem much more feasible to recover this investment in a timely manner than if sales are currently $2 million per store per year.

ABC Analysis/Pareto's Law

In Chapter 1, we used the abbreviation ABC for activity-based costing. Here, ABC analysis is used to denote a tool for classifying items or activities according to their relative importance. This concept also will be discussed in greater depth in conjunction with inventory management in Chapter 5.

ABC Analysis Described

The logic behind ABC classification is that some customers and products are more beneficial to a firm than others: beneficial in terms of profitability, sales revenues, segment growth rates, or other factors deemed important by corporate management. Using profitability as an example, the most profitable customer-product combinations should receive the most attention and, hence, higher customer service levels. Profitability should be measured according to a product's contribution toward fixed costs and profits.

Like ABC analysis, **Pareto's law** notes that many situations are dominated by relatively few critical elements. For example 80 percent of the bottlenecks in the logistics system may be caused by the failure of one carrier. This concept is also commonly referred to as the

The "80/20" Rule

80/20 rule. Table 2–1 illustrates how the importance of customers can be combined with the importance of products to establish customer service levels that are the most beneficial to a firm. This matrix can be interpreted as follows (using profitability as the relevant factor):

Customer-Product Contribution Matrix

1. Products in category A are the most profitable, followed by B, C, and D. The products in category A usually represent a small percentage of the firm's product line. The products in category D, on the other hand, are the least profitable and probably make up about 80 percent of the firm's product line.

---

[20]If the time period to recover the investment was greater than one year, the increased sales should be discounted to reflect the time value of money; that is, the concept that money received in the future is less valuable than money received today, or in the near term.

TABLE 2–1   A Customer-Product Contribution Matrix

	Product			
Customer Classification	*A*	*B*	*C*	*D*
I	1	2	6	10
II	3	4	7	12
III	5	8	13	16
IV	9	14	15	19
V	11	17	18	20

Source: Adapted from Bernard J. La Londe and Paul H. Zinszer, *Customer Service: Meaning and Measurement* (Chicago: National Council of Physical Distribution Management, 1976), p. 181.

TABLE 2–2   Making the Customer-Product Contribution Matrix Operational

Priority Range	*In-Stock Availability Standard (%)*	*Order Cycle Time Standard (Hours)*	*Order Completeness Standard (%)*
1–5	100%	48 hrs.	99%
6–10	95	72	97
11–15	90	96	95
16–20	85	120	93

Source: Adapted from Bernard J. La Londe and Paul H. Zinszer, *Customer Service: Meaning and Measurement* (Chicago: National Council of Physical Distribution Management, 1976), p. 182.

2. Customers in category I are the most profitable, but are few in number, maybe 5 to 10. Category V are the least profitable customers, accounting for the majority of the firm's customers.

3. The most profitable customer-product combination occurs when customers in category I buy products in category A. The next most profitable combines B products with category I customers, then category II customers with A products, and so on. Management will use some logical approach in ranking the various customer and product combinations. An example of one such approach is illustrated in Table 2–1.

An organization can use the data in Table 2–1 in setting customer service policies, as illustrated in Table 2–2. For example, the standards for customer-product combinations in priority range 1–5 may be 100 percent in-stock product availability, 48 hours' order cycle time, and 99 percent of all orders shipped complete (i.e., no partial shipments).

Again, if profitability is the relevant measure of customer and product importance, this method recognizes the need to provide the most profitable customers with the highest service levels in order to encourage customer loyalty and thus repeat business. Those less-profitable accounts can be made more attractive to the firm by reducing the service levels, which makes them less costly to service and therefore more profitable.

Consistency of Service Is Important Irrespective of the Service Level

A lower level of customer service does not mean that the service provided is less consistent. In other words, whatever the service level, 100 percent consistency of service is provided whenever possible. Consistency is important to all customers, irrespective of size or type. However, the important issue is that it is usually less expensive for a firm to deliver lower levels of customer service (e.g., lead time) with high consistency than it is to provide higher levels of service with low consistency; for example, a 72-hour order cycle time with high consistency is less expensive to the provider firm than a 48-hour order cycle time with low consistency.

As a generic example, it may be possible for a firm to develop several strategies that allow it to reduce its logistics costs while providing an acceptable level of customer service. Generally, the longer the order cycle time, the less inventory a firm must carry. As we will see later in this book, less inventory increases a firm's profits through reductions in inventory carrying costs. Also, it may be possible to obtain lower rates when transportation carriers are given more time to deliver products. As long as consistent service is provided to customers, most firms can plan ahead, knowing that order cycle times will be longer.

Gillette Implements a Multieschelon Customer Service Program

The principle is illustrated by Gillette, a global producer of razors and other personal care products. Gillette requires that small, **less-than-truckload (LTL)** customer orders be received by a certain day and time to be processed that week. These orders are then pooled and shipped with other orders destined for a particular geographical area. This is referred to as scheduled delivery.

The benefit of this approach is that Gillette can fill a truck, which lowers its transportation cost. It also reduces the absolute transit time and the variability in transit time, because the truck is going to one general area and dropping off products, or delivering to a regional carrier in the market for local delivery, rather than having many stops in dispersed areas. If customers miss the order deadline, they are given the option of waiting until the next week or having their order shipped LTL. Most opt to wait, for the cost and service reasons mentioned above.

The key to developing a customer-product contribution matrix that meets the needs of both the customer and the firm is knowing how customers define service, identifying which service components are most important, and determining how much customer service to provide. Customer service audits are often conducted to obtain this information prior to a firm establishing any kind of policy relating to customer-product profitability and customer service levels.

The Customer Service Audit

A customer service audit is used as a means of evaluating the level of service a company is providing and as a benchmark for assessing the impact of changes in customer service policies. The objectives of the audit are to (1) identify critical customer service elements, (2) identify how performance of those elements is controlled, and (3) assess the quality and capabilities of the internal information system.

Objectives of a Customer Service Audit

The audit typically includes four distinct stages:

- External customer service audit.
- Internal customer service audit.

- Identifying opportunities and methods for improvement.
- Establishing customer service levels.

Each of these stages is discussed below. While the stages tend to occur sequentially, there is some overlap between stages.

The External Customer Service Audit.   The external audit should be the starting point in an overall customer service audit, one that examines both internal and external factors. The key goals of the external audit are to:

Goals of an External Customer Service Audit

- Identify the elements of customer service that customers believe are important in their buying decision.
- Determine the customer's perception of the service being offered by the firm and each major competitor.

The first step is to determine which service elements the customer perceives as important. This should be accomplished using an interview format with a sample of the firm's customers. Interviewing can provide insights into customer service issues of which the firm may otherwise be unaware. Some of the key customer service elements to a retailer assessing a manufacturer might be the consistency of order cycle time, absolute length of the order cycle, whether the supplier uses EDI, the number of orders shipped complete, back-order policies of the firm, billing procedures, and backhaul policies. Because many service variables differ by industry, it is important to survey customers in order to establish their service requirements.

The Marketing Function Must Be Included in the Audit Process

It is beneficial to involve the marketing function in the external customer service audit for a number of reasons. First, marketing often has the major decision-making authority in terms of making customer service trade-offs within the marketing mix. Also, the marketing function can provide useful insights into a better understanding of customer needs and the incorporation of the most relevant issues in the design of any instruments used to collect customer data. A high level of involvement will create buy-in, so that more support will be provided by the marketing function when it later implements the audit findings.

If the organization does not have a corporate market research department to assist in the customer service audit, it could hire an outside research firm or consultant, or contact a local university where an undergraduate or MBA class, a professor, or doctoral candidate may be willing to carry out such research. Using an outside party often increases the response rate and reduces the response bias.

Once the important customer service elements have been identified, the next major step is to develop a questionnaire to gain feedback from a statistically valid and representative group of the firm's customers.

Using a Questionnaire to Obtain Customer Feedback

The questionnaire is used to determine the relative importance of various customer service elements, other marketing mix elements, and measures of the perceived performance of the firm and its major competitors on each element. Ideally, the organization would like to perform very well on those elements that customers and potential customers evaluate as the most important. This enables management to develop strategies by customer segments while considering the strengths and weaknesses of specific competitors.

It is important that the questionnaire ask about customers' relative market share with each supplier, as well as their overall perception/satisfaction with their supplier(s). This will allow the firm to examine the relationship between its sales and its performance as perceived by customers.

The questionnaire also should explore customers' expected levels of performance on key issues now and in the future. Demographic data will allow the firm to assess perceived performance differences according to geographical region, customer type, and other relevant dimensions.

For best results and validity, the questionnaire should be pretested with a small sample of customers to ensure that no critical issues have been missed and that customers are able to understand and answer the questions.

The External Audit Enables the Firm to Identify Service Problems and Opportunities

The results obtained from the customer service survey can reveal both opportunities and potential problems. The variables that receive the highest importance ratings from customers should be the focus of analysis and action. For example, if a firm scores significantly higher than competitors on key ratings, it could use those findings in their promotional mix—and perhaps generate increased sales revenues. If an organization scores significantly lower than competitors on important service variables or big gaps exist between desired performance and actual performance, it faces potentially significant problems. Without some corrective action, market share could erode if competitors take advantage of a firm's weaknesses.

Importance Ratings Cannot Be Used Alone

It would appear that the variables that receive the highest ratings should play the greatest role in share of business. However, this may not always be the case for a number of reasons:

- All of an industry's major suppliers may be performing at "threshold" levels or at approximately equal levels, which makes it difficult to distinguish among suppliers.
- Variables for which there are significant variances in vendor performance may be better predictors of market share than the variables described above.
- Customers may rate a variable as extremely important, but there may be few or no suppliers providing satisfactory levels of service for that variable. Such variables offer opportunities to provide differential service in the marketplace.
- A variable may be rated low in importance with a low variance in response. In addition, there may be no single supplier providing adequate service levels. Therefore, customers do not recognize the advantages of superior service for that variable. If one supplier improved performance, it could lead to gains in market share.[21]

The organization should look simultaneously at the importance of various elements and its position relative to competing suppliers. If customers perceive the supplier's performance to be poor on some attributes relative to management's beliefs on organization performance, management should determine whether it is measuring the firm's perfor-

---

[21]Jay U. Sterling and Douglas M. Lambert, "Establishing Customer Service Strategies within the Marketing Mix," *Journal of Business Logistics* 8, no. 1 (1987), pp. 1–30.

Corrective Actions Resulting from the Service Audit

mance the same way that customers are and, if not, adjust measurements to align with customer measures.

If the actual performance is better than customers believe it to be, management should determine how to educate customers and to inform them of actual performance. This might include providing the sales force with monthly or quarterly performance reports by customer that salespeople would review with each of their accounts.

The internal customer service audit can be conducted while the external customer service audit is occurring.

The Internal Customer Service Audit.   The internal customer service audit reviews the firm's current service practices. This provides a benchmark for assessing the impact of changes in customer service levels. As such, the internal customer service audit should address the following issues:

Internal Audit Questions

- How is customer service currently measured within the firm?
- What are the units of service measurement?
- What are the service performance standards or objectives?
- What is the current level of attainment: results versus objectives?
- How are these measures derived from the firm's information and/or the order processing systems?
- What is the internal customer service reporting system?
- How do each of the functional areas of the business (e.g., logistics, marketing) perceive customer service?
- What are the relationships between these functional areas in terms of communication and control?[22]

Goal of the Internal Audit

The major goal of the internal audit is to measure gaps between the firm's service practices and customer requirements. Customers' perceptions of current service levels also should be determined, because they may perceive service as worse than it really is. If that is the case, customers' perceptions should be the focus of change through education and promotion, rather than changing the firm's service levels.

Another key area to assess in the internal customer service audit is the communication flows from the customer to the company, and communication flows within the company, including the measurement and reporting of service performance. Communication is a major factor in determining how well customer service–related issues are understood. Without excellent internal communications, customer service tends to be reactive and problem focused, rather than proactive.[23]

Communication between the customer and the organization relates primarily to the order-ship-receive cycle. The seven major issues are order entry, postorder entry inquiry/change, delivery, postdelivery reports of any shipment-related problems, billing, post-billing discrepancies, and payment-related issues. The audit can help determine the effectiveness of the communications.

---

[22]Ibid., p. 52.
[23]La Londe and Zinszer, *Customer Service,* p. 168.

Management Interviews Are a Good Source of Information

Management interviews are an important source of information. Interviews should be conducted with managers responsible for all logistics activities and activities with which logistics interacts, such as accounting/finance, sales/marketing, and production. The interviews should examine:

- Definition of responsibilities.
- Size and organizational structure.
- Decision-making authority and process.
- Performance measurements and results.
- Definition of customer service.
- Management's perception of how customers define customer service.
- Company plans to alter or improve customer service.
- Intrafunctional communications.
- Interfunctional communications.
- Communications with key contacts such as consumers, customers, transportation carriers, and suppliers.

In addition, management should give its assessment of customer service measurement and reporting. This should include not only assessment of how current systems measure performance, but also how the firm interfaces with customers on service-related issues.

Identifying Potential Solutions.   The external service audit enables management to identify problems with the firm's customer service and marketing strategies. Used in combination with the internal service audit, it may help management adjust these strategies and vary them by segment in order to increase profitability. But if management wants to use such information to develop customer service and marketing strategies for optimal profitability, it must use these data to benchmark against competitors.

The most meaningful competitive benchmarking occurs when customer evaluations of competitors' performance are compared with each other and with customers' evaluations of the importance of supplier attributes. Once management has used this type of analysis to determine opportunities for gaining a competitive advantage, every effort should be made to identify best practice; that is, the most cost-effective use of technology and systems regardless of the industry in which it has been successfully implemented. Noncompetitors are much more likely to share their knowledge and, through such contacts, it is possible to uncover potential opportunities.[24]

A Methodology for Competitive Benchmarking

A methodology for competitive benchmarking can be demonstrated from the data contained in Table 2–3. The analysis involves a comparison of the performance of the major manufacturers in the office furniture industry. The first step is to generate a table with evaluations of the level of importance for each of the variables and the performance

---

[24]For more information on this approach, see Douglas M. Lambert and Arun Sharma, "A Customer-Based Competitive Analysis for Logistics Decisions," *International Journal of Physical Distribution and Logistics Management* 20, no. 1 (1990), pp. 17–24.

TABLE 2–3   Importance and Performance of Office Furniture Manufacturers on Selected Customer Service Attributes

Rank	Variable Number	Variable Description	Overall Importance—All Dealers		Dealer Evaluations of Manufacturers										
					Mfr. 1		Mfr. 2		Mfr. 3		Mfr. 4		Mfr. 5		Mfr. 6	
			Mean	SD	Mean	SD	Mean	SD	Mean	SD	Mean	SD	Mean	SD	Mean	SD
1	9	Ability of manufacturer to meet promised delivery date (on-time shipments)	6.4	0.8	5.9	1.0	4.1	1.6	4.7	1.6	6.6	0.6	3.7	1.8	3.3	1.6
2	39	Accuracy in filling orders (correct product is shipped)	6.4	0.8	5.6	1.1	4.7	1.4	5.0	1.3	5.8	1.1	5.1	1.2	4.4	1.5
3	90	Competitiveness of price	6.3	1.0	5.1	1.2	4.9	1.4	4.5	1.5	5.4	1.3	4.4	1.5	3.6	1.8
4	40	Advance notice on shipping delays	6.1	0.9	4.6	1.9	3.0	1.6	3.7	1.7	5.1	1.7	3.0	1.7	3.1	1.7
5	94	Special pricing discounts available on contract/project quotes	6.1	1.1	5.4	1.3	4.0	1.7	4.1	1.6	6.0	1.2	4.7	1.5	4.5	1.8
6	3	Overall manufacturing and design quality of product relative to the price range involved	6.0	0.9	6.0	1.0	5.3	1.3	5.1	1.2	6.5	0.8	5.2	1.3	4.8	1.5
7	16	Updated and current price data, specifications, and promotion materials provided by manufacturer	6.0	0.9	5.7	1.3	4.1	1.5	4.8	1.4	6.3	0.9	4.9	1.7	4.3	1.9
8	47	Timely response to requests for assistance from manufacturer's sales representative	6.0	0.9	5.2	1.7	4.6	1.6	4.4	1.6	5.4	1.6	4.2	2.0	4.3	1.7

continued

TABLE 2–3 *continued*

Rank	Variable Number	Variable Description	Overall Importance—All Dealers Mean	SD	Mfr. 1 Mean	SD	Mrf. 2 Mean	SD	Mfr. 3 Mean	SD	Mfr. 4 Mean	SD	Mrf. 5 Mean	SD	Mfr. 6 Mean	SD
							Dealer Evaluations of Manufacturers									
9	14	Order cycle consistency (small variability in promised versus actual delivery; that is, vendor consistently meets expected date)	6.0	0.9	5.8	1.0	4.1	1.5	4.8	1.4	6.3	0.9	3.6	1.7	4.4	1.7
10	4b	Length of promised order cycle (lead times (from order submission to delivery) for base line/in-stock ("quick ship") product	6.0	1.0	6.1	1.1	4.5	1.4	4.9	1.5	6.2	1.1	4.3	1.7	3.7	2.0
11	54	Accuracy of manufacturer in forecasting and committing to estimated shipping dates on contract/project orders	6.0	1.0	5.5	1.2	4.0	1.6	4.3	1.4	6.3	1.1	3.8	1.7	3.5	1.6
12	49a	Completeness of order (% of line items eventually shipped complete)—made-to-order product (contract orders)	6.0	1.0	5.5	1.2	4.3	1.2	4.7	1.3	6.0	1.1	4.4	1.4	4.0	1.6
...																
43	45	Free WATS line provided for entering orders with manufacturer	5.3	1.5	3.6	2.5	4.8	2.0	3.4	2.6	3.5	2.6	2.0	1.5	3.8	1.9
...																
50	33a	Price range of product line offering (e.g. low, medium, high price levels) for major vendor	5.0	1.3	4.4	1.5	4.6	1.6	5.1	1.5	5.2	1.4	4.3	1.6	3.9	1.6
...																
101	77	Store layout planning assistance from manufacturer	2.9	1.6	4.2	1.7	3.0	1.5	3.4	1.6	4.7	1.6	3.0	1.4	3.4	1.2

Note: Mean (average score) based on a scale of 1 (not important) through 7 (very important).

Source: Adapted from Jay U. Sterling and Douglas M. Lambert, "Customer Service Research: Past, Present and Future," *International Journal of Physical Distribution and Materials Management* 19, no. 2 (1989), p. 19.

evaluations of all firms within the industry. The next step is to compare the importance score of each service attribute to customer evaluations of each manufacturer's performance.

Table 2–3 shows that one of the most important attributes identified by customers, "ability to meet promised delivery date," received a score of 6.4 (out of 7.0) in overall importance. Manufacturer 1's perceived performance of 5.9 is significantly less than the mean importance score of 6.4 as well as the perceived performance of manufacturer 4 (6.6). Therefore, manufacturer 1 must improve its performance to meet customer requirements and achieve competitive parity.

The variable "advance notice on shipping delays," rated 6.1 in overall importance, presents a different situation. None of the manufacturers were perceived to be meeting customer expectations. Therefore, if manufacturer 1 wished to improve its performance in this area, it could use this as a source of performance differentiation compared with that of its competitors, and perhaps gain a competitive advantage.

On the other hand, the variable "free inward WATS [Wide-Area Telecommunications Service] telephone lines for placing orders with manufacturers" was ranked as 43rd in overall importance. No manufacturer received a high evaluation for its performance on this service. This indicated that customers did not perceive the advantages of this attribute because the service was not presently available from any manufacturer. If a competitor were to change its order entry procedures to allow customers the ability to telephone their orders without cost, then two things could happen: (1) Customers would likely change their opinion of the advantages of this capability and consequently increase their perceptions of the importance of free WATS service; (2) the supplier that first introduced this service could achieve a definite, long-term competitive advantage.

Indeed, this is precisely what happened in the office furniture industry. One of the major manufacturers implemented an on-line, interactive order entry system utilizing free inward WATS service. Within three years, this capability became a norm for all of the major firms in the industry. Therefore, when looking for ways to improve customer service, it is equally critical to look at both important and relatively unimportant services because conditions change over time.

This highlights the notion that customers may not really know what they want because it has never been offered to them. By improving on performance of current parameters, companies are sentenced to "keeping up with the competition." Yet, history shows that the real winners are those who see an opportunity first and stake out a leadership position, taking on risk on investing in the future before it arrives.[25] It is the unexploited, unserved market that holds real growth opportunities.

Service Performance Standards and the Measurement of Performance

Establishing Customer Service Levels.   The final steps in the audit process are the actual establishment of service performance standards and the ongoing measurement of performance. Management must set target service levels for segments based on factors such as the type of customer, geographic area, channel of distribution, and product line. It must communicate this information to all employees responsible for implementing service

---

[25]Gary Hamel and C. K. Prahalad, "Seeing the Future First," *Fortune,* Sept. 5, 1994, pp. 64–70.

policies while also developing compensation programs that encourage employees to reach the firm's customer service objectives. Formal reports that document performance are a necessity.

Finally, management must repeat the process periodically to ensure that the firm's customer service policies and programs reflect current customer needs. The collection of customer information over time is the most useful element in guiding overall corporate strategy and the specific strategies of the various functional areas within the firm.

Developing and Reporting Customer Service Standards

Once management has determined which elements of customer service are most important, it must develop standards of performance. Designated employees should regularly report results to the appropriate levels of management. Customer service performance can be measured and controlled by:

Measuring and Controlling Customer Service Performance

- Establishing quantitative standards of performance for each service element.
- Measuring actual performance for each service element.
- Analyzing variance between actual services provided and the standard.
- Taking corrective action as needed to bring actual performance into line.[26]

Customer cooperation is essential for the company to obtain information about speed, dependability, and condition of the delivered product. To be effective, customers must be convinced that service measurement and monitoring will help improve future service. Whirlpool does extensive measurement of ERX, with which it has formed a partnership to improve its customer service. This relationship is discussed in Box 2–2.

Figure 2–4 contains a number of possible measures of service performance. The emphasis any firm places on individual elements must be based on what customers believe is important. Service elements such as inventory availability, meeting delivery dates, order status, order tracing, and back-order status require good communication between firms and their customers.

Order processing offers significant potential for improving customer service because many companies have not kept pace with technological developments in that field. Con-

Automated Order Processing Improves Customer Service

sider the possibilities for improved communications if customers can either phone their orders to customer service representatives who have CRTs or input orders on their own computer terminals. Immediate information on inventory availability can be provided and product substitution can be arranged when a stockout occurs. Customers also can be given target delivery dates for their orders.

Figure 2–5 gives examples of customer service standards. The standards chosen should be those that best reflect what customers actually require, rather than what management thinks they need. Designated employees should measure and compare service

---

[26]William H. Hutchinson, Jr., and John F. Stolle, "How to Manage Customer Service," *Harvard Business Review* 46, no. 6 (Nov.–Dec. 1968), pp. 85–96; and Fuller, O'Conor, and Rawlinson, "Tailored Logistics," pp. 87–94.

Box 2–2

Whirlpool and ERX: Partners in Customer Service

In the early 1990s, Whirlpool Corporation, a leading manufacturer of major household appliances, became concerned about the low levels of on-time delivery performance to its dealers. It desired improved customer service, but believed that an outside expert would be able to do a better job. After all, it saw its own core competency in manufacturing high-quality, reliable appliances. Thus, Whirlpool was looking for an organization that could provide it with full logistics service for its finished product—from warehousing to final delivery and setup.

To meet Whirlpool's needs, a joint venture was established with Mark VII, Inc., and Elston Richards Warehousing Company, forming ERX. ERX obtained six of the eight Quality Express locations. Quality Express is a national delivery network designed to serve over 10,000 retailers and 50,000 construction sites. This system involves eight regional distribution centers which hold inventory. Inventory is then shipped to one of 48 locations *only* as needed to fill orders. Thus, the locations do not hold inventory, but serve as cross-docking sites. Whirlpool is responsible for all of the fixed distribution center costs and the leases for the trucks. It wants ERX

to focus on customer service, not assets. To better meet customers' needs and lower customers' inventory requirements, Whirlpool decreased its minimum order quantity from about a third of a truckload to five or six pieces. Now customers place smaller, more frequent orders. This levels demand considerably, which makes it much easier for Whirlpool to plan its own production and inventory needs. Thus, Whirlpool can focus on what it does best: manufacturing.

ERX is an important link to customer service and customer satisfaction. The delivery drivers unload the trucks and can handle returns, claims, and even reimburse the dealer. They also can unload and uncarton the product. Customer service also has improved in more tangible ways. Order cycle time has been reduced from over five days to one day in most cases, and two days in remote areas. On-time delivery has gone from 85 percent to over 99 percent, and damage has been reduced. This innovative relationship has benefited both Whirlpool and ERX.

Source: From Jay U. Sterling, "Managing Long-Term Partnership Alliances: How to Succeed and Fail," *Proceedings of the Annual Conference of the Council of Logistics Management*, Oct. 16–19, 1994, pp. 301–11.

performance to the standard, and report this information to management on a regular and timely basis.

The firm's order processing and accounting information systems can provide much of the information necessary for developing a customer-product contribution matrix and meaningful customer service management reports. We will discuss some of these important interfaces in Chapter 3, "Logistics Information Systems."

Impediments to an Effective Customer Service Strategy

Many companies have ineffective or inconsistent customer service strategies, policies, or programs. Sometimes even the best of firms may have difficulty in overcoming the various barriers or impediments that can hinder the implementation of successful customer service processes.

Examples of Customer Service Impediments

Failing to target specific market segments based on the services they require can be a costly mistake. Management sometimes hesitates to offer different levels of *customer service* for fear of violating antitrust laws. Service differentials are often viewed much like price

FIGURE 2–4

Possible measures of customer service performance

Pretransaction elements
- Advice on nonavailability
- Quality of sales representatives
- Regular calls by sales reps
- Monitors customer stock levels
- Consults on new product/package development
- Reviews product depth and breadth regularly
- Communicates target delivery dates

Transaction elements
- Ordering convenience
- Acknowledgement of orders
- Credit terms offered
- Handling of queries
- Frequency of delivery
- Order cycle time
- Order cycle time reliability
- On-time deliveries
- Shipment delays (cycle variance)
- Ability to handle emergency orders
- Orders filled completely
- Order status information
- Order tracing capability
- Backorder percentages
- Availability/fill-rate percentages
- Shipment shortages
- Product substitutes

Posttransaction elements
- Accuracy of invoices
- Returns/adjustments
- Damage (concealed and visible)
- Well stacked pallets
- Easy to read "use by dates" on packaging
- Quality of packaging for in-store display

FIGURE 2–5

Examples of customer service standards

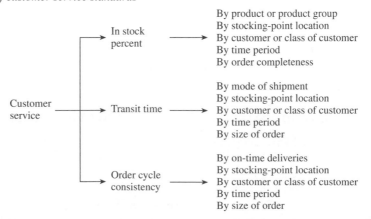

In stock percent
- By product or product group
- By stocking-point location
- By customer or class of customer
- By time period
- By order completeness

Transit time
- By mode of shipment
- By stocking-point location
- By customer or class of customer
- By time period
- By size of order

Order cycle consistency
- By on-time deliveries
- By stocking-point location
- By customer or class of customer
- By time period
- By size of order

differentials that must be cost justified. However, most firms do not have the necessary cost information to do so.[27] Nevertheless, management can segment markets based on customers' evaluations of the importance of marketing services and can obtain the necessary financial data to determine the costs of serving such markets through a variety of research techniques.

Salespeople Can Create Unrealistic Customer Expectations

Salespeople can create unrealistic customer service expectations by promising faster delivery of orders to "make the sale." But most customers value reliability and consistency in filling orders more than speed of delivery. Consequently, attempting to decrease the order cycle on an ad hoc basis typically increases transportation costs resulting from the need to expedite shipments. Order-assembly costs can rise because of the disruption of normal work flows that occur in "rush" situations. Also, the so-called domino effect might occur. When salespeople override customer service policies on shipping dates, lead times, shipping points, modes of transportation, and units of sale, they disrupt the orders of other customers and cause an increase in logistics costs throughout the system.[28]

A firm's customer service standards and performance expectations are affected substantially by the competitive environment and perceived traditional industry practices. Consequently, it is vital that management understands industry norms, expectations, and the costs required to provide high levels of customer service.

Evidence suggests, however, that many firms do not measure the cost-effectiveness of service levels and have no effective way of determining competitive service levels. Information is fed back into the company through a sales organization that is frequently concerned with raising service levels or through industry anecdotes and outraged customers. The net result of this information feedback is that firms may overreact to imprecise cues from the marketplace or even from within their own firms.[29]

Considering the vast sums of money firms spend on research and development and advertising, it makes little sense for a company not to adequately research the levels of customer service necessary for profitable long-range business development.

Finally, the economic environment of the 1980s and 1990s has caused top management to push for higher inventory turnover rates. As highlighted in the press, this is still a major source of effort today.[30] This emphasis may lead to lower levels of customer service.

Global Customer Service Issues

The global perspective focuses on seeking common market demands worldwide, rather than cutting up world markets and treating them as separate entities with very different product needs.[31] On the other hand, different parts of the world have different service

---

[27]See Ellram, *Total Cost Modeling in Purchasing.*

[28]Douglas M. Lambert, James R. Stock, and Jay U. Sterling, "A Gap Analysis of Buyer and Seller Perceptions of the Importance of Marketing Mix Attributes," in *Enhancing Knowledge Development in Marketing,* ed. William Bearden et al. (Chicago: American Marketing Association, 1990), p. 208.

[29]La Londe, Cooper, and Noordewier, *Customer Service,* p. 29.

[30]Shawn Tully, "Raiding a Company's Hidden Cash," *Fortune,* Aug. 22, 1994, pp. 82–87.

[31]Martin Christopher, "Customer Service Strategies for International Markets," *Annual Proceedings of the Council of Logistics Management* (Oak Brook, IL: Council of Logistics Management, 1989), p. 327.

Global

Surviving and Thriving in an Era of Unprecedented Change: A Japanese Case Study

Japan's entire wholesaling industry is under extreme pressure these days, pushing companies like Ryoshoku, the country's second largest food wholesaler, to reinvent themselves. Economic conditions are driving retail price discounting, large format retail stores are emerging, discount chains are growing more popular, and market power is shifting to consumers and retailers. These factors are turning wholesalers' attention to meeting demands for lower supply chain costs.

Further complicating the picture, large retailers have increased the amount of direct trade between themselves and large manufacturers, in some cases squeezing out the wholesaler altogether. The American transplant, Toys "Я" Us Japan, has been a highly visible pioneer in reducing costs through bypassing traditional wholesaling channels and purchasing directly from the manufacturer. Moreover, large retailers have invested in point-of-sale data capture and analysis capabilities, reducing their reliance on wholesalers for these services. To meet these challenges and to maintain and increase market share, leading wholesalers are strengthening and expanding value-added services . . . particularly emphasizing information services, retail support, and logistics.

Faced with these changes and prospects for continued distribution system restructuring in Japan,

Ryoshoku is positioning itself to thrive in these uncertain times. Aiming to bridge the gap between manufacturers and retailers . . . it is developing market-based transfer/consolidation centers to provide its retail customers with frequent and efficient full-truckload, multiple-vendor deliveries to stores. This combined delivery service is designed to offer the same flexible small-lot, just-in-time service demanded by stores without all the inefficiencies, let alone the traffic congestion and pollution problems, of unconsolidated deliveries. Ryoshoku has invested in nine regional distribution centers to provide flexible unit picking and order assembly services.

To provide these sophisticated and constantly evolving logistics services, Ryoshoku has set up an independent logistics organization that has equal status as the marketing, sales, and information systems groups. Leveraging the company's strong culture of innovation and technology, the new logistics organization is pursuing efficient consumer response (ECR)–based partnerships along the supply chain and expanding information systems links to retailer storefronts and suppliers' operations.

Source: David Frentzel, "Surviving and Thriving in an Era of Unprecedented Change: Case Studies of Four Agile Japanese Companies," *Logistics!* a publication of Mercer Management Consulting (Fall 1995), pp. 11–12.

needs related to information availability, order completeness, expected lead times, and so on.[32] In addition, the local congestion, infrastructure, communications, and time differences may make it impossible to achieve high levels of customer service. The service provided by market should match local customer needs and expectations to the greatest degree possible.

---

[32]For some global examples, see Mauro Caputo and Valeria Mininno, "Internal, Vertical and Horizontal Logistics Integration in Italian Grocery Distribution," *International Journal of Physical Distribution and Logistics Management* 26, no. 9 (1996), pp. 64–90; Jae-Il Kim, "Logistics in Korea: Current State and Future Directions," *International Journal of Physical Distribution and Logistics Management* 26, no. 10 (1996), pp. 6–21; and Andrei N. Rodnikov, "Logostics in Command and Mixed Economies: The Russian Experience," *International Journal of Physical Distribution and Logistics Management* 24, no. 2 (1994), pp. 4–14.

Coca-Cola Services Japan and the United States

For example, Coca-Cola provides very different types of service in Japan than in the United States. Coca-Cola delivery drivers in Japan focus on providing merchandising in supermarkets, help in processing bills in small "mom and pop" operations, and respond to signals from communication systems in vending machines, so that time is not wasted delivering to full machines.[33] This creates the most efficient and effective customer service policy, rather than simply duplicating domestic patterns worldwide. The latter strategy could be both ineffective and expensive.

Improving Customer Service Performance

Effective Customer Service Strategies Require a Thorough Understanding of Customers and the Service Process

The levels of customer service a firm achieves often can be improved through one or more of the following actions: (1) thoroughly researching customer needs, (2) setting service levels that make realistic trade-offs between revenues and expenses, (3) making use of the latest technology in order processing systems, and (4) measuring and evaluating the performance of individual logistics activities.

An effective customer service strategy *must* be based on an understanding of how customers define *service*. The internal and external customer service audits previously discussed were utilized to obtain customer inputs into service strategies, plans, and programs. As described above, Coca-Cola has identified the distinctive logistics needs of its customers.[34]

Once the firm has determined their customers' view of service, management must select a customer service strategy that advances the firm's objectives for long-term profits, return on investment, or other relevant measures of performance. The optimum level of customer service is the one that obtains and retains the most profitable customers.

Order processing systems can have a major impact on customer service levels and perceptions (see Chapter 3). Many firms have antiquated order processing systems. The primary benefit of automating them is to reduce the order cycle time. Given that most customers prefer a consistent delivery cycle to a shorter one, it usually is unnecessary—even unwise—to reduce the order cycle time for customers. But by using the additional time internally for planning, the company can achieve savings in transportation, warehousing, inventory carrying costs, production planning, and purchasing.

Automation improves customer service by providing the following benefits to the customer:

- Better product availability.
- More accurate invoices.
- The ability to lower safety stock levels and their associated inventory carrying costs.
- Improved access to information on order status.

---

[33]Fuller, O'Conor, and Rawlinson, "Tailored Logistics," p. 88.

[34]For a discussion of logistics competitive advantage, see Ronald Henkoff, "Deliveriing the Goods," *Fortune,* Feb. 28, 1994, pp. 64–78.

In short, automated order processing systems enhance the firm's ability to perform all of the transaction and posttransaction elements of customer service. The benefits of improved logistics systems are demonstrated by the following example:

P&G and Wal-Mart Improve Customer Service

Procter & Gamble (P&G) now receives daily data by satellite on Wal-Mart's Pampers (disposable diapers) sales and forecasts and ships orders automatically. As a result, Wal-Mart can maintain smaller inventories and still cut the number of times it runs out of Pampers. And P&G has increased its proportion of on-time deliveries to 99.6 percent from 94 percent. P&G has gone from being a vendor that was maybe the least desirable to deal with to one of the most desirable. The results have been astonishing. P&Gs volume at Wal-Mart grew by more than 40 percent, or by more than $200 million.[35]

Finally, the development of an effective customer service program requires the establishment of customer service standards that do the following:

Customer Service Standards Are Necessary

- Reflect the customer's point of view.
- Provide an operational and objective measure of service performance.
- Provide management with cues for corrective action.[36]

Management also should measure and evaluate the impact of individual logistics activities—transportation, warehousing, inventory management, production planning, purchasing, and order processing—on customer service. Designated employees should report achievements regularly to the appropriate levels of management. Management should compare actual performance to standards and take corrective action when performance is inadequate. For management to be successful and efficient, a firm needs timely information. It also is necessary to hold individuals accountable for their performance because information alone does not guarantee improved decision making.

The success of a firm is no longer based exclusively on selling products; instead it is the value-added services provided that can create a differential and sustainable competitive advantage.[37] Logistics can be an important source of such service-based advantage.

Summary

This chapter opened with a definition of customer service. Although the importance of the individual elements of customer service varies from company to company, we reviewed the common elements that are of concern to most companies. We also saw the necessity for a customer service strategy consistent with corporate and marketing strategies. The successful implementation of the integrated logistics management concept depends on management's knowledge of the costs associated with different system designs, and of the relationship between system design and customer service levels. We saw how management can obtain better knowledge of the costs and revenues associated with different levels of customer service, and how it can implement cost/service trade-offs.

---

[35]Zachary Schiller, "Stalking the New Consumer," *Business Week,* Aug. 28, 1989, p. 62.

[36]La Londe and Zinszer, *Customer Service,* p. 180.

[37]Rahul Jacob, "Why Some Customers Are More Equal than Others," *Fortune,* Sept. 19, 1994, pp. 215–24.

Creative Solutions

Quality in Logistics

Total quality principles and tools have been woven into the very fabric of how we do business at Procter & Gamble. In my view, two of the most powerful aspects of total quality within P&G have been in process improvement and measurement systems.

Process improvement taught us that all parts of logistics are interrelated processes, not stand-alone functions. In response to this, P&G completely reorganized the company, creating a new organization—Product Supply. We broke down the traditional organizational hierarchy of manufacturing, engineering, distribution, and purchases. This has had a tremendous positive effect on the way we interact with each other and on how we view our work.

We also introduced measurement systems to virtually every process within Product Supply. For example, all over the world, P&G employees are measuring customer satisfaction through tracking of "perfect orders." Total order management, as we know it, monitors our logistics performance from the time an order is generated until it is billed to the customer.

This quality thinking is building a high degree of reliability throughout our entire delivery system. These measures are included in our carrier performance standards and shared openly with our carriers. This helps them gain a clear understanding of our strategies and what is expected from them. The top carriers soon develop their own measures and present this to us on a regular basis.

We have learned that data are the most powerful tools we have. Without data, you are just another person with an opinion.

Source: Dennis M. Whan, "Quality in Logistics," *Transportation and Distribution* 34, no. 7 (July 1993), p. 33.

The customer service audit is a method of determining the existing service levels, determining how performance is measured and reported, and appraising the impact of changes in customer service policy. Firms should conduct both internal and external service audits. Surveys are one means of finding out what management and customers view as important aspects of customer service.

Although customer service may represent the best opportunity for a firm to achieve a sustainable competitive advantage, many firms implement customer service strategies that are simply duplicates of those implemented by their major competitors. The audit framework represented in this chapter can be used by management to collect and analyze customer and competitive information.

We saw that there are some common roadblocks to an effective customer service strategy as well as some ways to improve performance. In the next chapter, we will present the influence of information technology on the efficiency and effectiveness of the logistics function.

Suggested Readings

Anderson, Eugene W.; Claes Fornell; and Donald R. Lehmann. *Economic Consequences of Providing Quality and Customer Satisfaction,* Report No. 93–112. Boston: Marketing Science Institute, 1993.

Byrne, Pat. "Improve the Customer Service Cycle." *Transportation and Distribution* 33, no. 6 (June 1993), pp. 66–67.

Catalano, Doug, and Bill Read. "Customer Service: A Process Approach." *Perspectives,* a publication of CSC Consulting (1994), pp. 1–7.

"A Compendium of Research in Customer Service." *International Journal of Physical Distribution and Logistics Management* 24, no. 4 (1994), pp. 1–68.

Copacino, William. "A New Way to Look at Your Customers." *Traffic Management* 30, no. 4 (Apr. 1994), pp. 29–30.

"An Energized Process for Improving Customer Service." *NAPM Insights,* Apr. 1992, pp. 9–11.

Frentzel, David. "Needs-Based Customer Segmentation." *Japan Institute of Logistics System Journal,* May–June 1995, pp. 49–53.

Fuller, Joseph; James O'Conor; and Richard Rawlinson. "Tailored Logistics: The Next Advantage." *Harvard Business Review* 94, no. 3 (May–June 1994), pp. 87–94.

Harrington, Lisa. "Logistics Unlocks Customer Satisfaction." *Transportation and Distribution* 36, no. 5 (May 1995), pp. 41–44.

Henkoff, Ronald. "Delivering the Goods." *Fortune,* Feb. 28, 1994, pp. 64–78.

Jacob, Rahul. "Why Some Customers Are More Equal than Others," *Fortune,* Sept. 19, 1994, pp. 215–24.

Kyj, Myroslaw J. "Customer Service as a Competitive Tool." *Industrial Marketing Management* 16 (1987), pp. 225–30.

La Londe, Bernard J., and Martha C. Cooper. *Partnerships in Providing Customer Service: A Third-Party Perspective.* Oak Brook, IL: Council of Logistics Management, 1989.

La Londe, Bernard J.; Martha C. Cooper; and Thomas G. Noordewier. *Customer Service: A Management Perspective.* Oak Brook, IL: Council of Logistics Management, 1988.

Lewis, James P. "Think like Your Customers." *Transportation and Distribution* 34, no. 7 (July 1993), pp. 26–28.

Mathe, Herve, and Roy D. Shapiro. "Managing the Service Mix: After Sale Service for Competitive Advantage." *The International Journal of Logistics Management* 1, no. 1 (1990), pp. 44–50.

Pine, B. Joseph, II; Don Peppers; and Martha Rogers. "Do You Want to Keep Your Customers Forever?" *Harvard Business Review* 95, no. 2 (Mar.–Apr. 1995), pp. 103–14.

Power, Christopher; Lisa Driscoll; and Earl Bohn. "Smart Selling: How Companies Are Winning Over Today's Tougher Customer." *Business Week,* Aug. 3, 1992, p. 46.

Sharma, Arun; Dhruv Grewal; and Michael Levy. "The Customer Satisfaction/Logistics Interface." *Journal of Business Logistics* 16, no. 2 (1995), pp. 1–21.

Sterling, Jay U., and Douglas M. Lambert. "Customer Service Research: Past, Present and Future." *International Journal of Physical Distribution and Materials Management* 19, no. 2 (1989), pp. 3–23.

———. "Establishing Customer Service Strategies within the Marketing Mix." *Journal of Business Logistics.* 8, no. 1 (1987), pp. 1–30.

Walther, George R. "Upside Down Marketing." Audio-Tech Business Book Summaries 3, no. 5, sect. 1 (Mar. 1994), p. 4.

Questions and Problems

1. Customer service can be defined as an activity, a performance measure, or a corporate philosophy. What are the advantages and disadvantages of each of these types of definitions? How would you define customer service?

2. Explain the importance of the pretransaction, transaction, and posttransaction elements of customer service.

3. Explain why customer service should be integrated with other components of the marketing mix when management develops the firm's marketing strategy.

4. Explain how ABC analysis can be used to improve the efficiency of the customer service activity.

5. Why is the customer service audit important when establishing a firm's customer service strategy?

6. Why does automation of the order processing system represent such an attractive opportunity for improving customer service? How is this service improvement accomplished?

7. What are some ways that management can improve the firm's customer service performance?

8. Why is it important to use pretransaction, transaction, and posttransaction customer service elements to identify and develop customer service measures? Discuss specific examples of measures in each category.

THE DISTRIBUTION CHALLENGE!
PROBLEM: A CHILLING DILEMMA

The company is a maker of lightweight commercial air-conditioning units, the kind that goes on the roofs of strip malls or restaurants. We'll call it Arctic Atmospheres, Inc. Approximately 85 percent of its sales are replacement models, which means that the company relies heavily on repeat customers.

An air conditioner usually breaks down with little or no warning. Often the customer's livelihood depends on finding a replacement within a day or two—never mind who the provider is. "It's like an earthquake," notes Bob Sabath, vice president of Mercer Management Consulting. "You know it's going to happen in the next five years—you just don't know if it's tomorrow."

Arctic Atmospheres brought in Mercer Management to help optimize the company's distribution network and revive sales. At the time it had 16 distribution centers and warehouses around the country, stocking 45 different models.

Mercer's first idea was to shrink the network to four or five strategically placed warehouses, each with extensive inventory. That would have chopped 22 percent off Arctic's costs, but would have made rapid delivery tough. An Arctic vice president of marketing argued that the company should go in the opposite direction and expand to 24 locations with a full range of products. That would have been prohibitively expensive.

In the end, Arctic's solution combined local availability with minimal stocks. Which way did the company go?

What Is Your Solution?

Source: "Distribution: The Challenge," *Distribution* 95, no. 8 (Aug. 1996), p. 104.

Logistics Information Systems

Chapter Outline

Chapter Objectives

- To provide an overview of the ways that computers can be used in logistics operations.
- To show how the order processing system can influence the performance of logistics activities.
- To show how the order processing system can form the core of logistics information systems at both a tactical and strategic level, supporting customer service goals.
- To discuss the role of information technology in supporting time-based competition.
- To identify uses of advanced information technologies, such as decision support systems (DSSs), artificial intelligence (AI), and expert systems (ES), in logistics.

Introduction

Information Technology Will Affect the Growth and Development of Logistics

Computer and information technology has been utilized to support logistics for many years. It grew rapidly with the introduction of microcomputers in the early 1980s. Information technology is seen as the key factor that will affect the growth and development of logistics.[1]

The order processing system is the nerve center of the logistics system. A customer order serves as the communications message that sets the logistics process in motion. The speed and quality of the information flows have a direct impact on the cost and efficiency of the entire operation. Slow and erratic communications can lead to lost customers or excessive transportation, inventory, and warehousing costs, as well as possible manufacturing inefficiencies caused by frequent production line changes. The order processing and information system forms the foundation for the logistics and corporate management information systems. It is an area that offers considerable potential for improving logistics performance.

Computers Are Used to Support Logistics Activities

Organizations of all types are utilizing computers to support logistics activities. This is especially true for companies thought to be on the "leading edge," that is, leaders in their industry. Such firms are heavy users of computers in order entry, order processing, finished goods inventory control, performance measurement, freight audit/payment, and warehousing. A recent study of world-class logistics practices cited logistics information systems as a key to competitiveness.[2]

Definition of Decision Support System (DSS)

Going beyond "transaction processing and tracking," **decision support systems (DSSs)** are computer-based and support the executive decision-making process. The DSS is an integrative system of subsystems that has the purpose of providing information to aid a decision maker in making better choices than would otherwise be possible.

To support time-based competition, organizations are increasingly using information technologies as a source of competitive advantage. Systems such as quick response (QR), just-in-time (JIT), and efficient consumer response (ECR) are integrating a number of information-based technologies in an effort to reduce order cycle times, speed responsiveness, and lower supply chain inventory.

In addition, more sophisticated applications of information technology such as decision support systems, artificial intelligence, and expert systems are being used directly to support decision making in logistics. The chapter will begin with the customer order cycle, which is at the heart of logistics information systems.

Customer Order Cycle

Components of a Typical Customer Order Cycle

The **customer order cycle** includes all of the elapsed time from the customer's placement of the order to the receipt of the product in an acceptable condition and its place-

---

[1]Bernard J. La Londe and James M. Masters, "The 1996 Ohio State University Survey of Career Patterns in Logistics," *Proceedings of the Annual Conference of the Council of Logistics Management* (Oct. 20–23, 1996), pp. 115–38.

[2]Global Logistics Research Team, Michigan State University, *World Class Logistics: The Challenge of Managing Continuous Change* (Oak Brook, IL: Council of Logistics Management, 1995), pp. 137–64.

FIGURE 3–1

Total order cycle: a customer's perspective

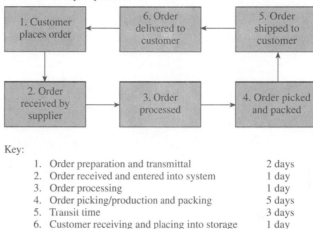

Key:

1.	Order preparation and transmittal	2 days
2.	Order received and entered into system	1 day
3.	Order processing	1 day
4.	Order picking/production and packing	5 days
5.	Transit time	3 days
6.	Customer receiving and placing into storage	1 day
	Total order cycle time	13 days

ment in the customer's inventory. The typical order cycle consists of the following components: (1) order preparation and transmittal, (2) order receipt and order entry, (3) order processing, (4) warehousing picking and packing, (5) order transportation, and (6) customer delivery and unloading.

Figure 3–1 illustrates the flow associated with the order cycle. In this example taken from the customer's point of view, the total order cycle is 13 days. However, many manufacturers make the mistake of measuring and controlling only the portion of the order cycle that is *internal* to their firm. That is, they monitor only the elapsed time from receipt of the customer order until it is shipped. The shortcomings of this approach are obvious.

In the example presented in Figure 3–1, the portion of the total order cycle that is internal to the manufacturer (steps 2, 3, and 4) amounts to only 7 of the 13 days. This ratio is not unusual for companies that do not have an automated order entry and processing system. Improving the efficiency of the seven-day portion of the order cycle that is "controlled" by the manufacturer may be costly compared to eliminating a day from the six days not directly under the manufacturer's control. For example, it may be possible to reduce transit time by as much as one day by monitoring carrier performance and switching business to carriers with faster and more consistent transit times.

Advanced Order Processing Systems Can Reduce the Total Order Cycle

However, a change in the method of order placement and order entry may have the potential for the most significant reduction in order cycle time. An advanced order processing system could reduce the total order cycle by as much as two days. In addition, the improved information flows could enable management to execute the warehousing and transportation more efficiently, reducing the order cycle by another one or two days.

In Figure 3–1, we treated the performance of order cycle components as though no variability occurred. Figure 3–2 illustrates the variability that may occur for each component of the order cycle and for the total. For this illustration, we assume that each of the variable time patterns follows a normal statistical distribution. However, other statistical distributions

FIGURE 3–2

Total order cycle with variability

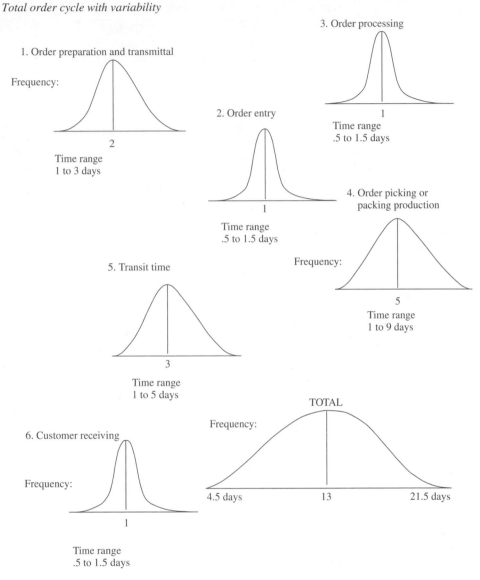

may actually be experienced. In our example, the actual order cycle could range from a low of 4.5 days to as many as 21.5 days, with 13 days as the most likely length. Variability in order cycle time is costly to the manufacturer's customer; the customer must carry extra inventory to cover for possible delays or lose sales as a result of stockouts.

Return to the example in Figure 3–2. If the average order cycle time is 13 days but can be as long as 21.5 days, the customer must maintain additional inventory equivalent to approximately eight days' sales just to cover variability in lead time. If daily sales

TABLE 3–1   Illustration of the Impact of Reduction in Order Cycle and Order Variability on Average Inventory

A. Situation 1: Base Case

Daily sales = 20 units

Order 13-day supply of inventory (20 units × 13 days = 260 units)

$$\frac{260 \text{ order quantity}}{2} = 130 \text{ units average cycle stock}$$

20 units per day × 8 days order cycle variability = 160 units safety stock

Average inventory = Average cycle stock + Safety stock

= 290 units

B. Situation 2: Reduce order cycle by 5 days to 8 days

8 days × 20 units daily sales = 160 unit order quantity

$$\frac{160 \text{ order quantity}}{2} = 80 \text{ units average cycle stock}$$

20 units per day × 8 days order cycle variability = 160 units safety stock

Average inventory = Average cycle stock + Safety stock

= 240 units

C. Situation 3: Reduce safety stock by 5 days due to reduction in variability to 3 days

$$\frac{260 \text{ order quantity}}{2} = 130 \text{ units average cycle stock}$$

20 units per day × 3 days order cycle variability = 60 units safety stock

Average inventory = Average cycle stock + Average safety stock

= 190 units

equal 20 units and the company's economic order quantity is 260 units—a 13-day supply—the average cycle stock is 130 units, one-half the order quantity. The additional inventory required to cover the order cycle variability of eight days is 160 units. Without even considering demand uncertainty, average inventory will increase from 130 units to 290 units because of the variability in the order cycle.

Which has the greatest impact on the customer's inventory—a five-day reduction in the order cycle or a five-day reduction in order cycle variability? Table 3–1 helps illustrate this scenario.

If the customer continued to order the economic order quantity of 260 units, a five-day reduction in the order cycle would result in little or no change in inventories as demonstrated in Table 3–1A. The customer simply waits five days longer before placing an order.

Table 3–1B shows that even if the customer orders 160 units every time instead of 260, making the average cycle stock 80 units instead of 130, safety stock of 160 units is still required to cover the eight days of variability. The result would be a reduction in total average inventory of 50 units, from 290 to 240 units.

**Order Cycle
Consistency Is
Preferred Over Fast
Delivery**

However, Table 3–1C demonstrates that a five-day reduction in order cycle variability would reduce safety stock by 100 units and result in an average inventory of 190 units. This example should make clear why order cycle *consistency* is preferred over fast delivery. Gaining competitive advantage based on reduced order cycle time is fruitless without consistent performance. Calculation of safety stock is described in Chapter 5.

In the next section, we will examine how customer orders enter the order processing function, and the typical path taken by a customer's orders.

How Do Customer Orders Enter the Firm's Order Processing Function?

**Customers Place
Orders in Many
Ways**

A customer may place an order in a number of ways. Historically, customers handwrote orders and gave them to salespeople, mailed them to the supplier, or telephoned them to the manufacturer's order clerk, who then wrote it up. Today, it is more common for a customer to telephone orders to a supplier's customer service representative, who is equipped with a computer terminal networked to the supplier's database.

This type of system allows the customer service representative to determine if the ordered products are available in inventory, and to deduct orders automatically from inventory so that items are not promised to another customer. This improves customer service because if there is a stockout on the item, the representative can inform the customer of product availability and perhaps arrange product substitution while the customer is still on the telephone. In addition, this type of system almost completely eliminates the first two days of the order cycle described in Figure 3–1.

**Electronic Order
Entry**

Electronic methods, such as an electronic terminal with information transmitted by telephone lines, and computer-to-computer hookups such as electronic data interchange (EDI), are commonplace today. These methods support the maximum speed and accuracy in order transmittal and order entry. Generally, rapid forms of order transmittal require an initial investment in equipment and software. However, management can use the time saved in order transmittal to reduce inventories and realize opportunities in transportation consolidation, offsetting the investment.

**There Is a Direct
Trade-Off between
Inventory Carrying
Costs and
Communications
Costs**

There is a direct trade-off between inventory carrying costs and communications costs. In many channels of distribution, significant potential exists for using advanced order processing to improve logistics performance. However, the more sophisticated the communications system, the more vulnerable the company becomes to any internal or external communications malfunctions. With advanced order processing systems and lower inventory levels, safety stocks are substantially reduced, leaving the customer with minimal protection against stockouts that result from any variability in the order cycle time. In addition, customers expect immediate information regarding availability and shipping, and become frustrated when systems go down.

The Path of a Customer's Order

When studying a firm's order processing system, it is important to understand the information flow that begins when a customer places an order. Figure 3–3 represents one interpretation of the path that a customer's order might take. In the first step, shown at upper left, the customer recognizes the need for certain products and transmits an order to the supplier.

FIGURE 3–3

The path of a customer's order

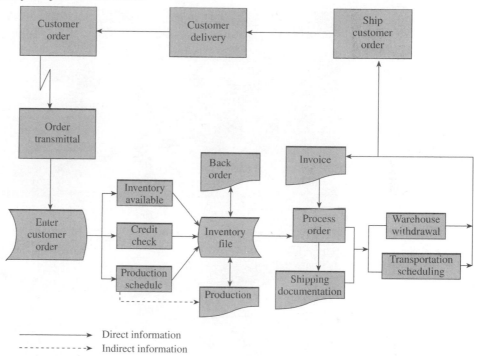

Once the order enters the order processing system, various checks are made to determine if (1) the desired product is available in inventory in the quantities ordered, (2) the customer's credit is satisfactory to accept the order, and (3) the product is scheduled for production if not currently in inventory. If these activities are performed manually, a great amount of time may be required, which can slow down (i.e., lengthen) the order cycle. The norm is that these activities are performed by computer in a minimal amount of time; often these activities can be performed simultaneously with other order cycle activities. The inventory file is then updated, product is back-ordered if necessary, and production is issued a report showing the inventory balance.

Management also can use the information on daily sales as an input to its sales forecasting package. Order processing next provides information to accounting for invoicing, acknowledgment of the order to send to the customer, picking and packing instructions to enable warehouse withdrawal of the product, and shipping documentation. When the product has been pulled from warehouse inventory and transportation has been scheduled, accounting is notified so that invoicing may proceed. All of these processes can be automated seamlessly to reduce additional input of data, and avoid the errors, paper shuffling, and nonvalue added of manual effort.

The primary function of the order processing system is to provide a communication network that links the customer and the manufacturer. In general, greater inconsistency is

A dedicated group of service representatives utilizes the latest computer and information technologies to provide customers with high levels of service.

Order Processing Systems Link Customers with the Company

associated with slower methods of order transmittal. Manual methods of order transmittal require more handling by individuals; consequently, there is greater chance of a communication error. Management can evaluate methods of order transmittal on the basis of speed, cost, consistency, and accuracy. As shown in Table 3–2, order transmittal should be as direct as possible; orders transmitted electronically instead of manually minimize the risk of human error.

The order processing system can communicate useful sales information to marketing (for market analysis and forecasting), to finance (for cash-flow planning), and to logistics or production. Finally, the order processing system provides information to those employees who assign orders to warehouses, clear customer credit, update inventory files, prepare warehouse picking instructions, and prepare shipping instructions and the associated documentation. In advanced systems, many of these activities are computerized.

TABLE 3–2   **Characteristics of Various Order Processing Systems**

Level	Type of Systems	Speed	Cost to Implement/ Maintain	Consistency	Accuracy
1	Manual	Slow	Low	Poor	Low
2	Phone in to customer service rep with a CRT	Intermediate	Intermediate	Good	Intermediate
3	Direct electronic linkage	Rapid	Investment high; operating cost low	Excellent	High

Advanced Order Processing Systems

The Process of Computerized Order Entry

No component of the logistics function has benefited more from electronic and computer technology than order entry and processing. Some advanced systems are so sophisticated that the orders are automatically generated when stock reaches the reorder point.

At the level of advanced order processing systems, shown as the second level in Table 3–2, customers and salespeople transmit orders to distribution centers or corporate headquarters by means of facsimile (fax) or a toll-free telephone number. The order clerk is equipped with a data terminal and can enter and access information on a real-time basis.

As soon as the order clerk enters the customer code, the order format (including the customer's name), billing address, credit code, and shipping address are displayed on the screen. The clerk receives the rest of the order information by fax or verbally and enters it on the terminal; it is displayed along with the header information.

Deviations from standard procedure, such as products on promotion, special pricing arrangements, and allocations, may be highlighted on the terminal (also referred to as the "screen") to ensure that the order clerk grants them special attention. The system can match order quantity against a list of minimum shipment quantities to ensure that the order meets the necessary specifications. If the customer is on the telephone, the clerk may then reread the order. When the order meets all criteria for accuracy and completeness, it is released for processing.

An Example of the Benefits of Computerized Order Entry

A major chemical company replaced a manual system with a system using terminal input similar to the one just described. Prior to the new order entry system, employees took orders over the telephone and recorded them on a form. The orders were then transferred to another form for data entry, and finally were batch-processed into the system. The cost of the terminal order entry system was justified by its savings over the previous manual system. As a result, sales increased by 23 percent with no increase in order processing costs. An additional benefit was that customer billing took place the day after the product was shipped, rather than five days later. This improved cash flow.

Baxter Healthcare Uses Advanced Order Processing Systems

Baxter Healthcare Corporation provides an example of how advanced order processing systems can be used to increase market share and profitability. Baxter manufactures its own products and also distributes products from over 2,000 other manufacturers, with a product line of more than 200,000 active stockkeeping units (SKUs). In the 1970s, the company established computer links with its customers and suppliers. Using terminals provided by Baxter, hospitals could enter orders directly to an assigned Baxter distribution center. In addition, customers could inquire about the availability of a product and determine anticipated availability dates on out-of-stock items.

As a result, hospitals were no longer required to orally communicate their orders to Baxter. This is shown as the third level in Table 3–2. The technology enabled Baxter to cut both its own and customer inventories, improve order fill rates, reduce cycle times, and receive better terms from suppliers because they could purchase in higher volumes. In addition, the company's market share increased dramatically. Even more important, Baxter often locked out rival distributors from its customers because competitors did not have direct communications with hospitals. Baxter continues to analyze industry data that it collects in order to spot order trends and customer needs more quickly.[3]

Becton Dickinson, a manufacturer of medical and surgical products, also has used level 3 advanced order processing/EDI to improve its cost and customer service (see Creative Solutions at the end of this chapter).

Inside Sales/Telemarketing

Inside sales/**telemarketing** is an extension of the advanced order processing systems we have discussed. It enables the firm to maintain contact with existing customers who are not large enough to justify frequent sales visits; increase contact with large, profitable customers; and efficiently explore new market opportunities.

Contacting Customers by Telephone

Customer contacts made by telephone from an inside sales group can achieve the desired market coverage in an economical, cost-effective manner. In addition, the use of data terminals for direct order input integrates inside sales with logistics operations. One of the major cost advantages of inside sales/telemarketing comes from the efficiencies of associated logistics.

One method of improving efficiency is to place all small customers on scheduled deliveries in order to allow for consolidation, thereby reducing transportation and other logistics costs. The expenditure for inside sales must be justified based on projected sales increases, and improved profitability and visibility with customers.

Electronic Data Interchange[4]

Electronic Data Interchange (EDI) Defined

Electronic data interchange (EDI) is the electronic, computer-to-computer transfer of standard business documents between organizations. EDI transmissions allow a document to be directly processed and acted upon by the receiving organization. Depending

---

[3]Catherine L. Harris, "Information Power," *Business Week,* Oct. 14, 1985, p. 109; and Tim Stevens, "R_x for Logistics," *Industry Week,* Sept. 18, 1995, p. 51.

[4]This section is adapted from Lisa M. Ellram and Laura M. Birou, *Purchasing for Bottom-Line Impact* (Burr Ridge, IL: Irwin Business One, 1995).

on the sophistication of the system, there may be no human intervention at the receiving end. EDI specifically replaces more traditional transmission of documents, such as mail, telephone, and even fax, and may go well beyond simple replacement, providing a great deal of additional information, as discussed later.

There are a couple of key points to note about the definition of EDI given above. First, the transfer is computer to computer, which means that fax transmissions do not qualify. Also, the transmission is of standard business documents/forms. Some of the purchasing-related documents that are currently being transmitted by EDI include purchase orders, material releases, invoices, electronic funds transfer (EFT) for payments, shipping notices, and status reports. Thus E-mail and sending information over the Internet, which is nonstandard, free-form data, does not fit the definition of EDI.

This section on EDI will discuss the issue of standards, various types of systems available, EDI benefits and potential problems, EDI implementation, and legal issues.

EDI Standards

For EDI to function properly, computer language compatibility is required. First, the users must have common communication standards. This means that documents are transmitted at a certain speed over particular equipment, and the receiver must be able to accept that speed from that equipment. But this is not enough. In addition, the users must share a common language or message standard or have conversion capabilities. This means that EDI trading partners must have a common definition of words, codes, and symbols; and a common format and order of transmission.

EDI Protocols

One issue is the multitude of EDI protocols in use today. Some are unique systems created by and for a particular company. Some standards have been adopted within a certain industry. The American National Standards Institute (ANSI) has proposed the use of the ANSI X12 standard, which is a form of EDI that supports virtually all standard customer-order associated documents. This standard, adapted from the Transportation Data Coordinating Committee, is supported by the National Association of Purchasing Management.

Many industry associations have established their own standards for EDI, which are to be used between members of firms within their industry. Examples of this include, but are not limited to, the grocery, automotive, retail, warehousing, chemical, and wholesale drug industries.

Types of EDI Systems

Value-Added Networks (VANs)

Several types and variations of EDI systems are in use today. The main types of systems are proprietary systems, **value-added networks (VANs),** and industry associations which were mentioned above. The difference between a proprietary system and a VAN is illustrated in Figure 3–4, and explained below.

"One-to-Many" Systems

Proprietary Systems.   Proprietary systems, also known as *one-to-many systems,* are aptly named, because they involve an EDI system which is owned, managed, and maintained by a single company. That company buys from, and is directly connected with, a number of suppliers. This situation works best when the company that owns the system is

FIGURE 3–4

FIGURE 3–4

Typical EDI configurations

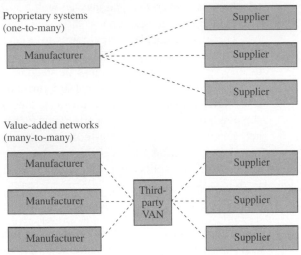

Source: GE Information Service, as reported in Lisa H. Harrington, "The ABCs of EDI," *Traffic Management* 29, no. 8 (Aug. 1990), p. 51.

relatively large and powerful, and can readily persuade key suppliers to become part of the network.

The advantage to the system owner is control. The disadvantages are that it may be expensive to establish and maintain internally, and suppliers may not want to be part of the system because it is unique and may require a dedicated terminal.

"Many-to-Many" Systems

Value-Added Networks. Value-added networks, also known as VANs, third-party networks, or *many-to-many systems,* appear to be the most popular choice for EDI systems. Under VANs, all of the EDI transmissions go through a third-party firm, which acts as a central clearinghouse.

For example, a buying firm sends a number of purchase orders (POs) which go to different suppliers through the VAN. The VAN sorts the POs by supplier and transmits them to the proper supplier. The real "value added" comes in when buyers and suppliers use incompatible communication and/or message standards. The VAN then performs translation "invisibly," so that the user does not need to worry about system compatibility with its trading partners. This represents a big advantage over one-to-many systems.

In addition, the users do not need expertise in EDI standards and issues, as many VANs provide *turnkey,* off-the-shelf systems. This can lower start-up costs and reduce start-up lead time.

Furthermore, a value-added network generally utilizes a "mailbox" feature. With the mailbox, orders and other documents are not transmitted automatically to the receiver when they arrive in the network. Instead, the receiver "picks up" the documents whenever it chooses. This may be at a regular time several times a day, to allow those sending the documents to plan accordingly. This gives the receiver flexibility, particularly if orders are placed or released to be filled at certain times. The user's system does not need to be cluttered with information that will not be acted upon immediately.

Yet another advantage of a VAN is that it can receive from and transmit to one-to-many systems. This means that the supplier who has a customer or customers that use proprietary systems does not need to have a dedicated terminal or direct linkage for each system. This capability of a VAN can increase the acceptability of networking with a customer who uses a proprietary system. Many major corporations, such as General Motors and Coca-Cola, have chosen the VAN route for EDI.[5]

Impact of Internet on VANs

EDI and the Internet

Using EDI over the Internet is rapidly becoming a reality. After initial software purchase and systems setup, EDI over the Internet is virtually "free," versus VAN transmission. There is an Internet Engineering Task Force made of prominent companies such as Compaq, Hewlett-Packard, Digital Corporation, Microsoft, and Oracle that is working to ensure the capability of EDI products on the Internet.[6]

Some major corporations such as NASA Goddard, AVEX Electronics and UNISYS are currently using the Internet for EDI on a regular basis. The revolution has begun—it is likely just a matter of time before the Internet completely replaces VANs.[7]

Benefits of EDI Implementation

It should be obvious from the above discussion that electronic data interchange is a complex system. However, once in place, EDI tends to be a very easy system with which to interface and communicate.

EDI Has Many Potential Benefits

The potential benefits of EDI are many (see Table 3–3). Most of these benefits are self-explanatory. The reduction in clerical work is a major benefit, reducing paperwork, increasing accuracy and speed, and allowing purchasing to shift its attention to more strategic issues.

The above improvements also should bring about a reduction in costs. One expert estimates that EDI can reduce the cost of processing a purchase order by 80 percent.[8] Other firms claim that they have been able to reduce their inventory dramatically owing to improved inventory accuracy and reduced order cycle time.

Specific EDI Applications

EDI at Oregon Steel Mills

Examples of EDI usage and its benefits include applications in manufacturing, merchandising, and service industries. Oregon Steel Mills, a small manufacturer of steel

[5]Mike Cassidy, "The Catalyst to Electronic Commerce," *EDI World,* Apr. 1996, pp. 14–16.

[6]Rik Drummond, "EDI over the Internet Inter-operability," *EDI World,* Apr. 1996, p. 8.

[7]Newton D. Swain, "Surfing for EDI Information," *EDI World,* Apr. 1996, p. 12; Howard Smith, "Caught in the Web," *EDI World,* July 1996, pp. 44–48.

[8]James Carbone, "Make Way for EDI," *Electronics Purchasing,* Sept. 1992, pp. 20–24.

TABLE 3–3   EDI Benefits

- Reduced paperwork to be created and filed
- Improved accuracy due to a reduction in manual processing
- Increased speed of order transmission and other data
- Reduced clerical/administrative effort in data entry, filing, mailing, and related tasks
- Opportunity for proactive contribution by purchasing because less time is spent on "clerical tasks"
- Reduced costs of order placement and related processing and handling
- Improved information availability due to speed of acknowledgments and shipment advises
- Reduced workload and improved accuracy of other departments through linking EDI with other systems, such as bar-coding inventory and electronic funds transfers (EFTs)
- Reduced inventory due to improved accuracy and reduced order cycle time

plate used in construction and military applications, implemented EDI in its traffic department. The firm, utilizing only PCs, transmitted bills of lading electronically to its major rail carriers. Errors were reduced, railcar tracing took minutes instead of hours, manpower requirements in the traffic department were reduced, and customer service levels improved.[9]

In the warehouse, EDI has proven to be extremely beneficial:

> Perhaps no development has had a greater impact on warehouse operations and information systems in the past two years than the requirements by major retailers and manufacturers that their suppliers provide trading partner specific bar-code labeling and EDI Advance Shipment Notices.[10]

EDI at Baxter Healthcare

The labor-intensive nature of the transportation sector and its heavy paperwork demands made the transport industry one of the first to turn to EDI. Baxter Healthcare uses EDI to communicate information on pickup and load status every 500 miles. The company notes that "all of our major carriers are set up on freight payment EDI and electronic funds transfer (EFT), and we are now evolving to self-invoicing, shipper-initiated billing."[11]

Also, Canadian National Railroad has used EDI to ease shipment movements between the United States and Canada.

EDI has become extremely important and widely used within the channels of distribution for consumer and industrial goods. Firms such as Eastman Kodak, Xerox, American Express, Ford, and Honda of America Manufacturing use EDI for the majority of their products moving within their respective channels of distribution.[12]

---

[9]"EDI Proves 'Godsend' to One-Man Department," *Traffic Management* 28, no. 8 (Aug. 1989), pp. 56–67.

[10]Stevens, "R_x for Logistics," p. 50.

[11]Ann Saccomano, "A Primer on Warehousing Information Technology," *Traffic World,* Apr. 1996, pp. 24–26.

[12]Michael Hammer and James Champy, *Reengineering the Corporation* (New York: HarperCollins, 1993), pp. 90–91.

Global

Canadian National Railroad Stays on Track with EDI

Canadian National Railroad (CNR) uses EDI to streamline its operations as well as to compete more effectively with the trucking industry. It sees EDI as essential to its core business processes. There is a cooperative industrywide effort in the rail industry to improve its reliability, accuracy, and timeliness with EDI. When the North American Free Trade Agreement (NAFTA) increased trade between the United States and Canada, EDI became the only viable solution for avoiding costly and needless border-crossing delays.

The U.S. and Canadian customs agencies strongly support EDI. They have adopted sophisticated procedures using EDI for allowing CNR trains to pass through customs without costly delays. For example, CNR has a "U.S. Customs Cargo Manifest"

transaction that contains information on the value, weight, commodity ownership, and other required data as required to meet U.S. and Canadian regulations. These data are also transmitted to the customs broker, who provides the invoice information that ensures the applicable duties are paid. The customs agents review the information in advance, determining whether to clear the shipment or stop it for inspection. Time is critical. If information is delayed and the train is stopped, it can cost CNR more than $10,000 for each hour delayed. This is particularly critical with perishable cargo.

Source: Paul Clarke and Carlson Henderson, "EDI Helps CNR Stay Right on Track," *EDI World,* Aug. 1996, pp. 20–25.

Electronic Mail and the Internet

A variation of EDI, **electronic mail,** also has become an important form of data transmission:

> Electronic mail involves electronic transmission of a variety of data. . . . EDI *always* involves one computer in contact with at least one other, usually transmitting specific documents such as invoices, waybills, or purchase orders.[13]

The electronic mail market is a multibillion dollar business that has exhibited tremendous growth during the past decade. Electronic mail usually occurs over the Internet. Many individuals and organizations subscribe to on-line Internet services, such as America on Line, Prodigy, and Gateway. This allows them access to many data sources and services (some for a fee), as well as allowing them to send E-mail to Internet users at other organizations throughout the world.[14] Many companies, such as MCI, solicit bids and interact regularly with suppliers on E-mail.

Electronic Mail at United Van Lines

One of the major reasons for the growth in E-mail, in addition to the speed and accuracy of its data transmission, is cost savings. United Van Lines of St. Louis has been using E-mail for a number of years and has achieved significant cost savings as a result. Under its previous manual systems, United Van Lines spent several dollars to transit a single communication. With electronic mail, the cost has been reduced to 30 cents a transmission.

[13]Ibid., p. 48.

[14]For an extensive listing of data sources see Harley Hahn and Rick Stout, *The Internet Yellow Pages* (Berkeley, CA: Osborne McGraw-Hill, 1994).

Integrating Order Processing and the Company's Logistics Management Information System

The order processing system sets many logistics activities in motion, such as:

Order Processing Sets Many Logistics Activities in Motion

- Determining the transportation mode, carrier, and loading sequence.
- Inventory assignment and preparation of picking and packing lists.
- Warehouse picking and packing.
- Updating the inventory file; subtracting actual products picked.
- Automatically printing replenishment lists.
- Preparing shipping documents (a bill of lading if using a common carrier).
- Shipping the product to the customer.

Other computerized order processing applications include maintaining inventory levels and preparing productivity reports, financial reports, and special management reports.

Order Processing and Information Flows

Processing an order requires the flow of information from one department to another, as well as the referencing or accessing of several files or databases, such as customer credit status, inventory availability, and transportation schedules. The information system may be fully automated or manual; most are somewhere in between.

Depending on the sophistication of the order processing system and the corporate management information system (MIS), the quality and speed of the information flow will vary, affecting the manufacturer's ability to provide fast and consistent order cycle times and to achieve transportation consolidations and the lowest possible inventory levels.

Generally, manual systems are very slow, inconsistent, and error prone. Information delays occur frequently. A manual system seriously restricts a company's ability to implement integrated logistics management, specifically, to reduce total costs while maintaining or improving customer service. Some common problems include the inability to detect pricing errors, access timely credit information, or determine inventory availability. Lost sales and higher costs combine to reduce the manufacturer's profitability.

Timely and Accurate Information Has Value

Indeed, timely and accurate information has value. Information delays lengthen the order cycle. Automating and integrating the order process frees time and reduces the likelihood of information delays. Automation helps managers integrate the logistics system and allows them to reduce costs through reductions in inventory and freight rates. The communications network is clearly a key factor in achieving least total cost logistics.

Basic Need for Information

How Is a Logistics Information System Used?

A logistics management information system is necessary to provide management with the ability to perform a variety of tasks, including the following:

- Penetrate new markets.
- Make changes in packaging design.
- Choose between common, contract, or private carriage.
- Increase or decrease inventories.
- Determine the profitability of customers.

- Establish profitable customer service levels.
- Choose between public and private warehousing.
- Determine the number of field warehouses and the extent to which the order processing system should be automated.

To make these *strategic decisions,* management must know how costs and revenues will change given the alternatives being considered.

Once management has made a decision, it must evaluate performance on a routine basis to determine (1) if the system is operating under control and at a level consistent with original profit expectations, and (2) if current operating costs justify an examination of alternative systems. This is referred to as *operational decision making.* The order processing system can be a primary source of information for both strategic and operational decision making.

Capabilities of an Advanced Order Processing System

An advanced order processing system is capable of providing a wealth of information to various departments within the organization. Terminals for data access can be made available to logistics, production, and sales/marketing. The system can provide a wide variety of reports on a regularly scheduled basis and status reports on request. It also can accommodate requests for a variety of data including customer order history, order status, and market and inventory position.

Designing the Information System

The Design of a Logistics Information System Begins with Customer Needs

The design of a logistics management information system should begin with a survey of the needs of both customers, and a determination of standards of performance for meeting these needs. Next, customer needs must be matched with the current abilities of the firm, and current operations must be surveyed to identify areas that will require monitoring and improvement.

It is important at this stage to interview various levels of management. In this way, the organization can determine what strategic and operational decisions are made, and what information is needed for decision making and in what form. Table 3–4 illustrates the various types of strategic and operational decisions that management must make within each of the functions of logistics.

The next stage is to survey current data processing capabilities to determine what changes must be made. Finally, a common database must be created and management reports designed, considering the costs and benefits of each. A good system design must support the management uses previously described and must have the capability of moving information from locations where it is collected to the appropriate levels of management.

Sources of Data for a Logistics Information System

Data for a logistics information system can come from many sources. The most significant sources of data for the common database are (1) the order processing system, (2) company records, (3) industry/external data, (4) management data, and (5) operating data. The type of information most commonly provided by each of these sources is shown in Figure 3–5.

Usually, the database contains computerized data files, such as the freight payment system, transportation history, inventory status, open orders, deleted orders, and standard costs for various logistics, marketing, and manufacturing activities. The computerized information

TABLE 3–4   Typical Strategic and Operational Decisions by Logistics Function

Decision Type	Customer Service	Transportation	Warehousing	Order Processing	Inventory
Strategic	Setting customer service levels	Selecting transportation models	Determination of number of warehouses and locations	Extent of mechanization	Replenishment systems
		Freight consolidation programs	Public vs. private warehousing		
		Common carriers vs. private trucking	Public vs. private warehousing		
Operational	Service level measurements	Rate freight bills	Picking	Order tracking	Forecasting
		Freight bill auditing	Packing	Order validation	Inventory tracking
		Claims administration	Stores measurement	Credit checking	Carrying— cost measurements
		Vehicle scheduling	Warehouse stock transfer	Invoice reconciliation	Inventory turns
		Rate negotiation	Staffing	Performance measurements	
		Shipment planning	Warehousing layout and design		
		Railcar management	Selection of materials- handling equipment		
		Shipment routing and scheduling	Performance measurements		
		Carrier selection			
		Performance measurements			

Source: American Telephone and Telegraph Company, *Business Marketing,* Market Management Division.

Figure 3–5

Key sources of information for the logistics database

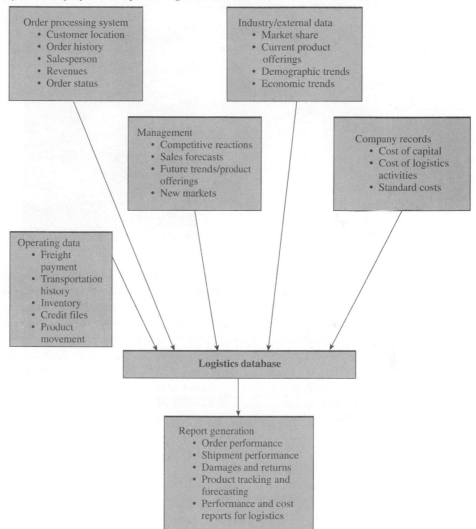

system must be capable of (1) data retrieval, (2) data processing, (3) data analysis, and (4) report generation.

Data retrieval is simply the capability of recalling data such as freight rates (in their raw form) rapidly and conveniently. **Data processing** is the capability to transform the data to a more useful form by relatively simple and straightforward conversion. Examples of data processing capability include preparation of warehousing picking instructions, preparation of bills of lading, and printing purchase orders.

Data analysis refers to taking the data from orders and providing management with information for strategic and operational decision making. A number of mathematical and

Following the lighted signals, an order selector picks the product, puts it into plastic totes, and sends it on the powered conveyor at the distribution center. A flashing light shows the item, quantity, and tote to be selected.

statistical models are available to aid a firm's management, including linear programming and simulation models. **Linear programming** is probably the most widely used strategic and operational planning tool in logistics management. It is an optimization technique that subjects various possible solutions to constraints that are identified by management.

Simulation

Simulation is a technique used to provide a model of a situation so that management can determine how the system is likely to change through the use of alternative strategies. The model is tested using known facts. Although simulation does not provide an optimal solution, the technique allows management to determine satisfactory solutions from a range of alternatives. A number of simulation models are available for purchase if the firm does not have the resources to develop its own.[15]

The last feature of an information system is **report generation**. Typical reports that can be generated from a logistics management information system include order performance reports; inventory management reports; shipment performance reports; damage reports; transportation administration reports; system configuration reports, which may contain the results of data analysis from mathematical and statistical models; and cost reports for logistics. Frito-Lay effectively uses an integrated logistics information system to support its operations (see the Technology box).

Financial Considerations

Start-Up Costs

Of course, it will be necessary to justify an advanced order processing system in terms of cost-benefit analysis. The costs of developing the system, *start-up costs,* can be justified by comparing the present value of improvement in cash flows associated with the new system

---

[15]See Richard C. Haverly and James F. Whelan, *Logistics Software* (New York: Andersen Consulting, 1996).

Technology

Frito-Lay: Integration of Information Systems Supports Integrated Logistics

Frito-Lay's $4-billion-a-year snack food operation boasts a supply pipeline bristling with more than 40 U.S. manufacturing plants, 28 over-the-road traffic centers, 2,000 distribution centers, 350,000 store-door accounts (delivery locations including multistore chain accounts), and 11,000 salespersons in the field armed with handheld computers to track micromarket-level retail data.

Delivering high volumes of limited shelf life products presents challenges for Ernest Harris, director of operations for Frito. "You've got to move quickly to get the product into consumers' hands. Our logistics plans require a lot of precision, understanding of market demand and rapid delivery methods

A Frito-Lay salesperson takes inventory of snacks to prepare a refill order for the store manager to sign.

like just-in-time . . . You just can't run a business today without information technology," said Harris.

The company has been bringing computerized manufacturing and logistics systems on-line since 1974. The current toolset includes distribution resource management and logistics modules from Cleveland Consulting Associates (Ohio) and Manugistics (Rockville, Maryland).

Harris told *Food Processing,* "What we're trying to do at Frito-Lay is look at the supply pipeline, at what consumers are doing on a daily basis, and use that information to drive operations all the way up through the supply chain." Product turns on store shelves, warehouses, distribution centers, and finished product inventories are all closely synchronized in a system that drives daily routing tactics as well as production planning.

The logistics management cycle doesn't stop with production planning. "After we decide what we're going to produce," said Harris, "we feed that information through the vehicle routing modules to schedule deliveries. And the same information is fed to the MRP II purchasing modules, to figure out how to replenish raw materials.

"The concept isn't magic . . . it's a matter of integrating information from the consumer all the way back through the supply chain. This ability to integrate that data and drive the company's decisions off that information is the key to supply chain management," said Harris.

Source: Bob Sperber, "Integrated Logistics: Turning Demand into Dollars," Food Processing, Apr. 1993, pp. 22–23.

to the initial investment. In most cases, cash flow will improve by changing to an advanced order processing system if the volume of orders processed is large. In smaller operations, however, this may not be true if the proposed system is more than the company needs.

Generally, the fixed costs associated with an advanced order processing system are higher than those incurred by a manual system. However, the variable costs per order are significantly less with the advanced system. We will expand upon this type of cost analysis in Chapter 13, which deals specifically with the calculation of logistics cost savings.

Using Logistics Information Systems to Support Time-Based Competition

As discussed in Chapter 2 in conjunction with customer service, customers are becoming increasingly demanding about their expectations of suppliers. Customers want consistent delivery times; consistent order cycles; and excellent communications regarding in-stock availability and expected shipment arrival. In short, customers are demanding integrated logistics systems supported by integrated logistics information systems.

These applications are aided by integrating a number of technologies, such as bar coding, EDI, and point-of-sale (POS) data gathering and transmission, and electronic funds transfer (EFT). Bar coding, POS technology, and TQM are described below. These technologies and techniques can be linked to support quick response or efficient consumer response (ECR), considerably reducing the total order cycle time.

Bar Coding

Bar codes can be seen on virtually all types of consumer packaged goods today. A **bar code** is a sequence of parallel bars of various widths, with varying amounts of space between the bars. The pattern and spacing of the bars convey information such as letters, numbers, and special characters. These bars are optically read by "scanning" them with a beam of light. The information contained in the bars is read directly into a computer, or stored and downloaded into the computer system at a later time.

Bar Coding at Texas Instruments

Bar coding can be useful in logistics applications. Texas Instruments has linked EDI and bar coding in the order placement and management of office supplies, with positive results. The firm reduced cash tied up in inventory by $2 million, freed up 40,000 square feet of warehouse space, reassigned 11 employees away from office supply control, and reduced cycle time by more than one-third. Further, by bar coding inbound shipments, the entire materials function can get more accurate accounts of actual receipts. The bar-code error rate has been estimated at from 1 in 10,000 to 1 in 1,000,000 compared with 1 in 25 or 30 for manually keyed data.[16]

Receiving also can be automated, which further contributes to cycle time reduction and data accuracy. These data can automatically be used by the accounts payable department for generating checks and reconciling invoices with purchase orders and receiving.

---

[16]Ed Hatchett, "Combining EDI with Barcoding to Automate Procurement," *1992 National Association of Purchasing Management Conference Proceedings* (Tempe, AZ: National Association of Purchasing Management, 1992), pp. 45–50.

Laser bar code readers track and route packages in an automated warehouse.

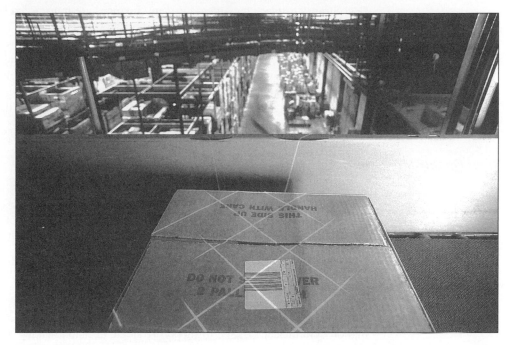

Thus, bar coding represents a logical extension of the organization's information systems and a linkage with EDI. This is illustrated in greater depth in the Technology box on Frito-Lay.

Bar-code technology is advancing rapidly. Two-dimensional bar codes are gaining acceptance, allowing the bar code to hold 100 times more data in the same space.[17]

Point-of-Sale Data

Point-of-sale (POS) data gathering is simply the scanning of bar codes of items sold, generally at the retail level. The data may be transmitted to the relevant supplier, who can replenish the inventory based on sales. This allows the retailer to "skip" order placement and to transfer responsibility directly to the supplier. This type of system is used by Wal-Mart. In other cases, the retailer may prefer to intervene and use POS data to place the order itself.

POS Data Gathering at Wal-Mart

Quick response (QR) and efficient consumer response (ECR) integrate the above technologies in an effort to speed time to market, thereby supporting time-based competition while reducing inventories and improving or maintaining customer service. For example, Levi Strauss & Company has integrated its customer order processing systems

Quick Response at Levi Strauss

---

[17]Saccomano, "A Primer on Warehousing Information Technology," pp. 24–26.

using a QR system called LeviLink.™ Retailers can order directly using EDI or allow Levi Strauss to place the orders for them. Invoices are transmitted by means of EDI, and customers can pay using electronic funds transfer.

The company has experienced increased sales with lower inventory levels, improving profits by 35 percent. Retailers benefit because LeviLink creates an electronic packing slip that can be verified by scanning bar-coded carton labels. This saves time in counting and matching paperwork such as the packing slip, invoice, and receiving document. Bar coding speeds stocking of products to shelves, freeing the retail employees to spend more time on the floor helping customers.[18]

Total Quality Management

Integrated information systems directly support an organization's total quality management (TQM) efforts by providing the customer with more accurate order fill. This occurs because the more automated the system, the less chance there is for human error. Such systems improve the quality of customer service by reducing order cycle time and improving order cycle consistency.

In addition, they create the ability to provide the customer with real-time information regarding inventory availability, order status, and shipment status. Thus, advanced logistics information systems support TQM.

While the types of systems described focus on day-to-day operations, logistics information systems can be used to support strategic decision making. Other systems, such as decision support systems (DSSs) and artificial intelligence (AI) provide a great deal of flexibility and support for logistics decisions based on logistics information. DSSs and AI are presented briefly in the next sections.

Decision Support Systems

Decision support systems (DSSs) encompass a wide variety of models, simulations, and applications that are designed to ease and improve decision making. These systems incorporate information from the organization's database into an analytical framework that represents relationships among data, simulates different operating environments (e.g., vehicle routing and scheduling), may incorporate uncertainty and "what-if" analysis, and uses algorithms or heuristics. DSSs actually present an analysis and, based upon the analysis, recommend a decision.

The artificial intelligence tools can be incorporated into DSSs, which may contain decision analysis frameworks, forecasting models, simulation models, and linear programming models. They can be used to assist in a wide variety of logistics decisions, such as evaluating alternative transportation options, determining warehouse location, and setting levels of inventory.

---

[18]Don Tapscott and Art Caston, *Paradigm Shift: The Promise of New Information Technology* (New York: McGraw-Hill, 1993), pp. 116–17.

FIGURE 3–6

Decision support system

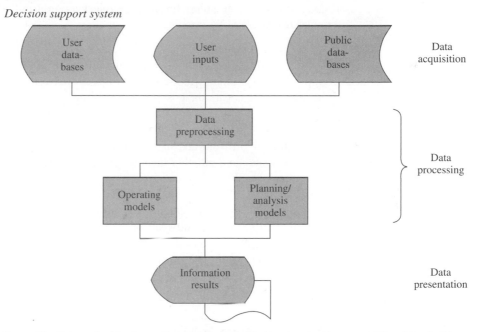

Source: Allan F. Ayers, *Decision Support Systems: A Useful Tool for Manufacturing Management* (King of Prussia, PA: K. W. Tunnell Company, 1985), p. 2.

While the use of DSSs is not currently widespread, it appears to be growing as the potential contribution becomes more understood, and computing costs continue to decline. Figure 3–6 shows the components of a DSS.

A DSS is applications oriented. More specifically, a DSS has the following objectives:

Objectives of a Decision Support System

- To assist logistics executives in their decision processes.
- To support, but not replace, managerial judgment.
- To improve the effectiveness of logistics decisions.[19]

Perhaps the most critical element of a DSS is the quality of the data used as input into the system. DSSs require information about the environment that is both internal and external to the organization. Thus, an important first step in DSS planning, implementation, and control is to have good external information. This is discussed in Chapter 15 in conjunction with strategic planning. Models are also needed to provide data analysis.

Modeling can be defined as the process of developing a symbolic representation of a total system. A model must accurately represent the "real world" and be managerially useful. The purpose of models has been described as:

The Purpose of Models

Essentially . . . to replicate reality and to assess the behavior of that reality if changes are introduced. A model supports, rather than replaces, the managerial decision-making process. By

---

[19]Eframin Turban, *Decision Support and Expert Systems* (New York: Macmillan, 1988), p. 8.

using a model, we are able to establish a current situation and then play "what-if" games. This "what-if" ability is significant. It allows us to quickly consider many different alternatives and test the outcome.[20]

Modeling at Pet Inc.   An interesting example of the use of logistics modeling in a corporate merger or acquisition occurred in 1989 when Pet Inc., a manufacturer of specialty foods, acquired Van de Kamp's Frozen Seafood. Before the acquisition was completed, Pet used its in-house logistics model to evaluate the cost and service implications. Within three days after the acquisition, all of Van de Kamp's orders were being processed on Pet systems and all products were being distributed through Pet's logistics system.

What's the payoff from this successful integration of systems and operations? From a quantitative standpoint, monthly inventories in 1989 dropped an average of nearly $1.5 million compared to the previous year. This was achieved despite a 10 percent increase in the number of cases sold.

Pet realized the highest inventory turnover rate in the company's history at 5.34. And the case-fill ratio has consistently hit the target of 98 percent. Notably, the distribution department accomplished this with no increase in manpower.[21] In the future, the company anticipates expanding its use of computer models to aid its marketing and logistics processes.

Artificial Intelligence and Expert Systems

Developed out of the field of computer science, **artificial intelligence (AI)** is

Artificial Intelligence (AI) Defined   concerned with the concepts and methods of inference by a computer and the symbolic representation of the knowledge used in making inferences. The term *intelligence* covers many cognitive skills, including the ability to solve problems, to learn, to understand language, and in general, to behave in a way that would be considered intelligent if observed in a human.[22]

AI is a comprehensive term encompassing a number of areas, including computer-aided instruction, voice synthesis and recognition, game-playing systems, natural language translators, robotics, and expert systems (ES).[23] While the number of AI applications is limited, the potential in logistics is staggering. AI has been used to model response time requirements for customer delivery; model transportation costs and times for various transportation modes, locations, and routings; determine which warehouses should serve which plants, with which products, and what inventory levels; model customer service response with various levels of reliability; and perform sensitivity analysis to determine how much inputs can vary without affecting the structure of the optimal solution.[24]

---

[20]John H. Campbell, "The Manager's Guide to Computer Modeling," *Business* 32, no. 4 (Oct.–Dec. 1982), p. 11.

[21]Francis J. Quinn, "A Model Distribution System," *Traffic Management* 29, no. 6 (June 1990), p. 34.

[22]Mary Kay Allen and Omar Keith Helferich, *Putting Expert Systems to Work in Logistics* (Oak Brook, IL: Council of Logistics Management, 1990), p. A6.

[23]Omar K. Helferich, Stephen J. Schon, Mary Kay Allen, Raymond L. Rowland, and Robert L. Cook, "Applications of Artificial Intelligence—Expert System to Logistics," *Proceedings of the Annual Conference of the Council of Logistics Management,* vol.1 (Oak Brook, IL: Council of Logistics Management, 1986) pp. 45–86.

[24]Paul S. Bender, "Using Expert Systems and Optimization Techniques to Design Logistics Strategies," *Proceedings of the Annual Conference of the Council of Logistics Management* (Oct. 16–19, 1994), pp. 231–39.

Of specific interest to logistics executives are the subareas of AI known as **expert systems (ES),** natural language recognition, and neural networks. An ES is defined as

Expert Systems (ES) Defined

> a computer program that uses knowledge and reasoning techniques to solve problems normally requiring the abilities of human experts. An expert system is an artificial intelligence (AI) program that achieves competence in performing a specialized task by reasoning with a body of knowledge about the task and the task domain.[25]

Expert systems are capable of being applied to a variety of problems in marketing and logistics, including interpretation, monitoring, debugging, repair, instruction, and control.[26] (See Box 3–1.) Examples of ES applications can be found in many industries.

Expert Systems at Xerox Corporation

Xerox Corporation, the multibillion-dollar office products equipment manufacturer and winner of the Malcolm Baldrige National Quality Award in 1989, has utilized expert systems to manage its vehicle routing and scheduling. Utilizing 70 to 80 trucks assigned to Xerox from five national motor carriers, the firm moves 250 million pounds of products in 12,000 truckload shipments annually to thousands of customers being serviced from three distribution centers located in California, Texas, and New York.[27]

Digital Equipment Corporation Uses Expert Systems

Digital Equipment Corporation, the computer manufacturer, has used an ES to reduce work-in-process cycle times from 35 to 5 days by better managing work in process inventory, and flows between operations. Eastman Kodak Company, the multinational firm that produces film and cameras, uses expert systems in its distribution centers to improve worker productivity in picking and palletizing products for shipment. For example, the training period for new employees was reduced from 6–12 weeks to 1–2 days.[28]

Five criteria aid decision makers in determining whether expert systems should be used to solve a particular logistics problem. If any of the criteria are met, an ES may be appropriate:

When Should an Expert System Be Used?

1. The task or problem solution requires the use of human knowledge, judgment, and experience.
2. The task requires the use of heuristic (e.g., rules of thumb) or decisions based on incomplete or uncertain information.
3. The task primarily requires symbolic reasoning instead of numerical computation.
4. The task is neither too easy (taking a human expert less than a few minutes) nor too difficult (requiring more than a few hours for an expert to perform).
5. Substantial variability exists in people's ability to perform the task. Novices gain competence with experience. Experts are better than novices at performing the task.[29]

Artificial Intelligence and EDI Work Together at Benneton

If an ES is appropriate, the next decision facing the logistics executive is whether the system can be economically justified and if EDI can be combined with other systems such as artificial intelligence (AI). At Benneton, the Italian clothing manufacturer, computers not only determine what will be included in upcoming production runs, but also designate optimum routing for all finished goods.

---

[25]Allen and Helferich, *Putting Expert Systems to Work in Logistics,* p. A10.

[26]See Paul Harmon and David King, *Expert Systems* (New York: John Wiley, 1985), p. 94.

[27]James Aaron Cooke, "Xerox's Drive for Logistics Quality," *Traffic Management* 29, no. 10 (Oct. 1990), pp. 50–53.

[28]Allen and Helferich, *Putting Expert Systems to Work in Logistics,* pp. 14, 44–45.

[29]Ibid., p. 115.

Box 3–1

What Is an Expert System? The Case of ABC Scientific

A good way to understand expert systems is to consider the case of ABC Scientific, a hypothetical company, which has problems similar to many existing wholesalers and retailers. Through a series of acquisitions and mergers, the company now maintains a vastly diversified product line of over 30,000 stockkeeping units (SKUs). The highly specialized products are documented in a catalog. The products are diverse in function and use, so it is difficult for any of ABC's employees to be familiar with them all.

ABC Scientific has a customer base distributed throughout the United States. More than 100 order entry and customer service representatives located at the corporate headquarters handle orders and customer inquiries. The majority of orders come in by telephone. The customers ordering the product rarely know exactly what they want, much less the ABC catalog model or part number. For example, a school might call to order a replacement light bulb for a piece of equipment in a physics laboratory. To select exactly the right bulb requires knowledge of several specifics, such as the general type, size, wattage, color, and usage. Selecting the right bulb is generally not a difficult task because light bulbs are familiar products. With a little training on what types of light bulbs ABC Scientific carries, most order clerks can determine the right questions to ask to select the right bulb for the job.

However, if the product is something completely unfamiliar, such as a complex piece of medical equipment, it is difficult for the clerks to know what questions to ask in order to determine whether ABC can satisfy the requirement. In this case, someone with specialized knowledge of medical equipment is required. For some medical items, ABC's catalog lists over 100 pages of different model numbers of the same type of item. This is further complicated by ABC's inventory of 30,000 stocked items.

With so many products and so many choices within product lines, it is nearly impossible for order entry personnel to possess expert knowledge of each product type. ABC would like to have an expert knowledgeable about each product readily available to answer any call, so that the customer receives immediate and accurate assistance, no matter

what product he or she is looking for. Without this expertise, the customer is likely to abandon ABC for a supplier who appears more knowledgeable and can provide better service. Equally displeasing to ABC management is the likelihood that the product was available on ABC's shelves, but the order clerk mistakenly told the customer it was not.

Further complicating the problem is the high turnover rate of order clerks and customer assistance personnel. Once an order clerk becomes familiar with a number of products, he or she may be promoted and vital knowledge about the company's inventory, customer buying habits, order cycle, and other order-related aspects could be lost.

The ideal solution to ABC's predicament must possess several key features. First, the solution should improve the effectiveness of ABC's personnel in advising the customer about the product best suited to his or her needs. This feature should result in increased revenues for ABC. ABC would earn a reputation as a company upon which a customer could rely for quick fulfillment of his or her needs, even when the customer does not thoroughly understand those needs. Second, a good solution should provide assistance in training new personnel and making them almost immediately proficient. Third, the solution must be responsive to the customer—a computerized solution with a 20-minute response time is inadequate when the customer is waiting on the telephone. Fourth, the solution must be cost effective. Finally, the solution must permit the knowledge of the existing order specialists to be captured and retained.

Expert systems technology matches all the requirements for an effective solution to ABC's problem. Expert systems mimic human experts and serve as intelligent advisors on specific areas of expertise. They are designed to deal with symbolic knowledge that would be required for this problem—knowledge about color, shape, and usage, among others. Further, they can reason with uncertain or conflicting information and missing details. Expert systems can store large amounts of facts and information, yet reach conclusions or provide advice by using shortcuts (referred to as "heuristics") to "think" about the problem.

Box 3–1 concluded

An ABC order clerk would probably use an expert catalog advisor on his or her personal computer. To facilitate the telephone conversation with the customer, the system might even have a speech interface as well as a keyboard interface. The clerk might begin an interactive consultation with the expert system by typing or saying the name of the product the customer required (e.g., light bulb). The system would then prompt the order clerk with questions to ask the user to determine which of ABC's products could best satisfy the demand. The figure below depicts an interactive consultation with the expert catalog advisor. The responses next to the > prompt are those that the order clerk provides to the system based on the customer's response. Note how easy it is to use and understand the system.

```
     Welcome to the ABC
      Catalog Advisor

What product type does the
customer require?
>> light bulb

What is the light bulb used
for?
>> a photo emitter

Who was the original
manufacturer of the photo
emitter?
>> Beckman Instruments
```

```
What is the model number of
this Beckman photo emitter?
>> unknown

Is the light emitter a
"professional" or "series
5000" unit?
>> unknown

Is the unit a floor model or a
desktop model?
>> desktop

Advice: Model No. 4367 best
meets the customer's needs.
Unit price is $1.67.
We have 450 in stock.

Do you wish to see alternate
light bulbs that also can
satisfy this requirement?
>> no

Does the customer wish to
place an order?
>>
```

Source: Mary Kay Allen and Omar Keith Helferich, *Putting Expert Systems to Work in Logistics* (Oak Brook, IL: Council of Logistics Management, 1990), pp. 22–24.

At each Benneton store, the point-of-sale cash registers maintain a running inventory of item sales, which they transmit by way of EDI to computers in branch offices. The branch offices, in turn, transmit the data to the central office computer, which uses AI and a modeling program to make decisions on production runs. If red sweaters are selling fast, the computer tells the manufacturing system to design and produce more red sweaters. The system then determines how the shipments will be routed to the stores, freeing the traffic department—which consists of only six people—to spend its time researching new routings and handling problems.[30]

---

[30]Marsha Johnston, "Electronic Commerce Speeds Benetton Business Dealings," *Software Magazine,* Jan. 1994, pp. 93–95.

Natural Language Recognition

Mead Corporation Uses Natural Language Processing

Mead Corporation, paper producer, has used the **natural language capabilities** of AI to make data stored within its computer system much more accessible. It used to be that a simple request like the past use of a commodity could take an hour, sorting through pages and pages of reports! Mead's Decision Support Department suggested that the firm create an on-line database that would be voice accessible, using natural language processing. With the advent of this system, the data can be accessed in three minutes rather than in an hour, simply by verbally asking the system a question. This has contributed tremendously to the productivity of the purchasing function as well as other areas within the firm.[31]

Neural Networks

Neural networks are still in the development stages. They can be considered an offshoot of expert systems because they aid in decision making through the use of logic and rules. A key difference is that neural networks actually create their own rules based on past decisions and outcomes, rather than relying on an "expert." Once developed, these systems will be excellent for any repetitive activity that requires analysis of large amounts of data, more than a human could process effectively. As such, neural networks could be used to alert management to potential problems in supplier performance patterns, quality, delivery, invoicing, and similar issues. Airlines are "training" neural networks to forecast passenger traffic.[32]

Database Management

Database Management Systems Must Perform Many Tasks

As previously mentioned, computers are excellent at managing data. A database management system allows application programs to retrieve required data stored in the computer system. The types of data stored were shown in Figure 3–5. A database management system must store data in some logical way, showing how different pieces of data are related, in order for retrieval to be efficient. This is a critical issue in logistics because of the large volume of data generated which may require analysis at a later date. For example, a buyer may want to see a history of transportation carriers with which it has placed orders for a particular item in the past six months.

---

[31]Gary M. Bramble, Bette Clark, and Robert Florimo, "Artificial Intelligence in Purchasing," *1990 National Association of Purchasing Management Conference Proceedings* (Tempe, AZ: NAPM, 1990), pp. 186–90.

[32]Joseph A Yacura, "Supply Line Management Information System," *1992 National Association of Purchasing Management Conference Proceedings* (Tempe, AZ: NAPM, 1992), pp. 343–48; Kyundo Nam and Thomas Schaefer, "Forecasting International Airline Passenger Traffic Using Neural Networks," *Logistics and Transportation Review* 31, no. 3 (Sept. 1995), pp. 239–51.

The database management system must be able to use the item number to reference the order and "pull up" the pertinent data. If the buyer sees that two suppliers have been used, the buyer may want the system to provide a transaction history with those suppliers over a given time period for all purchased items. The database management system must have the flexibility to sort data in a variety of ways that are meaningful to the user.

Relational database structures are popular today because they allow access to and sorting of data by relating the data to other data in many ways. This allows a great deal of flexibility. Increasingly, companies are using what is known as a **local area network (LAN).** This consists of a minicomputer linked to a number of microcomputers or terminals which allow access to a common database, software, and other systems features.[33] LANs give microcomputers the power of mainframe systems.

Regardless of the sophistication of the software and hardware, a system cannot provide good results if the data in the system are not accurate and timely. Thus, systems integrity is vital. If people do not use the system consistently (i.e., do not scan each barcoded item individually) the system will quickly be inaccurate. Once a system has data accuracy problems, it is very difficult, costly, and time consuming to correct.

Summary

In this chapter, we saw how the order processing system can directly influence the performance of the logistics function. We also examined how order processing systems can be used to improve customer communications and total order cycle time, or lead to substantial inventory reductions and transportation efficiencies. Information is vital for the planning and control of logistics systems, and we saw how the order processing system can form the basis of a logistics information system.

Today's computer technology and communication systems make it possible for management to have the information required for strategic and operational planning of the logistics function. The order processing system can significantly improve the quality and quantity of information for decision making.

Computers have become an invaluable aid to the logistics executive in making various operational and strategic decisions. Decision support systems, which are computer based, provide information for the decision-making process. The DSS has three components: data acquisition, data processing, and data presentation.

Computers are widely employed in many areas of logistics, including transportation, inventory control, warehousing, order processing, material handling, and so forth. Some of the most exciting areas of computerization are modeling, artificial intelligence (AI), and expert systems (ES). Improved database management contributes to the support of logistics decision making.

---

[33]Ellram and Birou, *Purchasing for Bottom-Line Impact,* p. 149.

Creative Solutions

Using EDI to Reengineer the Business Process between a Hospital Products Manufacturer and its Distributor

Becton Dickinson (BD) is a worldwide manufacturer of medical and surgical products, based in Franklin Lakes, New Jersey. To better understand the real benefits of EDI, BD has developed a model of EDI implementation that is useful in segmenting an EDI strategy and in prioritizing and allocating research and development (R&D) dollars (referring here to R&D used to develop EDI *service* products) and implementation resources.

The concepts and thinking behind Becton Dickinson's SPEED-COM LINK I process began in 1987 with a simple notion: Start with a clean sheet of paper and design a business based on the premise that the distributor and Becton Dickinson share *common business goals*. These business goals are:

- Improve the service level and service quality to end customers.
- Reduce channel costs by eliminating redundancies and nonvalue-adding functions, specifically the activities supporting rebates and end-of-quarter promotions.

These were novel concepts for their time, especially the ideas of "partnership" and shared business goals as opposed to the more prevalent notions of adversarial or, at best, arm's-length relationships and competing business goals. Also unusual for its time and even for today, was the willingness and openness of a manufacturer like Becton Dickinson to challenge the "accepted wisdom" of what had become over the years an institutionalized practice of rebates and of end-of-quarter promotions.

The design and testing of the SPEED-COM LINK I process was made in partnership with a major distributor and pharmaceutical wholesaler, Durr Fillauer (now known as Durr Medical, a division of Bergen Brunswig). Over the last four years, this process has been refined, expanded, and proven in practice. SPEED COM includes automatic order

entry by suppliers, as well as automatic order processing. However, it goes well beyond that to automate the entire order cycle.

The SPEED-COM LINK I process embodies the following principles in its business process.

- Elimination of quarterly promotions.
- Elimination of "rebates" as a cash-flow burden to the distributor and as an administrative burden to both.
- Alignment of the distributors' and Becton Dickinson's business processes by shifting the billing and cash flow cycle from point of purchase (by the distributor) to point of sale.
- Simplified payment process (one payment based on month-end statement, guaranteed accuracy of statement, not reason for deductions).
- Simplified billing terms and pricing rules.
- A "closed-loop" EDI process with the vision of an eventual paperless relationship with the elimination of purchase orders in LINK II.

In short, this is not just *another fix* for the rebate process. It is a fundamental change in the way business is done. The emphasis in this approach is to *do things right the first time:* Load the contract and prices right, bill the end customer right, manage the inventory right so as to achieve the desired service levels, bill the distributors right, and have the distributor pay Becton Dickinson the right (net) amount at the right time (upon sale to the end customer).

The benefits of the SPEED-COM LINK I (Level 3 EDI) relationship have been measured and validated independently by the distributor and BD. The table below highlights some of the major areas of benefits. While the process clearly improves the return on working capital for the distributor, the value

Creative Solutions concluded

to the partnership comes from building a long-term collaborative relationship. It is this relationship that fundamentally creates the environment for *change*— where both trading partners feel motivated and secure enough to think and act "outside the box," and to challenge and search alternatives to the way BD does business today. BD believes that if this is done (and it can be), everyone in the manufacturing/distribution loop can achieve the goals of reducing costs and improving service and, ultimately, driving toward the vision of "guaranteed service"—perfect service, every time!

BD's Link I Benefits

Category	Distributor	BD
1. Administrative/Process efficiencies	• Level product flow—no warehouse surges • Easier to reconcile	• Level plant/DC loading no shipping surges
2. Closed loop EDI process	• No paper handling • Greater end-to-end accuracy	• No paper handling • Greater end-to-end accuracy
3. Financial benefits	• Working capital reduction • Immediate capture of inventory profits and price increase	• No paper handling • Greater end-to-end accuracy
4. Quality improvement	• Improves dealer "Into-stock cost" accuracy—one price for all purchases • Easier payment process—statement based • Daily process maintains focus on accuracy • Improves quality of other processes—e.g., receiving discrepancies	• Easier/faster/more accurate payment application process—no deductions • Daily process maintains focus on accuracy, improves quality of other processes—e.g., delivery resolutions

Source: Naz Bhimji, "Using EDI to Re-engineer the Business Process between Hospital Manufacturer and Distributor," *EDI World,* Sept. 1994, pp. 40–42.

Suggested Readings

Allen, Mary K., and Omar Keith Helferich. *Putting Expert Systems to Work in Logistics.* Oak Brook, IL: Council of Logistics Management, 1990.

Bender, Paul S. "Using Expert Systems and Optimization Techniques to Design Logistics Strategies." *Proceedings of the Annual Conference of the Council of Logistics Management.* Cincinnati, OH: Oct. 16–19, 1994.

Carbone, James. "Make Way for EDI." *Electronics Purchasing,* Sept. 1992, pp. 20–24.

Carter, Joseph R., and Gary L. Ragatz. "Supplier Bar Codes: Closing the EDI Loop." *International Journal of Purchasing and Materials Management* 37, no. 3 (Summer 1991), pp. 19–23.

Cooke, James Aaron. "Computers Lead the Way to Total Inbound Control." *Traffic Management* 29, no. 1 (Jan. 1990), pp. 50–53.

Curry, Bruce, and Luiz Moutinho. "Expert Systems for Site Location Decisions." *Logistics Information Management* 4, no. 4 (1991), pp. 19–27.

Drummond, Rik. "EDI over the Internet Inter-operability." *EDI World,* Apr. 1996, p. 8.

Emmelhainz, Margaret A. *Electronic Data Interchange: A Total Management Guide,* 2d ed. New York: Van Nostrand Reinhold, 1995.

———. "Implementation of EDI in Logistics: An Introduction." *Proceedings of the Annual Conference of the Council of Logistics Management.* Oak Brook, IL: Council of Logistics Management, 1990.

Global Logistics Research Team, Michigan State University. *World Class Logistics: The Challenge of Managing Continuous Change.* Oak Brook, IL: Council of Logistics Management 1995.

Hahn, Harley, and Rick Stout. *The Internet Yellow Pages.* Berkeley, CA: Osborne McGraw-Hill, 1994.

Hatchett, Ed. "Combining EDI with Barcoding to Automate Procurement." *1992 National Association of Purchasing Management Conference Proceedings.* Tempe, AZ: National Association of Purchasing Management, 1992.

La Londe, Bernard J., and Martha C. Cooper. *Partnerships in Providing Customer Service: A Third-Party Perspective.* Oak Brook, IL: Council of Logistics Management, 1989.

Leenders, Michiel, and Harold E. Fearon. *Purchasing and Materials Management,* 10th ed. Burr Ridge, IL: Richard D. Irwin, 1993.

Mules, Glen R. J. "EDI Security and Control." *NAPM Insights,* June 1992, pp. 12–13.

Powers, Richard F. "Optimization Models for Logistics Decisions." *Journal of Business Logistics* 10, no. 1 (1989), pp. 106–21.

Schary, Philip B., and James Coakley. "Logistics Organization and the Information System." *The International Journal of Logistics Management* 2, no. 2 (1991), pp. 22–29.

Sheffi, Yosef. "The Shipment Information Center." *The International Journal of Logistics Management* 2, no. 2 (1991), pp. 1–12.

Skupsky, Donald S. "Keeping Records in the Electronic Age." *NAPM Insights,* May 1994, pp. 6–7.

Sriram, Ven, and S. Banerjee. "Electronic Data Interchange: Does Its Adoption Change Purchasing Policies and Procedures?" *International Journal of Purchasing and Materials Management* 30, no. 1 (1994), pp. 31–40.

Questions and Problems

1. How do wholesalers and retailers measure the order cycle provided to them by a manufacturer?

2. Explain the impact of order cycle variability on the inventory levels of wholesalers and retailers.

3. Discuss specifically how logistics performance is affected by the order processing system used.

4. What are the primary advantages associated with the implementation of an integrated, automated order processing system?

5. Electronic data interchange applications have experienced significant growth in recent years. Why do you believe this growth has occurred? What are the primary benefits of EDI? Do you think that the growth rate in EDI applications will be sustained? Why or why not?

6. How does the order processing system form the foundation of the logistics management information system?
7. How is the logistics management information system used to support planning of logistics operations?
8. Briefly describe the role of decision support systems in logistics decision making.
9. Identify areas of logistics that use expert systems (ES) and artificial intelligence (AI) to improve efficiency and effectiveness.

THE DISTRIBUTION CHALLENGE!
PROBLEM: EVE OF DESTRUCTION

Adobe Systems Inc. is a major producer of software for graphics and electronic publishing applications. It ships upward of 400,000 boxes a year—valued at more than $100 million—into the Pacific Rim, including Japan, Southeast Asia, India, Australia, and Latin America.

Like many software makers, Adobe does most of its overseas business through distributors, according to Larry C. Clopp, manager of international sales for the Pacific Rim. And it introduces regular updates of its most popular titles, rendering all previous versions obsolete.

But Adobe's method for taking back old software left much to be desired. It was getting requests from distributors to take back between 10,000 and 20,000 boxes a year, which were then shipped to California for destruction.

To discourage piracy, the company had to confirm the serial number of each returned title, then give it to a software recycler for erasure. However, Adobe was taking up to two months to credit distributors' accounts, so its distributors were hamstrung by severe reductions in their already thin credit lines.

Even worse, distributors were paying the cost—more than $2,500 per shipment—of sending the product by air back to the United States. Some became fed up by the process and sold the old software locally.

How can Adobe cut its processing time on returns in half, while sharply reducing administrative costs and ensuring product security?

What Is Your Solution?

Source: "Distribution: The Challenge," *Distribution* 95, no. 5 (May 1996), p. 72.

Inventory Concepts

Chapter Objectives

- To examine how the basic concepts of inventory management are applied.
- To illustrate how to calculate safety stocks.
- To show how production policies influence inventory levels.
- To demonstrate how inventories and customer service levels are interrelated.

Introduction

Inventory is a large and costly investment. Better management of corporate inventories can improve cash flow and return on investment. Nevertheless, most companies (retailers, wholesalers, and manufacturers) suffer through periodic inventory rituals; that is, crash inventory-reduction programs are instituted every year or so. However, the lack of comprehensive understanding of inventory management techniques and trade-offs often causes customer service levels to drop, so the programs are abandoned.[1]

Obviously, a better approach to inventory management is necessary. This chapter will provide the reader with the knowledge required to improve the practice of inventory management.

Basic Inventory Concepts

In this section, we will consider basic inventory concepts such as the reasons for holding inventory and various types of inventory.

Why Hold Inventory?

Inventory Serves Five Purposes

Formulation of an inventory policy requires an understanding of the role of inventory in production and marketing. Inventory serves five purposes within the firm: (1) It enables the firm to achieve economies of scale, (2) it balances supply and demand, (3) it enables specialization in manufacturing, (4) it provides protection from uncertainties in demand and order cycle, and (5) it acts as a buffer between critical interfaces within the channel of distribution.

Large Quantities Provide Several Advantages

Economies of Scale. Inventory is required if an organization is to realize economies of scale in purchasing, transportation, or manufacturing. For example, ordering large quantities of raw materials or finished goods inventory allows the manufacturer to take advantage of the per unit price reductions associated with volume purchases. Purchased materials have a lower transportation cost per unit if ordered in large volumes. This lower per unit cost results because less handling is required; for example, an order of 1 unit usually requires the same administrative handling as 1,000 units, and truckload and full railcar shipments receive lower transportation rates than smaller shipments of less-than-truckload (LTL) or less-than-carload (LCL) quantities.

Finished goods inventory makes it possible to realize manufacturing economies. Plant utilization is greater and per unit manufacturing costs are lower if a firm schedules long production runs with few line changes. Manufacturing in small quantities leads to short production runs and high changeover costs.[2]

---

[1]Hau L. Lee and Corey Billington provide an excellent overview of key issues in inventory management in, "Managing Supply Chain Inventory: Pitfalls and Opportunities," *Sloan Management Review* 33, no. 3 (Spring 1992), pp. 65–73.

[2]With newer manufacturing technology, some companies have been able to lower changeover costs by reducing the time and effort required to make the machine adjustments to accommodate producing smaller quantities of each product.

The production of large quantities, however, may require that some of the items be carried in inventory for a significant period of time before they can be sold. The production of large quantities also may prevent an organization from responding quickly to stock-outs, since large production runs mean that items are produced less frequently. The cost of maintaining this inventory must be "traded off" against the production savings realized.

Although frequent production changeovers reduce the quantity of inventory that must be carried and shorten the lead time that is required in the event of a stockout, they require time that could be used for manufacturing a product. In addition, at the beginning of a production run, the line often operates less efficiently due to fine-tuning the process and equipment settings.

Cost Trade-Offs

When a plant is operating at or near capacity, frequent line changes that create machine downtime may mean that contribution to profit is lost because there is not enough product to meet demand. In such situations, the costs of lost sales and changeovers must be compared to the increase in inventory carrying costs that would result from longer production runs. To respond to this, many companies, such as Honda of America Manufacturing, have made a major effort toward reducing changeover times.[3] This allows production of small lots, eliminating the penalty of higher setup costs.

Seasonal Inventories

Balancing Supply and Demand.   Seasonal supply or demand may make it necessary for a firm to hold inventory. For example, a producer of a premium line of boxed chocolates experiences significant sales volume increases at Christmas, Valentine's Day, Easter, and Mother's Day. The cost of establishing production capacity to handle the volume at these peak periods would be substantial. In addition, substantial idle capacity and wide fluctuations in the workforce would result if the company were to produce to meet demand when it occurs. The decision to maintain a relatively stable workforce and produce at a somewhat constant level throughout the year creates significant inventory buildup at various times during the year, but at a lower total cost to the firm. The seasonal inventories are stored in a freezer warehouse that was built adjacent to the plant.

On the other hand, demand for a product may be relatively stable throughout the year, but raw materials may be available only at certain times during the year (e.g., producers of canned fruits and vegetables). This makes it necessary to manufacture finished products in excess of current demand and hold them in inventory.

Specialization.   Inventory makes it possible for each of a firm's plants to specialize in the products that it manufactures. The finished products can be shipped to field warehouses where they are mixed to fill customer orders. The economies that result from the longer production runs and from savings in transportation costs more than offset the costs of additional handling. Companies such as Whirlpool Corporation have found significant cost savings in the operation of consolidation warehouses that allow the firm to specialize manufacturing by plant location. The specialization by facility is known as **focused factories.**[4]

---

[3]This information was obtained from David Curry, purchasing administrator of Honda of America Manufacturing.

[4]For a good description of "focused factories," see W. Skinner, "The Focused Factory," *Harvard Business Review* 52, no. 3 (May–June 1974), pp. 113–21.

Protection from Uncertainties.   Inventory is held as protection from uncertainties; that is, to prevent a stockout in the case of variability in demand or variability in the replenishment cycle. Raw materials inventories in excess of those required to support production can result from speculative purchases made because management expects a price increase or supply shortage, perhaps due to a potential strike. Another reason to hold raw materials inventory is to maintain a source of supply. Regardless of the reason for maintaining inventory, the costs of holding the inventory should be compared to the savings realized or costs avoided by holding it.

Work-in-Process Inventory

Work-in-process inventory is often maintained between manufacturing operations within a plant to avoid a shutdown if a critical piece of equipment were to break down, and to equalize flow, since not all manufacturing operations produce at the same rate. The stockpiling of work-in-process within the manufacturing complex permits maximum economies of production without work stoppage. Increasingly, organizations are focusing on rebalancing production processes to minimize or eliminate the need for work-in-process inventory. This is supportive of JIT manufacturing initiatives, presented in Chapters 9 and 10.

Inventory Planning Is Essential

Inventory planning is critical to successful manufacturing operations because a shortage of raw materials can shut down the production line or lead to a modification of the production schedule; these events may increase expenses or result in a shortage of finished product. While shortages of raw materials can disrupt normal manufacturing operations, excessive inventories can increase inventory carrying costs and reduce profitability. Organizations are working closely with suppliers and carriers to improve supply reliability, allowing a reduction in the amount of raw materials held to cover delivery uncertainty. Internal performance metrics may influence inventory investment, as shown in the General Mills example in the Creative Solutions box at the end of this chapter.

Balanced Inventory

Finally, finished goods inventory can be used as a means of improving customer service levels by reducing the likelihood of a stockout due to unanticipated demand or variability in lead time. If the inventory is balanced, increased inventory investment will enable the manufacturer to offer higher levels of product availability and less chance of a stockout. A balanced inventory is one that contains items in proportion to expected demand.

Inventory as a Buffer.   Inventory is held throughout the supply chain to act as a buffer for the following critical interfaces:

- Supplier-procurement (purchasing)
- Procurement-production
- Production-marketing
- Marketing-distribution
- Distribution-intermediary
- Intermediary-consumer/user

Inventory Is Held throughout the Supply Chain

Because channel participants are separated geographically, it is necessary for inventory to be held throughout the supply chain to successfully achieve time and place utility (see Chapter 1). Figure 4–1 shows the typical inventory positions in a supplier-manufacturer-

FIGURE 4–1

The logistics flow

FIGURE 4–1

The logistics flow

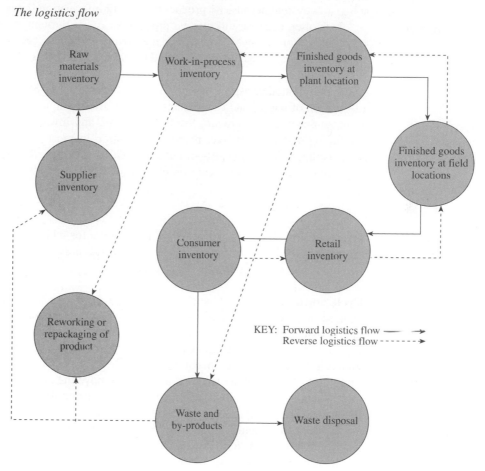

intermediary-consumer supply chain. Raw materials must be moved from a source of supply to the manufacturing location where they will be input into the manufacturing process. In many cases, work-in-process inventory will be necessary at the plant.

Once the manufacturing process has been completed, product must be moved into finished goods inventory at plant locations. The next step is the strategic deployment of finished goods inventory to field locations, which may include corporate-owned or leased distribution centers, public warehouses, wholesalers' warehouses, retail chain distribution centers, or delivery directly to the retail location. Inventory is then positioned to enable customer purchase. Similarly, the customer maintains an inventory to support individual or institutional consumption.

All of these product flows are the result of a decision by the ultimate consumer or user to purchase the product. The entire process depends on the information flow from

Reverse Logistics

the customer to the firm and to the firm's suppliers. Communication is an integral part of a logistics system because no product flows until information flows.

It is often necessary to move a product backward through the channel for a number of reasons. For example, a customer may return a product because it is damaged, or a manufacturer may need to recall a product because of defects. This is referred to as "reverse logistics."[5]

Finally, another aspect that promises to become a bigger factor in the future is the disposition of wastes and by-products. One specific example involves "bottle laws," such as those enacted in Michigan, Vermont, Oregon, and Iowa. As sensitivity to litter from packaging and concern over resource utilization increase, environmentalists and concerned citizens in other states—if not nationwide—are likely to push for such laws. These laws are being applied to a wide variety of packaging materials in Europe.

Types of Inventory

Inventories Can Be Classified Based on Why They Exist

Inventories can be classified based on the reasons for which they are accumulated. The categories of inventories include cycle stock, in-transit inventories, safety or buffer stock, speculative stock, seasonal stock, and dead stock.

Cycle Stock.   Cycle stock is inventory that results from replenishment of inventory sold or used in production. It is required in order to meet demand under conditions of certainty; that is, when the firm can predict demand and replenishment times (lead times). For example, if the rate of sales for a product is a constant 20 units per day and the lead time is always 10 days, no inventory beyond the cycle stock would be required. While assumptions of constant demand and lead time remove the complexities involved in inventory management, let's look at Figure 4–2 for an example to clarify the basic inventory principles. The example shows three alternative reorder strategies.

Since demand and lead time are constant and known, orders are scheduled to arrive just as the last unit is sold. Thus, no inventory beyond the cycle stock is required. The average cycle stock in all three examples is equal to half of the order quantity. However, the average cycle stock will be 200, 100, or 300 units depending on whether management orders in quantities of 400 (part A), 200 (part B), or 600 (part C), respectively.

In-Transit Inventories.   In-transit inventories are items that are en route from one location to another. They may be considered part of cycle stock even though they are not available for sale or shipment until after they arrive at the destination. For the calculation of inventory carrying costs, in-transit inventories should be considered as inventory at the place of shipment origin since the items are not available for use, sale, or subsequent reshipment.

Holding Inventory in Excess of Demand

Safety or Buffer Stock.   Safety or buffer stock is held in excess of cycle stock because of uncertainty in demand or lead time. Average inventory at a stockkeeping

---

[5]See Ronald Kopicki, Michael J. Berg, and Leslie Legg, *Reuse and Recycling— Reverse Logistics Opportunities* (Oak Brook, IL: Council of Logistics Management, 1993); and James R. Stock, *Reverse Logistics* (Oak Brook, IL: Council of Logistics Management, 1992).

FIGURE 4–2

The effect of reorder quantity on average inventory investment with constant demand and lead time

A. Order quantity of 400 units

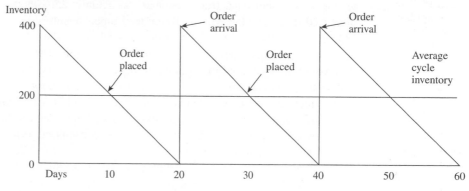

B. Order quantity of 200 units

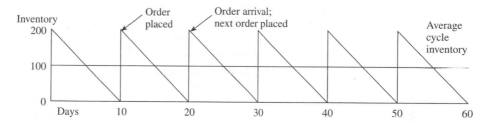

C. Order quantity of 600 units

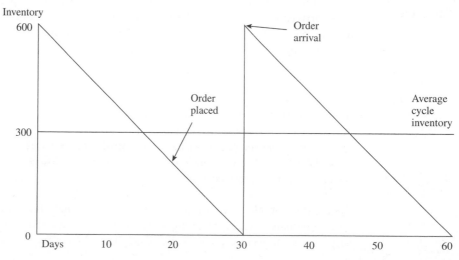

location that experiences demand or lead time variability is equal to half the order quantity plus the safety stock.

Inventory Levels Where Lead Times Are Constant but Demand Is Variable

In Figure 4–3, for example, the average inventory would be 100 units if demand and lead time were constant. But if demand was actually 25 units per day instead of the predicted 20 units per day with a 10-day lead time, inventory would be depleted by day 8 (200/25). Since the next order would not arrive until day 10 (order was placed on day zero), the company would be out of stock for two days. At 25 units of demand per day, this would be a stockout of 50 units in total. If management believed that the maximum variation in demand would be plus or minus 5 units, a safety stock of 50 units would prevent a stockout due to variation in demand. This would require holding an average inventory of 150 units (100 units average inventory + 50 units safety stock).

Inventory Levels Where Demand Is Constant but Lead Times Are Variable

Now consider the case in which demand is constant but lead time can vary by plus or minus two days (part B of Figure 4–3). If the order arrives 2 days early, the inventory on hand would be equal to a 12-day supply, or 240 units, since sales are at a rate of 20 units per day and 40 units would remain in inventory when the new order arrived. However, if the order arrived 2 days late, on day 12—which is a more likely occurrence—the firm would experience stockouts for a period of 2 days (40 units). If management believed that shipments would never arrive more than two days late, a safety stock of 40 units would ensure that a stockout due to variation in lead time would not occur if demand remained constant. This would require holding an average inventory of 140 units.

In most business situations, management must be able to deal with variability in demand and lead time. Forecasting is rarely accurate enough to predict demand, and demand is seldom, if ever, constant. In addition, transportation delays and supplier and production problems make lead time variability a fact of life. Consider part C of Figure 4–3, in which demand uncertainty (part A) and lead time uncertainty (part B) are combined.

Inventory Levels When Demand and Lead Times Are Variable

Combined uncertainty is the worst of all possible worlds. In this case, demand is above forecast by the maximum, 25 units instead of 20 units per day, and the incoming order arrives two days late. The result is a stockout period of four days at 25 units per day. If management wanted to protect against the maximum variability in both demand and lead time, the firm would need a safety stock of 100 units. This policy (no stockouts)would result in an average inventory of 200 units.

Good Forecasting Results in Less Safety Stock

In sum, variability in the order cycle requires safety stock. Since holding safety stock costs firms money, managers will try to reduce or eliminate variability. Forecasting can be used to better predict demand, resulting in less safety stock. Utilizing transportation carriers that provide consistent on-time deliveries will reduce lead time variability. Today, this concept is known as **time-definite delivery.** The goal is not necessarily to have the fastest delivery, but the most dependable, allowing safety stock reduction and the ability to plan more accurately.[6]

Speculative Stock. Speculative stock is inventory held for reasons other than satisfying current demand. For example, materials may be purchased in volumes larger than necessary in order to receive quantity discounts, because of a forecasted price increase or mate-

---

[6]Helen L. Richardson, "Trust Time-Definite, Reduce Inventory," *Transportation and Distribution* 35, no. 1 (Jan. 1994), pp. 41–44.

FIGURE 4–3

Average inventory investment under conditions of uncertainty

A. With variable demand

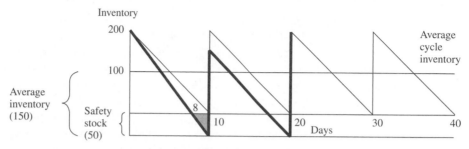

B. With variable lead time

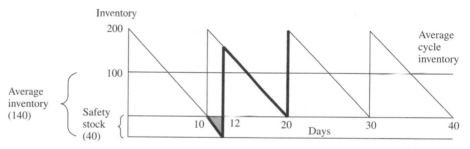

C. With variable demand and lead time

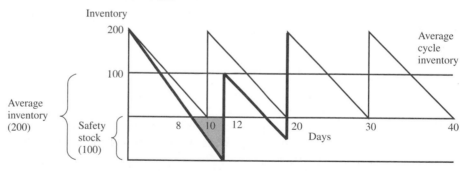

rials shortage, or to protect against the possibility of a strike. Production economies also may lead to the manufacture of products at times other than when they are in demand.

Seasonal Stock.   Seasonal stock is a form of speculative stock that involves the accumulation of inventory before a seasonal period begins. This often occurs with agricultural products and seasonal items. The fashion industry also is subject to seasonality with new fashions coming out many times a year. The back-to-school season is a particularly important time. See the Global box for a presentation of how Benetton tries to take some of the guess work out of demand for fashions.

Global

Benetton Uses Postponement to Improve Global Inventory Management

The concept of postponement—delaying commitment of the product to its final form until the last possible moment—can be an outstanding technique for responding to variability in customer demand. Benetton has only one distribution center—in Castrette, Italy—to serve stores in 120 countries. Benetton produces its most popular styles as "gray" goods, or undyed garments. When it sees what the actual demand pattern is for a certain sweater or pair of leggings by color, it can dye the gray goods quickly and speed them off to market. That way,

Benetton doesn't end up with too many aqua sweaters and not enough black sweaters. This allows Benetton to minimize its inventory while meeting customer demand and reducing end-of-season markdowns. Since it has only one distribution center and ships reorders based on actual demand, inventory is less likely to be located where it is not needed.

Source: Carla Rapoport and Justin Martin, "Retailers Go Global," *Fortune*, Feb. 20, 1995, pp. 102–8.

J. C. Whitney Company Makes Money from Selling Dead Stock

Dead Stock. Dead stock refers to items for which no demand has been registered for some specified period of time. Dead stock might be obsolete throughout a company or only at one stockkeeping location. If it is the latter, the items may be transshipped to another location to avoid the obsolescence penalty or mark down at their current location. An example of a company that has created a business by selling dead stock is J. C. Whitney Company. It sells parts for automobiles that are no longer produced, after the auto manufacturers get rid of their replacement part inventories. A company like Whitney sells them at higher prices (low volume, high margin).

Basic Inventory Management

Objectives of Inventory Management

Inventory is a major use of working capital. Accordingly, the objectives of inventory management are to increase corporate profitability through improved inventory management, to predict the impact of corporate policies on inventory levels, and to minimize the total cost of logistics activities while meeting customer service requirements.

Measures of Inventory Management Effectiveness

Methods of Decreasing Inventory-Related Costs

The key measure of effective inventory management is the impact that inventory has on corporate profitability. Effective inventory management can improve profitability by lowering costs or supporting increased sales.

Measures to decrease inventory-related costs include reducing the number of backorders or expedited shipments, purging obsolete or dead stock from the system, or improving the accuracy of forecasts. Transshipment of inventory between field warehouses and small-lot transfers can be reduced or eliminated by better inventory planning. Better

For most firms, dead stock is something to be avoided. However, for the J. C. Whitney Company, dead stocks of old, obsolete automobile parts have been turned into a business opportunity. Antique car restorers, old car enthusiasts, and automobile repair shops purchase many hard-to-find parts from J. C. Whitney because they aren't readily available elsewhere.

inventory management can increase the ability to control and predict how inventory investment will change in response to management policy.

Inventory Turnover   Inventory turnover is another measure of inventory performance. It is measured as:

$$\frac{\text{Annual dollar sales volume at cost}}{\text{Average dollar inventory investment}}$$

All else being equal, a higher number is preferred, indicating that inventory moves through the firm's operations quickly, rather than being held for an extensive period. For example, an item with annual sales of $500,000 valued at cost and an average inventory

Motorola combines EDI and JIT to reduce paperwork and dramatically increase inventory management performance.

investment of $100,000, would have a turnover of five times. Turnover should not be used as the only measure of inventory effectiveness, but should be combined with other measures that reflect customer service issues.

Fill Rate

Increased sales are often possible if high levels of inventory lead to better in-stock availability and more consistent service levels. Fill rate is a common measure of the customer service performance of inventory. As presented in Chapter 2, "Customer Service," fill rate is often presented as the percentage of units available when requested by the customer. A 96 percent fill rate means that 4 percent of requested units were unavailable when ordered by the customer. Low inventory levels can reduce fill rates, hurting customer service and creating lost sales. The Technology box presents some of the inventory measurements used by Motorola's Information Systems Group in reengineering its inventory management processes.

Finally, total cost integration should be the goal of inventory planning; that is, management must determine the inventory level required to achieve least total cost logistics, given the required customer service objectives.

Impact of Demand Patterns on Inventory Management

Whether inventory is "pulled" or "pushed" through a system and whether the demand is "dependent" or "independent" has implications for inventory management methods.

Pull versus Push Systems

Pull versus push systems are distinguished by the way the company's production is driven. If a company waits to produce products until customers demand it, that is a pull system. Customer demand "pulls" the inventory. If a firm produces to forecast or anticipated sales to customers, that is a "push" system. The firm is "pushing" its inventory into the market in anticipation of sales.

Technology

Reengineering Inventory Management at Motorola's Information Systems Group (ISG)

Motorola ISG recently revamped its inventory processes by combining EDI with JIT. In addition to drastically reducing the amount of paperwork in the procurement process, ISG is enjoying the following improvements in inventory performance:

- Reduced supplier cycle time from an average of six days to one, decreasing cycle stock needs.
- Reduced warehouse space by over 50 percent.
- Reduced total inventory by more than one-third.
- Eliminated the two-to-three-day lag between order receipt at ISG's warehouse and delivery to the production floor.
- Reduced raw material replenishment time from 40 days to 6 days.

ISG began its improved inventory management process by using EDI to reduce the order cycle times of its raw material suppliers thereby reducing inventory. With this accomplished, ISG added "auto order," to automatically release purchase orders when inventory reached a certain level. The next step was adding point-of-use delivery of materials directly to the location where the materials are used in manufacturing. This step reduced lead times and the buffer inventory between ISG's warehouse and production facilities.

Motorola ISG's next step is to move this system into place with its customers. This should further help ISG and its customers to reduce finished goods inventory and to speed up product lead times.

Source: Adapted from Joseph N. Salemi, "Just-in-Time EDI," *EDI World*, Jan. 1995, pp. 20–23.

Independent versus Dependent Demand

Independent versus dependent demand inventory focuses on whether the demand for an item depends on demand for something else. An independent demand item is a finished good, while dependent demand items are the raw materials and components that go into the production of that finished good. The demand for raw materials or components is "derived" based on the demand for the finished good. The need for dependent demand items doesn't have to be forecast; it can be calculated based on the production schedule of the finished good. The need for production of the finished good may be forecast or based on customer demand/orders.

Inventory managers must determine how much inventory to order and when to place the order. To illustrate the basic principles of reorder policy, let's consider inventory management under conditions of certainty. In reality, the more common situation is inventory management under uncertainty, but the management process will be similar in both instances.

Inventory Management under Conditions of Certainty

Components of Ordering Costs

Replenishment policy under conditions of certainty requires the balancing of ordering costs against inventory carrying costs.[7] For example, a policy of ordering large quantities

---

[7]When the supplier pays the freight cost.

infrequently may result in inventory carrying costs in excess of the savings in ordering costs. Ordering costs for products purchased from an outside supplier typically include (1) the cost of transmitting the order, (2) the cost of receiving the product, (3) the cost of placing it in storage, and (4) the cost of processing the invoice for payment.

In restocking its own field warehouses, a company's ordering costs typically include (1) the cost of transmitting and processing the inventory transfer, (2) the cost of handling the product if it is in stock, or the cost of setting up production to produce it, and the handling cost if the product is not in stock, (3) the cost of receiving at the field location, and (4) the cost of documentation. Remember that only direct out-of-pocket expenses should be included in ordering costs. Inventory carrying costs will be explained in detail in Chapter 5.

Economic Order Quantity.   The best ordering policy can be determined by minimizing the total of inventory carrying costs and ordering costs using the **economic order quantity (EOQ)** model. The EOQ is a "concept which determines the optimal order quantity on the basis of ordering and carrying costs. When incremental ordering costs equal incremental carrying costs, the most economic order quantity exists. It does not optimize order quantity and thus the shipment quantity, on the basis of total logistics costs, but only ordering and carrying costs."[8]

Two questions seem appropriate in reference to the example in Figure 4–2:

1. Should we place orders for 200, 400, or 600 units, or some other quantity?
2. What is the impact on inventory if orders are placed at 10-, 20-, or 30-day intervals, or some other time period? Assuming constant demand and lead time, sales of 20 units per day, and 240 working days per year, annual sales will be 4,800 units.[9] If orders are placed every 10 days, 24 orders of 200 units will be placed. With a 20-day order interval, 12 orders of 400 units are required. If the 30-day order interval is selected, 8 orders of 600 units are necessary. The average inventory is 100, 200, and 300 units, respectively. Which of these policies would be best?

Cost Trade-Offs in Calculating the EOQ

The cost trade-offs required to determine the most economical order quantity are shown graphically in Figure 4–4. By determining the EOQ and dividing the annual demand by it, the frequency and size of the order that will minimize the two costs are identified.

The EOQ Formula

The EOQ in units can be calculated using the following formula:

$$EOQ = \sqrt{\frac{2PD}{CV}}$$

where

P = The ordering cost (dollars per order)
D = Annual demand or usage of product (number of units)
C = Annual inventory carrying cost (as a percentage of product cost or value)
V = Average cost or value of one unit of inventory

[8]Kenneth B. Ackerman, *Words of Warehousing* (Columbus, OH: K. B. Ackerman Company, 1992), p. 28.
[9]For this example, it was assumed that the plant was closed for four weeks each year. In an industrial application, we would use the actual number of working days for the firm in question.

FIGURE 4–4

Cost trade-offs required to determine the most economical order quantity

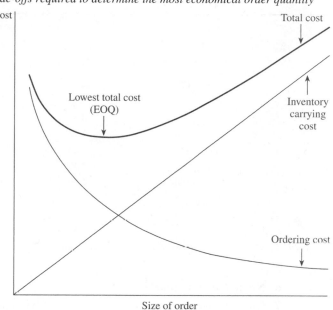

Now, using the EOQ formula, we will determine the best ordering policy for the situation described in Figure 4–2:

P = $40
D = 4,800 units
C = 25 percent
V = $100 per unit

$$EOQ = \sqrt{\frac{2(\$40)(4,800)}{(25\%)(100)}}$$

$$= \sqrt{\frac{384,000}{25}}$$

$$= 124 \text{ units}$$

If 20 units fit on a pallet, then the reorder quantity of 120 units would be established. This analysis is shown in Table 4–1.

The EOQ model has received significant attention and use in industry, but it is not without its limitations. The simple EOQ model is based on the following assumptions:

Assumptions of the EOQ Model

1. A continuous, constant, and known rate of demand.
2. Constant and known replenishment or lead time.
3. Constant purchase price independent of the order quantity or time.
4. Constant transportation cost independent of the order quantity or time.
5. The satisfaction of all demand (no stockouts are permitted).

TABLE 4–1 **Cost Trade-Offs Required to Determine the Most Economical Order Quantity**

Order Quantity	Number of Orders (D/Q)	Ordering Cost $P \times (D/Q)$	Inventory Carrying Cost $\frac{1}{2} Q \times C \times V$	Total Cost
40	120	$4,800	$500	$5,300
60	80	3,200	750	3,950
80	60	2,400	1,000	3,400
100	48	1,920	1,250	3,170
120	40	1,600	1,500	3,100
140	35	1,400	1,750	3,150
160	30	1,200	2,000	3,200
200	24	960	2,500	3,460
300	16	640	3,750	4,390
400	12	480	5,000	5,480

6. No inventory in transit.
7. Only one product in inventory or at least no interaction between products (independent demand items).
8. An infinite planning horizon.
9. No limit on capital availability.

It would be very unusual to find a situation where demand and lead time are constant, both are known with certainty, and costs are known precisely. However, the simplifying assumptions are of great concern only if policy decisions will change as a result of the assumptions made. The EOQ solution is relatively insensitive to small changes in the input data.

Referring to Figure 4–4, one can see that the EOQ curve is relatively flat around the solution point. This is often referred to as the "bathtub effect." Although the calculated EOQ was 124 units (rounded to 120), an EOQ variation of 20 or even 40 units does not significantly change the total cost (see Table 4–1).

Adjusting the EOQ for Volume Transportation Rates and Quantity Discounts

Adjustments to the EOQ. Typical refinements that must be made to the EOQ model include adjustments for volume transportation rates and for quantity discounts. The simple EOQ model did not consider the impact of these two factors. The following adjustment can be made to the EOQ formula so that it will consider the impact of quantity discounts and or freight breaks:[10]

$$Q^1 = 2\frac{rD}{C} + (1 - R)Q^0$$

---

[10]See Robert G. Brown, *Decision Rules for Inventory Management* (New York: Holt, Rinehart & Winston, 1967), pp. 205–6.

where

Q^1 = The maximum quantity that can be economically ordered to qualify for a discount on unit cost

r = The percentage of price reduction if a larger quantity is ordered

D = The annual demand in units

C = The inventory carrying cost percentage

Q^0 = The EOQ based on current price

Computing the EOQ: An Example

Using the modified EOQ formula, we will determine the best ordering policy for the Jymbob Manufacturing Company (a fictitious firm). Jymbob Manufacturing produced and sold a complete line of industrial air-conditioning units that were marketed nationwide through independent distributors. The company purchased a line of relays for use in its air conditioners from a manufacturer in the Midwest. It ordered approximately 300 cases of 24 units each, 54 times per year; the annual volume was about 16,000 cases. The purchase price was $8.00 per case, the order costs were $10.00 per order, and the inventory carrying cost was 25 percent. The relays weighed 25 pounds per case; Johnson Manufacturing paid the shipping costs. The freight rate was $4.00 per hundredweight (cwt) on shipments of less than 15,000 pounds, $3.90 per cwt on shipments of 15,000 to 39,000 pounds, and $3.64 per cwt on orders of more than 39,000 pounds. The relays were shipped on pallets of 20 cases.

First, it is necessary to calculate the transportation cost for a case of product without discounts for volume shipments. Shipments of less than 15,000 pounds—600 cases—cost $4.00 per cwt, or $1.00 ($4.00/100 lbs. × 25 lbs.) per case.

Therefore, without transportation discounts for shipping in quantities above 15,000 pounds, the delivered cost of a case of product would be $9.00 ($8.00 plus $1.00 transportation), and the EOQ would be:

$$EOQ = \sqrt{\frac{2PD}{CV}}$$

$$= \sqrt{\frac{(2)(\$10)(16,000)}{(.25)(\$9.00)}}$$

$$= \sqrt{\frac{320,000}{2.25}}$$

$$= 377, \text{ or } 380 \text{ rounded to nearest full pallet}$$

If the company shipped in quantities of 40,000 pounds or more, the cost per case would be $0.91 ($3.64/100 lbs. × 25 lbs.). The percentage price reduction r made possible by shipping at the lowest freight cost is:

$$r = \frac{\$9.00 - \$8.91}{\$9.00} \times 100 = 1.0\% \text{ reduction in delivered cost}$$

The adjusted EOQ is calculated as follows:

$$Q^1 = \frac{2(.01)(16,000)}{.25} + (1-.01)(380)$$

$$= 1,280 + 376$$

$$= 1,656, \text{ or } 1,660 \text{ rounded to the nearest full pallet}$$

While the largest freight break results in only a 1 percent reduction in the delivered cost of a case of the product, the volume of annual purchases is large enough that the EOQ changes significantly, from 380 cases to 1,660 cases. Calculations of the total annual costs at various order quantities are shown in Table 4–2.

It is also possible to include purchase discounts by adding an annual product cost column to Table 4–2 and adjusting the inventory carrying cost and total annual costs columns appropriately. Once again, the desired EOQ would be the order quantity that resulted in the lowest total cost.[11]

Fixed Order Point versus Fixed Order Interval Policy

Fixed Order Point The EOQ represents a **fixed order point** policy. Once the EOQ has been determined, we order a fixed quantity each time, based on the EOQ. Actual demand may cause the time between orders to vary. An order is placed when inventory on hand reaches a predetermined minimum level necessary to satisfy demand during the order cycle. The automated inventory control system normally generates an order or at least a management report when the reorder point is reached.

Fixed Order Interval Another reorder policy is the **fixed order interval** approach. Under this approach, inventory levels are reviewed at a certain, set time interval, perhaps every week. An order is placed for a variable amount of inventory, whatever is required to get the company back to its desired inventory level. This approach is common where many items are purchased from the same supplier. A weekly order may be placed to reduce ordering costs and take advantage of purchase volume discounts and freight consolidation.

Inventories and Customer Service

The establishment of a service level, and thus a safety stock policy, is a matter of managerial judgment. Management should consider factors such as customer relations, customer wants and needs, competitive service levels, and the ability of the firm to support continuous production processes.

In many companies, management improves customer service levels simply by adding safety stock because the cost of carrying inventory has often not been calculated for the firm or has been set arbitrarily at an artificially low level. Figure 4–5 illustrates the relationship between customer service levels and inventory investment. The calculations are shown in Table 4B–5 in Appendix B (at this time, ignore the broken line and arrows in Figure 4–5).

---

[11]For additional examples of special purpose EOQ models, refer to Richard B. Chase and Nicholas J. Aquilano, *Production and Operations Management,* 6th edition (Burr Ridge, IL: Richard D. Irwin, 1992).

TABLE 4–2   Cost Trade-Offs to Determine the Most Economical Order Quantity with Transportation Costs Included

A Possible Order Quantity	B Number of Orders per Year	C (A × $8) Purchase Price per Order	D Value of Orders per Year B × C	E Transportation Cost per Order	F Annual Ordering Cost	G Annual Transportation Cost	H Inventory Carrying Cost[d]	I Total Annual Costs
300	54	$2,400	$129,600	$300[a]	$540	$16,200	$338	$17,078
380	43	3,040	130,720	380[a]	430	16,340	428	17,198
400	40	3,200	128,000	400[a]	400	16,000	450	16,850
800	20	6,400	128,000	780[b]	200	15,600	898	16,698
1,200	14	9,600	134,400	1,170[b]	140	16,380	1,346	17,866
1,600	10	12,800	128,000	1,456[c]	100	14,560	1,782	16,442[e]
1,800	9	14,400	129,600	1,638[c]	90	14,742	2,005	16,837
2,000	8	16,000	128,000	1,820[c]	80	14,560	2,228	16,868

[a]Orders for less than 15,000 lbs. (600 cases) have a rate of $4.00/cwt which equals $1.00/case.

[b]Orders weighing between 15,000 lbs. and 39,000 lbs. (600 cases and 1,560 cases) have a rate of $3.90/cwt which equals $0.975/case.

[c]Orders weighing 40,000 lbs. or more (1,600 cases) have a rate of $3.64/cwt which equals $0.91/case.

[d]Inventory carrying cost = ½ (C + E) (25%).

[e]Lowest total cost.

To serve European customers better and more efficiently, 3M has consolidated its warehousing into five state-of-the-art distribution centers like this one in Juchen, Germany.

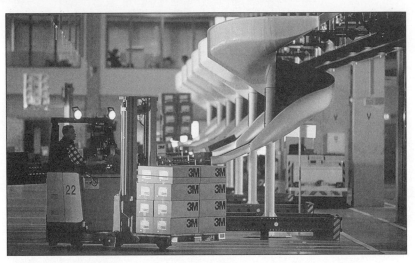

Although inventory investment figures will vary from situation to situation, relationships similar to those in the example will hold. As customer service levels move toward 100 percent, inventory levels increase disproportionately. It becomes obvious that customer service levels should not be improved solely by the addition of inventory. The need to develop an accurate inventory carrying cost for the purpose of planning should be clear.

Substituting Information for Inventory Carrying Costs

One way of resolving this problem is to substitute information for inventory carrying costs by using customers' point-of-sale scanner data to plan short-term production and restocking of customer inventory locations. Another possibility is to recognize the wide differences in demand levels and demand variation associated with each product and manage their inventories differently.

Managers often make the mistake of treating all products the same. Generally, a more economical policy is to stock the highest volume items at retail locations, high-and moderate-volume items at field warehouse locations, and slow-moving items at centralized locations. The centralized location may be a distribution center or a plant warehouse.

ABC Analysis

This type of multiechelon stocking procedure is referred to as **ABC analysis,** which will be discussed in Chapter 5. The broken line in Figure 4–5 shows how the relationship between inventory investment and customer service levels can be shifted, using some of these strategies.

Production Scheduling

Earlier in this chapter, we discussed how inventory levels can be influenced by production policies. The reverse also is true. In many cases, logistics policy changes—especially those that decrease inventory levels—can create significant increases in total production costs that are beyond the control of manufacturing management.

FIGURE 4–5

Relationship between inventory investment and customer service levels

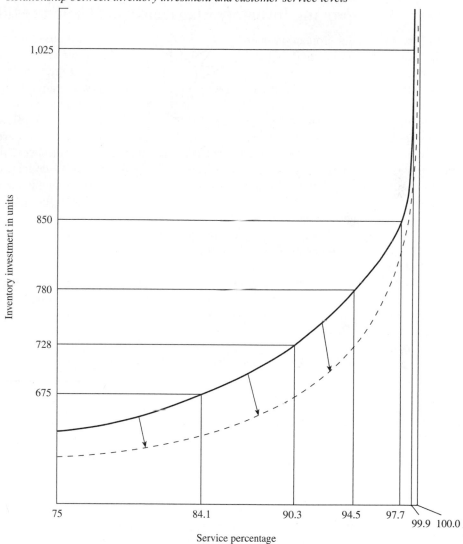

An inventory policy decision that reduces logistics costs by less than the increase in production setup cost results in lower overall profit performance for the company. This issue is presented in the Creative Solutions box in relation to General Mills. Logistics managers must be aware of the impact of their decisions on the efficiency of manufacturing operations and consider associated changes in manufacturing costs when establishing logistics policies.

Creative Solutions

Improving Inventory Management at General Mills

General Mills, Inc., had a production operations division that manufactured and distributed products for the several marketing divisions of the firm. Consequently, the logistics function received a sales forecast from marketing and, given the inventory deployment policies of company divisions and the objective to minimize total logistics costs, manufacturing was told how many units of each item to produce. Manufacturing then established a production schedule.

The system was not without its problems, however. Manufacturing performance was judged by comparing actual production costs to the cost arrived at by multiplying the various units produced by the standard manufacturing cost for each product. The standard cost was a full cost standard comprised of (1) direct materials, (2) direct labor, (3) variable overhead, and (4) fixed overhead. The overhead costs included production setup costs based on a projected number of setups for each product for the year and the estimated number of units produced during the year.

Logistics influenced the number of setups actually incurred by manufacturing, but the standard cost was not changed during the year to reflect this. Since the number of setups incurred would influence manufacturing performance, plant management resisted policies that would increase the projected number of setups. The solution was to maintain two separate standard costs for each product. One was a variable cost per unit, excluding a setup component, and the other was a standard setup cost for each product. Manufacturing performance was judged on the ability to manufacture a specified quantity efficiently. Logistics was charged with the responsibility of considering setup costs in the analysis when inventory policies were determined.

Source: Douglas M. Lambert and James R. Stock, *Strategic Logistics Management*, 3rd ed. (Burr Ridge, IL: Richard D. Irwin, 1993), pp. 423–24.

Summary

In this chapter and the accompanying appendixes, we examined the basic concepts of inventory management. The EOQ model was introduced, along with methods for adjusting it. In addition, we discussed demand and order cycle uncertainty. Appendixes 4–A, 4–B, and 4–C examine both types of uncertainty when calculating safety stock requirements. We saw that the traditional approach to improving customer service, increasing inventory investment, is costly. We closed with an overview of the impact of inventory investment on production scheduling. In the next chapter, we will further examine inventory concepts, focusing on inventory management techniques and the cost of holding inventory.

Suggested Readings

Berry, L. William; Thomas E. Vollman; and D. Clay Whybark. *Integrated Production and Inventory Management.* Burr Ridge, IL: BusinessOne Irwin, 1993.

Chambers, John C.; Satinder K. Mullick; and Donald D. Smith. "How to Choose the Right Forecasting Technique." *Harvard Business Review* 49, no. 4 (July–Aug. 1971), pp. 45–74.

Chase, Richard B., and Nicholas J. Aquilano. *Production and Operations Management,* 6th ed. Burr Ridge, IL: Richard D. Irwin, 1992.

Georgeoff, David M., and Robert G. Murdick. "Managers Guide to Forecasting." *Harvard Business Review* 64, no. 1 (Jan.–Feb. 1986), pp. 110–20.

Gill, Lynn E.; George Isoma; and Joel L. Sutherland. "Inventory and Physical Distribution Management." In James F. Robeson and Robert G. House, eds., *The Distribution Handbook.* New York: Free Press, 1985.

Graves, S. C.; A. H. G. Rinnooy Kan; and P. H. Zipkin. *Logistics of Production and Inventory.* Amsterdam: North-Holland, 1993.

Hau, Lee L., and Corey Billington. "Managing Supply Chain Inventories: Pitfalls and Opportunities." *Sloan Management Review* 33, no. 3 (Spring 1992), pp. 65–73.

Jain, C. L. "Myths and Realities of Forecasting." *Journal of Business Forecasting,* Fall 1990, pp. 18–29.

Richardson, Helen L. "Trust Time-Definite, Reduce Inventory." *Transportation and Distribution* 35, no. 1 (Jan. 1994), pp. 41–44.

Tersine, Richard J., and Michele G. Tersine. "Inventory Reduction: Preventive and Corrective Strategies." *The International Journal of Logistics Management* 1, no. 2 (1990), pp. 17–24.

Vander Duyn Schowten, Frank A.; Marc J. G. van Ejis; and Ruùd M. J. Heuts. "The Value of Information to Improve Management of a Retailer's Inventory." *Decision Sciences* 25, no. 1 (1994), pp. 1–14.

Zinn, Walter. "Developing Heuristics to Estimate the Impact of Postponement on Safety Stock." *The International Journal of Logistics Management* 1, no. 2 (1990), pp. 11–16.

Questions and Problems

1. Why is inventory so important to the efficient and effective management of a firm?

2. How does uncertainty in demand and lead time affect inventory levels?

3. How does the economic order quantity model mathematically select the most economical order quantity?

4. One of the product lines carried by Farha Wholesale Foods was a line of canned fruit manufactured by California Canners. Mr. Jones, the canned goods buyer, knew that the company did not reorder from its suppliers in a systematic manner and wondered if the EOQ model might be appropriate. For example, the company ordered 200 cases of fruit cocktail each week, and the annual volume was about 10,000 cases. The purchase price was $8 per case, the ordering cost was $15 per order, and the inventory carrying cost was 35 percent. California Canners paid the transportation charges, and there were no price breaks for ordering quantities in excess of 200

cases. Does the economic order quantity model apply in this situation? If so, calculate the economic order quantity.

5. Explain the basic differences between a fixed order point, fixed order quantity model, and a fixed order interval inventory model. Which is likely to lead to the largest inventory levels? Why?

6. Calculate the economic order quantity, the safety stock, and the average inventory necessary to achieve a 98 percent customer service level, given the following information:

   a. The average daily demand for a 25-day period was found to be:

Day	Units Demand	Day	Units Demand
1	8	14	9
2	5	15	10
3	4	16	5
4	6	17	8
5	9	18	11
6	8	19	9
7	9	20	7
8	10	21	7
9	7	22	6
10	6	23	8
11	7	24	10
12	8	25	11
13	12		

   b. There is no variability in order cycle.
   c. The ordering cost is $20 per order.
   d. The annual demand is 2,000.
   e. The cost is $100 per unit.
   f. The inventory carrying cost is 35 percent.
   g. The products are purchased FOB destination.

To Support Appendix

7. Recalculate your answer to question 6 given the following sample of replenishment cycles:

Replenishment Cycle	Lead Time in Days	Replenishment Cycle	Lead Time in Days
1	10	10	9
2	12	11	8
3	11	12	10
4	10	13	11
5	10	14	9
6	9	15	9
7	8	16	10
8	12	17	11
9	11	18	10

8. Given your calculations in questions 6 and 7, what will the actual fill rate be if management is willing to hold inventory equal to one week's sales as safety stock?

9. What is the cost saving to the customer resulting from a manufacturer's ability to reduce variability by two days, given the following information:

   a. Average sales of 40 cases per day.

   b. Purchase price per case of $45.

   c. Transportation cost per case of $5.

   d. Order cycle of 10 days.

   e. Inventory carrying cost of 40 percent.

   How does this compare with the cost saving associated with a two-day reduction in the order cycle with no change in order cycle variability?

10. As a member of the inventory planning team for Cook Department Stores, one of your primary responsibilities is to aid department managers with inventory decisions. The electronics department manager has come to your group with a desire to improve department inventory planning and profitability. The department stocks a VCR brand named Super View.

Super View Financial Data

Selling price/unit	$555
Cost of goods sold, including delivery costs at current level of operations and under current inventory policies	$495

Super View Sales Data

Representative 10-day sales (assume Cook Department Store is open 360 days a year):

Sales/Day	Number of Days (f)
1	2
2	2
6	2
10	2
16	2

Super View Lead-Time Data

Super View is supplied directly from Tokyo, Japan, by Sayonara Manufacturing.

Delivery pattern	Sample of 10 order cycles in days
Super View	9, 9, 42, 13, 22, 33, 11, 18, 36, 27

Current Super View Service and Inventory Policies

Order policy	EOQ: Orders are equal to the average demand that occur during average lead-time
Fill rate	99 percent

The following inventory carrying costs figures were collected:

Corporate opportunity of capital was 37% (pretax).	
Other costs:	
Inventory taxes	1.6%
Insurance	0.4%
Recurring storage	3.3%
Obsolescence	0.7%
Damage	2.0%

The manager has several questions regarding inventory policy:

a. Which of the of following Super View fill rates (99 percent, 95 percent, 91 percent, or 87 percent) will result in the highest annual profit?

TABLE 1   Daily Super View Sales

| | Branch Store | | | | |
Day	1	2	3	4	5
1	1	1	1	16	16
2	2	2	2	10	10
3	6	6	6	6	6
4	10	10	10	2	2
5	16	16	16	1	1
6	1	1	1	16	16
7	2	2	2	10	10
8	6	6	6	6	6
9	10	10	10	2	2
10	16	16	16	1	1
Average sales/store	7	7	7	7	
σ s/Store	5.81	5.81	5.81	5.81	5.81

b. Sayonara Manufacturing stated that for an additional 1.5 percent increase in price, it can hire more dependable international carriers to cut the lead-time standard deviation in half. Should the electronics department manager accept or reject the offer? (Assume their current 99 percent fill rate and ordering policies.)

c. There are five Cook Department Store branches in the Detroit area (see Table 1). Corporate management wants to compare the annual profitability of two strategies.

 (1) Provide a 99 percent fill rate for Super View by stocking the appropriate number of units of safety stock at each branch store.

 (2) Provide a 99 percent fill rate for Super View at the local area distribution center which serves all five branches, and expedite safety stock when needed to each individual branch at a total expediting cost of $150 per week.

Which strategy will be more profitable, assuming no lost sales if the second strategy is employed?

Appendixes

These appendixes contains some valuable, but slightly more advanced, calculations for dealing with inventory management under conditions of uncertainty. Detailed, step-by-step examples allow the reader to develop an excellent grasp of how to calculate safety stock requirements for desired levels customer service, and how to calculate fill rates. Questions 6–8 illustrate these concepts.

APPENDIX 4–A

INVENTORY MANAGEMENT UNDER UNCERTAINTY

As we have noted, managers rarely, if ever, know for sure what demand to expect for the firm's products. Many factors, including economic conditions, competitive actions, changes in government regulations, market shifts, and changes in consumer buying patterns, may influence forecast accuracy. Order cycle times also are not constant. Transit times vary; it may take more time to assemble an order or wait for scheduled production on one occasion than another, supplier lead times for components and raw materials may be inconsistent, and suppliers may not have the capability of responding to changes in demand.

Consequently, management has the option of either maintaining additional inventory in the form of safety stocks (see Figure 4–3) or risking a potential loss of sales revenue due to inventory stockouts. We must thus consider an additional cost trade-off: inventory carrying costs versus stockout costs.

The uncertainties associated with demand and lead time cause most managers to concentrate on *when* to order rather than how much to order. The order quantity is important to the extent that it influences the number of orders and consequently the number of times that the company is exposed to a potential stockout at the end of each order cycle. The point at which the order is placed is the primary determinant of the future ability to fill demand while waiting for replenishment stock. As presented in the chapter, order policy may be based on fixed order quantity or fixed interval. Figure 4A–1 illustrates these two methods.

A review of part A of Figure 4A–1 shows that replenishment orders are placed on days 15, 27, and 52, respectively, under the fixed order point, fixed order quantity model. In contrast, when the fixed order interval model is used (part B), orders are placed at 20-day intervals on days 15, 35, 55. With the fixed order interval model, it is necessary to forecast demand for days 20 through 40 on day 15, for days 40 through 60 on day 35, and so on. The fixed order interval system is more adaptive because management is forced to consider changes in sales activity and make a forecast for every order interval.

FIGURE 4A–1

Inventory management under uncertainty

A. Fixed-order point, fixed-order quantity model

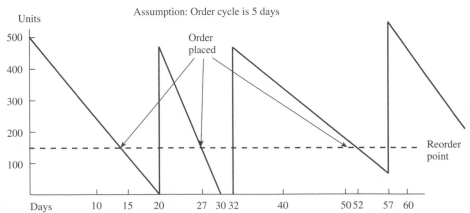

B. Fixed-order interval model

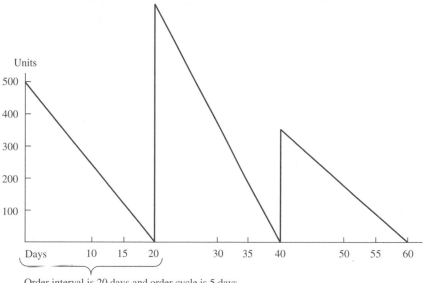

Order interval is 20 days and order cycle is 5 days

APPENDIX 4–B

CALCULATING SAFETY STOCK REQUIREMENTS

The amount of safety stock necessary to satisfy a given level of demand can be determined by computer simulation or statistical techniques. In this illustration, we address the use of statistical techniques. In calculating safety stock levels, it is necessary to consider the joint impact of demand and replenishment cycle variability. This can be accomplished by gathering statistically valid samples of data on recent sales volumes and replenishment cycles. Once the data are gathered, it is possible to determine safety stock requirements by using this formula:[12]

$$\sigma c = \sqrt{\overline{R}\left(\sigma S^2\right) + \overline{S}^2\left(\sigma R^2\right)}$$

where

σc = Units of safety stock needed to satisfy 68 percent of all probabilities (one standard deviation)

$\overline{R}$ = Average replenishment cycle

σR = Standard deviation of the replenishment cycle

$\overline{S}$ = Average daily sales

σS = Standard deviation of daily sales

---

[12]Robert Hammond of McKinsey and Company, Inc., as reported in Robert Fetter and Winston C. Dalleck, *Decision Models for Inventory Management* (Burr Ridge, IL: Richard D. Irwin, 1961), pp. 105–8. For a recent application of the formula in a simulation model, see Walter Zinn, Howard Marmorstein, and John Charnes, "The Effect of Autocorrelated Demand on Customer Service," *Journal of Business Logistics* 13, no. 1 (1992), pp. 173–92.

Assume that the sales history contained in Table 4B–1 has been developed for market area 1. From this sample, we can calculate the standard deviation of sales as shown in Table 4B–2. The formula is:

$$\sigma S = \sqrt{\frac{\Sigma f d^2}{n-1}}$$

where

σS = Standard deviation of daily sales

f = Frequency of event

d = Deviation of event from mean

n = Total observations

Applying this formula to the data yields a standard deviation of sales equal approximately to 20 units:

$$\sigma S = \sqrt{\frac{10,000}{25-1}}$$

$$= 20$$

This means that 68 percent of the time, daily sales fall between 80 and 120 units (100 units ± 20 units). A protection of two standard deviations, or 40 units, would protect against 95 percent of all events. In setting safety stock levels, however, it is important to consider only events that exceed the mean sales volume. Thus, a safety stock level of 40 units actually protects against almost 98 percent of all possible events (see Figure 4B–1). Given a distribution of measurements that is approximately bell-shaped, the mean, plus or minus one standard deviation, will contain approximately 68 percent of the measurements. This leaves 16 percent in each of the tails, which means that inventory sufficient to cover sales of one standard deviation in excess of mean daily sales will actually provide a customer service level of 84 percent. (If the sample does not represent a normal distribution, refer to a basic statistics book for an alternative treatment.)

The same procedure can be used to arrive at the mean and standard deviation of the replenishment cycle. Once this is accomplished, the formula shown previously can be used to determine safety stock requirements at a certain level of demand. For example, an analysis of replenishment cycles might yield the results shown in Table 4B–3. The standard deviation of the replenishment cycle is:

$$(\sigma R) = \sqrt{\frac{\Sigma f d^2}{n-1}}$$

$$= \sqrt{2.67}$$

$$= 1.634$$

The average replenishment cycle is:

$$\left(\overline{R}\right) = 10$$

The combined safety stock required to cover variability in both demand and lead time can be found using the formula:

$$\sigma c = \sqrt{\overline{R}\left(\sigma S^2\right) + S^2\left(\sigma R^2\right)}$$

$$= \sqrt{4,000 + 26,700} = \sqrt{30,700}$$

$$= 175 \text{ cases}$$

Thus, in a situation in which daily sales vary from 60 to 140 cases and the inventory replenishment cycle varies from 7 to 13 days, a safety stock of 175 cases will allow the manufacturer to satisfy 84 percent of all possible occurrences. To protect against 98 percent of all possibilities, 350

TABLE 4B–1   **Sales History for Market Area 1**

Day	Sales in Cases	Day	Sales in Cases
1	100	14	80
2	80	15	90
3	70	16	90
4	60	17	100
5	80	18	140
6	90	19	110
7	120	20	120
8	110	21	70
9	100	22	100
10	110	23	130
11	130	24	110
12	120	25	90
13	100		

TABLE 4B–2   **Calculation of Standard Deviation of Sales**

Daily Sales in Cases	Frequency (f)	Deviation from Mean (d)	Deviation Squared (d^2)	fd^2
60	1	−40	1,600	1,600
70	2	−30	900	1,800
80	3	−20	400	1,200
90	4	−10	100	400
100	5	0	0	0
110	4	+10	100	400
120	3	+20	400	1,200
130	2	+30	900	1,800
140	1	+40	1,600	1,600
$\overline{S} = 100$	$n = 25$			$\Sigma fd^2 = 10,000$

cases of safety stock are required. Table 4B–4 shows alternative customer service levels and safety stock requirements.

To establish the average inventory for various levels of customer service, we must first determine the EOQ. The projected yearly demand is found by multiplying the average daily demand by 250 working days,[13] which equals 25,000 cases (250 × 100). The inventory carrying cost was calculated to be 32 percent, the average value of a case of product was $4.37, and the ordering cost was $28.00. The average inventory required to satisfy each service level is shown in Table 4B–5.

---

[13]For this example, the average number of working days per year was assumed to be 250.

FIGURE 4B–1

Area relationships for the normal distribution

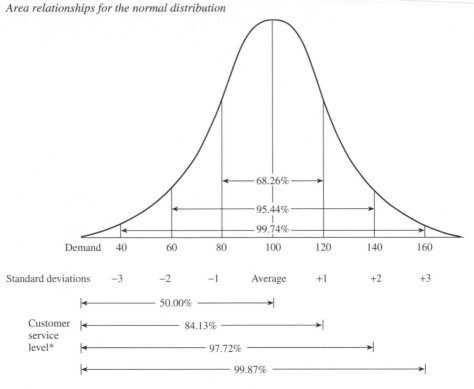

*As measured by the percentage of order cycles that will not suffer from stockouts. It is the probability that no stockout will occur during a replenishment cycle.

TABLE 4B–3   Calculation of Standard Deviation of Replenishment Cycle

Lead Times in Days	Frequency (f)	Deviation from Mean (d)	Deviation Squared (d²)	fd²
7	1	−3	9	9
8	2	−2	4	8
9	3	−1	1	3
10	4	0	0	0
11	3	+1	1	3
12	2	+2	4	8
13	1	+3	9	9
$\bar{R} = 10$	$n = 16$			$\Sigma fd^2 = 40$

TABLE 4B–4   **Summary of Alternative Service Levels and Safety Stock Requirements**

Service Levels (percent)	Number of Standard Deviations (C) Needed	Safety Stock Requirements (cases)
84.1	1.0	175
90.3	1.3	228
94.5	1.6	280
97.7	2.0	350
98.9	2.3	403
99.5	2.6	455
99.9	3.0	525

TABLE 4B–5   **Summary of Average Inventory Levels Given Different Service Levels**

Service Levels (percent)	Average Cycle Stock ($\frac{1}{2} \times EOQ$)	Safety Stock (units)	Total Average Inventory (units)
84.1	500	175	675
90.3	500	228	728
94.5	500	280	780
97.7	500	350	850
98.9	500	403	903
99.5	500	455	955
99.9	500	525	1,025

Note that the establishment of a safety stock commitment is really a policy of customer service and inventory availability. Although we have demonstrated a quantitative method of calculating safety stock requirements to protect the firm against stockouts at various levels of probability, additional calculations are necessary to determine the specific fill rate when stockouts occur. Fill rate represents the percentage of units demanded that are on hand to fill customer orders.

Calculating Fill Rate

Fill rate represents the magnitude of the stockout. If a manager wants to hold 280 units as safety stock, what will the fill rate be?[14]

The fill rate can be calculated using the following formula:

$$FR = 1 - \frac{\sigma c}{EOQ}\left[I(K)\right]$$

---

[14]This example was provided by Professor Robert L. Cook, Central Michigan University, Mount Pleasant, Michigan.

where

FR = Fill rate

σc = Combined safety stock required to consider both variability in lead time and demand (one standard deviation)

EOQ = Order quantity = 1,000 (in this example)

$I(K)$ = Service function magnitude factor (provided by Table 4B–6), based on desired number of standard deviations

K (the safety factor) is the safety stock the manager decides to hold divided by c. Returning to the question presented above, the manager's economic order quantity (EOQ) is 1,000. The safety stock determined by the manager is 280 units. Therefore, K is equal to 280 divided by 175, or 1.60. If K = 1.60, Table 4B–6 can be used to identify $I(K)$ = 0.0236 (see last column of Table 4B–6).

Now the fill rate can be calculated using the following formula:

$$FR = 1 - \frac{\sigma c}{EOQ}\big[I(K)\big]$$

$$= 1 - \frac{175}{1,000}(0.0236)$$

$$= 1 - .0041$$

$$= .9959$$

Thus, the average fill rate is 99.59 percent. That is, of every 100 units of product A demanded, 99.59 will be on hand to be sold if the manager uses 280 units of safety stock and orders 1,000 units each time.[15]

If the manager wants to know how much safety stock of product A to hold to attain a 95 percent fill rate, the same formula can be used:

$$FR = 1 - \frac{\sigma c}{EOQ}\big[I(K)\big]$$

$$I(K) = (1 - FR)\left(\frac{EOQ}{\sigma c}\right)$$

$$I(K) = (1 - 0.95)\left(\frac{1,000}{175}\right)$$

$$= (0.05)(5.714)$$

$$= 0.2857$$

Looking up the value for $I(k)$ in Table 4B–6, the corresponding K value is approximately 0.25. Since K is equal to the safety stock the manager decides to hold divided by c, the safety stock required to provide a 95 percent fill rate is 44 units (175×0.25).

---

[15]If demands, lead times, order quantities, or safety stocks change significantly, the fill rate percentage also will change.

Safety Factor K	Stock Protection (Single Tail)	Stockout Probability F(K)	Service Function (Magnitude Factor) Partial Expectation I(K)
0.00	0.5000	0.5000	0.3989
0.10	0.5394	0.4606	0.3509
0.20	0.5785	0.4215	0.3067
0.30	0.6168	0.3832	0.2664
0.40	0.6542	0.3458	0.2299
0.50	0.6901	0.3099	0.1971
0.60	0.7244	0.2756	0.1679
0.70	0.7569	0.2431	0.1421
0.80	0.7872	0.2128	0.1194
0.90	0.8152	0.1848	0.0998
1.00	0.8409	0.1591	0.0829
1.10	0.8641	0.1359	0.0684
1.20	0.8849	0.1151	0.0561
1.30	0.9033	0.0967	0.0457
1.40	0.9194	0.0806	0.0369
1.50	0.9334	0.0666	0.0297
1.60	0.9454	0.0546	0.0236
1.70	0.9556	0.0444	0.0186
1.80	0.9642	0.0358	0.0145
1.90	0.9714	0.0286	0.0113
2.00	0.9773	0.0227	0.0086
2.10	0.9822	0.0178	0.0065
2.20	0.9861	0.0139	0.0049
2.30	0.9893	0.0107	0.0036
2.40	0.9918	0.0082	0.0027
2.50	0.9938	0.0062	0.0019
2.60	0.9953	0.0047	0.0014
2.70	0.9965	0.0035	0.0010
2.80	0.9974	0.0026	0.0007
2.90	0.9981	0.0019	0.0005
3.00	0.9984	0.0014	0.0004
3.10	0.9990	0.0010	0.0003
3.20	0.9993	0.0007	0.0002
3.30	0.9995	0.0005	0.0001
3.40	0.9997	0.0003	0.0001
3.50	0.9998	0.0002	0.0001
3.60	0.9998	0.0002	
3.70	0.9999	0.0001	
3.80	0.9999	0.0001	
3.90	0.9999	0.0001	
4.00	0.9999	0.0001	

Source: Professor Jay U. Sterling, University of Alabama; adapted from Robert G. Brown, *Materials Management Systems* (New York: John Wiley, 1977), p. 429.

APPENDIX 4–C

DERIVATION OF ECONOMIC ORDER QUANTITY

This appendix illustrates the mathematical derivation of *EOQ* in Figure 4–4.

$$\text{Total annual cost } (TAC) = [\tfrac{1}{2}\,(Q) \times (V) \times (C)\,] + [(P) \times (D/Q)\,]$$

where
  Q = Average number of units in the economic order quantity during the order cycle

FIGURE 4C–1

Saw tooth diagram

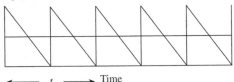

Units Q

$\longleftarrow\ t\ \longrightarrow$ Time

Mathematical solution:

$$\frac{d\,TAC}{dQ} = \frac{VC}{2} - \frac{PD}{Q^2}$$

$$\text{Set} = \text{Zero: } \frac{VC}{2} - \frac{PD}{Q^2}$$

$$\frac{VC}{2} = \frac{PD}{Q^2}$$

$$VCQ^2 = 2PD$$

$$Q^2 = \frac{2PD}{CV}$$

$$Q = \sqrt{\frac{2PD}{CV}}$$

Inventory Management

Chapter Objectives

- To explore how inventory investment influences corporate profit performance.
- To demonstrate how inventory management contributes to least total cost logistics.
- To calculate inventory carrying costs.
- To present ways to recognize poor inventory management.
- To illustrate methods to improve inventory management.
- To show how profit performance can be improved by systems that reduce inventories.

Introduction

Inventories Represent the Largest Investment for Many Firms

Inventories represent the largest single investment in assets for many manufacturers, wholesalers, and retailers. Inventory investment can represent over 20 percent of the total assets of manufacturers, and more than 50 percent of the total assets of wholesalers and retailers (see Table 5–1). Competitive markets of the past 20 years have led to a proliferation of products as companies have attempted to satisfy the needs of diverse market segments. Customers have come to expect high levels of product availability. For many firms, the result has been higher inventory levels.

With the growing popularity of just-in-time (JIT) manufacturing, the reduction of product life cycles, and an increased emphasis on time-based competition, firms who hold large amounts of inventory have been much criticized. However, as we will present in this chapter, inventory does serve some very important purposes. But carrying excessive levels of inventory is costly. Organizations frequently do not identify or capture all of the many costs associated with holding inventory.

Inventories Must Compete with Other Capital Investments for Available Funds

Since capital invested in inventories must compete with other investment opportunities available to the firm, and because of the out-of-pocket costs associated with holding inventory, the activity of inventory management is extremely important. Management must have a thorough knowledge of inventory carrying costs to make informed decisions about logistics system design, customer service levels, the number and location of distribution centers, inventory levels, where to hold inventory and in what form, transportation modes, production schedules, and minimum production runs. For example, ordering in smaller quantities on a more frequent basis will reduce inventory investment, but may result in higher ordering costs and increased transportation costs.

It is necessary to compare the savings in inventory carrying costs to the increased costs of ordering and transportation to determine how the decision to order in smaller quantities will affect profitability. See the Global box for an explanation of how one company centralized its global inventory to save money and improve performance. A determination of inventory carrying costs also is necessary for new product evaluation, the evaluation of price deals/discounts, make-or-buy decisions, and profitability reports. It is thus imperative to accurately measure a firm's inventory carrying costs.

Financial Aspects of Inventory Strategy

The quality of inventory management and the inventory policies a firm sets have a significant impact on corporate profitability and the ability of management to implement its customer service strategies at least total cost logistics.

Inventory and Corporate Profitability

Inventory Represents a Significant Portion of a Firm's Assets

Inventory represents a significant portion of a firm's assets. Consequently, excessive inventory levels can lower corporate profitability in two ways: (1) net profit is reduced by out-of-pocket costs associated with holding inventory, such as insurance, taxes, storage, obsolescence, damage, and interest expense, if the firm borrows money specifically to finance

TABLE 5–1 Selected Financial Data for Manufacturers, Wholesalers, and Retailers ($ millions)

Companies	Sales	Net Profits	Net Profits as a Percent of Sales	Total Assets	Inventory Investment	Inventories as a Percent of Assets
Manufacturers						
Abbott Laboratories	$ 11,013.0	$1,882.0	17.1%	$ 11,125.6	$ 1,238.0	11.1%
Campbell Soup	7,678.0	802.0	10.4	6,632.0	739.0	11.1
Clorox	2,217.8	222.1	10.0	2,178.9	138.9	6.4
Dresser Industries	6,561.5	257.5	3.9	5,150.2	913.6	17.7
Ford Motor	146,991.0	4,446.0	3.0	262,876.0	6,656.0	2.5
General Electric	79,179.0	7,280.0	9.2	272,402.0	4,473.0	1.6
General Mills	5,416.0	476.4	8.8	3,294.7	395.5	12.0
Goodyear Tire & Rubber	13,112.8	101.7	0.8	9,671.8	1,774.0	18.3
Harris Corp.	3,659.3	173.4	4.9	3,206.7	544.1	17.0
Honeywell	7,311.6	402.7	5.5	5,493.3	937.6	17.1
3M	14,236.0	1,526.0	10.7	13,364.0	2,264.0	16.9
Newell	2,872.8	256.5	8.9	3,005.1	509.5	17.0
Pfizer	11,306.0	1,929.0	17.1	14,567.0	1,589.0	10.8
Sara Lee	18,624.0	916.0	4.9	12,602.0	2,807.0	22.3
Xerox	19,521.0	1,206.0	6.2	26,818.0	2,676.0	10.0
Wholesalers and retailers						
Baxter International	5,438.0	669.0	12.3%	7,596.0	883.0	11.6%
Bergen Brunswig	9,942.7	73.5	0.7	2,489.8	1,221.0	49.0
Dayton Hudson	25,371.0	463.0	1.8	13,389.0	3,031.0	22.6
Fleming Companies	16,486.7	26.7	C.2	4,055.2	1,051.0	25.9
Kmart	31,437.0	(220.0)	(0.7)	14,286.0	6,354.0	44.5
Nordstrom	4,453.1	147.5	3.3	2,702.5	719.9	26.6
Sears, Roebuck	38,236.0	1,271.0	3.3	36,167.0	4,646.0	12.8
Super Value Stores	16,486.3	166.4	1.0	4,183.5	1,092.0	26.1
Wal-Mart Stores	106,147.0	3,056.0	2.9	39,501.0	15,897.0	40.2
Winn-Dixie	12,955.5	255.6	2.0	2,648.6	1,179.0	44.5

Source: These data are 1996 fiscal year financial results gathered from a number of public sources.

Global

Changing Inventory Holding Patterns to Improve Performance at Atlas Copco Tools

A change is taking place in distribution today: a movement away from "chains" of stocking locations to planned or centralized delivery systems that rely on an excellent information system to provide coordination. Atlas Copco Tools, a Swedish manufacturer of pneumatic hand tools, had two central distribution centers and more than 50 regional warehouses and subsidiaries in approximately 50 countries throughout the world. Each of these locations held inventory. Unfortunately, none seemed to hold the right inventory because:

- Product availability at sales subsidiaries averaged 70 percent.

- Lead time from the central distribution centers to the customer was two weeks.

- Lead time from production to central distribution centers was between 12 and 20 weeks.

- Capital tied up in inventory was 30 percent of annual sales revenue.

To combat this unsatisfactory performance, Atlas reconfigured its system, moving to a single central distribution center located in Belgium. All other stock points were eliminated. As a result of centralization, Atlas has:

- Reduced inventory by one-third.
- Reduced operating costs by $4 million a year.
- Substantially reduced its distribution labor force.
- Reduced average lead time within Europe from two weeks to 24–72 hours.

Thus, considering the trade-off between holding a great deal of inventory at multiple locations and centralizing distribution, Atlas found it could be more successful if it centralized.

Source: Philip B. Schary and Tage Skjøtt-Larsen, *Managing the Global Supply Chain* (Copenhagen: Handelshøjskolens, Forlag, 1995), pp. 225–28.

inventories; and (2) total assets are increased by the amount of the inventory investment, which decreases asset turnover, or the opportunity to invest in other more productive assets is foregone. In any case, the result is a reduction in return on net worth.

Inventory and Least Total Cost Logistics

Least total cost logistics is achieved by minimizing the total of the logistics costs illustrated in Figure 5–1 for a specified level of customer service. However, successful implementation of cost trade-off analysis requires that adequate cost data be available to management. Management should not set inventory levels and inventory turnover policies arbitrarily, but do so with full knowledge of inventory carrying costs, total logistics system costs, and necessary customer service policies.

Inventory Costs Impact Many Logistics Activities

The cost of carrying inventory has a direct impact not only on the number of warehouses that a company maintains, but on all of the firm's logistics policies, including stockouts and associated customer service costs. Inventory carrying costs are being traded off

FIGURE 5–1

Costs trade-offs required in a logistics system

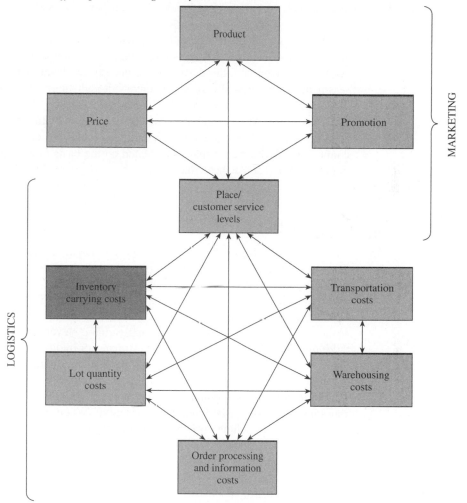

Marketing objective: Allocate resources to the marketing mix to maximize the long-run profitability of the firm. Logistics objective: Minimize total costs, given the customer service objective, where Total costs = Transportation costs + Warehousing costs + Order processing and information costs + Lot quantity costs + Inventory carrying costs.

Source: Adapted from Douglas M. Lambert, *The Development of an Inventory Costing Methodology: A Study of the Costs Associated with Holding Inventory* (Chicago: National Council of Physical Distribution Management, 1976), p. 7.

with other logistics costs, such as transportation and customer service. For example, given the same customer service level, firms with low inventory carrying costs will likely hold more inventory and use slower modes of transportation, such as railroads, because this provides the least total cost logistics.

High inventory carrying costs likewise result in a reduction in inventory investment and require faster means of transportation, such as motor or air carriers to minimize total costs while achieving the desired customer service level. Thus, without an accurate assessment of the costs of carrying inventory, it is difficult for a company to implement logistics policies that minimize costs.

In addition, knowledge of the cost of carrying inventory is required to accurately determine economic manufacturing quantities, economic order quantities, and sales discounts, all of which are usually calculated on the basis of estimated costs in the majority of companies that use these formulas.[1]

Inventory Carrying Costs

Inventory carrying costs are those costs associated with the amount of inventory stored. They are made up of a number of different cost components and generally represents one of the highest costs of logistics.[2] The magnitude of these costs and the fact that inventory levels are directly affected by the configuration of the logistics system shows the need for accurate inventory carrying cost data. Without such data, appropriate trade-offs cannot be made within the organization or the supply chain. Nevertheless, most managers who consider the cost of holding inventory use estimates or traditional industry benchmarks.

We have seen how inventory levels can affect corporate profit performance and have discussed the need for assessment of inventory carrying costs in logistics system design. Unfortunately, many companies have never calculated inventory carrying costs, even though these costs are both real and substantial. When inventory carrying costs are calculated, they often include only the current interest rate plus expenditures such as insurance and taxes. Many managers use traditional textbook percentages or industry averages. All of these approaches have problems.

Do Interest Rates Reflect the True Costs of Capital?

First, there are only a few special circumstances in which the current interest rate is the relevant cost of money (we will explore these shortly). Traditional textbook percentages also have serious drawbacks.

Most of the carrying cost percentages presented in published sources between 1951 and 1997 were about 25 percent. If 25 percent was an accurate number in 1951, how could it be accurate in 1997, when the prime interest rate fluctuated between 3 and 20 percent during that period?

There also is the method of using inventory carrying costs that are based on "benchmarking" with industry averages. For the most part, businesspeople seem to find comfort

---

[1]We described these formulas in Chapter 4, "Inventory Concepts."

[2]This section draws heavily from Douglas M. Lambert, *The Development of an Inventory Costing Methodology: A Study of the Costs Associated with Holding Inventory* (Chicago: National Council of Physical Distribution Management, 1976).

in such numbers, but many problems are inherent with this practice. For example, would the logistics executive of a cosmetics manufacturer want to compare his or her firm to Avon, a company that sells its products door to door; Revlon, a company that sells its products through major department stores; or—even worse—use an average of the two companies? The last approach would compare the executive's firm to a nonentity—no company at all.

Even if two companies are very similar in terms of the manufacture and distribution of their products, the availability of capital may lead to two different inventory strategies; that is, one firm may experience shortages of capital—capital rationing—while the other may have an abundance of cash. If capital is short, the cost of money for inventory decisions may be 35 percent pretax, which is the rate of return the company is earning on new investments. If capital is plentiful, the cost of money may be 8 percent pretax, which is the interest rate the company is earning on its cash. If both of these companies are well managed, the company whose cost of money is 8 percent will have more inventory.

As presented above, the lower the cost of money, the more attractive it is to increase inventory levels. The company with the 35 percent cost of money will have lower inventories by making different trade-offs such as incurring production setup costs more frequently, choosing more expensive transportation modes, or reducing customer service levels. Each company may have what represents least total cost logistics, and yet one may turn its inventories 6 times a year and the other 12 times. However, if either company were to change any component of its logistics system in order to match the other's performance, total costs could increase and return on net worth could decrease.

Calculating Inventory Carrying Costs

Inventory Carrying Costs Should Include Only Those Costs That Vary with the Quantity of Inventory

Because each company faces a unique operating environment, each company should determine its own logistics costs and strive to minimize the total of these costs, given its customer service objectives. *Inventory carrying costs should include only those costs that vary with the quantity of inventory* and that can be categorized into the following groups: (1) capital costs, (2) inventory service costs, (3) storage space costs, and (4) inventory risk costs. The elements to be considered in each of these categories are identified in Figure 5–2.

Capital Costs on Inventory Investment.   Holding inventory ties up money that could be used for other types of investments. This holds true for both internally generated funds and capital obtained from external sources, such as debt from banks and insurance companies or from the sale of common stock. Consequently, the company's **opportunity cost of capital,** the rate of return that could be realized from some other use of the money, should be used to accurately reflect the true cost involved. Virtually all companies seek to reduce inventory because management recognizes that holding excessive inventory provides no value added to the firm. The company must consider what rate of return it is sacrificing on the cash invested in inventory.

Some companies differentiate among projects by categorizing them according to risk and looking for rates of return that reflect the perceived level of risk. For example, management could group projects into high-, medium-, and low-risk categories. High-risk

FIGURE 5–2

Normative model of inventory carrying cost methodology

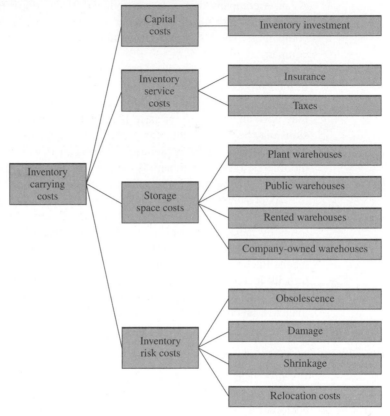

Source: Douglas M. Lambert, *The Development of an Inventory Costing Methodology: A Study of the Costs Associated with Holding Inventory* (Chicago: National Council of Physical Distribution Management, 1976), p. 68.

projects, such as investments in new products or technology, may have a desired rate of return of 25 percent after tax. Investment in new product inventory should reflect that higher perceived risk level.

Medium-risk projects may be required to obtain an 18 percent after-tax return while low-risk projects, which may include such investments as warehouses, private trucking, and inventory of established, stable product lines, might be expected to achieve an after-tax return of 10 percent. Keep in mind that all inventory carrying cost components must be stated in pretax numbers because all of the other costs in the trade-off analysis, such as transportation and warehousing, are reported in pretax dollars.

In some very special circumstances, such as the fruit-canning industry, short-term financing may be used to finance the seasonal buildup of inventories. Fruit must be packaged as it is harvested to meet all customer demand through the end of the next growing season. In this situation, the inventory buildup is short term and the actual cost of borrowing is the acceptable cost of money.

Once management has established the cost of money, it must determine the out-of-pocket (cash) value of the inventory for which the inventory carrying cost is being calculated. For wholesalers or retailers, the out-of-pocket value of the inventory is the current replacement cost of the inventory, including any freight costs paid, or the current market price if the product is being phased out. For manufacturers, the relevant cost is only the cost directly associated with producing the inventory and making it available for sale. Thus, it is necessary to know whether the company is using direct costs to determine the inventory value or using some form of absorption costing.

Direct Costing

Direct costing is a method of cost accounting based on separating costs into fixed and variable components. For management planning and control purposes, the fixed-variable cost breakdown provides more information than that obtained from current financial statements designed for external reporting. Under direct costing, the fixed costs of production are excluded from inventory values. Therefore, inventory values more closely reflect the out-of-pocket cost of their replacement. With **absorption costing** (otherwise

Absorption Costing

known as full costing or full absorption costing), the traditional approach used by most manufacturers, fixed manufacturing overhead is included in the inventory value.

In addition to the distinction between direct costing and absorption costing, companies may value inventories based on actual costs or standard costs. Thus, there are four distinct costing alternatives:

1. **Actual absorption costing** includes actual costs for direct material and direct labor, plus predetermined variable and fixed manufacturing overhead.
2. **Standard absorption costing** includes predetermined direct material and direct labor costs, plus predetermined variable and fixed manufacturing overhead.
3. **Actual direct costing** includes actual costs for direct material and direct labor, plus predetermined variable manufacturing overhead; it excludes fixed manufacturing overhead.
4. **Standard direct costing** includes predetermined costs for direct material and direct labor, plus predetermined variable manufacturing overhead; it excludes fixed manufacturing overhead.[3]

The preceding material on methods of inventory valuation supports the conclusion that using industry averages for inventory carrying costs is not a good policy. This is so because the various component percentages may not be calculated using comparable inventory valuation systems.

The situation is complicated even further if one considers the various methods of accounting for inventory for tax purposes. Most manufacturing companies use one of the following three methods:

FIFO

1. **First-in, first-out (FIFO).** Stock acquired earliest is assumed to be sold first, leaving stock acquired more recently in inventory.

---

[3]Students who want to read more about direct and absorption costing and the methods of accounting for inventory should refer to Charles T. Horngren, George Foster, and Srikant M. Datar, *Cost Accounting: A Managerial Emphasis,* 9th ed. (Englewood Cliffs, NJ: Prentice Hall, 1997); or John G. Burch, *Cost and Management Accounting: A Modern Approach* (St. Paul, MN: West, 1994).

FIGURE 5–3

Inventory positions in the logistics system

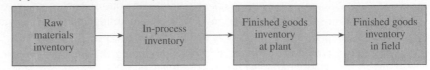

Assumption: A one-time increase (decrease) in finished goods inventory results in a one-time increase (decrease) in raw materials purchased.

LIFO

2. **Last-in, first-out (LIFO).** Sales are made from the most recently acquired stock, leaving items acquired in the earliest time period in inventory.

Average Cost

3. **Average cost.** This method could be a moving average in which each new purchase is averaged with the remaining inventory to obtain a new average price, or a weighted average in which the total cost of the opening inventory plus all purchases is divided by the total number of units.

For the purposes of calculating inventory carrying costs, it is immaterial whether the company uses LIFO, FIFO, or average cost for inventory valuation. To determine the value of the inventory for calculating carrying costs, multiply the number of units of each product in inventory by the standard or actual direct (variable) costs of manufacturing (or purchasing) the product and moving it to the storage location.

The current manufacturing or purchase costs are relevant for decision making because these are the costs that will be incurred if inventories are increased. Likewise, if products are held in field locations, the transportation cost incurred to move them there and the variable costs of moving them into storage become part of the cost of inventory. These costs are in addition to direct labor costs, direct material costs, and the variable manufacturing overhead.

The implicit assumption is that a reduction in finished goods inventory will lead to a corresponding reduction in inventory throughout the system (see Figure 5–3). That is, a one-time reduction in finished goods inventory results in a one-time reduction in raw materials purchases, as inventory is pushed back through the system.

In summary, inventory requires capital that could be used for other corporate investments; by having funds invested in inventory, a company forgoes the rate of return that it could obtain in such investments. Therefore, the company's opportunity cost of capital should be applied to the investment in inventory. The cost of capital should be applied to the out-of-pocket cost investment in inventory.

Inventory Service Costs. **Inventory service costs** are comprised of ad valorem (personal property) taxes and fire and theft insurance paid as a result of holding the inventory. Taxes vary depending on the state in which inventories are held. Tax rates can range from zero in states where inventories are exempt to as much as 20 percent of the assessed value. In general, taxes vary directly with inventory levels. Many states exempt inventories from taxation if they are placed into storage for subsequent shipment to customers in another state. With proper planning, a company can minimize this component when establishing a warehousing network. The cost of extra movement from a tax-exempt state, to the state where the product will be consumed must be considered in trade-off analysis.

Insurance rates are not strictly proportional to inventory levels because insurance is usually purchased to cover a certain value of product for a specified time period. Nevertheless, an insurance policy will be revised periodically based on expected inventory level changes. In some instances, an insurance company will issue policies in which premiums are based on the monthly amounts insured. Insurance rates depend on the materials used in the construction of the storage building, its age, and considerations such as the type of fire prevention equipment installed.

The actual dollars spent on insurance and taxes during the past year can be calculated as a percentage of that year's inventory value and added to the cost-of-money component of the carrying cost. If budgeted figures are available for the coming year, they can be used as a percentage of the inventory value based on the inventory plan—the forecasted inventory level—in order to provide a future-oriented carrying cost. In most cases, there will be few if any significant changes from year to year in the tax and insurance components of the inventory carrying cost.

Costs Associated with Warehousing

Plant Warehouse Costs

Public Warehouse Costs

Storage Space Costs.   Storage space costs relate to four general types of facilities: (1) plant warehouses, (2) public warehouses, (3) rented or leased (contract) warehouses, and (4) company-owned (private) warehouses.

Plant warehouse costs are primarily fixed. If any costs are variable, they are usually variable with the amount of product that moves through the facility, **throughput,** and not with the quantity of inventory stored. If some variable costs, such as the cost of taking inventory or any other expenses, change with the level of inventory, management should include them in inventory carrying costs. Fixed charges and allocated costs are not relevant for inventory policy decisions. If the firm can rent out the warehouse space or use it for some other productive purpose instead of using it for storing inventory, an estimate of the appropriate opportunity costs would be appropriate.

Public warehouse costs are usually based on the amount of product moved into and out of the warehouse (handling charges) and the amount of inventory held in storage (storage charges). In most cases, handling charges are assessed when the products are moved into the warehouse and storage charges are assessed on a periodic basis (e.g., monthly). Usually, the first month's storage must be paid when the products are moved into the facility. In effect, this makes the first month's storage a handling charge since it must be paid on every case of product regardless of how long it is held in the warehouse.

The use of public warehouses is a management policy decision because it may be the most economical way to provide the desired level of customer service without incurring excessive transportation costs. For this reason, handling charges, which represent the majority of costs related to the use of public warehouses, should be considered as throughput costs; that is, they should be thought of as part of the warehousing cost category of the cost trade-off analysis, and not part of inventory carrying costs. Only charges for *warehouse storage* should be included in inventory carrying costs because these are the public warehouse charges that will vary with the level of inventory.

Where a throughput rate (handling charge) is given based on the number of inventory turns, it is necessary to estimate the storage cost component by considering how the

Inventory control in a food manufacturing plant storage facility.

throughput costs per case will change if the number of inventory turns changes. Of course, the public warehouse fees that a company pays when its inventory is placed into field storage should be included in the value of its inventory investment.

Rented or leased warehouse space is normally contracted for a specified period of time. The amount of space rented is based on the maximum storage requirements during the period covered by the contract. Thus, warehouse rental charges do not fluctuate from day to day with changes in the inventory level, although rental rates can vary from month to month or year to year when a new contract is negotiated. Most costs, such as rent payment, the manager's salary, security costs, and maintenance expenses, are fixed in the short run. But some expenses, such as warehouse labor and equipment operating costs, vary with throughput. During the term of the contract, few if any costs vary with the amount of inventory stored.

All of the costs of leased warehouses could be eliminated by not renewing the contract and are therefore a relevant input for logistics decision making. However, operating costs that do not vary with the quantity of inventory stored, such as those outlined in the preceding paragraph, should not be included in the carrying costs. Rather, these costs belong in the warehousing cost category of the cost trade-off analysis. The inclusion of fixed costs, and those that are variable with throughput in inventory carrying costs, has no conceptual basis. Such a practice is simply incorrect and will result in erroneous decisions.

Private Warehouse Costs

The costs associated with *company-owned* or **private warehouses** are primarily fixed, although some may vary with throughput. All operating costs that can be eliminated by closing a company-owned warehouse or the net savings resulting from a change to public warehouses should be included in warehousing costs, not inventory carrying costs. Only those costs that vary with the quantity of inventory belong in inventory carrying costs. Typically, these costs are negligible in company-owned warehouses.

In most warehouses, the costs associated with order picking, put-away, and inventory control are significant because of the labor necessary to perform these tasks. Most of these costs vary with throughput and not inventory levels.

Inventory Risk Costs.   Inventory risk costs vary from company to company, but typically include charges for (1) obsolescence, (2) damage, (3) shrinkage, and (4) relocation of inventory.

Cost of Obsolescence

   Obsolescence cost is the cost of each unit that must be disposed of at a loss because it can no longer be sold at a regular price. In essence, it is the cost of holding products in inventory beyond their useful life. Obsolescence cost is the difference between the original cost of the unit and its salvage value, or the original selling price and the reduced selling price if the price is lowered (marked down) to move the product. Generally, obsolescence costs are buried in the "cost of goods manufactured" account or the "cost of goods sold" account instead of being shown as a separate item on profit-and-loss statements. Consequently, managers may have some difficulty arriving at this figure. However, it is a relevant cost of holding inventory, especially as product life cycles decrease.

Damage Costs

   Damage costs incurred during shipping should be considered a throughput cost, since they will continue regardless of inventory levels. Damage attributed to a public warehouse operation is usually charged to the warehouse operator if it is above a specified maximum amount. Damage is often identified as the net amount after claims.

Shrinkage Costs

   Shrinkage costs have become an increasingly important problem for American businesses. Many authorities think inventory theft is a more serious problem than cash embezzlement. Theft is far more common, involves far more employees, and is hard to control. Shrinkage also can result from poor record keeping, or shipping wrong products or quantities to customers. In the case of agricultural products, natural ores, or similar items that are shipped in bulk, shrinkage may result from loss in weight or spillage that occurs during transportation and handling. However, shrinkage costs may be more closely related to company security measures than inventory levels, even though they definitely will vary with the number of warehouse locations. Thus, management may find it more appropriate to assign some or all of these costs to the warehouse locations than to the amount of inventory.

Relocation Costs

Relocation costs are incurred when inventory is transshipped from one warehouse location to another to avoid obsolescence. For example, products that are selling well in the Midwest may not be selling on the West Coast. By shipping the products to the location where they will sell, the company avoids the obsolescence cost but incurs additional transportation costs. Transshipments to avoid obsolescence or markdowns are the result of having too much inventory, and the cost should be included in inventory carrying costs. Often, transshipment costs are not reported separately, but are simply included in transportation costs. In such cases, a managerial estimate or a statistical audit of freight bills can isolate the transshipment costs.

The frequency of these types of shipments will determine which approach is more practical in any given situation. That is, if such shipments are rare, the percentage component of the carrying cost will be very small and a managerial estimate should suffice. The Technology box describes how one firm misused technology in relocating product, and actually increased its inventory expense!

In some cases, firms may incur transshipment costs as a result of inventory stocking policies. For example, if inventories are set too low in field locations, stockouts may occur and may be rectified by shipping product from the nearest warehouse location that has the items in stock. The transportation costs associated with transshipment to avoid stockouts are a result of decisions that involve trade-offs among transportation costs, warehousing costs, inventory carrying costs, or stockout costs. They are transportation costs and should not be classified as inventory carrying costs.

Because managers do not always know just how much of the costs of damage, shrinkage, and relocation are related to the amount of inventory held, they may have to determine mathematically if a relationship exists. For example, a cost for damage may be available, but the amount of this cost attributed to the volume of inventory may be unknown.

Damage can be a function of such factors as throughput, general housekeeping, the quality and training of management and labor, the type of product, the protective packaging used, the material handling system, the number of times that the product is handled, how it is handled, and the amount of inventory (which may lead to damage as a result of overcrowding in the warehouse). To say which of these factors is most important and how much damage each one accounts for is extremely difficult.

Even an elaborate reporting system may not yield the desired results, as employees may try to shift the blame for the damaged product. The quality of damage screening during the receiving function, and the possible hiding of damaged product in higher inventories until inventories are reduced, may contribute to the level of damage reported, regardless of the cause.

Technology

To Use Technology Properly, You Must Understand It!

A U.S.-based cigarette manufacturer had devised a system whereby it ordered corrugated shipping containers based on the amount of product shipped. For some unexplained reason, however, its inventory of corrugated cases was growing. Where was the bug in the system?

Federal regulations require that cigarette production must be accounted for every 24 hours to allow for proper accounting and taxation. To comply with this law without disrupting production, an operator would log in to the inventory management system and "receive" finished pallet loads of cigarettes into the imaginary "location 99." When actually physically moved, the boxes were "relocated" to the correct inventory location.

The firm hired a systems specialist, who discovered that the ordering system was the source of the problem. The operator on one shift did not know how

to "relocate" product; he could only ship. Thus, he shipped the product twice—first into location 99, then into the actual physical warehouse. This created two "shipments" on the system, which drove the excessive corrugated orders. When asked why he did this, the operator replied it was the only way to move product on the system. When informed that he could, and should, relocate the product, the employee claimed that nobody ever showed him that!

Thus, it is not enough to have a good inventory system; you have to ensure that people know how to use it! When new people come on board, they are often trained poorly, if at all, by existing employees. This is an important lesson in proper use of any technology.

Source: Adapted from Tom Andel, "Inventory Horror Stories," *Transportation and Distribution,* Buyer's Guide Issue (July 1995), pp. BG3–BG6.

An Example from the Consumer Packaged Goods Industry

Table 5–2 summarizes the methodology that should be used to calculate inventory carrying costs. The model is *normative,* because using it will lead to a carrying cost that accurately reflects a firm's costs. Now let's examine an actual application of the methodology for a manufacturer of packaged goods.

Using the methodology summarized in Table 5–2, we calculate costs for the following four basic categories: (1) capital costs, (2) inventory service costs, (3) storage space costs, and (4) inventory risk costs.

Capital Costs

Capital Costs.   The opportunity cost of capital should be applied only to the out-of-pocket investment in inventory. The *out-of-pocket investment* is the direct variable expense incurred up to the point at which the inventory is held in storage. Using the company's inventory plan and standard variable product cost for the coming year, it is possible to calculate the average inventory for each product. This can be determined for each storage location and for the total system.

Next, the average transportation and warehousing cost per case of product is added to the variable manufactured cost. This is necessary because the transportation and warehousing costs are out-of-pocket costs. If any warehousing costs are incurred moving product into storage in field locations, these costs should be added on a per case basis to the standard variable manufactured cost. When public warehousing is used, any charges

TABLE 5–2 Summary of Data Collection Procedure Showing Source of Data

Classification	Step No.	Cost Category	Explanation
Cost of inventory	1	Average inventory valued at variable costs delivered to the distribution center.	Want only variable costs; fixed costs remain the same regardless of inventory levels.
Capital cost	2	Cost of money	The cost of money invested in inventory; the return should be comparable to other investment opportunities.
Inventory service costs	3	Taxes	Personal property taxes paid on finished goods inventory.
	4	Insurance	Insurance paid on inventory investment
Storage space costs	5	Variable storage	Include only those costs that are variable with the amount of inventory stored.
Inventory risk costs	6	Obsolescence	Obsolescence due to holding inventory
	7	Shrinkage	Shrinkage related to volume of inventory
	8	Damage	Damage directly attributable to the level of inventory held
	9	Relocation costs	Only relocation costs that result to avoid obsolescence
Financial calculations	10	Total carrying costs percentage	Calculate the numbers generated in steps 3 to 9 as a percentage of average inventory, and add to cost of money (step 2).
	11	Total carrying cost dollars	Multiply total carrying cost percentage (step 10) by average value of inventory (step 1).

paid at the time products are moved into the facility should be added on a per case basis to all products held in inventory. In corporate facilities, only the variable out-of-pocket costs of moving the products into storage should be included.

The company had $10 million in average system inventory valued at full manufactured cost. Annual sales were $175 million, or approximately $125 million at manufactured cost. The inventory value based on variable manufacturing costs and the forecasted product mix was $7 million—the average annual inventory held at plants and field locations in order to achieve least cost distribution. The variable costs associated with transporting the strategically deployed field inventory and moving it into public warehouses totaled $800,000. Therefore, the average system inventory was $7.8 million when valued at variable cost delivered to the storage location. All of the remaining inventory carrying cost components should be calculated as a percentage of the variable delivered cost ($7.8 million) and added to the capital cost percentage.

Table 5–3 shows how the carrying cost calculation must be adjusted if the carrying cost percentage is going to be applied to full costs rather than variable costs. If variable costs are 78 percent of full cost and the cost of money is 30 percent before taxes or 15 percent after taxes, and the inventory shown on management reports is valued at $10 million

TABLE 5–3   Adjusting the Cost of Money to Fit the Method of Inventory Valuation

Method A	
Inventory at full cost	$10,000,000
Variable cost is 78% of full cost	× 78%
Inventory at variable cost	$7,800,000
Pretax cost of money is 30%	× 30%
Cost of money associated with the inventory investment	$ 2,340,000
Method B	
Pretax cost of money	30%
Variable cost is 78% of full cost	× 78%
Adjusted cost of money	× 23.4%
Inventory at full cost	$10,000,000
Adjusted cost of money	× 23.4%
Cost of money associated with the inventory investment	$ 2,340,000

at full cost, a manager could take 78 percent of this amount and then apply the 30 percent cost of money. This would yield a capital cost of $2.34 million.

Another alternative is to adjust the cost of money at the time the inventory carrying cost is developed. By taking 78 percent of the 30 percent cost of money, the *adjusted* cost of money, 23.4 percent, can be applied to the inventory value shown at full value on the management reports. This method also yields a capital cost of $2.34 million. If full cost is used and the cost of money is appropriately adjusted, all remaining cost components should be calculated as a percentage of the full cost inventory value.

To establish the opportunity cost of capital—the minimum acceptable rate of return on new investments—an interview was conducted with the company's comptroller. Due to capital rationing, the current hurdle rate on new investments was 15 percent after taxes, 30 percent before taxes (Table 5–4, step 2). A pretax cost of money is required because all of the other components of inventory carrying cost and the other categories in logistics cost trade-off analysis, such as transportation and warehousing, are pretax numbers.

Inventory Service Costs

Inventory Service Costs.   Return to the example of the manufacturer of packaged goods, with system inventories of $7.8 million valued at variable cost delivered to the storage location. Taxes for the year were $90,948, which is 1.17 percent of the $7.8 million inventory value; this figure was added to the 30 percent capital cost (see Table 5–4, step 3). Insurance costs covering inventory for the year were $4,524, which is 0.06 percent of the inventory value (step 4).

Storage Space Costs

Storage Space Costs.   The storage component of the public warehousing cost was $225,654 for the year, which equals 2.89 percent of the inventory value (Table 5–4, step 5). Variable storage costs in plant warehouses should include only those costs that are variable with the amount of inventory stored. The vast majority of plant warehousing expenses were fixed in nature. Those costs that were variable fluctuated with the amount of product moved into and out of the facilities (throughput) and were not variable with inventory levels. Consequently, variable storage costs were negligible in plant warehouses.

TABLE 5–4   Summary of Data Collection Procedure

Step No.	Cost of Category	Source	Explanation	Amount (current study)
1.	Cost of money	Comptroller	This represents the cost of having money invested in inventory. The return should be comparable to other investment opportunities.	30% pretax
2.	Average monthly inventory valued at variable costs delivered to the distribution center	1. Standard cost data—comptroller's department 2. Freight rates and product specs are from distribution reports 3. Average monthly inventory in cases from printout received from sales forecasting	Only want variable costs since fixed costs go on regardless of the amount of product manufactured and stored—follow steps outlined in body of report	$7,800,000 valued at variable cost delivered to the DC (variable manufactured cost equaled 70% of full manufactured cost). Variable cost FOB the DC averaged 78% of full manufactured cost
3.	Taxes	The comptroller's department	Personal property taxes paid on inventory	$90,948 which equals 1.17%
4.	Insurance	The comptroller's department	Insurance rate/$100 of inventory (at variable costs)	$4,524 which equals 0.06%
5.	Recurring storage (public warehouse)	Distribution operations	This represents the portion of warehousing costs that are related to the volume of inventory stored.	$225,654 annually which equals 2.89%
6.	Variable storage (plant warehouses)	Transportation services	Only include those costs that are variable with the amount of inventory stored.	Nil
7.	Obsolescence	Distribution department reports	Cost of holding product inventory beyond its useful life	0.800 percent of inventory
8.	Shrinkage	Distribution department reports	Only include the portion attributable to inventory storage.	$100,308 which equals 1.29%
9.	Damage	Distribution department reports	Only include the portion attributable to inventory storage.	
10.	Relocation costs	Not available	Only include relocation costs incurred to avoid obsolescence.	Not available
11.	Total inventory carrying costs	Calculate the numbers generated in steps 3, 4, 5, 6, 7, 8, 9, and 10 as a percentage of average inventory valued at variable cost delivered to the distribution center, and add them to the cost of money (step 1).		36.21%

Source: Douglas M. Lambert and Robert H. Quinn, "Profit Oriented Inventory Policies Require a Documented Inventory Carrying Cost," *Business Quarterly* 46, no. 3 (Autumn 1981), p. 71.

Inventory Risk Costs

Inventory Risk Costs. Obsolescence cost was being tracked in this company and represented 0.80 percent of inventory for the past 12 months (step 7).

Shrinkage and damage costs were not recorded separately. Regression analysis would have been a possible means of isolating the portion of these costs that were variable with inventories. However, management was confident that no more than 10 percent of the total shrinkage and damage, $100,308, was related to inventory levels. Therefore, a managerial estimate of 10 percent was used. This was equal to 1.29 percent of the inventory value of $7.8 million (steps 8 and 9).

Relocation costs, incurred transporting products from one location to another to avoid obsolescence, were not available. Management said that such costs were incurred so infrequently that they were not recorded separately from ordinary transportation costs.

Total inventory carrying costs. When totaled, the individual percentages gave an inventory carrying cost of 36.21 percent. Thus, management would use a 36 percent inventory carrying cost when calculating cost trade-offs in the logistics system.

Up to this point, we have assumed that the company has a relatively homogeneous product line; that is, similar products are manufactured at each plant location, shipped in mixed quantities, and stored in the same facilities. Consequently, if the company has a 12-month inventory plan and standard costs are available, a weighted-average inventory carrying cost can be used for all products and locations. This figure would require updating on an annual basis when the new inventory plan, updated standard costs, and the budgeted expenditures for insurance, taxes, storage, and inventory risk costs become available.

Management at General Mills calculated an inventory carrying cost for each location where products were stored, and found considerable variation.[4] Since the costs have to be collected by storage location, minimal additional effort is required to fine-tune the numbers for decisions about a specific location or type of inventory. If the differences are minimal, the weighted-average inventory carrying cost will be sufficient.

In companies with heterogeneous product lines, however, inventory carrying costs should be calculated for each individual product. For example, bulk chemical products cannot be shipped in mixed quantities or stored in the same tanks. For this reason, transportation and storage costs should be included on a specific product/location basis, instead of on the basis of average transportation and storage costs as one would use for homogeneous products.

The previous example should clarify the methodology and how it can be applied. At this point, you should be able to calculate an inventory carrying cost percentage for a company.

The Impact of Inventory Turnover on Inventory Carrying Costs

In Chapter 1 we saw that, in many firms, management attempts to improve profitability by emphasizing the need to improve inventory turnover. But pushing for increased inventory turnover without considering the impact on total logistics system costs may actually lead

[4]William R. Steele, "Inventory Carrying Cost Identification and Accounting," *Proceedings of the Sixteenth Annual Conference of the National Council of Physical Distribution Management* (Chicago, IL: National Council of Physical Distribution Management, 1979), pp. 75–86.

TABLE 5–5   The Impact of Inventory Turns on Inventory Carrying Costs

Inventory Turns	Average Inventory	Carrying Cost at 40 Percent	Carrying Cost Savings
1	$750,000	$300,000	—
2	375,000	150,000	$150,000
3	250,000	100,000	50,000
4	187,500	75,000	25,000
5	150,000	60,000	15,000
6	125,000	50,000	10,000
7	107,143	42,857	7,143
8	93,750	37,500	5,357
9	83,333	33,333	4,167
10	75,000	30,000	3,333
11	68,182	27,273	2,727
12	62,500	25,000	2,273
13	57,692	23,077	1,923
14	53,571	21,428	1,649
15	50,000	20,000	1,428

Source: Douglas M. Lambert and Robert H. Quinn, "Profit Oriented Inventory Policies Require a Documented Inventory Carrying Cost," *Business Quarterly* 46, no. 3 (Autumn 1981), p. 65.

to decreased profitability.[5] Often, management expects inventory turns to increase each year. If the company is inefficient and has too much inventory, increasing inventory turns will lead to increased profitability. In the absence of a systems change, however, continued improvements in inventory turns may eventually result in the firm cutting inventories below the optimal level.

As shown in Table 5–5, if a logistics system is currently efficient and the goal is to increase turns from 11 to 12, the annual savings in carrying costs would be $2,273. Care must be taken that the costs of transportation, lot quantity, warehouse picking, and order processing and information do not increase by more than this amount; that lower customer service levels do not result in lost profit contribution in excess of the carrying cost savings; or that some combination of the above does not occur.

The Relationship between Inventory Carrying Costs and Inventory Turnover

Figure 5–4 illustrates the relationship between inventory carrying costs and the number of inventory turnovers. The example shows that improvements in the number of inventory turns has the greatest impact if inventory is turned less than six times a year. Indeed, beyond eight turns the curve becomes relatively flat. Increasing inventory turns from five to six times generates the same savings in inventory carrying costs as improving them from 10 to 15 times. When establishing inventory turnover objectives, it is necessary to fully document how each alternative strategy will increase the other logistics costs and to compare this with the savings in inventory carrying costs.

---

[5]This example is adapted from Douglas M. Lambert and Robert H. Quinn, "Profit Oriented Inventory Policies Require a Documented Inventory Carrying Cost," *Business Quarterly* 46, no. 3 (Autumn 1981), pp. 64–65.

FIGURE 5–4

Relationship between inventory turns and inventory carrying costs

Inventory carrying costs

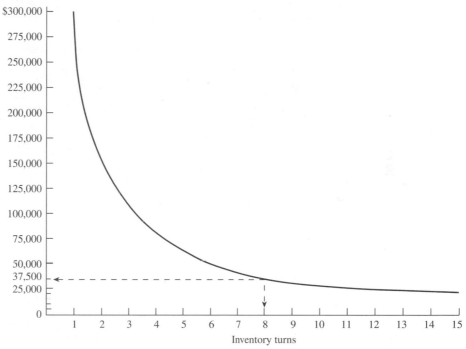

Source: Douglas M. Lambert and Robert H. Quinn, "Profit Oriented Inventory Policies Require a Documented Inventory Carrying Cost," *Business Quarterly* 46, no. 3 (Autumn, 1981), p. 65.

For a number of management decisions, it may be useful to calculate inventory carrying costs on a per unit basis. The inventory carrying costs associated with each item sold can vary dramatically between high-turnover items and low-volume, low-turn items. The previous analysis of inventory carrying costs and inventory turns is repeated, using a carrying cost per unit example to illustrate this point.

For example, if the manufacturer's selling price of an item to a retailer is $100, the retailer sells the item for $150, giving it a potential contribution of $50 before costs. If the annual inventory carrying cost is 30 percent, the monthly cost to carry the item in inventory is $2.50 ($30 ÷ 12). Annual turns of one (12 months in inventory) would consume $30 in carrying costs, whereas two turns a year would cost $15, four turns, $7.50 and eight turns, $3.75 (see Figure 5–5). It is not uncommon for some specialty items in a retail store to turn less than once a year. This can easily place an otherwise profitable retailer into a loss position.

One inventory turn a year would result in a charge of $30.00 in inventory carrying costs for every unit sold. On the other hand, 15 turns per year would result in a charge of only $2.00 per unit, while 30 turns would be $1.00! This example should make it clear how inventory turns affect the profitability of each item sold. Next, we will review methods for improving the profitability of products by better managing their inventories.

FIGURE **5–5**

Annual inventory carrying costs compared to inventory turnovers

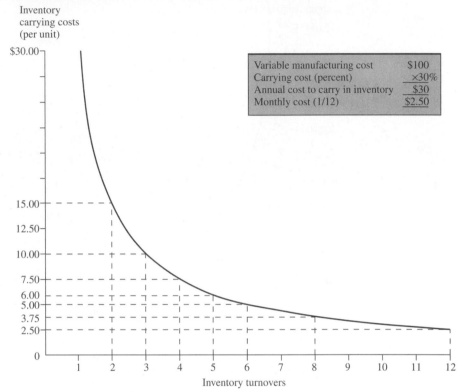

Source: Jay U. Sterling and Douglas M. Lambert, "Segment Profitability Reports: You Can't Manage Your Business without Them," unpublished manuscript, 1992.

Symptoms of Poor Inventory Management

This section deals with how to recognize improper management of inventories. Recognition of problem areas is the first step in determining where opportunities exist for improving logistics performance. If a firm is experiencing continuing problems associated with inventory management, a change in processes or systems may be in order.

The following symptoms may be associated with poor inventory management:

Symptoms Associated with Poor Inventory Management

1. Increasing numbers of back-orders.
2. Increasing dollar investment in inventory with back-orders remaining constant.
3. High customer turnover rate.
4. Increasing number of orders canceled.
5. Periodic lack of sufficient storage space.
6. Wide variance in turnover of major inventory items between distribution centers.

7. Deteriorating relationships with intermediaries, as typified by dealer cancellations and declining orders.
8. Large quantities of obsolete items.

In many instances inventory levels can be reduced by one or more of the following steps:

Methods for Reducing Inventory Levels

1. Multiechelon inventory planning. ABC analysis is an example of such planning.
2. Lead time analysis.
3. Delivery time analysis. This may lead to a change in carriers or negotiation with existing carriers.
4. Elimination of low turnover and/or obsolete items.
5. Analysis of pack size and discount structure.
6. Examination of procedures for returned goods.
7. Encouragement/automation of product substitution.
8. Installation of formal reorder review systems.
9. Measurement of fill rates by stockkeeping units (SKUs).
10. Analysis of customer demand characteristics.
11. Development of a formal sales plan and demand forecast by predetermined logic.
12. Expand view of inventory to include inventory management and information sharing at various levels in the supply chain.
13. Reengineering inventory management practices (include warehousing and transportation) to realize improvements in product flow.

In many companies, the best method of reducing inventory investment is to reduce order cycle time by using advanced order processing systems (see Chapter 3). If the order cycle currently offered to customers is satisfactory, the time saved in the transmittal, entry, and processing of orders can be used for inventory planning. The result will be a significant reduction in inventory.

Improving Inventory Management

Inventory management can be improved by using one or more of the following techniques: ABC analysis, forecasting, inventory models, and advanced order processing systems.

ABC Analysis

Pareto Principle

In his study of the distribution of wealth in Milan, Villefredo Pareto (1848–1923) found that 20 percent of the people controlled 80 percent of the wealth. The concept that critical issues, wealth, importance, and so on are concentrated among a few is termed **Pareto's law.** This applies in our daily lives—most of the issues we face have little importance, but a few are critical, long-term issues—and it certainly applies to inventory systems.[6]

---

[6]Richard B. Chase and Nicolas J. Aquilano, *Production and Operations Management,* 6th ed. (Burr Ridge, IL: Richard D. Irwin, 1992).

This type of ABC analysis should not be confused with activity based costing, also abbreviated as ABC (see Chapter 13). The logic behind ABC analysis is that 20 percent of the firm's customers or products account for 80 percent of the sales and perhaps an even larger percentage of profits. The first step in ABC analysis is to rank products by sales or, preferably, by contribution to corporate profitability if such data are available. The next step is to check for differences between high-volume and low-volume items that may suggest how certain items should be managed.

Inventory Levels Increase with the Number of Storage Locations

Inventory levels increase with the number of stockkeeping locations.[7] By stocking low-volume items at a number of logistics centers, the national demand for these products is divided by the number of locations. Each of these locations must maintain safety stock. If one centralized location had been used for these items, the total safety stock would be much lower. For example, if only one centralized warehouse is used and sales are forecast on a national basis, a sales increase in Los Angeles may offset a sales decrease in New York. However, safety stock is required to protect against variability in demand, and there is greater variability in demand when we forecast demand by regions. The total system inventory will increase with the number of field warehouse locations because the variability in demand must be covered at each location.

When a firm consolidates slow-moving items at a centralized location, transportation costs often increase. However, these costs may be offset by lower inventory carrying costs and fewer stockout penalties. Customer service can be improved through consolidation of low-volume items by decreasing the probability of experiencing a stockout. ABC analysis is a method for deciding which items should be considered for centralized warehousing.

An Example of ABC Analysis

At this point let's consider an example of ABC analysis.[8] An analysis of sales volume by product reveals that A items account for 5 percent of all items and contribute 70 percent to sales, B items account for 10 percent of items and add a further 20 percent to sales, while C items account for 65 percent of the remaining items but contribute only 10 percent to sales. The last 20 percent of the items have no sales whatsoever during the past year (see Figure 5–6). This statistical distribution is almost always found in companies' inventories.[9] The "degree of concentration of sales among items will vary by firm, but the shape of the curve will be similar."[10]

For A items, a daily or continuous review of inventory status might be appropriate; B items might be reviewed weekly while the C items should receive the least attention. Different customer service levels could be established for each category of inventory. An order fill rate of 98 percent might be set for A items, 90 percent for B items, and 85 percent for C items. This policy would result in an overall customer service level of 95 percent, as shown in Table 5–6. By focusing attention on the A items, management places greater emphasis on the products that contribute the most to sales and profitability.

---

[7]While average inventory at each facility decreases as the number of warehouse locations increases, total system inventory (all facilities) increases.

[8]This example is adapted from William C. Copacino, "Moving beyond ABC Analysis," *Traffic Management* 33, no. 3 (Mar. 1994), pp. 35–36; and Lynn E. Gill, "Inventory and Physical Distribution Management," in *The Distribution Handbook,* ed. James F. Robeson and Robert G. House (New York: Free Press, 1985), pp. 664–67.

[9]It is referred to as *log normal distribution.*

[10]Gill, "Inventory and Physical Distribution Management," p. 664.

FIGURE 5–6

ABC parts classification

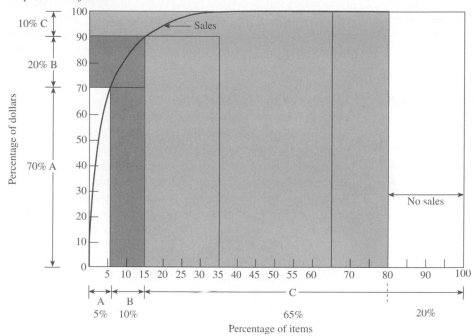

Source. Lynn E. Gill, "Inventory and Physical Distribution Management," in *The Distribution Handbook,* ed. James F. Robeson and Robert G. House (New York: Free Press, 1985), p. 665. Copyright © 1985 by The Free Press, a Division of Macmillan, Inc. Reprinted by permission of the publisher.

TABLE 5–6   Customer Service Levels Using ABC Analysis

Category	Percent of Sales	Customer Service Level (%)	Weighted Customer Service Level (%)
A	70	98	68.6
B	20	90	18.0
C	10	85	8.5
	100	Overall service level	95.1

Source: Lynn E. Gill, "Inventory and Physical Distribution Management," in *The Distribution Handbook,* ed. James F. Robeson and Robert G. House (New York: Free Press, 1985), p. 664. Copyright © 1985 by The Free Press, a Division of Macmillan, Inc. Reprinted by permission of the publisher.

Similarly, the amount of safety stock is less when lower volume items are stocked in fewer locations. If the firm made use of 20 distribution centers, A items might be stocked in all 20 warehouses, B items in 5 regional warehouses, and C items stocked only at the factory. Although transportation costs for B and C items are greater, the inventory reductions are usually more than enough to make a selective stocking policy worthwhile. Management can experiment with alternative inventory policies for their impact on customer service and profitability.

Forecasting

Surveying Buyer Intentions

Forecasting the amount of each product that is likely to be purchased is an important aspect of inventory management. One forecasting method is to *survey buyer intentions,* using mail questionnaires, telephone interviews, or personal interviews. These data can be used to develop a sales forecast. This approach is not without problems, however. It can be costly and the accuracy of the information may be questionable.

Judgment Sampling

Another approach is to solicit the opinions of salespeople or known experts in the field. This method, termed **judgment sampling,** is relatively fast and inexpensive. However, the data are subject to the personal biases of the individual salespeople or experts.

Most companies simply project future sales based on past sales data. Because most inventory systems require only a one- or two-month forecast, short-term forecasting is acceptable. A number of techniques are available to aid the manager in developing a short-term sales forecast.[11] A method for developing the forecast is shown in Figure 5–7. Rather than trying to forecast at the stockkeeping unit (SKU) level, which would result in large forecasting errors, management can improve forecast accuracy significantly by forecasting at a much higher level of aggregation.

For example, in Figure 5–7 a forecasting model is used to develop the forecast at the total company or product line level. The next step is to break that forecast down by product class and SKU based on past sales history. The inventory is then "pushed out" from the central distribution center to branch or regional distribution centers using one of the following methods:

- Going rate—the rate of sales that the SKU is experiencing at each location.
- Weeks/months of supply—the number of weeks/months of sales based on expected future sales that management wishes to hold at each location.
- Available inventory—currently available inventory less back-orders.

The only certainty in developing a forecast is that the forecast will not be 100 percent accurate. For this reason, many firms are developing time-based strategies that focus on reducing the total time from sourcing of materials to delivery of the final product. The shorter this time period can be made, the less critical forecasting becomes, because the firm can respond more quickly to changes in demand. Time-based competitive strategies will be discussed throughout the text. We will examine the most frequently used forecasting techniques in Chapter 12, providing a description of each technique and its advantages and disadvantages.

Firms are increasingly moving toward "demand pull" production where they replenish inventory based on actual customer demand/sales. Box 5–1 discusses how Nabisco has improved its forecasting using **continuous replenishment (CR),** in which daily sales data are combined with forecast data.

Order Processing/Inventory Systems

Many companies have not undertaken comprehensive and ongoing analysis and planning of inventory policy because of a lack of time and information. Many times a poor communica-

---

[11]For excellent in-depth coverage of various forecasting methods, see Branko Pecar, *Business Forecasting for Management* (London: McGraw-Hill, 1994).

FIGURE 5–7

Building a forecast

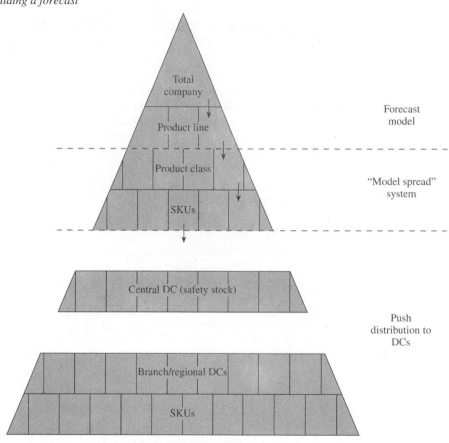

Source: Professor Jay U. Sterling, University of Alabama. Used with permission.

tions system is a contributing factor. A primary goal of inventory management is to achieve an optimum balance between inventory carrying costs and customer service. The essential task of determining the proper balance requires continuous and comprehensive planning. It hinges on the availability of information. Communications make information available.

An automated and integrated order processing system that utilizes up-to-date customer demand data and is linked to forecasting and production scheduling can reduce the time needed to perform certain elements of the order cycle and to reduce information lags in order processing and inventory replenishment. Cycle time reductions in the performance of these activities can be used for inventory planning, assuming the current order-cycle time is satisfactory to the manufacturer's customers. In this way, the firm can gain substantial cost savings by reducing its levels of safety stock. Kendall Healthcare has used this approach (see Box 5–2).

In addition, an automated and integrated logistics information system can reduce message errors and unexpected time delays. This facilitates better decision making and improves internal coordination in the firm.

Box 5–1

Nabisco Uses Continuous Replenishment to Manage Inventory

In a presentation to the Council of Logistics Management Annual Conference in Washington, D.C., Deborah Lentz, Nabisco's Director of Operations and Quick Response, focused on using continuous replenishment to support Nabisco's efficient consumer response (ECR) efforts.

Lentz defined continuous replenishment (CR) as:

. . . the managing of customer inventories and order process to reduce inventory and its related costs throughout the supply chain. It means sharing information and forming a partnership to minimize costs and optimize productivity and effectiveness.

Nabisco begins the CR process by exchanging historical sales data with retailers and wholesalers to use as an input for forecasting. It then receives transmission of actual sales/store demand from distribution centers (DCs) and stores on a daily basis. Nabisco also monitors inventory levels at each DC, and develops an order based on forecast, demand inventory balances, customer service objectives, and stock and turn objectives.

Nabisco has found many benefits from continuous replenishment, including improved flow of inventory requirements, which leads to an increase in in-stock position at the DC and at the store level; higher sales because of fewer stockouts, reduced lead time, increased consumer loyalty, and better customer service; higher inventory turns resulting in lower inventory and lower operating costs; and better product freshness and reduced markdowns due to the increase in inventory turns.

Additionally, increased inventory turns could lead to better cash flow for the customer because the product could turn before it is paid for.

Some successes that Nabisco and its partners have experienced include reduced inventories at one of Nabisco's customers from 10 weeks to 2 and, at another customer, increased inventory turns from 6 turns per year to 26. Nabisco sees additional opportunities to gain further effectiveness and to reap more benefits. Those include the standardization of varying input data and a focus on the entire supply chain. This means that a detailed understanding of a customer's business process is required to ensure that the data are used properly to prevent the creation of inaccurate orders.

The second opportunity concentrates on the supply chain: The **supply chain** is the flow of inventory from a manufacturer's production facility to its distribution center, to the customer's distribution center, to the retail store, and then on to the consumer. Currently, Nabisco's CR focuses on only a portion of the supply chain—the movement from the manufacturer's warehouse to the customer.

CR provides actual demand or point-of-sale data that can be used as input into a manufacturer's forecasting system. Until enough critical mass participates, however, CR data cannot be used to adequately affect the production process. Thus, a reduction in raw materials may not be realized and in some instances, with the onset of reduced lead times, inventory levels in a manufacturer's distribution center may actually increase.

Source: Deborah J. Lentz, "Efficient Consumer Response," *Proceedings of the Annual Conference of the Council of Logistics Management* (Oak Brook, IL: Council of Logistics Management, 1993), pp. 325–34.

With full, up-to-the-second information on orders, raw materials inventory and production scheduling can be better managed. The distribution center can meet customer commitments without increasing inventories. The firm can prepare more accurate invoices, invoice customers sooner, and receive payments more quickly and with fewer reconciliations. Reduced inventories and faster invoicing improve cash flow. Inventory management is improved by placing vital information into the hands of decision makers and providing them with the necessary time to use this information in planning inventory strategies.

Box 5–2

Integrating Systems to Improve Inventory Management at Kendall Healthcare Products

Kendall Healthcare Products has increased its logistics performance in a number of areas by improving the integration of its information systems, particularly its production and distribution systems. In addition, it has up-to-date customer demand information (continuous replenishment) to drive its production scheduling. The results have been impressive in all aspects of inventory performance. Kendall has:

- Improved its on-time order fill rate from the low- to mid-80 percent level to 98 percent.

- Cut 15 days from on-hand inventory.

- Improved forecast accuracy by 41 percent.

- Increased unit fill rate by 15 percent.

These changes were possible because Kendall viewed its operations from the perspective of a systems approach, recognizing that a change in one aspect of its logistics processes (i.e., using up-to-date, actual customer sales data) would have repercussions throughout the company's logistics systems.

To further improve its inventory performance and customer service, Kendall is planning key customers' warehouse inventory and carrying out their replenishment.

By reducing last-minute rush orders, everyone wins. Both Kendall and the customers enjoy reduced inventory and increased turns.

Source: Tom Andel, "Expanding Demand for Cycle Time Compression," *Transportation and Distribution* 35, no. 10 (Oct. 1994), pp. 95–96ff.

Impact of an Inventory Reduction on Corporate Profit Performance

Inventory Reductions Impact ROI and Profits

Inventory reductions have far-reaching implications on organizational **return on investment (ROI)** and profitability. Suppose, for example, that through the implementation of EDI, an organization can reduce its required cycle stock by $5 million. This will reduce the order transmission time without reducing lead time to its customers. What are some of the effects this would have? This is illustrated in Table 5–7.

First, profitability is improved due to a reduction in inventory carrying costs. With an incremental annual inventory carrying cost percentage of 30 percent, company X had a $1.5 million reduction in inventory carrying costs (30 percent × $5 million inventory reduction). This went right to the bottom line to improve pretax profit by $1.5 million. The pretax profit margin would thus go up from 4.0 percent to 5.5 percent as the company increases earnings on the same sales dollars.

Return on assets would also go up because the company could make the same return (profit) with fewer assets. It changes from 10.0 percent to 13.8 percent. Second, inventory turnover would go up because average inventory would be lower on the same sales dollars. Analysts like to see such numbers. Here, the figure goes from 4.3 percent to 6.7 percent! Improved inventory management has been the key to long-term profit improvements in the heavy equipment manufacturing sector. The Creative Solutions box at the end of the chapter explains why.

TABLE 5–7   Select Company X Financial Data for Analysis Purposes

	Before Inventory Reduction	After Inventory Reduction
Income Statement ($ millions)		
Sales	$100.0	$100.0
Cost of goods sold (COGS)	60.0	60.0
Gross margin	40.0	40.0
Operating variable	18.0	16.5
Operating fixed	18.0	18.0
Pretax profit	$ 4.0	$ 5.5
Balance Sheet ($ millions)		
Current assets inventory	$ 14.0	$ 9.0
Other	8.0	8.0
Total	22.0	17.0
Fixed assets	18.0	23.0
Total assets	$ 40.0	$ 40.0
Profit Margin		
Profit/sales	$4/$100 = 4%	$5.5/$100 = 5.5%
Return on Assets		
Profit/total assets	$4/$40 = 10%	$5.5/$40 = 13.8%
Inventory Turnover		
COGS/inventory	$60/$14 = 4.3 times	$60/$9 = 6.7 times

Many other ratios of improvements could be calculated in this simple example. If the company took its savings and invested it in assets that could improve production, marketing, or research and development to generate increased sales, even more changes could be seen.

Summary

In this chapter, we saw how to determine the impact of inventory investment on a firm's corporate profit performance. We examined the way in which inventory policy affects least total cost logistics, and described a methodology that can be used to calculate inventory carrying costs. We looked at the relationship between inventory turnover and inventory carrying costs. It should now be apparent that inventory is a costly investment. The chapter concluded with an explanation of techniques to use to improve inventory man-

Creative Solutions

Heavy Equipment Manufacturers Use Inventory Management to Improve Profitability

Heavy equipment manufacturers—makers of tractors, combines, cotton-pickers, and other large farming equipment—have not performed well for many years. A number of factors, such as volatile business cycles, persistent overcapacity, and slow to no growth have made this industry a poor prospect. In 1996, however, these firms experienced increased profitability. Why?

Sales were up slightly—3–4 percent annually—but the big reason was increased margins on sales, up to about 13 percent compared with 7 percent in the early 1990s. The key to the improvement in margins was improved inventory management. Jean-Pierre Rosso, Case Corporation's chairman and chief executive officer, noted: "We're now finding that we can run the business with fewer assets, lower costs, and a lot more flexibility."

In the past, when business was booming, equipment dealers would load up with enough inventory to cover 8 to 10 months of sales. This left them unable to respond quickly when demand began to decline. As a result, equipment would be deeply discounted to stimulate demand.

Deere and Company and other major equipment manufacturers are encouraging dealers to hold no more than four months of inventory. The manufacturers are also keeping stocks down. In 1988, stock on hand was 10 percent of cost of goods sold, even though sales were strong.

These companies have recognized the importance of excellent inventory management for the long-term profitability and even the viability of their companies. There were 20 major players in farm equipment 12 years ago; today there arc five. Cutting inventory at all levels in the supply chain allows manufacturers and dealers to respond much more quickly in this extremely cyclical industry.

Source: Peter Elstrom, "Heavy Equipment Gets into Gear," *Business Week,* Aug. 5, 1996, p. 29.

agement, and a method to determine the impact of an inventory reduction on corporate profit performance. In the next chapter, we will see how a knowledge of materials management can improve logistics performance.

Suggested Readings

Andel, Tom. "Inventory Horror Stories." *Transportation and Distribution,* Buyer's Guide Issue (July 1995), pp. BG3–BG6.

Burch, John G. *Cost and Management Accounting: A Modern Approach.* St. Paul, MN: West, 1994.

Copacino, William C. "Moving beyond ABC Analysis." *Traffic Management* 33, no. 3 (Mar. 1994), pp. 35–36.

Farris, M. Theodore, II. "Utilizing Inventory Flow Models with Suppliers." *Journal of Business Logistics* 17, no. 1 (1996), pp. 35–61.

Grenoble, William L., IV. "Inventory Control." In James F. Robeson and William C. Copacino, eds., *The Logistics Handbook.* New York: Free Press, 1994, pp. 372–90.

Hsleh, Pei Jung. "New Developments in Inventory and Materials Management." *Logistics Information Management* 5, no. 2 (1992), pp. 32–41.

Krupp, James A. "Measuring Inventory Management Performance." *Production and Inventory Management Journal* 35, no. 4 (1994), pp. 1–6.

Lambert, Douglas M. *The Development of an Inventory Costing Methodology: A Study of the Costs Associated with Holding Inventory*. Chicago: National Council of Physical Distribution Management, 1976.

Lambert, Douglas M., and John T. Mentzer. "Inventory Carrying Costs: Current Availability and Uses." *International Journal of Physical Distribution and Materials Management* 9, no. 6 (1979), pp. 256–71.

Loar, Tim. "Patterns of Inventory Management and Policy: A Study of Four Industries." *Journal of Business Logistics* 13, no. 2 (1993), pp. 69–82.

Scanlon, Patrick. "Controlling Your Inventory Dollars." *Production and Inventory Management Journal* 34, no. 4 (1993), pp. 33–35.

Shank, John K., and Vijay Govindarajan. *Strategic Cost Management: The New Tool for Competitive Advantage*. New York: Free Press, 1993.

"What Level of Inventory Should be Held?" *Logistics Information Management* 4, no. 2 (1992), pp. 50–55.

Questions and Problems

1. Explain how excessive inventories can erode corporate profitability.

2. Many businesspeople rely on industry averages or textbook percentages for the inventory carrying cost that they use when setting inventory levels. Why is this approach wrong?

3. How would you determine the cost of capital to be used in inventory decisions?

4. How would you determine the cash value of a manufacturer's finished goods inventory investment? How would this differ for a wholesaler or retailer?

5. What is the difference between the transportation cost component of logistics cost trade-off analysis and the transportation cost included in the inventory valuation (cash value)?

6. What problems do you foresee in gathering the cost information required to calculate a company's inventory carrying costs?

7. Describe the circumstances under which inventory carrying costs can vary within a given manufacturing company. Explain why total inventory carrying costs decrease, but at an ever-slower rate, as inventory turnovers increase. Consider raw materials, goods in process, and furnished goods inventories in your answer.

8. Calculate the inventory carrying cost percentage for XYZ Company, given the following information:

   • Finished goods inventory is $26 million, valued at full manufactured cost.

   • Based on the inventory plan, the weighted-average variable manufactured cost per case is 70 percent of the full manufactured cost.

- The transportation cost incurred by moving the inventory to field warehouse locations was $1.5 million.
- The variable handling cost of moving this inventory into warehouse locations was calculated to be $300,000.
- The company is currently experiencing capital rationing, and new investments are required to earn 15 percent after taxes.
- Personal property tax paid on inventory was approximately $200,000.
- Insurance to protect against loss of finished goods inventory was $50,000.
- Storage charges at public warehouses totaled $450,000.
- Variable plant storage was negligible.
- Obsolescence was $90,000.
- Shrinkage was $100,000.
- Damage related to finished goods inventory levels was $10,000.
- Transportation costs associated with the relocation of field inventory to avoid obsolescence was $50,000.

9. What are some of the key symptoms of poor inventory management?
10. Describe ABC analysis of inventory, and how it can be used to improve inventory management.

THE DISTRIBUTION CHALLENGE!
PROBLEM: ONE FOR THE BOOKS

This Challenge has already become a logistics textbook classic—which isn't surprising, considering that Stanford University Professor Hau Lee was involved in the solution. It concerns high-tech giant Hewlett-Packard (HP), one of the world's leaders in the production of computer printers.

The problem cropped up in 1990, two years after HP introduced its popular line of DeskJet printers. In that brief time, sales topped more than 600,000 units valued at $400 million. Already, however, HP was running into serious inventory snags, particularly with service to its European customers.

Production took place in the Vancouver, Washington, regional headquarters of the company's personal printer group. The printers were shipped to Europe by water. Unfortunately, that resulted in long lead times, making it tough for HP to accurately forecast demand.

HP found itself running short of production for certain customers while at the same time renting trailers outside the European distribution center to handle excess inventories.

Matters were further complicated because each destination country had its own power-supply requirements based on prevailing voltage levels, and manuals had to be in the local language. Figuring out how much product to ship to each market was proving next to impossible for Vancouver.

A number of options were available to HP. It could devise a complicated new methodology for projecting safety stocks. It could increase inventory in Europe, causing a further glut of product in some areas. It could cut inventory, angering customers and sales offices even more. It could set up manufacturing in Europe, an expensive move that might not be justified by sales volumes. Or it could ship by air, another pricey option.

What Is Your Solution?

Source: "Distribution: The Challenge," *Distribution* 95, no. 4 (Apr. 1996), p. 68.

Managing Materials Flow

Chapter Outline

Chapter Objectives

- To identify the activities of materials management.
- To examine the concept of total quality management (TQM).
- To identify and describe a variety of materials management philosophies and techniques, including Kanban/just-in-time (JIT), MRP, and DRP.

Introduction

Scope of Materials Management

As defined in this book, logistics management is concerned with the efficient flow of raw materials, in-process inventory, and finished goods from point of origin to point of consumption. An integral part of the logistics management process is **materials management,** which encompasses the administration of raw materials, subassemblies, manufactured parts, packing materials, and in-process inventory.[1] In a formal sense, implementation of a materials management organization will have "a single-manager responsible for the planning, organizing, motivating, and controlling of all those activities and principally concerned with the flow of materials into an organization."[2]

Materials management is critical to the total logistics process. Although materials management does not directly interface with the final customer, decisions made in its portion of the logistics process will directly affect the level of customer service offered, the ability of the firm to compete with other companies, and the level of sales and profits the firm is able to achieve in the marketplace.

Without efficient and effective management of inbound materials flow, the manufacturing process cannot produce products at the desired price and at the time they are required for distribution to the firm's customers. Thus, it is essential that the logistics executive understand the role of materials management and its impact on the company's cost-service mix. In a manufacturing setting, not having the proper materials when needed can cause manufacturing processes to slow down or even shut down, which can result in stockouts.

Poor materials management can result in stockouts at retail, causing customers to seek substitutes or shop elsewhere. In a service such as health care, lack of needed materials may delay testing or vital patient treatment, causing at least inconvenience and, at worst, threatening patient health.

The Role of Materials Management Has Expanded

As organizations have developed and matured, the role of materials management has expanded to meet the challenges of market-driven, rather than production-driven, economies. Table 6–1 identifies some of the differences between the traditional role played by materials management within firms and the contemporary environment in which materials will be brought into firms' production processes.

While many things, such as the need to reduce costs and provide high levels of customer service, will remain important, materials management will be characterized by a changing set of priorities and issues: global orientation, shorter product life cycles, lower levels of inventories, electronic data processing, and a market-oriented focus.

This chapter identifies the various components of materials management, and describes how to effectively manage materials flows within a manufacturing environment. We will examine specific management strategies and techniques used in the planning, implementation, and control of materials flows within organizations.

---

[1]See Joseph L. Cavinato, "Materials Management," in James F. Robeson and William C. Copacino, *The Logistics Handbook* (New York: Free Press, 1994), pp. 325–26.

[2]Michael Leenders and Harold E. Fearon, *Purchasing and Materials Management,* 10th ed. (Burr Ridge, IL: Richard D. Irwin, 1993), p. 5.

TABLE 6–1   **Materials Management: Old and New Thinking**

	Old Thinking	*New Thinking*
Market	Seller's market; low competition; restricted export	Buyer's market; keen competition; global oriented
Products	Small assortment; long life cycle; low technology	Wide assortments; short life cycle; high technology
Production	Full capacity load; low flexibility; large lot sizes; long lead times; low costs; make instead of buy	Full capacity load; high flexibility; low lot sizes; short lead times; low costs; buy instead of make
Service level	High service level; high inventories; slow logistics process; slow transport time	High service level; low inventories; quick logistics process; quick transport time
Information technology	Manual data processing; paper administration	Electronic data processing; paperless factory
Enterprise strategy	Production oriented	Market oriented

Source: Hans F. Busch, "Integrated Materials Management," *International Journal of Physical Distribution and Materials Management* 18, no. 7 (1988), p. 28.

Scope of Materials Management

Materials management is typically comprised of four basic activities:

Materials Management Activities

1. Anticipating materials requirements.
2. Sourcing and obtaining materials.
3. Introducing materials into the organization.
4. Monitoring the status of materials as a current asset.[3]

Functions performed by materials managers include purchasing, inventory control of raw materials and finished goods, receiving, warehousing, production scheduling, and transportation. The definition of materials management used in this chapter views the activity as an organizational system with the various functions as interrelated, interactive, subsystems.

The objectives of materials management are to solve materials problems from a total company viewpoint [optimize] by coordinating performance of the various materials functions, providing a communications network, and controlling materials flow.[4]

The specific objectives of materials management are closely tied to the firm's main objectives of achieving an acceptable level of profitability or return on investment (ROI), and remaining competitive in an increasingly competitive marketplace.

---

[3]Ibid.

[4]Ibid.

Figure 6–1

The objectives of integrated materials management

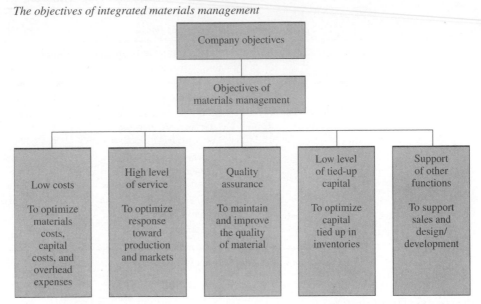

Source: Yunus Kathawala and Heino H. Nauo, "Integrated Materials Management: A Conceptual Approach," *International Journal of Physical Distribution and Materials Management* 19, no. 8 (1989), p. 10.

Figure 6–1 highlights the major objectives of materials management: low costs, high levels of service, quality assurance, low level of tied-up capital, and support of other functions. Each objective is clearly linked to overall corporate goals and objectives. Thus, trade-offs among the objectives must be made using a broad perspective of materials flow throughout the total system, from source of supply to the ultimate customer.[5]

Materials management encompasses a variety of logistics activities. The primary differences between the process of materials management and that of finished goods distribution are that the items handled in materials management are incoming finished goods, raw materials, component parts, and subassemblies to be further processed or sorted before being received by the final customer. The recipient of the materials management effort is the production or manufacturing group and other internal customers, not the final customer.

Integral aspects of materials management include purchasing and procurement, production control, inbound traffic and transportation, warehousing and storage, management information system (MIS) control, inventory planning and control, and salvage and scrap disposal.

---

[5]Yunus Kathawala and Heino H. Nauo, "Integrated Materials Management: A Conceptual Approach," *International Journal of Physical Distribution and Materials Management* 19, no. 8 (1989), p. 10.

Purchasing and Procurement

The acquisition of materials has been, and will continue to be, an important aspect of materials management:

> The rapidly changing supply scene, with cycles of abundance and shortages, and varying prices, lead times, and availabilities, provides a continuing challenge to those organizations wishing to obtain a maximum contribution from this area.[6]

Purchasing and Procurement Are Not the Same

The terms *purchasing* and *procurement* are often used interchangeably, although they do differ in scope. **Purchasing** generally refers to the actual buying of materials and those activities associated with the buying process. Procurement is broader in scope and includes purchasing, traffic, warehousing, and all activities related to receiving inbound materials. These topics are discussed in detail in Chapter 10, "Purchasing," and will not be examined here.

Production Control

Production control is an activity traditionally positioned under manufacturing, although a few firms place it under logistics. Its position in the firm's organizational chart is not crucial so long as both manufacturing and logistics have input into the production planning and control activities.

Production Affects Logistics in Two Significant Ways

Production affects the logistics process in two significant ways. First, production activity determines the quantity and type of finished goods that are produced. This in turn influences when and how the products are distributed to the firm's customers. Second, production directly determines the company's need for raw materials, subassemblies, and component parts used in the manufacturing process. Therefore, production control decisions are often jointly shared by manufacturing and logistics.

Inbound Logistics

Materials management is concerned with product flows into the firm. Much like the firm's target markets, manufacturing requires satisfactory levels of customer service which depend on the ability of materials management to effectively coordinate with a variety of functions, including traffic and transportation, warehousing and storage, and MIS control.

One of the most important activities of materials management is working with the logistics function to manage inbound traffic and transportation. Like their counterparts responsible for finished goods, materials managers must be aware of the available transport modes and combinations, government regulations that affect the firm's transportation carriers, private versus for-hire carrier issues, leasing, evaluation of mode/carrier performance, and the cost-service trade-offs involved in the inbound movement of product.[7]

---

[6]Leenders and Fearon, *Purchasing and Materials Management,* p. 2.

[7]For a discussion of inbound consolidation strategies as a facet of materials management activities, see Frank P. Buffa, "Inbound Consolidation Strategy: The Effect of Inventory Cost Rate Changes," *International Journal of Physical Distribution and Materials Management* 18, no. 7 (1988), pp. 3–14.

The control and flow of inbound materials into a pulp and paper mill is a large and complex logistics operation.

Differences between Inbound and Outbound Transportation

Three major differences exist between the administration of inbound and outbound transportation. First, the market demand that generates the need for outbound movement is generally uncertain and fluctuating. The demand that concerns materials managers originates with the production scheduling activity and tends to be more predictable and stable; thus, materials managers do not encounter the same types of problems as their counterparts in the outbound traffic area.

Second, the materials manager is more likely to be concerned with bulk movements of raw materials or large shipments of parts and subassemblies. In addition, raw materials and parts have different handling, loss, or damage characteristics which will affect mode/carrier selection and evaluation. Third, firms may exercise less control over their inbound transportation because purchasing procedures tend to look at "total delivered price" where the transportation cost is not separately identified. Thus, a separate analysis of inbound costs is not performed as often or in as much depth, and significant cost savings are potentially possible.

Warehousing and Storage

Raw materials, components parts, and subassemblies are placed in storage until they are required by the production process. Unlike the warehousing of finished goods, which usually occurs in the field, items awaiting use in production are usually stored on-site, that is, at the point of manufacture; or they are delivered on an "as needed" basis by a just-in-time (JIT) supplier.

Warehousing and Storage Costs Are Very Important to Materials Managers

If a JIT delivery system is utilized, the need for inbound warehousing is greatly minimized or eliminated altogether. If the JIT system is not used, and warehouses are used for the storage of inbound materials, the materials manager is usually much more concerned with warehousing and inventory costs because they account for a larger percentage of product value.

In addition, the warehousing requirements for raw materials and other items are usually quite different. For example, open or outside storage is possible with many raw materials, such as iron ore, sand and gravel, coal, and other unprocessed materials. Also, damage or loss due to weather, spoilage, or theft is minimal with raw materials because of their unprocessed state or low value per pound.

Data and Information Systems

Information Needed by Materials Managers

The materials manager needs direct access to the organization's information system to properly administer materials flow into and within the organization. The types of information needed include demand forecasts for production, names of suppliers and supplier characteristics, pricing data, inventory levels, production schedules, transportation routing and scheduling data, and other financial and marketing facts. Additionally, materials management supplies input into the firm's MIS. Data on inventory levels for materials, delivery schedules, pricing, forward buys, and supplier information are a few of the inputs provided by materials management.

Integrated materials management has a multitude of data to process, a task that would not be possible without EDP-supported systems. Numerous software packages for individual functional elements of integrated materials management have been developed during the last few years. These are packages tailored for particular branches of industry and particular company sizes.[8]

The Importance of Information Technology

Thus, modern information technology will offer opportunities for the fast and safe transmission and processing of extensive amounts of data, both internally for users within the company and externally for suppliers and customers. Paperless communication is coming to the forefront whereby routine tasks in order processing and scheduling will be decisively facilitated.[9] As a result, new information technology offers great opportunities for linking the planning, control, and processing functions of materials management that hitherto were performed independently, thereby creating the foundation for the establishment of integrated materials management.[10]

The proliferation of computerized information systems and databases, coupled with electronic data interchange (EDI), will make this facet of materials management even more significant in the future.

Inventory Planning and Control

Inventory planning and control of raw materials, component parts, subassemblies, and goods-in-process are just as important as the management of finished goods inventory. Many of the concepts discussed in Chapters 4 and 5, such as ABC analysis, inventory carrying costs, and economic order quantity (EOQ), are directly applicable to materials management.

---

[8]Richard C. Haverly and James F. Whelan, *Logistics Software* (New York: Andersen Consulting, 1996).

[9]Ken Sobel-Feldman and Ken Mewes, "Information Management: Challenges and Opportunities," *Fortune,* Oct. 17, 1994, special advertising section.

[10]Kathawala and Nauo, "Integrated Materials Management," p. 14.

Materials Disposal

One of the most important areas of materials management that a firm often overlooks or considers minor is the disposal of scrap, surplus, recyclable, or obsolete materials. During the last few years, this area, referred to as **reverse logistics,** has gained significant importance because of increased public awareness of the environment, more stringent government legislation, and a better recognition of the opportunities it offers in return.[11]

The Importance of Scrap and Waste Materials

Many materials can be salvaged and sold to other companies. It is estimated that annual sales of scrap and waste materials in the United States total billions of dollars. For example, a film-processing firm had been selling the residual chemicals and materials that were by-products of its operations for relatively low prices. The firm invested in a machine that could separate the waste materials into its various components. While the company was still able to sell some of the components to the same salvage firm that had previously been performing the separation process, one of the residues produced was silver, which the company subsequently sold to a precious metals dealer for a handsome profit. The separator machine purchased by the company paid for itself in less than two years.

Almost all firms produce surplus materials as by-products of their operations. In addition to the normal packaging materials associated with products (e.g., cartons, pallets, shrink-wrap, baling wire), this material can result from overoptimistic sales forecasts, changes in product specifications, errors in estimating materials usage, losses in processing, and overbuying due to forward buys or quantity discounts on large purchases.

The basic tasks of the disposal function include a disposal classification based on whether something can be reused and the possibility of environmental pollution it bears. As a result of legal requirements and technical conditions, the hazard represented by some waste products is being recognized by firms. Additionally, increased public awareness of the environment has highlighted the importance of reverse logistics issues. Therefore, it is absolutely necessary to assign the responsibility for waste disposal to a central department that must report to the materials management function.[12]

This aspect of materials management is likely to become much more important in the future.[13] Figure 6–2 shows an advertisement that illustrates an alternative to traditional disposal methods.

Forecasting

Predicting the future is important because it allows logistics executives to primarily be proactive rather that reactive. Every area of logistics is affected in some way by the fore-

---

[11]E. J. Muller, "The Greening of Logistics," *Distribution* 90, no. 1 (Jan. 1991), pp. 26–34 and Ronald Kopicki, Michael J. Berg, and Leslie Legg, *Reuse and Recycling—Reverse Logistics Opportunities* (Oak Brook, IL: Council of Logistics Management, 1993).

[12]Kopicki, Berg, and Legg, *Reuse and Recycling—Reverse Logistics Opportunities,* pp. 53–86.

[13]See James R. Stock, *Reverse Logistics* (Oak Brook, IL: Council of Logistics Management, 1992); and "Environmental Aspects of Logistics," *International Journal of Physical Distribution and Logistics Management* 25, no. 2 (1995), special issue, pp. 1–68.

casting process; that is, conducting or developing forecasts, providing information to be used in forecasting, or receiving forecasting results and implementing necessary actions. While other activities of logistics are more actively involved in the forecasting process, materials management utilizes forecasts employed in MRP and DRP (discussed later in this chapter) efforts, and is indirectly affected by the forecasts developed (and the subsequent actions taken) by others (e.g., inventory planning, purchasing, and demand forecasting). **Forecasting** attempts to predict the future through quantitative or qualitative methods, or some combination of both. The essence of forecasting is to aid in logistics decision making.[14]

Why Forecast?

A study of the forecasting practices of a large number of companies indicated that the most widely cited reasons for engaging in forecasting included:

1. Increasing customer satisfaction.
2. Reducing stockouts.
3. Scheduling production more efficiently.
4. Lowering safety stock requirements.
5. Reducing product obsolescence costs.
6. Managing shipping better.
7. Improving pricing and promotion management.
8. Negotiating superior terms with suppliers.
9. Making more informed pricing decisions.[15]

Effective and efficient materials management requires many types of forecasts, including:

Types of Forecasts

• *Demand forecast.* Investigation of the firm's demand for the item, to include current and projected demand, inventory status, and lead times. Also considered are competing current and projected demands by industry and product end use.

• *Supply forecast.* Collection of data about current producers and suppliers, the aggregate projected supply situation, and technological and political trends that might affect supply.

• *Price forecast.* Based on information gathered and analyzed about demand and supply. Provides a prediction of short- and long-term prices and the underlying reasons for those trends.[16]

Additionally, forecasts can be short term, midrange, or long term. Typically, firms would use all three types of forecasting.

---

[14]A historical overview of forecasting and numerous examples are provided in Leslie Bernard Trustrum, F. Robert Blore, and William James Paskins, "Using Demand Forecasting Models," *Marketing Intelligence & Planning,* 5, no. 3 (1987), pp. 5–15.

[15]Glen Galfond, Kelly Ronayne, and Christian Winkler, "State-of-the-Art Supply Chain Forecasting," *PW Review,* Nov. 1996, p. 3.

[16]Leenders and Fearon, *Purchasing and Materials Management,* p. 457.

Forecasting Time Frames

• **Long-term forecasts** usually cover more than three years and are used for long-range planning and strategic issues. These will be performed in broad terms; that is, sales by product line or division, throughput capacity by ton per period or dollars per period.

• **Midrange forecasts** usually range from one to three years and address budgeting issues and sales plans. Again, these might predict more than demand.

• **Short-term forecasts** are most important for the operational logistics planning process. They project demand into the next several months and, in some cases, more than a year ahead. These are needed in units, by actual items to be shipped, and for finite periods of time—monthly or perhaps weekly.[17]

The firm may utilize a variety of forecasting techniques, ranging from those based on general market information (from suppliers, sales force, customers, and others) to highly sophisticated computer algorithms. The specific technique or approach a firm selects should be appropriate for the unique characteristics of the company and its markets.[18] Just-in-time systems, materials requirements planning (MRP I), manufacturing resource planning (MRP II), distribution requirements planning (DRP I), and distribution resource planning (DRP II) systems also can improve the efficiency of inventory planning and control. We will briefly describe these systems later in this chapter.

Total Quality Management

Total quality management (TQM) and reengineering are concepts that gained much attention and popularity in the 1980s and 1990s. TQM has been defined as:

TQM Defined

A philosophy and a set of guiding principles that represent the foundation of a continuously improving organization. TQM is the application of quantitative and human resources to improve the materials services supplied to an organization, all the processes within the organization, and the degree to which the needs of the customer are met—now and in the future. TQM integrates fundamental techniques, existing improvement efforts, and technical tools under a disciplined approach focused on continuous improvement.[19]

TQM has particular relevance and importance to materials flow within logistics. Many leading authorities have championed the importance of quality in business, including W. Edwards Deming and Philip B. Crosby.[20] Additionally, the Malcolm Baldrige National Quality Award program of the U.S. Department of Commerce has helped shape

---

[17]Allan F. Ayers, "Forecasting: Art or Reality?" *Transportation and Distribution,* 35, no. 6 (June 1994), pp. 29–30.

[18]David M. Georgoff and Robert G. Murdick, "Manager's Guide to Forecasting," *Harvard Business Review* 64, no. 1 (Jan.–Feb. 1986), pp. 110–20.

[19]U.S. Department of Defense, Office of the Deputy Assistant Secretary of Defense for TQM, *Total Quality Management: A Guide for Implementation,* DOD 5000.51-G, Washington, DC, Aug. 23, 1989.

[20]Howard S. Gitlow and Shelly J. Gitlow, *The Deming Guide to Quality and Competitive Position* (Englewood Cliffs, NJ: Prentice Hall, 1987); and Philip B. Crosby, *Quality Is Free* (New York: McGraw-Hill, 1979).

FIGURE 6–2

Alternative to traditional excess inventory disposal

Source: Used by permission of Educational Assistance Ltd., a nonprofit organization.

TABLE 6–2 **Traditional Management and TQM Comparison**

Traditional Management	Total Quality Management
Looks for "quick fix"	Adopts a new management philosophy
Firefights	Uses structured, disciplined operating methodology
Operates the same old way	Advocates "breakthrough" thinking using small innovations
Randomly adopts improvement efforts	"Sets the example" through management action
Focuses on short term	Stresses long-term, continuous improvement
Inspects for errors	Prevents errors
Throws resources at a task	Uses people to add value
Motivated by profit	Focuses on the customer
Relies on programs	A new way of life

Source: James H. Saylor, "What Total Quality Management Means to the Logistician," *Logistics Spectrum* 24, no. 4 (Winter 1990), p. 20.

corporate thinking on quality issues. Traditional concepts about quality have been modified and enhanced to form the TQM approach outlined in Table 6–2.

The TQM approach stresses long-term benefits resulting from continuous improvements to systems, programs, products, and people. Improvements most often result from a combination of small innovations. A structured, disciplined operating methodology is used to maximize customer service levels. Sometimes, however, significant changes are required to bring about system improvements. If so, reengineering might have to occur.

Reengineering and TQM

The concept of **reengineering** deals with "starting with a clean slate"; that is, taking systems and processes, and rethinking and redesigning them in order to create significant improvements in quality, cost, speed, and service.[21]

Table 6–3 identifies the relationships between TQM and logistics.[22] Underlying the specific items listed in the table is the notion that quality is a philosophy of doing business. It is like the marketing concept, cost trade-off analysis, and the systems approach, in that each provides a way of doing business that influences how individuals, departments, and companies plan, implement, and control marketing and logistics activities.

Therefore, all people involved in logistics must understand their role in delivering a level of quality to suppliers, internal operations, and customers. TQM focuses on continuous improvement through employee involvement and top-level management support. Studies have shown that quality is more important than cost within materials management, especially in outsourcing and supplier selection decisions.[23]

---

[21]For a comprehensive discussion of reengineering concepts, see Michael Hammer and James Champy, *Reengineering the Corporation* (New York: HarperCollins, 1993); and James Champy, *Reengineering Management: The Mandate for New Leadership* (New York: HarperCollins, 1995).

[22]For a discussion of this topic as it relates to logistics, see the *International Journal of Physical Distribution and Logistics Management* 23, no. 7 (1993), special issue on "JIT in Logistics."

[23]Arnold Maltz, "The Relative Importance of Cost and Quality in the Outsourcing of Warehousing," *Journal of Business Logistics* 15, no. 2 (1994), pp. 45–62.

TABLE 6–3   **Direct Relationship between TQM and Logistics**

TQM	Logistics
Provides a TQM management environment	Uses systematic, integrated, consistent, organizationwide perspective for satisfying the customer
Reduces chronic waste	Emphasizes "doing it right the first time"
Involves everyone and everything	Involves almost every process
Nurtures supplier partnerships and customer relationships	Knows the importance of supply partnerships
	Keys to customer relations. Customer relations are directly dependent on training, documentation, maintenance, supply support, support equipment, transportation, manpower, computer resources, and facilities
Creates a continuous improvement system	Uses logistics support analysis to continuously improve the system
Includes quality as an element of design	Influences design by emphasizing reliability, maintainability, and supportability, using the optimum mix of manpower and technology
Provides constant training	Provides constant technical training for everyone
Leads long-term continuous improvement efforts geared to prevention	Focuses on reducing life cycle costs by quality improvements geared to prevention
Encourages teamwork	Stresses the integrated efforts of everyone
Satisfies the customer	Places the customer first

Source: James H. Saylor, "What Total Quality Management Means to the Logistician," *Logistics Spectrum* 24, no. 4 (Winter 1990), p. 22.

Examples of TQM Implementation in Materials Management

Implementation of TQM within the materials management environment has resulted in significant benefits and improvements for many companies. McDonnell Douglas Corporation employed TQM concepts and reduced scrap by 58 percent. Boeing Ballistic Systems Division reduced the lead time on parts and materials by 30 percent and reduced material shortages from 12 percent to zero. AT&T reduced product defect rates and total process time by 30 percent and 46 percent, respectively. Hewlett-Packard Company reduced scrap by 75 percent and its product failure rate by 60 percent through TQM improvements.[24] (See Global box for a discussion of international quality standards.)

In summary, TQM and logistics are interrelated. "Managing logistics without incorporating the costs of quality is just as shortsighted as looking at the management of quality

---

[24]See Joe W. Meredith and Benjamin S. Blanchard, "Concurrent Engineering: Total Quality Management in Design," *Logistics Spectrum* 24, no. 4 (Winter 1990), pp. 31–40; and R. I. Winner, J. P. Pennell, H. E. Bertrand, and M. G. Slusarczuk, *The Role of Concurrent Engineering in Weapons System Acquisition,* IDA Report R-338 (Alexandria, VA: Institute for Defense Analyses, Dec. 1988).

without considering the role of logistics."[25] Thus, it is important that the flow of materials be administered and controlled utilizing the concepts of TQM.

Administration and Control of Materials Flow

Like all of the functions of logistics, materials management activities must be properly administered and controlled. This requires some methods to identify a firm's level of performance. Specifically, a firm must be able to *measure, report,* and *improve* performance.

Measuring the Performance of Materials Management

In measuring the performance of materials management, a firm should examine a number of elements, including supplier service levels, inventory, prices paid for materials, quality levels, and operating costs.[26]

Service levels can be measured using several methods, including order cycle time and fill rate for each supplier and the number of production delays caused by materials being out of stock. This and related topics were examined in Chapter 2.

Inventory is an important aspect of materials management. It can be controlled by considering the amount of slow-moving inventory and comparing actual inventory levels and turnover with targeted and historical levels, for example. Chapters 4 and 5 examined these issues.

Materials *price level* measures include gains and losses resulting from forward buying, a comparison of prices paid for major items over several time periods, and a comparison of actual prices paid for materials with targeted prices.

Measures that can be used in the area of *quality control* are the number of product failures caused by defects in materials and the percentage of materials rejected from each shipment from each supplier.

As an overall measure of performance, management can compare the *actual budget* consumed by materials management to the *targeted budget* determined at the beginning of the operating period. This and related topics will be examined in Chapter 13, "Methods to Control Logistics Performance."

Operating Reports Developed by Materials Management

Once the company has established performance measures for each component in the materials management process, data must be collected and results reported to individuals in decision-making positions. The major operating reports that should be developed by materials management include (1) market and economic conditions and price performance, (2) inventory investment changes, (3) purchasing operations and effectiveness, and (4) operations affecting administration and financial activities. Table 6–4 presents a summary of these reports.

---

[25]James M. Kenderdine and Paul D. Larson, "Quality and Logistics: A Framework for Strategic Integration," *International Journal of Physical Distribution and Materials Management* 18, no. 6 (1988), p. 9; also see S. J. Brill, "A Quality Approach to Logistics," *Proceedings of the Conference on the Total Logistics Concept* (Pretoria, South Africa, June 4–5, 1991).

[26]For an in-depth discussion of materials management control procedures, see Donald W. Dobler and David N. Burt, *Purchasing and Materials Management,* 5th ed. (New York: McGraw-Hill, 1990), pp. 600–22.

Global

Certifying Quality with ISO 9000

"ISO 9000? Total quality management? Quality assurance? Quality system? Quality policy? Depending upon whom you ask, these terms can conjure up many different and sometimes conflicting definitions.

Since 1987 one set of standards, the ISO 9000 series, has attempted to define a single definition for "quality" and a "quality system." The ISO 9000 series is a set of five international standards that establish the minimum requirements for an organization's quality system.

The five standards were authored by the International Organization for Standardization, headquartered in Geneva, Switzerland. Contrary to popular belief, ISO is not an acronym for the International Organization for Standardization. ISO is the official nickname, derived from *isos,* a Greek word meaning "equal."

The standards themselves are numbered ISO 9000, 9001, 9002, 9003, and 9004. The ISO 9000 series was adopted by the United States as the ANSI/ASQC Q90 series of standards. ANSI is the American National Standards Institute while ASQC is the American Society for Quality Control.

Each of the five standards has a particular application, explained below:

- ISO 9000/Q90 specifies the guidelines for selection and use of the other series standards.

- ISO 9001/Q91 specifies a quality system model for use by organizations that design/develop, produce, install, and service a product.
- ISO 9002/Q92 specifies a quality system model for use by organizations that produce and install a product or service.
- ISO 9003/Q93 specifies a quality system model for use by organizations that include final inspection and testing.
- ISO 9004/Q94 provides a set of guidelines for an organization to develop and implement a quality system, and interpret the standards of the other series.

When a firm becomes ISO 9000 certified, it proves to an independent assessor that it meets all the requirements of either ISO 9001/Q91, ISO 9002/Q92, or ISO 9003/Q93. Generally, ISO 9000 certification is good for a period of three years.

Source: Lance L. Whitacre, *ISO 9000: Certifying Quality in Warehousing and Distribution* (Oak Brook, IL: Warehousing Education and Research Council, March 1994), pp. 5–6.

The organization must look for opportunities for reengineering and continuous improvement based on a comparison of actual with desired performance. To initiate improvements, the materials manager can address some key questions:

Key Questions Important to Materials Management

1. What is the means of communication between materials management and production? What issues are communicated and how often?
2. What is our suppliers' involvement in the process of materials forecasting and inventory management?
3. What sort of relationships do we have with our suppliers? Are they eager to serve us and meet our needs, even in times when supplies are allocated?
4. Who schedules production runs? On what basis are production runs scheduled?

TABLE 6–4 **Operating Reports That Should Be Developed by Purchasing and Materials Management Functions**

Market and Economic Conditions and Price Performance

- Price trends and changes for the major materials and commodities purchased. Comparisons with:
  1. Standard costs where such accounting methods are used
  2. Quoted market prices
  3. Target costs as determined by cost analysis
- Changes in demand-supply conditions for the major items purchased; effects of labor strikes or threatened strikes
- Lead time expectations for major items

Inventory Investment Changes

- Dollar investment in inventories, classified by major commodity and materials groups
- Days' or months' supply, and on order, for major commodity and materials groups
- Ratio of inventory dollar investment to sales dollar volume
- Rates of inventory turnover for major items

Purchasing Operations and Effectiveness

- Cost reductions resulting from purchase research and value analysis studies
- Quality rejection rates for major items
- Percentage of on-time deliveries
- Number of out-of-stock situations that caused interruption of scheduled production
- Number of change orders issued, classified by cause
- Number of requisitions received and processed
- Number of purchase orders issued
- Employee workload and productivity
- Transportation costs

Operations Affecting Administration and Financial Activities

- Comparison of actual departmental operating costs to budget
- Cash discounts earned and cash discounts lost
- Commitments to purchase, classified by types of formal contracts and by purchase orders, aged by expected delivery dates
- Changes in cash discounts allowed by suppliers

Source: Michael R. Leenders and Harold E. Fearon, *Purchasing and Materials Management,* 10th ed.(Burr Ridge, IL: Richard D. Irwin, 1993), p. 467.

5. How frequently is scheduling performed and updated?
6. How do the policies or procedures of materials management impact other parts of the organization?

These questions relate to how the product is produced and how inventories are controlled. Computers also are used to improve materials management performance. Systems that have gained acceptance in many firms are Kanban/just-in-time (JIT), MRP, and DRP.

Kanban/Just-in-Time Systems

Kanban and just-in-time systems have become much more important in manufacturing and logistics operations in recent years. **Kanban,** also known as the **Toyota Production System (TPS),** was developed by Toyota Motor Company during the 1950s and 1960s. The philosophy of Kanban is that parts and materials should be supplied at the very moment they are needed in the factory production process. This is the optimal strategy, from both a cost and service perspective. The Kanban system can apply to any manufacturing process involving repetitive operations (see Box 6–2).

JIT Extends Kanban

Just-in-time (JIT) systems extend Kanban, linking purchasing, manufacturing, and logistics. The primary goals of JIT are to minimize inventories, improve product quality, maximize production efficiency, and provide optimal customer service levels. It is basically a philosophy of doing business. Box 6–1 shows how Harley-Davidson used JIT concepts to significantly improve its operations.

JIT has been defined in several ways, including the following:

JIT Defined

• As a production strategy, JIT works to reduce manufacturing costs and to improve quality markedly by waste elimination and more effective use of existing company resources.[27]

• A philosophy based on the principle of getting the right materials to the right place at the right time.[28]

• A program that seeks to eliminate nonvalue-added activities from any operation with the objectives of producing high-quality products (i.e., "zero defects"), high productivity levels, and lower levels of inventory, and developing long-term relationships with channel members.[29]

At the heart of the JIT system is the notion that waste should be eliminated. This is in direct contrast to the traditional "just-in-case" philosophy in which large inventories or safety stocks are held just in case they are needed. In JIT, the ideal lot size or EOQ is one unit, safety stock is considered unnecessary, and any inventory should be eliminated.

Toyota Pioneers Kanban and JIT

Perhaps the best-known example of Kanban and JIT systems is the approach developed by Toyota. The company identified problems in supply and product quality through reduction of inventories, which forced problems into the open. Safety stocks were no longer available to overcome supplier delays and faulty components, thus forcing Toyota to eliminate "hidden" production and supply problems.

The same type of procedure has been applied to many companies in the United States. The advantage to the system becomes evident when we see that raw materials can be reduced by 75 percent with JIT implementation.[30] Not every component can be

---

[27]Amrik S. Sohal, Liz Ramsay, and Danny Samson, "JIT Manufacturing: Industry Analysis and a Methodology for Implementation," *International Journal of Physical Distribution and Logistics Management* 23, no. 7 (1993), pp. 4–21.

[28]Snehemay Banejee and Damodar Y. Golhar, "EDI Implementation: A Comparative Study of JIT and Non-JIT Manufacturing Firms," *International Journal of Physical Distribution and Logistics Management* 23, no. 7 (1993), pp. 22–31.

[29]Larry C. Giunipero and Waik K. Law, "Organizational Support for Just-in-Time Implementation," *The International Journal of Logistics Management* 1, no. 2 (1990), pp. 35–36.

[30]Sohal et al., "JIT Manufacturing," p. 13.

Box 6–1

Harley-Davidson Embraces Just-in-Time (JIT) and TQM Concepts

Harley-Davidson, the only domestic producer of large motorcycles in the United States, began to seriously study and implement TQM and supporting techniques in the early 1980s. Harley was pushed to the verge of bankruptcy by tough competition from Honda and Yamaha, whose products had a reputation for better quality. To support the emphasis on TQM, Harley-Davidson implemented just-in-time (JIT) manufacturing which, like TQM, emphasizes continuous improvement. These complementary philosophies forced the firm to review virtually every one of its products and processes for improvement. It reconfigured its entire manufacturing process, using computer-aided design (CAD) to support the design of engines and other components, and invested in updated equipment and process improvements in areas such as painting and plating. It also reconfigured its production process into "work cells," combining like activities together.

Harley-Davidson utilizes JIT manufacturing and logistics to produce and distribute its many sizes and styles of motorcycles.

Materials management also played a key role in Harley-Davidson's TQM effort. Materials personnel at the company worked to reduce the number of suppliers from about 500 to 200. A smaller supplier base made quality improvements more manageable to implement, and eased the detection, tracking, and solution of quality problems. Materials personnel also worked with suppliers to get small quantities of defect-free parts and components delivered directly to the production line. This required a major effort to improve and develop suppliers. Harley has since gained a reputation for excellence in supplier development.

The materials management area worked to develop special containers to store parts for assembly. These containers serve as a "kanban," limiting the number of parts in inventory only to those in the container. These reusable containers are designed to prevent component damage and support TQM through inventory reduction.

The inbound transportation aspect of materials management was also affected. Harley formed its own inbound transportation company to handle JIT deliveries of critical parts and components. It has made significant process improvements, such as dropping a truck trailer off at a carrier's terminal and letting suppliers fill the trailer for JIT delivery. If a supplier misses the deadline, that supplier must pay for air freight to get the goods to Harley-Davidson on time.

This company illustrates that TQM and JIT are broad, complementary philosophies. The approaches cannot be used in isolation (e.g., focusing only on production); instead, they show how greater benefits can be achieved when various functions work together and support each others' efforts.

Source: Compiled from William T. Turk, "Management Accounting Revitalized: The Harley-Davidson Experience," *Journal of Cost Management* 3, no. 4 (1990), pp. 28–36; "Born to Be Real," *Industry Week*, Aug. 2, 1993, pp. 14ff; and Gary Shitsker, "Harley-Davidson: Struggling with Success," *Forbes*, May 24, 1993, pp. 45–46.

handled by the Kanban or JIT approaches, but the systems work very well for items that are used repetitively.

Many firms have successfully adopted the JIT approach. Companies in industries such as metal products, automobile manufacturing, electronics, and food and beverage have implemented JIT and realized a number of benefits, including:

Benefits Resulting from Implementing JIT

- Productivity improvements and greater control between various production stages.
- Diminished raw materials, work in process, and finished goods inventory.
- A reduction in manufacturing cycle times.
- Dramatically improved inventory turnover rates.[31]

In general, JIT produces benefits for firms in four major areas: improved inventory turns, better customer service, decreased warehouse space, and improved response time. In addition, reduced distribution costs, lower transportation costs, improved quality of supplier products, and a reduced number of transportation carriers and suppliers can result from the implementation of JIT.[32]

Some specific examples of firms that have achieved success through JIT include Rank Xerox Manufacturing (Netherlands) and Ford Motor Company. As the largest Xerox company outside the United States, Rank Xerox (a joint venture between Xerox Corporation and Britain's Rank Corporation) produces and refurbishes midvolume copier equipment for distribution throughout the world. Throughout most of the 1980s, Rank Xerox implemented a JIT program.

As part of the JIT program, the firm also installed an automated materials handling system and information processing system. Production procedures were modified at the same time. As a result of the JIT program and other system changes, Rank Xerox realized the following specific benefits:

1. Its supplier base was reduced from 3,000 to 300.
2. Ninety-eight percent on-time inbound delivery was achieved, with 70 percent of materials arriving within an hour of the time they were needed.
3. Warehouse stock was reduced from a three-month to a half-month supply.
4. Overall material costs were reduced by more than 40 percent.
5. Most inbound product inspection stations were eliminated because of higher-quality materials from suppliers.
6. Reject levels for defective or inferior materials fell from 17.0 percent to 0.8 percent.
7. Positions for 40 repack people were eliminated because of standardized shipment-packaging criteria.
8. Inbound transportation costs were reduced by 40 percent.
9. On-time inbound delivery performance was improved by 28 percent.[33]

---

[31]Ibid., pp. 12–13.

[32]Francis J. Quinn, Robert C. Lieb, and Robert A. Millen, "Why U.S. Companies Are Embracing JIT," *Traffic Management* 29, no. 11 (Nov. 1990), p. 33.

[33]Lisa H. Harrington, "Why Rank Xerox Turned to Just-in-Time," *Traffic Management* 27, no. 10 (Oct. 1988), pp. 82–87.

Just-in-time manufacturing and logistics support provides delivery of automobile sunroofs in 136 minutes, instead of two weeks.

Problems Associated with Implementing JIT

Other companies that have successfully introduced JIT into their operations include Brunswick, Cummins Engine, General Motors, Textron, 3M, and Whirlpool. While JIT offers a number of benefits, it may not be suitable for all firms. It has some inherent problems which fall into three categories: production scheduling (plant), supplier production schedules, and supplier locations.

When leveling of the production schedule is necessary due to uneven demand, firms will require higher levels of inventory. Items can be produced during slack periods even though they may not be demanded until a later time. Finished goods inventory has a higher value because of its form utility; thus, there is a greater financial risk resulting from product obsolescence, damage, or loss.

However, higher levels of inventory, coupled with a uniform production schedule, can be more advantageous than a fluctuating schedule with less inventory. In addition, when stockout costs are great because of production slowdowns or shutdowns, JIT may not be the optimal system. JIT reduces inventory levels to the point where there is little if any safety stock, and parts shortages can adversely affect production operations.

Supplier production schedules are a second problem with JIT. Success of a JIT system depends on suppliers' ability to provide parts in accordance with the firm's production schedule. Smaller, more frequent orders can result in higher ordering costs and must be taken into account when calculating any cost savings due to reduced inventory levels. When a large number of small lot quantities are produced, suppliers incur higher production and setup costs. Generally, suppliers will incur higher costs, unless they are able to achieve the benefits associated with implementing similar systems with their suppliers.

Supplier locations can be a third problem. As distance between the firm and its suppliers increases, delivery times may become more erratic and less predictable. Shipping costs increase as less-than-truckload (LTL) movements are made. Transit time variability can cause inventory stockouts that disrupt production scheduling; when this is combined with higher delivery costs on a per unit basis, total costs may be greater than the savings in inventory carrying costs.

Other problem areas that can become obstacles to JIT, especially in implementation, are organizational resistance, lack of systems support, inability to define service levels, a lack of planning, and a shift of inventory to suppliers.[34] Overcoming these and the previously discussed problems requires cooperation and integration within and between companies.

Implications of JIT for Logistics Integration

JIT has numerous implications for logistics executives. First, proper implementation of JIT requires that the firm fully integrate all logistics activities. Many trade-offs are required, but without the coordination provided by integrated logistics management, JIT systems cannot be fully implemented.

Transportation in a JIT System

Second, transportation becomes an even more vital component of logistics under a JIT system. In such an environment, the demands placed on the firm's transportation network are significant and include a need for shorter, more consistent transit times; more sophisticated communications; the use of fewer carriers with long-term relationships; a need for efficiently designed transportation and materials handling equipment; and better decision-making strategies relative to when private, common, or contract carriage should be used.

Warehousing in a JIT System

Third, warehousing assumes an expanded role as it assumes the role of a consolidation facility instead of a storage facility. Since many products come into the manufacturing operation at shorter intervals, less space is required for storage, but there must be an increased capability for handling and consolidating items. Different forms of materials handling equipment may be needed to facilitate the movement of many products in smaller quantities. The location decision for warehouses serving inbound materials needs may change because suppliers are often located closer to the manufacturing facility in a JIT system.

JIT systems are usually combined with other systems that plan and control material flows into, within, and out of the organization. MRP and DRP are often used to implement the JIT philosophy. They will be presented in the following sections.

---

[34]See Louis Guist, "Just-in-Time Manufacturing and Materials Handling Trends," *International Journal of Physical Distribution and Logistics Management* 23, no. 7 (1993), pp. 32–38.

Box 6–2

Kanban Card Procedure

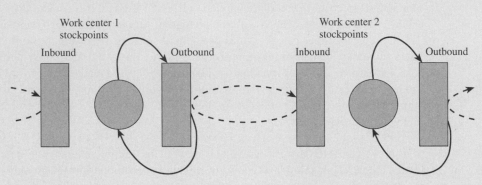

- - -   Move card path. When a container of parts
is selected for use from an inbound stockpoint,
the move card is removed from the container
and taken to the outbound stockpoint of the
preceding work center as authorization to
pick another container of parts.

———   Production card path. When a container of
parts is picked from an outbound stockpoint,
the production card is removed and left
behind as authorization to make a standard
container of parts to replace the one taken.

"Kanban" literally means "signboard" in Japanese. The system involves the use of cards (called "kanbans") that are attached to containers which hold a standard quantity of a single part number. There are two types of kanban cards: "move" cards and "production" cards.

When a worker starts to use a container of parts, the move card, which is attached to it, is removed and is either sent to or picked up by the preceding or feeding work center (in many cases this is the supplier). This is the signal—or "sign"—for that work center to send another container of parts to replace the one now being used. This replacement container has a production card attached to it which is replaced by the "move" card before it is sent. The production card then authorizes the producing work center to make another container full of parts. These cards circulate respectively within or between work centers or between the supplier and the assembly plant.

For Kanban to work effectively, these rules must be observed:

1. Only one card can be attached to a container at any one time.
2. The using (or following) work center must initiate the movement of parts from the feeding (or preceding) work center.
3. No fabrication of parts is allowed without a kanban production card.
4. Never move or produce other than the amount indicated by the kanban card.
5. Kanban cards must be handled on a first-in, first-out (FIFO) basis.
6. Finished parts must be placed at the location point indicated on the kanban card.

Because each kanban card represents a standard number of parts being made or used within the production process, the amount of work-in-process inventory can easily be controlled by controlling the number of cards on the plant floor. Japanese managers, by simply removing a card or two, can test or strain the system and reveal bottlenecks. Then they have a problem they can address themselves to—an opportunity to improve productivity, the prime goal of Kanban.

Source: "Why Everybody Is Talking about 'Just-in-Time'," *Warehousing Review* 1, no. 1 (Oct. 1984), p. 27. Reprinted with permission from *Warehousing Review,* 1984 Charter Issue; The American Warehouse Association (publisher), 1165 N. Clark, Chicago, IL 60610.

JIT II

JIT II applies JIT concepts to the purchasing function by having a representative of the supplier locate at the buying organization's facility. Developed by Bose Corporation, this approach improves mutual understanding between the buyer and supplier, reduces waste and redundancy of efforts, improves supplier responsiveness, and creates a positive working environment.[35] This concept will be discussed in Chapter 10, "Purchasing."

MRP Systems

MRP has been used to signify systems called **materials requirements planning (MRP I)** and **manufacturing resource planning (MRP II).** Introduced first, MRP I developed into MRP II with the addition of financial, marketing, and purchasing aspects.

Components of a MRP I System

MRP I became a popular concept in the 1960s and 1970s. From a managerial perspective, MRP I consists of (1) a computer system, (2) a manufacturing information system, building on inventory, production scheduling, and administering all inputs to production, and (3) a concept and philosophy of management.[36]

When to Use MRP I

MRP I is a computer-based production and inventory control system that attempts to minimize inventories while maintaining adequate materials for the production process. MRP I systems are usually employed when one or more of the following conditions exist:

• When usage (demand) of the material is discontinuous or highly unstable during a firm's normal operating cycle. This situation is typified by an intermittent manufacturing or job shop operation, as opposed to a continuous-processing or mass-production operation.

• When demand for the material depends directly on the production of other specific inventory items or finished products. MRP [I] can be thought of as primarily a component fabrication planning system, in which the demand for all parts (materials) is dependent on the demand (production schedule) for the parent product.

• When the purchasing department and its suppliers, as well as the firm's own manufacturing units, possess the flexibility to handle order placements or delivery releases on a weekly basis.[37]

Advantages of MRP I Systems

MRP I systems offer many advantages over traditional systems, including:

• Improved business results (i.e., return on investment, profits)
• Improved manufacturing performance results
• Better manufacturing control
• More accurate and timely information
• Less inventory
• Time-phased ordering of materials
• Less material obsolescence

---

[35]For a comprehensive discussion of JIT II principles and implementation, see Lance Dixon and Anne Millen Porter, *JIT II: Revolution in Buying and Selling,* (Newton, MA: Cahners, 1994).

[36]Larry Ritzman and Lee Krajewski, *Operations Management,* 3rd ed. (Reading, MA: Addison Wesley, 1994).

[37]Ibid.

- Higher reliability
- More responsiveness to market demand
- Reduced production costs

Disadvantages of MRP I Systems

MRP I does have a number of drawbacks which should be examined by any firm considering adopting the system. First, MRP I does not tend to optimize materials acquisition costs. Because inventory levels are kept to a minimum, materials must be purchased more frequently and in smaller quantities. This results in increased ordering costs.

Higher transportation bills and higher unit costs are incurred because the firm is less likely to qualify for large volume discounts. The company must weigh the anticipated savings from reduced inventory costs against the greater acquisition costs resulting from smaller and more frequent orders.

Another disadvantage of MRP I is the potential hazard of a production slowdown or shutdown that may arise because of factors such as unforeseen delivery problems and materials shortages. The availability of safety stocks gives production some protection against stockouts of essential material. As safety stocks are reduced, this level of protection is lost.

A final disadvantage of MRP I arises from the use of standardized software packages, which may be difficult to accommodate within the unique operating situations of a given firm. Firms buying off-the-shelf software often will have to modify it, so that it meets their specific needs and requirements.

The master production schedule serves as the major input into the MRP I system (see Figure 6–3A). Other inputs include the bill-of-materials file and the inventory records file. The bill-of-materials file contains the component parts of the finished product, identified by part number. The inventory records file maintains a record of all inventory on hand and on order. It also keeps track of due dates for all component parts.

Reports generated from MRP I systems include planning reports that can be used to forecast inventory and specify future requirements, performance reports for identifying and determining whether actual and programmed item lead times and actual and programmed quantity usages and costs agree, and exception reports, which point out discrepancies such as errors, late or overdue orders, excessive scrap, or nonexistent parts.[38]

While MRP I is still being used by many firms, it has been updated and expanded to include financial, marketing, and logistics elements. This newer version is called manufacturing resource planning, or MRP II.

MRP II Described

MRP II includes the entire set of activities involved in the planning and control of production operations. It consists of a variety of functions of modules (see Figure 6–3B) and includes production planning, resource requirements planning, master production scheduling, materials requirements planning (MRP I), shop floor control, and purchasing.[39]

---

[38]Leenders and Fearon, *Purchasing and Materials Management,* p. 211.

[39]See R. John Aalbregtse and Roy L. Harmon, "Production and Manufacturing Resource Planning in a Just-in-Time Environment," in *The Logistics Handbook,* James F. Robeson and William C. Copacino, eds. (New York: Free Press, 1994), pp. 427–42; Karl A. Hatt, "What's the Big Deal about MRP II?" *Winning Manufacturing* 5, no. 2 (1994), pp. 1–2; and John F. Magee, William C. Copacino, and Donald B. Rosenfield, *Modern Logistics Management: Integrating Marketing, Manufacturing, and Physical Distribution* (New York: John Wiley, 1985), p. 150.

FIGURE 6–3A

Elements of an MRP I system

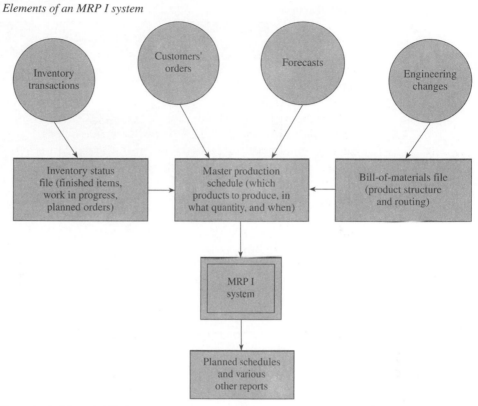

Source: Amrik Sohal and Keith Howard, "Trends in Materials Management," *International Journal of Physical Distribution and Materials Management* 17, no. 5 (1987), p. 11.

**Advantages of
MRP II Systems**

The advantages of MRP II include:

- Inventory reductions of one-fourth to one-third
- Higher inventory turnover
- Improved consistency in on-time customer delivery
- Reduction in purchasing costs due to fewer expedited shipments
- Minimization of workforce overtime[40]

These advantages typically result in savings to a firm beyond the initial costs of implementing MRP II. Costs can easily exceed $750,000 during the first year of setup, although smaller companies may spend as little as $250,000. Therefore, the benefits of MRP II must be tangible and sizable.

---

[40]For further discussion of benefits, see Peter Duchessi and Charles M. Schaniger, "MRP II: A Prospectus for Renaissance," *Operations Research* 34, no. 3 (1994), pp. 325–51; and "Benefits Multiply with MRP II," *Modern Materials Handling* 48, no. 7 (July 1993), pp. 60–65.

FIGURE 6–3B

MRP II system

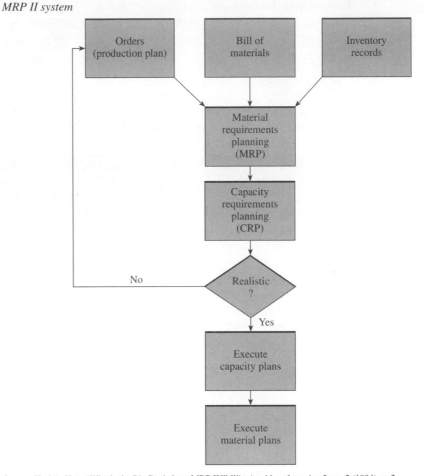

Source: Karl A. Hatt, "What's the Big Deal about MRP II?" *Winning Manufacturing* 5, no. 2 (1994), p. 2.

Warren Communications Implements MRP II

Some firms have achieved impressive results. Warren Communications, a division of General Signal Corporation, markets power supplies used in telephone systems. The company installed an MRP II system and estimated first-year savings of $850,000, with most of the savings coming from reductions in inventory and more efficient use of personnel and equipment.[41]

---

[41]"MRP II: A Framework for Factory Management," *Dun's Business Month Special Report* 123, no. 2 (Feb. 1984), pp. O, U.

DRP Systems

DRP Defined

Distribution requirements planning (DRP I) has been defined as "the application of MRP principles to the distribution environment, integrating the special needs of distribution . . . [it] is a dynamic model that looks at a time-phased plan of events that affect inventory."[42]

> **Distribution resource planning (DRP II)** is an extension of distribution requirements planning (DRP I). Distribution requirements planning applies the time-phased DRP I logic to replenish inventories in multiechelon warehousing systems. Distribution resource planning extends DRP I to include the planning of key resources in a distribution system—warehouse space, manpower levels, transport capacity (e.g., trucks, railcars), and financial flows.[43]

An extension of DRP I, DRP II uses the needs of distribution to drive the master schedule, controlling the bill of materials, and ultimately, materials requirements planning.[44] In essence, DRP I and DRP II are outgrowths of MRP I and MRP II, applied to the logistics activities of a firm.

Uses of DRP-Generated Information

Companies use DRP-generated information to project future inventory requirements. Specifically, the information is used to:

- Coordinate the replenishment of SKUs coming from the same source (e.g., a company-owned or vendor's plant).
- Select transportation modes, carriers, and shipment sizes more cost efficiently.
- Schedule shipping and receiving labor.
- Develop a master production schedule for each SKU[45]

See the Technology box for an enumerated list of the benefits of information.

DRP II and Forecasting

Figure 6–4 depicts the DRP II system schematically. Although not shown in the figure, accurate forecasts are essential ingredients for successful DRP II systems. "A DRP[II] system translates the forecast of demand for each SKU [stockkeeping unit] at each warehouse and distribution center into a time-phased replenishment plan. If the SKU forecasts are inaccurate, the plan will not be accurate."[46]

An example of how DRP II works in a hypothetical company is shown in Box 6–3. The logic would be much the same for real firms.

---

[42]R. Neil Southern, *Transportation and Logistics Basics* (Memphis, TN: Continental Traffic Publishing, 1997), p. 228.

[43]Magee, et al., *Modern Logistics Management,* p. 150.

[44]Ho Chrwan-jyh, "An Examination of a Distribution Resource Planning Problem: DRP System Nervousness," *Journal of Business Logistics* 13, no. 2 (1993), pp. 125–42.

[45]Alan J. Stenger, "Distribution Resource Planning," in *The Logistics Handbook,* James F. Robeson and William C. Copacino, eds. (New York: Free Press, 1994), p. 392.

[46]Mary Lou Fox, "Closing the Loop with DRP II," *Production and Inventory Management Review* 7, no. 5 (May 1987), pp. 39–41.

Technology

Seven Benefits of Information Technology

Here are seven ways that information technology can make you a more effective logistics manager.

1. **Greater accuracy.** Through elimination of manual data entry, information technology minimizes errors and gives you more accurate information. This in turn translates to better management decisions.

2. **More economy.** By streamlining and automating data entry and exchange, technology delivers accurate information at a far lower cost than manual approaches.

3. **Faster.** Bar-code scanners, EDI systems, satellite-tracking programs, and the like transmit information instantaneously—far faster than a letter, fax, or even a telephone call.

4. **Higher visibility.** Today's logistics technology gives you a systemwide view of your operations. Powerful software programs, for example, can afford an instant overview of the inventory picture across warehouses, retail units, or sales territories.

5. **Immediate availability.** Technology gives logistics professionals instant access to information they need to manage their distribution centers, track their shipments, run their fleets, and audit freight bills.

6. **Tighter customer focus.** Fast communication of accurate, timely information is a key to customer satisfaction. Information technology is the enabler of this critical activity.

7. **Higher productivity.** By taking the manual, repetitive tasks out of the work equation, information technology frees up people to be a lot more innovative, customer-oriented, and productive.

Source: "Logistics Technology Takes Off!" *Traffic Management* 34, no. 10 (Oct. 1995), p. S-4.

The Logistics/Manufacturing Interface

Joint Logistics/ Manufacturing Planning and Decision Making Are Vital

Systems such as Kanban, JIT, MRP, and DRP require that the logistics and manufacturing activities of a firm work together closely. Without a cooperative effort, the full advantages of systems like JIT can never be realized. Conflicts, both real and perceived, must be minimized. This requires joint logistics/manufacturing planning and decision making. There are a number of areas in which cooperation is necessary and great improvements can be made. The following actions can be of significant benefit:

• Logistics must reduce replenishment lead times to increase manufacturing flexibility and reduce order fulfillment lead times.

• Manufacturing and logistics must work together in the production scheduling area to reduce production planning cycle time. Logistics can provide input into production scheduling and system requirements.

• Manufacturing and logistics strategies, such as shortening of lead times, setup times, and production run sizes must be used to minimize average inventory levels and stockouts.

• Logistics must develop strategies to reduce supplier lead times for parts and supplies.

FIGURE 6–4

Distribution resource planning (DRP II)

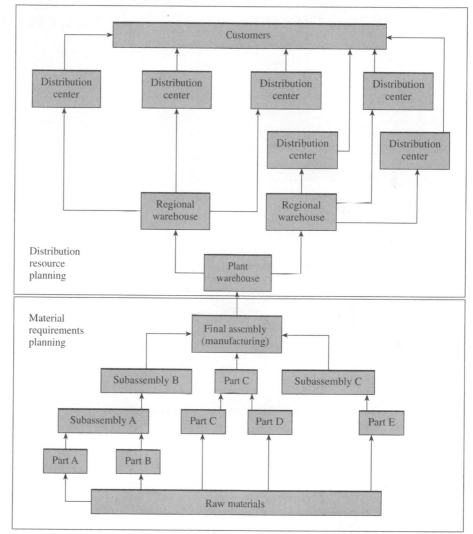

Source: "How DRP Helps Warehouses Smooth Distribution," *Modern Materials Handling* 39, no. 6 (Apr. 9, 1984), p. 53. *Modern Materials Handling,* copyright 1984 by Cahners Publishing Company, Division of Reed Holdings, Inc.

• Logistics must adopt the philosophy that slow movers (i.e., products with low inventory turnover ratios) should be produced only after orders are received, rather than held in stock.

Many other areas of logistics/manufacturing interface exist. It is important that each functional area of the firm examine its role in the JIT, MRP, or DRP system and identify how it can work individually and jointly to optimize the firm's strategic position (see Creative Solutions box).

Box 6–3

How DRP II Forecasts Demand: A Case History

BOSTON DISTRIBUTION CENTER
On hand balance: 352   Lead time: 2 weeks
Safety stock: 55   Order quantity: 500

	Past due	Week							
		1	2	3	4	5	6	7	8
Gross requirements		50	50	60	70	80	70	60	50
Scheduled receipts						500			
Projected on hand	352	302	252	192	122	542	472	412	362
Planned orders				500					

CHICAGO DISTRIBUTION CENTER
On hand balance: 220   Lead time: 2 weeks
Safety stock: 115   Order quantity: 800

	Past due	Week							
		1	2	3	4	5	6	7	8
Gross requirements		115	115	120	120	125	125	125	120
Scheduled receipts		800							
Projected on hand	220	905	790	670	550	425	300	175	855
Planned orders							800		

SAN DIEGO DISTRIBUTION CENTER
On hand balance: 140   Lead time: 2 weeks
Safety time: 2 weeks   Order quantity: 150

	Past due	Week							
		1	2	3	4	5	6	7	8
Gross requirements		20	25	15	20	30	25	15	30
Scheduled receipts						150			
Projected on hand	140	120	95	80	60	180	155	145	110
Planned orders				150					

CENTRAL SUPPLY FACILITY
On hand balance: 1250
Safety stock: 287
Lead time: 3 weeks
Order quantity: 2200

	Past due	Week							
		1	2	3	4	5	6	7	8
Gross requirements	0	0	0	650	0	0	800	0	0
Scheduled receipts									
Projected on hand	1250	1250	1250	600	600	600	2000	2000	2000
Master sched-rcpt							2200		
Master sched-start				2200					

→ To material requirements planning schedule ──────→

MMH, Inc., has three distribution centers (DCs) located across the United States, and a central supply facility at its manufacturing plant in Quebec, Canada. Here's how their distribution resource planning (DRP[II]) system works over an eight-week period:

The Boston DC has a safety stock level set at 55 units of widgets. When stock goes below that level, the DC sends out an order for 500 more widgets. The lead time for shipment from the central facility to the Boston DC is two weeks.

The DRP display for the Boston DC shows the demand forecast, called *gross requirements,* for eight weeks. Starting with an on-hand balance of 352 widgets, the DC forecasts that it will have only 42 widgets during week 5 (the 122 widgets on hand minus the 80 in gross requirements).

This is below the safety stock level, so DRP initiates a planned order of 500 widgets during week 3 (week 5 minus the lead time). Stock comes, as forecasted, and the DC is back to safe operating levels.

Widgets are a high-volume seller in Chicago, so the Chicago DC has a higher gross requirement than the Boston DC. It also orders more widgets at a time.

The DRP display for the Chicago DC shows that 800 widgets are already in transit (scheduled receipts) and due to arrive in week 1. They do, and the next order, for 800 widgets, is placed in week 6 to satisfy the upcoming below-safety stock condition in week 8.

Through experience, the San Diego DC expresses their safety stock as safety time (two weeks).

Examining the DRP display, the DC realizes that without replenishment, 30 widgets (60–30) would be remaining

Box 6–3 concluded

in week 5, five widgets (30 – 25) in week 6, and a negative on-hand balance of 10 (5 – 15) in week 7. So, the DC initiates a planned order for 150 widgets in week 3—week 7 minus the safety time minus the lead time (four weeks total).

The DRP display for the central supply facility is similar to that for the DCs; however, it displays recommendations for the master schedule in terms of the start and receipt of manufacturing orders.

The gross requirements in the facility are caused by the DCs; the Boston and San Diego DCs produced de-

mands for a total of 650 widgets in week 3, while Chicago DC produced demands for 800 widgets in week 6. The facility finds it will have a negative on-hand balance in week 6. Therefore it initiates a master schedule order in week 3 of 2,200 widgets to cover the shortage.

Source: "How DRP Helps Warehouses Smooth Distribution," *Modern Materials Handling* 39, no. 6 (Apr. 9, 1984), p. 57. *Modern Materials Handling,* copyright 1984 by Cahners Publishing Company, Division of Reed Holdings, Inc.

Creative Solutions

Excellence in Logistics Strategies

Sequent Computer Systems has a Preferred Logistics Supplier Program which concentrates its business with a small number of high-performing suppliers. A commodity team manages the program.

"We have a formal program for order fulfillment reduction," says Sequent's Martha McMahon, worldwide logistics manager. It's a team effort within the organization and focuses on the areas of supply of materials and materials management.

Another area of focus is linking with customers in the field. Sequent's "prelim" order program allows the company to see what potential orders are coming in and anticipate its material needs.

The third area is staff education. "It's important for everyone to understand what the goals are, why

the goals have been set up, and how to monitor the progress on achieving those goals to keep everyone informed."

Sequent has achieved a significant reduction of order-to-shipment time from 35 days down to 7.5 days, which exceeds industry best in class by 10 days. Spare parts can be made available to customers within two to four hours if their computer goes down. Significant cost savings have resulted from the program: over $350,000 for the year and an inventory reduction of $3 million. On-time delivery is averaging 98 percent with preferred suppliers.

Source: Sarah A. Bergin, "Recognizing Excellence in Logistics Strategies," *Transportation and Distribution* 37, no. 10 (Oct. 1996), p. 50.

Summary

This chapter examined the broad areas of materials flow. We explored the functions of purchasing and procurement, production control, inbound logistics, warehousing and storage, data and information systems, inventory planning and control, and materials disposal. The relationships between materials management and total quality management

(TQM) were discussed. The TQM process was examined and some examples of its implementation were presented.

The administration and control of materials flow requires that firms measure, report, and improve performance. Concepts and approaches being used or developed include Kanban/just-in-time, MRP I and MRP II, and DRP I and DRP II systems. Each system has been implemented by a variety of firms, with significant results. Advances in computer technology have enabled many of the systems to be implemented successfully in manufacturing, retailing, and service firms. The impact on logistics has been substantial.

Suggested Readings

Daugherty, Patricia J., and Michael S. Spencer. "Just-in-Time Concepts: Applicability to Logistics/Transportation." *International Journal of Physical Distribution and Logistics Management* 20, no. 7 (1990), pp. 12–18.

Daugherty, Patricia J.; Dale S. Rogers; and Michael S. Spencer. "Just-in-Time Functional Model: Empirical Test and Validation." *International Journal of Physical Distribution and Logistics Management* 24, no. 6 (1994), pp. 20–26.

Demmy, W. Steven, and Arthur B. Petrini. "MRP II + JIT + TQM + TOC: The Path to World Class Management." *Logistics Spectrum* 26, no. 3 (Fall 1992), pp. 8–13.

"Evolution Continues in MRP II Type Systems: New Functionality for Flexible Enterprise Management." *Manufacturing Systems* 12, no. 7 (July 1994), pp. 32–35.

Dixon, Lance, and Anne Millen Porter. *JIT II: Revolution in Buying and Selling* (Newton, MA: Cahners, 1994).

Galfond, Glenn; Kelly Ronayne; and Christian Winkler. "State-of-the-Art Supply Chain Forecasting." *PW Review,* Nov. 1996, pp. 1–12.

Garreau, Alain; Robert Lieb; and Robert Millen. "JIT and Corporate Transport: An International Comparison." *International Journal of Physical Distribution and Logistics Management* 21, no. 1 (1991), pp. 42–47.

Germain, Richard; Cornelia Droge; and Nancy Spears. "The Implications of Just-in-Time for Logistics Organization Management and Performance." *Journal of Business Logistics* 17, no. 2 (1996), pp. 19–34.

Henn, Carl L. "Logistics for a Better World." *Logistics Spectrum* 25, no. 3 (Fall 1991), pp. 3–9.

Ho, Samuel K. M. "Is the ISO 9000 Series for Total Quality Management?" *International Journal of Quality & Reliability Management* 11, no. 9 (1994), pp. 74–89.

Lam, Karen D. "The Future of Total Quality Management (TQM)." *Logistics Spectrum* 24, no. 4 (Winter 1990), pp. 45–48.

Masters, James M.; Greg M. Allenby; and Bernard J. La Londe. "On the Adoption of DRP." *Journal of Business Logistics* 13, no. 1 (1992), pp. 47–67.

Mozeson, Mark H. "What Your MRP II Systems Cannot Do." *Industrial Engineering* 23, no. 12 (Dec. 1991), pp. 20–24.

Oliver, Nick. "JIT: Issues and Items for the Research Agenda." *International Journal of Physical Distribution and Logistics Management* 20, no. 7 (1990), pp. 3–11.

Snehemay, Banejee, and Damodar Y. Golhar. "EDI Implementation: A Comparative Study of JIT and Non-JIT Manufacturing Firms." *International Journal of Physical Distribution and Logistics Management* 23, no. 7 (1993), pp. 22–31.

Sohal, Amrik S.; Liz Ramsay; and Danny Samson. "JIT Manufacturing: Industry Analysis and a Methodology for Implementation." *International Journal of Physical Distribution and Logistics Management* 23, no. 7 (1993), pp. 4–21.

Swenseth, Scott R., and Frank P. Buffa. "Just-in-Time: Some Effects on the Logistics Function." *The International Journal of Logistics Management* 1, no. 2 (1990), pp. 25–34.

Von Flue, Johann L. "The Future with Total Quality Management." *Logistics Spectrum* 24, no. 1 (Spring 1990), pp. 23–27.

Waters-Fuller, Niall. "The Benefits and Costs of JIT Sourcing: A Study of Scottish Suppliers." *International Journal of Physical Distribution and Logistics Management* 26, no. 4 (1996), pp. 35–50.

Zipkin, Paul H. "Does Manufacturing Need a JIT Revolution?" *Harvard Business Review* 91, no. 1 (Jan.–Feb. 1991), pp. 40–50.

Questions and Problems

1. How does total quality management (TQM) differ from traditional management? How can TQM be applied to logistics?

2. Briefly describe the concept of just-in-time (JIT) and its relationship to logistics.

3. Discuss the role of suppliers in a JIT system. Identify areas where potential conflicts may occur.

4. Briefly discuss how forecasting can be used in materials management. Identify the general uses according to the (*a*) type of forecast and (*b*) the time frame of the forecast.

5. MRP and DRP are computer systems in materials management and manufacturing. Describe the types of situations where MRP and DRP can be effectively and/or efficiently used in a firm.

Transportation

Chapter Outline

Chapter Objectives

- To examine transportation's role in logistics and its relationship to marketing.
- To describe alternative transport modes, intermodal combinations, and other transportation options.
- To examine the impact of deregulation on carriers and shippers.
- To examine the issues of transportation cost and performance measurement.
- To examine international dimensions of transportation.
- To identify major transportation management activities of carriers and shippers.
- To identify areas where computer technology is important.

Introduction

This chapter provides an overview of the transportation function and its importance to logistics. We will examine alternative transportation modes and intermodal combinations. We also describe key transportation management issues of shippers and carriers, transportation cost and performance measurement, and the role of computers.

U.S. Transportation Costs $455 Billion Yearly

Efficient transportation systems are the hallmark of industrialized societies. The transportation sector of most industrialized economies is so pervasive that we often fail to comprehend the magnitude of its impact on our way of life. In 1996, U.S. transportation expenditures were approximately $455 billion of the nation's total logistics costs, which were estimated to be $797 billion.[1]

Since 1970, the transportation sector has grown considerably. Figure 7–1 shows that since 1981, national freight transportation costs have been growing more slowly than the gross domestic product (GDP).[2]

FIGURE 7–1

Freight transportation outlays compared to GDP

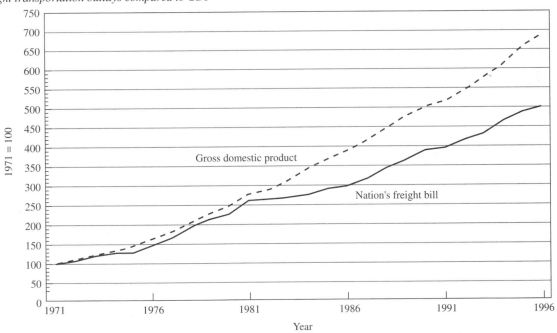

Source: Robert V. Delaney, "CLI's State of Logistics Annual Report," press conference at the National Press Club, Washington, DC (June 2, 1997), fig. 15.

---

[1]Robert V. Delaney, "CLI's State of Logistics Annual Report," press conference at the National Press Club, Washington, DC (June 2, 1997), p. 4.

[2]Deregulation of motor and rail transportation in 1980 resulted in transportation efficiencies.

Time and Place Utility

Transportation Provides Value-Added through Place Utility

Transportation physically moves products from where they are produced to where they are needed. This movement across space or distance adds value to products. This value-added is often referred to as **place utility.**

Time utility is created by warehousing and storing products until they are needed. Transportation is also a factor in time utility; it determines how fast and how consistently a product moves from one point to another. This is known as **time-in-transit** and *consistency of service,* respectively.

If a product is not available at the precise time it is needed, there may be expensive repercussions, such as lost sales, customer dissatisfaction, and production downtime, when the product is being used in the manufacturing process. Transportation service providers such as CSX, Federal Express (FedEx), Leaseway Transportation, Ryder Integrated Logistics, and United Parcel Service (UPS) have achieved success because they are able to provide consistent time-in-transit and thus increase the time and place utility of their customers' products.

Transportation/Logistics/Marketing Interfaces

Transportation moves products to markets that are geographically separated and provides added value to customers when the products arrive on time, undamaged, and in the quantities required. In this way, transportation contributes to the level of customer service, which is one of the cornerstones of customer satisfaction: an important component of the marketing concept.

Because transportation creates place utility and contributes to time utility—both of which are necessary for successful marketing efforts—the availability, adequacy, and cost of transportation impact business decisions seemingly unrelated to managing the transportation function itself; that is, what products should be produced, where should they be sold, where should facilities be located, and where should materials be sourced?

For Many Firms Transportation Is the Largest Logistics Cost

Transportation is one of the largest logistics costs and may account for a significant portion of the selling price of some products. Low value-per-pound products such as basic raw materials (e.g., sand and coal) are examples. Transportation costs for computers, business machines, and electronic components may be only a small percentage of the selling price. Generally, the efficient management of transportation becomes more important to a firm as inbound and outbound transportation's share of product cost increases. Even with high-value products, expenditures for transportation are important although the percentage of selling price may be low, primarily because the total cost of transportation in absolute terms is significant.

Factors Influencing Transportation Costs and Pricing

In general, factors influencing transportation costs/pricing can be grouped into two major categories: product-related factors and market-related factors.

Product-Related Factors.   Many factors related to a product's characteristics influence the cost/pricing of transportation. They can be grouped into the following categories:

1. Density.
2. Stowability.
3. Ease or difficulty of handling.
4. Liability.

Density

Density refers to a product's weight-to-volume ratio. Items such as steel, canned foods, building products, and bulk paper goods have high weight-to-volume ratios; they are relatively heavy given their size. On the other hand, products such as electronics, clothing, luggage, and toys have low weight-to-volume ratios and thus are relatively lightweight given their size. In general, low-density products—those with low weight-to-volume ratios—tend to cost more to transport on a per pound (kilo) basis than high-density products.

Stowability

Stowability is the degree to which a product can fill the available space in a transport vehicle. For example, grain, ore, and petroleum products in bulk have excellent stowability because they can completely fill the container (e.g., railcar, tank truck, pipeline) in which they are transported. Other items, such as automobiles, machinery, livestock, and people, do not have good stowability, or cube utilization. A product's stowability depends on its size, shape, fragility, and other physical characteristics.

Ease or Difficulty of Handling

Related to stowability is the *ease or difficulty of handling* the product. Difficult-to-handle items are more costly to transport. Products that are uniform in their physical characteristics (e.g., raw materials and items in cartons, cans, or drums) or that can be manipulated with materials-handling equipment require less handling expense and are therefore less costly to transport.

Liability

Liability is an important concern. Products that have high value-to-weight ratios are easily damaged, and are subject to higher rates of theft or pilferage, cost more to transport. Where the transportation carrier assumes greater liability (e.g., with computer, jewelry, and home entertainment products), a higher price will be charged to transport the product.

Other factors, which vary in importance depending on the product category, are the product's hazardous characteristics and the need for strong and rigid protective packaging. These factors are particularly important in the chemical and plastics industries.

Market-Related Factors.   In addition to product characteristics, important market-related factors affect transportation costs/pricing. The most significant are:

1. Degree of intramode and intermode competition.
2. Location of markets, which determines the distance goods must be transported.
3. Nature and extent of government regulation of transportation carriers.
4. Balance or imbalance of freight traffic into and out of a market.
5. Seasonality of product movements.
6. Whether the product is transported domestically or internationally.

Each of these factors affects the costs and pricing of transportation. These topics will be examined later in this chapter. In addition, there are important service factors that need to be considered.

Transportation Impacts Customer Service

Customer service is a vital component of logistics management. While each activity of logistics management contributes to the level of service a company provides to its customers, the impact of transportation on customer service is one of the most significant. The most important transportation service characteristics affecting customer service levels are:

- Dependability—consistency of service.
- Time-in-transit.
- Market coverage—the ability to provide door-to-door service.
- Flexibility—handling a variety of products and meeting the special needs of shippers.
- Loss and damage performance.
- Ability of the carrier to provide more than basic transportation service (i.e., to become part of a shipper's overall marketing and logistics programs).

Each mode of transport—motor, rail, air, water, and pipeline—has varying service capabilities. In the next section, we will examine each mode in terms of its economic and service characteristics.

Carrier Characteristics and Services

Any one or more of five transportation modes—motor, rail, air, water, and pipeline—may be selected to transport products. In addition, intermodal combinations are available: rail-motor, motor-water, motor-air, and rail-water. Intermodal combinations offer specialized or lower cost services not generally available when a single transport mode is used. Other transportation options that offer a variety of services to shippers include freight forwarders, shippers' associations, intermodal marketing companies (or shippers' agents), third-party logistics service providers, parcel post, and air express companies.

Motor

The motor carrier, or trucking industry, is comprised of $121 billion (52 percent) for private fleets, $66 billion (29 percent) for-hire truckload, $23 billion (10 percent) package and express delivery, and $20 billion (9 percent) less-than-truckload shipments.[3] Motor carriers transport over 75 percent of the tonnage of agricultural products such as fresh and frozen meats, dairy products, bakery products, confectionery items, beverages, and consumer tobacco products. Many manufactured products are transported primarily by motor carriers, including amusement, sporting, and athletic goods; toys; watches and clocks; farm machinery; radios and television sets; carpets and rugs; clothing; drugs; and office equipment and furniture. Most consumer goods are transported by motor carrier. Motor carriage offers fast, reliable service with little damage or loss in transit.

Motor Carriers Provide Fast and Reliable Service

Domestically, motor carriers compete with air for small shipments and rail for large shipments.[4] Efficient motor carriers can realize greater efficiencies in terminal, pickup,

---

[3]Delaney, "State of Logistics Annual Report," fig. 19.

[4]Smaller shipments transported by motor carriers are referred to as less-than-truckload (LTL), which is any quantity of freight weighing less than the amount required for the application of a truckload rate.

The dock area of the Food Marketing Division of SuperValu Stores in Ft. Wayne, Indiana, is where some of the 750 truckloads representing 1,600 shipments leave weekly to serve the division's 220 diverse retailer customers.

and delivery operations, which enables them to compete with air carriers on **point-to-point service**[5] for any size shipment if the distance involved is 500 miles or less.

Motor carriers compete directly with railroads for truckload (TL) shipments that are transported 500 miles or more. However, rail is the dominant mode when shipment sizes exceed 100,000 pounds. Motor carriers dominate the market for smaller shipments.[6]

The average length of haul for motor carriers is approximately 500 miles. Some national carriers have average hauls that are much longer while some intracity carriers may average only a few miles. LTL shipments are generally shorter hauls than TL shipments, but significant variability exists.

Motor Carriers Are Flexible and Versatile

Motor carriers are very flexible and versatile. The flexibility of motor carriers is made possible by a network of over 4 million miles of roads, thus enabling them to offer point-to-point service between almost any origin-destination combination. This gives motor carriers the widest market coverage of any mode. Motor carriers are versatile because they can transport products of varying sizes and weights over any distance.

Virtually any product can be transported by motor carriers, including some that require carrier equipment modifications.. Their flexibility and versatility have enabled them

---

[5]Point-to-point service refers to a single transport mode picking products up at origin and delivering them to their final destination. No additional transport modes are necessary.

[6]Shipments transported by motor carriers are referred to as truckload (TL) and less-than-truckload (LTL). When the terms were first developed, truck capacities were near 10,000 pounds, so this became the "norm" for designating the break point between a TL and LTL shipment. A TL amount was 10,000 pounds or more, while a LTL shipment was anything less than 10,000 pounds. Because the physical capacity of trucks has increased over the years, the amount that can be transported by truck has grown considerably. Today, LTL is any quantity of freight weighing less than the amount required for the application of a truckload rate.

to become the dominant form of transport (based on the amount of freight transported as measured in dollars) in the Americas and in many other parts of the world. Many motor carriers, particularly those involved in just-in-time programs, operate on a scheduled timetable. This results in very short and reliable transit times.

The amount of freight transported by motor carriers has steadily increased over the years. Motor carriage has become an important part of the logistics networks of most firms because the characteristics of the motor carrier industry are more compatible than other transport modes with the service requirements of the firms' customers. As long as it can provide fast, efficient service at rates between those offered by rail and air, the motor carrier industry will continue to prosper.

Baxter Healthcare, a large hospital supply company, presently outsources its truck-load transportation in order to utilize its carrier's expertise and efficiency, and to stream-line its operations (see Box 7–1).

Rail

In countries such as Austria, the People's Republic of China, and the former republics of the Soviet Union and Yugoslavia, rail is the dominant mode of transport. In the United States, most of the freight (in dollar terms) once shipped by rail has been shifted to motor carriers. Some traffic has been lost to water and pipeline carriers, which compete with railroads for bulk commodities. However, railroads carry the largest share of inter-city ton-miles and in 1995, this total was 1,276 billion ton-miles, or 18.29 million railcar loadings.[7] A ton-mile is one ton of freight moving a distance of one mile.

Railroads have an average length of haul of approximately 763 miles.[8] While rail service is available in almost every major metropolitan center in the world and in many smaller communities, the rail network is not nearly as extensive as the highway network.

Rail Lacks the Versatility and Flexibility of Motor Carriers

Rail transport lacks the versatility and flexibility of motor carriers because it is limited to fixed track facilities. As a result, railroads—like air, water, and pipeline transport—provide terminal-to-terminal service rather than point-to-point service unless companies have a rail siding at their facility, in which case service would be point to point.

Rail Costs Are Low

Rail transport generally costs less (on a weight basis) than air and motor carriage.[9] For many shipments, rail does not compare favorably with other modes on loss and damage ratios. Compared to motor carriers, it has disadvantages in terms of transit time and frequency of service, although railroads have improved significantly in these areas since deregulation of the U.S. rail industry in 1980.

Many trains travel on timetable schedules, but depart less frequently than motor carriers.[10] If a shipper has strict arrival and departure requirements, motor carriers usually

---

[7]"TM News Capsule," *Traffic Management* 35, no. 2 (Feb. 1996), p. 14.

[8]*Railroad Facts* (Washington, DC: Association of American Railroads, 1993), p. 3.

[9]In some transportation lanes and markets, motor carriers have been very price competitive with rail. In a few instances, motor carriers have been able to match or even undercut the rates charged by railroads.

[10]For a discussion of scheduled railroad service, see Peter Bradley, "It's about Time!" *Traffic Management* 34, no. 12 (Dec. 1995), pp. 37–39.

Box 7–1

Outsourcing Truckload Fleet Helps Baxter Healthcare Cut Supply Chain Costs

As the world's leading manufacturer and distributor of hospital and medical-related products, Baxter Healthcare of Deerfield, Illinois, is caught squarely in the middle of the ongoing overhaul of the U.S. health care system. To come out on top of this massive industry reengineering, Baxter relies on its logistics partners for help in streamlining its total medical supply chain, adding value, and cutting costs. In several important areas of its business, Baxter relies on outsourcing partners to handle the entire activity.

One partner is Schneider National/Schneider Dedicated. In 1993, Schneider took over Baxter's inbound truckload fleet operation. That operation provided inbound transport of 25 percent of the company's truckload shipments to production plants and replenishment centers. Baxter Healthcare made the decision to outsource its over-the-road private fleet (90 units at that time) in the summer of 1993. "When we stepped back and looked at the fleet," recalls Timothy Houghton, director of corporate transportation for Baxter Healthcare, "we decided that running a truckload (TL) carrier was not a core competency for us. We realized we couldn't possibly compete with national TL carriers.

"Our company philosophy," notes Houghton, "is that if we're not the number one or number two player in every market we service, then we get out of it. That's part of our commitment to taking cost out of the health care chain."

Leveraging Volumes

Houghton's analysis of Baxter's total inbound volumes indicated that the company not only was inefficient in its TL fleet operations, but also was not leveraging its inbound volumes with its for-hire carriers.

"We're a high-volume TL shipper, but we were using more than 100 truckload carriers—in addition to our private fleet—to handle inbound movements. We weren't leveraging our potential buying power," Houghton says.

"We also were spending an inordinate amount of time trying to keep track of and manage all those carriers."

To resolve this situation, Baxter first identified those lanes which could operate as closed loops (with full front-and-back-hauls), segregated them, and gave that business to Schneider Dedicated. "We operate about 95 units in our dedicated fleet, and have a loaded-mile factor of 94 percent," the distribution executive reports.

Then, the company concentrated the remaining 75 percent of its inbound TL business with a handful of core carriers, thereby obtaining better rates and service.

Schneider's tightly focused dedicated operation serves only those lanes where fully loaded round trips are possible. As a result, the operation is extremely cost effective, undercutting regular for-hire truckload rates by 15–25 percent, according to Houghton. At the same time, Schneider provides the high-quality service Baxter needs to keep its production plants running smoothly.

Greater Flexibility

Cost savings aren't the only benefit Baxter realizes from its Schneider operation. The new arrangement offers much more flexibility. "We were locked into the number of units and number of drivers," recalls Houghton. Dedicated contract carriage solved these problems, allowing Baxter complete flexibility to adjust fleet size to company demand. For example, if the company needs 10 additional units for the last two weeks in June, Houghton simply notifies Schneider and the units are slotted. "With the Schneider arrangement," says Houghton, "we get the best of all possible worlds."

In little more than a year, Schneider Dedicated saved Baxter 25 percent.

Source: *Outsourced Logistics Report,* Special Preview Issue, 1994, pp. 1–2.

TOFC and COFC Services

have a competitive advantage over railroads. Some of this rail disadvantage may be overcome through the use of trailer-on-flatcar (TOFC) or container-on-flatcar (COFC) service, which offer the economy of rail or water movements combined with the flexibility of trucking. TOFC and COFC eliminate much of the inventory penalty associated with rail transportation. Most logistics executives refer to TOFC and COFC as piggyback service.

Truck trailers or containers are delivered to the rail terminals, where they are loaded on flatbed railcars. Containers may be single or double stacked; that is, one or two containers on a single railcar.[11] At the destination terminal, they are off-loaded and delivered to the consignee, the customer who receives the shipment. We will examine these services in greater detail later in this chapter.

Railroads suffer in comparison to motor carriers in equipment availability. Railroads use their own as well as each other's railcars, and at times this equipment may not be located where it is most needed. Railcars may be unavailable because they are being loaded, unloaded, moved within railroad sorting yards, or undergoing repair. Other cars may be standing idle or lost within the vast rail network.

Recent Developments Aid Rail Utilization

A number of developments in the rail industry have helped to overcome some of these utilization problems. Advances have included computer routing and scheduling; the upgrading of equipment, roadbeds, and terminals; improvements in railcar identification systems; railcars owned or leased by the shipper; and the use of **unit trains** or dedicated through-train service between major metropolitan areas (i.e., nonstop shipments of one or a few shippers' products).[12]

Railroads own most of their car fleet, with the remainder leased or owned by shippers. Shippers that own or lease cars are typically heavy users of rail transport and are especially sensitive to railcar shortages that occur because of unique market or competitive conditions.

During the late 1980s, railroads recaptured some of the traffic previously lost to trucks, pipelines, and water carriers. The relative energy-efficiency advantage of railroads over motor carriers, deregulation of the rail industry, and the continuing trend toward consolidation through mergers and acquisitions hold promise for a brighter future for this transport mode.

Air

Domestically, air carriers transport less than 1 percent of ton-mile traffic in the United States. Revenues of scheduled air carriers from movement of freight were about $16 billion in 1993, but this represented only a small percentage of the total U.S. freight bill.[13]

Air Freight Is Used Primarily as a Premium Service

Although increasing numbers of shippers are using air freight for regular service, most view air transport as a premium, emergency service because of its higher cost. But when an item must be delivered to a distant location quickly, air freight offers the

---

[11]Helen L. Richardson, "Shippers and Carriers Win with Doublestack," *Transportation and Distribution* 30, no. 12 (Nov. 1989), pp. 22–24.

[12]Unit trains are trains of great length carrying a single product in one direction. Commodities transported by unit trains have included coal, grains, U.S. mail, automobiles, fruits, and vegetables.

[13]U.S. Bureau of the Census, *Statistical Abstract of the United States: 1995,* 115th ed. (Washington, DC: U.S. Government Printing Office, 1995), p. 625.

quickest time-in-transit of any transport mode. For most shippers, however, these time-sensitive shipments are relatively few in number or frequency.

Modern aircraft have cruising speeds of 500 to 600 miles per hour and are able to travel internationally. The average length of haul domestically is more than 800 miles, although international movements may be thousands of miles.[14]

For most commercial airlines, freight is incidental to passenger traffic, and is carried on a space-available basis. United Airlines led the way in cargo revenue for passenger airlines in 1995, with $757 million, followed closely by Northwest Airlines with $751 million.[15]

To a great extent, domestic air freight competes directly with motor carriers, and to a much lesser degree with rail carriers. Where countries are separated by large expanses of water, the major competitor for international air freight is water carriage.

Air carriers generally handle high-value products. Air freight usually cannot be cost-justified for low-value items, because the high price of air freight would represent too large a percentage of the product cost. Customer service considerations may influence the choice of transport, but only if service issues are more important than cost issues.

Air transport provides frequent and reliable service and rapid time-in-transit, but terminal and delivery delays and congestion may appreciably reduce some of this advantage. On a point-to-point basis over short distances, motor transport often matches or outperforms the total transit time of air freight. It is the *total* transit time that is important to the shipper rather than the transit time from terminal to terminal.

Despite the limitations of air carriers, the volume of air freight has grown over the years and it shows continuing growth even in the face of higher rates. Undoubtedly, as customers demand higher levels of service and as international shipments increase, air freight will have a potentially greater role in the distribution plans of many firms.

Water

Water transportation can be broken down into several distinct categories: (1) inland waterway, such as rivers and canals, (2) lakes, (3) coastal and intercoastal ocean, and (4) international deep sea. In the United States, water carriage competes primarily with rail and pipeline, since the majority of commodities carried by water are semiprocessed or raw materials transported in bulk. It is concentrated in low-value items (e.g., iron ore, grains, pulpwood products, coal, limestone, and petroleum) where speed is not critical.

The Importance of Water Carriage Varies around the World

Other than in ocean transport, water carriers are limited in their movement by the availability of lakes, rivers, canals, or intercoastal waterways. Reliance on water carriage depends to a greater or lesser degree on the geography of the particular location. In the United States, for example, approximately 467 billion revenue freight ton-miles ($21 billion), or around 15 percent of the total intercity freight, is moved by water.[16] In northern and central Europe, water carriage is much more important because of the vast system of

---

[14]*Air Transport 1994,* p. 16.

[15]Marcia Jedd, "Shedding the Stepchild Image," *Distribution* 95, no. 8 (July 1996), p. 58.

[16]*Statistical Abstract of the United States: 1995,* p. 626.

Barge traffic on the Mississippi River near St. Louis, Missouri.

navigable waterways, the accessibility to major population centers provided by water routes, and the relatively shorter distances between origins and destinations. In the Netherlands, Belgium, and Luxembourg, waterways account for 20 percent of all freight transported.[17]

The average length of haul varies tremendously depending on the type of water transport. For international ocean movements, the length of haul can be many thousands of miles. Generally, water is the dominant mode in international shipping. Domestically, movements are of shorter lengths, depending on the length of navigable waterways and lakes.

Water carriage is perhaps the most inexpensive method of shipping high-bulk, low-value commodities. However, because of the inherent limitations of water carriers, it is unlikely that water transport will gain a larger role in domestic commerce, although international developments have made marine shipping increasingly important.

VLCCs

The development of **very large crude carriers (VLCCs),** or supertankers, has enabled marine shipping to assume a vital role in the transport of petroleum between oil-producing and oil-consuming countries. Because of the importance of energy resources to industrialized nations, water carriage will continue to play a significant role in the transportation of energy resources. In addition, container ships have greatly expanded the use of water transport for many products.

Many domestic and most international shipments involve the use of containers. The shipper in one country places cargo into an owned or leased container at its facility or at

[17]Kevin A. O'Laughlin, James Cooper, and Eric Cabocel, *Reconfiguring European Logistics Systems* (Oak Brook, IL: Council of Logistics Management, 1993), p. 38.

point of origin.[18] Then the container is transported by rail or motor carriage to a water port for loading onto a container ship. After arrival at the destination port, it is unloaded and tendered to a rail or motor carrier in that country and subsequently delivered to the customer or consignee. The shipment leaves the shipper and arrives at the customer's location with no or minimal handling of the items within the container.

Containers Are Important in Global Commerce

The use of containers in intermodal logistics reduces staffing needs, minimizes in-transit damage and pilferage, shortens time in transit because of reduced port turnaround time, and allows the shipper to take advantage of volume shipping rates.

The largest ocean water carriers are Sea-Land Service, Evergreen Line, Maersk, Hanjin Shipping, and APL Limited. These companies utilize both container and general cargo ships. The container ships are very large; newer vessels are able to carry the equivalent of 6,000 twenty-foot containers.[19] Often, a carrier will form alliances with other ocean carriers to maximize market coverage and customer service levels.[20] See the Global box on the birth of containers.

Pipeline

Pipelines are able to transport only a limited number of products, including natural gas, crude oil, petroleum products, water, chemicals, and slurry products.[21] Natural gas and crude oil account for the majority of pipeline traffic. Oil pipelines transport approximately 18.4 percent of all domestic intercity freight traffic measured in ton-miles. In Europe and Japan, pipeline movements are relatively insignificant, although in the Commonwealth of Independent States (CIS), large amounts of product are moved using this form of transport.[22]

There are over 440,000 miles of intercity pipeline in the United States. The average length of haul is under 500 miles except for the 800-mile Trans-Alaska Pipeline System.[23] Pipelines offer the shipper an extremely high level of service dependability at a relatively low cost. Pipelines are able to deliver their product on time because of the following factors:

Characteristics of Pipeline Transportation

- The flows of products within the pipeline are monitored and controlled by computer.
- Losses and damages due to pipeline leaks or breaks are extremely rare.
- Climatic conditions have minimal effects on products moving in pipelines.

---

[18]Containers typically are 8 feet high, 8 feet wide, and of various lengths (e.g., 53 ft., 48 ft., 45 ft., 40 ft., 20 ft.) and are compatible conventional motor or rail equipment. A common transport statistic is the TEU, a 20-foot container equivalent.

[19]Robert J. Bowman, "Stormy Weather," *Distribution* 95, no. 8 (July 1996), pp. 72, 74.

[20]Toby B. Gooley, "Will Mega-Alliances Mean Mega-Benefits for Shippers?" *Logistics Management* 35, no. 5 (May 1996), pp. 65A–69A.

[21]Slurry is usually thought of as a solid product that is suspended in a liquid, often water, which can then be transported easily.

[22]*Statistical Abstract of the United States: 1995,* p. 626; O'Laughlin, Cooper, and Cabocel, *Reconfiguring European Logistics Systems,* p. 72.

[23]Donald F. Wood and James C. Johnson, *Contemporary Transportation,* 4th ed. (New York: Macmillan, 1993), pp. 147, 152.

Global

The Birth of Containers

On April 26, 1996, an anniversary of some significance occurred for Sea-Land Service Inc. The company marked the 40th anniversary of its first sailing—and with it the birth of containerization. On April 26, 1956, a small former tanker called the *Ideal X* set sail from Port Newark in New

York Harbor with containers on board, bound for Texas. Now a unit of CSX Transportation, Sea-Land is one of the largest containerized shipping companies in the world.

Source: "Management Update," *Logistics Management* 35, no. 6 (June 1996), p. 3.

TABLE 7–1   Estimated Distribution of Intercity Freight Ton-Miles in the United States

Mode	1993 (billions of ton-miles)	Percentage of Total			
		1993	*1980*	*1960*	*1940*
Rail	1,183	38%	38%	44%	61%
Motor	871	28	22	22	10
Air	12	<1	<1	<1	<1
Inland waterway	467	15	16	17	19
Oil pipeline	572	18	24	17	10
Total	3,105	100%	100%	100%	100%

Source: U.S. Bureau of the Census, *Statistical Abstract of the United States: 1995,* 115th ed. (Washington, DC: U.S. Government Printing Office, 1995), p. 626.

- Pipelines are not labor-intensive; therefore, strikes or employee absences have little effect on their operations.

The advantages in cost and dependability that pipelines have over other transport modes have stimulated shipper interest in moving other products by pipeline. Certainly, if a product is or can be in liquid, gas, or slurry form, it can be transported by pipeline. As the costs of other modes increase, shippers may give additional consideration to pipelines as a mode of transport for nontraditional products.

Each mode transports a large amount of freight, as shown in Tables 7–1 (United States) and 7–2 (Europe). The particular mode a shipper selects depends on the characteristics of the mode coupled with the needs of the company and its customers. Table 7–3 summarizes the economic and service characteristics of the five basic modes of transport.

TABLE 7–2   European Freight Movements (in Billion Ton-Kilometers)—1989

	Road[a]	Rail[b]	Inland Waterway[b]	Sea-going	Inland Pipeline
European Community					
Belgium	31.0[c]	8.0[c]	5.3	—	1.0
Denmark	9.2[c]	1.7	0	2.0[c]	1.6[c]
FR of Germany	124.2	60.0[c]	54.0	0.6[c]	8.8[c]
France	116.7	52.3[c]	7.0[c]	—	31.0[c]
Greece	12.5[c]	0.6[c]	0	—	—
Irish Republic	4.0[c]	0.6[c]	—	—	—
Italy	165.0[c]	20.0[c]	0.1	36.0[c]	9.0[c]
Luxembourg	0.2[c]	0.7	0.4	0	—
Netherlands	22.1[c]	3.1	36.0	—	4.6
Portugal	12.05[c]	1.7	—	—	—
Spain	143	11.9	—	28.0[c]	4.8[c]
United Kingdom	134.3	17.0	0.3	56.2	9.1
Other Europe					
Austria	8.0[c]	11.2[c]	1.8[c,d]	0	5.3
Czechoslovakia	23.8	72.0	4.8[d]	0	9.0[c]
German DR[f]	16.9	59.0	2.3	—	4.3
Hungary	13.4	19.8	2.1[d]	0	3.4
Sweden	22.6[c]	19.2	0	8.0[c]	—
Switzerland	7.5[c]	8.2	0.1	0	1.1
Yugoslavia	25.0[c,e]	25.9	8.8	—	3.4
Rest of the World					
Japan	260.0[c]	23.0[c]	0	2405	—
United States	1,200.0[c]	1,500.0[c]	550.0[c]	900.0[c]	9205
Soviet Republics	510.0[c]	4,000.0[c]	239.6	—	1,422

[a]In vehicles above a size threshold which (for EC countries) may not exceed 3.5 tons net or 6 tons gross vehicle weight.
[b]Carried by national and foreign vehicles.
[c]Estimated from previous years.
[d]Transport by national shipping undertaken at home and abroad.
[e]For hire and reward only.
[f]Now unified with the Federal Republic of Germany

Source: Kevin A. O'Laughlin, James Cooper, and Eric Cabocel, *Reconfiguring European Logistics Systems* (Oak Brook, IL: Council of Logistics Management, 1993), p. 72.

Third Parties

Third parties are companies similar to channel intermediaries that provide linkages between shippers and carriers. Often, third parties do not own transportation equipment themselves; instead, they partner with a number of carriers who provide the necessary equipment to transport their shipments. There are several types of third parties, including

TABLE 7–3   Comparison of U.S. Domestic Transportation Modes

	Motor	*Rail*	*Air*	*Water*	*Pipeline*
Economic Characteristics					
Cost	Moderate	Low	High	Low	Low
Market coverage	Point-to-point	Terminal-to-terminal	Terminal-to-terminal	Terminal-to-terminal	Terminal-to-terminal
Degree of competition (number of competitors)	Many	Few	Moderate	Few	Few
Predominant traffic	All types	Low–moderate value, moderate high density	High value, low–moderate density	Low value, high density	Low value, high density
Average length of haul (in miles)	515	617	885	376 to 1,367	276 to 343
Equipment capacity (tons)	10 to 25	50 to 12,000	5 to 125	1,000 to 60,000	30,000 to 2,500,000
Service Characteristics					
Speed (time-in-transit)	Moderate to fast	Moderate	Fast	Slow	Slow
Availability	High	Moderate	Moderate	Low	Low
Consistency (delivery time variability)	High	Moderate	High	Low to moderate	High
Loss and damage	Low	Moderate	Low	Low to moderate	Low
Flexibility (adjustment to shipper's needs)	High	Moderate	Moderate to high	Low to moderate	Low

transportation brokers, freight forwarders (domestic and foreign), shippers' associations or cooperatives, intermodal marketing companies (shippers' agents), and third-party logistics service providers.

Transportation Brokers.   **Transportation brokers** are companies that provide services to both shippers and carriers by arranging and coordinating the transportation of products. They charge a fee to do so, which usually is taken as a percentage of the revenue collected by the broker from the shipper. The broker in turn pays the carrier.[24]

Functions of Transportation Brokers

Shippers with minimal traffic support, or no traffic department at all, can use brokers to negotiate rates, oversee shipments, and do many of the things the shipper may not be able to do because of personnel or resource constraints. In these instances, the broker partially replaces some of the firm's own traffic department. The broker does not completely replace the traffic function; it merely assumes some of the transportation functions.

---

[24]James C. Johnson and Kenneth C. Schneider, "Licensed Transportation Brokers: Their Joys and Frustration," *Transportation Journal* 34, no. 4 (Summer 1995), pp. 38–51.

Small- and medium-sized shippers are the major users of transportation brokers, although larger firms utilize them in smaller markets.

Functions of Freight Forwarders

Freight Forwarders. **Freight forwarders** purchase transport services from various carriers, although in some instances they own the equipment themselves. For example, the most successful air freight forwarders typically purchase and operate their own equipment, rather than relying on other air carriers. Freight forwarders consolidate small shipments from a number of shippers into large shipments moving into a certain region at a lower rate. Because of consolidation efficiencies, these companies can offer shippers lower rates than the shippers could obtain directly from the carrier.[25] Often, the freight forwarder can provide faster and more complete service because they are able to tender larger volumes to the carrier.

Freight forwarders can be classified as domestic or international, depending on whether they specialize in shipments within a country or between countries. They can be surface or air freight forwarders. If they are involved in international shipments, freight forwarders will provide documentation services, which is especially vital for firms with limited international marketing experience.

Often, freight forwarders and transportation brokers are viewed similarly, but there are important differences:

Differences between a Freight Forwarder and a Transportation Broker

- A forwarder is the shipper to a carrier and the carrier to a shipper.
- A broker is neither shipper nor carrier, but an intermediary between the two.
- A forwarder can arrange for transportation of freight by any mode.
- A broker can arrange for freight transportation only by a motor carrier.
- A forwarder is exempt from federal government oversight.
- A broker must be licensed by the Surface Transportation Board.
- A forwarder is primarily liable to a shipper for cargo loss and damage.
- A broker is not usually liable for cargo loss and damage, although many do provide this coverage.[26]

Functions of Shippers' Associations

Shippers' Associations. In their operations, shippers' associations are much like freight forwarders, but they differ in terms of perception by regulatory authorities. A shippers' association can be defined as a nonprofit cooperative that consolidates small shipments into truckload freight for member companies.

Shippers' associations primarily utilize motor and rail carriers for transport. Because small shipments are much more expensive to transport (on a per pound or per unit basis) than large shipments, companies band together to lower their transportation costs through consolidation of many small shipments into one or more larger shipments. The members of the shippers' association realize service improvements.

Shippers' associations also can handle truckload shipments by purchasing large blocks of flatbed railcars at discount rates. They then fill the available railcars with the

---

[25]Consolidation refers to taking a number of small shipments and combining them into a single larger shipment.

[26]Mitchell E. MacDonald, "Broker vs. Forwarder," *Traffic Management* 31, no. 6 (June 1992), p. 62.

trailers on flatcars (TOFCs) of member companies. Both parties benefit as a result. Shippers are charged lower rates than they could get by themselves (shipping in smaller quantities), while the railroads realize better equipment utilization and the economies of large, direct-route piggyback trains.

Functions of IMCs

Intermodal Marketing Companies (or Shippers' Agents).   **Intermodal marketing companies (IMCs),** or shippers' agents, act much like shippers' associations or cooperatives. They specialize in providing piggyback services to shippers and are an important intermodal link between shippers and carriers. As the use of intermodal transportation increases in the future, shippers' agents will grow in importance as they purchase large quantities of TOFC/COFC services at discount and resell them in smaller quantities.

Third-Party Logistics Service Providers.   This sector is growing very rapidly. As illustrated in Box 7–2, Sears (mass merchandise retailer) and Menlo Logistics (third-party logistics service provider) have established a mutually beneficial relationship; Menlo provides significant transportation support for Sears LTL 1.2 billion pounds of freight annually.[27]

The Use of Third Parties Is Increasing

With the increasing emphasis on supply chain management, more companies are exploring the third-party option. For some firms, dealing with one third-party firm who will handle all or most of their freight offers a number of advantages, including the management of information by the third party, freeing the company from day-to-day interactions with carriers, and having the third party oversee hundreds or even thousands of shipments. Activities such as freight payment and dedicated contract carriage have been administered by third parties for many years. However, additional transportation and logistics activities are being outsourced. In some instances, some comapnies have outsourced large parts of their logistics operations to third parties.

Brokers, freight forwarders, shippers' associations, intermodal marketing companies, and third-party logistics service providers can be viable shipping options for a firm in the same way that the five basic modes and intermodal combinations can. The logistics executive must determine the optimal combination of transport alternatives for his or her company.

In addition to the preceding alternatives, many companies find that other transport forms can be used to distribute their products. Small-package carriers such as Federal Express (FedEx), United Parcel Service (UPS), and parcel post are important transporters of many time-sensitive products. These entities use a combination of transport modes, especially air. The U.S. domestic air freight market consists of 60 percent express, 25 percent passenger carriers, and 15 percent mail. The growth rate in this sector has been robust, averaging about 10 percent a year.[28]

---

[27]Thomas A. Foster, "How Sears Leverages Its LTL," *Distribution* 91, no. 9 (Sept. 1992), pp. 46, 49–50. For additional examples of the use of third parties, see James Aaron Cooke, "Third Time's a Charm!" *Logistics Management* 35, no. 3 (Mar. 1996), pp. 85–87; James Aaron Cooke, "Three 'Takes' on Third Party," *Logistics Management* 35, no. 5 (May 1996), pp. 53–55; and Toby B. Gooley, "Why GM Pushed Inbound Shipments Back Out the Door," *Traffic Management* 34, no. 6 (June 1995), pp. 49–52.

[28]John Bell, "Express Meets Time-Definite," *Distribution* 95, no. 8 (July 1996), p. 62.

Box 7–2

How Sears Leverages Its LTL Transportation

No shipper has embraced the third-party logistics concept more completely than Sears. In 1990, the merchandising giant spun off its own transportation and logistics operations as a separate company called Sears Logistics Services (SLS) to handle the needs of the Sears Merchandising Group and to take on other customers.

SLS in turn has contracted with third-parties to handle certain operations involved with warehousing, intermodal operations, customs brokerage, and, most recently, less-than-truckload (LTL) transportation.

This relationship with Menlo Logistics, a subsidiary of Consolidated Freightways (CF), is designed to handle about 1.2 billion pounds of LTL traffic each year from Sears 4,000 suppliers to SLS's network of distribution centers, and a limited amount of outbound LTL to Sears catalog stores throughout the country.

"Our overall transportation strategy is to leverage our freight to the density economics of a limited number of carriers," says Jim Comerford, vice president of transportation for SLS.

"We realized our problem was similar to what faced an LTL carrier with terminals all over the country," said Comerford. "Since major LTL carriers are adept at dealing with networks operating up to 200 to 300 terminals, we decided it made sense to talk to LTL-oriented companies to solve our problem."

Menlo won the bid and started planning with SLS in November 1991. Menlo started managing the LTL operations in December, and by January 6, 1992, Menlo was in full charge of managing all of Sears LTL movements from 4,000 vendors to SLS locations all over the country.

Menlo's primary function is to manage all LTL operations. The CF family of carriers handle the majority of the freight. CF MotorFreight receives about 58 percent. The four Con-Way carriers share approximately 29 percent. Twenty-one carriers not affiliated with CF handle about 13 percent of the LTL freight.

Menlo brings LTL vendor shipments to Sears' five catalog merchandise centers (CMCs) and eight retail replenishment centers (RRCs) as well as selected outbound movement from SLS's 46 cross-docking centers (CDCs) to remote areas.

"It is their responsibility to get the best rate on the lane and to determine which carrier will handle what freight,"

says Comerford. Menlo's financial success depends on its getting the best rates, because it earns its money in this partnership by performing as a property broker licensed by the Interstate Commerce Commission. Menlo receives payment from SLS and pays the carriers. Anything left over is revenue for Menlo. Menlo has four people at SLS headquarters in Itasca, Illinois, running the LTL operations.

The Menlo partnership results in a number of operational advantages for SLS, as shown below.

Twelve Ways SLS and Menlo Improve Logistics Performance

1. Increase land density by adjusting vendor shipping schedules.
2. Improve vendor packaging and shipping characteristics.
3. Find ways to avoid accessorial charges; that is, additional charges of carriers for services such as box car loading/unloading, transit stop-off, inspection, repackaging, etc.
4. Produce videotapes to teach SLS employees how to handle outbound loading better.
5. Train carrier employees so they know how to deal with SLS.
6. Use CF imaging technology to prepare proof of deliveries and handle claims.
7. Use EDI to create a paperless environment.
8. Have Menlo review Hazmat documentation to comply with all regulations without overdocumenting shipments.
9. Adjust SLS shipping zones to the operating boundaries of CF MotorFreight to improve efficiency of serving vendors.
10. Have Menlo help SLS inventory and dispose of trailers no longer needed for the terminal freight handling operation.
11. Gain carriers' commitment to stage trailers at RRCs.
12. Develop compatible logistics programs with large vendors unwilling to participate in Sears' freight collect program.

Source: Thomas A. Foster, "How Sears Leverages Its LTL," *Distribution* 91, no. 9 (Sept. 1992), pp. 46, 49–50.

Small-Package Carriers

For companies such as electronics firms, catalog merchandisers, cosmetic companies, and textbook distributors, small-package carriers can be important transportation options. During 1995, six million shipments were sent by means of small-package carriers. Growth rates for this transport sector are expected to average 10 to 15 percent per year.[29]

Shipping with the U.S. Postal Service

Parcel Post.   The U.S. Postal Service provides both surface and air parcel post services to companies shipping small packages. The advantages of parcel post are low cost and wide geographical coverage, both domestically and internationally. Disadvantages include specific size and weight limitations, variability in transit time, higher loss and damage ratios than other forms of shipment, and inconvenience because packages must be prepaid and deposited at a postal facility. Mail-order houses are probably the most extensive users of parcel post service.

Federal Express Transports 2.2 Million Packages Every Day

Air Express Companies.   Characterized by high levels of customer service, the air express industry has significantly expanded since its inception in 1973. The Federal Express Corporation, one of the best-known examples of an air express company, illustrates how the concept of supplying rapid transit with very high consistency has paid off. In 1995, FedEx had worldwide revenues of $9.4 billion (profits of $298 million). This represented 2.2 million daily express packages, transported on 496 aircraft, and supported by 35,900 vehicles and more than 94,000 employees.[30] Because some firms need to transport certain products quickly, the air express industry is able to offer overnight (or second day) delivery of small parcels to many locations throughout the world.

Many carriers have experienced a drop in order quantities as their customers aim to reduce inventory by ordering more frequently and in smaller quantities. This has increased the demand for air express–type services.[31] Competition is fierce among the "giants" of the industry, including FedEx, UPS, TNT Worldwide, Airborne Express, and DHL Airways.[32] As long as there is a need to transport products quickly and with very high levels of consistency, the air express companies will continue to provide a valuable service for many shippers.

Intermodal Services

In addition to the five basic modes of transport, a number of intermodal combinations are available to the shipper. The more popular combinations are trailer-on-flatcar (TOFC) and container-on-flatcar (COFC). Intermodal movements combine the cost and/or service advantages of two or more modes in a single product movement.

---

[29]John Bell, "Expanding a Small World," *Distribution* 95, no. 8 (July 1996), p. 56.

[30]Federal Express, *1995 Annual Report,* p. 1.

[31]Helen L. Richardson, "Will Shrinking Shipments Shrink Profits?" *Transportation and Distribution* 36, no. 3 (Mar. 1995), p. 45.

[32]See Brian P. Analla and Marilyn M. Helms, "Worldwide Express Small Package Industry," *Transportation Quarterly* 50, no. 1 (Winter 1996), pp. 51–64; and "FedEx, UPS Set Sights on LTL Freight," *Logistics Management* 35, no. 6 (June 1996), pp. 45–47.

A truck chassis is positioned to receive a container from a doublestack train in Chicago, Illinois. The truck can move the cargo directly to a retail store or other user.

Piggyback (TOFC/COFC).   In piggyback service, a motor carrier trailer or a container is placed on a rail flatcar and transported from one terminal to another. Axles can be placed under the containers, so they can be delivered by a truck. At the terminal facilities, motor carriers perform the pickup and delivery functions. Piggyback service thus combines the low cost of long-haul rail movement with the flexibility and convenience of truck movement.

Since 1976 shippers have increased their use of piggyback service by 200 percent. In 1994 there were 8.1 million intermodal shipments, with 1995 and 1996 shipments approximating the same levels.[33] Figure 7–2 shows the shift in freight between highway and intermodal traffic.

Truck and rail partnerships to support intermodalism, such as the one begun in 1989 between the Santa Fe Railroad and J. B. Hunt Transportation Services, are relatively common.[34] The railroad carries freight on the long haul, and the trucking company picks up and delivers between the customer and railroad. Seventy-seven percent of intermodal users agree that such alliances have a positive impact on transportation options available to them.[35]

---

[33]Robert J. Bowman, "Hitting the Wall," *Distribution* 95, no. 8 (July 1996), p. 52.

[34]Mitchell E. MacDonald, "Intermodal Battles a Perception Problem," *Traffic Management* 29, no. 5 (May 1990), p. 32.

[35]Martha Spizziri, "Intermodal Overcomes the Obstacles," *Traffic Management* 33, no. 4 (Apr. 1994), pp. 39–42.

FIGURE 7–2

Freight shift to intermodal transportation

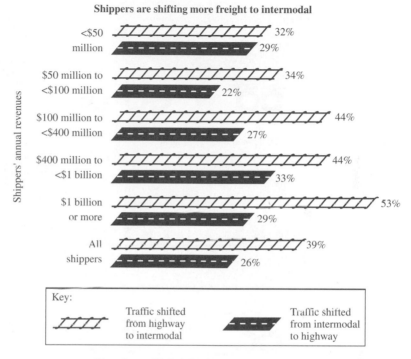

Shippers are shifting more freight to intermodal

More than a third of the shippers surveyed diverted freight from highway to intermodal in 1993.

Source: Adapted from Martha Spizziri, "Intermodal Overcomes the Obstacles," *Traffic Management,* 33, no. 3 (Apr. 1994), p. 39.

Roadrailers

Roadrailers.   An innovative intermodal concept was introduced in the late 1970s. **Roadrailers,** or trailertrains as they are sometimes called, combine motor and rail transport in a single piece of equipment. As shown in Figure 7–3, the roadrailer resembles a conventional motor carrier (truck) trailer. However, the trailer has both rubber truck tires and steel rail wheels. Over highways, tractor power units transport the trailers in the normal way, but instead of placing the trailer on a flatcar for rail movement, the wheels of the trailer are retracted and the trailer rides directly on the rail tracks.

The advantages of this intermodal form of transport are that rail flatcars are not required and that the switching time to change wheels on the trailer is less than loading and unloading the trailer from the flatcar. The major disadvantages of roadrailers are the added weight of the rail wheels, which reduces fuel efficiency and results in higher movement costs in addition to the higher cost of the equipment. The disadvantages have tended to outweigh the advantages, resulting in very low usage of this intermodal option. If technology improvements can reduce the cost of this transport option, usage is likely to increase.

FIGURE 7–3

Selected forms of intermodal transportation

1. Trailer on flatcar (TOFC)

2. Trailer and tractor on flatcar

3. Roadrailer

4. Container on flatcar (COFC)

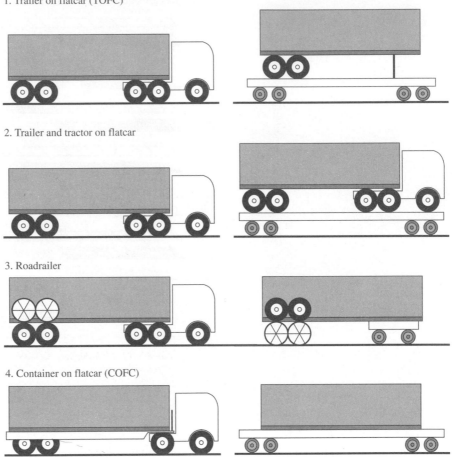

Miscellaneous Intermodal Issues. Many other intermodal combinations are possible. In international commerce, for example, the dominant modes of transportation are air and water. Both include intermodal movements through the use of containers and truck trailers. Combinations of air-sea, air-rail, truck-sea, and rail-sea are used globally.

As an example: "By shipping cargo by ocean from . . . Japan to Seattle, then transferring it to a direct flight to Europe from Seattle-Tacoma Airport, Asian exporters reap substantial benefits. They can cut their transit times from 30 days for all-water service to about 14 days, and slash freight costs by up to 50 percent compared with all-air service."[36]

[36]Toby B. Gooley, "Air Freight Hits the Rails," *Logistics Management* 35, no. 3 (Mar. 1996), p. 112A.

Between 1980 and 1995, intermodal freight movements increased steadily, often at double-digit growth rates.[37] While that growth rate has now plateaued, intermodal movements by carriers and intermodal marketing companies (IMCs) continue to be important means of transporting products domestically and internationally. While overall industry growth may have stabilized, many shippers and carriers are exploring expanded usage of this form of transport.

Briggs & Stratton Utilizes Intermodal Transport

Briggs & Stratton Corporation, a $1 billion Milwaukee-based manufacturer of internal combustion engines used in lawn tractors, mowers, and other equipment, exports 2,000 intermodal containers a year. The company makes just-in-time deliveries to Europe, where it competes against Honda. Because intermodal service has become more reliable, Briggs & Stratton is able to meet tight delivery schedules.[38]

Global Issues

International freight transportation can involve any of the five basic modes of transportation, although air and water carriage are perhaps the most important. Motor and rail carriage are the most important freight movements *within* nations.

Managers of firms involved in international markets must be aware of the services, costs, and availability of transport modes within and between the countries where their products are distributed. For example, air and water transportation directly compete for transoceanic shipments. Management must consider many factors when it compares the two alternatives.

International Transportation Is More Expensive Than Domestic Transportation

Within countries, differences can exist because of taxes, subsidies, regulations, government ownership of carriers, geography, and other factors. Because of government ownership or subsidies to railroads in Europe, rail service benefits from newer or better maintained equipment, track, and facilities. Japan and Europe utilize water carriage to a much larger degree than the United States or Canada due to the length and favorable characteristics of coastlines and inland waterways.

In general, international transportation costs represent a much higher fraction of merchandise value than domestic transportation costs. This is primarily due to the longer distances involved, administrative requirements, and related paperwork that must accompany international shipments.[39]

Intermodal transportation is much more common in international movements. Even though rehandling costs are higher than for single-mode movements, cost savings and service improvements can result. There are three basic forms of international intermodal distribution, described as follows:

Landbridge

Landbridge is a service in which foreign cargo crosses a country en route to another country. For example, European cargo en route to Japan may be shipped by ocean to the

---

[37]Peter Bradley, "Intermodal Falls Off the Fast Tract," *Traffic Management* 35, no. 2 (Feb. 1996), p. 26.

[38]"Special Report: Think Global, Go International," *International Business* 6, no. 3 (Mar. 1993), p. 61.

[39]Paul S. Bender, "International Logistics," in *The Distribution Management Handbook,* ed. James A. Tompkins and Dale Harmelink (New York: McGraw-Hill, Inc., 1994), pp. 8.5–8.6.

FIGURE 7–4

International distribution shipping options

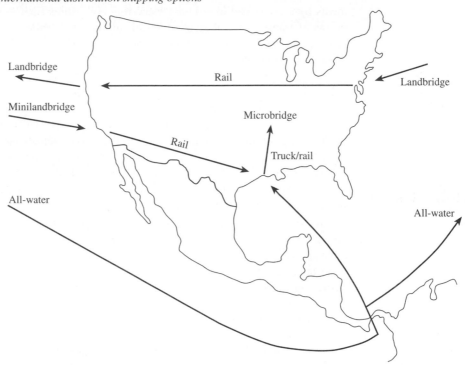

Source: David L. Anderson, "International Logistics Strategies for the Eighties," *Proceedings of the Twenty-Second Annual Conference of the National Council of Physical Distribution Management,* 1984, p. 363. Used by permission of the Council of Logistics Management.

East Coast of the United States, then moved by rail to the West Coast, and from there shipped by ocean to Japan.

Minilandbridge

Minilandbridge (MLB) (also called *minibridge*) is a special case of landbridge, where foreign cargo originates or terminates at a point within the United States.

Microbridge

Microbridge is a relatively new service being provided by ports on the West Coast. In contrast with minibridge, this service provides door-to-door rather than port-to-port transportation. The big advantage of microbridge is that it provides a combined rate, including rail and ocean transportation, in a single tariff that is lower than the sum of the separate rates (see Figure 7–4).[40]

A comparison of single-mode and intermodal movements between the Far East and the U.S. East Coast demonstrates the advantages of the latter. If we compare an all-water movement with a minilandbridge movement for comparable shipments, the costs are

---

[40]Paul S. Bender, "The International Dimension of Physical Distribution Management," in *The Distribution Handbook,* ed. James A. Robeson and Robert G. House (New York: Free Press, 1985), pp. 791–92.

approximately the same. But MLB is significantly faster, thus offering the opportunity to reduce order cycle times and to improve customer service levels.

In making traffic and transportation decisions, the logistics manager must know and understand the differences between the domestic and international marketplace. Modal availability, rates, regulatory restrictions, service levels, and other aspects of the transportation mix may vary significantly from one market to another.

Regulatory Issues

There are two major areas of transportation regulation: economic and safety. All freight movements are subject to safety regulation, but not all are subject to economic regulation. The regulation of the transportation sector has had an enormous impact on the logistics activities of carriers and shippers. We will briefly describe economic and safety regulation, legal forms of transportation, and the impact of deregulation on shippers and carriers.

Forms of Regulation

Transportation Is Governed by Both Economic and Safety Regulations

Historically, transportation regulation has developed along two lines. The first, and perhaps the most publicized in recent years, is *economic* regulation. Economic regulation affects business decisions such as mode/carrier selection, rates charged by carriers, service levels, and routing and scheduling. *Safety* regulation deals with labor standards, working conditions for transportation employees, shipment of hazardous materials, vehicle maintenance, insurance, and other elements relating to public safety.

The 1970s, 1980s, and 1990s have been periods of **deregulation** in North America, Europe, and elsewhere throughout the world. At the same time, safety regulation has been increasing in terms of its scope and breadth. In the United States, all transport modes are regulated (economic and safety) by the Department of Transportation (DOT) and are subject to a variety of laws such as the Occupational Safety and Health Act (OSHA) of 1970, the Hazardous Materials Transportation Uniform Safety Act (1990), and the National Environmental Policy Act (1969). An important part of the responsibilities of a logistics or transportation executive is to keep abreast of regulatory changes because of their potential impact on the firm's operations.

U.S. Transportation Modes Have Mostly Been Deregulated

In recent years, the role of various U.S. transportation agencies in administering the regulatory environment has changed. Since the early 1970s, the trend has been toward decreasing economic regulation of transportation. Four of the five basic modes of transport have been deregulated at the federal level.

Transportation is also regulated at the state level. It is beyond the scope of this book to examine the myriad of state regulations that exist, but carriers and shippers must be familiar with all regulations in states where they operate.

Legally Defined Forms of Transportation

In addition to classifying alternative forms of transportation by mode, carriers can be classified on the basis of the four legal forms: common, contract, exempt, and private carriers. The first three forms are for-hire carriers, and the last is owned by a shipper. **For-hire carriers** transport freight belonging to others and are subject to various federal, state, and local statutes and regulations. For the most part, private carriers transport their own goods and supplies in their own equipment and are exempt from most regulations, except for those dealing with safety and taxation.

Deregulation has reshaped how logistics executives view the transport modes, particularly the legal forms of transportation. In principle, these legal designations no longer exist because of deregulation. For example, the distinction between common and contract motor carriers was eliminated by the Trucking Industry Regulatory Reform Act of 1994 (TIRRA). However, the terms are used within the industry and do provide some guidance with respect to transportation type.

Common Carriers

Common Carriers. **Common carriers** offer their services to any shipper to transport products, at published rates, between designated points. To operate legally, they must be granted authority from the appropriate federal regulatory agency. With deregulation, common carriers have significant flexibility with respect to market entry, routing, and pricing. Common carriers must offer their services to the general public on a nondiscriminatory basis; that is, they must serve all shippers of the commodities which their equipment can feasibly carry. A significant problem facing common carriers is that the number of customers cannot be predicted with certainty in advance. Thus, future demand is uncertain. The result has been that many common carriers have entered into contract carriage.

Contract Carriers

Contract Carriers. A **contract carrier** is a for-hire carrier that does not hold itself out to serve the general public; instead, it serves a limited number of shippers under specific contractual arrangements. The contract between the shipper and the carrier requires the carrier to provide a specified transportation service at a specified cost. In most instances, contract rates are lower than common carrier rates because the carrier is transporting commodities it prefers to carry for cost and efficiency reasons. An advantage is that transport demand is known in advance.

Exempt Carriers

Exempt Carriers. An **exempt carrier** is a for-hire carrier that transports certain products such as unprocessed agricultural and related products (e.g., farm supplies, livestock, fish, poultry, and agricultural seeds). Carriers of newspapers also are given exempt status. The exempt status was originally established to allow farmers to transport their products using public roads; however, it has been extended to a wider range of products transported by a variety of modes. In addition, local cartage firms operating in a municipality or a "commercial zone" surrounding a municipality are exempt.

Generally, exempt carrier rates are lower than common or contract carriage rates. Because very few commodities are given exempt status, the exempt carrier is not a viable form of transport for most companies. In reality, because transportation deregulation has eliminated pricing regulations, almost all carriers can be considered exempt from pricing restrictions.

Private Carriers

Private Carriers. A **private carrier** is generally not for-hire and is not subject to federal economic regulation. Private carriage means that a firm is providing transportation primarily for its own products. As a result, the company must own or lease the transport equipment and operate its own facilities. From a legal standpoint, the most important factor distinguishing private carriage from for-hire carriers is the restriction that the transportation activity must be incidental to the primary business of the firm.

Private carriage has had an advantage over other carriers because of its flexibility and economy. The major advantages of private carriage have been related to cost and service. With deregulation, common and contract carriage can often provide excellent service levels at reasonable costs. Later in this chapter, we will examine the private versus for-hire transportation decision and discuss more fully the pros and cons of private carriage.

Impact of Deregulation

Economic Deregulation Has Been the Trend

The degree to which the transportation sector has been regulated has varied over the years. Since 1977, the trend in the United States has been toward less economic regulation. Airlines were the first transport mode to be extensively deregulated, with the amendment of the Federal Aviation Act in 1977 followed by the passage of the Airline Deregulation Act of 1978. Railroads and motor carriers were next, with the passage of the Staggers Rail Act and the Motor Carrier Act, both in 1980. In 1984, the Shipping Act partially deregulated ocean cargo carriers. Further deregulation occurred through the Negotiated Rates Act of 1993, Trucking Industry Regulatory Reform Act (TIRRA) of 1994, Federal Aviation Administration Authorization Act of 1994 (including Section 601 that affected motor carriers), and the ICC Termination Act of 1995.

Deregulation of the major transportation modes has had a significant impact on motor, rail, air, and water carriers, and the shippers who use their services. Freight transportation has moved into a new age. The next decade promises to be an exciting time for carriers and shippers. We will begin by examining the motor carrier industry.

Motor Carrier Act of 1980

Motor.   The Motor Carrier Act of 1980 substantially reduced the amount of economic regulation of interstate trucking. The act specifically addressed restrictions on market entry, routing, *intercorporate* hauling, contract carriage, rates, and transportation brokers.

As a result of this legislation, motor carriers have had to be cost-efficient in order to survive. For example, in the less-than truckload (LTL) market between 1980 and 1989, approximately one-half of the largest motor carriers declared bankruptcy. The shakeout of unprofitable and inefficient motor carriers that characterized the first 10 years after deregulation (1980–1989) has passed and, since 1990, the motor carrier industry has exhibited much more stability.

As a by-product of a more competitive environment, there have been significant developments in the offerings of rates and services. Rates for truckload (TL) and LTL have declined since 1984. Energy costs and other factors may cause these rates to increase, but the trend will likely continue downward (or perhaps stabilize) over the long term. Deregulation removed constraints on motor carriers' product, service, and price offerings, and new price and service trade-offs emerged. As mentioned previously, significant additional deregulation has occurred during the 1990s.

Let's look more closely at this legislation.

Economic Deregulation in the 1990s

• **Negotiated Rates Act of 1993.** It is common practice for carriers and shippers to negotiate rates for transportation services. However, when motor carriers fail to properly file the negotiated rate with the ICC (now replaced by the Surface Transportation Board) or when tariff provisions cancel tariff discounts under certain conditions, difficulties occur. The receiver or trustee of a bankrupt motor carrier frequently hires an auditor to search the carrier's records for discrepancies between the rates billed and collected and the rates on file. If the former are lower, the receiver or trustee can file a collection action to recover the difference from the shipper. Usually the shipper will refuse to pay the claim, on the grounds that both the shipper and the carrier had agreed to the lower rate in a valid agreement. The large number of motor carrier bankruptcies in the 1980s brought on numerous collection actions.[41] The law provided mechanisms for the resolution of claims relating to negotiated rates.[42]

• **Trucking Industry Regulatory Reform Act of 1994 (TIRRA).** Carriers no longer must file their rates with the Interstate Commerce Commission or its replacement, the Surface Transportation Board. Only household goods movers must file their rates.

• **Federal Aviation Administration Authorization Act of 1994 (Section 601).** The law preempts state laws and regulations relating to prices, routes, and services of motor carriers. In essence, it eliminated intrastate regulations of transportation.[43]

• **ICC Termination Act of 1995.** Eliminated the Interstate Commerce Commission and placed transportation regulation under the Surface Transportation Board (STB) of the Department of Transportation.

As a result of TIRRA and the ICC Termination Act, the following notable changes in trucking regulation occurred:

The Results of Motor Carrier Deregulation

1. The distinction between common and contract carriers was eliminated. All motor carriers now are allowed to enter into contracts or to provide transportation that is not covered by contracts. The common carrier obligation to provide service on reasonable request remains.

2. All remaining motor carrier tariff filing and rate regulations are repealed, except for those affecting noncontiguous domestic trade and individual household goods movements.

3. The STB has broad exemption authority except with regard to cargo loss and damage, insurance, safety fitness, and antitrust immunity.

4. Responsibility for motor carrier registration is transferred to the DOT. New carriers no longer must seek a certificate of operating authority. Safety fitness and financial responsibility are the only requirements for registering.[44]

As a result of the most recent deregulation of motor carriers, the industry has seen the expansion of intrastate service by LTL carriers, introduction of a variety of new

---

[41]Small Business Legislative Council, *The Business Guide to the Negotiated Rates Act of 1993* (Park Ridge, IL: American Warehouse Association, 1993), p. 2.

[42]For a discussion of this act in some detail, see William J. Augello, *Doing Business under the New Transportation Law: The Negotiated Rates Act of 1993* (Huntington, NY: Transportation Claims and Prevention Council, 1994).

[43]Ray Bohman, "The Brave New World of Tariff-Free Pricing," *Traffic Management* 34, no. 6 (June 1995), pp. 41–45.

[44]Peter Bradley, "The ICC Fades Away, But Regulation Never Dies," *Traffic Management* 35, no. 2 (Feb. 1996), p. 14.

intrastate pricing options, simplification of carrier service offer sheets and related charges, a switch from tariffs to pricing agreements with individual shippers, increased use of "spot pricing" where pricing concessions are given to shippers in special circumstances, more innovative carrier pricing approaches, and increased offerings of new carrier services.

Rail.   Deregulation has had a significant impact on the railroads. Between 1975 and 1987, the number of railroad companies with operating revenues over $50 million (called Class I railroads) increased the ton-miles of freight by one-third. During the same period, track miles declined by 30 percent, freight cars by 25 percent, locomotives by 29 percent, and the number of railroad employees by 49 percent.[45]

Because of their increased rate flexibility and ability to enter into long-term contracts with shippers, railroads have offered a variety of cost-service packages, greatly increasing their customer focus.[46] Most rail rates are negotiated and the number of rail-shipper contracts is increasing, so that contract carriage is the dominant method of shipping products by rail.

The Trend Toward Megacarriers

Since 1980, the trend has been toward large regional railroads, or megacarriers. The largest U.S. railroads (Burlington Northern/Santa Fe Railway Co., CSX Transportation, Norfolk Southern, Union Pacific/Southern Pacific) transport the bulk of all rail shipments.[47] Mergers have allowed significant economies of scale as well as the ability to provide single-line rates between many origin-destination pairs.

Specific deregulation of the rail industry includes the Staggers Rail Act and the ICC Termination Act.

• **Staggers Rail Act of 1980.** Removed much of the federal regulatory agency control over rail rates. The Interstate Commerce Commission has since been replaced by the Surface Transportation Board. The act established a zone of rate flexibility for carriers and reduced the importance of rate bureaus. Authorized long-term railroad contracts between shippers and carriers.

• **ICC Termination Act of 1995.** Eliminated the Interstate Commerce Commission and placed transportation regulation under the Surface Transportation Board (STB) of the Department of Transportation (DOT). Notable elements of the law include:

1. Rail mergers will be reviewed by the STB, which has a 15-month time limit to do so.

2. Eliminated tariff filing and most contract filing for railroads, except for agricultural products. Carriers are required to give 20 days' advance notice of rate increases or changes in service terms.[48]

---

[45]"The Staggers Rail Act: Why It Was Passed . . . What It Has Accomplished," Association of American Railroads Publication No. AAR6-040389 (1989), p. 8.

[46]Lewis M. Schneider, "New Era in Transportation Strategy," *Harvard Business Review,* 63, no. 2 (Mar.–Apr. 1985), p. 122.

[47]Kurt Hoffman, "Wild and Woolly," *Distribution* 95, no. 8 (July 1996), pp. 44–48.

[48]Bradley, "The ICC Fades Away," p. 14.

Air.   With the amending of the Federal Aviation Act in 1977, followed by the passage of the Airline Deregulation Act of 1978, the airline industry became the first transport mode to be substantially deregulated in the United States. For the most part, the impact of deregulation on air carriers (including passengers and freight) has been mixed. Operating profits of the airline industry have been erratic.[49] The industry's unstable financial performance has been due in part to competitive pressures, general economic conditions, industry pricing practices, fluctuations in the cost of jet fuel, and equipment updating. However, deregulation itself has had a significant effect on the airline industry.

The major airline deregulation can be summarized as follows:

• **Amendment of the Federal Aviation Act in 1977.** Removed federal rate and operating authority regulations from all-cargo aircraft operations, including all-cargo airlines, FedEx, and any all-cargo operation of regularly scheduled airlines. Size restrictions on all-cargo aircraft were eliminated.

• **Airline Deregulation Act of 1978.** Deregulated the airline passenger industry, which in turn affected the freight transportation operations of scheduled airlines. The primary impacts were on passenger traffic with secondary impacts on freight traffic. All market entry and rate controls were eliminated.

• **Federal Aviation Administration Authorization Act of 1994.** Exempts air intermodal carriers from economic regulation by the individual states.

Water.   The final mode of transportation to be deregulated was the maritime shipping industry. The Shipping Act of 1984 was the principal vehicle for changing the regulatory environment in which ocean carriers operated. Ocean common carriers, or *liners,* are regulated by the Federal Maritime Commission.

• **Shipping Act of 1984.** Partially deregulated the ocean transport industry. Allowed carriers to pool or apportion traffic, allot ports and regulated sailings, publish port-to-port or point-to-point rates, and enter into confidential service contracts with shippers. Allowed shippers to form nonprofit groups to obtain volume rates.

Shipping Conferences

Ocean carriers have traditionally formed groups called **conferences** for the purpose of establishing rates, deciding which ports to serve, agreeing upon the pooling or consolidating of cargo, and allocating revenues among participating carriers. Conferences were originally given limited antitrust immunity under the Shipping Act of 1916; the Shipping Act of 1984 gave them greater immunity.

Point-to-Point Rates

Liner rates can be adjusted up or down to meet shipper needs and market conditions without undue difficulty. The ability to publish point-to-point rates has facilitated intermodal movements, such as landbridge (ocean-land-ocean movement), microbridge, (inland location-seaport-ocean movement), and minilandbridge (ocean via ship—land via rail movement). As in the rail and trucking industries, contract carriage in the ocean transport sector will continue to increase in the future.

In many instances, shippers have benefited from the economic deregulation of motor, rail, air, and ocean cargo carriers. Thus, the trend for the foreseeable future is likely to be

---

[49]"Uncertain Weather Patterns Ahead," *Distribution* 93, no. 6 (July 1994), pp. 49–54.

further deregulation of the transportation sector. While any projections of future deregulation would be imprecise, it is certain that shippers and carriers will work together more closely than ever before.

Carrier Pricing and Related Issues

Several pricing issues are important in transportation. They involve how rates are developed in general and how specific rates are determined by a carrier to transport a shipment between an origin and destination point. Rates and rate determination will be overviewed, followed by a description of the issues relating to the specific rates carriers charge. The most significant approaches **free-on-board (FOB)** pricing. Also relevant are the availability of quantity discounts and allowances provided to the buyer by the carrier or shipper.

FOB or "Free on Board"

Rates and Rate Determination

Cost-of-Service Pricing

Two forms or methods of transportation pricing can be utilized: cost of service and value of service. **Cost-of-service pricing** establishes transportation rates at levels that cover a carrier's fixed and variable costs, plus allowance for some profit. Transportation costs can vary within the cost-of-service pricing approach because of two major factors: distance and volume. Naturally, this approach is appealing because it establishes the lower limit of rates. However, it has some inherent difficulties.

First, a carrier must be able to identify its fixed and variable costs. This involves a recognition of the relevant cost components and an ability to measure these costs accurately. Many carrier firms are unable to measure costs precisely. Second, this approach requires that fixed costs be allocated to each freight movement (shipment). As the number of shipments increase, the fixed costs are spread over a larger number of movements, and thus the fixed cost per unit becomes smaller. As the number of shipments decreases, the fixed cost per unit becomes larger. As a result, the allocation of fixed costs changes the price based on the volume of shipments. Clearly, this method creates problems.

Value-of-Service Pricing

A second method of transportation pricing is **value-of-service pricing.** This approach is based on charging what the market will bear; and is based on the demand for transportation services and the competitive situation. This approach establishes the upper limit on rates. The rates set will maximize the difference between revenues received and the variable cost incurred for carrying a shipment. In most instances, competition will determine the price charged.

Line-Haul Rates

Accessorial Charges

Categories of Rates.   There are two types of charges assessed by carriers: **line-haul rates,** which are charged for the movement of goods between two points that are not in the same local pickup and delivery area, and **accessorial charges,** which cover all other payments made to carriers for transporting, handling, or servicing a shipment. Line-haul rates can be grouped into four types: (1) class rates, (2) exception rates, (3) commodity rates, and (4) miscellaneous rates.

Class Rates

Class rates reduce the number of transportation rates required by grouping products into classes for pricing purposes. A product's specific classification is referred to as its class rating. A basic rate would be Class 100, with higher numbers representing more expensive rates and lower numbers less expensive rates. The charge to move a specific product classification between two locations is referred to as the *rate*. By identifying the class rating of a product, the rate per hundredweight (100 pounds) between any two points can be determined.

Exception Rates

Exception rates, or exceptions to the classification, provide the shipper with rates lower than the published class rates. This type of rate was introduced in order to provide a special rate for a specific area, origin-destination, or commodity when competition or volume justified the lower rate. When an exception rate is published, the classification that normally applies is changed.

Commodity Rates

Commodity rates apply when a large quantity of a product is shipped between two locations on a regular basis. These rates are published on a point-to-point basis without regard to product classification.

Contract Rates

Contract rates and freight-all-kinds (FAK) rates include other rates that apply in special circumstances. For example, contract rates are those negotiated between a shipper and carrier. They are formalized through a written contractual agreement between the two parties. These types of rates are increasing in usage because of the growth of contract carriage.

Freight-all-Kinds (FAK) Rates

Freight-all-kinds (FAK) rates have developed in recent years and apply to shipments instead of products. They tend to be based on the costs of providing the transportation service; the products shipped can be of any type. The carrier provides the shipper with a rate per shipment based on the weight of the products being shipped. FAK rates have become very popular with companies such as wholesalers and manufacturers that ship a variety of products to retail customers on a regular basis.

Since deregulation, with carriers no longer having to file their rates with rate bureaus[50] and other entities, carriers have been developing numerous contracts with shippers as well as discounting many rates. These actions have tended to blur the distinctions between the various rate classifications.

FOB Pricing

The FOB pricing terms that are offered by sellers to buyers have a significant impact on logistics generally and transportation specifically. For example, if a seller quotes a delivered price to the buyer's retail store location, the total price includes not only the cost of the product, but the cost of moving the product to the retail store. This rather simple illustration highlights a number of important considerations for the buyer or consignee (i.e., the recipient of the product being distributed).

---

[50]Prior to 1980, rate bureaus established and published the overwhelming number of common carrier rates for motor, rail, and domestic water carriers. Since deregulation of the major transport modes, most rates have been established or changed by individual carriers and shippers in consort, rather than through rate bureaus. Rate bureaus no longer exercise control over the actual setting of rates.

FIGURE 7–5

Terms of sale and corresponding buyer and seller responsibilities

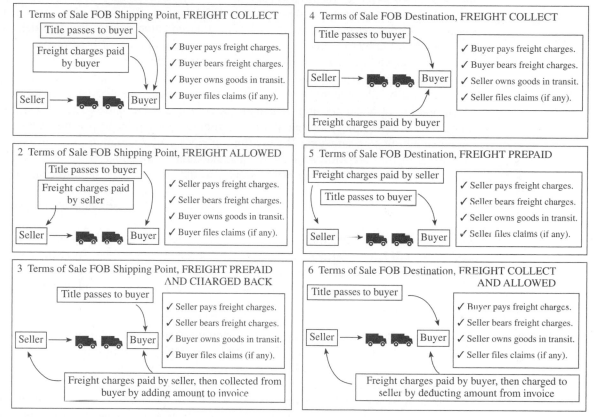

Source: Harold Fearon, Donald Dobler, and Ken Killen, *The Purchasing Handbook,* National Association of Purchasing Management, 1993, McGraw-Hill.

Why FOB Terms are Important

1. The buyer knows the final delivered price prior to the purchase.

2. The buyer does not have to manage the transportation activity involved in getting the product from the seller's location to the buyer's.

3. The buyer typically will not control the transportation decision, so it is possible that a mode or carrier could be selected by the seller that might be disadvantageous to the buyer (e.g., due to poor service levels provided by the mode/carrier).

While it is easier from a management perspective to purchase products FOB destination, the lack of control of the transportation function can cause problems for the purchaser (e.g., the carrier selected by the shipper might provide poor service in your area, or only make deliveries at certain times which may not correspond to your ideal time to receive shipments). Buyers should always know the specifics about all shipments that include delivery to ensure that best decisions are being made on their behalf.

Figure 7–5 provides a simple overview of the major types of FOB pricing methods and their implications for buyers and sellers.

Delivered Pricing

In a **delivered pricing system,** buyers are given a price that includes delivery of the product. As mentioned in the discussion of FOB pricing, this form of pricing is, in essence, FOB destination. The seller secures the transportation mode/carrier and delivers the product to the buyer. This option can be advantageous to one or both parties of the transaction, depending on which variation of delivered pricing is used by the seller.

For example, assume that two manufacturers compete for business in a market area. Manufacturer A is located in the market area, sells its product for $2.50 a unit, and earns a contribution of $0.50 per unit. If manufacturer B incurs the same costs exclusive of transportation costs, but is located 400 miles from the market, $0.50 per unit represents the maximum that manufacturer B can afford to pay for transportation to the market. If two forms of transportation available to manufacturer B are equal in terms of performance characteristics, the higher-priced service would have to meet the lower rate to be competitive.

Variations include zone pricing, basing point pricing, and uniform delivered pricing.

Zone Pricing

Zone Pricing. **Zone pricing** is a method that categorizes geographic areas into zones. Each zone will have a particular delivery cost associated with it. The closer the zone to the seller, the lower the delivery cost; the farther away, the higher the delivery charge. Depending upon the buyer's location in a particular zone, some buyers will be paying more for delivery on a per mile basis than others.

Basing-Point Pricing

Basing-Point Pricing. In a **basing-point pricing** system, the seller selects one or more locations that serve as points of origin. Depending on which point of origin is selected by the seller, the buyer will pay delivery costs from that point to the buyer's location. The seller will often use a manufacturing plant, distribution center, port, free trade zone, and so forth as a basing point. This method can be good or bad for the buyer, depending on which basing point is selected. For example, a manufacturer may have a distribution center located in the same state as the buyer, but use the location of the corporate office located in another state as the basing point. The product may or may not actually originate at the basing-point location.

Quantity Discounts

Cumulative versus Noncumulative Quantity Discounts

Quantity discounts can be cumulative or noncumulative. **Cumulative quantity discounts** provide price reductions to the buyer based on the amount of purchases over some prescribed period of time. **Noncumulative quantity discounts** are applied to each order and do not accumulate over a time period.

From a transportation perspective, buyers purchasing products under a cumulative quantity discount system can order smaller quantities, paying the higher transportation costs for smaller shipments, and still gain a cost advantage (i.e., the additional cost of transportation is less than the cost savings resulting from the quantity discount).

On the other hand, if a noncumulative quantity discount is applied, buyers must purchase sufficient quantities in order to obtain truckload (TL) or carload (CL) rates for larger shipments. While transportation costs on a per item or per pound basis will be less for larger shipments, buyers will incur additional costs (e.g., warehousing and inventory carrying costs), which must be considered when they place larger, but fewer, orders with sellers. These issues will be addressed in later chapters.

In today's business environment, managers must be very responsive to customer demand in the marketplace. The trend is for companies to purchase smaller quantities more often and as quickly as possible, so it is more advantageous for buyers to have a cumulative quantity discount applied.

Allowances

Sometimes, sellers will provide price reductions to buyers that perform some of the delivery function. For example, when using a delivered pricing system, the seller assumes all costs of delivery and adds those costs to the price of the product. If the buyer is willing to assume some of the delivery functions, the seller will often provide some **allowances,** or price reductions, to the buyer.

The most common allowances are provided for customer pickup of the product or unloading of the carrier vehicle upon delivery at the customer's location. These services cost the seller money and if the buyer is willing to perform these functions, the seller can provide a price concession.

The important element in making the right decisions about taking advantage of allowances is to know the costs associated with each delivery function. The allowance should be equal to, or greater than, the costs to the buyer for assuming these responsibilities.

Pricing and Negotiation

Shippers are concentrating more business with fewer carriers[51] and placing greater emphasis on negotiated pricing.[52] The goal of the negotiation process is to develop an agreement that is mutually beneficial, recognizes the needs of the parties involved, and motivates them to perform. Because most negotiations are based on cost-of-service pricing, carriers should have precise measures of their costs. Only when all costs are considered can carriers and shippers work together to reduce the carriers' cost base.

US West and CF MotorFreight Form an Alliance

US West has been very aggressive in developing an alliance with CF MotorFreight, its national LTL carrier. It began by looking at its total cost of doing business with carriers, going beyond simply transportation price. The goal of the relationship is to reduce

---

[51]For a discussion of this trend and other issues relating transportation to customer service, see Bernard J. La Londe, Martha C. Cooper, and Thomas G. Noordewier, *Customer Service: A Management Perspective* (Oak Brook, IL: Council of Logistics Management, 1988).

[52]For a managerial discussion of carrier-shipper negotiation issues, see Joseph V. Barks, "Who's Getting a Bad Deal?" *Distribution* 93, no. 3 (Mar. 1994), pp. 34–38; Jack Barry, "Advanced Negotiating: Preparation Is the Key," *Distribution* 87, no. 6 (June 1988), pp. 54–56; Roger J. Bowman, "Rick and Reward: How Shippers Are Negotiating the Best Possible Transportation Deals in a Time of Radical Change," *Distribution* 95, no. 4 (Apr. 1996), pp. 42–49; and Joseph Cavinato, "Tips for Negotiating Rates," *Distribution* 90, no. 2 (Feb. 1991), pp. 66–68.

the total cost of doing business. US West and CF work together to take costs out of the supply chain. Since the beginning of the relationship in August 1993, US West's base transportation rate has gone down 15 percent.[53] For an additional example, see the Creative Solutions box at the end of this chapter.

Logistics and Traffic Management

The strategies of carriers and shippers are inextricably interrelated. Transportation is an integral component of logistics strategy. Carriers must understand the role of transportation in a firm's overall logistics system, and firms must understand how carriers aid them in satisfying customer needs at a profit.

Some of the logistics issues relating to transportation will be described in the following section. The administration of transportation activities is referred to as **traffic management** and includes major issues such as inbound and outbound transportation, carrier-shipper contracts, strategic partnerships and alliances, private carriage/leasing, mode/carrier selection, routing and scheduling, service offerings, and computer technology.

Inbound and Outbound Transportation

Transportation Impacts Customer Service Levels and Costs

Transportation is one of the most significant areas of logistics management because of its impact on customer service levels and the firm's cost structure. Inbound and outbound transportation costs can account for as much as 10 percent, 20 percent, or more of the product's price. Firms in medium- and high-cost business sectors will be especially conscious of the transportation activity. Effective traffic management can achieve significant improvements in profitability.[54]

To be effective, the traffic function must interface with other departments within and outside of the logistics area. Areas of interface include accounting (freight bills); engineering (packaging, transportation equipment); legal (warehouse and carrier contracts); manufacturing (just-in-time deliveries); purchasing (expediting, supplier selection); marketing/sales (customer service standards); receiving (claims, documentation); and warehousing (equipment supply, scheduling).

The transportation executive has many and varied duties, including selecting the best modes of transportation, choosing specific carriers, routing and scheduling of company-owned transport equipment, consolidation of shipments, filing claims with carriers, and negotiating with carriers.

The carrier-shipper relationship is an important one; it directly affects the transportation executive's ability to manage successfully.

---

[53]Peter A. Buxbaum, "Winning Together," *Transportation and Distribution* 36, no. 4 (Apr. 1995), pp. 47–50.

[54]James Aaron Cooke, "Should You Control Your Inbound?" *Traffic Management* 32, no. 2 (Feb. 1993), pp. 30–33.

Carrier-Shipper Contracts

In 1996, 3M Company awarded CF MotorFreight a three-year contract as its primary LTL carrier for inbound and outbound shipments for all of its U.S. locations. Approximately 200 million pounds of freight will be handled by CF MotorFreight.[55]

Advantages of Carrier-Shipper Contracts

The advantages of contracting are numerous. Contracts permit the shipper to exercise greater control over the transportation activity, typically at a lower cost. They assure predictability and guard against fluctuation in rates. In addition, contracting provides the shipper with service level guarantees and allows the shipper to use transportation to gain a competitive advantage.

Carrier-shipper contracts can prove valuable to both parties, but it is important that the contract include all of the relevant elements that apply to the shipping agreement. Because the transportation contract is a legal document and therefore binding, it should not be entered into casually. The exact format for each carrier-shipper contract will vary, depending on factors such as: the mode/carrier involved, the type of shipping firm, the products to be transported, and the level of competition.[56]

Carrier–Shipper Alliances

An effective logistics network requires a cooperative relationship between shippers and carriers on both a strategic and an operational level. When this cooperation takes place, the shipper and carrier may become part of a partnership or alliance.[57] Companies that have implemented the concept include Black and Decker, GTE, McKesson, Procter & Gamble, Xerox, and 3M.

In many instances, shippers and carriers do not act in concert because of differences in perceptions, practice, or philosophy. Sometimes the notion that "we never did it that way before" impedes cooperation and synergism. Such differences result in inefficiencies in the transportation system and conflicts between shippers and carriers.

In essence, a successful alliance is more than simply a set of plans, programs, and methods. Like the marketing concept and like customer service, a willingness to form a partnership is a philosophy that permeates the entire organization. It is a way of life that becomes a portion of the way a firm conducts its business.

---

[55]"Doing Business," *Logistics Management* 35, no. 6 (June 1996), p. 23.

[56]A. T. Kearney, Inc., *A Shipper's Approach to Contract Logistics,* no. 44 (Chicago: A. T. Kearney, 1995); Charles D. Braunschweig, Michael R. Crum, and Benjamin J. Allen, "Evolution of Motor Carrier Contracting," *Transportation Quarterly* 49, no. 2 (Spring 1995), pp. 99–115; and Helen L. Richardson, "Contracts Build Relationships," *Transportation and Distribution* 34, no. 11 (Nov. 1993), pp. 53–56.

[57]Edward J. Marien, "Structuring the Shipper/Carrier Relationship," *Transportation and Distribution* 36, no. 7 (July 1995), pp. 60–62; Steven E. Leahy, Paul R. Murphy, and Richard F. Poist, "Determinants of Successful Logistical Relationships: A Third-Party Provider Perspective," *Transportation Journal* 35, no. 2 (Winter 1995), pp. 5–13; and David L. Sparkman, "Promises Clash with Reality in Logistics Partnerships," *Transport Topics,* no. 3140 (Oct. 9, 1995), pp. 5–8.

Private Carriage

A private carrier is any transportation entity that moves products for the manufacturing or merchandising firm that owns it. While the equipment may transport products of other firms in some cases, private carriers were established primarily to haul the products of their own companies. Each year, private fleets handle more than half of intercity motor freight tonnage in manufactured goods. Private fleet volume is expected to grow by nearly 10 percent by the year 2005.[58]

Private carriage should not be viewed strictly as a transportation decision; it also is a financial decision. There are two stages in evaluating the financial considerations of private carriage. The first involves a comparison of current cost and service data of the firm's for-hire carriers with that of a private operation. The second is to devise a plan of implementation and procedure for system control.

The feasibility study should begin with an evaluation of the current transportation situation, along with corporate objectives regarding potential future market expansion. Objectives should include a statement outlining past, current, and desired service levels, as well as a consideration of the business environment, including legal restrictions and the general economic trends.

A Cost-Benefit Analysis Is Necessary to Evaluate the Private Carriage Option

A firm must perform a cost-benefit analysis to determine whether it should use private carriage. Any financial analysis should consider the time value of money. The company must calculate the net cash inflows (cash inflows minus cash outflows) for the life of the investment decision and discount them, using the company's minimum acceptable rate of return on new investments. The sum of these discounted cash flows must be compared with the initial capital requirement to determine if the investment is financially sound.

If the company makes the decision to engage in private carriage, its next step is to devise a plan of implementation and a procedure for system control. Implementation begins with a review of the structure of the organization or group responsible for operating the private fleet. Management assigns the activities to be performed to groups or individuals, and formulates a timetable for phasing in the project. Because of the risk involved, most firms begin with a low level of activity, followed by intermediate reviews of results and subsequent modification of the plan. The process is repeated until the firm achieves full implementation.

Control of private carriage should emphasize the measurement of performance against standards, with the ability to identify specific problem areas. If management desires to use a total cost approach in order to charge cost against the product and customer, it can calculate a cost per mile, identifying the fixed costs associated with distribution of the product and then adding the variable costs per mile. This information may be useful to compare budgeted with actual expenditures, or to compare the figures for the private fleet operation with those of common or contract carriers.

The future of private trucking can hold tremendous promise for shippers that are able to take advantage of its benefits.[59] For others, for-hire carriers offer the most opportunities. The most likely scenario is that shippers will utilize a mixture of private and for-hire options.

---

[58]"Management Update," *Logistics Management* 35, no. 6 (June 1996), pp. 3, 5.

[59]See Terence A. Brown and Janet Greenlee, "Private Trucking after Deregulation: Managers' Perceptions," *Transportation Journal* 35, no. 1 (Fall 1995), pp. 5–14.

Mode/Carrier Selection Decision Process

Economic and resource constraints, competitive pressures, and customer requirements mandate that firms make the most efficient and productive mode/carrier choice decisions possible. Because transportation affects customer service, time-in-transit, consistency of service, inventories, packaging, warehousing, energy consumption, pollution caused by transportation, and other factors, traffic managers must develop the best possible mode/carrier strategies.

Four separate and distinct decision stages occur in the mode/carrier selection decision: (1) problem recognition, (2) search process, (3) choice process, and (4) postchoice evaluation.

Problem Recognition

Problem Recognition. The **problem recognition** stage of the mode/carrier choice process is triggered by a variety of factors, such as customer requirements, dissatisfaction with an existing mode, and changes in the distribution patterns of a firm. Typically, the most significant factors are related to service. In circumstances where the customer does not specify the transport mode, a search is undertaken for feasible alternatives.

Search Process

Search Process. In the **search process,** transportation executives scan a variety of information sources to aid them in making optimal mode/carrier decisions. Possible sources include past experience, carrier sales calls, company shipping records, and customers of the firm. Once the desired information is gathered, the decision becomes one of using the information obtained to select the optimal mode or carrier alternative.

Choice Process

Choice Process. The **choice process** involves the selection of an option from the several modes and carriers available. Using information previously gathered in the selection process, the transportation executive determines which of the available options best meets the firm's customer service requirements at an acceptable cost. Generally, service-related factors are the major determinants of mode/carrier choice. For example, Table 7–4 identifies a number of selection criteria used in the evaluation of motor carriers.

There are similarities across modes in terms of the most important attributes used to select and evaluate carriers. Attributes such as on-time pickups and deliveries, prompt response to customer inquires, consistent transit times, and competitive rates seem to be important irrespective of the mode or carrier being considered.[60]

The transportation executive selects the mode or carrier that best satisfies the decision criteria, and the shipment is sent by that option. When a similar decision may arise in the future, such as a repeat order from a customer, management may establish an order routine, so that the same choice process will not have to be repeated. Order routines eliminate the inefficiencies associated with making the same decision repeatedly.

---

[60]For a discussion of factors used in selecting other transportation modes and related transportation services, see Edward A. Morash and Roger J. Calantone, "Rail Selection, Service Quality, and Innovation," *Journal of the Transportation Research Forum* 32, no. 1 (1991), pp. 205–15; Paul R. Murphy and James M. Daley, "A Comparative Analysis of Port Selection Factors," *Transportation Journal* 34, no. 1 (Fall 1994), pp. 15–21; Paul R. Murphy and Patricia K. Hall, "The Relative Importance of Cost and Service in Freight Transportation Choice before and after Deregulation: An Update," *Transportation Journal* 35, no. 1 (Fall 1995), pp. 30–38; and "What Do Air Shippers Want?" *Traffic Management* 31, no. 7 (July 1992), pp. 65–67.

TABLE 7–4   **The Most Important Attributes Considered in the Selection and Evaluation of LTL Motor Carriers**

Attribute Description	Importance Mean*
Honesty of dispatch personnel	6.5
On-time pickups	6.5
On-time deliveries	6.5
Competitive rates	6.5
Accurate billing	6.4
Assistance from carrier in handling loss and damage claims	6.4
Prompt action on complaints related to carrier service	6.4
Honesty of drivers	6.4
Prompt response to claims	6.4
Carrier's general attitude toward problems and complaints	6.3
Prompt availability of status information on delivery	6.3
Consistent (reliable) transit times	6.3

*Respondents were asked to indicate on a seven-point scale how important the attribute was in selecting a LTL motor carrier. The scale ranged from 1 (not important) to 7 (very important).

Source: Adapted from Douglas M. Lambert, M. Christine Lewis, and James R. Stock, "How Shippers Select and Evaluate General Commodities LTL Motor Carriers," *Journal of Business Logistics* 14, no. 1 (1993), p. 135.

Postchoice Evaluation

Postchoice Evaluation.   Once management has made its choice of mode or carrier, it must institute some evaluation procedure to determine the performance level of the mode/carrier. Depending on the individual firm, the **postchoice evaluation** process may be extremely detailed or there may be no evaluation at all. For the majority of firms, the degree of postchoice evaluation lies somewhere between the two extremes. It is rare that a company does not at least respond to customer complaints about its carriers, and this is one form of postchoice evaluation. Many firms use other techniques, such as cost studies, audits, and reviews of on-time pickups and delivery performance. Some will statistically analyze the quality of carrier service attributes, such as on-time performance and loss-damage ratios.

Mode and carrier selection is becoming much more important as shippers reduce the number of carriers with whom they do business and develop core carriers. By leveraging freight volumes to get bigger discounts and higher levels of service, shippers are able to reduce their transportation costs. At the same time, carriers benefit by having to deal with fewer shippers, each shipping larger volumes of product consistently over longer periods of time.

Carrier Selection at Square D

Square D [an electrical equipment manufacturer] reports that [it] has successfully reduced the number of carriers it uses. Five years ago, as many as 1,500 carriers were involved in moving company goods. Today, 55 handle 98 percent of the freight. The savings also have been substantial . . . The program saved $3.5 million in transportation costs when first implemented three years ago. Today, the company's annual transportation costs have stabilized at a three-year-old level, while the volume of freight moved steadily increases.[61]

---

[61]Mitchell E. MacDonald, "Why Shippers Are Cutting Carriers," *Traffic Management* 29, no. 4 (Apr. 1990), p. 49.

Routing and Scheduling

Considering the significant capital investments in equipment and facilities, along with operating expenses, carriers recognize the importance of good routing and scheduling in achieving acceptable levels of company profit and customer service. In recent years, these areas have become much more significant because of increased competition and deregulation, and a number of economic factors (e.g., fuel, labor, and equipment).

Routing and Scheduling Benefits to Carriers

Carriers can achieve sizable benefits by optimizing their routing and scheduling activities. For example, by prescheduling shipments into specific market areas while simultaneously reducing the frequency of delivery, a vehicle's load factor can be increased. The result is a cost savings to the carrier. A reduction in the frequency of pickups and deliveries can result in a reduced level of transportation necessary to deliver the same amount of goods. Thus, the cost of transportation is reduced and productivity is increased.[62]

Other examples include the use of fixed routes instead of variable routes for some shipments, and changing customer delivery hours. If customers can accept shipments at off-peak hours, the carrier will have a larger delivery time window and thus can improve vehicle utilization and reduce equipment cost on a per delivery basis.[63]

In general, the benefits to a carrier of improved routing and scheduling include greater vehicle utilization, higher levels of customer service, lower transportation costs, reduced capital investment in equipment, and better management decision making.

Routing and Scheduling Benefits to Shippers

For the shipper, cost and service improvements can result from better routing and scheduling. For example, Baskin-Robbins, an ice-cream maker with 2,500 stores in the United States, computerized its fleet routing and scheduling, resulting in a 10 percent reduction in truck fleet miles, which translated into an annual cost savings of $180,000.[64]

Service Offerings

In the traditional areas of service—pickup and delivery, claims, equipment availability, time-in-transit, and consistency of service—competitive pressures from the marketplace have worked to improve service levels. Carriers have had to develop customer service packages that meet the needs of increasingly demanding customers. Such improvements have benefited shippers and have required carriers to maximize their efficiency and productivity in order to remain profitable.

Customer Service at MollerMaersk Line and Sea-Land Service

Examples of carriers providing higher levels of traditional transportation services can be found in all modes. In 1991 the international ocean marine carriers A. P. Moller-Maersk Line and Sea-Land Service (a division of CSX) began a vessel-sharing plan in order to improve service levels. The plan reduced the number of ships deployed and increased the number of transpacific sailings to five per week. At the same time, Maersk and Sea-Land continued to compete against each other.[65]

[62]A. T. Kearney, Inc., *Measuring and Improving Productivity in Physical Distribution Management* (Chicago: National Council of Physical Distribution Management, 1984), pp. 176, 178.

[63]Ibid., p. 182.

[64]"Routing Software Prevents Scheduling Meltdown," *Logistics Management* 35, no. 6 (June 1996), p. 85-S.

[65]Elizabeth Canna, "The Maersk/Sea-Land Deal," *American Shipper* 33, no. 5 (May 1991), p. 43.

CSX Becomes a Logistics Service Provider

Carriers have begun to expand into nontraditional areas such as warehousing, logistics consulting, import-export operations, and facility location analysis. In effect, the transportation carrier has become a logistics service firm. For example, CSX Corporation, with $10.5 billion in annual revenues, offers one-stop shipping that includes trains, trucks, barges, ocean containers, intermodal services, and distribution warehouses. The operating companies of CSX include CSX Transportation (rail), Sea-Land Service (ocean), American Commercial Lines (barge), CSX Intermodal (intermodal), and Customize Transportation (contract logistics).[66]

The trend will continue as carriers expand their traditional and nontraditional service offerings. In addition, competitive pressures will force overall carrier service levels to improve.

Computer Technology

The use of computers has become widespread in logistics, especially in the area of traffic management.[67] For example:

Examples of Computerization

- Con-Way Transportation services uses 12-inch optical storage disks, each of which will store about 60,000 documents. These disks are housed on-line, allowing instant retrieval of documents up to six months old.[68]
- Conrail provides free computer software and training to help small railroads with which it interchanges traffic to establish electronic data interchange (EDI) systems.[69]
- *Fortune* magazine reported that "new cellular technology now allows vehicles equipped with radio modems and a cellular jack in a truck to transmit data much like a regular telephone jack in an office. Drivers simply plug a laptop computer into the modem and send data."[70]
- Glass manufacturer Pittsburgh Plate Glass (PPG) has computerized its carrier management activities to the extent that it has been able to reduce its transportation carriers from 252 to a core group of 42 which handle an average of 8,000 to 9,000 shipments a month, at a lower overall cost and with higher service levels.[71]
- CF MotorFreight's error rate in billing went from 4.0 percent to 1.1 percent since implementing EDI.[72]

Generally, computerized transportation activities can be categorized into four groups: transportation analysis, traffic routing and scheduling, freight rate maintenance and auditing, and vehicle maintenance.

---

[66]CSX Corporation, *1995 Annual Report,* pp. 1–16.

[67]For an overview of the types of computer hardware and software and how they are used by companies in traffic management activities, see "Caution! Computers at Work," *Traffic Management* 34, no. 9 (Sept. 1995), pp. 48–49.

[68]Lisa H. Harrington, "Motor Carrier Productivity: Improvements Make a Difference," *Transportation and Distribution* 35, no. 9 (Sept. 1994), pp. 30–34.

[69]"Conrail Giving Software to Small Railroads," *On Track* 4, no. 14 (July 17–31, 1990), p. 2.

[70]Lisa H. Harrington, "The Future of Truck Transportation," *Fortune,* Apr. 3, 1995, special advertising supplement.

[71]Mitchell E. MacDonald, "A High-Tech Formula for Truckload Management," *Traffic Management* 33, no. 5 (May 1994), p. 38.

[72]Buxbaum, "Winning Together," p. 50.

Four Groups of Computerized Transportation Activities

Transportation Analysis.   This software allows management to monitor costs and service by providing historical reporting of key performance indicators such as carrier performance, shipping modes, traffic lane utilization, premium freight usage, and backhauls.

Traffic Routing and Scheduling.   Software in this area provide features such as the sequence and timing of vehicle stops, route determination, shipping paperwork preparation, and vehicle availability.

Freight Rate Maintenance and Auditing.   These software systems maintain a database of freight rates used to rate shipments or to perform freight bill auditing. They compare actual freight bills with charges computed from the lowest applicable rates in the database. The systems can then pay, authorize payment, or report on exceptions.

Vehicle Maintenance.   Features commonly provided by these packages include vehicle maintenance scheduling and reporting.[73]

The degree and scope of computer usage will vary from firm to firm and by transportation activity. Despite these variations, it is clear that the computer has had a significant impact on traffic management and will have an even greater impact in the future. The Technology box describes how several transportation companies are using the World Wide Web.

Technology

More Traffic Jumps on the Web

More transportation carriers are developing or expanding their sites on the World Wide Web or other Internet sites. Some recent developments in the industry include:

• *Consolidated Freightways* (CF) has developed six Web sites, including one tailored to customers and investors. At this site, **http://www.cnf.com**, CF provides a history of the company and financial information such as stock price and earnings. At another site, **http://www/freight.com**, information is provided to the media.

• *Emery Worldwide* has a home page, **http://www.emery-world.com**, which provides information on the firm's products, services, and technology.

• *Burlington Air Express,* with its Web site at **http://www.bax-world.com**, gives information on freight status, carrier locations, global logistics, special services, pricing and timetables. It also allows customers to communicate with the company by means of E-mail.

• *Roadway Express* provides information on Roadway products and services, press releases, and financial data. A "Guestbook" page allows visitors to leave comments at its Web site, **http://www.roadway.com**.

Source: "More Traffic Jumps on the Web," *Logistics Management* 35, no. 6 (June 1996), p. 25.

---

[73]Richard C. Haverly and James F. Whelan, *Logistics Software* (New York: Andersen Consulting, 1996), p. 9.

Transportation Productivity Issues

Both shippers and carriers are concerned with improving transportation productivity. Such improvements are absolutely vital to the success of the logistics system.[74]

Areas in which transportation productivity can be improved can be categorized into three groups:

Three Types of Productivity Improvements

1. Improvements in the transportation system's design and its methods, equipment, and procedures.
2. Improvements in the utilization of labor and equipment.
3. Improvements in the performance of labor and equipment.[75]

Each of the following groups offer examples of possibilities for productivity improvement:

- Group 1—inbound consolidation, company operates over-the-road trucking, local pickup and delivery operations, and purchases for-hire transportation.
- Group 2—breakbulk operations, backhaul use of fleet, routing and scheduling systems, tracing and monitoring systems, customer delivery hours, shipment consolidation and pooling, and driver utilization.
- Group 3—standards for driver activity, first-line management improvements, establishment of a transportation database, incentive compensation to encourage higher productivity and safety, and programs to increase fuel efficiency.[76]

From a shipper's perspective, some of the most common types of data that measure carrier effectiveness and efficiency include claims and damage ratios, transit time variability, on-time pickup and delivery percentages, cost per ton-mile, billing accuracy, and customer complaint frequency. In many firms, the data do not appear on a formal report, and carrier performance is therefore examined informally.

Carriers employ similar measures, although they view them from the perspective of a provider rather than a receiver of services. Some carriers measure dollar contributions by traffic lane, shipper, salesperson, or terminal. Those measures are used primarily for internal performance evaluations, but they may be provided to customers in special situations such as rate negotiations or partnership arrangements. The exact format for data collection is not as important as the need to have the information available in some form.

---

[74]For examples of several transportation productivity improvements, see Lisa H. Harrington, "Motor Carrier Productivity: Improvements Make a Difference," *Transportation and Distribution* 35, no. 9 (Sept. 1994), pp. 30–34.

[75]A. T. Kearney, Inc., *Measuring and Improving Productivity,* p. 174.

[76]Ibid., pp. 174–85.

Creative Solutions

Goodyear Tire & Rubber Company Takes a New Approach to Carrier Productivity

Before 1992, Goodyear took a hard-line approach to negotiating with transportation providers, focusing only on rates. The negotiation process was really an "annual rate battle" that consumed a great deal of time in terms of preparation and the actual negotiation process. Then Richard Adante, vice president of materials management for Goodyear realized how unproductive this approach was. "We realized there could be strength in sharing information," he says, "and developing a relationship where each party knew more about the other's operation . . . we realized that how we worked impacted their business and cost structure."

Goodyear thus developed the following negotiating strategy:

1. Establish three-year, firm price LTL contracts.
2. Consolidate domestic LTL carriers, giving preferred carriers greater volume.
3. Pursue open-book negotiations with each party, studying the processes of each for ways to reduce total system costs.

While this innovative approach was initially not well received by carriers, Yellow Freight System responded. The two firms established a joint steering committee to reduce costs, agreeing that it would be dissolved after one year if either side was dissatisfied. They worked together to establish key indicators of the success of the relationship. The chosen indicators included:

- Yellow Freight's operating ratio.
- Percent of on-time delivery compared with Yellow Freight's average.
- Average days in transit.
- Transfer data: cost per bill, per cwt.
- Pickup and delivery cost data: per bill, per cwt.

The relationship has progressed very positively. The two-way information sharing and joint management of continuous improvement efforts have created a commitment to the project and the relationship.

Source: Adapted from E. J. Muller, "A New Paradigm for Partnerships," *Distribution,* 93 no. 1 (Jan. 1994), pp. 45–48.

Summary

In this chapter, we examined the role of transportation in logistics. The five basic transport modes were described, including intermodal combinations, third-party providers, and small-package carriers.

Transportation regulation and deregulation issues were briefly presented in order to gain a perspective on today's competitive environment. The regulatory environment is one of open competition, with shippers and carriers having significant freedom to negotiate prices, service levels, and other transportation aspects.

Transportation pricing issues were examined, including rates and rate determination, categories of rates, FOB pricing, delivered pricing, quantity discounts, allowances, and pricing-negotiation issues.

We described transportation management in terms of the importance of the carrier-shipper interface and some of the specific functions of management. Important perspectives included inbound and outbound transportation, carrier-shipper contracts, carrier-shipper alliances, private carriage, mode/carrier selection, routing and scheduling, service offerings, computer technology, and transportation productivity.

Suggested Readings

Buxbaum, Peter A. "Winning Together." *Transportation and Distribution* 36, no. 4 (Apr. 1995), pp. 47–50.

Carter, Joseph L.; Bruce G. Ferrin; and Craig R. Carter. "The Effect of Less-than-Truckload Rates on the Purchase." *Transportation Journal* 34, no. 3 (Spring 1995), pp. 35–47.

Cavinato, Joseph L. *Transportation-Logistics Dictionary,* 3rd ed. Washington, DC: International Thomson Transport Press, 1989.

Cooke, James Aaron. "3PLs Look toward More Realistic Growth." *Distribution,* 35, no. 12 (Dec. 1996), pp. 29–32.

Cook, Peter N. C. "Value-Added Strategies in Marketing." *International Journal of Physical Distribution and Logistics Management* 20, no. 5 (1990), pp. 20–24.

Corbett, Michael F. "Outsourcing: How Industry Leaders Are Reshaping the American Corporation." *Fortune,* Oct. 16, 1995, Special Advertising Supplement.

Daugherty, Patricia J., and Michael S. Spencer. "Just-in-Time Concepts: Applicability to Logistics/Transportation." *International Journal of Physical Distribution and Logistics Management* 20, no. 7 (1990), pp. 12–18.

D'Este, Glen. "An Event-Based Approach to Modelling Intermodal Freight Systems." *International Journal of Physical Distribution and Logistics Management* 26, no. 6 (1996), pp. 5–16.

Ernst & Whinney. *Transportation Accounting and Control: Guidelines for Distribution and Financial Management.* Oak Brook, IL: National Council of Physical Distribution Management, 1983.

Forsythe, Kenneth H.; James C. Johnson; and Kenneth C. Schneider. "Traffic Managers: Do They Get Any Respect?" *Journal of Business Logistics* 11, no. 2 (1990), pp. 87–100.

Foster, Thomas A. "Rough Going for LTL Carriers." *Distribution* 91, no. 9 (July 1992), pp. 12–18.

Garreau, Alain; Robert Leib; and Robert Millen. "JIT and Corporate Transport: An International Comparison." *International Journal of Physical Distribution and Logistics Management* 21, no. 1 (1991), pp. 42–47.

Gooley, Toby B. "How to Choose a Third Party." *Traffic Management* 32, no. 10 (Oct. 1993), pp. 85A–87A.

Kasarda, John D. "Transportation Infrastructure for Competitive Success." *Transportation Quarterly* 50, no. 1 (Winter 1996), pp. 35–50.

La Londe, Bernard J.; James M. Masters; Arnold B. Maltz; and Lisa R. Williams. *The Evolution, Status, and Future of the Corporate Transportation Function.* Louisville, KY: American Society of Transportation and Logistics, 1991.

McConville, Daniel J. "Private Fleet Leasing: Two Sides to Teamwork." *Distribution* 96, no. 3 (Mar. 1997), pp. 40–46.

Min, Hokey, and Martha Cooper. "A Comparative Review of Analytical Studies on Freight Consolidation and Backhauling." *Logistics and Transportation Review* 26, no. 2 (June 1990), pp. 149–69.

Mohring, Herbert, ed. *The Economics of Transport,* vols. 1 and 2. Brookfield, VT: Edward Elgar, 1994.

Muller, E. J. "A New Paradigm for Partnerships." *Distribution* 93, no. 1 (Jan. 1994), pp. 45–48.

Murphy, Paul R., and Patricia K. Hall. "The Relative Importance of Cost and Service in Freight Transportation Choice before and after Deregulation: An Update." *Transportation Journal* 35, no. 1 (Fall 1995), pp. 30–38.

Richardson, Barbara C. "Transportation Ethics." *Transportation Quarterly* 49, no. 2 (Spring 1995), pp. 117–126.

Richardson, Helen L. "Will Shrinking Shipments Shrink Profits?" *Transportation and Distribution* 36, no. 3 (Mar. 1995), pp. 45–50.

Rinehart, Lloyd M., and David J. Closs. "Implications of Organizational Relationships, Negotiator Personalities, and Contract Issues on Outcomes in Logistics Negotiations." *Journal of Business Logistics* 12, no. 1 (1991), pp. 123–44.

Spizziri, Martha. "Intermodal Overcomes the Obstacles." *Distribution* 33, no. 4 (Apr. 1994), pp. 39–42.

Temple, Baker, and Sloane, Inc. *Creating Profitability: The Sales and Marketing Challenge.* Alexandria, VA: Sales and Marketing Council of the American Trucking Association, 1985.

Theurmer, Karen. "Multimodal Carriers at Your Service." *Intermodal Shipping* 29, no. 7 (Sept. 1994), pp. 28–31.

Tompkins, James A., and Dale Harmelink, eds. *The Distribution Management Handbook.* New York: McGraw-Hill, 1994.

Trunick, Perry A. "Air Cargo Needs Positive Action." *Transportation and Distribution* 35, no. 9 (Sept. 1994), pp. 53–58.

Vantine, José G., and Claudirceu Marra. "Logistics Challenges and Opportunities Within MERCOSUR." *The International Journal of Logistics Management* 8, no. 1 (1997), pp. 55–66.

Vantuono, William C. "Roadrailer Hits the Big Time." *Railway Age* 195, no. 10 (Oct. 1994), pp. 49–52.

Waller, David G.; Robert L. D'Avanzo; and Douglas M. Lambert. *Supply Chain Directions for a New North America.* Oak Brook, IL: Council of Logistics Management, 1995.

Waters, C. D. J. "Computer Use in the Trucking Industry." *International Journal of Physical Distribution and Logistics Management* 20, no. 9 (1990), pp. 24–31.

Questions and Problems

1. What are time utility and place utility? How does the transportation function add utility to products?

2. Briefly discuss the five transport modes, based on their economic and service characteristics.

3. Discuss the role and functions of brokers in the transportation system.

4. Trailer-on-flatcar (TOFC) and container-on-flatcar (COFC) intermodal combinations are referred to as piggyback movements. Describe piggyback movements from the perspectives of cost, service, and availability, and identify their major strengths and weaknesses.

5. Identify the three types of for-hire transportation carriers. Briefly define and describe the characteristics of each. Identify the impact, if any, that deregulation has had on each of them.

6. What is the difference between cost-of-service and value-of-service pricing in transportation? How does each affect the rates charged by carriers?

7. How has the deregulation of transportation affected carrier pricing?

8. Most transportation executives believe that service factors are generally more important than cost factors in causing firms to switch from one transport mode to another. Under what circumstances would service factors be more important than cost factors?

9. In the evaluation of transportation modes, *consistency of service* is significantly more important to shippers than *time-in-transit.* What is the difference between the two terms? Identify some reasons why shippers consider consistency of service more important. In your answer, be sure to consider the impact on inventory levels.

10. Private carriage should not be viewed strictly as a transportation decision—it also is a financial decision. Briefly explain the reasons that underlie this statement.

THE DISTRIBUTION CHALLENGE!
PROBLEM: PEAKS AND VALLEYS

A problem faced by seasonal shippers is how to handle short-term surges of supply while keeping freight costs low.

One of the clients of third-party Mark VII Logistics Services is a food processor that requires large amounts of raw materials which are not especially delicate. Huge amounts of the product move from Florida to plants in the northeastern United States over a six-week period, by second-day delivery or faster. One week, the shipper could move between 200 and 230 loads. The next, shipment volume will be zero.

Prior to Mark VII, the shipper had handled the problem in-house. Its strategy consisted of coordinating the shipments through produce brokers, and the price wasn't cheap. If it wanted capacity, the shipper would have to match what truckers were getting for moving higher-value perishables. And because most movements during that time of year were headed north, shippers were expected to cover the carriers' backhaul costs—almost $2 a mile.

Although the shipper's product was of relatively low value, its equipment needs were strict. It required refrigerated or insulated trailers—48 inches long by 102 inches wide at the minimum—equipped with satellite communications. In addition, it needed to haul between 5 and 20 loads a week from the destination plant to local consignees. And it wanted only one or two carriers to handle the whole job.

By bringing more truckers into the market, Mark VII could boost capacity and challenge the existing pricing structure. But how does one entice a high-quality carrier to enter a traffic lane for just six weeks? And how could Mark VII meet its customer's service demands while reducing freight costs? (*Hint:* The solution consisted of more than a change of mode.)

What Is Your Solution?

Source: "Distribution: The Challenge," *Distribution* 95, no. 9 (Sept. 1996), p 80.

Chapter Outline

Chapter Objectives

- To show why warehousing is important in the logistics system.
- To identify the major types or forms of warehousing.
- To examine the primary functions of warehousing.
- To compare public and private warehousing from a financial perspective.
- To identify the factors that affect the size and number of warehouses.
- To examine the warehouse site selection decision from macro- and microperspectives.
- To describe the factors that affect warehouse layout and design.
- To describe global warehousing issues.
- To provide an overview of the importance of productivity and accounting/control issues in warehouse management.

Introduction

Warehousing Links Producers and Customers

Warehousing is an integral part of every logistics system. There are an estimated 750,000 warehouse facilities worldwide, including state-of-the-art, professionally managed warehouses, as well as company stockrooms, garages, self-store facilities, and even garden sheds.[1] Warehousing plays a vital role in providing a desired level of customer service at the lowest possible total cost (see Figure 8–1). Warehousing activity is an important link between the producer and the customer. Over the years, warehousing has developed from a relatively minor facet of a firm's logistics system to one of its most important functions.

We can define **warehousing** as that part of a firm's logistics system that stores products (raw materials, parts, goods-in-process, finished goods) at and between point of origin and point of consumption, and provides information to management on the status, condition, and disposition of items being stored. The term **distribution center (DC)** is sometimes used, but the terms are not identical. **Warehouse** is the more generic term.

Warehouses and Distribution Centers Are Not the Same

Warehouses store all products, DCs hold minimum inventories and predominantly high-demand items. Warehouses handle most products in four cycles [receive, store, ship, and pick], DCs handle most products in two: receive and ship. Warehouses perform a minimum of value-added activity, DCs perform a high percentage of value adding, including possible final assembly. Warehouses collect data in batches, DCs collect data in real-time. Warehouses focus on minimizing the operating cost to meet shipping requirements, DCs focus on maximizing the profit impact of meeting customer delivery requirements.[2]

With an increasing interest in improving inventory turns and reducing time to market, the role of distribution increasingly focuses on filling orders rapidly and efficiently.

Effective warehouse management involves a thorough understanding of the functions of warehousing, the merits of public versus private warehousing, and the financial and service aspects of warehousing decisions. Managers need knowledge of the methods that can improve warehousing performance and a strategy for locating warehousing facilities at optimal locations.

Strategic versus Operational Warehousing Decisions

Warehousing decisions may be strategic or operational. *Strategic* decisions deal with the allocation of logistics resources over an extended time in a manner consistent and supportive of overall enterprise policies and objectives. They can take either long-range or project-type forms.

An example of a long-range strategic decision is the choice of a logistics system design. A project-type decision might deal with consolidation of branch warehouses into a regional distribution center. Other examples of typical strategic questions include the following:

- Should warehousing be owned, leased, rented, or some combination of these?
- Should the warehousing functions be "spun off"; that is, contracted out to a third-party provider?
- Should the company install new materials handling equipment or continue to hire more labor?

---

[1]Richard J. Sherman, "The Warehouse Systems Market: Fragmented or Segmented?" *The Report on Supply Chain Management,* June 1996, p. 3.

[2]Richard L. Dawe, "Reengineer Warehousing," *Transportation and Distribution* 36, no. 1 (Jan. 1995), p. 102.

FIGURE 8–1

Cost trade-offs required in a logistics system

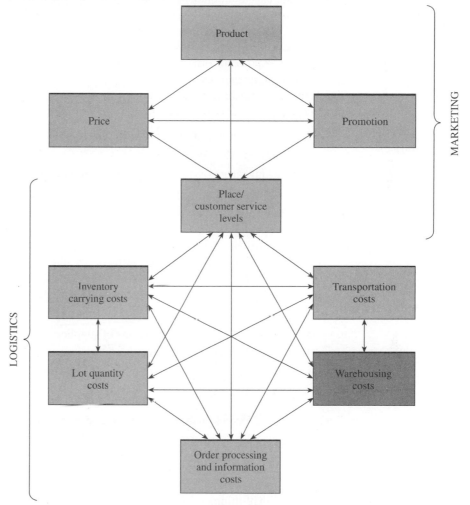

Marketing objective: Allocate resources to the marketing mix to maximize the long-run profitability of the firm.
Logistics objective: Minimize total costs given the customer service objective where Total costs = Transportation costs + Warehousing costs + Order processing and information costs + Lot quantity costs + Inventory carrying costs.

Source: Adapted from Douglas M. Lambert, *The Development of an Inventory Costing Methodology: A Study of the Costs Associated with Holding Inventory* (Chicago, IL: National Council of Physical Distribution Management, 1976), p. 7.

Operational decisions are used to manage or control logistics performance. Typically, these decisions are routine in nature and involve time spans of one year or less. They relate to the coordination and performance of the logistics system. For example, a warehouse manager would be concerned with how to best utilize labor in the shipping department. Due to the short time horizon involved, these decisions have more certainty than strategic decisions.

Nature and Importance of Warehousing

Warehousing has traditionally provided storage of products (referred to as inventory) during all phases of the logistics process. Two basic types of inventories can be placed into storage: (1) raw materials, components, and parts (physical supply); and (2) finished goods (physical distribution). Also, there may be inventories of goods-in-process and materials to be disposed of or recycled, although in most firms these constitute only a small portion of total inventories.

Why do companies hold inventories in storage? Traditionally, the warehousing of products has occured for one or more of the following reasons:

Why Should a Firm Have Inventories?

1. Achieve transportation economies.
2. Achieve production economies.
3. Take advantage of quantity purchase discounts and forward buys.
4. Maintain a source of supply.
5. Support the firm's customer service policies.
6. Meet changing market conditions (e.g., seasonality, demand fluctuations, competition).
7. Overcome the time and space differentials that exist between producers and consumers.
8. Accomplish least total cost logistics commensurate with a desired level of customer service.
9. Support the just-in-time programs of suppliers and customers.
10. Provide customers with a mix of products instead of a single product on each order.
11. Provide temporary storage of materials to be disposed of or recycled (i.e., reverse logistics).

Several Uses of Warehousing.   Figure 8–2 identifies some of the uses of warehousing in both the physical supply and physical distribution systems. Warehouses can be used to support manufacturing, to mix products from multiple production facilities for shipment to a single customer, to breakbulk or subdivide a large shipment of product into many smaller shipments to satisfy the needs of many customers, and to combine or consolidate a number of small shipments into a single higher-volume shipment.[3]

Warehousing is used increasingly as a "flow-through" point rather than a "holding" point, or even bypassed (e.g., scheduled deliveries direct to customers), as organizations increasingly substitute information for inventory, purchase smaller quantities, and use warehouses as "consolidation points" to receive purchased transportation rates and service levels.

Pull versus Push Systems in Warehousing

The traditional method [of distribution] is a push system. Production plans are based on capabilities and capacities of the plant, and product is produced in the expectation that it will sell. When it is produced faster than it can be sold, it is stockpiled at plant warehouses. If sales cannot be accelerated, then the plant will be slowed down until supply moves into balance with

---

[3]An exhaustive listing of logistics definitions is given in Joseph L. Cavinato, ed., *Transportation-Logistics Dictionary,* 3rd ed. (Washington, DC: International Thomson Transport Press, 1989).

FIGURE 8–2

Uses of warehousing in physical supply and physical distribution

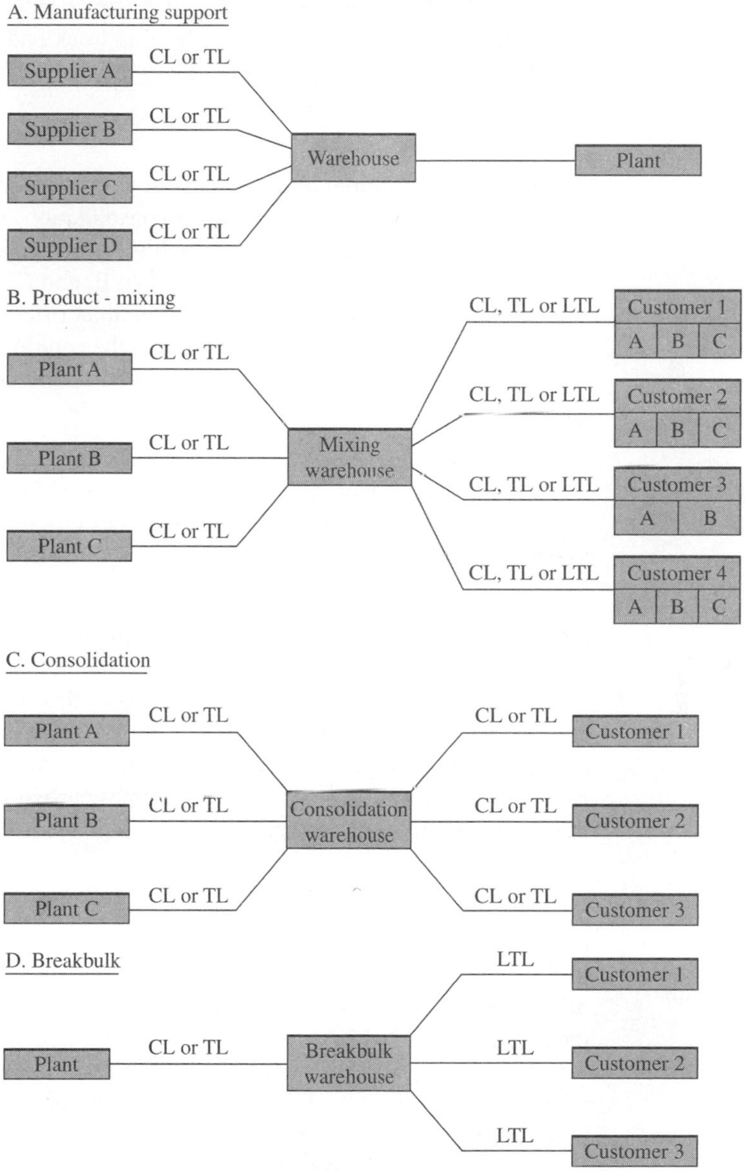

A. Manufacturing support

B. Product - mixing

C. Consolidation

D. Breakbulk

demand. In this system, warehousing serves to absorb excess production. Today's pull system depends on information. It is based on a constant monitoring of demand. . . . With a pull system, there is no need for a reservoir. Instead, the warehouse serves as a flow-through center, offering improved service by positioning inventory closer to the customer.[4]

---

[4]Kenneth B. Ackerman, "Push versus Pull," *Warehousing Forum* 11, no. 7 (June 1996), p. 3.

Manufacturing Support. In supporting manufacturing operations, warehouses often play the important role of inbound consolidation points for the receipt of shipments from suppliers. As shown in Figure 8–2, part A, firms order raw materials, parts, components, or supplies from various suppliers, who ship truckload (TL) or carload (CL) quantities to a warehouse located in close proximity to the plant. Items are transferred from the warehouse to the manufacturing plant(s).

Product Mixing

Product Mixing. From a physical distribution or outbound perspective, warehouses can be used for product mixing, outbound consolidation, or breakbulk. Product mixing (see Figure 8–2, part B) often involves multiple plant locations (e.g., plant A, plant B, and plant C) that ship products (e.g., products A, B, and C) to a central warehouse. Each plant manufactures only a portion of the total product offering of the firm. Shipments are usually made in large quantities (TL or CL) to the central warehouse, where customer orders for multiple products are combined or mixed for shipment.

Outbound Consolidation

Consolidation. When a warehouse is used for outbound consolidation (see Figure 8–2, part C), TL or CL shipments are made to a central facility from a number of manufacturing locations. The warehouse consolidates or combines products from the various plants into a single shipment to the customer.

Breakbulk Warehouses

Breakbulk. Breakbulk warehouses (see Figure 8–2, part D) are facilities that receive large shipments of product from manufacturing plants. Several customer orders are combined into a single shipment from the plants to the breakbulk warehouse. When the shipment is received at the warehouse, it is broken down into smaller LTL shipments which are sent to customers in the geographical area served by the warehouse. As illustrated in Box 8–1, breakbulk operations are sometimes carried out by using transportation innovations rather than warehousing.

Relationships between Warehousing and Transportation

Warehousing and Transportation. Transportation economies are possible for both the physical supply system and the physical distribution system. In the case of physical supply, small orders from a number of suppliers may be shipped to a consolidation warehouse near the source of supply; in this way, the producer can achieve a TL or CL shipment to the plant, which normally is situated at a considerably greater distance from the warehouse. The warehouse is located near the sources of supply so that the LTL rates apply only to a short haul, and the volume rate is used for the long haul from the warehouse to the plant.

Warehouses are used to achieve similar transportation savings in the physical distribution system. In the packaged goods industry, manufacturers often have multiple plant locations, with each plant manufacturing only a portion of the company's product line. Such plants are often referred to as *focused factories.*

Usually, these companies maintain a number of **field warehouse** locations from which mixed shipments of the entire product line can be made to customers. Shipments

Box 8–1

Warehousing in the High-Fashion Goods Industry

Fashion is a very perishable commodity . . . a hot-selling fashion item is a loser . . . unless it is on the selling floor precisely when it is most in fashion. In some cases, that can be as little as 7 to 10 days.

Saks Fifth Avenue operates 69 stores served by two distribution centers. One is in Yonkers, New York, close to Saks's flagship store on New York City's Fifth Avenue. The second is in Ontario, California, well situated to serve the trendy Southern California market.

Neither of these operations is in any sense a warehouse . . . Items generally move through these centers on a 24-hour turnaround. There is an emphatic realization . . . that every hour that a rack of $800 dresses sits in a distribution center can represent a lost sale and lost profit.

Speedy transit starts at the beginning of the pipeline. About 80 percent of Saks's imported items move into one of these centers by air freight. Imports move to one of the distribution centers based on the region where they originate: Yonkers handles the European imports and Ontario covers the Far East.

Items are exchanged between the two centers by air freight, with a dedicated flight in each direction between New York and Los Angeles every business day.

The distribution centers then serve their local stores with a combination of air freight and trucking.

Source: Bruce Vail, "Logistics, Fifth Avenue Style," *American Shipper* 36, no. 8 (Aug. 1994), p. 49.

from plants to field warehouses are frequently made by rail in full carload quantities of the products manufactured at each plant. Orders for customers, comprised of various items in the product line, are shipped by truck at TL or LTL rates. The use of field warehouses results in lower transportation costs than direct shipments to customers. Savings are often significantly larger than the increased costs resulting from warehousing and the associated increase in inventory carrying costs.

Relationships between Warehousing and Production

Warehousing and Production.   Short production runs minimize the amount of inventory held throughout the logistics system by producing quantities near to current demand, but they carry increased costs of setups and line changes.[5] If a plant is operating near or at capacity, frequent line changes may leave the manufacturer unable to meet product demand. If so, the cost of lost sales—the lost contribution to profit on unrealized sales—could be substantial.

On the other hand, the production of large quantities of product for each line change results in a lower per unit cost on a full-cost basis and more units for a given plant capacity. However, long production runs lead to larger inventories and increased warehouse requirements. Consequently, production cost savings must be balanced with increased logistics costs in order to achieve least total cost.

---

[5]These costs can vary widely and depend on the level of technology employed in the manufacturing process. Newer, high-tech production equipment can be changed from one product to another with little downtime and very little cost.

Traditionally, warehousing was necessary if a company was to take advantage of quantity purchase discounts on raw materials or other products. Not only is the per unit price lower as a result of the discount, but if the company pays the freight, transportation costs will be less on a volume purchase because of transportation economies. Similar discounts and savings can accrue to manufacturers, retailers, and wholesalers. Once again, however, those savings must be weighed against the added inventory costs incurred as a result of larger inventories.

Increasingly, companies operating with a JIT manufacturing philosophy are negotiating with their suppliers to receive cumulative quantity discounts. Thus, they receive the lower rate based on total yearly order volume rather than individual order size.

Holding inventories in warehouses may be necessary to maintain a source of supply. For example, the timing and quantity of purchases is important in retaining suppliers, especially during periods of shortages. It may be necessary to hold an inventory of items that are in short supply as a result of damage in transit, vendor stockouts, or a strike against one of the company's suppliers.

Warehousing and Customer Service

Warehousing and Customer Service.   Customer service policies, such as a 24-hour delivery standard, may require a number of field warehouses in order to minimize total costs while achieving the standard. Changing market conditions may make it necessary to warehouse product in the field, primarily because companies are unable to accurately predict consumer demand and the timing of retailer or wholesaler orders. By keeping some excess inventory in field warehouse locations, companies can respond quickly to meet unexpected demand. In addition, excess inventory allows manufacturers to fill customer orders when shipments to restock the field warehouses arrive late.

Warehousing and Least Total Cost Logistics

Warehousing and Least Total Cost Logistics.   The majority of firms utilize warehousing to accomplish least total cost logistics at some prescribed level of customer service, considering the trade-offs shown in Figure 8–1. Factors that influence a firm's warehousing policies include:

- The industry.
- The firm's philosophy.
- Capital availability.
- Product characteristics such as size, perishability, product lines, substitutability, and obsolescence rates.
- Economic conditions.
- Competition.
- Seasonality of demand.
- Use of just-in-time programs.
- Production process in use.[6]

---

[6]For a discussion of many of the changes taking place in business which are affecting the roles of warehousing in logistics, see Kenneth B. Ackerman, "21st Century Business Theory and Warehouse Operations," *Warehousing Forum* 10, no. 6 (May 1995), pp. 1–2; and "Warehousing: Coping with the Challenge of Change," *Modern Materials Handling* 50, no. 6 (May 1995), pp. 12–13.

Types of Warehousing

In general, firms have a number of warehousing alternatives. Some companies may market products directly to retail customers (called **direct store delivery**), thereby eliminating warehousing in the field. Mail-order catalog companies, for example, utilize warehousing only at a point of origin, such as sales headquarters or plant.

Cross-Docking

Cross-Docking.   Another alternative is to utilize cross-docking concepts, whereby warehouses serve primarily as "distribution mixing centers." Product arrives in bulk and is immediately broken down and mixed in the proper range and quantity of products for customer shipment. In essence, the product never enters the warehouse. This topic will be described more fully in the next section.

Cross-docking is becoming popular among retailers, who can order TL, then remix and immediately ship to individual store locations. Products usually come boxed for individual stores from the supplier's location. For example, Laney & Duke, Hanes's third-party warehousing company in Jacksonville, Florida, tickets merchandise, places it on hangers, and boxes it up for individual Wal-Mart stores to replace items sold. The trailer leaves Jacksonville for the Wal-Mart DC where product is cross-docked to trucks for stores. At stores, the boxes are opened and garments are immediately ready to hang on display racks.

Most firms warehouse products at some intermediate point between plant and customers. When a firm decides to store product in the field, it faces two warehousing options: rented facilities, called *public warehousing,* or owned or leased facilities, called *private warehousing.*

Contract Warehousing

Contract Warehousing.   Another option exists, termed **contract warehousing,** which is a variation of public warehousing. Contract warehousing is an arrangement between the user and provider of the warehousing service. It has been defined as:

> . . . a long-term mutually beneficial arrangement which provides unique and specially tailored warehousing and logistics services exclusively to one client, where vendor and client share the risks associate with the operation. [There is a] focus on productivity, service and efficiency, not the fee and rate structure itself.[7]

Firms must examine important customer service and financial considerations to choose between public and private warehousing. For example, operating costs for a public warehouse tend to be higher because the warehouse will attempt to operate at a profit; it may also have selling and advertising costs. However, a firm makes no initial investment in facilities when it uses public warehousing. From a customer service perspective, private warehousing can generally provide higher service levels because of its more specialized facilities and equipment, and its better familiarity with the firm's products, customers, and markets.

---

[7]Kenneth B. Ackerman, "Contract Warehousing—Better Mousetrap, or Smoke and Mirrors?" *Warehousing Forum,* 8 no. 9 (Aug. 1993), p. 1; see also William G. Sheehan, "Contract Warehousing: The Evolution of an Industry," *Journal of Business Logistics* 10, no. 1 (1989), p. 31; and Thomas W. Speh, et al., *Contract Warehousing: How It Works and How to Make It Work Effectively* (Oak Brook, IL: Warehousing Education and Research Council, 1993).

The two options must be examined closely. In some instances, innovative public warehouses can provide higher levels of service owing to their expertise and strong competitive drive to serve the customer.[8]

Types of Public Warehouses

Public Warehouses.   There are many types of public warehouses, including: (1) general merchandise warehouses for manufactured goods, (2) refrigerated or cold storage warehouses, (3) bonded warehouses, (4) household goods and furniture warehouses, (5) special commodity warehouses, and (6) bulk storage warehouses. Each type provides users with a broad range of specialized services.

General Merchandise Warehouse.   The *general merchandise warehouse* is probably the most common form. It is designed to be used by manufacturers, distributors, and customers for storing almost any kind of product.

Refrigerated Warehouses.   *Refrigerated or cold storage warehouses* provide a temperature-controlled storage environment. They tend to be used for preserving perishable items such as fruits and vegetables. However, a number of other items (e.g., frozen food products, some pharmaceuticals, photographic paper and film, and furs) require this type of facility.

Bonded Warehouses

Bonded Warehouses.   Some general merchandise or special commodity warehouses are known as **bonded warehouses.** These warehouses undertake surety bonds from the U.S. Treasury and place their premises under the custody of an agent of the Treasury. Goods such as imported tobacco and alcoholic beverages are stored in this type of warehouse, although the government retains control of the goods until they are distributed to the marketplace. At that time, the importer must pay customs duties to the Internal Revenue Service. The advantage of the bonded warehouse is that import duties and excise taxes need not be paid until the merchandise is sold, so that the importer has the funds on hand to pay these fees.

Household Goods Warehouses

Household Goods Warehouses.   *Household goods warehouses* are used for storage of personal property rather than merchandise. The property is typically stored for an extended period as a temporary layover option. Within this category of warehouses, there are several types of storage alternatives. One is the open storage concept. The goods are stored on a cubic-foot basis per month on the open floor of the warehouse. Household goods are typically confined to this type of storage. A second kind of storage is private room or vault storage, where users are provided with a private room or vault to lock in and secure goods. A third kind, container storage, provides users with a container into which they can pack goods. Container storage affords better protection of the product than open storage.

Special Commodity Warehouses

Special Commodity Warehouses.   *Special commodity warehouses* are used for particular agricultural products, such as grains, wool, and cotton. Ordinarily each of these warehouses handles one kind of product and offers special services specific to that product.

---

[8]For a brief overview of the three general types of warehousing (private, public, and contract), see American Warehouse Association, "Three Warehousing Choices: Private, Public, and Contract," *Logistics Today* 1, no. 2 (1993), pp. 1–3.

**Bulk Storage
Warehouses**

Bulk Storage Warehouses.   *Bulk storage warehouses* provide tank storage of liquids and open or sheltered storage of dry products such as coal, sand, and chemicals. These warehouses may provide services such as filling drums from bulk or mixing various types of chemicals with others to produce new compounds or mixtures.

Warehousing Operations: Three Functions

Warehousing serves an important role in a firm's logistics system. In combination with other activities, it provides the firm's customers with an acceptable level of service. The obvious role of warehousing is to store products, but warehousing also provides break-bulk, consolidation, and information services. These activities emphasize product flow rather than storage.

Fast and efficient movement of large quantities of raw materials, component parts, and finished goods through the warehouse, coupled with timely and accurate information about the products being stored, are the goals of every logistics system. These goals have received increasing attention from the top management of many organizations (see Box 8–2).

**Three Functions of
Warehousing**

Warehousing has three basic functions: movement, storage, and information transfer. Recently, the movement function has been receiving the most attention as organizations focus on improving inventory turns and speeding orders from manufacturing to final delivery (see Figure 8–3).

Movement

The movement function can be further divided into several activities, including:

- Receiving
- Transfer or putaway
- Order picking/selection
- Cross-docking
- Shipping[9]

The *receiving* activity includes the actual unloading of products from the transportation carrier, the updating of warehouse inventory records, inspection for damage, and verification of the merchandise count against orders and shipping records.

Transfer or *putaway* involves the physical movement of the product into the warehouse for storage, movement to areas for specialized services such as consolidation, and movement to outbound shipment. Customer *order selection* or *order picking* is the major movement activity and involves regrouping products into the assortments customers desire. Packing slips are made up at this point.

Cross-docking bypasses the storage activity by transferring items directly from the receiving dock to the shipping dock (see Figure 8–4). A pure cross-docking operation would avoid putaway, storage, and order picking. Information transfer would become paramount because shipments require close coordination.

---

[9]See James A. Tompkins et al., *Facilities Planning,* 2nd. ed. (New York: John Wiley, 1996), pp. 389–450.

Box 8–2

How Moore Keeps Its Operations in Top Form

A Canadian corporation headquartered in Toronto, Moore Business Forms and Systems manufactures custom business forms and documents. Corporate sales in 1994 topped $2.3 billion.

To serve customers in the United States, Moore operates 18 U.S. distribution centers. Although some 75 percent of products are shipped directly from the factory to the purchaser, another 25 percent go into storage for later shipment.

Moore developed six critical measurements designed to maximize warehouse efficiency and effectiveness while maintaining a high level of customer service. The six-element program (referred to as the RSVP program) consists of the following:

1. *Safety*—zero safety incidents or accidents; the OSHA employee logbooks that report accidents are used for evaluation.
2. *Shipping Errors*—zero shipping errors in the firm's pick and pack activities (i.e., ship exactly what was ordered to the customer); financial statement information indicates whether orders have been filled completely.
3. *On-Time Shipments*—delivery of freight precisely when requested because customers are operating JIT operations; warehouse records on shipping performance are used for evaluation.

4. *Customer Problems*—customer feedback is periodically requested for every shipment, and summary statistics are compiled for management review.
5. *Cost per Line Shipped*—based on the number of items shipped in a period, the company came up with a cost per line and measures that expense against a preestablished objective; financial statements and the firm's computerized inventory system measure costs in this area.
6. *Total Warehouse Expenses*—an overall measure of warehouse efficiency which determines whether workers kept warehousing costs in line with company standards and projections.

At the end of each quarter, Moore measures each warehouse's performance against the criteria and issues bonuses to the employees, managers, and directors. During 1994, more than a third of the warehouses met all six objectives. At the end of the year, 99.6 percent of Moore's customers rated their service level as good or better.

Source: James Aaron Cooke, "How Moore Keeps Its Operations in Top Form," *Traffic Management* 34, no. 9 (Sept. 1995), pp. 23–27.

Cross-docking has become commonplace in warehousing because of its impact on costs and customer service. For example, approximately 75 percent of food distribution involves the cross-docking of products from supplier to retail food stores.[10] Eliminating the transfer or putaway of products reduces costs and the time goods remain at the warehouse, thus improving customer service levels.[11]

[10]"Grocery Warehouses Turn to Cross-Docking," *Traffic Management* 34, no. 2 (Feb. 1995), p. 77-S.

[11]A large literature overviews cross-docking. The interested reader is directed to the following sources: Tom Andel, "Define Cross-Docking before You Do It," *Transportation and Distribution* 35, no. 11 (Nov. 1994), pp. 93–98; *Cross-Docking in the '90s,* Monograph Series no. M0020 (Raleigh, NC: Tompkins Associates, n.d.); Lisa Harrington, "Cross-Docking Takes Costs Out of the Pipeline," *Distribution* 92, no. 9 (Sept. 1993), pp. 64–66; "Implementing a Cross-Docking Program," *Distribution Center Management* 30, no. 5 (May 1995), p. 3; and James T. Westburgh, "Cross-Docking in the Warehouse—An Operator's View," *Warehousing Forum* 10, no. 9 (Aug. 1995), pp. 1–3.

FIGURE 8–3

Typical warehouse functions and flows

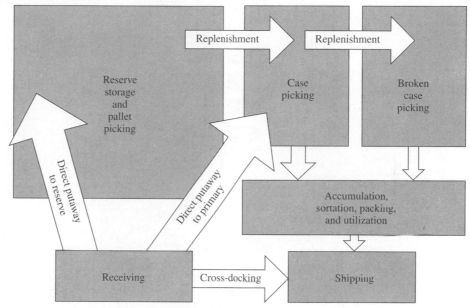

Source: James A. Tompkins et al., *Facilities Planning,* 2nd ed. (New York: John Wiley, 1996), p. 392.

Cross-docking should be considered as an option by firms meeting two or more of the following criteria:

When Should Cross-Docking Be Considered?

- Inventory destination is known when received.
- Customer is ready to receive inventory immediately.
- Shipment to fewer than 200 locations daily.
- Daily throughput exceeds 2,000 cartons.
- More than 70 percent of the inventory is conveyable.
- Large quantities of individual items received by firm.
- Inventory arrives at firm's docks prelabeled.
- Some inventory is time sensitive.
- Firm's distribution center is near capacity.
- Some of the inventory is prepriced.[12]

Shipping, the last movement activity, consists of product staging and physically moving the assembled orders onto carrier equipment, adjusting inventory records, and checking orders to be shipped. It can consist of sortation and packaging of items for specific customers. Products are placed in boxes, cartons, or other containers, placed on pallets, or shrinkwrapped (i.e., the process of wrapping products in a plastic film), and are marked with information necessary for shipment, such as origin, destination, shipper, consignee, and package contents.

---

[12]"Receiving Is Where Efficiency Starts," *Modern Materials Handling* 50, no. 5 (Mid-Apr. 1995), p. 9.

FIGURE 8-4

Two examples of cross-docking

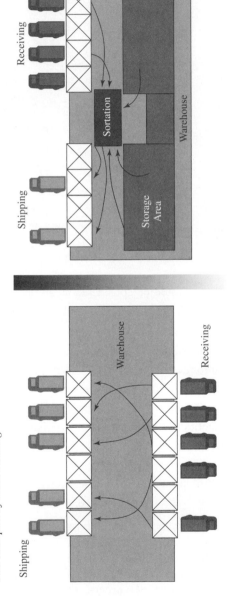

Under a cross-docking system, palletloads can be moved directly across the warehouse floor from receiving to shipping (left). Boxes, however, first must pass through a sortation system (right).

Source: James Aaron Cooke, "Cross-Docking Rediscovered," *Traffic Management* 33, no. 11 (Nov. 1994), p. 51.

Storage

Temporary Storage

Storage, the second function of warehousing, can be performed on a temporary or a semipermanent basis. *Temporary storage* emphasizes the movement function of the warehouse and includes only the storage of product necessary for basic inventory replenishment. Temporary storage is required regardless of the actual inventory turnover. The extent of temporary inventory storage depends on the design of the logistics system and the variability experienced in lead time and demand. A goal of cross-docking is to utilize only the temporary storage function of the warehouse.

Semipermanent Storage

Semipermanent storage is the storage of inventory in excess of that required for normal replenishment. This inventory is referred to as buffer or safety stock. The most common conditions leading to semipermanent storage are (1) seasonal demand, (2) erratic demand, (3) conditioning of products such as fruits and meats, (4) speculation or forward buying, and (5) special deals such as quantity discounts.

Information Transfer

Information transfer, the third major function of warehousing, occurs simultaneously with the movement and storage functions. Management always needs timely and accurate information as it attempts to administer the warehousing activity. Information on inventory levels, throughput levels (i.e., the amount of product moving through the warehouse), stockkeeping locations, inbound and outbound shipments, customer data, facility space utilization, and personnel is vital to the successful operation of a warehouse. Organizations are relying increasingly on computerized information transfer utilizing electronic data interchange (EDI) and bar coding to improve both the speed and accuracy of information transfer.

In spite of numerous attempts by firms to reduce the flow of paperwork, the amount of paperwork is still significant. For this reason and many others, management in many firms has attempted to automate the clerical function whenever possible. The developments in electronic communications have been instrumental in reducing the clerical activities in all aspects of warehousing.

Successful completion of all of the warehousing activities already mentioned eliminates the need for *checking.* However, errors and mistakes do occur within any warehouse operation, usually making it necessary to conduct a check of previous activities. In some instances, this activity can be minimized in operations where employees are empowered to perform quality control at their respective levels within the warehouse. This activity may be performed by teams, instead of individuals.

It is important to eliminate any inefficiencies in movement, storage, and information transfer within the warehouse. These can occur in a variety of forms:

Examples of Warehousing Inefficiencies

- Redundant or excessive handling.
- Poor utilization of space and cube.
- Excessive maintenance costs and downtime due to obsolete equipment.
- Dated receiving and shipping dock conditions.
- Obsolete computerized information handling of routine transactions.

The competitive marketplace demands more precise and accurate handling, storage, and retrieval systems, as well as improved packaging and shipping systems. It is vital for a warehouse operation to have the optimal mix of manual and automated handling systems. These issues are presented in more depth in Chapter 9. The next section compares and contrasts private and public warehousing.

Public versus Private Warehousing

One of the most important warehousing decisions a company makes is whether to use public (rented) or private (owned or leased) facilities. To make the proper decision from a cost and service standpoint, the logistics executive must understand the advantages and disadvantages, as well as the financial implications, of each alternative.[13]

Contract warehousing is a variant of public warehousing in which the organization has a contractual relationship to utilize a certain amount of space and services in a facility or facilities over a set time period. This arrangement gives the warehouser more stability and certainty in making investments and planning for the future.

Advantages and Disadvantages of Public Warehousing

Advantages.   The benefits that may be realized if a firm uses public warehouses rather than privately owned or leased warehouses include: (1) conservation of capital: (2) the ability to increase warehouse space to cover peak requirements; (3) reduced risk; (4) economies of scale; (5) flexibility; (6) tax advantages; (7) specific knowledge of costs for storage and handling; and (8) potential minimization of labor disputes.

Conservation of Capital

Conservation of Capital.   One of the major advantages of public warehouses is that they require no capital investment from the user. The user avoids the investment in buildings, land, and materials handling equipment, as well as the costs of starting up the operation and hiring and training personnel.

Adjusts for Seasonality

Use of Space to Meet Peak Requirements.   If a firm's operations are subject to seasonality, the public warehouse option allows the user to rent as much storage space as needed to meet peak requirements. A private warehouse, on the other hand, has a constraint on the maximum amount of product that can be stored because it cannot be expanded in the short term. Also, it is likely to be underutilized during a portion of each year. Since most firms experience variations in inventory levels because of seasonality in demand or production, sales promotions, or other factors, public warehousing offers the distinct advantage of allowing storage costs to vary directly with volume.

Reduced Risk

Reduced Risk.   Companies normally plan for a distribution facility to have a life span of 20 to 40 years. By investing in a private warehouse, management assumes the risk that

---

[13]See James Aaron Cooke, "Getting the Right Fit," *Traffic Management* 34, no. 2 (Feb. 1995), Warehousing and Distribution Supplement, pp. 78–80.

changes in technology or in the volume of business will make the facility obsolete. With public warehousing, the user firm can switch to another facility in a short period of time, often within 30 days.

Economies of Scale

Economies of Scale.   Public warehouses are able to achieve economies of scale that may not be possible for some firms. Because public warehouses handle the requirements of a number of firms, their volume allows the employment of a full-time warehousing staff. In addition, building costs are nonlinear, and a firm pays a premium to build a small facility. Additional economies of scale can be provided by using more expensive, but more efficient, materials handling equipment and by providing administrative and other expertise.

Public warehouses often can offer a number of specialized services more economically than a private warehouse. These specialized services include the following:

• Broken-case handling, which is breaking down manufacturers' case quantities to enable orders for less-than-full-case quantities to be filled.

• Packaging of manufacturers' products for shipping. Exel Logistics, a public warehousing and logistics services firm, has performed a variation of this service for the California Growers Association. Product was shipped to the Atlanta distribution center in "brights"—cans without labels—and the labels were put on the product at the warehouse as orders were received from customers.

• Consolidation of damaged and recalled products for shipment to the manufacturer in carload or truckload quantities. In addition to the documentation and prepacking that may be necessary, the public warehouse can perform the *reworking* (repair, refurbishing) of damaged product.

• Equipment maintenance and service.

• Stock spotting of product for manufacturers with limited or highly seasonal product lines. **Stock spotting** involves shipping a consolidated carload of inventory to a public warehouse just prior to a period of maximum seasonal sales.

• A breakbulk service whereby the manufacturer combines the orders of different customers in a particular market and ships them at the carload or truckload rate to the public warehouse. There the individual orders are separated and local delivery is provided.

Economies of scale result from the consolidation of small shipments with those of noncompetitors who use the same public warehouse. The public warehouse consolidates orders of specific customers from the products of a number of different manufacturers on a single shipment. This results in lower shipping costs and reduced congestion at the customer's receiving dock. Customers who pick up their orders at the public warehouse are able to obtain the products of several manufacturers with one stop, if the manufacturers all use the same facility.

Greater Flexibility

Flexibility.   Another major advantage offered by public warehouses is flexibility. Owning or holding a long-term lease on a warehouse can become a burden if business conditions necessitate changes in locations. Public warehouses require only a short-term contract and, thus, short-term commitments. Short-term contracts available from public warehouses make it easy for firms to change field warehouse locations because of changes in the marketplace (e.g., population shifts), the relative cost of various transport modes, volume of a product sold, or the company's financial position.

In addition, a firm that uses public warehouses does not have to hire or lay off employees as the volume of business changes. A public warehouse provides the personnel required for extra services when they are necessary, without having to hire them on a full-time basis.

Tax Advantages

Tax Advantages.   In some states, a firm can have an advantage if it does not own property in the state. Ownership means that the firm is doing business in the state and is thus subject to various state *taxes*. These taxes can be substantial. If the company does not currently own property in a state, it may find it advantageous to use a public warehouse.

Some states do not charge property taxes on inventories in public warehouses; this tax shelter applies to both regular warehouse inventories and storage-in-transit inventories. A **free-port** provision enacted in some states allows inventory to be held for up to one year, tax-free. The manufacturer pays no real estate tax. The public warehouse pays real estate taxes and includes this cost in its warehouse rates, but the cost is smaller on a per unit throughput basis because the cost is allocated among all of the clients using the public warehouse.

Knows Exact Warehousing Costs

Knowledge of Exact Storage and Handling Costs.   When a company uses a public warehouse, it knows the exact storage and handling costs because it receives a bill each month. The user can forecast costs for different levels of activity because the costs are known in advance. Firms that operate their own facilities often find it extremely difficult to determine the fixed and variable costs of warehousing precisely.

A public warehouse may be very flexible and adaptable in terms of meeting an organization's special requirements. For example, PRISM Team Services, a San Francisco area warehouser in the food industry, emphasizes value-added services such as just-in-time delivery, plant production support, and export shipping.[14]

Can Minimize Labor Disputes

Insulation from Labor Disputes.   The courts have ruled that a labor union does not have the right to picket a public warehouse when the union is involved in a labor dispute with one of the customers of that warehouse. Thus, using a public warehouse has the advantage of insulating the manufacturer's distribution system from a labor dispute.

Disadvantages.   A number of disadvantages are associated with the use of public warehousing.

Communication Problems

Communication Problems.   Effective communication may be a problem with public warehouses because not all computer terminals and systems are compatible. A warehouse operator may hesitate to add another terminal for only one customer. In addition, the lack of standardization in contractual agreements makes communication regarding contractual obligations difficult.

---

[14]Ann Saccamano, "California Warehouse Operator Emphasizes Tailored Services, sans Bells and Whistles," *Traffic World,* May 8, 1995, pp. 66–67.

Lack of Specialized Services	*Lack of Specialized Services.* The space or specialized services desired may not always be available in a specific location. Many public warehouse facilities provide only local service and are of limited use to a firm that distributes regionally or nationally. A manufacturer that wants to use public warehouses for national distribution may find it necessary to deal with several different operators and monitor several contractual agreements.
Space May Not Be Available	*Shortage of Space.* Public warehousing space may not be available when and where a firm wants it. Shortages of space do occur periodically in selected markets, which can have an adverse affect on the logistics and marketing strategies of a firm.

Advantages and Disadvantages of Private Warehousing

	Advantages. The advantages associated with private warehousing will now be described.
Degree of Control	*Control.* In private warehousing, the company that owns the goods can exercise a greater degree of control. The firm has direct control of and responsibility for the product until the customer takes possession or delivery, which allows the firm to integrate the warehousing function more easily into its total logistics system.
Flexibility	*Flexibility.* With warehouse control comes a greater degree of flexibility to design and operate the warehouse to fit the needs of customers and the characteristics of the product. Companies with products requiring special handling or storage may not find public warehousing feasible. The firm must utilize private warehousing or ship the product directly to customers. The warehouse can be modified through expansion or renovation to facilitate product changes, or it can be converted to a manufacturing plant or branch office location.
Less Costly over the Long Term	*Less Costly.* Private warehousing can be less costly over the long term. Operating costs can be 15 to 25 percent lower if the company achieves sufficient throughput or utilization. The generally accepted industry norm for the utilization rate is 75 to 80 percent. If a firm cannot achieve at least 75 percent utilization, it generally would be more appropriate to use public warehousing.
Better Use of Human Resources	*Better Use of Human Resources.* By employing private warehousing, a firm can make better use of its human resources. There is greater care in handling and storage when the firm's own workforce operates the warehouse. Some public warehouses allow their clients to use their own employees in the handling and storage of products. The company can utilize the expertise of its technical specialists.
Tax Benefits	*Tax Benefits.* A company also can realize tax benefits when it owns its warehouses. Depreciation allowances on buildings and equipment reduce taxes payable.

Sears services its U.S. retail stores with several large distribution centers located strategically throughout the country.

Intangible Benefits

Intangible Benefits.   There may be certain intangible benefits associated with warehouse ownership. When a firm distributes its products through a private warehouse, it can give the customer a sense of permanence and continuity of business operations. The customer sees the company as a stable, dependable, and lasting supplier of products. However, customers are more concerned with on-time delivery of products and remote warehousing sites can provide similar service levels if managed properly. The Creative Solutions box at the end of the chapter shows how Lincoln Electric achieved better distribution and thus better service for its customers through its distribution centers.

Disadvantages.   A number of disadvantages are associated with the use of private warehousing.

Lack of Flexibility

Lack of Flexibility.   Many experts feel that the major drawback of private warehousing is the same as one of its main advantages—flexibility. A private warehouse may be too costly because of its fixed size and costs. Regardless of the level of demand the firm experiences, the size of the private warehouse is restricted in the short term. A private facility cannot expand and contract to meet increases or decreases in demand. When demand is low, the firm must still assume the fixed costs as well as the lower productivity linked to unused warehouse space. The disadvantage can be minimized if the firm is able to rent out part of its space.

If a firm uses only private warehouses, it loses flexibility in its strategic location options. If a company cannot adapt to rapid changes in market size, location, and preferences it may lose a valuable business opportunity. Customer service and sales could fall if a private warehouse cannot adapt to changes in the firm's product mix.

Financial Constraints   *Financial Constraints.*   Because of the high costs involved, many firms are simply unable to generate enough capital to build or buy a warehouse. A warehouse is a long-term, often risky investment (which later may be difficult to sell because of its customized design). The hiring and training of employees, and the purchase of materials handling equipment makes start-up a costly and time-consuming process. And, depending on the nature of the firm, return on investment may be greater if funds are channeled into other profit-generating opportunities.

Rate of Return   *Rate of Return.*   A further consideration in the decision is the rate of return that the private warehouse alternative will provide. At a minimum, the investment in a corporate-owned warehouse should generate the same rate of return as the firm's other investments. Most companies find it advantageous to use some combination of public and private warehousing. Private warehouses are used to handle the basic inventory levels required for least cost logistics in markets where the volume justifies ownership. Public warehouses are used where volume is insufficient to justify ownership or to store peak requirements.

Public warehouses typically charge on the basis of cases, pallets, or hundredweight stored or handled. When the volume of activity is sufficiently large, public warehousing charges exceed the cost of a private facility, making ownership more attractive.[15]

Facility Development

One of the more important decisions a logistics executive faces is how to develop an optimal warehousing network for the firm's products and customers. Such a decision encompasses a number of significant elements. Management must determine the size and number of warehouses, and ascertain their location. Each warehouse must be laid out and designed properly in order to maximize efficiency and productivity.

Size and Number of Warehouses

Two issues that must be addressed are the size and number of warehouse facilities. These are interrelated decisions because they typically have an inverse relationship; that is, as the *number* of warehouses increases, the average *size* of a warehouse decreases.

Size of a Warehouse.   Many factors influence how large a warehouse should be. First, it is necessary to define how size is measured. In general, size can be defined in terms of

---

[15]For a discussion of these and other issues concerning public and private warehousing, as well as criteria to consider in selecting between the various warehousing options, see Cooke, "Getting the Right Fit," pp. 78–80; James Aaron Cooke, "How to Pick a Public Warehouse," *Traffic Management,* Jan. 1994, Warehousing and Distribution Supplement pp. 14–16; C. Alan McCarrell, "Monitoring Public Warehouses," *Warehousing Forum* 8, no. 4 (Mar. 1993), pp. 1–4; Hugh L. Randall, "Contact Logistics: Is Outsourcing Right for You?" in *The Logistics Handbook,* ed. James F. Robeson and William C. Copacino (New York: Free Press, 1994), pp. 508–16; and William G. Sheehan, "Criteria for Judging a Public Warehouse," *Warehousing Forum* 11, no. 5 (Apr. 1996), p. 3.

square footage or cubic space. Most public warehouses still use square footage dimensions in their advertising and promotional efforts.

Unfortunately, square footage measures ignore the capability of modern warehouses to store merchandise vertically. Hence, the cubic space measure was developed. Cubic space refers to the total volume of space available *within* a facility. It is a much more realistic size estimate than square footage because it considers more of the available usable space in a warehouse. Some of the most important factors affecting the size of a warehouse are:

Factors Affecting Warehouse Size

- Customer service levels.
- Size of market or markets served.
- Number of products marketed.
- Size of the product or products.
- Materials handling system used.
- Throughput rate.
- Production lead time.
- Economies of scale.
- Stock layout.
- Aisle requirements.
- Office area in warehouse.
- Types of racks and shelves used.
- Level and pattern of demand.

As a company's service levels increase, it typically requires more warehousing space to provide storage for higher levels of inventory. As the market served by a warehouse increases in number or size, additional space is required. When a firm has multiple products or product groupings, especially if they are diverse, it needs larger warehouses to maintain at least minimal inventory levels of all products. In general, greater space requirements are necessary when products are large; production lead time is long; manual materials handling systems are used; the warehouse contains office, sales, or computer activities; and demand is erratic and unpredictable.

Warehouse Size Is Related to the Materials Handling Equipment Used

To illustrate, consider the relation of warehouse size to the type of materials handling equipment used.[16] As Figure 8–5 shows, the type of forklift truck a warehouse employs can significantly affect the amount of storage area necessary to store product. Because of different capabilities of forklift trucks, a firm can justify the acquisition of more expensive units when it is able to bring about more effective utilization of space. The four examples in Figure 8–5 show that warehouse layout and warehouse handling systems, one of the topics described in Chapter 9, are interwined.

The simplest type of forklift truck, the counterbalanced truck, requires aisles that are 10 to 12 feet wide. At $30,000, it is the least expensive forklift. The turret truck requires aisles only 5 to 7 feet wide to handle the same amount of product, but it costs $65,000 or

---

[16]Examples can be found in Clyde E. Witt, "Multi-Million Dollar Facelift for Exchange Service," *Material Handling Engineering* 43, no. 8 (Aug. 1988), pp. 47–53; "How to Implement Robotic Palletizing," *Material Handling Engineering* 43, no. 7 (July 1988), pp. 61–64; and Clyde E. Witt, "Publisher Creates Textbook Case for Distribution," *Material Handling Engineering* 43, no. 3 (Mar. 1988), pp. 41–47.

FIGURE 8–5

Narrow-aisle trucks can reduce floor space

Type of truck	Deep reach	Turret	Reach-fork	Counter-balanced
Area required	5,550 sq. ft.	3,070 sq. ft.	6,470 sq. ft.	10,000 sq. ft.
Aisle width	102 inches	66 inches	96 inches	144 inches
Floor space saved	45%	70%	33%	————

Source: James Aaron Cooke, "When to Choose a Narrow-Aisle Lift Truck," *Traffic Management* 28, no. 12 (Dec. 1989), p. 55.

more.[17] The warehouse decision maker must examine the cost trade-offs for each of the available systems, and determine which alternative is most advantageous from a cost-service perspective.

Demand Fluctuations Impact Warehouse Size

Demand also has an impact on warehouse size. Whenever demand fluctuates significantly or is unpredictable, inventory levels generally must be higher. This results in a need for more space and thus a larger warehouse. All the warehousing space need not be private. Many firms utilize a combination of private and public warehousing. Figure 8–6 shows the relationship between demand and warehouse size.

The hypothetical firm depicted in Figure 8–6 utilizes private warehousing to store 36,000 units of inventory. This results in full utilization of its facilities all year, with the exception of July and August. For months when inventory requirements exceed private warehousing space, the firm rents short-term storage space from one or more public warehouses. In essence, the firm develops private facilities to accommodate a maximum level of inventory of 36,000 units.

Inventory velocity (as measured by turnover) and the maximization of "direct deliveries" to customers (bypassing a regional or wholesaler's warehouse) can have a great impact on the size of a warehouse. Whirlpool Corporation developed a computer program to simulate these two characteristics, as well as the cubic warehousing space requirements of its total channel network, including wholesale distributors. The company calculated the square footage required for each of its factory-controlled and wholesale warehouses. It added space to the base requirements of each of its major product categories in order to

---

[17]See Edward H. Frazelle and James M. Apple, Jr., "Materials Handling Technologies," in *The Logistics Handbook,* ed. James F. Robeson and William C. Copacino, (New York: Free Press, 1994), p. 560.

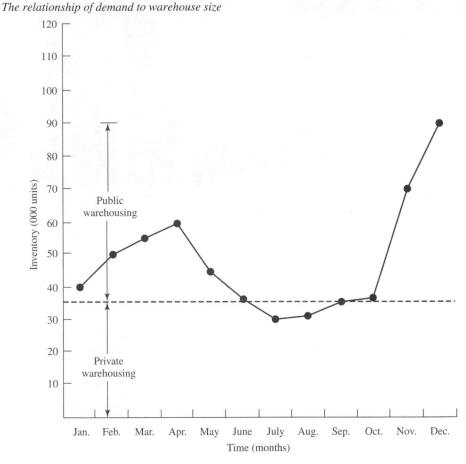

Figure 8–6

The relationship of demand to warehouse size

provide for aisles and docks, and unused (empty) vertical and horizontal storage bays. By manipulating planned sales volumes, inventory turns, and orders shipped directly to dealers, Whirlpool was able to accurately project future warehousing needs.[18]

Four Factors Influence the Number of Warehouses

Number of Warehouses.   Four factors are significant in deciding on the number of warehousing facilities: cost of lost sales, inventory costs, warehousing costs, and transportation costs. Figure 8–7 depicts these cost areas except for cost of lost sales.

Cost of Lost Sales

Cost of Lost Sales.   Although lost sales are extremely important to a firm, they are the most difficult to calculate and predict, and they vary by company and industry. If the **cost of lost sales** appeared in Figure 8–7, it would generally slope down and to the right. The degree of slope, however, would vary by industry, company, product, and customer.

---

[18]Illustration provided by Professor Jay U. Sterling, University of Alabama, and former director of logistics planning for Whirlpool Corporation.

Figure 8–7

Relationship between total logistics cost and the number of warehouses

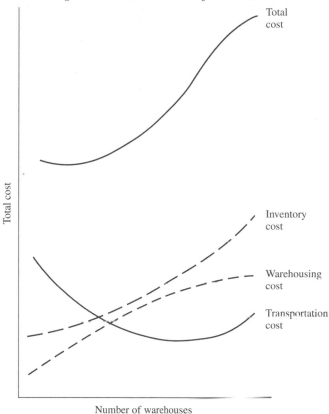

The remaining components of Figure 8–7 are more consistent across firms and industries.

Inventory Costs

Inventory Costs.   Inventory costs increase with the number of facilities because firms usually stock a minimum amount (e.g., safety stock) of all products at every location, although some companies have specific warehouses dedicated to a particular product or product grouping. This means that both slow and fast turnover items are stocked; thus, more total space is required.

Warehousing Costs

Warehousing Costs.   Warehousing costs increase, because more warehouses mean more space to be owned, leased, or rented, but they decrease after a number of warehouses are brought on-line, particularly if the firm leases or rents space. Public and contract warehouses often offer quantity discounts when firms acquire space in multiple locations.

Transportation Costs

Transportation Costs.   Transportation costs initially decline as the number of warehouses increase, but they eventually curve upward if too many facilities are employed owing to the combination of inbound and outbound transportation costs. A firm must be concerned with the total delivered cost of its products, not simply the cost of moving products to warehouse locations. In general, the use of fewer facilities means lower inbound transport costs due to bulk shipments from the manufacturer or supplier.

After the number of warehouses increases to a certain point, the firm may not be able to ship its products in such large quantities and may have to pay a higher rate to the transportation carrier. Local transportation costs for delivery of products from warehouses to customers may increase because of minimum charges that apply to local cartage.

If the cost of lost sales is not included, the slopes shown in Figure 8–7, taken together, indicate that fewer warehouses are better than many warehouses. However, customer service is a critical element of a firm's marketing and logistics systems. In general, if the cost of lost sales is very high, a firm may wish to expand its number of warehouses or use scheduled deliveries. There are always cost-service trade-offs. Management must determine the optimal number of warehouses given the desired customer-service level.

Value of Computers.   Computers can help minimize the firm's number of warehouses by improving warehouse layout and design, inventory control, shipping and receiving, and the dissemination of information. Coupled with more efficient warehouses, the substitution of information for inventories tends to reduce the number of warehouses needed to service a firm's customers. In essence, the more responsive the logistics system, the less need there is for warehousing.

Location Analysis

Where Is the Best Place to Locate a Warehouse?

Where would be the best place to build a warehouse that would service the greatest number of U.S. consumers? Bloomington, Indiana, would be closer, on average, to the U.S. population than any other location.[19] If a firm wished to locate facilities closest to its potential customers, using one or more warehouses in their logistics network, a number of sites would be possible. Table 8–1 identifies the best locations given various warehouse configurations.

The site-selection decision can be approached from macro and micro perspectives. The macro perspective examines the issue of where to locate warehouses geographically within a general area so as to improve the sourcing of materials and the firm's market offering (improve service and/or reduce cost). The micro perspective examines factors that pinpoint specific locations within the large geographic areas.

Macro Approaches.   In one of the best-known macro approaches to warehouse location, Edgar M. Hoover, an American location theorist, identified three types of location strategies: (1) market positioned, (2) production positioned, and (3) intermediately positioned.[20] The **market-positioned strategy** locates warehouses nearest to the final customer. This maximizes customer service levels and enables a firm to utilize transportation economies—TL and CL shipments—from plants or sources to each warehouse location.

Market-Positioned Warehouses

---

[19]"10 Best Warehouse Networks for 1997," Chicago Consulting Information Sheet, undated.
[20]Edgar M. Hoover, *The Location of Economic Activity* (New York: McGraw-Hill, 1948), p. 11.

TABLE 8–1   10 Best Warehouse Networks for 1997
Warehouse Networks Closest to the U.S. Population

Number of Warehouses in the Network	Shortest Average Distance to the U.S. Population (miles)	Best Warehouse Location		
One	788	Bloomington, IN		
Two	483	Chillicothe, OH	Mojave, CA	
Three	372	Allentown, PA	Paducah, KY	Mojave, CA
Four	316	Caldwell, NJ Mojave, CA	Cincinnati, OH	Dallas, TX
Five	261	Summit, NJ Dallas, TX	Macon, GA Mojave, CA	Chicago, IL
Six	234	Summit, NJ Dallas, TX	Macon, GA Pasadena, CA	Chicago, IL Tacoma, WA
Seven	218	Caldwell, NJ Rockford, IL Tacoma, WA	Macon, GA Tacoma, WA	Mansfield, OH Pasadena, CA
Eight	200	Caldwell, NJ Mansfield, OH	Gainesville, GA Rockford, IL	Lakeland, FL Dallas, TX
Nine	186	Caldwell, NJ Mansfield, OH Alhambra, CA	Gainesville, GA Rockford, IL Oakland, CA	Lakeland, FL Dallas, TX Tacoma, WA
Ten	173	Caldwell, NJ Mansfield, OH Denver, CO Tacoma, WA	Gainesville, GA Rockford, IL Long Beach, CA	Lakeland, FL Palestine, TX Oakland, CA

Best Networks: The service a warehouse network can provide is the time it takes to deliver products to customers. This depends on the distance from the network to them. The above networks are "best" because they are the *lowest possible average distance* to the U.S. population. Of course, an individual company's warehouse network should be designed to be low cost and to serve their specific customers (which may be different from the U.S. population).

Example: In the best two-warehouse network above with locations at Chillicothe, OH, and Mojave, CA, shipments to everyone in the United States would range from very short distances to hundreds of miles. The *average* distance is 483 miles. Furthermore, this is the lowest possible average distance in *any* two-warehouse network.

Source: Chicago Consulting, Chicago, IL.

The factors that influence the placement of warehouses near the market areas served include transportation costs, order cycle time, the sensitivity of the product, order size, local transportation availability, and levels of customer service offered.

Production-Positioned Warehouses

The **production-positioned strategy** locates warehouses in close proximity to sources of supply or production facilities. These warehouses generally cannot provide the same level of customer service as market-positioned warehouses; instead, they serve as collection points or mixing facilities for products manufactured at a number of different plants.

For multiproduct companies, transportation economies result from consolidation of shipments into TL or CL quantities. The factors that influence the placement of warehouses close to the point of production are perishability of raw materials, number of products in the firm's product mix, assortment of products ordered by customers, and transportation consolidation rates.

Intermediately Positioned Warehouses

The **intermediately positioned strategy** places warehouses at a midpoint location between the final customer and the producer. Customer service levels are typically higher for intermediately positioned warehouses than they are for the production-positioned facilities and lower than for market-positioned facilities. A firm often follows this strategy if it must offer high customer service levels and if it has a varied product offering manufactured at several plant locations.

Von Thünen's Model

Another macro approach includes the combined theories of a number of well-known economic geographers. Many of these theories are based on distance and cost considerations. Johan Heinrich von Thünen (1783–1850), German agriculturalist, called for a strategy of facility location based on cost minimization.[21] Specifically, when locating points of agricultural production, he argued that transportation costs should be minimized to result in maximum profits for farmers. Von Thünen's model assumed that market price and production costs would be identical (or nearly so) for any point of production. Since farmer profits equal market price less production costs and transportation costs, the optimal location would have to be the one that minimized transportation expenditures.

Weber's Model

Alfred Weber, a German economist, also developed a model of facility location based on cost minimization.[22] According to Weber, the optimal site was one that minimized "total transportation costs—the costs of transferring raw materials to the plant and finished goods to the market."[23] Weber classified raw materials into two categories according to their effect on transportation costs: location and processing characteristics. Location referred to the geographical availability of the raw materials. Few constraints would exist on facility locations for items that had wide availability.

Processing characteristics were concerned with whether the raw material increased, remained the same, or decreased in weight as it was processed. If the processed raw material decreased in weight, facilities should be located near the raw material source because transportation costs of finished goods would be less with lower weights. Conversely, if processing resulted in heavier finished goods, facilities should be located closer to the final customers. If processing resulted in no change in weight, a location close to raw material sources or to markets for finished goods would be equivalent.

Hoover's Model

Other economic geographers included the factors of demand and profitability in the location decision. **Hoover's model** considered both cost and demand elements, and stressed cost minimization in determining an optimal location. In addition, Hoover identified that transportation rates and distance were not linearly related; that is, rates increased with distance, but at a decreasing rate. The tapering of rates over greater distances supported placement of warehouses at the end points of the channel of distribution, rather that at some intermediate location. In that regard, Hoover did not fully agree with Weber's location choices.

---

[21]See *Von Thünen's Isolated State,* C. M. Warnenburg, trans., and Peter Hall, ed. (Oxford: Pergamon Press, 1966).

[22]See Alfred Weber, *Theory of the Location of Industries,* trans. Carl J. Friedrich (Chicago: University of Chicago Press, 1929).

[23]John J. Coyle, Edward J. Bardi, and C. John Langley, Jr., *The Management of Business Logistics,* 6th ed. (St. Paul, MN: West, 1996) p. 474.

Greenhut's Model   Melvin Greenhut, an American location theorist, expanded upon the work of his predecessors by including factors specific to the company (e.g., environment, security) and profitability elements in the location choice. According to Greenhut, the optimal facility location was one that maximized profits.[24]

Center-of-Gravity Approach   Another approach, the **center-of-gravity approach,** is simplistic in scope, and locates facilities based on transportation costs. This approach locates a warehouse or distribution center at a point that minimizes transportation costs for products moving between a manufacturing plant and the markets.

Envision two pieces of rope tied together with a knot and stretched across a circular piece of board, with unequal weights attached to each end of the rope. Initially, the knot would be located in the center of the circle. Upon the release of the weights, the rope would shift to the point where the weights would be in balance. Adding ropes with varying weights would result in the same shifting of the knot (assuming the knots were all in the same place). If the weights represented transportation costs, then the position where the knot would come to rest after releasing the weights would represent the center of gravity or position where transportation costs would be minimized.[25] The approach provides general answers to the warehouse location problem, but it must be modified to take into account factors such as geography, time, and customer service levels.

Micro Approaches.   From a micro perspective, more specific site-selection factors must be examined.[26] If a firm wants to use private warehousing, it must consider:

Some Important Site-Selection Factors
- Quality and variety of transportation carriers serving the site.
- Quality and quantity of available labor.
- Labor rates.
- Cost and quality of industrial land.
- Potential for expansion.
- Tax structure.
- Building codes.
- Nature of the community environment.
- Costs of construction.
- Cost and availability of utilities.
- Cost of money locally.
- Local government tax allowances and inducements to build.

---

[24]See Melvin L. Greenhut, *Plant Location in Theory and in Practice* (Chapel Hill: University of North Carolina Press, 1956).

[25]For a similar discussion of the center-of-gravity approach, see Philip B. Schary, *Logistics Decisions* (Chicago: Dryden Press, 1984), p. 423.

[26]For a comprehensive discussion of the warehouse location decision, see "A Guide to Site Selection in the '90s," *Traffic Management* 34, no. 9 (Sept. 1993), Warehousing and Distribution Supplement, pp. 22–23; Thomas L. Freese, "Site Selection," in *The Logistics Handbook,* ed. James F. Robeson and William C. Copacino (New York: Free Press, 1994), pp. 604–31; Tan Miller, "Learning about Facility Location Models," *Distribution* 92, no. 5 (May 1993), pp. 47–50; and Robert Pano, "Pull Out the Stops in Your Network," *Transportation and Distribution* 35, no. 8 (Aug. 1994), pp. 38–39.

If the firm wants to use public warehousing, it will be necessary to consider:

Public Warehousing Considerations

- Facility characteristics.
- Warehouse services.
- Availability and proximity to motor carrier terminals.
- Availability of local cartage.
- Other companies using the facility.
- Availability of computer services and communications.
- Type and frequency of inventory reports.[27]

The site-selection process is interactive, progressing from the general to the specific. It may be formalized or informal, centralized at the corporate level, decentralized at the divisional or functional level, or some combination of each. It is important that management follow some type of logical process that recognizes many trade-offs when making a location decision.

Many nonquantitative and political factors may take on great importance in the warehouse locating decision. An example is shown for Target (a discount department store) in Box 8–3.

Related to the location of facilities is the decision to design an optimal structure that maximize efficiency and effectiveness. This is the warehouse layout and design decision.

Warehouse Layout and Design

Where should products/materials be located in the logistics system and, more particularly, within the warehouse? With an average warehouse containing about 22,000 stockkeeping units (SKUs), this consideration has a critical effect on system efficiency and productivity.[28] A good warehouse layout can (1) increase output, (2) improve product flow, (3) reduce costs, (4) improve service to customers, and (5) provide better employee working conditions.[29]

Benefits of Good Warehouse Layout

The optimal warehouse layout and design for a firm will vary by the type of product being stored, the company's financial resources, competitive environment, and needs of customers. In addition, the warehouse manager must consider cost trade-offs between labor, equipment, space, and information.

For example (see Figure 8–5), the purchase of more expensive, yet more efficient, materials handling equipment can affect the optimal size of a warehouse facility. Installation of an expensive conveyor system to reduce labor costs and raise productivity can affect the configuration of a warehouse. Considering all of the possible factors and their combinations, it is imperative that the firm use a logical and consistent decision strategy

---

[27]See "Basic Tools for Locating a Site," *Plants, Sites and Parks,* Sept.–Oct. 1989, pp. 46–63; and Freese, "Site Selection," pp. 604–31.

[28]Philippe R. Hebert, "Manage Inventory? Better Find it First!" *Transportation and Distribution,* July 1995, Buyers Guide Issue, p. 8.

[29]Greg Owens and Robert Mann, "Materials Handling System Design," in *The Distribution Handbook,* ed. James F. Robeson and William C. Copacino (New York: Free Press, 1994), pp. 519–45; see also "Layout Principles That Upgrade Materials Flow," *Modern Materials Handling* 41, no. 13 (Fall 1986), pp. 25–27.

Box 8–3

Target Stores Discover There is More to Site Selection Than Running the Right Models

In choosing a location for a major distribution center to serve the Chicago region, Target Stores considered 55 sites in three states. It did all of the right things: considered proximity to market, transportation costs, labor availability, and tax incentives offered by each community. It narrowed the pool of prospects to three sites, then chose an industrial park in Oconomowoc, Wisconsin. What Target didn't anticipate was landing in the middle of a battle between politicians over environmental concerns.

Target had gone through all the necessary legal and environmental processes to break ground on the Wisconsin site. Yet the environmental groups weren't satisfied. What about groundwater runoff? What about air pollution and congestion from truck and employee traffic? These groups believed the Target project was rushed—"ramrodded" through the state with minimal public awareness or input. To complicate matters further, a neighboring town was protesting this development because of an old battle with Oconomowoc on water and sewer lines. Wisconsin politicians were upset about the impact that this battle would have on the state's "aggressive pro-business attitude."

What did Target learn from this process? Target management would have taken more time to meet in advance with local groups if they had realized the extent of these concerns. Second, going through all the "right" steps in the political process—dealing with regulators and local governments—is not enough. Third, citizens in small towns such as Oconomowoc, population 7,000, are even more sensitive to the impact of a new facility in their town. Adding more housing, schools, roads, and general infrastructure might change the atmosphere of the town in a manner that would be viewed unfavorably by current residents. Local businesses might feel threatened that their longtime employees may be stolen away by the new employer in town.

Once a facility is in place, its long-range success and viability depends on maintaining and enhancing its good citizenship. Target is committed to this policy. As part of this commitment, it donates 5 percent of its pretax income each year to communities where it has facilities. This story has a happy ending. The Oconomowoc facilities were built and are operational. A great deal of expense and delay could have been avoided by involving the community and concerned citizens and groups in the process at an earlier stage.

Source: Adapted from Tom Andel, "Site Selection: How to Avoid Rough Landings," *Transportation and Distribution* 34, no. 8 (Aug. 1993), pp. 30–35.

to develop an optimal warehousing system for itself. Whatever layout the company finally selects for its warehouse, it is vital that all available space be utilized as fully and efficiently as possible.[30]

Randomized Storage   **Randomized Storage.**   Randomized and dedicated storage are two examples of how products can be located and arranged. **Randomized storage,** or **floating slot storage,** places items in the closest available slot, bin, or rack. The items are retrieved on a first-in, first-out (FIFO) basis. This approach maximizes space utilization, although it necessitates longer travel times between order-picking locations. Randomized systems often employ a computerized automatic storage and retrieval system (AS/RS) which minimizes labor and handling costs.

---

[30]"Storage/Staging: Planning Pays Off," *Modern Materials Handling* 50, no. 5 (Mid-April 1995), pp. 12–15.

Good warehouse layout and design often involve the use of automated equipment, such as a conveyor system to handle large numbers of products packaged in cartons.

Dedicated Storage

Dedicated Storage.   Another example is **dedicated storage,** or **fixed-slot storage.** In this approach, products are stored in permanent locations within the warehouse. This tends to be common in manual labor situations where employee performance improves as employees learn each product's location. Three methods can be used to implement the dedicated storage approach, including storing items by (1) part number sequence, (2) usage rates, or (3) activity levels (e.g., grouping products into classes or families based on how fast products move in and out of storage).[31]

Products Can Be Grouped by Compatibility

In terms of overall warehouse layout, products may be grouped according to their compatibility, complementarity, or popularity. **Compatibility** refers to whether products can be stored together harmoniously. For example, pharmaceuticals cannot be stored with bagged agricultural chemicals because of U.S. Food and Drug Administration regulations. Many years ago before the development of newer paints, it was discovered that automobile tires and consumer appliances could not be stored together. Apparently, chemical vapors given off by the tires reacted with the pigments in the appliance paint, resulting in slight color changes. Appliances had to be repainted or sold at a discount.

Products Can Be Grouped by Complementarity

Complementarity refers to how often products are ordered together and therefore stored together. Computer disk drives and monitors, pens and pencils, and desks and chairs are examples of complementary products that are usually stored in close proximity

Products Can Be Grouped by Popularity

Popularity relates to the different inventory turnover rates or demand rates of products. Another term used for this turnover rate is *velocity*. Items that are in greatest demand should be stored closest to shipping and receiving docks. Slow-moving items should be stored elsewhere. In a food wholesaler's warehouse, for example, nonrefrigerated basic food items are stored close to the outbound shipping area, whereas slow movers are located in more remote areas of the warehouse.

---

[31]For a brief discussion of random and dedicated storage, see Hebert, "Manage Inventory? Better Find it First!" pp. 7–9.

Using the computer, it is possible to group products within a warehouse, so that the following objectives are met:[32]

• Fast movers are placed nearest the outbound truck docks. This minimizes the distances traveled daily by materials handling equipment.

• Slow movers are located at points farthest from outbound shipping docks. This ensures that lengthy horizontal moves by materials handling equipment are minimized.

• Remaining areas in the warehouse are reserved for products received in periodic batches, those requiring rework before shipping, those that are compatible with fast-moving products, and backup overflow from fast-moving areas.

• Aisles are redesigned to facilitate the most efficient flow of products to and from dock areas.

• Storage areas are configured to match the velocity and dimensions of each major product, rather than designing all storage bins, racks, and floor storage areas in the same dimensions. This facilitates the maximum use of available cubic space, because products are not only matched to the width of each slot, but also to the depth and height of each storage slot.

The entire area of facilities development—size and number of warehouses, location analysis, warehouse layout and design—is an important, yet complex, part of warehouse management. In recent years, computers have played a much more significant role as logistics executives attempt to optimize warehouse operations. With increased globalization, many firms now face the issue of international warehousing.

International Dimensions of Warehousing

Products must be stored at some point prior to their final consumption. Depending on the particular conditions in effect in each foreign market, products may be stored at different points within the channel of distribution.

In the European Union (EU), Philips, a large multinational electronics firm, must store and warehouse a variety of products at factories throughout Europe.

Warehousing in the EU

> Philips has poured impressive sums into the establishment of superautomated international distribution centers, or "Eurostores," for each of its product divisions.
>
> A typical Eurostore is that of Philips's Lighting Division, located in the Dutch city of Roosendaal. Its preeminent features are an immense high-bay warehouse and an all-encompassing computer system that runs the entire operation on an ORFO (order of forwarding) basis. The Eurostore is a study in quiet, rhythmic efficiency, with human management evident only at critical monitoring locations.[33]

If a firm is involved in exporting, it may store items domestically and ship them only after it receives orders. Thus, no foreign storage is necessary.

---

[32]For a discussion of how computers can be used in warehouse space utilization, see Richard A. Parrott, "Automated Space Planning for Warehousing," *Transportation and Distribution* 33, no. 7 (July 1992), pp. 54, 56; and Tompkins et al., *Facilities Planning*, pp. 418–34.

[33]Joseph V. Barks, "Strategies for International Distribution," *Distribution* 84, no. 5 (May 1985), p. 69.

If distributors or other intermediaries are used, inventories will have to be stored or warehoused at other locations within the channel. The ability of the manufacturer or supplier to push the inventory down the channel of distribution varies from market to market, depending on the size of the channel intermediaries, customer inventory policies, demand for the product by final consumers, storage costs, and customer service levels necessary to serve each market.

In Japan and most European countries, the retail network is composed of a great number of small shops, each having little capacity for inventory storage. As a result, these shops order frequently from distributors, manufacturers, or other channel intermediaries. The burden of storage is carried by the manufacturer or other channel members instead of by the retailer. In the United States, where retail stores are fewer in number but much larger, the storage function is more easily shifted from the channel intermediaries directly to the retailer.

The Quality and Availability of Warehousing Varies Widely

When an international firm needs warehousing facilities in a foreign market, it may find an abundance of sophisticated, modern warehouses in some industrial nations. In Japan, for example, many companies use high-cube automated warehousing. On the other hand, storage facilities in many developing countries may be nonexistent or limited in availability or sophistication. In the latter instance, the product package or shipping container may have to serve the warehousing purpose. Third-party providers such as CTI, Exel, GATX, and Ryder Integrated Logistics have begun operations in Latin America and Asia at the request of their North American customers.

In the United States, many public warehouses provide services such as consolidation and breakbulk, customer billing, traffic management, packaging, and labeling. Public warehouses in many foreign markets also may provide services in addition to storage.[34]

Like all logistics activities, the warehousing and storage activity must be administered differently in each foreign market. The logistics executive is responsible for recognizing how the storage activity differs and adjusting the firm's strategy accordingly.

Warehouse Productivity Measurement

To obtain maximum logistics efficiency, each component of the logistics system must operate at optimal levels. This means that high levels of productivity must be achieved, especially in the warehousing area. Productivity gains in warehousing are important to the firm in terms of reduced costs and to its customers in terms of improved customer service levels (see the Global box).

Productivity Defined

Productivity has been defined in many ways, but most definitions include the notions of real outputs and real inputs, utilization, and warehouse performance. One study defined those elements as follows:

• *Productivity is the ratio of real output to real input.* Examples are cases handled per labor-hour and lines selected per equipment-hour.

• *Utilization is the ratio of capacity used to available capacity.* Examples are the percent of pallet spaces filled in a warehouse and employee-hours worked versus employee-hours available.

---

[34]For an example from Mexico, see Russ Dixon, "Logistics in Mexico: The Warehouse Solution," *Export Today* 9, no. 6 (July–Aug. 1993), pp. 38–39.

Global

BBN Communications Serves Customers Worldwide

BBN Communications of Cambridge, Massachusetts, manufactures high-value telecommunications and networking equipment, "including components that allow a firm's satellite offices to combine all computer traffic on a local area network and communicate with the home office to share information." The firm searched for ways to improve service levels to customers located in North America and Europe.

"BBN Communications' remote warehousing solution relies on same-day shipping and delivery of . . . components. BBN has established sites in London and Stuttgart for warehousing its high-value materials. London currently is the larger of the two sites.

"Not only do these sites build a comfort level for the parts managers, but also they make life easier on the BBN sales staff. . . There are hidden dollar sav-

ings to using a location within the [EU] for warehousing parts. One never knows to which country a part might be sent and it is impractical to establish warehouses in every country. By establishing parts centers within the [EU], BBN pays duties only once on materials shipped into [another country] and stored at a parts bank.

"So successful has the European parts bank been [that the company] is considering establishment of a similar depot in Asia . . . either Singapore or Hong Kong—to take advantage of the duty free ports there, again bringing cost savings into the warehousing and distribution network."

Source: Renee Sall, "Case Study: BBN Communications," *Export Today* 9, no. 6 (July–Aug. 1993), p. 45.

• *Performance is the ratio of actual output to standard output (or standard hours earned to actual hours).* Examples are cases picked per hour versus standard rate planned per hour, and actual return on assets employed versus budgeted return on assets employed.[35]

Any working definition of productivity probably includes all three components because they are interrelated. Most firms utilize a variety of measures. Firms tend to use more sophisticated productivity measures over time.

A multitude of warehouse productivity measures are used although they can be grouped into major categories such as labor cost per unit handled, amount of space needed to store each unit, and frequency of errors.[36] Performance data must be available and used as the basis for corrective action and proactive improvement.

You Can't Manage What You Don't Measure

The general management notion that "you can't manage what you don't measure" is an important warehousing performance concept. Some of the most important areas of

Risk

---

[35]A. T. Kearney, Inc., *Measuring and Improving Productivity in Physical Distribution* (Oak Brook, IL: National Council of Physical Distribution Management, 1984), p. 188; see also Douglas Lambert, "Logistics Cost, Productivity, and Performance Analysis," in *The Logistics Handbook,* ed. James F. Robeson and William C. Copacino (New York: Free Press, 1994), pp. 289–91.

[36]Kenneth B. Ackerman, "Meeting the 'Process Needs' of Warehousing," *Warehousing Forum* 9, no. 5 (Apr. 1994), pp. 1–3.

measurement that highlight problems or opportunities include customer service (e.g., shipping performance, error rates, order cycle time), inventory accuracy (e.g., the quantity of each SKU is correct at all warehouse locations), space utilization (e.g., having the right inventory, square foot or cube utilization of facilities), and labor productivity (e.g., throughput rates).[37]

It is not enough to merely identify problem areas; rather, it is vital that the firm take appropriate actions to improve poor performance whenever possible. A company should develop decision strategies to handle most problem areas before the problems develop. This is the essence of contingency planning. Once issues are pinpointed, the firm can institute various controls or corrective actions to improve warehouse productivity.

Improving Warehouse Productivity

Because warehousing is such a significant component of the logistics process in terms of its cost and service impacts, logistics executives are acutely aware of the need to improve warehouse productivity. Productivity can be improved in many ways, including methods-related, equipment-related, systems-related, and training/motivation-related programs.[38]

Methods-Related Programs

Methods-related programs consider alternative processes for achieving desired results. They include those involving warehouse cube utilization, warehouse layout and design, methods and procedures analysis, batch picking of small orders, combined putaway/picking, wrap packaging,[39] inventory cycle counting, product line obsolescence, standardized packaging, and warehouse consolidation.

Equipment-Related Programs

Equipment-related programs include the use of new technology such as optical scanners, automatic labeling devices, computer generated putaway and pick lists, automated materials handling equipment, communications devices, computers and automated storage/retrieval systems (AS/RSs), carousels, and conveyors. The Technology box shows how a grocery chain used a radio-frequency system to track its products.

---

[37]*The Journey to Warehousing Excellence,* Monograph Series no. M0003 (Raleigh, NC: Tompkins Associates, n.d.), p. 22; see also Kenneth B. Ackerman, "Benchmarking and the Holy Grail," *Warehousing Forum* 11, no. 2 (Jan. 1996), pp. 1–2; and "How to Benchmark Warehouse Operations," *Distribution* 91, no. 9 (Sept. 1992), pp. 60–64.

[38]This material was paraphrased from A. T. Kearney, Inc., *Measuring and Improving Productivity in Physical Distribution,* pp. 227–34. Used with permission of the Council of Logistics Management, formerly the National Council of Physical Distribution Management.

[39]Wrap packaging includes shrink and stretch film used to protect the product from the elements and to replace rigid, generally corrugated, packaging.

Technology

Radio to the Rescue

"Software can be a real space saver in the warehouse today. Especially when it's combined with a radio-frequency (RF) system to track product instantly. At least that's what West Coast grocery chain Smart and Final discovered.

Faced with a space shortage, the company installed a radio-frequency inventory management system to provide a 'real time' fix on its inventory. Thanks to that up-to-the-minute information about stock on hand, the company was able to use warehouse space better. . . How much better? Smart and Final estimates that the radio-frequency inventory management system brought about a 10 to 15 percent increase in space utilization.

The West's oldest and largest grocery retailer, Smart and Final earned roughly $1 billion last year [1995]. The Los Angeles–based company, which operates a chain of approximately 150 nonmembership warehouse stores up and down the West Coast, ships more than 400 outbound loads of dry goods and health and beauty care products weekly from its distribution center in Los Angeles. A private fleet delivers product to the stores and picks up some inbound shipments on backhauls as well. The company moves freight seven days a week, shipping full trailerloads whenever possible.

Due to growing business, however, the company faced a space shortage at its distribution center three years ago. It had begun considering relocating to a new warehouse when managers decided that a real-time inventory software system just might do the trick. [The company] purchased a radio-frequency (RF) control system that would enhance the company's existing computer system. In an RF setup, workers scan bar-coded items. The scanned data then are fed continuously via radio waves to a computer that monitors stock level and location.

As impressive as the inventory-related improvements may be, they're not the whole story. For one thing, the radio-frequency inventory system also has increased productivity by 25 percent. Today, the center completely turns its inventory 26 times a year.

But most importantly of all, the system increased space utilization at Smart and Final's distribution center to such a degree that a new warehouse is no longer needed."

Source: James Aaron Cooke, "Radio to the Rescue," *Logistics Management* 35, no. 4 (Apr. 1996), pp. 59–62.

Systems-Related Programs

Systems-related programs include the use of router/location systems, geographic or zone picking, and random location of products in the warehouse. These are systems related because they directly affect the way that different components of the logistics system interact.

Training/Motivation-Related Programs

Training/motivation-related programs include employee training, management development programs, work teams,[40] incentive systems, and awards recognition. These programs

[40]Toby B. Gooley, "Team Spirit," *Traffic Management* 34, no. 9 (Sept. 1993), Warehousing and Distribution Supplement, pp. 14–16.

can improve warehouse productivity by empowering those closest to the activity to make improvements in operations.

The preceding approaches can be implemented individually or in combination. Most firms utilize several methods simultaneously to improve warehouse productivity.

Financial Dimensions of Warehousing

Financial control of warehousing is closely tied to logistics productivity and corporate profitability.[41] Before the various activities of warehousing can be properly integrated into a single unified system, management must be aware of the risks and costs of each activity.

Many warehouse decisions involve risk. The risks can be of many types, but all eventually will result in some impact on costs or revenues. For example, making a capital investment in automated storage and retrieval systems increases both risk and the level of expected return on investment.[42] Firms must be able to justify such investments financially. The more quickly the cost of the equipment can be recovered, the less risk associated with the decision. Financial accounting and control techniques are very important in assessing the risks and rewards associated with warehousing decisions.

Activity-Based Costing

Activity-Based Costing (ABC)

One approach that has proven successful in the financial control of warehousing activities is *activity-based costing (ABC)*. Accurate and timely financial data allow warehouse executives to properly plan, administer, and control warehousing activities. Traditional costing systems, in place at many firms, often do not provide financial data in the proper form for use in making warehousing decisions. Frequently, it is difficult to identify how warehousing costs impact overall corporate profitability and how changes in costs in one area affect costs in another. Some companies are implementing ABC in order to have better warehousing cost information.

With ABC, costs are determined by specific products, services, or customers (see Chapter 13). It utilizes a two-stage process. The first stage assigns resource costs according to the amount of each resource consumed in performing specific warehousing activities. The second stage assigns warehousing activity costs to the products, services, or customers consuming the activities.

Proponents of ABC state that it unbundles traditional cost accounts and shows how resources are consumed. Figure 8–8 compares the two approaches.[43]

---

[41]Morton T. Yeomans, "Using Warehouse Information," in *The Logistics Handbook,* ed. James F. Robeson and William C. Copacino (New York: Free Press, 1994), pp. 632–43.

[42]James D. Krasner, "Satisfying the Chief Financial Officer," *Warehousing Forum* 10, no. 7 (June 1995), pp. 1–2.

[43]Terrance L. Pohlen, "Activity Based Costing for Warehouse Managers," *Warehousing Forum* 9, no. 5 (May 1994), pp. 1–3; see also Lisa Ellram et al., "Understanding the Implications of Activity-Based Costing for Logistics Management," *Proceedings of the Annual Conference of the Council of Logistics Management* (Oak Brook, IL: Council of Logistics Management, 1994), pp. 11–25.

FIGURE 8–8

A comparison of traditional costing and activity-based costing

General ledger view of warehousing costs	
Storage and handling	$40.1
General and administration	30.9
Trucking and delivery	14.5
Freight consolidation	2.4
Value-added services	3.3
Total	**$91.2**

Activity-based view of warehousing costs	
Dry storage	$25.0
Refrigerated storage	8.1
Receiving	20.0
Shipping	18.8
Billing	3.2
Delivery	6.0
Packaging/stenciling	1.8
Freight consolidation	3.0
Material handling equipment	5.3
Total	**$91.2**

Source: Terrance L. Pohlen, "Activity Based Costing for Warehouse Managers," *Warehousing Forum* 9, no. 5 (May 1994), p. 1.

Levels of Sophistication in Warehouse Accounting and Control

Companies are often at various levels of sophistication in terms of warehouse accounting and control. Four levels have been identified:

Four Levels of Sophistication in Warehouse Accounting and Control

Level I.   Warehouse costs are allocated in total, using a single allocation base.

Level II.   Warehouse costs are aggregated by major warehouse function (e.g., handling, storage, and administration) and are assigned using a separate allocation base for each function.

Level III.   Warehouse costs are aggregated by major activity within each function (e.g., receiving, putaway, order pick) and are allocated using a separate base for each activity.

Level IV.   Costs are categorized in matrix form, reflecting each major activity, natural expense, and type of cost behavior. Separate allocations are developed for each cost category, using bases that reflect the key differences in warehousing characteristics among cost objectives.[44]

Accounting and control require having the right kind of financial data available when and where they are needed, and in a form that is usable by as many functional areas of the firm as possible. Ultimately, these data are essential to making the necessary cost-service trade-offs within the warehousing activity and between other logistics functions.

---

[44]Ernest and Whinney, *Warehouse Accounting and Control: Guidelines for Distribution and Financial Managers* (Oak Brook, IL: National Council of Physical Distribution Management, 1985), p. 50. Used with permission of the Council of Logistics Management, formerly the National Council of Physical Distribution Management.

Creative Solutions

Less Warehousing, Better Distribution

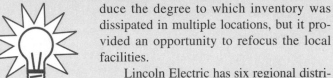

Lincoln Electric is the world's leading manufacturer of welding equipment and supplies, as well as a major producer of electric motors. The company used to have 36 to 40 small warehouses scattered around the country. Pricing policies were designed to encourage large orders that would simplify manufacturing and shipping to end users and stocking distributors.

Because the firm's local warehouses were not large enough to carry a complete stock to supply the growing needs of the distribution network, the company decided to consolidate its distribution in a much smaller number of larger, well-stocked regional distribution centers.

The first distribution center (DC) was set up in Cleveland, Ohio, toward the end of 1989. New DCs were added to cover the rest of the country and corresponding local warehouses were closed when they became redundant. Not only did the consolidation re-

Lincoln Electric utilizes six U.S. and two Canadian regional distribution centers to store its many products, such as electric motors, welding equipment, and supplies.

duce the degree to which inventory was dissipated in multiple locations, but it provided an opportunity to refocus the local facilities.

Lincoln Electric has six regional distribution centers located across the United States and two in Canada. Others are planned for Philadelphia and Mexico, as well as parts of Europe and South America. The U.S. distribution centers range in size from 30,000 to 100,000 square feet and are operated by staffs that vary from three to about a dozen employees.

To get up and running faster, the operations of some new DCs were contracted out, although each has at least one Lincoln Electric employee at the location.

By working more effectively with its distributors and helping them serve their end users better, Lincoln Electric is able to meet the broader needs of the entire arc welding market more effectively. Independent welding distributors can carry a lower level of inventory and rely on a Lincoln Electric DC to provide most items their customers need, usually in 24 to 72 hours.

With minimal delay, customers receive more of the products they need to keep operating. Distributors can provide better customer service and turn inventories more often while maintaining smaller stocks and relying on the distribution centers for backup.

By improving the way it serves customers, Lincoln Electric gains greater efficiency, increased sales, and positive customer relations.

Source: John J. Hach, "Less Warehousing, Better Distribution," *Transportation and Distribution*, 36, no. 3 (Mar. 1995), pp. 108–15.

Summary

In this chapter, we described the importance of warehousing and distribution in the logistics system. Economies of scale, costs, and customer service are the most important considerations. The types of options available to a firm include public (rented) and private (owned or leased) warehousing.

The major functions of warehousing are movement, storage, and information transfer. Firms may choose to perform these functions utilizing public or private warehousing. Each option has advantages and disadvantages which must be understood so that optimal warehousing decisions are made.

Facility development is a large part of warehouse management. Decisions relating to the size and number of warehouses, the location of the facilities, and layout and design have significant impact on a firm's ability to satisfy its customers and make a profit. We described various methods, techniques, and approaches relative to each decision area. That led us to explore some important management issues relating to warehouse productivity, accounting, and control.

In the next chapter, we will examine the issues of materials handling, packaging, and computerization in warehousing. With a knowledge of key warehousing decisions, it will be possible to more fully understand the role of these parameters in the logistics system.

Suggested Readings

Ackerman, Kenneth B. "The Deming Management Message: It Can Work in Your Warehouse!" *Warehousing Forum* 11, no. 4 (Mar. 1996), pp. 1–2.

Ackerman, Kenneth B. "Leadership in the 21st Century Warehouse." *Warehousing Forum* 7, no. 6 (May 1992), pp. 1–3.

Ackerman, Kenneth B. *Warehousing Profitably: A Manager's Guide.* Columbus, OH: Ackerman, 1994.

Baker, C. M. "Case Study: Development of National Parts Distribution Center." *Proceedings of the Conference on the Total Logistics Concept.* Pretoria, South Africa: University of Pretoria, 1991.

Ballou, Ronald H., and James M. Masters. "Commercial Software for Locating Warehouses and Other Facilities." *Journal of Business Logistics* 14, no. 2 (1993), pp. 71–107.

Bancroft, Tony. "Strategic Role of the Distribution Center: How to Turn Your Warehouse into a DC." *International Journal of Physical Distribution and Logistics Management* 21, no. 4 (1991), pp. 45–47.

Britt, Frank F. "A Profit Center Approach to Warehousing." *WERC Research Paper.* Oak Brook, IL: Warehousing Education and Research Council, 1990.

Copacino, William C. "How Warehousing Provides a Competitive Edge." *Warehousing Forum* 6, no. 10 (Sept. 1991), pp. 1–4.

"Getting the Right Fit." *Traffic Management* 34, no. 2 (Feb. 1995), Warehousing and Distribution Supplement, pp. 785–805.

Gooley, Toby B. "ISO 9000 Is Coming!" *Traffic Management* 34, no. 10 (Oct. 1995), Warehousing and Distribution Supplement, pp. 77–80.

Gordon, Jay. "Smart Life Truck Fleet Management." *Distribution* 91, no. 5 (May 1992), pp. 70–76.

Harmon, Roy L. *Reinventing the Warehouse: World Class Distribution Logistics.* New York: Free Press, 1993.

Ho, Peng-Kuan, and Jossef Perl. "Warehouse Location under Service-Sensitive Demand." *Journal of Business Logistics* 16, no. 1 (1995), pp. 133–62.

Maltz, Arnold B. "The Relative Importance of Cost and Quality in the Outsourcing of Warehousing." *Journal of Business Logistics* 15, no. 2 (1994), pp. 45–62.

Maltz, Arnold B. "Warehouse Systems and the Year 2000: What You Need to Do NOW!" *WERC Special Report,* Jan. 1997.

McGinnis, Michael A. "Basic Economic Analysis for Warehouse Decisions." *WERC Research Paper.* Oak Brook, IL: Warehousing Education and Research Council, 1990.

Murphy, Paul R., and Richard F. Poist. "In Search of Warehousing Excellence: A Multivariate Analysis of HRM Practices." *Journal of Business Logistics* 14, no. 2 (1993), pp. 145–64.

Robeson, James F., and William C. Copacino, eds. *The Logistics Handbook.* New York: Free Press, 1994.

Rogers, Dale S., and Patricia J. Daugherty. "Warehousing Firms: The Impact of Alliance Involvement." *Journal of Business Logistics* 16, no. 2 (1995), pp. 249–69.

Setting Continuous Improvement Priorities in Warehouse Operations. Monograph Series no. M0016. Raleigh, NC: Tompkins Associates, n.d.

Speh, Thomas W. *How to Determine Total Warehouse Costs.* Sarasota, FL: DCW-USA, 1990.

Speh, Thomas W., and James A. Blomquist. "The Financial Evaluation of Warehouse Options: An Examination and Appraisal of Contemporary Practices," *WERC Research Paper.* Oak Brook, IL: Warehousing Education and Research Council, 1988.

Speh, Thomas W.; Rachel Numann; Chris Rittberger; Renee West; and David Eric Williams. "A Guide for Establishing Warehouse Job Descriptions." *WERC Research Paper,* 2nd ed. Oak Brook, IL: Warehousing Education and Research Council, 1997.

Stock, James R. "Managing Computer, Communication and Information Technology Strategically: Opportunities and Challenges for Warehousing." *Logistics and Transportation Review* 26, no. 2 (June 1990), pp. 32–54.

Stock, James R. "Strategic Warehousing: Bringing the 'Storage Game' to Life." *WERC Research Paper.* Oak Brook, IL: Warehousing Education and Research Council, 1988.

Tompkins, James A. "Enhancing the Warehouse's Role through Customization." *WERC Special Report,* Feb. 1997.

Tompkins, James A., and Dale Harmelink, eds. *The Distribution Management Handbook.* New York: McGraw-Hill, 1994.

Traveling the Road of Logistics: The Evolution of Warehousing and Distribution. Chicago: American Warehousemen's Association, 1991.

Van Oudheusden, Dirk L., and Peter Boey. "Design of an Automated Warehouse for Air Cargo: The Case of the Thai Air Cargo Terminal." *Journal of Business Logistics* 15, no. 1 (1994), pp. 261–85.

"Warehousing: Coping with the Challenge of Change." *Modern Materials Handling* 50, no. 6 (May 1995), pp. 12–13.

Questions and Problems

1. Warehousing is used for the storage of inventories during all phases of the logistics process. Since inventory carrying costs can be so high, why is it necessary for a firm to store inventories of any kind?

2. What are the differences between *private* and *public* warehousing? What are the advantages and disadvantages of each type?

3. What is meant by a cost trade-off analysis within the context of warehousing? Give two examples of the cost trade-offs involved in a firm's decision to use a combination of public and private warehousing rather than public or private warehousing alone.

4. What are the three basic functions of warehousing? Briefly describe each.

5. Identify and describe some of the more important factors that affect the specific size of a firm's warehouse or warehouses.

6. What are the differences between the following types of facility location strategies: (*a*) market positioned, (*b*) production positioned, and (*c*) intermediately positioned?

7. How can layout and design affect warehouse efficiency and productivity?

8. Productivity has been defined as the ratio of real output to real input. In terms of the warehousing function, how could a firm measure the productivity level of its storage facilities?

9. Discuss the reasoning behind the following statement: "Financial control of warehousing is closely tied to logistics productivity and corporate profitability."

THE DISTRIBUTION CHALLENGE!
PROBLEM: HOW ARE WE DOING?

Spicers Paper Inc. was faced with an elemental problem of measuring basic productivity.

Spicers is a distributor of high-end paper products to the printing industry. Based in Australia, it has sales of about $1 billion, a third of which are in the United States, according to Richard Maron, general manager of distribution and warehousing at U.S. headquarters in Santa Fe Springs, California.

The Spicers operation is fairly complex. Working out of six locations in the western United States, it ships product in a variety of ways, including cartons, skids, boxes, and gigantic rolls. But when Maron arrived, he had no way of assessing the productivity of its warehouse or delivery personnel.

A more diversified company might have launched an elaborate program for measuring operations down to the minute, then spilled the data onto reams of spreadsheets and management reports. Spicers didn't have that luxury, says Maron. It needed something cheap, simple, accurate—and fast.

Maron was given 30 days or less to come up with a way to measure productivity at each of the U.S. warehouses. The reporting requirements could take no more than 20 minutes out of the 10- to 11-hour days of the warehouse managers. Exactly what information would you require from the warehouse managers, what formulas would you use, and how would you chart it?

What Is Your Solution?

Source: "Distribution: The Challenge," *Distribution* 95, no. 6 (June 1996), p. 60.

Chapter Objectives

- To provide an overview of the various types of automated and nonautomated materials handling systems.
- To examine the role of warehousing in a just-in-time (JIT) environment.
- To identify the role of packaging in the warehouse operation.
- To demonstrate the important role of computer technology in materials management.

309

Introduction

If one views warehousing as a means of achieving a competitive advantage, traditional perspectives of warehousing as merely storing and managing inventories are replaced by new paradigms that include information flows as well as inventories. In the new mission of warehousing, computerization, information, and automation become essential ingredients in logistics success.

This chapter integrates some of the key components that affect warehousing decisions. Some companies tend to view the warehousing decisions described in Chapter 8 (private versus public, location, size and number) as separate from decisions about warehouse automation, materials handling systems, packaging, and warehouse computerization. Yet, these decisions are very intertwined, as we will demonstrate in this chapter.

Materials Handling Equipment

The Materials Handling Institute, an industry trade association for manufacturers of materials handling equipment and systems, has estimated that:

Materials Handling Expenditures Exceed $50 Billion Annually

> The hardware and software used to move, store, control, contain, and unitize materials in factories and warehouses exceeds $50 billion annually. Much of the growth in size and variety of the market is fueled by major changes in the requirements of warehouse and distribution operations (e.g., reduced order cycle times, reduced inventory levels, reduced order sizes, SKU proliferation).[1]

Materials handling equipment and systems often represent a major capital outlay for an organization. Like the decisions related to the number, size, and location of warehouses, materials handling can affect many aspects of the firm's operations.

Manual or Nonautomated Materials Handling Systems

Manual or nonautomated materials handling equipment has been the mainstay of the traditional warehouse and will likely continue to be important even with the move toward automated warehousing. Such equipment can be categorized according to the functions performed; that is, storage and order picking, transportation and sorting, and shipping.

Examples of Storage and Order-Picking Equipment

Storage and Order-Picking Equipment.   Storage and order-picking equipment includes racks, shelving, drawers, and operator-controlled devices (e.g., forklift trucks). Manual systems provide a great deal of flexibility in order picking, because they use the most flexible handling system (i.e., people).

Table 9–1 explains the many types of racks, shelving, and drawers most often used in a warehouse. Storage racks normally store palletized or unitized loads. In most instances, some type of operator-controlled device places the load into the storage rack.

---

[1]Edward H. Frazelle and James M. Apple, Jr., "Materials Handling Technologies," in *The Logistics Handbook,* ed. James F. Robeson and William C. Copacino (New York: Free Press, 1994), p. 547.

Manufacturing processes and unit loads in the textile industry are unique. Materials handling equipment can be used for simplified order picking within a storage/retrieval system designed and developed to handle rolled goods.

Table 9–1 presents the type of materials stored, the benefits, and other information about each item. Figures 9–1 through 9–5 illustrate what these items look like.

The storage racks illustrated in Figures 9–1A and 9–1B are found in most warehouse facilities as either permanent or temporary fixtures for storage of products. They would be considered "standard" or "basic" components of a warehouse. All these storage racks are easily accessible by materials handling equipment such as forklift trucks.

Gravity Flow Storage Racks

Gravity flow storage racks (see Figure 9–2) are often used to store high-demand items. Products that are of uniform size and shape are well suited for this type of storage system. Items are loaded into the racks from the back, flow to the front of the racks which are sloped forward, and are then picked from the front of the system by order-picking personnel.

Bin Shelving Systems

For small parts, bin shelving systems are useful. Figure 9–3 illustrates a typical bin configuration. Items are handpicked, so the height of the system must be within the physical reach of employees. Typically, the full cube of each bin cannot be used, so some wasted space exists. Bin shelving systems are relatively inexpensive compared with other storage systems, but they have limited usefulness beyond storage of small parts.

Modular Storage Drawers and Cabinets

The modular storage drawers and cabinets shown in Figure 9–4 are used for small parts. Similar in function to bin shelving systems, they require less physical space and allow items to be concentrated into areas that are easily accessed by employees. The drawers are pulled out and items are selected. Fasteners, nuts and bolts, and other small parts and components are often stored in this manner. By design, modular storage drawers must be low to the floor and often less than five feet in height to allow access by employees picking items from the drawers.

TABLE 9–1   Storage Guidelines for the Warehouse

	Equipment	Type of Materials	Benefits	Other Considerations
M A N U A L	Racking: Conventional pallet rack	Pallet loads	Good storage density, good product security	Storage density can be increased further by storing loads two deep
	Drive-in racks	Pallet loads	Fork trucks can access loads, good storage density	Fork truck access is from one direction only
	Drive-through racks	Pallet loads	Same as above	Fork truck access is from two directions
	High-rise racks	Pallet loads	Very high storage density	Often used in AS/R systems, may offer tax advantages when used in rack-supported building
	Cantilever racks	Long loads or rolls	Designed to store difficult shapes	Each different SKU can be stored on a separate shelf
	Pallet stacking frames	Odd-shaped or crushable parts	Allow otherwise unstackable loads to be stacked, saving floor space	Can be disassembled when not in use
	Stacking racks	Odd-shaped or crushable parts	Same as above	Can be stacked flat when not in use
	Gravity-flow racks	Unit loads	High-density storage, gravity moves loads	FIFO or LIFO flow of loads
	Shelving	Small, loose loads and cases	Inexpensive	Can be combined with drawers for flexibility
	Drawers	Small parts and tools	All parts are easily accessed, good security	Can be compartmentalized for many SKUs
	Mobile racking or shelving	Pallet loads, loose materials, and cases	Can reduce required floor space by half	Come equipped with safety devices
A U T O M A T E D	Unit Load AS/RS	Pallet loads, and a wide variety of sizes and shapes	Very high storage density, computer controlled	May offer tax advantages when rack-supported
	Car-in-lane	Pallet loads, other unit loads	High storage density	Best used where there are large quantities of only a few SKUs
	Miniload AS/RS	Small parts	High storage density, computer controlled	For flexibility, can be installed in several different configurations
	Horizontal carousels	Small parts	Easy access to parts, relatively inexpensive	Can be stacked on top of each other
	Vertical carousels	Small parts and tools	High storage density	Can serve dual role as storage and delivery system in multifloor facilities
	Man-ride machines	Small parts	Very flexible	Can be used with high-rise shelving or modular drawers

This table is a general guide to the types of available storage equipment and where each is best used in the warehouse. Each individual storage application should be studied in detail with the equipment supplier before any equipment is specified.

Source: "Storage Equipment for the Warehouse," *Modern Materials Handling, 1985 Warehousing Guidebook* 40, no. 4 (Spring 1985), p. 53. *Modern Materials Handling,* Copyright 1985 by Cahners Publishing Company, Division of Reed Holdings, Inc.

FIGURE 9–1A

Nonautomated storage units—storage racks

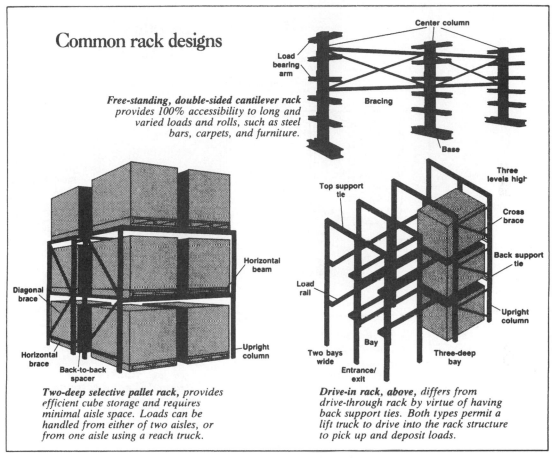

Common rack designs

Free-standing, double-sided cantilever rack provides 100% accessibility to long and varied loads and rolls, such as steel bars, carpets, and furniture.

Two-deep selective pallet rack, provides efficient cube storage and requires minimal aisle space. Loads can be handled from either of two aisles, or from one aisle using a reach truck.

Drive-in rack, above, differs from drive-through rack by virtue of having back support ties. Both types permit a lift truck to drive into the rack structure to pick up and deposit loads.

"Fixed" and "Movable" Storage Systems

The storage systems described previously are classified as "fixed" systems because they are stationary. Others can be classified as "movable" because they are not in fixed positions. The bin shelving systems shown in Figure 9–3 can be transformed from a fixed to a movable system (see Figure 9–5). In the bin shelving mezzanine, wheels on the bottom of the bins follow tracks in the floors, allowing the bins to be moved and stacked together when not being accessed. This allows maximum utilization of space, because full-width aisles are not needed between each bin.

Products are picked from the various storage systems, using some order-picking approach. In a manual system, the personnel doing the order picking go to the location of the items, walking with a cart or riding a mechanized cart. In many cases, the order picker retrieves items from a flow-through gravity storage rack (see Figure 9–2).[2]

---

[2]For a discussion of various storage and handling equipment, see James A. Tompkins, "Measuring Warehousing Performance: How Are You Doing?" *Proceedings of the Annual Conference of the Council of Logistics Management* (Oak Brook, IL: Council of Logistics Management, 1994), pp. 437–49.

Figure 9–1B

Nonautomated storage units—storage racks

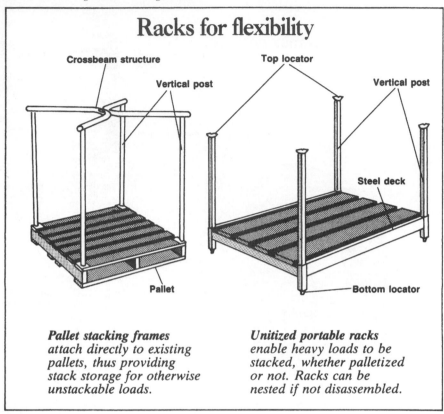

Racks for flexibility

Pallet stacking frames attach directly to existing pallets, thus providing stack storage for otherwise unstackable loads.

Unitized portable racks enable heavy loads to be stacked, whether palletized or not. Racks can be nested if not disassembled.

Source: "The Trends Keep Coming in Industrial Storage Racks," *Modern Materials Handling,* 40, no. 9 (Aug. 1985), pp. 54–55. *Modern Materials Handling,* Copyright 1985 by Cahners Publishing Company, Division of Reed Holdings, Inc.

Transporting and Sorting Items

Transportation and Sorting.   The order picker can use a large selection of powered and nonpowered equipment for transporting and sorting items located in the racks, shelves, and drawers. Examples of this type of apparatus include forklift trucks, platform trucks, hand trucks, cranes, and carts.

Manual sorting of items is a very labor-intensive part of warehousing. It involves separating and regrouping picked items into customer orders. Personnel physically examine items and place them onto pallets or slipsheets, or into containers for shipment to customers. This is a time-consuming process subject to human error. As a result, most firms attempt to minimize manual sorting.

Shipping Products

Shipping of products to customers involves preparing items for shipment and loading them onto the transport vehicle. The powered and nonpowered equipment previously described are used for this purpose. Pallets, palletizers, strapping machines, and stretch wrappers also are important.[3]

---

[3]See S. M. Bhardwaj, *The Pallet Storage System Selection Process* (Oak Brook, IL: Warehousing Education and Research Council, 1990).

FIGURE 9–2

Gravity flow rack

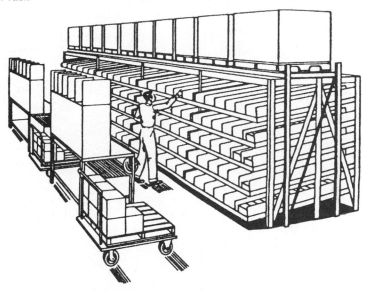

Source: Department of the Navy, Naval Supply Systems Command, Publication 529. From Edward H. Frazelle, *Small Parts Order Picking: Equipment and Strategy* (Oak Brook, IL: Warehousing Education and Research Council, 1988), p. 3. Reprinted with permission.

FIGURE 9–3

Bin shelving systems

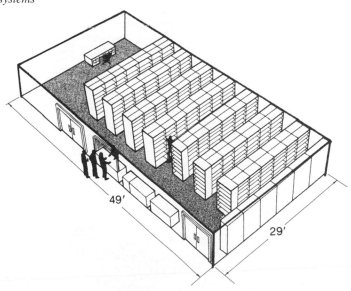

Source: Edward H. Frazelle, *Small Parts Order Picking: Equipment and Strategy* (Oak Brook, IL: Warehousing Education and Research Council, 1988), p. 1. Reprinted with permission.

FIGURE 9–4

Modular storage drawers and cabinets

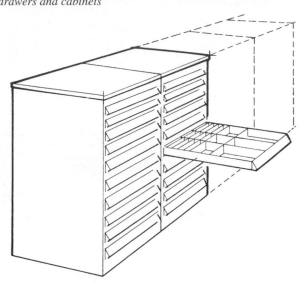

Source: Department of the Navy, Naval Supply Systems Command, Publication 529. From Edward H. Frazelle, *Small Parts Order Picking: Equipment and Strategy* (Oak Brook, IL: Warehousing Education and Research Council, 1988), p. 2. Reprinted with permission.

FIGURE 9–5

Bin shelving mezzanine

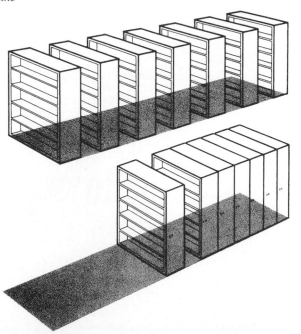

Source: Courtesy of White Storage & Retrieval Systems. From Edward H. Frazelle, *Small Parts Order Picking: Equipment and Strategy* (Oak Brook, IL: Warehousing Education and Research Council, 1988), p. 8. Reprinted with permission.

FIGURE 9–6

The modern shipping and receiving dock

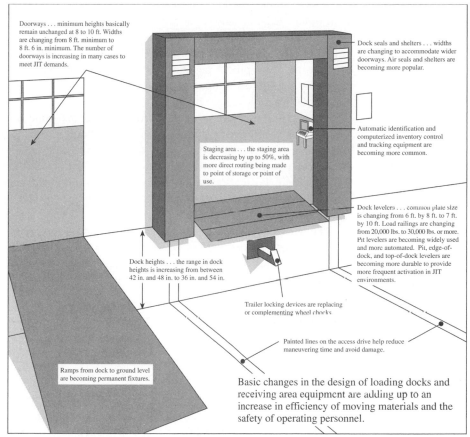

Doorways . . . minimum heights basically remain unchanged at 8 to 10 ft. Widths are changing from 8 ft. minimum to 8 ft. 6 in. minimum. The number of doorways is increasing in many cases to meet JIT demands.

Dock seals and shelters . . . widths are changing to accommodate wider doorways. Air seals and shelters are becoming more popular.

Automatic identification and computerized inventory control and tracking equipment are becoming more common.

Staging area . . . the staging area is decreasing by up to 50%, with more direct routing being made to point of storage or point of use.

Dock levelers . . . common plate size is changing from 6 ft. by 8 ft. to 7 ft. by 10 ft. Load railings are changing from 20,000 lbs. to 30,000 lbs. or more. Pit levelers are becoming widely used and more automated. Pit, edge-of-dock, and top-of-dock levelers are becoming more durable to provide more frequent activation in JIT environments.

Dock heights . . . the range in dock heights is increasing from between 42 in. and 48 in. to 36 in. and 54 in.

Trailer locking devices are replacing or complementing wheel chocks.

Painted lines on the access drive help reduce maneuvering time and avoid damage.

Ramps from dock to ground level are becoming permanent fixtures.

Basic changes in the design of loading docks and receiving area equipment are adding up to an increase in efficiency of moving materials and the safety of operating personnel.

Source: "Docks and Receiving—Where It All Begins," *Modern Materials Handling, 1985 Warehousing Guidebook* 40, no. 4 (Spring 1985), p. 36. *Modern Materials Handling,* Copyright 1985 by Cahners Publishing Company, Division of Reed Holdings, Inc.

In addition, the shipping and receiving activity requires equipment for handling outbound and inbound transportation vehicles. Therefore, shipping and receiving docks are important elements of the material handling process. For example, new highway regulations increasing the amount of weight a truck trailer can haul, and regulations allowing wider and longer trailers, have placed new demands on shipping and receiving docks. Some of the changes that have occured are shown in Figure 9–6, which represents a modern shipping and receiving dock. As stated previously, manual or nonautomated equipment is often used in combination with automated equipment.

Automated Materials Handling Systems

Automated storage and retrieval systems (AS/RS), carousels, case-picking and item-picking equipment, conveyors, robots, and scanning systems have become commonplace in warehouses. As a result, many firms have been able to achieve improvements in materials handling efficiency and productivity.

For example, the Park Seed Company in South Carolina, the largest family-owned mail order seed company in the world, must be able to fill customers' orders within 24 to 36 hours during the peak season of December to April. Because of increasing business, the firm replaced its 125-year-old wooden bin system with automated horizontal carousels. As a result, the lines picked per hour per operator increased five times while labor was reduced by one-third. Compared to the old system, picking speed increased from 180 to 950–1,000 lines picked per hour.[4]

Automated Storage and Order-Picking Equipment

Automated equipment can be grouped into the same categories used to describe nonautomated equipment: storage and order-picking, transportation and sorting, and shipping. Table 9–1 listed examples of automated storage and order-picking equipment. Bausch & Lomb, Chek Lap Kok Airport (Hong Kong), Compaq, General Electric, Nike, Packard Bell, Posten PaketFrakt (Sweden), Rothmans Tobacco (Netherlands), Toyota, and many other firms have employed automated systems with great success. The Global box describes Packard Bell's integrated solution to materials handling.

Toyota Automates Its Warehouse

The Toyota Marketing Company's Parts Distribution Center in South Africa was partially automated between 1984 and 1991 at a cost of $5.6 million. Additional storage and handling facilities were added; new receiving, binning, and order processing systems were introduced; and a high-rise bulk warehouse was constructed. The benefits were significant:

- Order processing productivity increased 300 percent.
- Product damage rates declined by 50 percent.
- Stock accuracy and service rates improved by 65 percent.
- The work of three clerks was eliminated and an additional three clerks were reassigned to more essential tasks.[5]

Automated Storage and Retrieval Systems (AS/RS)

Among the most important storage and order-picking equipment are automated storage and retrieval systems (AS/RS). In comparison with manual systems, an AS/RS provides reduced labor cost and floor space, while increasing inventory accuracy. An AS/RS is applicable to virtually all types of products and many warehouse configurations.[6]

Advantages of Automated Systems

Advantages of Automated Systems.   Automated systems can provide several benefits for warehouse operations. Table 9–2 lists some of the most important benefits of automated systems as identified by users. Generally, the benefits can be categorized into operating cost savings, improved service levels, and increased control through more and better information.

---

[4]Ed Romaine, "How One Company Increased Its Pick Rate," *Parcel Shipping & Distribution* 2, no. 4 (July–Aug. 1995), pp. 27–28.

[5]C. M. Baker, "Case Study: Development of National Parts Distribution Center," *Proceedings of the Conference on the Total Logistics Concept* (Pretoria, South Africa, 1991).

[6]For several examples of order-picking systems and approaches, see *The Warehouse Manager's Guide to Effective Orderpicking,* Monograph Series no. M0008 (Raleigh, NC: Tompkins Associates, n.d.).

Global

Providing Integrated Solutions through Computers and Automation

At Packard Bell's facility in Angers, France, computers are assembled on a last minute basis before delivery to the final customer. This strategy required a materials handling system with the responsiveness to operate in a JIT environment.

The system consists of five kitting (assembly) stations, 32 modular and interchangeable conveyor workstations where the computers are assembled and tested, and an in-line burn-in testing system.

At the kitting stations, a paperless, pick-to-light system speeds picking and ensures that the kits are error-free by guiding workers through the process by means of a series of light displays mounted to flow racks.

To minimize work-in-process inventory and streamline the workflow, the assembly area operates on a pull strategy. While the system automatically determines the workflow (through a bar code on the transport trays), product is not released from a workstation until the destination location is free to accept it.

Source: "Total Solutions: Problem Solving with Materials Handling Systems," *Modern Materials Handling* 50, no. 7 (June 1995), p. 22.

Computer control of an automated storage and retrieval system (AS/RS) ensures proper rotation of stock in a pharmaceutical warehouse.

TABLE 9–2   **Benefits of Automated Materials Handling Systems**

Benefit	Percent of Respondents That "Agree" or "Strongly Agree"
Labor cost reduction	98.8%
Ability to increase output rate	95.2
Improvement in consistency of service	92.1
Reduction in materials handling	92.1
Increased accuracy level	89.5
Service availability	87.0
Improvement in speed of service	81.0

Source: Kofi Q. Dadzie, and Wesley J. Johnston, "Innovative Automation Technology in Corporate Warehousing Logistics," *Journal of Business Logistics,* 2, no. 1 (1991), p. 76.

Disadvantages of Automated Systems

Disadvantages of Automated Systems.   However, automated systems are not without disadvantages. Typical problems faced by firms choosing to automate materials handling operations include the following:

- Initial capital cost.
- Downtime or unreliability of equipment/maintenance interruptions.
- Software-related problems (e.g., poor documentation, incompatibility, failure).
- Capacity problems.
- Lack of flexibility to respond to changing environment.
- Maintenance costs.
- User interface and training.
- Worker acceptance.
- Obsolescence.[7]

Types of Equipment.   The initial capital outlay is usually the most significant obstacle. For example, a miniload AS/RS (see Figures 9–7 and 9–8), where a storage/retrieval (S/R) machine travels horizontally and vertically simultaneously in a storage aisle, transporting containers to and from an order-picking station at one end of the system, generally costs between $150,000 and $300,000 per aisle.[8]

An Example of Unit Load AS/RSs

When the unit to pick is a full pallet or similar large load, the AS/RS offers complete automation from storage to retrieval in minimal space. Unit-load AS/RSs are installed up to 100 feet high with aisles only inches wider than the load to be stored. The S/R machines operate at speeds much faster than industrial trucks and travel simultaneously in horizontal and vertical directions. They

---

[7]Kofi Q. Dadzie and Wesley J. Johnston, "Innovative Automation Technology in Corporate Warehousing Logistics," *Journal of Business Logistics* 12, no. 1 (1991), p. 72.

[8]Edward H. Frazelle, *Small Parts Order Picking: Equipment and Strategy* (Oak Brook, IL: Warehousing Education and Research Council, 1988), p. 6.

FIGURE 9–7

Miniload AS/RS

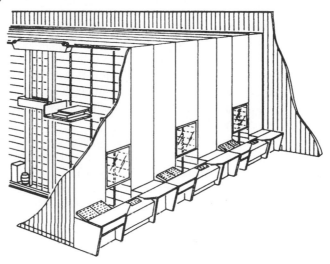

Source: Department of the Navy, Naval Supply Systems Command, Publication 529. From Edward H. Frazelle, *Small Parts Order Picking: Equipment and Strategy* (Oak Brook, IL: Warehousing Education and Research Council, 1988), p. 6. Reprinted with permission.

FIGURE 9–8

Minimizing inventory at Apple Computer with a flexible miniload AS/RS

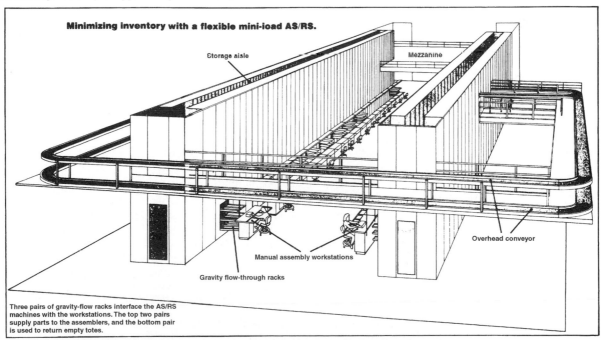

Source: "Mini-Load AS/RS Trims Inventory, Speeds Assembly," *Modern Materials Handling* 39, no. 13 (Sept. 21, 1984), pp. 48–49. *Modern Materials Handling,* Copyright 1984 by Cahners Publishing Company, Division of Reed Holdings, Inc.

are used when inventories, throughput, and space costs are high. In totally automated systems, AS/RSs are supplied by conveyors, automated guided vehicles, or electrified monorail systems.[9]

Carousels.   A form of AS/RS is the carousel. Carousels are mechanical devices that house and rotate items for order picking. The most frequently utilized carousel configurations are the horizontal and vertical systems.

Horizontal Carousels   A horizontal carousel (see Figure 9–9) is a linked series of rotating bins of adjustable shelves driven on the top or bottom by a drive motor. Rotation takes place on an axis perpendicular to the floor at approximately 80 feet a minute. Costs for horizontal carousels begin at $5,000 a unit.[10]

Vertical Carousel   A vertical carousel is a horizontal carousel turned on its end and enclosed in sheet metal (see Figure 9–10). Like horizontal carousels, an order picker operates one or multiple carousels. The carousels are indexed either automatically by way of computer control or manually by the order picker operating a keypad on the carousel's work surface. The cost of a vertical carousel begins at $10,000.[11]

The transportation and sorting activities are typically performed in combination with storage and order picking. The three pieces of transportation equipment most frequently used are conveyors, automatic guided vehicle systems (AGVS), and operator-controlled trucks or tractors.

Conveyors.   Sorting equipment can be specialized, such as a tilt-tray sorter with built-in diverting mechanisms, or it can be assembled from other components, such as conveyors and diverters.[12]

Pic 'N' Save Uses a Conveyor Sorting System to Handle 100 Cases Per Minute   Pic 'N' Save Corporation has developed a conveyor sorting system that handles over 100 cases per minute. The company has shipped up to 68,000 cases in one working day— a high level of productivity under normal conditions, but even more outstanding for Pic 'N' Save because the firm rarely has the same item in stock more than once. The company buys close-out goods (e.g., overruns, discontinued items, style changes) from manufacturers and therefore has a wide variety of merchandise in inventory. Case goods are stored in a reserve storage area and are then moved to a picking area four levels high. After being picked, items move to a merge area where they are sorted and shipped.[13]

Automatic Guided Vehicle Systems (AGVSs)   *Automatic Guided Vehicle Systems (AGVSs).*   **Automatic guided vehicle systems (AGVSs)** are "battery-powered driverless vehicles that are controlled by computers for task assignment, path selection, and positioning."[14] AGVSs are often used in automated warehouse operations involving AS/RSs. The benefits of AGVSs include "lower handling costs, reduced handling-related product damage, improved safety, the ability to interface

[9]*Warehouse Manager's Guide to Effective Orderpicking,* p. 21.

[10]Edward H. Frazelle and James M. Apple, Jr., "Materials Handling Technologies," in *The Logistics Handbook,* ed. James F. Robeson and William C. Copacino (New York: Free Press, 1994), p. 574.

[11]Frazelle, *Small Parts Order Picking,* pp. 4–5; Frazelle and Apple, "Materials Handling Technologies," p. 575.

[12]"Transportation and Sorting—Keys to Throughput," *Modern Materials Handling, 1985 Warehousing Guidebook* 40, no. 4 (Spring 1985), p. 75.

[13]"How We Sort Up to 135 Cases per Minute," *Modern Materials Handling* 40, no. 6 (May 1985), pp. 60–63.

[14]David R. Olson, "Material Handling Equipment," in *The Distribution Management Handbook,* ed. James A. Tompkins and Dale Harmelink (New York: McGraw-Hill, 1994), pp. 19, 17.

FIGURE 9–9

Horizontal carousels

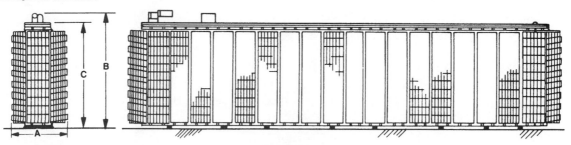

A. End elevation

B. Side elevation

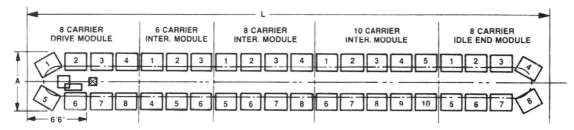

C. Plan view

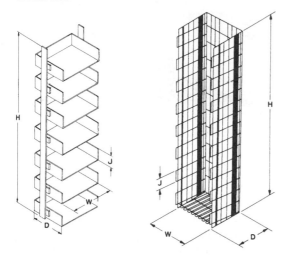

D. Sheet metal
carrier and shelves

E. Wire carrier
and shelves

Source: Courtesy of SPS Technologies, Inc. From Edward H. Frazelle, *Small Parts Order Picking: Equipment and Strategy* (Oak Brook, IL: Warehousing Education and Research Council, 1988), p. 4. Reprinted with permission.

Figure 9–10

Vertical carousel

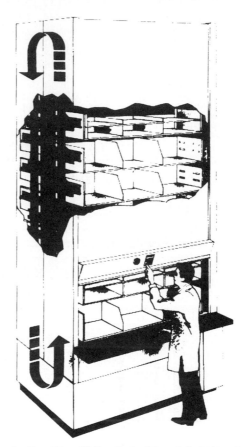

Source: Courtesy of Kardex Systems, Inc. From Edward H. Frazelle, *Small Parts Order Picking: Equipment and Strategy* (Oak Brook, IL: Warehousing Education and Research Council, 1988), p. 5. Reprinted with permission.

with other automated systems, and reliability."[15] Automated guided vehicles (AGVSs) cost about $30,000 for a single model at the low end of the scale and about $70,000 for a more advanced model.[16]

Maybelline Uses AS/RS and AGVSs to Pick 90,000 Items

Maybelline, a cosmetics manufacturer, utilizes a combination system that includes an AS/RS and AGVSs. The automated systems have increased the number of items picked each day by over 50 percent. On busy days, approximately 90,000 items are picked. Figure 9–11 shows the Maybelline operation and describes some of the specifics of the systems being used.[17]

---

[15]Les Gould, "Selecting an AGVS: New Trends, New Designs," *Modern Materials Handling* 50, no. 6 (May 1995), pp. 42–43.

[16]James Aaron Cooke, "Should You Automate Your Warehouse?" *Traffic Management* 34, no. 11 (Nov. 1993), pp. 6-S through 8-S.

[17]Gary Forger, "How Maybelline Ships Smaller, More Frequent Orders," *Modern Materials Handling* 50, no. 7 (June 1995), pp. 48–50.

Robots.   The robot is another type of equipment used in many phases of materials handling. Robots have been used in the manufacturing process for some time, but advances in robotics technology have expanded their use to a larger number of applications.[18] It is likely that materials handling robots will have steady growth in many application areas (see Figure 9–12).

Shipping Automation

Automation in the shipping area also has occurred. The two aspects of the shipping activity that have been most affected by automation are packaging and optical scanning. We have previously described pass-through and rotary stretchwrapping machines, and will further address packaging later in this chapter.

Computerized Documentation

Computerized Tracking and Information Systems.   Another aspect of shipping automation is documentation. As other components of the warehouse become automated, firms need to computerize their tracking and information systems. A. B. Oxford Cold Storage Company in Melbourne, Australia, utilizes radio frequency portable data terminals and barcode scanning to manage frozen and refrigerated food storage.[19] Items entering the warehouse are bar-code scanned and assigned storage locations by the computer. The data collected become part of the warehouse information system, which is used for a variety of purposes, including the preparation of business-related documentation.

Many companies are utilizing various computerized documentation procedures. Whether such technology is being used by Avia Presto of Holland (air freight cargo handling), the Royal Marines of Britain, or the Barrow-upon-Soar site of British Gypsum Plaster production),[20] firms are recognizing the benefits of automating the materials handling process, including increased productivity, better space utilization, higher customer service levels; reduced operating expenses; and improved flow of materials.[21]

The type and scope of benefits a company receives will vary according to product characteristics, labor intensity of the operation, existing customer service levels, and present level of company expertise.

---

[18]For a discussion of the use of robots in a typical materials handling environment, see "Smooth WIP Flow with the Right Handling," *Modern Materials Handling* 50, no. 5 (Apr. 1995), pp. 23–26.

[19]For a thorough discussion of radio frequency data communication in warehousing, see Bruce Richmond, *Radio Frequency Data Communication for Warehousing and Distribution* (Oak Brook, IL: Warehousing Education and Research Council, July 1993); "RF Pacesetter Applies Hands-On Handling Experience," *Logistics and Materials Handling* 3, no. 7 (Feb. 17, 1995), pp. 21–24.

[20]Moyette Marrett-Gibbons, "Freight Flies Faster with Bar Code," *ID Systems* 4, no. 7 (Sept. 1996), pp. 46–49; Paul Quinn, "Bar Code Moves Military Munitions," *ID Systems* 4, no. 7 (Sept. 1996), pp. 42–44, 54; British Gypsum news release, Feb. 25 1993.

[21]For examples, see Tom Andel, "Automatic Data Identification: For Your Own Good," *Transportation & Distribution* 34, no. 10 (Oct. 1993), pp. 76–88; James Aaron Cooke, "Getting Your Money's Worth from Auto ID," *Traffic Management,* Mar. 1992, Warehousing and Distribution Supplement pp. 17–19; Gary Forger, "Our System Eliminates Errors and Cuts Our Customers' Costs," *Modern Materials Handling* 50, no. 6 (May 1995), pp. S-10 through S-11; and "Wrap It All Up the Right Way in Shipping," *Modern Materials Handling* 50, no. 5 (Apr. 1995), pp. 31–34.

FIGURE 9–11

Utilizing AS/RS and AGVSs at Maybelline

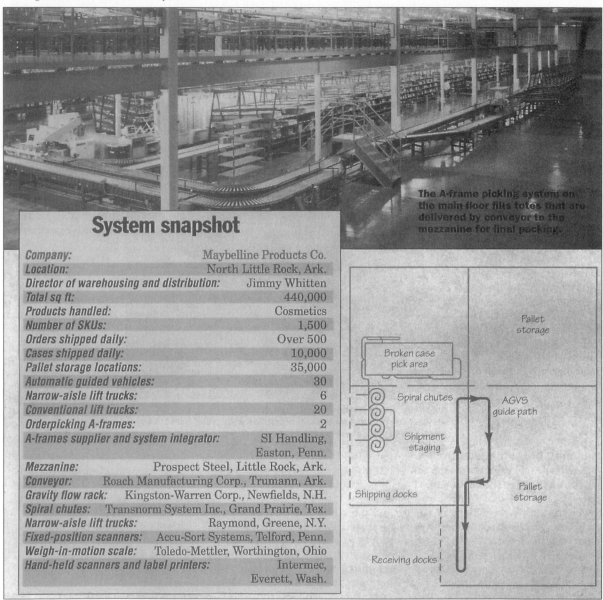

The A-frame picking system on the main floor fills totes that are delivered by conveyor to the mezzanine for final packing.

System snapshot

Company:	Maybelline Products Co.
Location:	North Little Rock, Ark.
Director of warehousing and distribution:	Jimmy Whitten
Total sq ft:	440,000
Products handled:	Cosmetics
Number of SKUs:	1,500
Orders shipped daily:	Over 500
Cases shipped daily:	10,000
Pallet storage locations:	35,000
Automatic guided vehicles:	30
Narrow-aisle lift trucks:	6
Conventional lift trucks:	20
Orderpicking A-frames:	2
A-frames supplier and system integrator:	SI Handling, Easton, Penn.
Mezzanine:	Prospect Steel, Little Rock, Ark.
Conveyor:	Roach Manufacturing Corp., Trumann, Ark.
Gravity flow rack:	Kingston-Warren Corp., Newfields, N.H.
Spiral chutes:	Transnorm System Inc., Grand Prairie, Tex.
Narrow-aisle lift trucks:	Raymond, Greene, N.Y.
Fixed-position scanners:	Accu-Sort Systems, Telford, Penn.
Weigh-in-motion scale:	Toledo-Mettler, Worthington, Ohio
Hand-held scanners and label printers:	Intermec, Everett, Wash.

Source: Gary Forger, "How Maybelline Ships Smaller, More Frequent Orders," *Modern Materials Handling* 50, no. 7 (June 1995), p. 49.

FIGURE 9–12

Robots in the warehouse

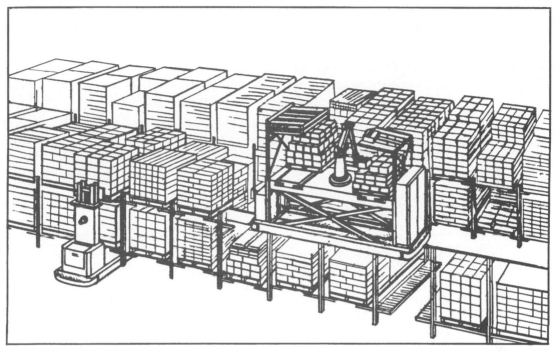

Artist's conception of guided vehicles and robotics in the warehouse. An automatically guided and programmed lift truck is shown stacking a load into a pallet rack. The robot is shown on a floor-supported vehicle capable of raising and lowering; the robot is picking from gravity flow racks and building pallet loads.

Source: "Warehousing Flexibility Aided by Robots," *Material Handling Engineering,* 40, no. 9 (Sept. 1985), p. 103. Reproduced by permission of The St. Onge Company, York, PA.

Warehousing in a Just-in-Time Environment

As manufacturing and merchandising firms adopt and implement just-in-time (JIT) programs, logistics components such as warehousing will be directly affected. Because JIT stresses reduced inventory levels and more responsive logistics systems, greater demands are placed on warehousing to maximize both efficiency and effectiveness. Examples of these demands include the following:[22]

JIT Places Additional Demands on Warehousing and Materials Handling

- *Total commitment to quality.* Warehouse employees must perform their tasks (inbound and outbound) at levels specified by customers.
- *Reduced production lot sizes.* Items are packaged in smaller lots, and warehouse deliveries are smaller and in mixed pallet quantities.

---

[22]See Robin G. Stenger and Robert E. Murray, "Using Warehousing Operations to Support a Just-In-Time Manufacturing Program," *WERC Technical Paper No. 20* (Oak Brook, IL: Warehousing Education and Research Council, 1987), pp. 1–2; and Louis Giust, "Just-in-Time Manufacturing and Material-Handling Trends," *International Journal of Physical Distribution and Logistics Management* 23, no. 7 (1993), pp. 32–38.

- *Elimination of nonvalue-added activities.* Nonessential and inefficient physical movement and handling activities are identified and eliminated, resulting in improved facilities layout and warehouse operating efficiencies.
- *Rapid flowthrough of materials.* Because JIT stresses low or even zero inventory, emphasis is placed on the mixing function of the warehouse rather than storage.

Zytec Corporation Utilizes JIT in Its Warehouse

Zytec Corporation, a manufacturer of power supplies for computers and medical equipment, successfully utilized its warehousing operations to support a JIT manufacturing system. Prior to implementing JIT, the firm's warehousing situation was described as follows:

> The raw materials and purchased parts warehouse at Zytec was out of control. Boxes of parts clogged every aisle and spilled into two additional buildings. The computer on-hand balances were seldom correct, destroying MRP [materials requirements planning] credibility. Unable to trust the system, purchasing agents bought excess inventory to protect against stockouts. Lines were shut down due to parts "lost in the crib" and then worked overtime when hot parts were expedited. Three inventory analysts worked 13-hour days to correct on-hand balances verified by two full-time cycle counters, yet no improvements were visible.[23]

After identifying the problems and causes of the warehousing inefficiencies, process and procedural changes were implemented that resulted in a raw materials inventory reduction of $5 million ($8.8 million to $3.8 million) and an increase in inventory accuracy from 98.5 to 99.6 percent. Only one facility was needed instead of the three that had been required.

Rio Bravo Electricos Uses JIT in Mexico

Rio Bravo Electricos, a firm in Juarez, Mexico, that assembles electric wiring harnesses for General Motors vans, supplies its 36 subassembly and assembly lines with parts every two hours or so. A wiring harness can be assembled in one hour within Rio Bravo's JIT environment.[24]

Delphi Packard Electric Systems and Its JIT Distribution Center

Similarly, Delphi Packard Electric Systems, a manufacturer of wiring harnesses, uses JIT in its El Paso, Texas, distribution center to move 99 percent of its product out of the facility within 24 hours. Since the late 1980s, the number of outbound shipments and stockkeeping units has increased annually at the distribution center while the amount of storage space has shrunk.[25] A brief overview of Delphi Packard's JIT distribution center is shown in Figure 9–13.

Packaging

Packaging is an important warehousing and materials management concern, one that is closely tied to warehouse efficiency and effectiveness. The best package increases service, decreases cost, and improves handling. Good packaging can have a positive impact on layout, design, and overall warehouse productivity.

---

[23]Stenger and Murray, "Using Warehousing Operations to Support a Just-In-Time Manufacturing Program," p. 2.

[24]Karen A. Auguston, "Feeding the JIT Pipeline from Across the Border," *Modern Materials Handling* 50, no. 6 (May 1995), pp. 34–35.

[25]Karen A. Auguston, "A Focus on Throughput Scores a JIT Success," *Modern Materials Handling* 50, no. 6 (May 1995), pp. 36–38.

FIGURE 9–13

A layout designed for quick handling, high throughput

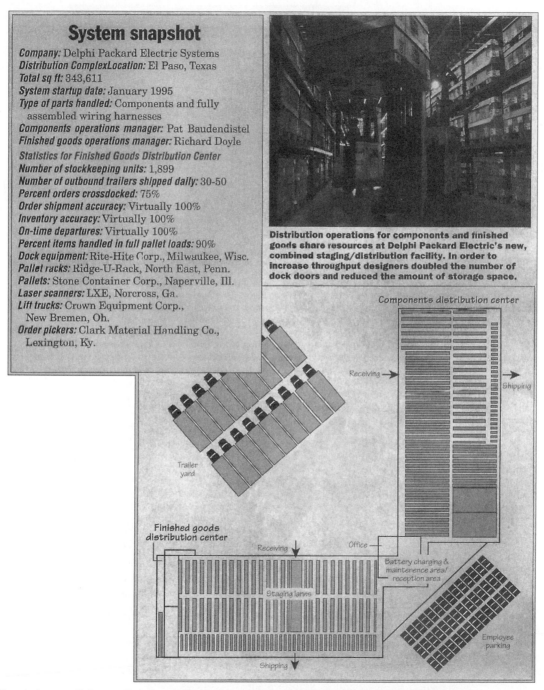

System snapshot

Company: Delphi Packard Electric Systems
Distribution ComplexLocation: El Paso, Texas
Total sq ft: 343,611
System startup date: January 1995
Type of parts handled: Components and fully
   assembled wiring harnesses
Components operations manager: Pat Baudendistel
Finished goods operations manager: Richard Doyle

Statistics for Finished Goods Distribution Center
Number of stockkeeping units: 1,899
Number of outbound trailers shipped daily: 30-50
Percent orders crossdocked: 75%
Order shipment accuracy: Virtually 100%
Inventory accuracy: Virtually 100%
On-time departures: Virtually 100%
Percent items handled in full pallet loads: 90%
Dock equipment: Rite-Hite Corp., Milwaukee, Wisc.
Pallet racks: Ridge-U-Rack, North East, Penn.
Pallets: Stone Container Corp., Naperville, Ill.
Laser scanners: LXE, Norcross, Ga.
Lift trucks: Crown Equipment Corp.,
   New Bremen, Oh.
Order pickers: Clark Material Handling Co.,
   Lexington, Ky.

Distribution operations for components and finished goods share resources at Delphi Packard Electric's new, combined staging/distribution facility. In order to increase throughput designers doubled the number of dock doors and reduced the amount of storage space.

Source: Karen A. Auguston, "A Focus on Throughput Scores a JIT Success," *Modern Materials Handling* 50, no. 6 (May 1995), p. 37.

Stretchable tape from 3M holds drums and boxes on warehouse pallets securely, while generating far less waste than commonly used plastic wraps.

Functions of Packaging

Packaging Serves Two Basic Functions: Marketing and Logistics

Packaging serves two basic functions: marketing and logistics. In its marketing function, the package provides customers with information about the product and promotes the product through the use of color and shape.

> The [package] is the "silent sales [person]," and it is the final interface between the company and its consumers. . . Consumers generally choose to buy from the image they perceive that a product has, and what they perceive is heavily influenced by the cues given on the product's packaging: brand name, color and display.[26]

From a logistics perspective, the function of packaging is to organize, protect, and identify products and materials. In performing this function, packaging takes up space and adds weight. Industrial users of packaging strive to gain the advantages packaging offers while minimizing the disadvantages, such as added space and weight. We are getting closer to that ideal in several types of packaging, including corrugated containers, foam-in-place packaging, stretchwrapping, and strapping. The environmental aspects of packaging are important because of reverse logistics (see Box 9–1).

---

[26]Rod Sara, "Packaging as a Retail Marketing Tool," *International Journal of Physical Distribution and Logistics Management* 20, no. 8 (1990), p. 30.

Packaging Performs Six Logistics Functions

More specifically, packaging performs six functions:

1. *Containment.* Products must be contained before they can be moved from one place to another. If the package breaks open, the item can be damaged or lost, or contribute to environmental pollution if it is a hazardous material.

2. *Protection.* To protect the contents of the package from damage or loss from outside environmental effects (e.g., moisture, dust, insects, contamination).

3. *Apportionment.* To reduce the output from industrial production to a manageable, desirable "consumer" size; that is, translating the large output of manufacturing into smaller quantities of greater use to customers.

4. *Unitization.* To permit primary packages to be unitized into secondary packages (e.g., placed inside a corrugated case); the secondary packages are unitized into a stretch-wrapped pallet, and ultimately into a container that is loaded with several pallets. This reduces the number of times a product must be handled.

5. *Convenience.* To allow products to be used conveniently; that is, with little wasted effort by customers (e.g., blister packs, dispensers).

6. *Communication.* The use of unambiguous, readily understood symbols such as a UPC (Universal Product Code).[27]

The package should be designed to provide the most efficient storage. Good packaging interfaces well with the organization's materials handling equipment and allows efficient utilization of storage space as well as transportation cube and weight constraints.

Effects of Packaging on Costs and Customer Service

An Example of Cost Savings through Packaging

In the past, packaging trade-offs were frequently ignored or downplayed in logistics decision making. Like all logistics decisions, packaging impacts both costs and customer service levels. From a cost perspective, suppose a company uses a carton that is 12" × 12" × 8" instead of a carton that measures 12" × 12" × 16". Assume the smaller carton costs $0.30 less and requires less loose fill, which can save a half cubic foot of dunnage costing $0.50. In this example, that is a savings of $0.80 per carton. Multiplied by hundreds, thousands, or millions of packages distributed during a year, the savings add up quickly.[28]

At the same time that costs are reduced, service levels are improved because customers are able to obtain more of the same amount of product in less space, enabling them to achieve cost savings. The customer is likely to realize fewer partial or split shipments from suppliers because more products can be placed on the transport vehicle that makes the delivery.

Saving Money through Efficient and Effective Packaging. Packaging is becoming a more visible issue with the current environmental concerns about recycling and the reuse

---

[27]Gordon L. Robertson, "Good and Bad Packaging: Who Decides?" *International Journal of Physical Distribution and Logistics Management* 20, no. 8 (1990), pp. 38–39.

[28]Toby B. Gooley, "Is There Hidden Treasure in Your Packaging?" *Logistics Management* 35, no. 12 (Dec. 1996), p. 23.

of packaging.[29] Investing in efficient and effective packaging can save a company money in the following ways:

Benefits of Good Packaging

- Lighter packaging may save transportation costs.
- Careful planning of packaging size/cube may allow better space utilization of warehousing and transportation.
- More protective packaging may reduce damage and requirements for special handling.
- More environmentally conscious packaging may save disposal costs and improve the company's image.
- Use of returnable containers provides cost savings as well as environmental benefits through the reduction of waste products.[30]

Ways Packaging Changes Cut Costs and Improve Customer Service. The following are specific examples of cost savings and customer service improvements resulting from packaging modifications.

- A frozen-foods supplier and a baked-goods company saved $3 million and $1 million, respectively, on annual freight costs with redesigned packaging that better fit standard pallets. Both companies could put more product on a pallet and more pallets in each truck, greatly reducing the number of truckloads.
- A pharmaceuticals company cut freight costs by 25 percent on one product line by reducing the amount of packaging used, and it did so without compromising product protection.
- An electronic components manufacturer changed the packaging on some products to reflect the average quantities ordered by customers. "Customers liked the larger quantities, and the reduced number of packages per order improved inventory and order accuracy, and reduced packaging and transportation costs."[31]

Box 9–1 describes some of the trade-offs between packaging materials and other logistics aspects as a result of Green Marketing and environmental concerns.

Factors Influencing Package Design

Factors Governing Good Package Design. Good package design is influenced by (1) standardization, (2) pricing (cost), (3) product or package adaptability, (4) protective level, (5) handling ability, (6) product packability, and (7) reusability and recyclability. With the growth in automation and computerization of warehousing, the ability to utilize "high" storage space and convey information are key. The importance a firm places on each factor, as well as the cost-service trade-offs it makes, varies by company, industry, and geographic location.

---

[29]John H. Sheridan, "Pollution Prevention Picks Up Steam," *Industry Week,* Feb. 17, 1992, p. 48; and Tom Andel, "Don't Recycle When You Can Recirculate," *Transportation and Distribution* 31, no. 9 (Sept. 1991), pp. 68–72.

[30]For a discussion of returnable containers, see Tom Andel, "Conversion to Returnables Wins Believers," *Transportation & Distribution* 36, no. 9 (Sept. 1995), pp. 94–100; and Leo Kroon and Gaby Vrijens, "Returnable Containers: An Example of Reverse Logistics," *International Journal of Physical Distribution and Logistics Management* 25, no. 2 (1995), pp. 56–68.

[31]Ibid., p. 20.

Box 9–1

Green Manufacturing Has Major Implications for Logistics

Design for disassembly is a hot new trend in manufacturing. The goal is to design, develop, and produce product with the goal of reducing the waste created when the product reaches the end of its useful life. That could involve recycling, refurbishing, or safely disposing of a product and its components. It has major implications for how a company designs its logistics and purchasing systems.

Germany has been the leader in the green movement by requiring manufacturers to "take back" their product's packaging. To address this requirement, manufacturers banded together to form a private company that collects, recycles, and disposes of packaging material. In the first two years of implementation, this has reduced the amount of waste due to packaging materials by 4 percent.

It has major implications for materials handling equipment and packaging design. For example, companies have been designing product to use less packaging. Colgate and several other manufacturers are now using a de-

sign for a toothpaste tube that stands on the cap. Thus, no box is needed.

Hewlett-Packard has designed workstations in a "green" way, which has many implications for logistics. Instead of using internal metal "frames" to hold the parts in place, HP uses a polypropylene foam chassis with cutouts for each component and connection. This is so effectively protective that external packaging can be reduced—by as much as 30 percent. The product is lighter, which reduces transportation cost. Disassembly time has been reduced by 90 percent.

As components are reused, new ways of transporting, storing, and handling the unusable materials and inventory need to be found. Logistics will play a key role in this process.

Source: Gene Bylinsky, "Manufacturing for Reuse," *Fortune*, Feb. 6, 1995, pp. 102–12.

Packaging and Logistics Cost Trade-Offs

Due to differences in the cost and physical characteristics of products, a food processor, for example, is more concerned than a computer manufacturer with having a package that minimizes shipping and storage costs. A computer manufacturer emphasizes the protective aspects of packaging because of the fragile, expensive nature of computer systems.

Another illustration would be a company that completed construction of a fully automated warehouse. Managers of such a facility would be very concerned with handling ability, cube utilization, and the ability to convey information so that it could be "read" by the equipment.

On the other hand, a company doing business in Germany would be concerned with reusability and recyclability aspects of packaging because of Germany's strict environmental laws. The packaging decision is truly one that requires the use of a systems approach in order to understand the true "total cost" picture.

Examples of the packaging and logistics cost trade-offs are shown in Table 9–3. There are many important interfaces between packaging and activities, such as transportation, inventory, warehousing, and information systems.[32]

---

[32]For specific company examples, see "Foam Protection Serves Electronic Parts Well," *Transportation & Distribution* 29, no. 3 (Mar. 1989), pp. 57–58; Ronald Kopicki, Michael J. Berg and Leslie Legg, *Reuse and Recycling—Reverse Logistics Opportunities* (Oak Brook, IL: Council of Logistics Management, 1993); and Paul R. Murphy, Richard F. Poist and Charles D. Braunschweig, "Role and Relevance of Logistics to Corporate Environmentalism: An Empirical Assessment," *International Journal of Physical Distribution and Logistics Management* 25, no. 2 (1995), pp. 5–19.

TABLE 9–3 **Packaging Cost Trade-Offs with Other Logistics Activities**

Logistics Activities	Trade-Offs
Transportation	
Increased package information	Decreases shipment delays; increased package information decreases tracking of lost shipments.
Increased package protection	Decreases damage and theft in transit, but increases package weight and transport costs.
Increased standardization	Decreases handling costs, vehicle waiting time for loading and unloading; increased standardization; increases modal choices for shipper and decreases need for specialized transport equipment.
Inventory	
Increased product protection	Decreases theft, damage, insurance; increases product availability (sales); increases product value and carrying costs.
Warehousing	
Increased package information	Decreases order filling time, labor cost.
Increased product protection	Increases cube utilization (stacking), but decreases cube utilization by increasing the size of the product dimensions.
Increased standardization	Decreases material handling equipment costs.
Communications	
Increased package information	Decreases other communications about the product such as telephone calls to track down lost shipments.

Source: Professor Robert L. Cook, Department of Marketing and Hospitality Services Administration, Central Michigan University, Mt. Pleasant, MI, 1991.

Of course, other factors influence the product package, such as the channel of distribution and institutional requirements. This often is true in retail channels. For example, when compact disks (CDs) first came out, retailers were concerned whether they could utilize the racks they were using for albums. And, there was concern about potential pilferage because of the small size of the CDs. A larger, environmentally unfriendly package was chosen as a way to address those concerns.[33]

Procter & Gamble (P&G) has examined the full implications of the packaging decision. The company developed a program called Direct Product Profitability[34] which identified product costs through the entire channel of distribution, including those associated with packaging. Some of the results achieved by P&G included the following:

Packaging Changes Implemented at Procter & Gamble

- An Ivory shampoo bottle was redesigned in a squarer configuration that took up less space and saved distributors 29 cents per case.

---

[33]Example provided by Dr. William A. Cunningham, Air Force Institute of Technology, Wright-Patterson Air Force Base, Ohio.

[34]Martin Christopher, "Integrating Logistics Strategy in the Corporate Financial Plan," in *The Logistics Handbook,* ed. James F. Robeson and William C. Copacino (New York: Free Press, 1994), pp. 255–57.

Box 9–2

Carriers Get into the Packaging Act

It may surprise some shippers, but carriers can be excellent sources of information on packaging improvements. Some large trucking companies and small-package carriers offer package testing, analysis, and consulting either as a free service to customers or on a fee-for-service basis.

For example, United Parcel Service, CF MotorFreight, and Federal Express all have package-testing laboratories. Their packaging engineers employ standard testing methods to determine whether shippers' packaging will withstand the rigors of transportation. Federal Express, for example, employs about 50 packaging engineers in the United States. United Parcel Service operates four packaging labs in the United States and Canada. CF Motor-Freight has a lab at its company headquarters.

It makes sense for carriers to get involved with packaging. By assisting shippers with their packaging concerns, carriers can reduce loss and damage rates and claims payments. They also benefit when changes in package size allow for better pallet and trailer utilization.

Carrier-operated laboratories are independent in the sense that they have no ties to the packaging manufacturers. Dozens of independent package-testing labs have been certified as conforming to specified testing standards by government agencies (e.g., Department of Transportation) and industry groups such as the International Safe Transit Association (ISTA) and the National Motor Freight Traffic Association (NMFTA). These groups can provide shippers with a list of certified testing facilities.

Source: Toby B. Gooley, "Is There Hidden Treasure in Your Packaging?" *Logistics Management* 35, no. 12 (Dec. 1996), p. 20.

- Tide powder detergent was reformulated so that P&G was able to shrink the size of the box without reducing the number of washings per box. P&G was able to pack 14 boxes in a case instead of 12, thus reducing handling and storage costs.[35] Later the firm introduced an even smaller package that allowed for a comparable number of wash loads but reduced the case size.

Packaging, warehouse handling systems, and warehousing operations are interrelated within the firm's logistics system, and all must be managed effectively (Box 9–2 has examples). The effectiveness of these systems can be enhanced with an excellent information system.

Computer Technology, Information, and Warehouse Management

Computers and Warehouse Management

We saw in Chapter 8 that the basic functions of warehousing were movement, storage, and information transfer. In each of those areas, the use of computer technology has become widespread. Warehousing is moving toward greater computer utilization. The fully computerized warehouse will likely have a structure similar to that shown in Figure 9–14, where all activities of the warehouse interface with the system, including receiving, quality control, storage, order picking, error control, packing, and shipping. Significant

[35]"Packaging/Handling Interaction Gets a Boost," *Material Handling Engineering* 40, no. 3 (Mar. 1985), p. 48.

FIGURE 9–14

Computers throughout the warehouse

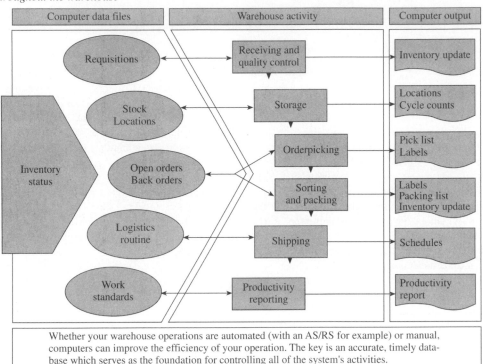

Computer data files	Warehouse activity	Computer output

Whether your warehouse operations are automated (with an AS/RS for example) or manual, computers can improve the efficiency of your operation. The key is an accurate, timely database which serves as the foundation for controlling all of the system's activities.

Source: "Increase Productivity with Computers and Software," *Modern Materials Handling, 1986 Warehousing Guidebook* 41, no. 4 (Spring 1986), p. 68. *Modern Materials Handling,* copyright 1986 by Cahners Publishing Company, Division of Reed Holdings, Inc.

advantages will result, including improved customer service, lower costs, and more efficient and effective operations.

Associated Grocers Automates Its Distribution Center

Associated Grocers of Colorado, Inc., has a computerized system that controls a variety of racking, conveyor, and automatic identification equipment in its distribution center.[36] Approximately 6,000 SKUs of dry grocery products are stored in the facility. Employees pick merchandise from a pick module (rack storage area) and manually apply bar-code labels to the items. They place the items on a belt conveyor, where they are moved to a merge and sorting area on an upper mezzanine. Bar-code readers divert items to the proper conveyor lane, which transports them to floor level.[37] There they are palletized and loaded into trucks for delivery to customers. With the exception of the manual order-picking activity, almost all of the process is controlled by computer. Box 9–3 ex-

---

[36]"How We Use Computers to Manage Distribution," *Modern Materials Handling* 40, no. 5 (Apr. 1985), p. 78.

[37]For an overview of various applications of bar codes, see James Aaron Cooke, "Bar Code or Perish!" *Traffic Management* 34, no. 9 (Sept. 1993), pp. 10-S through 13-S; *Data Acquisition and Bar Coding Strategies to Address Today's Challenges,* Monograph Series no. M0013 (Raleigh, NC: Tompkins Associates Inc., n.d.); and "2-D Bar Codes: One Step Closer to Use on Shipping Labels," *Modern Materials Handling* 50, no. 6 (May 1995), pp. S-5 through S-7.

Box 9–3

Texas Instruments Uses Bar Coding to Reduce Warehouse Space

Bar coding can be an essential link to inventory management. For example, Texas Instruments has linked electronic data interchange (EDI) and bar coding in the order placement and management of office supplies, with positive results. The company reduced the amount of cash tied up in inventory by $2 million, freed up 40,000 square feet of warehouse space, reassigned 11 office supply control employees, and reduced cycle time by more than one-third.

By bar coding inbound shipments, purchasing and the entire materials function can achieve more accurate accounts of actual receipts. The bar-code error rate has been quoted between 1 in 10,000 and 1 in 1 million, versus 1 in 25 or 30 for manually keyed data. Receiving also can be automated, which further contributes to cycle time reduction. These data can automatically be used by the accounts payable department for generating checks and reconciling invoices with purchase orders and receiving. Thus, bar coding represents a logical extension of the organization's information systems and an excellent linkage with EDI.

Source: Ed Hatchett, "Combining EDI with Bar Coding to Automate Procurement," *1992 NAPM* (Tempe, AZ: National Association of Purchasing Management, 1992), pp. 45–50.

plains how bar coding has been a key link in improving warehouse efficiency for Texas Instruments.

Malasia Airlines Uses Bar Coding to Manage Cargo

Malaysia Airlines, Southeast Asia's largest airline company, was the first Asia-Pacific air carrier to implement advanced bar-code and client-server technology in cargo tracking and warehouse operations.[38] Other companies in diverse industries—toy retailing, blood-testing laboratories, textbook manufacturing—are utilizing similar technology to improve materials handling efficiency and effectiveness.[39]

Importance of Information in Warehouse Management

Information is the key to successful warehouse management. However, many warehousing operations exhibit symptoms resulting from a lack of information. Not many warehouse managers operate in a total information vacuum, but many information gaps exist in warehousing operations.

The importance of information in warehouse management is significant. Accurate and timely information allows a firm to minimize inventories, improve routing and scheduling of transportation vehicles, and generally improve customer service levels. A typical warehouse management system achieves these improvements in three ways:

1. Reducing direct labor.
2. Increasing materials handling equipment efficiency.
3. Increasing warehouse space utilization.[40]

---

[38]"Airline Adopts Barcoding," *Logistics and Materials Handling* 4, no. 2 (Apr. 21, 1995), p. 39.

[39]See "Accurate Data Cuts Warehouse Costs by $1 Million Annually," *Modern Materials Handling* 50, no. 6 (May 1995), p. S-17; "Barcodes to Track Blood," *Logistics and Materials Handling* 4, no. 2 (Apr. 21, 1995), p. 41; and "Tracking What's Hot in Toys," *Logistics and Materials Handling* 4, no. 2 (Apr. 21, 1995), p. 40.

[40]For discussions of warehouse management systems (WMSs), see John M. Hill, "The Elements of a Successful WMS," *Transportation & Distribution* 36, no. 7 (July 1995), pp. 80–84; "Warehouse Management Software: Using Good Data to Beat the Clock," *Modern Materials Handling* 50, no. 6 (May 1995), p. S-19; and "The Wide, Wide World of WMS," *Traffic Management* 34, no. 8 (Aug. 1995), pp. 61-S through 63-S.

Technology

Parts to Go!

Thirty minutes doesn't sound like much of a wait for a part. But for workers on Hewlett-Packard's JIT production line, it was too long.

Employees at the company's Camas, Washington, production facility assemble the computer maker's popular low-cost, high-performance ink-jet printers. Some of the parts they need for the high-speed, high-volume assembly operations are available in an on-site warehouse. Others must be ordered from an off-site facility 12 miles away that holds inventories of screws, plastic parts, and electrical components.

The answer turned out to be a warehouse-management system (WMS) software package called Stockmaster. . . The WMS tracks the movement of inbound materials through the warehouse setup and into production.

Besides tracking inbound inventory, Stockmaster determines which specific parts will be pulled in response to a demand order from the factory.

To coordinate this stocking activity, Hewlett-Packard actually runs two separate Stockmaster systems that talk to one another. One WMS runs the on-site warehouse and materials-distribution system. The other oversees the off-site warehouse.

Throughout the process, Stockmaster knows each part's inventory levels, storage location, and even location in transit between warehouses. As a result, more than 90 percent of orders now get to the production line 10 minutes after they are requested.

Source: James Aaron Cooke, "Parts to Go!" *Logistics Management* 35, no. 4 (Apr. 1996), p. 87-S.

Local Area Networks (LANs)

Networks are communications systems that allow transmission of data between a number and variety of devices such as terminals, word processors, bar-code readers, robots, conveyors, automatic guided vehicles, and AS/RSs. A local area network (LAN), whose devices are located in close proximity to one another, is typically used in warehousing. Figure 9–15 shows an example of a local area network.

Many approaches are possible to setting up a LAN system. No matter which approach a firm uses, the objectives are the same: to provide better control over information flows and to allow the warehouse facility to maximize its effectiveness and efficiency. Due to direct connection and a common database, information feeds and flows directly to the next. This reduces redundant data entry, excessive paperwork and the potential for error.

Summary

In this chapter, we described warehousing materials handling, automation, packaging issues, JIT warehousing, and computerization. All of these factors are closely related and interact in creating efficient, effective warehousing and materials handling operations. They support the decisions related to warehouse facilities presented in Chapter 8.

FIGURE 9–15

A local area network (LAN) example

What you gain: a sharing of hardware, software, and data

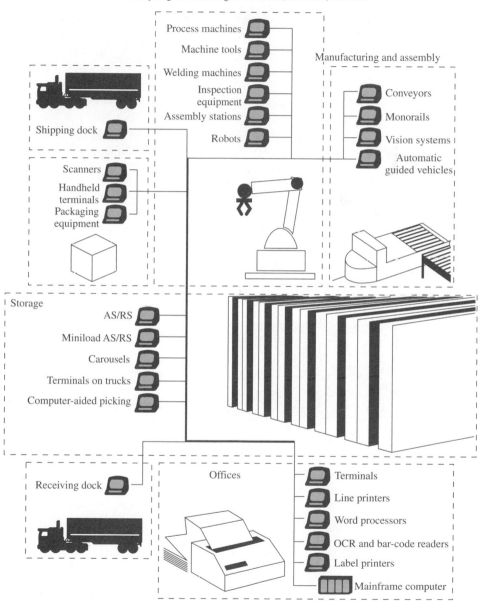

A local area network (LAN) can link computers and computerlike devices, from different manufacturers, each with their own communications protocols. This means that imcompatible equipment can "talk" with each other and share resources like mass memory storage and processors. And, as a result, a variety of computerized handling equipment and systems can be electronically connected into an integrated manufacturing operation.

Source: "Local Area Networks—The Crucial Element in Factory Automation," *Modern Materials Handling* 39, no. 7 (May 7, 1984), p. 51. *Modern Materials Handling,* Copyright 1986 by Cahners Publishing Company, Division of Reed Holdings, Inc.

Creative Solutions

A Call to Greatness

Ameritech's South Bend, Indiana, 390,000-square-foot distribution center (ADC) is considered world class and has been recognized by *Warehousing Management* as one of the greatest DCs ever built. In 1996, Ameritech's distribution center (ADC) received the designation "Warehouse of the Year."

The company stocks 35,000 SKUs and handles 6,200 inbound trucks and 5,400 outbound trucks. Its leading product is cellular telephones, but it also handles fiber optic cable, circuit boards, pagers, and cable television products. When consolidating its 20 DCs into a single facility several years ago,

Using state-of-the-art technology, Ameritech efficiently and effectively handles 35,000 SKUs in a single distribution center located in South Bend, Indiana.

Ameritech contacted John Deere, United Stationers, and Exel Logistics, and used the information about DCs at those firms to develop its present facility.

Products are received at the DC, scanned into the Ameritech computer system, and placed directly into storage. Most vendors supply products with bar codes that identify the product, quantity, and purchase order.

Using radio frequency technology, products move from the receiving dock to their respective storage location within two hours. Items that are not palletized are placed on conveyors where the bar code is scanned, diverting products to the appropriate storage area. There, a worker puts the item away and puts the storage location into the computer.

When product orders are received (almost all customer orders are received electronically), pick tickets are printed in location sequence by the computer, so that that the picker can make one pass down each aisle of the warehouse, thus reducing travel and cycle time. When products are picked, a pick-to-light system is used. Items are placed in totes and moved by conveyor to the appropriate truck loading docks. In sum, the system provides a 99.75 percent selection accuracy level and a 97.8 percent order fill rate (counted as an order completely filled).

Products are shipped to 2,600 customer locations in Ohio, Indiana, Michigan, Illinois, and Wisconsin. On-time delivery averages 99.6 percent.

Source: Cindy H. Muroff, "A Call to Greatness," *Warehousing Management* 3, no. 5 (Sept.–Oct. 1996), pp. 18–22.

Within a warehouse, manual (nonautomated) or automated materials handling equipment can be employed. Standard equipment can be categorized by the function it performs: storage and order picking, transportation and sorting, or shipping. Automated equipment includes items such as automated storage and retrieval systems (AS/RS), carousels, conveyors, robots, and scanning systems.

Packaging decisions affect warehousing, promotion, transportation, information transfer, and a number of other key logistics decisions. Environmental concerns about packaging, recyclability, and reusability are becoming more important.

Computer technology has had a significant impact on warehousing by improving the speed and accuracy of movement storage and information transfer. This material coupled with that in previous chapters prepares us for the examination of the role of procurement in the logistics process in Chapter 10.

Suggested Readings

Ackerman, Kenneth B. "The Changing Role of Warehousing." *Warehousing Forum* 8, no. 12 (Nov. 1993), pp. 1–4.

Ackerman, Kenneth B. "Receiving and Shipping Systems." In *The Distribution Management Handbook.* James A. Tompkins and Dale Harmelink, eds. New York: McGraw-Hill, 1994.

Ackerman, Kenneth B. *Warehousing Profitably: A Manager's Guide.* Columbus, OH: Ackerman Publications, 1994.

Andel, Tom. "The Environment's Right for a Packaging Plan." *Transportation & Distribution* 34, no. 11 (Nov. 1993), pp. 66–74.

Andel, Tom. "Pallets Take New Directions." *Transportation & Distribution* 33, no. 1 (Jan. 1992), pp. 32–34.

Cooke, James Aaron. "How to Choose the Lift Truck That's Right for You." *American Public Warehouse Register,* 14th ed. (1995), pp. 34–35.

Dadzie, Kofi Q., and Wesley J. Johnston. "Innovative Automation Technology in Corporate Warehousing Logistics." *Journal of Business Logistics* 12, no. 1 (1991), p. 76–90.

Forger, Gary. "We Turned an AS/RS into a Materials Control Center." *Modern Materials Handling* 50, no. 7 (June 1995), pp. 54–55.

Fraedrich, John, and John Cherry. "New Technology: Its Effects on International Distribution Systems of LDCs." *International Journal of Physical Distribution and Logistics Management* 23, no. 2 (1993), pp. 15–24.

Frazelle, Edward H., and James M. Apple, Jr. "Materials Handling Technologies." In *The Logistics Handbook.* James F. Robeson and William C. Copacino, eds. New York: Free Press, 1994.

Gray, Victor, and John Guthrie. "Ethical Issues of Environmental Friendly Packaging." *International Journal of Physical Distribution and Logistics Management* 20, no. 8 (1990), pp. 31–36.

Guist, Louis. "Just-in-Time Manufacturing and Material Handling Trends." *Logistics Information Management* 6, no. 1 (1993), pp. 16–23.

Harman, Roy L. *Reinventing the Warehouse: World Class Distribution Logistics.* New York: Free Press, 1993.

Harrington, Lisa. "Cross-Docking Takes Costs out of the Pipeline." *Distribution Logistics* 92, no. 9 (Sept. 1993), pp. 64–66.

Lancioni, Richard A. and Rajan Chandran. "The Role of Packaging in International Logistics." *International Journal of Physical Distribution and Logistics Management* 20, no. 8 (1990), pp. 41–43.

Moore, Alicia Hills, and Karen Nickel Anhalt. "Manufacturing for Reuse." *Fortune,* Feb. 6, 1995, pp. 102–12.

Muroff, Cindy. "Cost-Added Services." *Distribution* 92, no. 9 (Sept. 1993), pp. 77–79.

Nofsinger, John B. "Storage Equipment." In *The Distribution Management Handbook.* James A. Tompkins and Dale Harmelink, eds. New York: McGraw-Hill, 1994.

Olson, David R. "Material Handling Equipment." In *The Distribution Management Handbook.* James A. Tompkins and Dale Harmelink, eds. New York: McGraw-Hill, 1994.

Owens, Greg, and Robert Mann. "Materials Handling System Design." In *The Logistics Handbook.* James F. Robeson and William C. Copacino, eds. New York: Free Press, 1994.

Speh, Thomas W.; Jane C. Haley; Kelly A. Logan; and Mindy S. West. *A Guide for Evaluating and Implementing a Warehouse Bar Code System.* Oak Brook, IL: Warehousing Education and Research Council, 1992.

Stilwell, E. Joseph; R. Claire Canty; Peter W. Kopf; and Anthony M. Montrone. *Packaging for the Environment: A Partnership for Progress.* New York: AMACOM, 1991.

Stock, James R. "Managing Computer, Communication and Information Technology Strategically: Opportunities and Challenges for Warehousing." *Logistics and Transportation Review* 26, no. 2 (June 1990), pp. 32–54.

Tompkins, James A. "Measuring Warehousing Performance: How Are You Doing?" *Proceedings of the Annual Conference of the Council of Logistics Management,* 1994, pp. 437–49.

Traveling the Road of Logistics: The Evolution of Warehousing and Distribution. Chicago: American Warehouseman's Association, 1991.

"Try to Plan in Orderpicking Productivity." *Modern Materials Handling* 50, no. 5 (Apr. 1995), pp. 19–22.

Twede, Diana, ed. *Logistical Packaging Innovation Symposium Proceedings,* May 20–21, 1991.

"Warehousing: A Review for Management." *Distribution* 90, no. 3 (Mar. 1991), pp. 90–100.

Questions and Problems

1. Compare the advantages and benefits of automated materials handling systems with those of manual systems.

2. What are some potential pitfalls of automated materials handling? How do they affect the growth of automation in warehousing?

3. Discuss the relationship between warehousing and JIT.

4. Packaging serves two basic functions: marketing and logistics. Identify the role of packaging in each of these functions.

5. What marketing and logistics conflicts might occur in consumer goods packaging decisions? Use trade-off analysis to show how those conflicts might be analyzed and resolved.

6. What are some of the key trends and their implications in warehousing automation and computerization?

THE DISTRIBUTION CHALLENGE!
PROBLEM: A BREAK IN THE CHAIN

Sun Microsystems Computer Company shares a distribution problem with its high-tech competitors: security of product in transit. All companies labor to keep a close eye on their high-value goods, but Sun wasn't content with the way things were going.

Losses were occurring at some point in the lengthy distribution chain, but Sun didn't know exactly where, according to Bob Boehm, manager of North American logistics. Crafty thieves were opening cartons, removing a portion of the contents, then resealing the cartons. Especially vulnerable were memory upgrades which can easily be separated from other items.

Most of the time, the shortage wouldn't be detected until the goods got to an irate customer. Sun would have to rush a replacement shipment to the customer and bear the additional cost. Worse, air carriers weren't compensating for losses even close to the full amount. Wayne Brown, process analyst of corporate security, says carriers typically guarantee shipments by weight, not value. With insurance deductibles running at $50,000 or more, that places the onus for theft prevention squarely on the back of the shipper.

Sun needed an inexpensive way to detect where the losses were occurring and to help put a stop to them. What would you do?

What Is Your Solution?

Source: "Distribution: The Challenge," *Distribution* 95, no. 11 (Nov. 1996), p. 80.

Purchasing

Chapter Objectives

- To show how better management of purchasing activities can lead to increased profitability.
- To identify the activities that must be performed by the purchasing function.
- To describe the impact of just-in-time production on purchasing.
- To present issues in purchasing cost management.
- To illustrate the role of partnering in supplier relationship management.

Introduction

Manufacturing Purchasing Agents Buy More Than $1.5 Trillion Worth of Goods Each Year

In the United States, purchasing agents for manufacturing firms buy more than $1.5 trillion worth of goods each year.[1] How well this money is spent is an issue of considerable concern to companies. When one reflects that purchases consistently represent the largest single expense of doing business, it becomes evident that there is a pressing need for reliable measures of purchasing efficiency and effectiveness.[2]

The purchasing area within many organizations is undergoing many changes, including broadening its responsibilities, which is often reflected in departmental name changes. The group that used to be called purchasing may now be called, to name a few, procurement, sourcing, strategic sourcing, supply management, strategic supply management, supplier management, or materials management.

Along with the name changes has come a growing recognition of the importance of purchasing activities to the success of an organization, and a growth and shift in the types of activities performed by the sourcing area. The shifts in purchasing's activities and recognition mirror shifts in the status and responsibility of logistics activities in general.

While the sheer dollar volume of purchases is impressive, it is just as significant to note that the value of purchases averages approximately 57 percent of sales in manufacturing industries.[3] Purchase value also is significant in the service sector. For example, purchases average about 15 percent of revenues at investment firms like Salomon Brothers and Merrill Lynch.[4]

The Role of Purchasing in the Supply Chain

As presented more fully in Chapter 14, supply chain management is an integration of business processes from end user through original suppliers that provide products, services, and information that add value to customers.[5] Figure 10–1 illustrates how purchasing (or in its expanded role, procurement) supports supply chain management.

Purchasing Is Primarily Responsible for Inbound Flows into an Organization

Purchasing is responsible primarily for inbound, or upstream, channel activities, whereas logistics spans both inbound and outbound relationships and material flows. The specific activities for which purchasing is frequently responsible are presented next.

---

[1]U.S. Bureau of the Census, *1989 Annual Survey of Manufacturers* (Washington, DC: U.S. Government Printing Office, 1990), pp. 1–5, 1–10, and Appendix; as reported in Michiel R. Leenders and Harold E. Fearon, *Purchasing and Materials Management,* 10th ed. (Burr Ridge, IL.: Richard D. Irwin, 1993), pp. 7–8.

[2]Portions of this chapter are adapted from Lisa M. Ellram and Laura M. Birou, *Purchasing for Bottom Line Impact* (Burr Ridge, IL: Business One Irwin, 1995).

[3]Leenders and Fearon, p. 9.

[4]Shawn Tully, "Purchasing's New Muscle," *Fortune,* Feb. 20, 1995, p. 76.

[5]The International Center for Competitive Excellence, University of North Florida, 1994.

FIGURE 10–1

Supply chain management

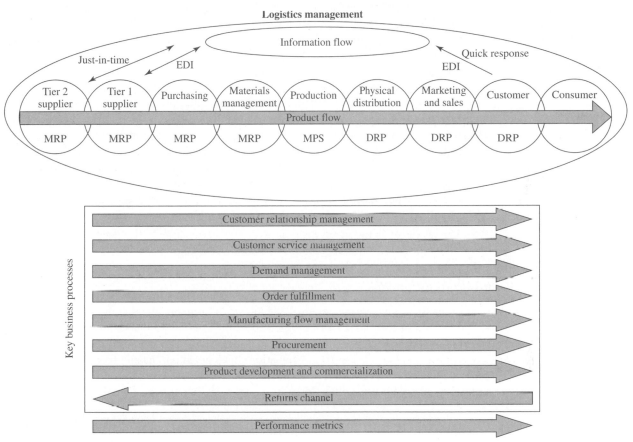

Source: The International Center for Competitive Excellence, University of North Florida.

Purchasing Activities

Purchasing was once looked upon primarily as a service function. As such, its responsibility was to meet the needs of the manufacturing function or other internal functions for which it was buying. It was not the responsibility of purchasing to question those needs, forge long-term relationships with suppliers, or to understand the needs of the end customer.

This perspective severely limited the contribution that purchasing could make to the firm. In this scenario, purchasers had to focus primarily on a narrow set of activities to serve the needs of the internal interfaces, such as production, marketing, operations, and others who needed to procure something from outside the organization. The scope of purchasing activities was defined and limited by those inside the organization.

Purchasing focused on getting the right product or service to the right place at the right time—in the right quantity, in the right condition or quality, and from the right supplier at the right price. While this may sound like a broad range of responsibilities, it really was not because the internal client[6] was defining what was "right" at each step.

An Example of Purchasing Performed Incorrectly

While purchasing played a key role in keeping the operation running smoothly by ensuring a reliable source of supply, this was not always accomplished at the lowest total cost. In many cases, purchasing may have contributed directly to the bottom line of the organization by reducing prices paid to suppliers.

Many organizations still see this as the focal point for purchasing. For example, José Ignacio Lopez, former purchasing head for General Motors Corporation, aggressively pitted suppliers against each other for short-term price gains during 1992–1993. With tight capacity in 1994–1995, many auto industry suppliers put service to GM as their lowest priority, withholding new ideas and parts in favor of other customers.[7] This operational perspective focused on short-term, day-to-day purchasing details, rather than the big picture. Clearly, the proper purchasing perspective must be the systems approach: to look at how purchasing can support the organization's broader goals.

Typically, purchasing was not seen as an activity of strategic importance. It involved following a series of prescribed steps, which included writing up a purchase order, contacting suppliers for pricing, and sometimes following up on a supplier who failed to deliver.

Development of the Purchasing Function

The purchasing function has gradually evolved. As organizations increasingly automate and outsource many activities, the funds spent on external purchases increase compared to those on labor. Thus, purchasing activities have been receiving more attention.

For the past 30 years or so, organizations have given purchasing more leeway in performing its activities. In some cases, purchasers have taken the initiative in broadening their roles in order to contribute more fully to the organization as a whole.

Purchasing Is the Largest Single Function at AT&T

You can spend your days trimming inventories and tweaking labor productivity, but if you think purchasing is a bore best left to ink-stained clerks in basement cubicles, you're misusing your time. Listen to William Marx, AT&T's executive vice president for telephone products: "Purchasing is by far the largest single function at AT&T. Nothing we do is more important."[8]

In many ways, purchasing today stands at a crossroads in its development. Many activities that were once the mainstream of purchasing are being eliminated and automated. Activities such as purchase order placement, expediting, matching documents, and calling to check stock have either been eliminated or are now possible on-line with electronic data interchange (EDI).

---

[6]Internal clients are those within the company, often in other functional areas, with whom purchasing interfaces. Customers or external customers represent those who purchase the good or service from the firm.

[7]See Tully, "Purchasing's New Muscle," pp. 76–77; and Arjan R. van Weele, "Partnership Revisited: The New Reality of Performance Based Purchasing," *Proceedings for the First Worldwide Research Symposium on Purchasing and Supply Chain Management* (Tempe, AZ: National Association of Purchasing Management, 1995), pp. 38–48.

[8]Tully, "Purchasing's New Muscle," p. 75.

While elimination of routine clerical activities frees up time, enabling purchasing to play a more proactive role in the firm, purchasers must recognize and seize the opportunity or they may face job elimination in an environment where downsizing and reengineering are common occurrences.

An important part of recognizing opportunities comes from understanding the organization's strategic goals and direction, so that purchasing can support those goals. It also comes from understanding the important role that purchasing plays in helping the organization achieve total customer satisfaction.

The Role of Purchasing in Total Customer Satisfaction

The major objective of any business is to create value for the owners. Many managers recognize that this can be accomplished more successfully by focusing on "serving the customer" or "providing a service to the customer." This reflects the realization that if they do not serve the customer effectively by meeting some otherwise unfulfilled need, the firm will cease to exist. This is not a change in the marketing concept, but a better implementation of the concept.

Purchasing Impacts Customer Service and Customer Satisfaction

Traditionally, purchasing has been separated from the firm's final customers, or end users. However, the receipt of high-quality, reliable goods and services on a timely basis at a reasonable cost often directly affects customer satisfaction. The relationship is illustrated in Figure 10–2.

An organization cannot provide its ultimate customers with better quality goods and services than it receives from its suppliers. If a supplier is late with a delivery or has quality problems, the quality and availability of the product or service to the customer will be affected unless the firm carries higher inventory. In such cases, the supplier increases the total cost of the product or service.

Purchasing Must Understand Customer Needs

It is important that purchasers understand the needs of their organization's customers. This understanding will allow purchasing to make the "right" decisions to meet the organization's needs. The skills required and tasks performed by purchasing are very similar for buyers in the retail, manufacturing, government, and service sectors.[9]

The Strategic Role of Purchasing

The strategic role of purchasing is to perform sourcing-related activities in a way that supports the overall objectives of the organization. Purchasing can make many contributions to the strategic success of the organization through its key role as one of the organization's boundary-spanning functions.

---

[9]Eugene W. Muller, *Job Analysis: Identifying the Tasks of Purchasing* (Tempe, AZ: Center for Advanced Purchasing Studies, 1992), p. 6.

FIGURE 10–2

Total customer satisfaction depends on supplier performance

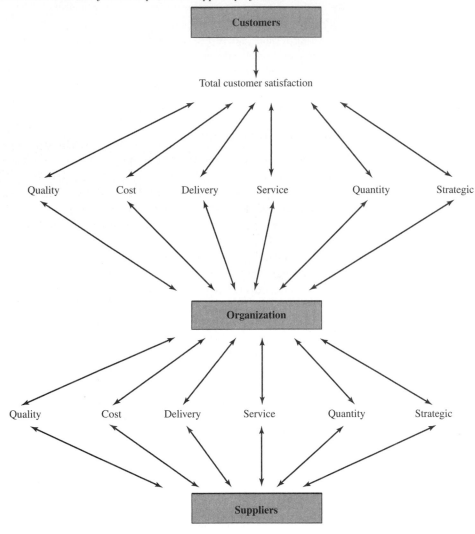

Source: Michiel Leenders, and Anna Flynn, *Value Driven Purchasing: Managing the Key Steps in the Acquisition Process* (Burr Ridge, IL: Irwin Professional Publishing, 1994) p. 3.

Access to External Markets. Through external contacts with the supply market, purchasing can gain important information about new technologies, potential new materials or services, new sources of supply, and changes in market conditions.

By communicating this competitive intelligence, purchasing can help reshape the organization's strategy to take advantage of market opportunities. The Creative Solutions box at the end of this chapter illustrates the important strategic role that purchasing can play in the public sector.

The timely arrival of inbound raw materials, such as the phosphate ores shown in this photograph, is important to the manufacture and distribution of finished goods, such as fertilizers.

Supplier Development and Relationship Management.   Purchasing can help support the organization's strategic success by identifying and developing new and existing suppliers. Getting suppliers involved early in the development of new products and services or modifications to existing offerings can reduce development times. The idea of time compression—getting to market quickly with new ideas—can be very important to the success of those ideas and perhaps to the organization's position as a market leader or innovator.

Among the primary purchasing activities that influence the ability of the firm to achieve its objectives are supplier selection, evaluation and ongoing management (sourcing), total quality management, and purchasing planning and research.

The Role of Purchasing Is Operational and Strategic

Relationship to Other Functions.   Virtually every department within an organization relies on the purchasing function for some type of information or support. Purchasing's role ranges from a support role to a strategic function. To the extent that purchasing provides value to other functional areas, it will be included in important decisions and become involved early in decisions that affect purchasing. Being well informed allows the purchasing function to better anticipate and support the needs of other functional areas. This support in turn leads to greater recognition and participation.

Purchasing often has the same functional reporting relationship as logistics, which is helpful for coordinating materials management. Purchasing and logistics need to work closely in coordinating inbound logistics and associated material flows. The following sections apply to purchases of goods and services; they apply equally to purchasing of logistics services and managing relationships with logistics service providers.

Supplier Selection and Evaluation

It Is Extremely Important to Select the Right Suppliers

In the acquisition process, perhaps the most important activity is selecting the best supplier from among a number of suppliers that can provide the needed materials. The buying process is complex because of the variety of factors that must be considered when making a purchase. The process includes both decision makers and decision influencers, who combine to form the **decision-making unit.** Increasingly, organizations are using cross-functional teams to make important decisions. The use of teams is described more fully in Chapter 12, which deals with organizational structures.

Figure 10–3 shows some of the many information flows between purchasing and other internal functions that may affect the supplier selection and evaluation system. These flows exist at many levels, from dealing with users on order commitments, to verifying contractual terms with the legal department, to ensuring adequate materials availability, to supporting marketing's sales promotions.

Five-Step Purchasing Process of Managing Supplier Relationships

Figure 10–4 shows a basic, five-step purchasing process for managing supplier relationships from the identification of a need to make a purchase through ongoing evaluation and follow-up. Purchasing managers may consider a broad range of factors when making the purchasing decision. These may include issues such as lead time, on-time delivery performance, ability to expedite, price competitiveness, and postpurchase sales support.[10]

Purchase Categories. There are six major purchase categories in most companies: (1) component parts, (2) raw materials, (3) operating supplies, (4) support equipment, (5) process equipment, and (6) services. These may be routine, ongoing purchases or nonroutine purchases that may require special attention because they represent a new buy, an infrequent purchase, a major acquisition or if there are problems or major opportunities (strategic, cost savings) associated with the buy.

In the 1980s and 1990s, increased concern for productivity improvements and cost reduction caused management attention to focus on the purchasing function and on the development of closer ties with a reduced number of suppliers.[11] To determine the impact of supplier performance on productivity, performance must be measured and evaluated (see phase 5 in Figure 10–4). Next, the data can be used to identify those suppliers with

---

[10]For a more complete description of supplier selection factors and associated issues, see Donald W. Dobler and David N. Burt, *Purchasing and Supply Management,* 6th ed. (New York: McGraw-Hill, 1996), pp. 238–60.

[11]Robert E. Spekman, "Strategic Supplier Selection: Understanding Long-Term Buyer Relationships," *Business Horizons,* July–Aug. 1988, pp. 75–81; and William F. Given, "Improving Your Supplier Relationship," *NAPM Insights,* Sept. 1994, pp. 8–9.

FIGURE 10–3

Overview of internal information flows from purchasing

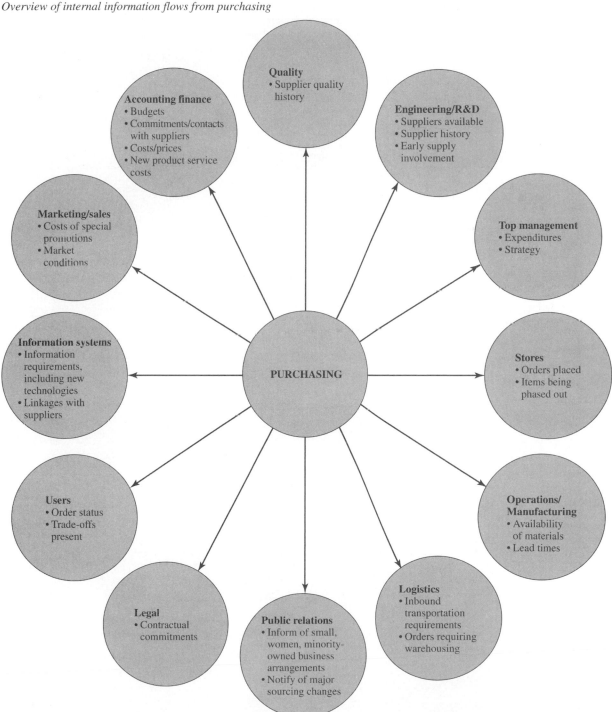

Source: Adapted from Lisa M. Ellram and Laura M. Birou, *Purchasing for Bottom Line Impact* (Burr Ridge, IL: Irwin Professional Publishing, 1995), p. 74.

FIGURE 10–4

Five phases in the selection development and management of purchasing relationships

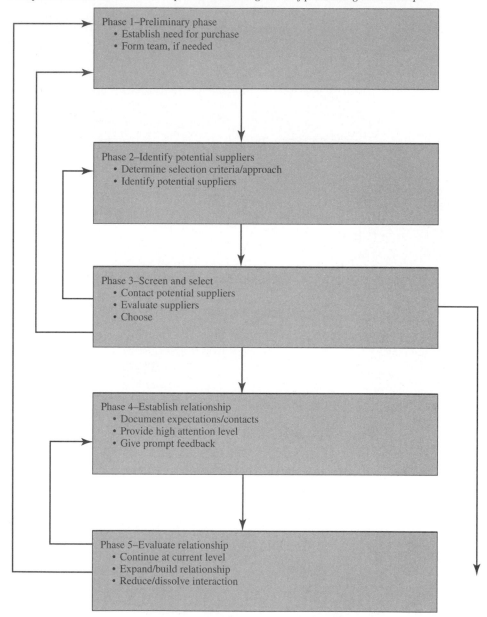

Source: Lisa M. Ellram, "A Managerial Guideline for the Development and Implementation of Purchasing Partnerships," *International Journal of Purchasing and Materials Management* 31, no. 2 (1995), p. 12.

TABLE 10–1   Evaluating Suppliers in a Typical Manufacturing Firm

Factor	Rating of Supplier (1 = Worst Rating: 5 = Highest Rating) 1 2 3 4 5		Importance of Factor to Your Firm (0 = No Importance; 5 = Highest Importance) 0 1 2 3 4 5		Weighted Composite Rating (0 = Minimum; 25 = Maximum)
Supplier A		×		=	
Product reliability					
Price					
Ordering convenience					
•					
•					
•					
After-sale service					
Total for supplier A					_____
Supplier B					
Product reliability					
Price					
Ordering convenience					
•					
•					
•					
After-sale service					
Total for supplier B					_____
Supplier C					
Product reliability					
Price					
Ordering convenience					
•					
•					
•					
After-sale service					
Total for supplier C					_____

Decision rule: Select the supplier with highest composite rating.

whom the firm wishes to develop long-term relationships, to identify problems so that corrective action can be taken, and to realize productivity improvements.[12]

Evaluating Suppliers.   A variety of evaluation procedures are possible; there is no best method or approach for all firms. Most important, always use consistent procedures to increase the objectivity of the process. Table 10–1 presents an example of an evaluation procedure.

[12]Thomas C. Harrington, Douglas M. Lambert, and Martin Christopher, "A Methodology for Measuring Vendor Performance," *Journal of Business Logistics* 12, no. 1 (1991), p. 83.

In the purchse of bulk commodities such as coal, price, and on-time delivery capability are important factors in supplier selection.

Develop a List of Supplier Evaluation Factors

The manager must identify all potential suppliers for the items being purchased. The next step is to develop a list of factors to evaluate each supplier. These should complement the factors used earlier in supplier selection. Once the factors have been determined, the performance of individual suppliers should be evaluated on each factor (e.g., product reliability, price, ordering convenience). Table 10–1 uses a five-point scale (1 = worst rating; 5 = highest rating), but other scales may be used.

Relative Importance of Each Evaluation Factor

Prior to evaluating suppliers, management must determine the relative importance of the factors to its particular situation, and assign each a weight. For example, if product reliability were of paramount importance to the firm, it would be given the highest importance rating. If price were not as important as product reliability, management would assign price a lower importance rating. A factor of no importance to the firm would be assigned a zero.[13]

The next step is to develop a weighted composite measure for each factor by multiplying the supplier's evaluation by the factor's importance. The addition of the composite scores for each supplier provides an overall rating that can be compared to the ratings of other suppliers. The higher the composite score, the more closely the supplier meets the needs and specifications of the procuring company. Going through the process itself is

---

[13]Some factors may be of no importance to the firm in one type of buying situation, but of moderate or high importance at other times. Therefore, it is necessary that all potentially critical factors be included in the rating form in order to eliminate the need for a different form for each buying situation.

one of the major benefits of this approach. This forces management to formalize the important elements of the purchasing decision and to question existing methods, assumptions, and procedures.

An Example of Supplier Performance Evaluation

Implementation of a supplier performance evaluation methodology in a company that assembled kits for the health care industry resulted in a reduction in the number of suppliers, closer relationships with remaining suppliers, and a 34 percent reduction in component inventories within the first few months.[14] After two full years of using the quarterly performance reports, buyers had reduced component inventories by more than 60 percent.

Formal Supplier Selection Process Is Optimal

Selecting Suppliers.   Selecting the right suppliers has an immediate and long-term impact on the firm's ability to serve its customers. A formal selection process, similar to the formal evaluation process presented in the previous section, is advisable.

The supplier selection process is more difficult when materials are being purchased in international markets or for international operations. Firms buy raw materials, components, and subassemblies from foreign sources because of cost and availability issues.

Some of the complexities of doing business internationally are presented in Chapter 11, "Global Logistics." The Global box demonstrates how Kodak worked to develop a better approach to manage the purchase of important equipment across its worldwide operations.

Rewards Associated with Proper Supplier Selection and Evaluation

The rewards associated with the proper selection and evaluation of suppliers can be significant. As we saw in Chapter 1, logistics cost savings can be leveraged into substantial improvements in profits. Similarly, purchasing activities can have positive effects on the firm's profits. Not only will a reduction in the cost of materials increase the profit margin on every unit manufactured and sold, but the lower cost logistics associated with the materials purchased will reduce the investment in inventories by decreasing the cost per unit and the number of units in inventory.

In addition, customer service improvements are possible because the manufacturing process can operate smoothly, with no slowdowns or shutdowns. Since effective purchasing management results in the acquisition of high-quality materials, there is less likelihood that customers will return finished goods due to product failure.

Total Quality Management

The Purchase Price of an Item Is Only One Element of the Total Cost

Although cost is an important consideration in materials acquisition, so is quality management. The initial purchase price of an item is only one element of the total cost. For example, some items are easier to work with than others and can save production costs. Materials of higher quality may require fewer fabrication processes or have a longer life span, resulting in lower overall product costs or higher prices for finished products. Companies must achieve some balance between the components of the acquisition process—namely, price, cost, and value received.[15]

---

[14]Harrington, Lambert, and Christopher, "A Methodology for Measuring Vendor Performance," pp. 97–98.

[15]For a comprehensive discussion of total cost issues in purchasing, see Lisa M. Ellram, *Total Cost Modeling in Purchasing* (Tempe, AZ: Center for Advanced Purchasing Studies, 1994).

Global

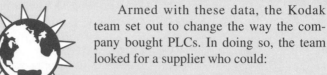

Kodak Uses Total Cost Analysis to Leverage Global Purchases through Computers and Automation

Eastman Kodak, a leader in the imaging industry, was faced with a difficult situation in managing its purchase of programmable logic controllers (PLCs). PLCs are the "brains" that run the equipment, materials flow, and related processes in a manufacturing facility. Kodak had no companywide standard for the type of PLC purchased, so each plant in each country purchased whatever technology it wanted. The purchase generally was based on the lowest price. A self-empowered, worldwide team of buyers and engineers was formed to explore how Kodak could reduce its costs. The team agreed that "price" was only a small part of total cost, and set out to prove this by performing a total cost of ownership analysis on PLCs. It discovered that price was truly the tip of the iceberg, as shown in the total cost breakdown below.

	% of Purchase Price
Purchase price	100%
Engineering costs	75
Installation costs	100
Commissioning costs	12
Parts and service costs	15
Maintenance costs	50
Training costs	5
Retirement costs	10
Total as a percent of current purchase price	367%

Armed with these data, the Kodak team set out to change the way the company bought PLCs. In doing so, the team looked for a supplier who could:

- Provide worldwide coverage on a number of products and services.
- Maximize savings in the nonprice categories/overall value.
- Agree to annual price negotiations instead of project-by-project negotiations.
- Understand partnering and willingly "partner."
- Provide a match between the portfolio of products and services offered and Kodak's existing installed equipment.

The results have been greater than expected. In the affected product classes (e.g., PLCs, drives, motors and industrial controls), 74 percent was spent with world sources in 1994, compared with 54 percent in 1993. The supplier base has been reduced between 20 and 59 percent, depending on the site. Price and other cost categories listed above were reduced by 25 percent in the first six months of operation of the agreements, significantly exceeding original estimates.

Source: Lisa Ellram and Owen Edis, "A Case Study of Successful Partnering Implementation," *Journal of Purchasing and Materials Management* 32, no. 4 (Fall 1996), pp. 10–18.

After the required quality level has been determined and specifications developed, usually by manufacturing, it becomes purchasing's responsibility to secure the proper materials. The correct quality specification must be given to suppliers. The supplier that offers the best cost-quality combination that meets the specifications should be selected.

The firm should never pay higher prices to obtain materials with quality levels greater than those specified by manufacturing unless justifiable marketing or logistics reasons exist for doing so. Purchasing materials that needlessly exceed quality specifications adds unnecessary costs to products.[16]

One way that firms might ensure quality is through inspection of incoming materials parts. But, this is costly and time consuming. Inspection requires human resources, space, and perhaps test equipment. In addition, incoming inventory is tied up or delayed awaiting inspection. For these reasons, purchasing managers have turned to **supplier certification.** In the certification process, the supplier's quality levels and processes are closely evaluated by members of the buying firm. If they "pass," the buying organization no longer inspects that supplier's incoming material.

Supplier Certification Is Better Than Inspection Programs

Quality is even more critical for firms pursuing a JIT philosophy, where little or no inventory is held. Improper quality in a JIT environment can shut down processes immediately, creating excessive costs and delays.

Just-in-Time

Just-in-time (JIT) manufacturing is more a philosophy of doing business than a specific technique. The JIT philosophy focuses on the identification and elimination of waste wherever it is found in the manufacturing system. The concept of continuous improvement becomes the central managerial focus.

Results of JIT Implementation

Typically, JIT implementation involves the initiation of a "pull" system of manufacturing (matching production to known demand) and the benefits include: significant reductions of raw material, work-in-process, and finished goods inventories; significant reductions in throughput time; and large decreases in the amount of space required for the manufacturing process.

A company implementing JIT can usually make the greatest improvement in the area of quality. The JIT focus on the elimination of waste includes the supplier, with the aim of reducing waste and cost throughout the entire supply chain. If a manufacturer decides it will no longer carry a raw materials inventory and that henceforth its suppliers must carry this inventory, the supply chain cost is reduced because inventory with lower value added is being held.

Compaq Utilizes JIT

One example of this is Compaq, which requires its suppliers to hold a certain amount of inventory at a warehouse near Compaq's production facilities, so suppliers can respond quickly in case of problems. It is preferable that this inventory be eliminated altogether because while those additional inventory carrying costs may be borne in the short term by the seller, eventually they may be passed on to the buyer in the form of higher prices. The supplier needs to reduce its own manufacturing and supplier lead times. The major differences between "traditional" and JIT purchasing are summarized in Table 10–2.

Difficulties in Implementing JIT

Difficulties in Implementing JIT.   One of the most frequently cited reasons for difficulty in the implementation of JIT is a lack of cooperation from suppliers, due to the

---

[16]Donald W. Dobler and David N. Burt, *Purchasing and Supply Management,* 6th ed. (New York: McGraw-Hill, 1996), pp. 160–76.

TABLE 10–2   **Differences between the Traditional Approach and the JIT Approach in Purchasing**

Purchasing Activity	Traditional Approach	JIT Approach
Supplier selection	Minimum of two suppliers; price is central	Often one local supplier; frequent deliveries
Placing the order	Order specifies delivery time and quality	Annual order; deliveries made as needed
Change of orders	Delivery time and quality often changed at the last moment	Delivery time and quality fixed, quantities are adjusted within predetermined margins if necessary
Follow-up of orders	Many phone calls to solve delivery problems	Few delivery problems thanks to sound agreements; quality and delivery problems are not tolerated
Incoming inspection	Inspection of quality and quantities of nearly every delivered order	Initial sample inspections; later, no inspections necessary
Supplier assessment	Qualitative assessment; delivery deviations of up to 10% are tolerated	Deviations are not accepted; price is fixed based on open calculation
Invoicing	Payment per order	Invoices are collected and settled on a monthly basis

Source: A. J. van Weele, *Purchasing Management: Analysis, Planning and Practice* (New York: Chapman and Hall, 1994) p. 132.

changes required in the supplier's system. In addition to changing from traditional quality control inspection practices to the implementation of statistical process control, the supplier is asked to manufacture in quantities that may differ from the usual lot sizes and to make frequent deliveries of small lots with precise timing. The supplier and buyer are normally required to provide each other with access to their master production planning system, shop floor schedule, and material requirements planning system.

Communication Is the Key to Successful JIT

Importance of Buyer-Supplier Communication.   Under JIT, close and frequent buyer-supplier communication is essential. Suppliers are given long-range insight into the buyer's production schedule. Often, this look ahead spans months, but the schedule for the nearest several weeks is frozen. This allows the supplier to acquire raw materials in a stockless production mode and to supply the buyer without inventory buildups. Suppliers provide daily updates of progress, production schedules, and problems. Purchasers and suppliers must cooperate and have a trusting relationship in order to convert supply chains to JIT operations.

Supplier selection, single sourcing, supply management, and supplier communication become critical issues for purchasing and materials managers in implementing JIT. Issues relating to supplier selection include quality-control methods, supplier proximity, manufacturing flexibility, and lead time reliability.

JIT manufacturers and their suppliers generally develop close collaborative relationships supported by long-term, single-source contracts. The concept of partnering, described in further detail later in the chapter, is often applied to the JIT buyer-supplier relationships.

Following supplier selection, careful supplier performance measurement and management often lead to supplier certification—a designation reserved for those suppliers whose quality, on-time delivery, and reliability have proven acceptable over long periods of time.

JIT Programs at Ethyl Corporation

At the Ethyl Corporation, purchasing managers are responsible for knowing supply lead times. Since there is little room for storage of materials for this petrochemical and pharmaceutical intermediary, the company operates in a JIT mode to accommodate weekly manufacturing schedules. Using experience, sales forecasts, and historical usage as a basis, monthly or quarterly forecasted requirements are easier to predict. A rolling four-quarter forecast for material prices is used and forecasts are tracked for accuracy.[17]

The Functioning of the Purchasing Department Changes under JIT

Under JIT, the purchasing department has significantly changed from the processing of orders to a focus on supplier selection and long-term contract negotiation. Many times these close communications are supported by electronic data interchange (EDI) capabilities to facilitate the timely and accurate transmittal of information. The remaining sections apply to purchasing in general, and are critical to support the success of JIT purchasing.

Purchase Agreements

JIT in Japan

JIT purchasing is facilitated by an even, repetitive master production schedule. Repetitive manufacture of products evens out the demand for individual parts. The steady demand for parts has an impact on shipping quantities, containers, and purchasing paperwork. In Japan, JIT purchase agreements usually involve little paperwork. The purchase order may specify price and overall quantity, but the supplier will deliver in accordance with a schedule or with daily production needs, which are telephoned from the buying plant. The JIT purchase agreement does not permit variability. In most cases, the buyer expects and receives the exact quantity. Having a purchase agreement in place saves much time in negotiating and pricing each order.

Value Analysis

Value Analysis Described

In the United States, **value analysis** is a respected purchasing practice that may receive more attention as a result of the interest in JIT purchasing. When negotiating a purchase agreement, the supplier receives the buyer's specifications and provides a bid price. If the price is too high, the buyer may visit the supplier's plant to review its processes. The objective is to identify areas where the supplier's costs exceed the value added and, if possible, to modify the minimal specifications in order to reduce the supplier's cost and the bid price.

"Loose" Engineering Specifications/Early Supplier Involvement

U.S. engineers tend to specify tolerances for almost every design feature for which parts are purchased. The Japanese place more importance on how the item actually performs

---

[17]Joel D. Wisner, "Forecasting Techniques for Today's Purchaser," *NAPM Insights,* Sept. 1991, p. 23.

than on conformance to tight design specifications. The supplier is permitted to innovate on the premise that the supplier is the expert.

Early Supplier Involvement Programs

The concept of getting the supplier involved in the design process is often called **early supplier involvement** (ESI). This concept has been applied successfully by companies like Bose, Chrysler (in the introduction of the Neon), and Harley Davidson. **Concurrent engineering** is a type of early supplier involvement where the engineers in the buying and selling firms work together on product development or product improvement.

The benefits of closer coordination on engineering and quality matters are significant. Engineers and quality control people may pay frequent visits to a supplier's plant to answer engineering questions and identify potential quality problems before they surface. Xerox Corporation utilizes these practices with its key suppliers, resulting in better supplier quality, responsiveness, and competitiveness.

Control of Inbound Transportation

Inbound freight decisions such as delivery and routing are frequently left to the supplier's traffic department. This is often the case 372
when materials are purchased "FOB shipping point" and the buyer owns the goods and absorbs the inventory carrying costs from the date of shipment.[18]

JIT Purchasing Requires Steady, Reliable Incoming Deliveries

JIT purchasing requires steady, reliable incoming deliveries. The objective is to avoid excessive inventory carrying costs for materials that arrive early and to avoid disruptions in manufacturing operations when goods arrive late. Therefore, the buying firms must become involved in selecting both the transportation mode and the specific carrier. For example, CTI and Ryder Integrated Logistics review manufacturers production schedules, notify the supplier of requirements, schedule pickup of the materials, pick up and time-sequence the materials, and deliver them directly to the JIT production line.[19]

Supplier Development

Supplier development has been defined as:

Supplier Development Defined

A systematic organizational effort to create and maintain a network of competent suppliers and to improve various supplier capabilities that are necessary for the buying organization to meet its increasing competitive challenges.[20]

Sometimes organizations find that their current suppliers are unable to support stringent JIT quality and delivery requirements. Such organizations may search for other suppliers or work with suppliers to develop the skills needed to support JIT. Supplier development efforts are increasing as organizations form longer-term relationships with suppliers. Chrysler's philosophy toward supplier development is presented in Box 10–1. Chrysler is an example of a company that was performing very poorly until it adopted

---

[18]FOB. terms were presented in Chapter 7.

[19]Information obtained from CTI and Ryder Integrated Logistics.

[20]*NAPM Dictionary* (Tempe, AZ: National Association of Purchasing Management, 1993), p. 22.

Box 10–1

Supplier Development: The Extended Enterprise at Chrysler

Chrysler utilizes horizontal, cross-functional teams organized around a "platform" or car model. External suppliers are an integral part of that team, which has helped Chrysler to improve productivity and speed new product development. By utilizing its suppliers' ideas in the design stages, Chrysler has been able to incorporate the latest technology and to speed products to market.

Going beyond this, the "extended enterprise" concept at Chrysler encompasses all tiers of suppliers. It encourages noncompeting suppliers to share their best practices to help them become more globally competitive. Chrysler manages the total supply chain from raw material suppliers (steel/resin), secondary suppliers (stampers/molders), to first-tier suppliers of components. Communication is the key in joint coordination and effective working relationships among supply chain members. This communication is possible because of the mutual trust among members of the Chrysler supply chain.

Suppliers can expect that Chrysler will work within a long-term, "evergreen" relationship based on shared goals. In turn, Chrysler expects suppliers to provide technological innovations and to reinvest profits in their business through research and development and improved infrastructure.

In 1990, Chrysler launched a program to actively encourage supplier feedback and suggestions. Since that time, it has received about 10,000 ideas that have generated over $1 billion in annual savings. These are not simply cost avoidances or one-time ideas, but permanent, bottom-line improvements.

Working closely with suppliers to create mutually beneficial relationships has strengthened both Chrysler and its suppliers. As a result, Chrysler's entire supply chain is more competitive globally.

Source: Adapted from Thomas T. Stalkamp, "Beyond Reengineering: Developing the Extended Enterprise," *NAPM Insights,* Feb. 1995, p. 76.

innovative purchasing, logistics, and practices such as JIT, supplier development, and early supplier involvement.

JIT II

JIT II is an innovative type of purchasing relationship which aims JIT principles at the purchasing function. Like JIT, JIT II attempts to eliminate waste, redundancy, and excess paperwork, and to improve quality, responsiveness, and innovation in the purchasing arena. It represents a type of alliance relationship between a buying and selling organization. The term *JIT II* was coined by Bose Corporation to describe this type of relationship.[21] The steps in developing JIT II are shown in Box 10–2.

JIT II at Bose Corporation

In JIT II, the supplier places one of its employees, called an "in-plant," in the buying company's office, replacing a purchaser, planner, and salesperson. In addition to colocation, the concurrent engineering and continuous improvement aspects of JIT II

[21]Lance Dixon and Anne Porter Millen, *JIT II: Revolution in Buying and Selling* (Newton, MA: Cahners, 1994), pp. 9–15.

Box 10–2

Steps in JIT II Information Flow

Steps 1, 2: Supplier reassigns its sales representative to new duties, and customer reassigns its purchaser.

Step 3: In full JIT II implementation, the customer reassigns its material planner to new duties.

Step 4: Supplier replaces purchaser, planner, and salesperson with a full-time professional at the customer's location. At Bose Corporation, supplier professionals are called "in-plants." Although supplier replaces purchaser with an in-plant rep, this step actually assists existing purchasing personnel as more people address the overall department workload.

Step 5: The in-plant representative works 40 hours a week at the customer's location, usually in its purchasing department.

Step 6: Customer empowers the in-plant within its planning and purchasing systems. The in-plant works directly from the customer's MRP (or similar) system, and uses the customer's purchase order to place material orders on his or her own company. Note: The customer typically prohibits the in-plant from placing purchasing orders with other companies.

Step 7: Customer provides the in-plant with an employee badge (or equivalent), providing free access to customer engineering and manufacturing personnel. When not planning and ordering material, the in-plant practices concurrent engineering by working with the customer's design engineering staff.

Step 8: Customer and supplier understand that many more steps lie ahead. JIT II will cause change in both organizations.

Source: *Purchasing,* May 6, 1993, p. 17.

distinguish it from other supplier relationships. One of the companies with which Bose has established this in-plant relationship is G&F Industries, an injection molder. The in-plant representative places orders, practices concurrent engineering, and has full access to all of Bose's facilities, information, and employees. The supplier benefits include greater integration with the customer, improved communications, more efficient administrative processes, and savings on "sales effort."[22]

Purchasing Research and Planning

Research and Planning Are Becoming More Important

Uncertainty in the business environment is making the purchasing decisions for key items more complex and the effects of these decisions more long lasting. Important environmental considerations include uncertainty of supply and dependence on foreign sources for key commodities, price increases on key commodities, extended and variable lead times, energy shortages or price increases, government regulation such as environmental laws, and increasing worldwide competition.

[22]Ibid., pp. 143–50 and 159–60.

The changing environment makes it necessary for purchasing management to do a more effective job of researching the supply market. Purchasing needs to provide information about supply conditions, (e.g., availability, lead times, prices, technology) to different groups within the firm, including top management, logistics, engineering, design, manufacturing, and marketing. This information is important when formulating long-term strategy and making short-term decisions. Key materials for which availability, pricing, and quality problems may occur should be identified, so that action plans can be developed before problems become critical and costly.

Strategic Planning for Purchasing

Strategic planning for purchasing involves the identification of critical purchases, supply market analysis, risk assessment, and strategy development and implementation. It is important to determine whether materials problems or shortages might jeopardize current or future production of new or existing products, whether materials quality can be expected to change, whether prices are likely to increase or decrease, and the appropriateness of forward buying. Management should develop specific plans to ensure an uninterrupted flow of materials.

Identifying Critical Purchases

Typical criteria to use in identifying critical purchases are percentage of product cost, percentage of total purchase expenditure, and use on high-margin end items. Criteria used for determining the risk in the supply market include number of suppliers, availability of raw materials to suppliers, supplier cost and profitability needs, supply capacity, and technological trends. The more critical the purchase and the riskier the supply market, the greater attention the purchase requires.

Risk Assessment

Risk assessment requires that the purchaser determine the probability of best or worst conditions occurring. Supply strategies like those shown in Table 10–3 should be developed for the predicted events. Asking these questions for any given strategy or situation can help purchasing ensure that they have considered the important issues.[23] Implementation of a particular strategy requires the involvement of top management and integration with the firm's overall business plan.

Purchasing Cost Management

Cost Saving Opportunities in Purchasing

Given the large percentage of the firm's dollars that purchasing spends, purchasing departments must manage and reduce costs. Purchasing can use a number of methods to reduce administrative costs, purchase prices, and inventory carrying costs, but the most prevalent are purchase cost reduction programs, price change management programs, volume leverage (time or quantity) contracts, systems contracts and stockless purchasing, and establishing long-term relationships with suppliers.

Purchasing savings have the same sort of profit leverage effect as logistics cost savings (see Figure 1–2 in Chapter 1). If top management calls for a set percentage of cost

---

[23]For further discussion of purchasing research and planning, see A. J. van Weele, *Purchasing Management: Analysis, Planning and Practice* (New York: Chapman and Hall, 1994), pp. 97–176; Leenders and Fearon, *Purchasing and Materials Management,* pp. 448–63; and Joel Adamson, "Strategic Planning and Procurement," *NAPM Insights,* May 1991, pp. 10–11.

TABLE 10–3 Supply Strategy Questions

1. *What?* Make or buy Standard vs. special Quality vs. cost	Multiple vs. sole source High vs. low supplier turnover Supplier relations Supplier certification Supplier ownership
2. *Quality?* Quality vs. cost Supplier involvement	8. *How?* Systems and procedures Computerization
3. *How much?* Large vs. small quantities (inventory)	Negotiations Competitive bids Fixed bids
4. *Who?* Centralize or decentralize Quality of staff Top management involvement	Blanket orders/open orders Systems contracting Blank check system Group buying
5. *When?* Now or later Forward buy	Materials requirements planning Long-term contracts Ethics Aggressive or passive
6. *What price?* Premium Standard Lower Cost-based Market-based Lease/make/buy	Purchasing research Value analysis 9. *Why?* Objectives congruent Market reasons Internal reasons
7. *Where?* Local, regional Domestic international Large vs. small	*a.* Outside supply *b.* Inside supply

Source: Michiel E. Leenders and Harold E. Fearon, *Purchasing and Materials Management,* 10th ed. (Burr Ridge, IL: Richard D. Irwin, 1993), p. 643.

Profit Leverage Impact

reduction in all areas of spending, the potential impact of purchasing is large. Because purchasing spends such a large percentage of a firm's revenue, a 10 percent cost reduction in purchase expenditures has a much greater impact than a 10 percent reduction in labor or overhead expenses (see Table 10–4).

Cost-Reduction Programs

An effective cost-reduction program by purchasing requires top management support, clear definition of goals, visibility of savings to top management, measurement of savings, reporting on the process and its results, and incorporation of cost-reduction goals in the individual performance appraisal process.

TABLE 10–4   Cost as a Percentage of a Firm's Total Revenue

Cost of Goods	Percent
Labor	5
Purchased materials	55
Overhead	10
Total	70%

A 10% reduction in costs in each category will bring about:	Total reduction
Labor	.5%
Materials	5.5
Overhead	1.0
Total	7.0%

Requirements of a Successful Cost Reduction Program

For a cost-reduction program to succeed, top management must communicate the need for cost-saving accomplishments in both good and bad economic times. The program must define cost-reduction objectives adequately, so that accomplishments can be measured and performances evaluated.

In many firms, for example, a "cost reduction" is defined as a decrease in prior purchase price. This means a cost reduction occurs only when the firm is paying a lower price. Cost avoidance is the amount that *would* have been paid less the amount actually paid. The distinction between cost savings and cost avoidance is shown in Table 10–5.

Cost-reduction and avoidance programs may include any of the following:

- Supplier development.
- Development of competition.
- Requirement of supplier cost reduction.
- Early supplier involvement in new product design and design changes.
- Substitution of materials.
- Standardization.
- Make-or-buy analysis.
- Value analysis, including supplier involvement.
- The reduction of scrap.
- A change in tolerances.
- Improvement of payment terms and conditions.
- Volume buying.
- Process changes.

The appropriateness of each technique will vary with the purchase situation and type of supplier relationship.

TABLE 10–5   **Cost Savings versus Cost Avoidance**

	Per Unit Cost
Scenario 1—Cost savings:	
Current price paid	$20.00
New price	19.00
Cost savings	$1.00
Scenario 2—Cost avoidance:	
Current price paid	$20.00
New price quoted by supplier	25.00
Price obtained from alternate supplier	22.00
Cost savings	
Current price paid	$20.00
New price actually paid	22.00
Cost savings [Actually a $2.00 price increase]	–$2.00
Cost avoidance	
New price quoted	$25.00
New price actually paid	22.00
Cost avoidance	$3.00

Price Change Management

Purchasing managers must challenge supplier price increases and not treat them as pass-through costs. It is important to work with suppliers to restrict price increases to a reasonable and equitable level. Furthermore, purchasing should establish a systematic method of handling all price increase requests from suppliers. At a minimum, the system should require:

Handling Price Increase Requests from Suppliers

- Determination of the reason for the price change request.
- Specification of the total dollar value impact on the firm.
- Justification of the price change by suppliers.
- Review of the price change by management.
- Strategies to deal with price increases.
- Alternatives for reducing other price elements or improving processes to offset the price increase.

Purchasing should work with the supplier to offset price increases through other improvements, such as reduced delivery lead times, better service, or other opportunities. To restrict price increases, management should require price protection clauses and advance notification of 30, 60, or 90 days for price increases. As part of a program of price change management, purchasing should determine the impact of engineering changes on product costs before it recommends making these changes.

Forward Buying versus Speculative Buying

Frequently, conditions such as potential supply constrictions or inflationary markets cause purchasing managers to buy more of a product than is required for current consumption. This practice, called **forward buying,** serves to protect the organization from anticipated shortages or to delay the impact of rising prices. The trade-off of course is increased inventory carrying costs. When using this strategy, the purchasing manager must evaluate the trade-off between inventory carrying cost increases and the risk of supply constriction or increased prices. This was the case with Ethyl Corporation.

Ethyl Corporation Engages in Forward Buying

The Ethyl Corporation, a petrochemical and pharmaceutical company, forecasts raw materials needs and prices in its purchasing department. An economist at Ethyl creates a quarterly outlook based on major economic indicators to aid in the purchase of materials. Steven Moore, director of commercial services reported:

> During the period leading up to the conflict in the Persian Gulf, we saw a major increase in petroleum-based raw material prices; we predicted this price increase and we were able to benefit from advance purchases of these materials.[24]

Speculative Buying

Speculative buying refers to purchases made not for internal consumption, but to resell at a later date for profit. Speculative goods may be the same as goods purchased for consumption, but the quantities purchased will be in excess of current or future needs. An example occurs in the diverting of retail goods.

Companies may offer special discounts to retailers only in certain areas of the country. Retailers will buy substantial quantities of goods to ship to other locations or even to sell to other retailers in different parts of the country where the discount is unavailable. The retailer makes a profit by selling for more money or saving enough money to offset the increased freight and handling costs. The fundamental intent is to take advantage of expected increases in price to profit from the resale of the goods.

Volume Contracts

Volume contracts are a way to leverage purchase requirements over time, between various business units or locations in the company, or on different line-item requirements. As a result of combining purchases, the buyer's leverage with suppliers can lead to reductions in purchase prices and administrative costs. Cumulative volume discounts allow a buyer to combine purchase volume over time, getting lower prices with successive buys as it places additional orders throughout the year. More companies are using this approach to support smaller, more frequent buys in JIT purchasing.

Cumulative Discounts

In noncumulative discounts, the price is based on the amount of each order. A review of purchase prices for a particular item often identifies the opportunity for suppliers to provide quotes on a semiannual or contract basis. An increase in the purchase quantity can enable suppliers to reduce their costs and prices as a result of production or purchasing economies. In addition, the supplier may be willing to accept lower per unit margins on a higher volume of business.

---

[24]Wisner, "Forecasting Techniques," p. 23.

Past purchase patterns should be available from computer-generated requirement plans and from suppliers. Management needs to review the firm's purchase history systematically and regularly for new opportunities for volume contracting.

Stockless Purchasing

Stockless purchasing is a means of reducing materials-related costs such as unit purchase price, transportation, inventory, and administration. Contracts are arranged for a given volume of purchases over a specified period of time. The supplier provides products to individual plant locations as ordered, and payment is arranged through purchasing. Logistics is involved in the actual order release, which simplifies repetitive ordering considerably and lowers transaction costs.

Stockless purchasing implies that the firm does not carry inventory of purchased materials. While it may or may not result in "zero" inventory, the underlying principles of stockless purchasing support improved inventory management. The objectives of stockless purchasing are to:

Objectives of Stockless Purchasing

- Lower inventory levels.
- Reduce the supplier base.
- Reduce administrative cost and paperwork.
- Reduce the number of purchases of small dollar value and requisitions that purchasers have to handle, freeing up time for more important activities.
- Achieve volume leverage with suppliers, lowering costs and improving service.
- Provide for timely delivery of material directly to the user.
- Standardize purchase items where possible.
- Have supplier manage inventory and, in some cases, place orders.[25]

Stockless purchasing systems are best suited to frequently purchased items of low dollar value where administrative processing costs are relatively high compared with unit prices. In many cases, the combined administrative, processing, and inventory carrying costs may exceed the item's cost. Stockless purchasing may lead to larger supplier discounts, reduced processing costs, and increased product availability. An example of the effective use of stockless purchasing by Texas Instruments is illustrated in the Technology box.

The Concept of Integrated Supply

Going beyond systems contracts is the concept of **integrated supply.** Under this concept, a purchaser will combine all buys of like items with one supplier, further reducing administrative costs and increasing leverage. Examples of items well suited to integrated supply are office supplies, lab supplies, small tools, screws, nuts and bolts, and standard electrical components.[26]

---

[25]Lisa M. Ellram, *Fundamentals of Purchasing,* seminar workbook provided to the National Association of Purchasing Management, 1995.

[26]For more information on integrated supply, view the video, "Integrated Supply: A Special Supplier Relationship," available from the National Association of Purchasing Management, Tempe, AZ; Telephone: 800-888-6276.

Technology

Texas Instruments Simplifies Low-Dollar Purchases

In line with the concept of stockless purchasing, Texas Instruments (TI) has adopted an on-line electronic catalog that all employees can access for low-dollar purchases. This system, called Express Buying, is designed for low-dollar, high-volume purchases in order to reduce the administrative costs of procuring such items. Targeted toward purchases under $2,500, this system uses standard EDI documents, based on ANSI standards. The documents in the system include:

- Price/sales catalog (prepared by supplier).
- Purchase order.
- Purchase order acknowledgment.
- Shipment and billing notice.
- Purchase order change request.

A user can search for items in the catalog by using key words, TI or manufacturer part numbers, commodity classes, manufacturer, and supplier. A user also can use a paper catalog. Once the items are selected, the order is transmitted to the supplier by means of EDI, and the user receives an acknowledgment.

When the supplier fills the order, it transmits a shipment and billing notice. Upon receiving the shipment, TI's system compares the notice to the order received. If there is a match, TI's system creates an approved electronic invoice for accounts payable. That amount is vouchered for the next payment cycle.

The benefits of this approach are:

- Purchasers spend less time as "paper pushers" on small purchases.
- Data entry errors are reduced because manual data handling and re-entry is limited.
- The supply base can be consolidated, creating greater volume leverage.
- Order cycle time is reduced.
- Payment accuracy is increased.

This system has helped TI to better manage the "paper tiger" in purchasing.

Source: Adapted from Michael Bulkelley, "Express Buying Made Simple," *NAPM Insights,* May 1994, pp. 10–11.

Usually, the length of the contract for purchasing agreements varies from one to five years and includes price protection clauses. The purchaser should have the right to research the market to ensure that suppliers' unit prices are reasonable.

Managing Supplier Relationships

Supplier partnerships have become one of the hottest topics in interfirm relationships. Business pressures such as shortened product life cycles and global competition are making business too complex and expensive for one firm to go it alone. Despite all the interest in partnerships, a great deal of confusion still exists about what constitutes a partnership and when it makes the most sense to have one. This section will present a model that can be used to identify when a partnership is appropriate as well as the type of partnership that should be implemented.

While there are countless definitions for partnerships in use today, we prefer the definition that follows:

Partnership Defined

A partnership is a tailored business relationship based on mutual trust, openness, shared risk and shared rewards that yields a competitive advantage, resulting in business performance greater than would be achieved by the firms individually.[27]

Types of Partnerships[28]

Relationships between organizations can range from arm's length relationships (consisting of either one-time exchanges or multiple transactions) to vertical integration of the two organizations, as shown in Figure 10–5. Most relationships between organizations have been at arm's length where the two organizations conduct business with each other, often over a long period of time and involving multiple exchanges. However, there is no sense of joint commitment or joint operations between the two companies. In arm's length relationships, a seller typically offers standard products/services to a wide range of customers who receive standard terms and conditions. When the exchanges end, the relationship ends. While arm's length represents an appropriate option in many situations, there are times when a closer, more integrated relationship, called a partnership, would provide significant benefits to both firms.

A partnership is not the same as a joint venture or strategic alliance, which normally entails some degree of shared ownership across the two parties. Nor is it the same as vertical integration. Yet a well-managed partnership can provide benefits similar to those found in joint ventures or vertical integration. For instance, Pepsi chose to acquire restaurants such as Taco Bell, Pizza Hut, and KFC in order to ensure distribution of its products in these outlets. Coca-Cola has achieved a similar result without the cost of vertical integration through its partnership with McDonald's.

While most partnerships share some common elements and characteristics, there is no one ideal or "benchmark" relationship that is appropriate in all situations. Because each relationship has its own set of motivating factors as well as its own unique operating environment, the duration, breadth, strength, and closeness of the partnership will vary from **Three Types of** case to case and over time. Research has indicated that three types of partnerships exist.
Partnerships Exist

Type I. The organizations involved recognize each other as partners and, on a limited basis, coordinate activities and planning. The partnership usually has a short-term focus and involves only one division or functional area within each organization.

Type II. The organizations involved progress beyond coordination of activities to integration of activities. Although not expected to last "forever," the partnership has a long-term horizon. Multiple divisions and functions within the firm are involved in the partnership.

---

[27]Douglas M. Lambert, Margaret A. Emmelhainz, and John T. Gardner, "Developing and Implementing Supply Chain Partnerships," *The International Journal of Logistics Management* 7, no. 2 (1996), p. 2.

[28]This section and the following section are taken from Lambert, Emmelhainz, and Gardner, "Developing and Implementing Supply Chain Partnerships," pp.1–17.

Figure 10–5

Types of relationships

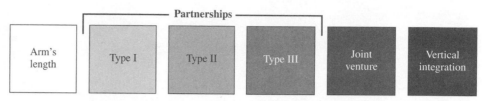

Source: Douglas M. Lambert, Margaret A. Emmelhainz, and John T. Gardner, "Developing and Implementing Supply Chain Partnerships," *The International Journal of Logistics Management* 7, no. 2 (1996), p. 2.

Type III.   The organizations share a significant level of integration. Each party views the other as an extension of their own firm. Typically no "end date" for the partnership exists.

The Majority of Relationships Will Be Arm's Length

Normally, a firm will have a wide range of relationships spanning the entire spectrum, the majority of which will not be partnerships but arm's length associations. Of the relationships that are partnerships, the largest percentage will be Type I, and only a limited number will be Type III partnerships. Type III partnerships should be reserved for those suppliers or customers who are critical to an organization's long-term success. The previously described relationship between Coke and McDonald's has been evaluated as a Type III partnership.

The Partnership Model

Drivers Provide the Motivation to Partner

The partnership model shown in Figure 10–6 has three major elements that lead to outcomes: drivers, facilitators, and components. **Drivers** are compelling reasons to partner. **Facilitators** are supportive corporate environmental factors that enhance partnership growth and development. **Components** are joint activities and processes used to build and sustain the partnership. Outcomes reflect the performance of the partnership.

Four Categories of Drivers

Drivers.   Both parties must believe that they will receive significant benefits in one or more areas and that these benefits would not be possible without a partnership. The primary potential benefits that drive the desire to partner include: (1) asset/cost efficiencies, (2) customer service improvements, (3) marketing advantage, and (4) profit stability/ growth (see Table 10–6 for examples).

While the presence of strong drivers is necessary for successful partnerships, the drivers by themselves do not ensure success. The benefits derived from the drivers must be sustainable over the long term. If, for instance, the marketing advantage or cost efficiencies resulting from the relationship can be easily matched by a competitor, the probability of long-term partnership success is reduced.

In evaluating a relationship, how does a manager know if there are enough drivers to pursue a partnership? First, drivers must exist for each party. It is unlikely that the drivers will be the same for both parties, but they need to be strong for both. Second, the drivers must be strong enough to provide each party with a realistic expectation of significant

Figure 10–6

The partnering process

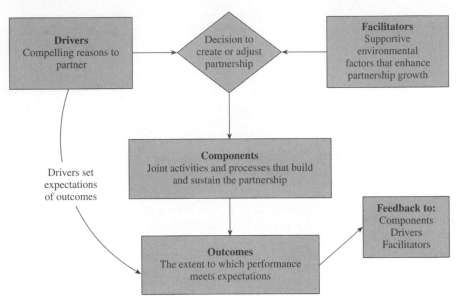

Source: Douglas M. Lambert, Margaret A. Emmelhainz, and John T. Gardner, "Developing and Implementing Supply Chain Partnerships," *The International Journal of Logistics Management* 7, no. 2 (1996), p. 4.

benefits through a strengthening of the relationship. Each party should independently assess the strength of its specific drivers.

Facilitators Measure Supportiveness of the Environment

Facilitators.   Drivers provide the motivation to partner. But even with a strong desire for building a partnership, the probability of success is reduced if the corporate environments are not supportive of a close relationship. Just as the relationship of a young couple with a strong desire to marry can be derailed by unsupportive in-laws, different communication styles, and dissimilar values, so can a corporate relationship be side-tracked by a hostile environment. On the other hand, a supportive environment that enhances integration of the two parties will improve the success of the partnership.

Facilitators are elements of a corporate environment that allow a partnership to grow and strengthen. They serve as a foundation for a good relationship. In the short run, facilitators can not be developed; they either exist or they don't. And the degree to which they exist often determines whether a partnership succeeds or fails. Facilitators include: (1) corporate compatibility, (2) similar managerial philosophy and techniques, (3) mutuality, and (4) symmetry (see Table 10–6 for details).

Four Catagories of Facilitators

Facilitators apply to the combined environment of the two potential partners. Therefore, unlike drivers, which are assessed by managers in each firm independently, facilitators should be assessed jointly. The discussion of corporate values, philosophies, and objectives often leads to an improved relationship even if no further steps toward building a partnership are taken. The more positive the facilitators, the better the chance of partnership success.

TABLE 10–6   Partnership Drivers, Facilitators, and Components

Partnership Drivers
- Asset/cost efficiency: What is the probability that this relationship will substantially reduce channel costs or improve asset utilization, for example, product costs, distribution costs savings, handling costs savings, packing costs savings, information handling costs savings, managerial efficiencies, and assets and devoted to the relationship?
- Customer service: What is the probability that this relationship will substantially improve the customer service level as measured by the customer, for example, improved on-time delivery, better tracking of movement, paperless order processing, accurate order deliveries, improved cycle times, improved fill rates, customer survey results, and process improvements?
- Marketing advantage: What is the probability that this relationship will lead to substantial marketing advantages, for example, new market entry, promotion (joint advertising, sales promotion), price (reduced price advantage), product (jointly developed product innovation, branding opportunities), place (expanded geographic coverage, market saturation), access to technology, and innovation potential?
- Profit stability/growth: What is the probability that this relationship will result in profit growth or reduced variability in profit, for example, growth, cyclical leveling, seasonal leveling, market share stability, sales volume, and assurance of supply?

Partnership Facilitators
- Corporate compatibility: What is the probability that the two organizations will mesh smoothly in terms of: (1) Culture, for example, both firms place a value on keeping commitments, constancy of purpose, employees viewed as long term assets, and external stakeholders considered important, and (2) business, for example, strategic plans and objectives consistent, commitment to partnership ideas, and willingness to change?
- Management philosophy and techniques: What is the probability that the management philosophy and techniques of the two companies will match smoothly, for example, organizational structure, use of TQM, degree of top management support, types of motivation used, importance of teamwork, attitudes toward "personnel churning," and degree of employee empowerment?
- Mutuality: What is the probability both parties have the skills and predisposition needed for mutual relationship building? Is management skilled at two-sided thinking and action, taking the perspective of the other company, expressing goals and sharing expectations, and taking a longer term view, for example, or is management willing to share financial information and integrate systems?
- Symmetry: What is the probability that the parties are similar on the following important factors that will affect the success of the relationship: relative size in terms of sales, relative market share in their respective industries, financial strength, productivity, brand image/reputation, and technological sophistication?

Partnership Components
- Planning (style, level, and content)
- Joint operating controls (measurement and ability to make changes)
- Communications (nonroutine and day-to-day: organization, balanced flow, and electronic)
- Risk/reward sharing (loss tolerance, gain commitment, and commitment to fairness)
- Trust and commitment to each other's success)
- Contract style (timeframe and coverage)
- Scope (share of partner's business, value added, and critical activities)
- Investment (financial, technology, and people)

Partnership Outcomes
- Global performance outcomes (enhancement of profits, leveling of profits over time)
- Process outcomes (improved service, reduced costs)
- Competitive advantage (market positioning, market share, access to knowledge)

Drivers and Facilitators Determine Partnership Type

If both parties realistically expect benefits from a partnership and if the corporate environments appear supportive, then a partnership is warranted. The appropriateness of any one type of partnership is a function of the combined strength of the drivers and facilitators. A combination of strong drivers and strong facilitators would suggest a Type III partnership, while low drivers and low facilitators suggest an armís length relationship.

While it might seem, from all of the press on the importance of integrated relationships and alliances, that managers should attempt to turn all of their corporate relationships into Type III partnerships, this is not the case. In partnering, more is not always better. The objective in establishing a partnership should not be to have a Type III partnership; rather it should be to have the *most appropriate* type of partnership given the specific drivers and facilitators. In fact, in situations with low drivers and/or facilitators, trying to achieve a Type III partnership is likely to be counterproductive. The necessary foundation is just not there. Having determined that a partnership of a specific type is warranted and should be pursued, the next step is to actually put the partnership into place. This is done through the components.

An assessment of drivers and facilitators is used to determine the potential for a partnership but the components describe the type of relationship that has actually been implemented.

Management Controls the Components

Components.   Components are the activities and processes that management establishes and controls throughout the life of the partnership. Components make the relationship operational and help managers create the benefits of partnering. Every partnership has the same basic components, but the way in which the components are implemented and managed varies. Components include: planning, joint operating controls, communications, risk/reward sharing, trust and commitment, contract style, scope, and financial investment. Table 10–6 summarizes the drives, facilitators, and components of partnership.

Outcomes Measure the Results

Outcomes and Feedback.   Whatever type of supplier partnership is implemented, the effectiveness of the relationship must be evaluated and possibly adjusted. The key to effective measurement and feedback is how well the drivers of partnership were developed at the outset. At this beginning point, the measurement and metrics of relating to each driver should have been made explicit. These explicit measures then become the standard in evaluation of the partnership outcomes. Feedback can loop back to any step in the model. Feedback can take the form of periodic updating of the status of the drivers, facilitators, and components.

Summary

In this chapter, we saw how better management of purchasing activities can lead to increased profitability. We described the activities such as supplier selection, evaluation, and management that must be performed by the purchasing function, and explored the implications of just-in-time and JIT II in purchasing. We examined various types of supplier relations and the role of purchasing in supply chain management, with an emphasis on various

Creative Solutions

Reengineering Purchasing at Public Utilities

Reengineering is not synonymous with "downsizing" or "right sizing." It involves completely reinventing processes, rather than simply reducing or streamlining efforts. In many organizations, the need for reengineering is particularly strong in purchasing as purchasing moves from clerical to strategic roles. It doesn't make sense to be more efficient performing current activities when the current tasks perhaps aren't even the right activities to perform.

This issue is particularly relevant in the utilities sector, which is being driven by deregulation and increased competition. A few of the utilities that have been leaders in reengineering are Santee Cooper (South Carolina), BHP Hawaii, Texas Utilities Fuel Company, Arizona Public Service Company, Illinois Power, and Florida Power and Light.

Increased competition in a deregulated environment has driven Santee Cooper. Wade C. Ferguson, a contract administrator for the utility, notes, "It would be foolish for any utility company not to be looking for reengineering opportunities." By reducing and eliminating paperwork wherever possible, Santee Cooper frees purchasers to "manage the supply chain, which is what we all think procurement should be all about."

It is crucial not to let reengineering efforts degenerate into cutbacks and downsizing. Thus, it is important to clearly identify the key purchasing processes and to ensure adequate support for these processes.

Santee Cooper used an external consultant to help chart processes, identify and eliminate nonvalue-added activities, and improve valued activities. The three areas of focus for purchasing were managing the complete purchase order cycle, requesting change orders, and administering a small dollar procurement charge card program.

Santee Cooper employees have formed teams to do process mapping of each activity. The consultant or other facilitator works with the team to identify and eliminate unnecessary processes or automate, redesign, or outsource as necessary. The use of an external consultant allows greater objectivity and the advantage of an outside perspective.

Reengineering of many logistics-related functions has been occurring in a variety of industries and service organizations, including public utilities such as Santee Cooper.

Source: Adapted from Cherish Calloway, "Reengineering in Action," *NAPM Insights,* Feb. 1995, pp. 37–40.

types of partnerships. Because the costs of purchased materials represent a significant cost of doing business, we devoted a considerable amount of attention to the management of purchasing cost. Effective logistics plays an important role in effective purchasing management. In addition, third-party logistics service providers are "suppliers" to the firm. Much can be learned from purchasing about better managing those relationships.

Suggested Readings

Dixon, Lance, and Anne Millen Porter. *JIT II: Revolution in Buying and Selling.* Newton, MA: Cahners, 1994.

Dobler, Donald W., and David N. Burt. *Purchasing and Supply Management,* 6th ed. New York: McGraw-Hill, 1996.

Festervand, Troy A., and David B. Meinert. "Purchasing Intelligence Systems in Small Manufacturing Firms: Present Status and Future Direction." *The International Journal of Logistics Management* 3, no. 1 (1992), pp. 37–45.

Gentry, Julie J. *Purchasing Involvement in Transportation Decision Making.* Tempe, AZ: Center for Advanced Purchasing Studies/National Association of Purchasing Management, 1991.

Harrington, Thomas C.; Douglas M. Lambert; and Martin Christopher. "A Methodology for Measuring Vendor Performance." *Journal of Business Logistics* 12, no. 1 (1991), pp. 83–104.

Heinritz, Stuart; Paul V. Farrell; Larry Giunipero; and Michael Kolchin, *Purchasing: Principles and Applications,* 8th ed. Englewood Cliffs, NJ: Prentice Hall, 1991.

Leenders, Michiel R., and Harold E. Fearon. *Purchasing and Supply Management,* 11th ed. Burr Ridge, IL: Richard D. Irwin, 1997.

Leenders, Michiel R., and Anna E. Flynn. *Value Driven Purchasing.* Burr Ridge, IL: Irwin Professional Publishers, 1995.

Newbourne, Paul T. "The Role of Partnerships in Strategic Account Management." *The International Journal of Logistics Management* 8, no. 1 (1997), pp. 67–74.

Raedels, Alan R., *Value Focused Supply Management.* Burr Ridge, IL: Irwin Professional Publishers, 1995.

Tersine, Richard J., and Albert B. Schwarzkopf. "Optimal Transition Ordering Strategies with Announced Price Increases." *The International Journal of Logistics Management* 2, no. 1 (1991), pp. 26–34.

Tully, Shawn. "Purchasing's New Muscle." *Fortune,* Feb. 20, 1995, pp. 75–83.

van Weele, Arjan J. *Purchasing Management.* New York: Chapman and Hall, 1994.

Questions and Problems

1. Explain why supplier selection and evaluation is frequently considered the most important activity in the purchasing function.

2. What are some of the reasons that purchasing is taking on a more strategic role in organizations?

3. Explain the concept of forward buying and its relationship to total cost trade-off analysis.

4. What are the major advantages of just-in-time purchasing? What are the possible difficulties in implementing a JIT system?
5. Why is cost measurement an important activity for purchasing management?
6. Why is it necessary for two firms to each have strong drivers if they are considering forming a partnership?
7. In the chapter it stated that the majority of a firm's relationships would be arm's length. Why do you think this would be the case?
8. Why are quality suppliers important to a firm? Why is this even more true in a JIT environment?

THE DISTRIBUTION CHALLENGE!
PROBLEM: THE CENTER OF ATTENTION

Let's examine the question of centralized distribution in global markets. This challenge comes from Paul Holman, global account manager of MSAS Cargo International.

His client was a U.S. manufacturer of consumer electronics—one with a big share of the burgeoning market for cellular phones. The item in question was the base station for a cell phone, a large unit that is mounted atop a building. The target market was India.

Parts were flown in from four locations: Chicago, Reading (England), Munich, and Helsinki. Destinations in India were Delhi, Bombay, and Madras. Among the pieces to be moved were large reels, antennas, and cables.

The entire 250-ton shipment had to be moved from multiple points of origin to India in about three weeks, requiring five 747 freighters. If that's not complicated enough, the customer wanted the various shipments consolidated at an airport outside India prior to their arrival under a master airway bill. The paperwork had to be letter-perfect.

"Indian Customs is very picky," notes Holman. "They'll impound the whole shipment if something's wrong."

Where would be the best location to combine the shipments onto a single aircraft bound for India? (Hint: There is no single right answer.)

What Is Your Solution?

Source: "Distribution: The Challenge," *Distribution* 95, no. 12 (Dec. 1996), p. 60.

Chapter Objectives

- To identify some of the controllable and uncontrollable factors that affect global logistics activities.
- To describe the major international distribution channel strategies—exporting, licensing, joint ventures, ownership, and importing.
- To highlight the elements involved in managing export shipments.
- To identify the organizational, financial, and managerial issues related to global logistics.

Introduction

One of the most important business developments in recent years has been the expansion of global industry. For an ever-growing number of firms, management is defining the marketplace globally. Table 11–1 identifies the world's largest industrial corporations. The companies may be headquartered in Asia, Europe, or North America, but their markets are international in scope.

For example, more than one-half of Procter & Gamble's $33 billion annual revenues in 1995 were generated from international operations. P&G products are sold in 140 countries. Over half of Hewlett-Packard's 1996 net revenues came from outside the

TABLE 11–1   The World's Largest Corporations, 1995

Rank	Company	Country	Industry	1995 Sales ($ millions)
1	Mitsubishi	Japan	Trading	184,365
2	Mitsui	Japan	Trading	181,519
3	Itochu	Japan	Trading	169,164
4	General Motors	U.S.	Motor vehicles	168,829
5	Sumitomo	Japan	Trading	167,531
6	Marubeni	Japan	Trading	161,057
7	Ford	U.S.	Motor vehicles	137,137
8	Toyota	Japan	Motor vehicles	111,052
9	Exxon	U.S.	Petroleum refining	110,009
10	Royal Dutch/Shell Group	U.K./Netherlands	Petroleum refining	109,834
11	Nissho Iwai	Japan	Trading	97,886
12	Wal-Mart Stores	U.S.	General merchandisers	93,627
13	Hitachi	Japan	Electronics	84,167
14	Nippon Life Insurance	Japan	Insurance	83,207
15	Nippon Telegraph	Japan	Telecommunications	81,937
16	AT&T	U.S.	Telecommunications	79,609
17	Daimler-Benz	Germany	Motor vehicles	72,256
18	IBM	U.S.	Computers	71,940
19	Matsushita Electric	Japan	Electronics	70,398
20	General Electric	U.S.	Electronics	70,028
21	Tomen	Japan	Trading	67,756
22	Mobil	U.S.	Petroleum refining	66,724
23	Nissan	Japan	Motor vehicles	62,569
24	Volkswagen	Germany	Motor vehicles	61,489
25	Siemens	Germany	Electronics	60,674

Source: "The Fortune Global 500, The Global 500 List," *Fortune,* 134, no.3, August 5, 1996, pp. F–1, F–15 through F–26, available on the Internet (http://pathfinder.com/fortune).

United States.[1] Other companies with more than 50 percent of their revenues coming from international sales include Exxon, IBM, Citicorp, Boeing, and Coca-Cola.

New markets are opening up and existing markets are expanding worldwide. The economies of the industrialized nations have matured; that is, their economic growth rates have slackened, so firms in those countries are seeking market opportunities abroad. A global financial network has developed that allows multinational enterprises to expand their operations. In addition, manufacturers have increased new material and component acquisitions from other countries (i.e., global sourcing). In sum, the world economy is becoming more interdependent.

Distribution Systems in Developing Countries

To support nondomestic markets a company must have a distribution system or network that satisfies the particular requirements of those markets. For example, the distribution systems in the developing countries of Africa, South America, or Asia are characterized by large numbers of channel intermediaries supplying an even larger number of small retailers. The systems in these nations are marked by inadequate transportation and storage facilities, a large labor force of mainly unskilled workers, and an absence of distribution support systems. In the developed countries (e.g., Japan, Canada, United States, and most of Western Europe), the distribution systems are highly sophisticated, have good transportation systems, high-technology warehousing, and a skilled labor force.

Distribution Systems in Developed Countries

In this chapter, we will describe some of the similarities and differences in the management of logistics in domestic and international environments (see Table 11–2). We will see how to assess the global logistics environment and how to develop meaningful logistics strategies in that environment.

International Distribution Channel Strategies

Many factors can influence a company's decision to enter international markets. They include:

Factors Influencing Companies to Enter Global Markets

- Market potential.
- Geographic diversification.
- Excess production capacity and the advantage of a low-cost position due to experience-curve economies and economies of scale.
- Products near the end of their life cycle in the domestic market could generate growth in the international market.
- Source of new products and ideas.
- Foreign competition in the domestic market.[2]

---

[1]See "The Fortune Global 500," *Fortune* 134, no. 3 (August 5, 1996), pp. F–1, F–15 through F–26, available on the Internet (http://pathfinder.com/fortune); and Greg Brown, "Education a Matter of Global Concern, Says P&G's Smale," *Mutual Interest,* Dec. 1990, p. 7; Hewlett-Packard's *1996 Annual Report,* available on the Internet (http://www.hp.com/go/computing).

[2]See Vern Terpstra and Ravi Sarathy, *International Marketing,* 7th ed. (Ft. Worth, TX: Dryden Press, 1997), p. 24.

TABLE 11–2   **Comparison of Domestic and International Logistics**

	Domestic	*International*
Cost	About 10.5% of U.S. GNP today	Estimated at 16% of world GNP today. Total global expenditure expected to reach $2 trillion by year 2000
Transport mode	Mainly truck and rail	Mainly ocean and air, with significant intermodal activity
Inventories	Lower levels, reflecting short-order, lead-time requirements and improved transport capabilities	Higher levels, reflecting longer lead times and greater demand and transit uncertainty
Agents	Modest usage, mostly in rail	Heavy reliance on forwarders, consolidators, and customs brokers
Financial risk	Minimal	High, owing to differences in currencies, inflation levels, and little recourse for default
Cargo risk	Minimal	High, owing to longer and more difficult transit, frequent cargo handling, and varying levels of infrastructure development
Government agencies	Primarily for hazardous materials, weight, safety laws, and some tariff requirements	Many agencies involved (e.g., customs, commerce, agriculture, transportation)
Administration	Minimal documentation involved (e.g., purchase order, bill of lading, invoice)	Significant paperwork. The U.S. Department of Commerce estimates that paperwork cost for an average shipment is $250.
Communication	Voice, paper-based systems adequate, with growing usage of electronic data interchange	Voice and paper costly and often ineffective. Movement toward electronic interchange but variations in standards hinder widespread usage.
Cultural differences	Relative homogeneity requires little product modification	Cultural differences require significant market and product adaptation.

Source: William W. Goldsborough and David L. Anderson, "The International Logistics Environment," in *The Logistics Handbook,* ed. James F. Robeson and William C. Copacino (New York: Free Press, 1994), p. 677.

Raw materials, components parts, or assemblies are additional reasons for a firm to enter international markets. For example, some raw materials, such as petroleum, bauxite, uranium, certain foodstuffs, are found only in certain geographic regions. A firm may locate a facility overseas or import an item for domestic use, and thereby become international in scope.

Companies that become involved in the international marketplace have many options available to them:

FIGURE 11–1

Major participants in an international logistics transaction

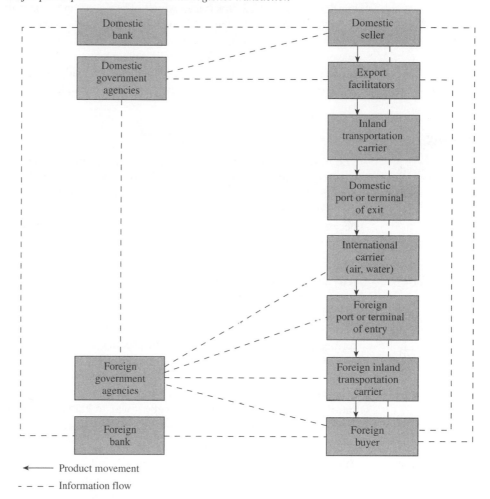

International Market Entry Strategies

- Exporting
- Licensing
- Joint ventures
- Ownership
- Importing
- Countertrade

Several options are available within each channel strategy. Figure 11–1 identifies some of the major participants in an international logistics transaction, including product and information flows.

Successful completion of the various logistics activities in the international distribution channel can contribute to the development of global markets in many ways, including door-to-door freight services which offer speed and reliability of delivery, and allow order lead times to be quoted accurately; reduced delivery costs through consolidation; expansion into new world markets which previously were out of reach; ability to offer a reasonable after-sales service or replacement policy to international markets; and, once captured, an overseas market may be held and expanded despite intense competition, because of high levels of customer service offered through distribution services.

Exporting

The most common form of distribution for firms entering international markets is exporting. **Exporting** refers to selling products in another country. Companies can hire independent marketing intermediaries (indirect exporting) or market their products themselves (direct exporting). Exporting requires the least amount of knowledge about foreign markets because domestic firms allow an international freight forwarder, distributor, trading company, or some other organization to carry out the logistics and marketing functions.

Advantages of Exporting

Advantages of Exporting.   Many advantages are associated with exporting, such as greater flexibility and less risk than other international distribution strategies. For example, no additional production facilities or logistics asset investment is needed in the foreign market because firms produce the product domestically and allow the exporting intermediary to handle distribution of the product abroad.

Without direct foreign investment, political uncertainties are less significant because firms are not concerned with the host country nationalizing their operations. Also, it is relatively easy to withdraw if the foreign market does not meet the profit or sales expectations of firms. Exporting is an excellent way to gain experience and test a market before firms expand their own production and marketing operations.

Disadvantages of Exporting

Disadvantages of Exporting.   Exporting is not without disadvantages. It is sometimes difficult for firms to compete with firms located in the foreign market. For example, **tariffs** (taxes assessed on goods entering a market), **import quotas** (limitations on the amount of goods that can enter a market), or unfavorable currency exchange rates may adversely affect the price or availability of imported goods.

In addition, domestic firms have little control over the pricing, promotion, or distribution of the product they export. Success in international markets depends to a large degree on the capability of **export intermediaries.**

Management must recognize that the export process is not as simple as it first appears. With or without the help of intermediaries, a firm must perform planning, package design, sales negotiation, financial monitoring, banking, insurance, and a variety of documentation. Logistics needs to be involved continually in the process from the planning stage. A firm involved in exporting often has to deal with a number of intermediaries who provide a variety of export services.

Licensing

Licensing Defined

Licensing involves agreements that allow a firm in one country (the licenser) "to use the manufacturing, processing, trademark, know-how, technical assistance, merchandising knowledge, or some other skill provided by the licenser located in another country."[3]

Advantages of Licensing

Advantages of Licensing.   Unlike exporting, licensing allows domestic firms more control over how they distribute their products, because distribution strategy is usually part of the preliminary discussions. The specific logistics functions are carried out by the licensees, using the established distribution systems of the foreign country.

Licensing is similar to exporting in that it does not require large capital outlays, thereby reducing risk and increasing flexibility. Licensing is a strategy frequently used by small- and medium-sized businesses. It can be an excellent approach if the foreign market has high tariff barriers or strict import quotas. The licenser is usually paid a royalty or a percentage of sales by the licensee.

Disadvantages of Licensing

Disadvantages of Licensing.   Although licensing does provide domestic firms with flexibility, it does not mean that licensing agreements can be terminated quickly. While the agreements with licensees may include termination or cancellation provisions, there is usually a time lag between the decision to terminate and the actual date of termination, typically longer than in an exporting situation.

A potentially serious drawback is that licensees can become future competitors. As licensees develop their own know-how and capabilities, they may end the licensing agreement and begin to compete with licensers.

Joint Ventures

Management may wish to exercise more control over the foreign firm than is available in a licensing agreement, but at the same time it may not want to establish a freestanding manufacturing plant or other facility in a foreign market. If so, the **joint venture** offers a compromise.

McDonald's Joint Venture in Japan

Box 11–1 presents McDonald's joint venture in Japan, showing how the U.S. firm retained some ownership control in Japan while using local management and adapting to local customs.

The risk is higher and the flexibility is lower for a company because an equity position is established in a foreign firm (in that firms's own country). The financial partnership, however, enables a company to provide substantial management input into the channel and distribution strategies of the foreign company. This increased management voice does place additional burdens on the domestic firm—namely, it requires a greater knowledge of the international markets the firm is trying to serve.

---

[3]David L. Anderson and Dennis Colard, "The International Logistics Environment," in *The Logistics Handbook,* ed. James F. Robeson and William C. Copacino (New York: Free Press, 1994), pp. 658–59.

Box 11–1

Adapting McDonald's to Japan's Market

"Sometime over the next 24 hours, while the rest of us merely work, eat, and sleep, McDonald's will open three more shiny new restaurants. One may be out in a fast-growing suburb of Salt Lake City, another in the pristine downtown of Singapore, and the third in the smoggy bustle of Warsaw where it will soon be flooded by smartly dressed young Poles hungry for a taste of America." McDonald's has more than 15,000 restaurants worldwide; the largest non-U.S. markets are Japan, Canada, Great Britain, Germany, Australia, and France.

Selling Big Macs in Japan

Next in sales to the U.S. operations is McDonald's Co. (Japan) Ltd. McDonald's Japan was established in May 1971 as a 50–50 joint venture by McDonald's Corporation and Fujita Shoten. McDonald's worldwide business policy—"local management over local stores"—was adopted in Japan. Beginning with only five restaurants, the partnership grew by 1982 to 347 outlets with annual sales of ¥70.3 billion. McDonald's Japan soon dominated the "food away from home" industry. By 1989, the company had 706 restaurants with annual sales of ¥162.7 billion. By 1994 the number had increased to 1,070, with the potential estimated at 6,100.

Catering to Japanese Preferences

The first McDonald's in Japan was a shop on the first floor of Ginza Mitsukoshi, a leading department store—a location very different from the popular drive-ins in the United States. McDonald's executives concluded that Japan at that point had not reached the automobile age so

evident in the United States. "According to our research, most customers just drop in a hamburger shop as they happen to pass by. To attract a large number, a good location is essential." The Ginza McDonald's attracted young people seeking the latest fashions; such consumers living outside Tokyo often came to the Ginza just to eat at McDonald's.

In 1977, the first drive-in McDonald's in Japan appeared; today, two-thirds of the new branches follow that design. Before the advent of McDonald's Co. Japan, there was no concept of "fast food." Few Japanese restaurants were as clean as McDonald's, nor was there a chain of restaurants serving staple meals at reasonable prices. "We are very proud of the fact that we developed a new restaurant concept that Japan never had before," said a company spokesperson. The new style is now widely accepted, no doubt because of the firm's dedication to qualities demanded by consumers—"Good Quality, Service, and Cleanliness."

Wherever one travels in the world, Big Macs have a consistent taste. (The product is so universal that *The Economist,* a British journal, uses a Big Mac index to compare general consumer prices around the world.) However, McDonald's amazing success in Japan with a thoroughly American product sold in an American style would probably have been impossible without the company's efforts to meet the unique demands of the Japanese market.

Sources: Andrew E. Serwer, "McDonald's Conquers the World," *Fortune,* Oct. 17, 1994, pp. 103–16; and William W. Goldsborough and David L. Anderson, "The International Logistics Environment," in *The Logistics Handbook,* ed. James F. Robeson and William C. Copacino (New York: Free Press, 1994), p. 655.

The joint venture may be the only method of market entry if management wishes to exercise significant control over the distribution of its products. This would be especially true if wholly owned subsidiaries are prohibited by the foreign government. Such restrictions occur more frequently in developing countries, which often attempt to promote internal industrial or retail development.[4]

Direct Ownership

Ownership Offers the Highest Reward but Comes with the Most Risk

Complete ownership of a foreign subsidiary offers the domestic firm the highest degree of control over its international marketing and logistics strategies. **Direct ownership** takes place through acquisition or expansion.

Advantages of Direct Ownership

Advantages of Direct Ownership.   Acquisition of a foreign facility can be advantageous because it minimizes the start-up costs: locating and building facilities, hiring employees, and establishing distribution channel relationships. Compared with other forms of market entry, ownership of a foreign subsidiary requires the most knowledge of a particular international market. The firm is totally responsible for marketing and distributing its product.

Direct ownership in the foreign market allows the company to compete more effectively on a price basis because it can eliminate the transportation costs incurred in shipments from domestic plants to foreign points of entry, customs duties, and other import taxes.

Disadvantages of Direct Ownership

Disadvantages of Direct Ownership.   Drawbacks include a loss of flexibility because the firm has a long-term commitment to the foreign market. Fixed facilities and equipment cannot be disposed of quickly if sales or profits decline, levels of competition increase, or other adversities occur.

The possibility of government nationalization of foreign-owned businesses is another drawback of direct ownership, especially in politically unstable countries. Additionally, exchange rate fluctuations change the relative value of foreign investments because they are valued in local (i.e., foreign) currency instead of currency of the owner's home country.

Firms Typically Use More Than One Market-Entry Strategy

Market-Entry Strategies.   In general, firms follow more than one market-entry strategy. Markets, product lines, economic conditions, and political environments change over time, so the optimal market-entry strategy may change. Furthermore, a good market-entry strategy in one country may not be good in another.

A firm considering exporting, licensing, joint venture, or ownership should establish a formal procedure for evaluating each alternative. Each market-entry strategy can be evaluated on a set of management-determined criteria. Each functional area of the firm (e.g., accounting, manufacturing, marketing, logistics) must be involved in establishing

---

[4]For a discussion of joint ventures in developing countries, see Dianne J. Cyr, "Implications for Learning: Human Resources Management in East-West Joint Ventures," *Organization Studies* 17, no. 2 (Spring 1996), pp. 207–26; Roger W. Mills and Gordon Chen, "Evaluating International Joint Ventures Using Strategic Value Analysis," *Long Range Planning* 29, no. 4 (1996), pp. 552–61; Anthony J. F. O'Reilly, "Establishing Successful Joint Ventures in Developing Nations: A CEO's Perspective," *Columbia Journal of World Business* 23, no. 1 (Spring 1988), pp. 65–71; and Gregory E. Osland and S. Tamer Cavusgil, "Performance Issues in US-China Joint Ventures," *California Management Review* 38, no. 2 (Winter 1996), pp. 106–30.

the criteria and their evaluation. A firm should decide on a method of international involvement only after it has made a complete analysis of each market-entry strategy.

Importing

Many firms will be involved in activities that bring raw materials, parts, components, supplies, or finished goods from sources outside the country. This may involve importing, countertrade, and duty drawbacks.

Importing involves the purchase and shipment of goods from an overseas source. Imported items can be used immediately in the production process or sold directly to customers. They can be transported to other ports of entry, stored in **bonded warehouses** (where goods are stored until import duties are paid), or placed in a **free trade zone** (where goods are exempted from customs duties until they are removed for use or sale).

Many firms utilize customshouse brokers for importing products into the United States. These brokers facilitate the movement of imported products and ensure the accuracy and completeness of import documentation. Customshouse brokers are licensed by the U.S. Customs Service of the Treasury Department.

> Many . . . brokers help clients choose modes of transportation and appropriate carriers . . . They also provide assistance to importers in assigning shipments the best routes. They handle estimates for landed costs, payments of goods through draft, letters of credit insurance, and re-delivery of cargo if there is more than one port of destination."[5]

Countertrade and Duty Drawbacks[6]

Countertrade Defined

The term **countertrade** applies to the requirement that a firm import something from a country in which it has sold something else.[7] In essence, countertrade is any transaction in which part of the payment is made in goods instead of money. The need for countertrade is driven by the balance of payments problems of a country and by weak demand for the country's products. A likely candidate for countertrade is a country with a shortage of foreign exchange or a shortage of credit to finance trade flows. Such a country will try to expand its exports or to develop markets for its new products.

Five Forms of Countertrade

Five Forms of Countertrade.   Five basic forms of countertrade exist: barter, buyback, compensation, counterpurchase, and switch.[8]

---

[5]R. Neil Southern, *Transportation and Logistics Basics* (Memphis, TN: Continental Traffic Service, 1997), p. 295.

[6]This section is taken from Lisa M. Ellram and Laura Birou, *Purchasing for Bottom Line Impact* (Burr Ridge, IL: Irwin Professional Publishing, 1995), p. 61.

[7]See Kwabena Anyane-Ntow and Santhi C. Harvey, "A Countertrade Primer: A Look at a Growing Trend That Demands Management Accountants' Attention," *Management Accounting* 76, no. 10 (Apr. 1995), pp. 47–50; and John N. Pearson and Laura B. Forker, "International Countertrade: Has Purchasing's Role Really Changed?" *International Journal of Purchasing and Materials Management* 31, no. 4 (Fall 1995), pp. 38–44.

[8]Kenton W. Elderkin and Warren E. Norquist, *Creative Countertrade* (Cambridge, MA: Ballinger, 1987), p. 152.

1. **Barter,** the simplest form of countertrade, occurs when goods of equal value are exchanged and no money is involved.

2. In **buyback** arrangements, the selling firm provides equipment or an entire plant, and agrees to buy back a certain part of the production. Many developing countries insist on buyback arrangements because they ensure access to Western technology and stable markets.

3. A **compensation** arrangement takes place when barter is specified as a percentage of the value of goods being traded to the value of the product being sold.

4. **Counterpurchase** involves transactions with more cash, smaller volumes of goods flowing to the multinational corporation over a shorter period of time, and goods unrelated to the original deal.

5. A **switch** transaction uses at least one third party outside the host country to facilitate the trade. The countertraded goods or the multinational enterprise's goods are sent through a third country for purchase in hard currency or for distribution.

While countertrade agreements may be complex, they do offer an opportunity to develop lower-cost sources of supply in the world marketplace. In some cases, they may provide the only means of market entry for the firm.

Duty Drawbacks

Duty Drawbacks.   Firms that import goods used in manufacturing or export products that contain imported materials can take advantage of drawbacks. A drawback, or **duty drawback,** is a refund of customs duties paid on imported items. As illustrated in Figure 11–2, duty drawbacks involve many steps and can be time consuming. However, duty drawbacks can provide significant cost savings for firms that take advantage of them.

Figure 11–2

How duty drawbacks work

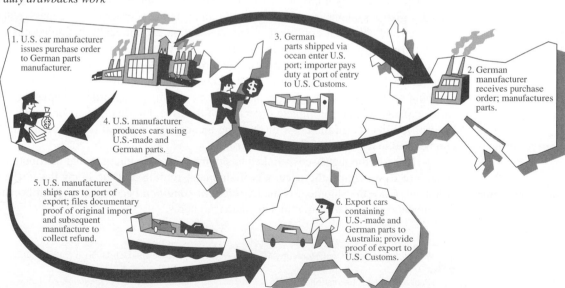

1. U.S. car manufacturer issues purchase order to German parts manufacturer.

2. German manufacturer receives purchase order; manufactures parts.

3. German parts shipped via ocean enter U.S. port; importer pays duty at port of entry to U.S. Customs.

4. U.S. manufacturer produces cars using U.S.-made and German parts.

5. U.S. manufacturer ships cars to port of export; files documentary proof of original import and subsequent manufacture to collect refund.

6. Export cars containing U.S.-made and German parts to Australia; provide proof of export to U.S. Customs.

Source: Adapted from Lisa H. Harrington, "How to Take Advantage of Duty Drawback," *Traffic Management* 28, no. 6 (June 1989), p. 121A.

Managing Global Logistics

Management of a global distribution system is much more complex than that of a purely domestic network. Managers must properly analyze the international environment, plan for it, and develop the correct control procedures to monitor the success or failure of the foreign distribution system. Figure 11–3 identifies some of the questions the international logistics manager must ask—and answer—about the firm's foreign logistics programs.

Key Issues in Global Logistics Decision Making

The questions can be classified into five categories: (1) environmental analysis, (2) planning, (3) structure, (4) plan implementation, and (5) control of the logistics program.[9]

The overall objective of the process diagrammed in Figure 11–3 is to develop the optimal logistics system for each international target market. This is achieved by examining the various characteristics of the foreign market and developing a set of alternatives or strategies that will fulfill the company's objectives. With a set of objectives or strategies, management can define the proper organizational and channel structures. Once these are established, management implements the distribution system. The final step is to measure and evaluate the performance of the system and to provide feedback to the strategic planning process for purposes of adjustment or modification of the system.

Cost-Service Trade-Off Analysis

Cost-Service Trade-Off Analysis

An integral part of the global logistics management process is cost-service trade-off analysis. Whether operations are domestic or international, the ability to properly identify, evaluate, and implement the optimal cost-service mix is always important to the firm and its customers. The only difference between domestic and international operations is in the emphasis placed on each cost and service element.

Some particularly important cost and service considerations concern the use of integrated logistics systems to effectively and rapidly manage order completeness, shipping accuracy, and shipment condition to any destination economically.[10] Global customers are no longer willing to settle for longer and less reliable order cycle times.

Order Completeness

Order completeness is much more important in international logistics, because the costs of back orders and expedited shipments are substantially higher. Processing and shipping costs must be weighed against the cost of improving order completeness. It is more expensive to ship complete orders all of the time, but this higher service level may be justified in view of the costs of shipping incomplete or partial orders. A similar logic can be used in the case of *shipping accuracy.*

Shipping Accuracy

Shipment Condition

Because of the higher costs linked to shipping errors in international distribution, it is important to maximize the accuracy of shipment routing and the items that make up a shipment. Once the shipment is made, *shipment condition* becomes important because of the time and cost entailed in replacing damaged items.

---

[9]Warren J. Keegan, *Global Marketing Management,* 5th ed. (Englewood Cliffs, NJ: Prentice Hall, 1995), p. 37.

[10]Paul S. Bender, "International Logistics," in *The Distribution Management Handbook,* ed. James A. Tompkins and Dale Harmelink (New York: McGraw-Hill, 1994), p. 87.

FIGURE 11–3

The global logistics management process

Key Questions for Analysis, Planning, and Control

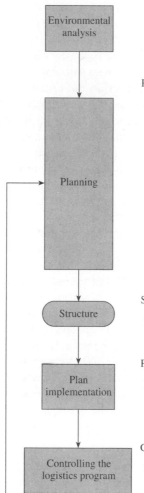

Environmental analysis

1. What are the unique characteristics of each national market? What characteristics does each market have in common with other national markets?

2. Should the firm cluster national markets for logistics operating and/or planning purposes?

Planning

3. Who should make logistics decisions?

4. What are our major assumptions about target markets? Are they valid?

5. What are the customer service needs of the target markets?

6. What are the characteristics of the logistics systems available to our firm in each target market?

7. What are our firm's major strengths and weaknesses relative to existing and potential competition in each target market?

8. What are our objectives, given the logistics alternatives open to us and our assessment of opportunity, risk, and company capability?

9. What is the balance of payments and currency situation in target markets? What will be their impact(s) on our firm's physical distribution system?

Structure

10. How do we structure our logistics organization to optimally achieve our objectives, given our skills and resources? What is the responsibility of each organizational level?

Plan implementation

11. Given our objectives, structure, and our assessment of the market environment, how do we develop effective operational logistics plans? Specifically, what transportation, inventory, packaging, warehousing, and customer service strategies do we have for each target market?

Controlling the logistics program

12. How do we measure and monitor plan performance? What steps should be taken to bring actual and desired results together?

Source: Adapted from Warren J. Keegan, *Global Marketing Management,* 5th ed., p. 37. Copyright 1995. Reprinted by permission of Prentice Hall, Inc., Englewood Cliffs, NJ.

Guidelines in Developing a Global Logistics Strategy

In developing a global logistics strategy, some general guidelines apply. The following list can be useful to firms in almost any international market:

**Guidelines for
Developing a Global
Logistics Strategy**

1. *Logistics planning should be integrated into the company's strategic planning process.* For example, DuPont, the $40 billion chemical giant, implemented supply chain management programs throughout its 30 major businesses operating in about 100 countries. The purpose of the programs is to focus more on markets and customers, including just-in-time delivery of chemicals and inputs to their product processes. To achieve these objectives, logistics personnel have been added to each business unit to assist in planning activities ranging from site location to customer delivery programs.

2. *Logistics departments need to be guided by a clear vision and must measure output regularly.* Baxter Healthcare Corporation, the $8 billion multinational company, is accomplishing this through its unique arrangement with Trammel Crow, the real estate management firm. In the late 1980s, Baxter set out to rationalize its logistics operations. Its goal was to increase the total space available to handle materials and products from 6.5 million square feet to 9 million square feet. Moreover, Baxter wanted to cut the number of cities in which it had a facility from 50 to 40, and to reduce the total number of facilities from 91 to 49. Baxter entered into a seven-year contract with Trammel Crow with the goal of saving $15 million. All relevant logistics cost and service parameters are measured, according to Jerry Arthur, Baxter's vice president of distribution staff operations. The system tracks savings per labor-hour, land cost savings, rental savings, revenue, and tax incentives. A formal steering committee comprised of members from both organizations meets quarterly to monitor performance and suggest improvements.

3. *Import-export management should try to ensure integrated management of all elements of the logistics supply chain from origin to destination.* This is especially important as major structural and regulatory changes are under way across the globe. Deregulation in transport in the United States and increasingly in other areas such as Europe, Mexico, and Japan permits negotiation of creative "door-to-door" service and price packages with carriers. This allows shippers to design and manage their supply chains, so that delivery can be tailored to customer specifications at a reasonable cost.

4. *Opportunities to integrate domestic and international operations should be pursued to leverage total company volumes with globally oriented carriers.* This usually requires a change in organizational thinking, but major opportunities exist for companies that can move in this direction. A good starting point is to make a list comparing domestic and international logistics activity.[11]

Managers who approach the global logistics process using the above guidelines, good judgment, and a determination to succeed are likely to do well. While the international marketplace may be undergoing rapid change, it is certainly manageable and offers exciting opportunities and challenges to firms seeking global markets.

Organizing for Global Logistics

Proper organization and administration of the logistics function is just as important internationally as it is domestically.

---

[11]William W. Goldsborough and David L. Anderson, "Import/Export Management," in *The Logistics Handbook,* ed. James F. Robeson and William C. Copacino (New York: Free Press, 1994), pp. 675–76.

To be competitive, companies must understand all facets of global sourcing and marketing . . . today's international logistics manager must be a well-trained, full-time professional, experienced in managing complex international logistics decisions.[12]

When a company enters the international marketplace, initially through exporting or licensing, the balance of power in the firm will continue to be held by domestic operations. Obviously, that is only proper in the early stages of development, but as foreign operations grow in sales and profits, and thus in importance, the international component of the business must be allowed to give more input into corporate decision making.

Should You Centralize or Decentralize Logistics Globally?

Many companies operating in the global marketplace centralize a large number of logistics activities while decentralizing others. For example, management of customer service tends to work best when it is under local control in the foreign market. On the other hand, material flows into the organization are often centralized, because technology can quickly overcome spatial distances. Most information systems tend to be centralized, which enables decision making across international boundaries.[13] Also, purchasing economies may occur with centralization.

The Global box discusses how Hoffman-La Roche organized its worldwide distribution system.

Financial Aspects of Global Logistics

A firm participating in global logistics faces a financial environment quite different from that of a strictly domestic firm. It has concerns about currency exchange rates, costs of capital, the effects of inflation on logistics decisions and operations, tax structures, and other financial aspects of performing logistics activities in foreign markets.[14]

Working Capital Considerations

Working Capital.   Global logistics activities require financing for working capital, inventory, credit, investment in buildings and equipment, and accommodation of merchandise adjustments that may be necessary. **Working capital** considerations are extremely important to the international firm owing to time lags caused by distance, border crossing delays, and government regulations. Typically, foreign operations require larger amounts of working capital than domestic operations.

Inventories

Inventories.   **Inventories** are an important aspect of global logistics: In general, higher levels of inventory are needed to service foreign markets because of longer transit times, greater variability in transit times, port delays, customs delays, and other factors.[15]

In addition, inventories can have a substantial impact on the international firm because of the rapid inflation that exists in some countries. It is important to use the proper

---

[12]Ibid., p. 674.

[13]Alan Braithwaite, "Integrating the Global Pipeline: Logistics Systems Architectures," unpublished paper, Logistics Consulting Partners, Colchester, U.K.; see also Jonathan Reynolds, "Retailing in Computer-Mediated Environments: Electronic Commerce across Europe," *International Journal of Retail and Distribution Management* 25, no. 1 (1997), pp. 29–37.

[14]Bender, "International Logistics," pp. 8.5–8.6.

[15]Goldsborough and Anderson, "Import/Export Management," p. 677.

Global

"Localized" Global Distribution

Hoffman-La Roche, the multinational pharmaceutical firm based in Switzerland, has steered a middle course between centralized and decentralized control of logistics for its vitamins and chemicals unit.

In 1996, the company gave responsibility for distribution and inventories of finished products to area marketing managers. At the same time, the company retained carrier selection, rate negotiation, raw materials supply, and intracompany shipments at its Basel headquarters. Hoffman-La Roche says the "localized" global distribution system is a way to stay close to the customer without surrendering the economies of central control.

The company has separate business units (or product divisions) and operates globally, with production facilities in both Europe and in the United States. The vitamins and fine-chemicals business unit has three regional areas: Europe, including Africa and the Middle East; North and South America; and the Far East, including Australia.

Before area managers were given responsibility for distribution and inventory, they already were responsible for marketing.

The headquarters office controls worldwide logistics and transportation of finished goods from production sites to a global distribution center at Venlo, the Netherlands; from the global center to area distribution centers within each of the three world areas; and from each area center to the area's customers.

In Europe, distribution from the area distribution center to customers is usually by truck and takes only one day at the vitamins and fine-chemicals division. In Asia, however, where ocean transportation is used, distribution can take up to two weeks.

Source: Philip Damas, "'Localized' Global Distribution," *American Shipper* 39, no. 2 (Feb. 1997), pp. 36, 38.

---

inventory accounting procedure because of the impact of inflation on company profits. The LIFO (last in-first out) method is probably the most appropriate strategy because the cost of sales is valued closer to the current cost of replacement.[16] The FIFO (first in-first out) method gives a larger profit figure than LIFO because old costs are matched with current revenues, although this will increase the tax liability.

In anticipation of higher costs caused by inflation or other factors, management of an international firm must weigh the cost trade-offs involved in the buildup of inventories. The trade-off is between the accumulation of excess inventory and inventory carrying costs on the one hand, and the reduction of carrying costs by holding less inventory on the other, which would require paying higher acquisition costs at a later date.

When management considers direct investment in facilities and logistics networks in the foreign market, the capital budgeting aspects of financial planning become important. As is the case in domestic operations, customers in the international sector do not tender payment to the shipper until the product is delivered. As you have read, many factors

---

[16]In periods of inflation, products in inventory will be carried at a much lower value than their current replacement cost.

FIGURE 11–4

How a letter of credit works

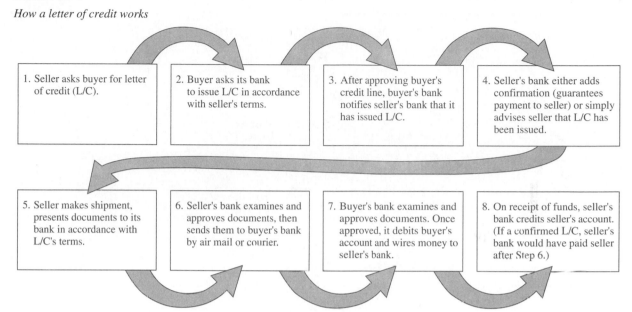

1. Seller asks buyer for letter of credit (L/C).

2. Buyer asks its bank to issue L/C in accordance with seller's terms.

3. After approving buyer's credit line, buyer's bank notifies seller's bank that it has issued L/C.

4. Seller's bank either adds confirmation (guarantees payment to seller) or simply advises seller that L/C has been issued.

5. Seller makes shipment, presents documents to its bank in accordance with L/C's terms.

6. Seller's bank examines and approves documents, then sends them to buyer's bank by air mail or courier.

7. Buyer's bank examines and approves documents. Once approved, it debits buyer's account and wires money to seller's bank.

8. On receipt of funds, seller's bank credits seller's account. (If a confirmed L/C, seller's bank would have paid seller after Step 6.)

Source: Adapted from James Aaron Cooke, "What You Should Know about Letters of Credit," *Traffic Management* 29, no. 9 (Sept. 1990), pp. 44–45.

might cause the foreign shipment to have a longer delivery time than a comparable domestic shipment. The exporter must be concerned with exchange rate fluctuations that may occur between the time the product is shipped, delivered to the consignee, and paid for by the customer.

Letters of Credit

Letters of Credit.   To ensure that international customers pay for products shipped to them, letters of credit are often issued. A **letter of credit** is a document issued by a bank on behalf of a buyer which authorizes payment for merchandise received. Payments are made to the seller by the bank instead of the buyer. Figure 11–4 shows how a letter of credit works.

> Although it might appear to be more the concern of the corporate financial department, it is crucial that logistics managers involved in international trade understand how letters of credit work. If they misinterpret information or fail to diligently follow the shipping instructions contained in the document, it could jeopardize the company's chances of receiving payment for the goods shipped.[17]

---

[17]James Aaron Cooke, "What You Should Know about Letters of Credit," *Traffic Management* 29, no. 9 (Sept. 1990), pp. 44–45. See also Chris Gillis, "Automated Letters of Credit," *American Shipper* 38, no. 2 (Feb. 1996), p. 52; Gordon Platt, "Benchmark Study Finds Letters of Credit Amassed More Than $1 Billion Last Year," *Journal of Commerce and Commercial* 410, no. 28840 (Oct. 30, 1996), p. 9C; and Ira Weissman, "Letters of Credit—Doing Business in a Global Market," *CPA Journal* 66, no. 1 (Jan. 1996), pp. 46–49.

FIGURE 11–5

The global logistics environment

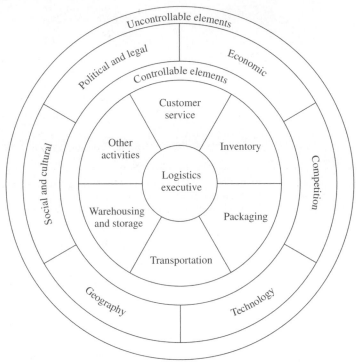

The Global Marketplace

All forms of entry into the international marketplace require an awareness of the variables that can affect a firm's distribution system. Some of these factors can be controlled by logistics executives. Others, unhappily, are not subject to control, but must still be dealt with in any international marketing undertaking. Figure 11–5 shows the environment in which the logistics executive operates.

Uncontrollable Elements.   Anything that affects the logistics strategy of the international firm, yet is not under the direct control and authority of the logistics manager, is an uncontrollable element. The major uncontrollable elements include:

- Political and legal systems of the foreign markets.
- Economic conditions.
- Degree of competition in each market.
- Level of distribution technology available or accessible.

- Geographic structure of the foreign market.
- Social and cultural norms of the various target markets.[18]

Examples of the Uncontrollable Environment

An uncontrollable environment is characterized by uncertainty and frequently by volatility. The logistics executive must make decisions within such an environment; for example, cost trade-offs, customer service levels, and pricing. To illustrate, shipping component parts instead of finished goods to a foreign market can result in payment of lower duties, although transportation costs may be higher.

Other examples include paying higher prices for a freight forwarder with lower damage rates, which may allow the firm to reduce packaging costs, or using a bonded warehouse instead of a private warehouse may result in higher customs supervision costs but lower overhead costs for storage. Such trade-offs are only a few of the many that the logistics executive must evaluate.

Firms are experiencing increasing competitive pressures from many sources. In the United States, manufacturers in a number of industries have found themselves at a competitive disadvantage compared with their Asian and European counterparts.

U.S. manufacturers have attempted to respond in several ways—manufacturing, research and development, and marketing, including logistics. Examples of innovative logistics strategies include:

Innovative Global Logistics Strategies

- *Rapid product introduction.* Bringing new products to market in record time across numerous regions.
- *Market focus.* Customizing design, packaging, and service offerings to meet varying consumer requirements.
- *Quick-response delivery.* Distributing sufficient product quantities to meet consumer demand as it occurs.
- *Expanded services.* Linking innovative, value-added services (e.g., product kitting or 24-hour customer hotlines) to product offerings.
- *Innovative channels.* Using minimal-echelon, store-direct (or consumer-direct) delivery systems to reach customers rapidly at lower cost.[19]

It is beyond the scope of this chapter to examine in detail each of the various uncontrollable factors in the global marketplace. A number of international marketing textbooks address these elements.[20] It is sufficient to say that the uncontrollable elements

---

[18]For a discussion of several uncontrollable elements, see James C. Cooper, "Logistics Strategies for Global Business," *International Journal of Physical Distribution and Logistics Management* 23, no. 4 (1993), pp. 12–23.

[19]Anderson and Colard, "International Logistics Environment," p. 647.

[20]See Gerald Albaum, Jesper Strandskov, Edwin Duerr, and Laurence Dowd, *International Marketing and Export Management* (Reading, MA: Addison-Wesley, 1994); Edward W. Cundiff and Mary Tharp Hilger, *Marketing in the International Environment,* 2nd ed. (Englewood Cliffs, NJ: Prentice Hall, 1988); Philip R. Cateora, *International Marketing,* 7th ed. (Burr Ridge, IL: Richard D. Irwin, 1990); and Michael R. Czinkota, Ilkka A. Ronkainen, and John J. Tarrant, *The Global Marketing Imperative* (Lincolnwood, IL: NTC Business Books, 1995).

affect the actions of the logistics executive and must be considered in the planning, implementation, and control of the firm's global distribution network.

Controllable Elements.   When a firm becomes involved in international operations, the scope of the logistics executive's responsibilities often expands to include international distribution activities. Although the logistics executive may have full international responsibility, others within the organization probably have some involvement. A 1995 survey by the Council of Logistics Management found that approximately 84 percent of all logistics executives polled had direct or advisory responsibility for their company's global logistics operations.[21]

Management of a firm involved in international distribution must try to administer the logistics components to minimize cost and provide an acceptable level of service to its customers. However, a firm's cost-service mix will vary in international markets.

International Distribution Is More Expensive

For example, logistics costs as a percentage of sales are much higher in Japan and the United States than in Europe.[22] When all factors are considered, international distribution is generally more expensive than domestic distribution. Increased shipping distances, documentation costs, larger levels of inventory, longer order cycle times, and other factors combine to increase the expense of international distribution. Today the cost of international logistics is estimated at 16 percent of world GNP.[23]

Customer Service Consistency Is Harder to Achieve Globally

Customer Service Strategies.   The same consistency of service that a firm provides its domestic customers is not as easily achieved internationally. Because international transportation movements tend to be longer and often require several different types of carriers, multiple transfers and handlings, and the crossing of many international boundaries, time in transit may vary significantly from one shipment to the next. As a result, firms tend to require larger amounts of inventory to meet safety and cycle stock requirements.

Customer service levels may be higher in international markets, such as Japan, where the order cycle time is generally shorter than in the United States. The geographical differences between the two countries, the physical facilities of many wholesalers and retailers, and financial considerations permit the majority of all consumer goods orders in Japan to be delivered in 24 hours or less. For that reason, many international firms operate owned facilities in foreign markets in order to compete effectively on a customer service basis.

Customer Service Costs Vary Widely

The cost of providing a specified level of customer service often varies between countries. A company must examine the service requirements of customers in each foreign market and develop a logistics package that best serves each area. Competition, specific customer needs, and other factors may cause a firm to incur higher logistics costs, which will result in lower profits. Therefore, top management must make a complete analysis of the situation.

---

[21]Bernard J. La Londe and James M. Masters, "The 1996 Ohio State University Survey of Career Patterns in Logistics," *Proceedings of the Annual Conference of the Council of Logistics Management* (Oak Brook, IL: Council of Logistics Management, Oct. 20–23, 1996), p. 126.

[22]See Bender, "International Logistics," pp. 8.15–8.19.

[23]Goldsborough and Anderson, "Import/Export Management," p. 677.

Hewlett-Packard Gains Competitive Advantage Internationally

Hewlett-Packard (HP) was able to gain a competitive advantage internationally by improving its level of customer service. HP implemented programs to tightly link R&D and manufacturing and has been successful in reducing the "concept-to-delivery" time. HP's logistics organizations have played a key role in this program.[24] Improving the order fulfillment process continues to be a key strategic initiative. Objectives have been set to dramatically reduce the cost of taking and processing customer orders, and transporting products to customers. Thus, logistics will continue to play a key role in HP's global strategy.[25]

Inventory Strategies.   Inventory control is particularly important to an international company and requires an awareness of the many differences between international and domestic inventory management systems.

Global Inventories

> International systems usually have more inventory points at more levels between suppliers and customers; thus multilevel inventory systems are more complex and more common than in domestic systems.
>
> In-transit inventories can be substantially higher than for a domestic operation with similar sales volume. This results from the larger number of locations and levels involved, and longer transportation times.[26]

Depending on the length of transit and delays that can occur in international product movements, a firm may have to supply its distributors or other foreign intermediaries with higher than normal levels of inventory. A typical domestic firm will have 25 to 30 percent of its assets in inventory, but firms engaged in international marketing can often have 50 percent or more of their assets in inventory. For high-value products, the inventory carrying costs as well as the amount of accounts receivable outstanding can be extremely high.

In markets where the firm's products are sold at retail, consumer shopping patterns can be extremely important in determining inventory strategies. Companies in the United States can usually exercise greater control over their inventories because they can influence the amount of product ordered by their customers through discounts. However, this may not be a viable strategy in some international markets.

Since conditions may vary in foreign markets, it is important for the firm to develop inventory policies and control procedures that are appropriate for each market area.

International Shipments Require Greater Protection

Packaging and Containerization.   International shipments require greater protection than domestic shipments, especially when they are not containerized. Other issues to consider include the handling of products, climate, potential for pilferage, communication and language differences, freight rates, customs duties, and the customer's requirements. The greater number of handlings of international goods increases the possibility of

---

[24]Anderson and Colard, "International Logistics Environment," pp. 669–70.

[25]Ibid., p. 670.

[26]Paul S. Bender, "The International Dimension of Physical Distribution Management," in *The Distribution Handbook,* ed. James F. Robeson and Robert G. House (New York: Free Press, 1985), pp. 785–86.

Containers being loaded or off-loaded from a ship in an Italian port.

damage.[27] Generally, the amount of damage and loss in international traffic movements is higher than in domestic movements. Therefore, global shippers must be much more concerned with the protective aspect of the package than their domestic counterparts.

The bottom line in all international packaging decisions is that the item should arrive at its destination undamaged. Logistics executives can help to ensure that goods arrive safely at their international destinations through the proper planning, implementation, and control of packaging decisions.[28]

Containers Are Widely Used Internationally

To facilitate product handling and protect the product during movement and storage, many firms have turned to the use of containers. Containers are widely used in international logistics, especially when water movements are part of the transport network.[29] Many companies have adopted standard container sizes (8 ft. × 8 ft. × 10 ft., 20 ft., 30 ft., or 40 ft.) that allow for intermodal movements.

---

[27]Diana Twede, "Packaging," in *The Logistics Handbook,* ed. James F. Robeson and William C. Copacino (New York: Free Press, 1994), pp. 457–58.

[28]For discussion of various packaging issues and some examples, see Tom Andel, "Out-of-the-Box Thinking: Packaging Design Is More Than Just the Formation of Fiberboard, Plastic, and Foam," *Transportation and Distribution* 37, no. 10 (Oct. 1996), pp. 104–7; L. W. Lye and H. Y. Yeong, "An Integrated Framework for Protective Packaging Design and Manufacture," *International Journal of Production Research* 32, no. 8 (1993), pp. 1837–41; and Gerard Prendergast and Leyland Pitt, "Packaging, Marketing, Logistics and the Environment: Are There Trade-Offs?" *International Journal of Physical Distribution and Logistics Management* 26, no. 6 (1996), pp. 60–72.

[29]For a discussion of how water ports handle ocean containers, see Toby B. Gilley, "Follow That Container!" *Traffic Management* 34, no. 9 (Sept. 1995), pp. 29–35.

Advantages of Containers.   The use of standardized materials handling equipment has become commonplace. The advantages of containers are numerous:

Advantages of Containers

- Costs due to loss or damage are reduced because of the protective nature of the container.
- Labor costs in freight handling are reduced because of the increased use of automated materials handling equipment.
- Containers are more easily stored and transported than other types of shipments, which results in lower warehousing and transportation costs.
- Containers are available in a variety of sizes, many of which are standardized for intermodal use.
- Containers are able to serve as temporary storage facilities at ports and terminals with limited warehousing space.

Disadvantages of Containers

Disadvantages of Containers.   On the other hand, containerization is not without disadvantages. The major problem is that ports or terminals with container facilities may not be available in certain parts of the world. Even when these facilities exist, they may be so overburdened with inbound and outbound cargo that long delays occur.

Another major problem with containerization is that large capital expenditures are required to initiate a container-based transportation network. Significant capital outlays for port and terminal facilities, materials handling equipment, specialized transport equipment, and the containers themselves are necessary before a firm can utilize containerization.

Labeling is related to the packaging component of global logistics. From a cost standpoint, labeling is of minor importance in international logistics. However, accurate labeling is essential to the timely and efficient movement of products across international borders. Important issues related to labeling include content, language, color, and location on the package.

Other Activities.   Each of the activities or functions of logistics must be performed in the international market. The difference between the domestic and foreign market is not *whether* the logistics activity should be performed, but *how* each activity should be carried out.

Sourcing of Materials

One activity where differences occur is in the sourcing of materials. Traditionally, firms obtained raw materials, parts, supplies, and components from domestic sources. In recent years there has been an accelerating trend toward international sourcing. For example, Canon uses some local sources of supply for products built outside of Japan; in its California facility, it uses 30 percent local sources, in Virginia less than 20 percent, and in Germany 40 percent.[30]

The concepts of **integrated logistics management,** the **systems approach,** and **cost trade-off analysis** are very important in international logistics. However, the relative importance of each logistics component may vary from market to market, along with the costs incurred in carrying out each activity. This results in different cost-service equations for each international market.

---

[30]Anderson and Colard, "International Logistics Environment," p. 666.

The best advice for the executive whose company is entering into international logistics for the first time is to obtain as much information as possible about business conditions and operating procedures in each market from as many data sources as possible.[31]

Each of the logistics activities of a company must be performed, although the task may be completed by one or more members of the international channel of distribution. The specific entities involved depend on the channel strategy selected.

Management of the Export Shipment

Many facilitator organizations are involved in the exporting activity. The types of organizations utilized most extensively are:

Export Companies

- Export distributor
- Customshouse broker
- International freight forwarder
- Trading company
- Non-vessel-operating common carrier (NVOCC)

Other facilitators are used, but to a much lesser degree. These include export brokers, export merchants, foreign purchasing agents, and others.[32]

Export Facilitators

A firm involved in exporting for the first time would likely use an export distributor, customshouse broker, international freight forwarder, or trading company.

Export Distributor. A company involved in international markets often employs the services of an export distributor (export management company). An **export distributor** (1) is located in the foreign market, (2) buys on its own account, (3) is responsible for the sale of the product, and (4) has a continuing contractual relationship with the domestic firm. The distributor frequently is granted exclusive rights to a specific territory. It may refrain from handling the products of competing manufacturers, or it may sell goods of other manufacturers to the same outlets.

Functions Performed by an Export Distributor

The distributor often performs some of the following functions:

- Managing channels of distribution and marketing/sales efforts.
- Handling customs clearances.
- Obtaining foreign exchange for payments to suppliers.

---

[31]For an example of how Unisys Corp. utilizes automated information systems to link its worldwide operations, see Lisa H. Harrington, "Traveling the Global Data Highway," *Traffic Management* 29, no. 4 (Apr. 1990), pp. 38–42.

[32]For a discussion of the decision-making process of selecting export facilitators, see Toby B. Gooley, "Do You Need an Export Intermediary?" *Traffic Management* 34, no. 9 (Sept. 1995), pp. 67A–69A.

- Maintaining inventories.
- Providing warehouse facilities.
- Managing transportation activities.
- Breaking bulk.
- Managing credit policies.
- Gathering market information.
- Providing after-the-sale services.

Functions Performed by a Customshouse Broker

Customshouse Broker.   The **customshouse broker** performs two critical functions: (1) facilitating product movement through customs and (2) handling the necessary documentation that must accompany international shipments.

The task of handling the large number of documents and forms that accompany an international shipments can be overwhelming for many firms. Coupled with differing customs procedures, restrictions, and requirements from country to country, the job of facilitating export shipments across international borders requires a specialist—the customshouse broker. In general, if a company is exporting to a number of countries with different import requirements or if the company has a large number of items in its product line (e.g., automotive parts, electronic components, food products), a customshouse broker should be a part of the firm's international distribution network.

Functions Performed by an International Freight Forwarder

International Freight Forwarder.   **International freight forwarders** perform a number of functions to facilitate trade for an international company.

- Speed the movement of goods from the site of production to the customer's location by using drop shipments, thus eliminating double handling.
- Receive advanced shipping notices which speed clearance of customs and rapid preparation of required documentation.[33]
- Arrange transportation and carrier routings.
- Coordinate product storage and pick-and-pack operations.
- Provide full-service logistics to their clients.

Nearly every international company utilizes the services of an international freight forwarder in order to coordinate activities at the destination.

Fritz Companies Provide Forwarder Services to Sears

The Fritz Companies, a U.S.-based customs broker and freight forwarder, provides a broad base of services for Sears, Roebuck & Company. In addition to performing standard customs brokerage for all Sears products imported from the Far East, Fritz negotiates and manages contracts with eastbound carriers out of Hong Kong and Singapore, books cargo, consolidates merchandise into container loads, manages cargo to Sears distribution facilities in the United States, and provides information regarding cargo disposition as cargo moves through the pipeline."[34]

---

[33]Goldsborough and Anderson, "Import/Export Management," p. 683.
[34]Ibid., p. 694.

Trading Company.   Most trading companies are primarily involved in exporting, but some engage in the import business as well. **Trading companies** match the seller with buyers of goods or services, and manage the export arrangements, paperwork, transportation, and foreign government requirements.

Export Trading Company Act

In the United States, export trading companies became more important as a result of legislation enacted in 1982. The **Export Trading Company Act** of that year allowed financial institutions (e.g., banks and bank holding companies) to own or participate in export trading companies. That affiliation helped to minimize cash flow, terms of payment, credit, and other financial problems related to the export business. In addition, the act allowed trading companies to export a wide range of services to support global trade.

Although trading companies are not used extensively by U.S. firms, they will continue to be an option as a result of the Export Trading Company Act.

NVOCCs

Non-Vessel-Operating Common Carrier (NVOCC).   The NVOCC, sometimes referred to as a NVO, "consolidates small shipments from different shippers into full container loads . . . and accepts responsibility for all details of the international shipment from the exporter's dock, including paperwork and transportation."[35] Figure 11–6 shows how these common carriers work.

Documentation

International documentation is much more complex than domestic documentation because each country has its own specifications and requirements. Errors in documentation can create long, costly delays in shipping. Nine of the most widely used documents are listed below.

Widely Used Export Documents

1. **Air waybill.** *Issued by:* Airline, consolidator.
Purpose: Each airline has its own air waybill form, but the format and numbering system have been standardized by the airline industry to allow computerization. Like the ocean bill of lading, the air waybill serves as contract of carriage between shipper and carrier.

2. **Certificate of origin.** *Issued by:* Exporter or freight forwarder on exporter's behalf.
Purpose: Required by some countries to certify the origin of product components. Used for statistical research or for assessing duties, particularly under trade agreements.

3. **Commercial invoice.** *Issued by:* Seller of goods.
Purpose: Invoice against which payment is made. Required for clearing goods through customs at destination.

4. **Dock receipt (D/R).** *Issued by:* Exporter or freight forwarder on exporter's behalf.
Purpose: No standard form, but the D/R must include shipment description, physical details, and shipping information. Used by both shipper and carrier to verify shipment particulars, condition, and delivery to carrier.

---

[35]Southern, *Transportation and Logistics Basics,* p. 297.

FIGURE 11–6

How NVOCCs work

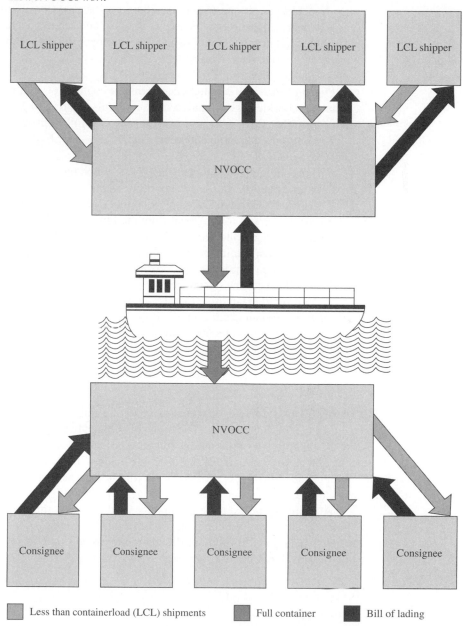

Source: Toby B. Estis, "NVOCCs: A Low-Cost Alternative for LCL Shippers," *Traffic Management* 27, no. 6 (June 1988), p. 87.

5. **Ocean bill of lading (B/L).** *Issued by:* Steamship line.

Purpose: Each carrier has its own bill of lading form. Serves as the contract of carriage between carrier and shipper, spelling out legal responsibilities and liability limits for all parties to the shipment. The B/L also can be used to transfer title to the goods to a party named in the document. Specifies shipment details, such as number of pieces, weight, destination, and so on.

6. **Packing list.** *Issued by:* Exporter.

Purpose: Provides detailed information of contents of each package in the shipment. Customs authorities at destination use this information during clearance and inspection procedures. The packing list also is invaluable when filing claims for damage or shortage.

7. **Shipper's export declaration (SED).** *Issued by:* Exporter or freight forwarder on exporter's behalf.

Purpose: Required by federal law for any commodity with a value over $2,500 or any shipment requiring validated export license.

8. **Sight, time drafts.** *Issued by:* Exporter or freight forwarder on exporter's behalf.

Purpose: Request for payment from the foreign buyer. Instructs buyer's bank to collect payment; when collected, the bank releases shipping documents to the buyer. The buyer's bank then remits to seller's bank. Sight drafts are payable on receipt at the buyer's bank. Time drafts extend credit; the foreign bank releases documents immediately, but collects payment later.

9. **Validated export licenses.** *Issued by:* U.S. Department of Commerce.

Purpose: Required for commodities deemed important to national security, foreign policy objectives, or protecting domestic supplies of strategic materials. The validated export license constitutes permission to export a specific product to a specific party.[36]

Terms of Trade

The **terms of shipment** or **terms of trade** are important information to be included on the actual export documents. The terms of shipment are much more important in international shipping than in domestic shipping because of the uncertainties and problems of control that accompany foreign traffic movements. These terms determine who is responsible for the various stages of delivery, who bears what risks, and who pays for the various elements of transportation.

A summary of the most commonly used terms of shipment in exporting from the United States is given below and in Table 11–3. In international trade, "incoterms" are the equivalent to FOB origin or destination terms and were developed and defined by the International Chamber of Commerce.[37]

---

[36]"Ten Key Trade Documents," *Traffic Management* 29, no. 9 (Sept. 1990), pp. 53, 55.

[37]For a discussion of the basics of international trade law and terms, see James Giermanski, "Can You Talk International Trade?" *Transportation and Distribution* 35, no. 7 (July 1994), pp. 34–36.

TABLE 11–3   **Who's Responsible for Costs under Various Terms?**

Cost Items/Terms	FOB (Free on Board) Inland Carrier at Factory	FOB (Free on Board) Inland Carrier at Point of Shipment	FAS (Free Alongside) Vessel or Plane at Port of Shipment	CIF (Cost, Insurance, Freight) at Port of Destination
Export packing*	Buyer	Seller	Seller	Seller
Inland freight	Buyer	Seller	Seller	Seller
Port charges	Buyer	Buyer	Seller	Seller
Forwarders' fee	Buyer	Buyer	Buyer	Seller
Consular fee	Buyer	Buyer	Buyer	Seller
Loading on vessel or plane	Buyer	Buyer	Buyer	Buyer†
Ocean freight	Buyer	Buyer	Buyer	Seller
Cargo insurance	Buyer	Buyer	Buyer	Seller
Customs duties	Buyer	Buyer	Buyer	Seller
Ownership of goods passes	When goods are on board an inland carrier (truck, rail, etc.) or in hands of inland carrier	When goods are alongside carrier or in hands of air or ocean carrier	When goods are on board air or ocean carrier at port of shipment	When goods are on board air or ocean carrier at port of shipment

*Who absorbs export packing? This charge should be clearly agreed upon. Charges are sometimes controversial.

†The seller has responsibility to arrange for consular invoices (and other documents requested by buyer's government). According to official definitions, buyer pays fees, but sometimes as a matter of practice, seller includes in quotations.

Source: Philip R. Cateora, *International Marketing,* 9th ed. (Burr Ridge, IL: Richard D. Irwin, 1996), p. 367.

Most Commonly Used Terms of Shipment

Ex Origin.   Origin should be identified as factory, plant, and so forth. The seller bears the costs and risks until the buyer is obligated to take delivery. The buyer pays for the documents, must take delivery of the shipment when specified, and must pay for any export taxes.

FOB (Free on Board) Inland Carrier.   The seller arranges for loading on the carrier's equipment. The seller provides a clean bill of lading and is responsible for loss or damage until goods have been placed on the inland vehicle.

FOB Vessel U.S. Port.   The price quoted covers all expenses involved in the delivery of goods upon the vessel designated at the port named. The buyer must give the seller adequate notice of sailing date, name of ship, and berth. The buyer bears additional costs resulting from the vessel being late or absent.

FAS (Free Alongside) Vessel U.S. Port.   Similar to FOB vessel, but certain additional port charges for the seller, such as heavy lift, may apply. The buyer is responsible for loss or damage while the goods are on a lighter (small barge) or within reach of the loading device. Loading costs are the responsibility of the buyer.

FOB Vessel Foreign Port.   The price quoted includes all transportation costs to the point where goods are off-loaded in the destination country. The seller is responsible for insurance to this point. The buyer assumes the risk as soon as the vessel is at the foreign port.

FOB Inland Destination.   The price quoted includes all costs involved in getting the goods to the named inland point in the country of importation.

C & F (Cost and Freight).   The price quoted includes all transportation to the point of destination. The seller pays export taxes and similar fees. The buyer pays the cost of certificates of origin, consular invoices, or other documents required for importation into the buyer's country. The seller must prove these, but at the buyer's expense. The buyer is responsible for all insurance from the point of vessel loading.

CIF (Cost, Insurance, and Freight).   The price quoted includes the cost of goods, transportation, and marine insurance. The seller pays all taxes or fees, as well as marine and war risk insurance. The buyer pays for any certificates or consular documents required for importation. Although the seller pays for insurance, the buyer assumes all risk after the seller has delivered the goods to the carrier.[38]

Free Trade Zones

Free trade zones (FTZs), sometimes referred to as **foreign trade zones,** are areas where companies may ship products to postpone or reduce customs duties or taxes. Products remaining in the FTZ are not subject to duties or taxes until they are reshipped from the zone into the country of destination. Firms often process, assemble, sort, and repackage the product within the FTZ before reshipment.[39] The facilities, services offered, and quality of FTZ management vary significantly. Management wishing to utilize a FTZ will have to explore each zone individually to determine its potential usefulness.[40]

---

[38]Thomas A. Foster, "Anatomy of an Export," *Distribution* 79, no. 10 (Oct. 1980), pp. 76–77. For a definition of these and other import-export terms, see "Export/Import Terms You Need to Know," *Traffic Management* 19, no. 9 (Sept. 1990), pp. 37–41.

[39]Dale A. Harmelink, "Distribution Network Systems: Planning, Design and Site Selection," in *The Distribution Management Handbook,* ed. James A. Tompkins and Dale Harmelink (New York: McGraw-Hill, 1994), pp. 4.18–4.19.

[40]For an examination of the role of FTZs in global marketing, see Tom Andel, "Site Here and Zone Out," *Transportation and Distribution* 37, no. 8 (Aug. 1996), pp. 52–54; William Armbruster, "The Competitive Edge," *Journal of Commerce and Commercial* 409, no. 28806 (Sept. 11, 1996), pp. 1C–2C; and Patriya S. Tansuhaj and James W. Gentry, "Firm Differences in Perceptions of the Facilitating Role of Foreign Trade Zones in Global Marketing and Logistics," *Journal of International Business Studies,* Spring 1987, pp. 19–33.

Logistics Characteristics of Global Markets[41]

Three major geographic regions account for the bulk of world economic activity and international trade: North America, Western Europe, and the Pacific Rim, which includes China and Japan. These three areas produce 80 percent of the world's economic output and account for 75 percent of world exports. For this reason, it is necessary to understand the foundations of business and logistics systems in those regions, and in other developing areas.

North America

NAFTA Integrates the Markets of Canada, the United States, and Mexico

The North American Free Trade Association (NAFTA) brings together the economies of Canada, the United States, and Mexico. In 1995, the flow of trade between the United States and Mexico exceeded $100 billion, of which $62 billion was from Mexico to the United States, and $45 billion was from the United States to Mexico. Between Canada and the United States, the flow of trade was over $260 billion in 1994.[42]

This area will have a larger population and domestic economic product than the European Union (EU) and the European Free Trade Association (EFTA) combined. South of the NAFTA countries is the rest of Latin America, a potential addition to NAFTA with a population of some 350 million.

The provisions of NAFTA are significant in that they directly impact a variety of logistics activities and affect how supply chains are structured when Canadian, U.S., and Mexican companies are involved. Some of the more substantive changes brought about by NAFTA include:

Changes Resulting from NAFTA

- Eliminates many tariff and nontariff barriers (by the year 2004, most tariffs will be eliminated).
- Enhances carriers' ability to operate across borders, especially between the United States and Mexico, where cross-border movements occur much more easily.
- Liberalizes foreign investment (allows U.S. and Canadian companies the right to establish firms in Mexico or to acquire existing Mexican companies).
- Standardizes customs initiatives, local content rules, and packaging and labeling requirements.[43]

Canada and the United States have the most advanced logistics infrastructure and systems in the world. North America offers a wide choice of suppliers in all transportation modes and very good, competitively priced warehousing facilities and ancillary services throughout the continent. Thus, the development of logistics strategies and operations are seldom limited by the physical facilities available.

---

[41]This section was taken from Bender, "International Logistics," pp. 8.14–8.19.

[42]Arnold B. Maltz, James R. Giermanski, and David Molina, "The U.S.–Mexico Cross-Border Freight Market: Prospects for Mexican Truckers," *Transportation Journal* 36, no. 1 (Fall 1996), p. 5; "NAFTA's Momentum," *Industrial Distribution Supplement,* May 1995, p. S3.

[43]David G. Waller, Robert L. D'Avanzo, and Douglas M. Lambert, *Supply Chain Directions for a New North America* (Oak Brook, IL: Council of Logistics Management, 1995), pp. 2–3.

Technology

NAFTA and Technology Combine to Cut Customs Delays

"Today, the documentation for more than 1.5 million motor carrier shipments into Canada is processed by customs before the freight even reaches the border, shortening the time spent releasing the freight when it arrives.

Five years ago, going into Mexico meant clearances that could take three or four days. Today, 90 percent of all goods from the United States are cleared by Mexican Customs at the border in 20 seconds or less.

The ultimate goal of [the United States, Canada, and Mexico] is to completely automate the customs clearance process. Canadian Customs is implementing Customs 2000 initiatives with the goal of making its customs system paperless by the year 2000. One initiative that has boosted the automation efforts in Canada has been implementation of the Pre-Arrival Review System (PARS) and the Inland Pre-Arrival Review System (INPARS). . . . Through PARS and INPARS, information on a shipment is sent from the carrier to the broker or designate who prepares the release documentation and forwards it to Canadian Customs for review and processing. These systems allow brokers to prepare release documentation for customs review prior to the freight's arrival. . . This allows paperwork errors to be corrected while the freight is en route instead of delaying the shipment after it arrives at the border.

Automation has helped Mexican Customs. . . Over the last five years, traffic volume through Mexican Customs has increased 300 percent while the agency has been able to reduce its staff by 60 percent through automation."

Source: Robert B. Carr, "Don't Let Borders Be Barriers," *Transportation and Distribution* 36, no. 3 (Mar. 1995), pp. 65–70.

In North America, it is possible to find common, contract, and private carriers offering transportation services by air, highway, railroad, pipeline, and water. In the United States and Canada, prices are negotiable in most cases, depending on freight type (e.g., hazardous materials, refrigerated goods) and product characteristics (e.g., annual volumes, seasonality, shipment size, type of product).

Unitization, in the form of pallets and slip sheets, and freight containerization have been commonplace for decades. Pallets have been standardized mostly along industry lines (e.g., grocery manufacturers). Containers, most 40 feet and longer in length, with some 20-foot containers, have served as the basis for the International Standards Organization's standards.

The use of electronic data interchange (EDI) to support logistics operations was pioneered in North America several decades ago, and the continent is the largest user of that technology in the world today. See the Technology box.

Many North American manufacturers, retailers, and logistics service providers are taking advantage of NAFTA opportunities. Those "leading-edge," or "best-practice," companies have adopted one or more of the following strategies:

**Strategies of
Leading-Edge
Companies as a
Result of NAFTA**

• **Customer service.** Best-practice companies manage key accounts in a consistent, coordinated manner in all three countries. They are working to create more uniform service levels across an integrated North American marketplace.

• **Manufacturing.** Best-practice companies modify their product development and manufacturing approaches to take advantage of market and tariff advantages inherent in NAFTA.

• **Channel design.** Best-practice companies establish market research groups in each North American country to facilitate distribution channel designs.

• **Sourcing.** Best-practice companies regularly revisit and revise their sourcing strategies. Increasingly, this means moving away from offshore vendors to suppliers in North America.

• **Distribution.** Best-practice companies establish core carrier programs with their major North American carriers. They develop cross-border shipping programs that include innovative freight consolidation and stacktrain approaches (referred to as "double stack" in Chapter 7). Finally, they establish a strong border presence to expedite cross-border product flow.

• **Sales and marketing.** Best-practice companies develop sales and marketing strategies targeted to specific markets and customers within North America.

• **Organization.** Best-practice companies create internal NAFTA units dedicated to managing business in the NAFTA trading area. They train their own people and their vendors on NAFTA rules and regulations.[44]

Many companies have taken advantage of the opportunities which NAFTA has provided, including Alamo Iron Works (distributor), Darco Southern (industrial products manufacturer), Loctite Corporation (industrial products manufacturer), NSK-RHP Canada (ball-bearing manufacturer), Rich Products (food products), and Yellow Freight (trucking).[45]

Maquiladora Operations.   Many firms throughout the world have become involved in global manufacturing; that is, they have manufacturing facilities located in various parts of the world. The major advantage of manufacturing products throughout the world is that a firm has greater opportunities to reduce the costs of production, especially the labor component. Additionally, the avoidance of border tariffs is a primary factor influencing firms to utilize maquiladoras.

Global manufacturers currently find many opportunities for production sharing and they are actively taking advantage of them. While American manufacturers have traditionally

---

[44]Ibid., p. 8.

[45]For a discussion of these, and other, companies that have benefited from NAFTA, see James H. Gilmore, "Designing a Distribution Strategy for Canada," *CCA White Paper* (Cleveland, OH: Cleveland Consulting Associates, n.d.); Toby B. Gooley, "How Rich Products Gets the Best of Both Worlds," *Traffic Management* 35, no. 2 (Feb. 1996), pp. 47–49; "NAFTA's Momentum," pp. S3–S12; and David Valdez, "Switch to Free Trade," *Transportation and Distribution* 36, no. 1 (Jan. 1995), pp. 53–58.

focused on the Pacific Rim countries when establishing production-sharing facilities, they are increasingly active in setting up production-sharing facilities in the Caribbean Basin, Mexico, South America, and even in some European countries.

Japanese firms have taken advantage of low-cost labor in other Pacific Rim countries and have begun establishing a presence in Mexico. Likewise, European companies have set up many production facilities in Mexico and are beginning to take advantage of the new production opportunities available in Eastern Europe.[46]

Maquiladoras Defined

The **maquiladora** is an example of production sharing or twin plant (also known as in-bound manufacturing), operation. Companies from throughout the world "set up assembly and manufacturing facilities along the Mexican side of the U.S.-Mexican border. The production sharing aspects . . . are encouraged by special tariff provisions that reduce the duties that would normally be assessed on materials that flow across the border."[47]

Maquiladora operations affect the costs of performing various logistics activities. Generally, costs for documentation, inventory, sourcing, and transportation are higher in maquiladoras than in domestic-only operations. Order-processing, packaging, and warehousing costs tend to be the same or slightly lower in maquiladoras.[48] Often, the logistics executive will see logistics costs increase when the firm is involved in maquiladora operations. However, because of the significantly lower labor costs in manufacturing, the total cost to the firm will be lower.

The logistics, as well as manufacturing, implications of maquiladoras need to be considered by any firm planning the establishment of twin plant operations. More than 2,100 maquiladora facilities have been developed, employing approximately half a million people, and that number is increasing each year.[49]

As firms evaluate international sourcing and manufacturing options in their search to gain competitive advantage, they will continue to find the maquiladora operation as a viable option. U.S. and Canadian firms exploring maquiladoras in Mexico may see their use diminish because of the implementation of NAFTA. With reduced tariffs, maquiladora operations will have to create more value added to remain viable.

Western Europe[50]

The European continent has undergone a major political and economic transformation since the early 1990s. This transformation must be clearly understood for businesses to operate successfully in it.

---

[46]Stanley E. Fawcett, "Logistics and Manufacturing Issues in Maquiladora Operations," *International Journal of Physical Distribution and Logistics Management* 20, no. 4 (1990), p. 13.

[47]Ibid.; see also Arnold Maltz, Linda Riley, and Kevin Boberg, "Purchasing Logistics Services in a Transborder Situation: Logistics Outsourcing in US-Mexico Co-production," *International Journal of Physical Distribution and Logistics Management* 23, no. 8 (1993), pp. 46–54; and Gustavo A. Vargas and Thomas W. Johnson, "An Analysis of Operational Experience in the US/Mexico Production Sharing (Maquiladora) Program," *Journal of Operations Management* 11, no. 1 (Mar. 1993), pp. 17–34.

[48]Fawcett, "Logistics and Manufacturing Issues in Maquiladora Operations," p. 17; see also U.S. International Trade Commission, *The U.S.-Mexican Border Industrialization Program: Use and Economic Impact of TSUS Items 806.3 and 807.0* (Washington, DC: U.S. Government Printing Office, 1988), p. 500.

[49]Waller, D'Avanzo, and Lambert, *Supply Chain Directions for a New North America,* p. 100.

[50]This section is taken from Bender, "International Logistics," pp. 8.15–8.17.

There are several major European regions, each one with clearly differentiated subregions. The most significant are the European Union (EU), the former Soviet Union (including Russia, the Ukraine, the Baltic republics), and Eastern Europe, which are discussed in the next section.

The EU groups 15 nations (Austria, Belgium, Denmark, Finland, France, Germany, Greece, Ireland, Italy, Luxembourg, Netherlands, Portugal, Spain, Sweden, and the United Kingdom) with a population of more than 350 million persons, and a gross regional product (analogous to the use of the term **gross domestic** product in the United States) similar to that of the United States. Several Eastern European countries are expected to join the EU in the future.[51]

The countries of the former Soviet Union, including Russia, and the former Soviet satellite nations of Eastern Europe are trying to effect a transition from centrally planned economies to free market economies. The concurrent political and economic turmoil is not likely to end in the near future. Their economic problems are compounded by political volatility that is disintegrating the region into a conglomerate of smaller, tribal nations. Many of these problems were not envisioned in the early days following the breakup of the Soviet Union.

Twelve of the 15 former Soviet republics belong to the Commonwealth of Independent States (CIS) of which 4 are in Europe: Russia, Ukraine, Belarus, and Moldova.[52] The CIS has a population of approximately 300 million people, with a per capita income less than half that of the United States, but with enormous reserves of natural resources and a well-educated population. Russia and the Ukraine are the economic backbone of the CIS and encompass most of its population.

Eastern Europe is made up of Poland, Czechoslovakia, Hungary, Romania, Bulgaria, Serbia, Croatia, Slovenia, Bosnia, Macedonia, Albania, and the Baltic states of Lithuania, Latvia, and Estonia. This region has a population of approximately 150 million persons with a low per capita income, adequate natural resources, and a well-educated population. This region has two economically different subregions: a relatively advanced one formed by Poland, Czechoslovakia, Hungary, and the Baltic states, and another, less advanced one, comprised of the rest.

Africa, especially North Africa, is economically important to Europe. It has substantial trade with Western Europe and has been the source of massive immigration.

Economic Issues for the New Century.   Into the 21st century, Western Europe will be the locomotive of the European economy. The following business-related issues are of major importance to companies operating in Western Europe:

Issues Important to Companies Operating in Western Europe

• *Common currency.* The conversion to a common currency, the **European Currency Unit (ECU).** While slow in coming, this will eliminate the costs and work of converting Europe's many currencies.

• *Tax equalization.* The equalization of personal and corporate taxes throughout the region. This will bring logistic costs to the forefront, as the critical ones necessary to establish facility locations.

---

[51]John L. Manzella, "No More Business as Usual," *Sky Magazine,* Apr. 1995, pp. 118–28.
[52]The Baltic republics of Estonia, Latvia, and Lithuania do not belong to the CIS.

• *Political homogenization.* The creation of uniform political institutions among all members. This will compound the benefits of tax equalization.

• *Standards homogenization.* In January 1993, the EU implemented some 1,500 safety, health, environmental, and quality standards. The ultimate goal is to establish some 10,000 standards in Europe. The new rules are being drafted by the European Committee for Standardization, better known by its French acronym, CEN, and the International Standards Organization (ISO).

Logistics Issues Facing Western Europe.   The developments affecting these issues will have major consequences for business in Western Europe, especially for logistics decisions concerning the location of plants and warehouses and the determination of their missions and areas of converge.

Pan-European Logistics Strategies

However, one fact is clear from the development of optimum logistics strategies on a Western European scale: The optimum number and location of plants and warehouses is substantially lower than that required to optimize the logistic networks of each individual country. Typical cost reductions obtained by optimum continental systems are 15 to 20 percent compared with optimum national systems. Thus, companies that streamline their logistics networks on a continental basis before their competitors will gain major competitive advantages. If those advantages are retained for a few years, they may become insurmountable to their competitors.

The economic heart of Western Europe is a rectangle with vertexes in London, Hamburg, Trieste, and Marseilles. Most production and consumption takes place within that area and is therefore of major logistics importance. This area contains major distribution centers to supply West European customers or secondary warehouses.

Other major considerations governing West European logistics are as follows.

Characteristics of Western European Logistics

1. *Customs and transit procedures.* The EU has eliminated customs and transit procedures among its members; thus, there is a free flow of goods between its members and the European Free Trade Association (EFTA).[53]

2. *Transportation deregulation.* The deregulation of the transportation industry should reduce transportation costs by 25 to 50 percent by the year 2000 and drastically reduce the optimum number of facilities required to meet customer service requirements economically.

3. *Transportation modes.* Trucks and pipelines account for the majority of tonnage transported in Europe. They will continue to gain tonnage at the expense of rail and coastal and inland water transportation, although for environmental reasons, the national railroads are waging a campaign to force more traffic to use rail. The result is likely to be an increase in intermodal transportation.

4. *Subcontracting of services.* Logistics services are increasingly being subcontracted to logistic service companies, rather than performed in-house. This trend is likely to accelerate as the average shipment size continues to decrease and the average shipping frequency to increase; consolidation provides substantial economies.

---

[53]EFTA members in 1996 were Iceland, Norway, Liechtenstein, and Switzerland. Many previous members of the EFTA have joined the EU.

Eurotunnel or "Chunnel"	5. *Eurotunnel.* The opening of the Eurotunnel (the "Chunnel") across the English Channel improved service and reduced transportation costs between the United Kingdom and Continental Europe. This has affected facility location decisions. 6. *Palletization.* Palletized freight is increasingly using the ISO standard pallet sizes.

Five Major Areas of Change in the European Union.   Changes in the EU are expected to have substantial impact on the marketing and manufacturing strategies of firms selling products in Europe. The anticipated changes will occur in five major areas: manufacturing, transportation, distribution channels, administration, and organization.[54]

Where Should Plants Be Located?	*Manufacturing.* Many firms have traditionally established plants in each country, but with the economic unification of Europe companies are establishing plants that can service multiple countries. With larger plants, greater economies of scale can be realized, which will have a variety of effects on logistics activities carried out in the channel of distribution due to the larger amounts of goods being produced. If firms maintain several plant locations, the focused factory concept could be implemented, with each plant specializing in one or a few product lines.
European Transport Deregulation	*Transportation.* Accompanying the unification of Western Europe on January 1, 1993, was the deregulation of transportation, particularly motor transport. As happened in the United States after the deregulation of transportation, customers in Europe are demanding more services. Transportation providers have become more competitive in pricing and more innovative in service.[55] Just as in the United States, a shakeout of the industry is anticipated.[56] The transport industry should experience financial improvement after a shakeout occurs. Freight consolidation opportunities should increase because of many factors, including deregulation, more optimal routing and scheduling opportunities, and the development of Pan-European (across Europe) services. In addition, the "Chunnel" links the United Kingdom with the rest of Europe and will facilitate additional freight transport between England and France.
Use of Channel Intermediaries	*Distribution Channels.* Within the European channel of distribution, there may be a decline in the use of channel intermediaries. With a single European market, separate channels will not be required for each country. Instead, larger wholesalers and distributors will develop. Vertical integration will occur, and direct marketing and distribution will

---

[54]The following section related to these five areas of change was adapted from Alan Braithwaite, "Achieving Outstanding Logistics Performance in Europe Post 1992," a paper presented at the Annual Conference of the Council of Logistics Management, Oct. 1991; for a more recent updating of European trends, see "European Logistics Trends and Strategies," a collaborative research study (1995) by The French Logistics Association (ASLOG), Cle 128, Digital Equipment, Berlin-based Zentrum fur Logistik und Unternehmensplanung, and the German Logistics Association (BVL).

[55]For an example of transportation changes occurring in Germany, see Patrick M. Byrne, Henner Klein, Stephan Hofstetter, and Niklas Hoppe, "Changes in Europe Transform German Logistics," *Transportation and Distribution* 36, no. 4 (Apr. 1995), pp. 53–55.

[56]Patrick M. Byrne, Johan C. Aurik, and Jan Van de Oord, "New Priorities in Logistics Services in Europe," *Transportation and Distribution* 35, no. 2 (Feb. 1995), pp. 45–58.

increase. The result will be less inventory within the system and a lowering of channel-wide logistics costs. How Xerox achieved logistics success in Europe is discussed in the Creative Solutions box at the end of this chapter.

Administration. The removal of customs procedures will result in greater efficiencies in transportation, packaging, and labeling. Technology improvements can be implemented throughout Europe instead of within individual countries. More centralization of order processing, inventory control, warehousing, and computer technology can occur with a unified Europe. However, a recent study indicated that inventory carrying and systems and administrative costs have grown from about one-third to about one-half of logistics costs since the EU was created. Thus, these areas are the focus of productivity improvements.[57]

Organization. Significant organizational changes are occurring in Europe. The centralization trend mentioned previously, and the organizational structures that recognize national boundaries to a lesser extent will result in pervasive changes in all industries.

In sum, the competitive situation in Western Europe will intensify. The penalties for poor performance will be greater, but the rewards much higher for those firms that can effectively implement optimal manufacturing, marketing, and logistics strategies in a unified European economy.

The Commonwealth of Independent States and Eastern Europe

During the early 1990s, significant changes took place in the Soviet Union (much of which reorganized itself as independent nations within the Commonwealth of Independent States) and throughout Eastern Europe. The fall of the Berlin Wall, in 1989, which had symbolized the separation of Communist from noncommunist Europe; the reunification of East and West Germany; political freedom in Poland, Hungary, and Czechoslovakia; and the independence movements of many of the republics in the former Soviet Union have reshaped political and commercial boundaries in Europe and Asia.

Tremendous opportunities and challenges face companies interested in entering the markets of the CIS and Eastern Europe (see Box 11–2). Excluding the CIS, the market potential of Eastern Europe has been estimated at over $1 trillion.[58] However, the attractiveness of individual country markets within Eastern Europe will vary significantly and will depend on several factors, including:

Factors Impacting the Attractiveness of Markets in Eastern Europe

- Degree of indebtedness.
- Development of the banking system.
- Level of productivity.

---

[57]Ibid.

[58]A.T. Kearney, Inc., *The Iron Curtain Rises: Investment Opportunities in East Central Europe,* management report (Jan. 1991), p. 3.

Some of the 1,049 farm combines manufactured by John Deere are loaded onto a ship bound for customers located in the Ukraine, a former Soviet republic located in eastern Europe.

- Quality of the workforce.
- Condition of the infrastructure.
- State of technology.
- Depth of managerial skills.
- Supply of production materials.
- Profit repatriation regulations.[59]

---

[59]Ibid., p. 6.

Box 11–2

Wanted: Creative, Do-It-Yourself Shippers

"With so many roadblocks—both figurative and literal—constantly being thrown in a shipper's way, it sometimes takes creative thinking and a can-do attitude to deliver a shipment in the former Soviet Union.

The experience of Houston-based IMC Maritime Group, a ship operator and project-cargo-management company, illustrates the do-it-yourself nature of shipping to the region. IMC had a contract to deliver more than 100,000 tons of oil-field equipment to the new Ardalin oil field in northwestern Siberia. But there were no roads to the remote site. How to get it there?

Because the tundra is waterlogged and mushy in the summer, the brutal Siberian winter was the only time when such heavy shipments could travel overland. IMC first chartered specially built icebreaker vessels to take the oversized shipments to icebound Archangel. IMC then used trucks to transfer the cargo to a staging area just north of the Arctic Circle. The final leg of the journey required the company to build its own roads to the site. Rather than dig up the fragile terrain, workers sprayed water over the tundra, forming enough layers of ice to support the heaviest pieces of equipment. The roads are temporary; they melt in summer and leave no permanent damage.

Koch Supplies Inc. of Kansas City, Missouri, has shown equal creativity in meeting the tough conditions in the former Soviet Union. Koch manufactures and distributes food-handling and -processing equipment. The company has designed a mobile meat-processing plant for sale in the CIS. All the necessary cutting, processing, and packaging equipment is fitted inside a 40-foot ocean container on a chassis with heavy-duty tires. 'All the buyer needs to do when it gets there is hook it up to gas or a generator and to a water supply,' explains project planner Jim Masterson.

Getting there is half the problem, of course, and Koch has found that intermodalism is the answer. Self-contained units move via piggyback from Kansas City to the East or West Coasts, depending on the final destination. From there, the container rolls onto a ship for delivery to the appropriate port, explains Benjamin Khayet, a Russian native who is Koch's export manager and translator for CIS projects. Once overseas, the trailer can continue either by rail or road as dictated by local conditions. 'We even shipped a unit to Frankfurt, and then drove it to Kazakhstan,' he recalls. The flexibility afforded by the intermodal container and chassis makes modern, sanitary food processing available in even the remotest locations, Khayer says. 'It's especially popular for processing reindeer meat in Siberia!' he says with a smile."

Source: Toby B. Gooley, "Shipping to the Wild, Wild East," *Traffic Management* 35, no. 1 (Jan. 1996), p. 70A.

From a logistics perspective, the CIS and Eastern Europe offer special challenges.[60] Most businesspeople traveling to those areas recognize the poor transportation infrastructures resulting from decades of Communist rule. Except in a few rare instances, the concepts of customer satisfaction and customer service are unknown. Sophisticated logistics techniques and the use of computerized order processing and information systems are impossible in most areas.

Because of the immense opportunities, many firms will decide that the benefits outweigh the costs. It will be a slow process, but the firms that penetrate the markets of Eastern Europe and the CIS will gain competitive advantage over firms that wait.

[60]For a discussion of Eastern European logistics operations, especially Hungary, see Attila Chikan, "Consequences of Economic Transition on Logistics: The Case of Hungary," *International Journal of Physical Distribution and Logistics Management* 26, no. 1 (1996), pp. 40–48.

The Pacific Rim: China

An advertisement by the California Department of Commerce titled "Asia: Mega-Market of the 1990s" in a special issue of *Fortune,* stated that the Pacific Rim was a $4 trillion market growing at $5 billion per week.[61] It is important to note for our discussion that Pacific Rim refers to countries on the Eastern Pacific—China, Japan, Malaysia, Australia, and New Zealand—because the United States, Canada, Mexico, and Chile, for example, are also countries on the Pacific Rim. Some statistics indicate the rising importance of the Pacific region:

The Rising Importance of the Pacific Rim

- Steel consumption is higher in the Pacific Rim region than in the United States and Europe.
- Within two years, Asia's demand for semiconductors will exceed that of the European Community (EC).[62]
- By the year 2000, the Pacific Rim economies will be bigger in total than those of the EC and about the same as those of North America.
- Asia is the world's largest market for cars, telecommunications equipment, paint, and many other products.
- Asian manufacturers, excluding Japan, have captured 25 percent of the world's market for personal computers.[63]

Firms that import from or export to the Pacific Rim of Asia, those outsourcing materials from the region, and those interested in entering markets there recognize that differences in economics, politics, and culture greatly influence business activities in specific Asian countries. Ranging from the affluence of Japan to the poverty of Indonesia and China, the region offers a myriad of immense problems and significant opportunities for companies.[64]

Firms marketing products to Japan, South Korea, Hong Kong, and other industrialized areas of the Pacific Rim will find logistics environments similar to those found in North America and the European Union. While cultures and politics are different, transportation infrastructures are developed, a variety of warehousing options exist, the use of automated systems is widespread, and customer service concepts are understood and accepted by logistics service providers.[65]

Logistics Is Difficult in China

This cannot be said about the developing countries of the Pacific Rim, such as China. In China, most logistics activities are handled by the government. The economy is

---

[61]Advertisement by the California Department of Commerce in a special issue of *Fortune,* Fall 1990, inside front cover.

[62]The European Union was called the European Community until 1994.

[63]Louis Kraar, "The Rising Power of the Pacific," special issue of *Fortune,* Fall 1990, pp. 8–9.

[64]See Justin Zubrod, Robert Tasiaux, and Alan Beebe, "The Challenges of Logistics within Asia," *Transportation and Distribution* 37, no. 2 (Feb. 1996), pp. 81–83.

[65]See "The Art of Distribution in Japan," *Traffic Management* 28, no. 12 (Dec. 1989), pp. 75A–79A; Paul S. Bender, "Japan's Distribution Revolution," *Traffic Management* 29, no. 4 (Apr. 1990), p. 61; and Anderson and Colard, "The International Logistics Environment," pp. 652–59.

characterized by materials shortages, planned distribution by the government, and a dual pricing system (i.e., planned prices and market prices).[66]

Firms penetrating the Chinese market will find great logistics difficulties. The process will be slow, requiring great patience both managerially and financially. However, conditions are changing for the better. For example, Lucent Technologies, Network Systems Division has been able to reduce the time to ship products from the United States to destinations within China to an average of 39 days; it used to take months. Relative to destinations within industrialized nations, the time is significantly longer.[67]

Business transactions in countries like China will not show significant payback for many years, and firms will not be able to utilize the same financial criteria in evaluating Chinese logistics efficiencies as they use in other parts of the world.

The Pacific Rim: Japan[68]

Japan remains the economic powerhouse of the Asian side of the Pacific Rim despite some signs of slowing in its economic growth rate. The Japanese distribution system is by far the most complex and inefficient of the industrialized countries, although that may be changing, as described in Box 11–3. This is a consequence of historical preferences given by the government to small business enterprises.

Government Involvement in Product Distribution

Most aspects of goods distribution in Japan are tightly controlled by the government. The recent affluence of Japan, coupled with complaints from foreign governments and companies that consider the system a major impediment to entering the Japanese market, have provoked political actions. These have resulted in the beginnings of major liberalization of the distribution system in Japan. However, distribution costs are so high that retail prices are several times their respective wholesale prices.

Although Japan is an archipelago comprising more than 5,000 islands, the bulk of its population lives on the four major islands of Hokkaido, Honshu, Kyushu, and Shikoku. Of these, the island of Honshu contains all the major cities and most of the population of Japan.

Characteristics of Japanese Logistics

Some of the major characteristics of Japanese logistics are as follows.

1. *Transportation modes.* Ninety percent of domestic tonnage is transported by truck, and this is likely to continue. Truck transportation requires licensing from the Ministry of Transport. Licenses distinguish between:

- Long-distance trucks, which carry loads between major regions; for example, from plants to distribution centers.
- Short-distance trucks, which carry loads within a region; for example, between a wholesaler and a retailer.

---

[66]See Sun Yao-jun and Li Kening, "Materials Distribution and Its Reform in China," *Asia Pacific International Journal of Business Logistics* 1, no. 2 (1988), pp. 8–9; and Anderson and Colard, "International Logistics Environment," pp. 652–59.

[67]Bill Mongelluzzo, "AT&T Network Finds Shipping to China a Test of Ingenuity: 39-Day Average Impresses Rivals," *Journal of Commerce and Commercial,* Oct. 27, 1995, p. 2B.

[68]This section is taken from Bender, "International Logistics," pp. 8.18–8.19.

Box 11–3

Is Japan Beginning to Adopt Western Supply Chain Management Concepts in Its Retail Distribution Systems?

A survey performed by Japan's Ministry of International Trade and Industry (MITI) in 1989 found that Japan averaged 2.21 wholesale steps between the producer and retailer. This compared to .73 in France, .90 in the former West Germany, and 1.0 in the United States. This heavy "middleman" structure has several effects: It increases prices to Japanese consumers, promotes inefficiency, and makes it extremely difficult for anyone new, such as foreign competitors, to break into the market. They have to establish a relationship with wholesalers in order to have a point of entry.

These long distribution channels are part of Japan's **Keiretsu** system, where manufacturers own full or partial shares in many of the retailers and wholesalers that are part of their channel. These channels are tightly controlled through interlocking directorates and secret meetings among channel members to plan the long-term strategy of the channel. Interpersonal relationships are very close and stable. Information flow is excellent, and transaction costs are relatively low due to the familiar, established network.

Things began to change in the early 1990s when Japan suffered an economic slump, making increased efficiency more important. As in the United States and Europe, power is shifting away from manufacturers to retailers. Large retailers don't want to deal with long channels that add costs to their processes. Direct sales and mail order have been growing faster than retail sales, causing retailers to want to become more competitive. As a result, innovative Japanese manufacturers have begun to respond, reducing the length of their channels. An example of this is KOA Soap. The firm used three levels of wholesalers in the 1960s and two levels, including its own exclusive wholesaler, in the 1970s and 1980s. In the 1990s, KOA Soap is using only its own exclusive wholesaler.

This could be a trend that further shakes up the Japanese retail sector. As distribution becomes simplified, it may be easier for foreign competitors to enter Japanese markets, and bring their own logistics innovations. Japanese consumers should come out the clear winners!

Sources: John Fahy and Fuyuki Taguchi, "Reassessing the Japanese Distribution System," *Sloan Management Review,* Winter 1995, pp. 49–61; and Lisa M. Ellram and Martha C. Cooper, "The Relationship between Supply Chain Management and Keiretsu," *The International Journal of Logistics Management* 4, no. 1 (1993), pp. 1–12.

- District trucks, which can carry loads anywhere, but whose routes must originate and terminate within a designated district and can carry goods only for a single shipper.
- Route trucks, which can carry loads along their licensed route for multiple shippers.

2. *Logistics heartland.* The main area for production in Japan is the triangle bound by the cities of Tokyo, Nagoya, and Osaka on the island of Honshu. It is about 500 kilometers from Tokyo to Osaka. The triangle includes the metropolitan area around Tokyo known as Kanto (including Yokohama and Kawasaki) and that around Osaka known as Kansai (including Kobe and Kyoto).

3. *Traffic congestion.* Traffic congestion on roads and highways is a critical problem in the triangle, especially in and around the major cities where traffic speed averages less than 15 kilometers per hour. For this reason, just-in-time systems require many small facilities or substantial fleets of small vehicles to meet customer requirements quickly, reliably, and economically.

4. *Distribution systems.* Distribution systems for varying products are usually diverse because of traditional differences in trade practices and channels of distribution.

5. *Distribution channels.* Nontraditional distribution channels, especially nonstore channels, are booming. They often represent the best way to introduce new products into the Japanese market. These channels include mail order, catalog sales, door-to-door sales, teleshopping, and vending machines.

6. *Shared distribution.* Shared distribution is common. Competitors delivering to the same stores share delivery facilities and trucks.

7. *Palletization.* Large companies tend to use ISO standard pallet sizes. These are not mandatory, and a proliferation of different pallet sizes complicates logistics operations significantly.

8. *Warehousing.* Business warehouses are supervised by the Ministry of Transport and regional Transport Bureaus. These distinguish between private, agricultural, cooperative, and public warehouses. Public warehouses are further classified into general-purpose, cold storage, open-air, storage tanks, floating storage (e.g., for logs), and dangerous goods warehouses. These are treated differently by the Ministry of Transport, which issues them permits.

Logistics practices in the rest of the Pacific Rim of Asia present significant national differences, although many countries in the region look to Japanese practices as a model.

Summary

More companies are expanding their operations into the international sector. As firms locate and service markets in various countries, they must establish logistics systems to provide the products and services that customers demand. While the components of a global logistics system may be similar to those in a domestic system, the management and administration of the international network can be vastly different.

To be a global company, management must be able to coordinate a complex set of activities—marketing, production, financing, procurement—so that least total cost logistics is realized. This will allow a firm to achieve maximum market impact and competitive advantage in its international target markets.

In this chapter, we examined some of the reasons firms expand into global markets. Companies that do so can become involved in exporting, licensing, joint ventures, direct ownership, importing, or countertrade. As part of the exporting process, we described the specific roles of the export distributor, customshouse broker, international freight forwarder, and trading company. In addition, we looked at the importance of documentation and the use of free trade zones.

The international logistics manager must administer the various logistics components in a marketplace characterized by a number of uncontrollable elements: political and legal, economic, competitive, technological, geographical, and social and cultural. Within the uncontrollable environment the manager attempts to optimize the firm's cost-service mix. A number of differences exist between countries in administering logistics activities.

Creative Solutions

Xerox's European Logistics Success

In Europe, Xerox meets its customers' needs for new product, suppliers, and maintenance through a central distribution center in Venray, the Netherlands. (Interestingly, the company's sophisticated logistics modeling analysis had located the theoretically best site for its European logistics operations only 20 miles from this existing facility.) Including older machines, Xerox estimates it must maintain a 100,000-item catalog to meet customer-support requirements. The company uses air transport for priority shipments. To meet the needs of a more unified Europe, Xerox has entered into long-term alliances with surface carriers that transport copiers and replacement parts. These contracts include provisions for a common tracking system for inventory management. Xerox estimates that 80 percent of all repairs and parts deliveries can be performed within one day, 98 percent by the second day, and 100 percent by the third day. The company's goal is to improve its performance to 98 percent within one day.

Xerox sees its European logistics systems as a model for those in the United States and, eventually, in all its markets around the globe. The company aims to establish a new manufacturing plant near its Venray distribution center. Its benchmarking approach focuses on qualitative measurements of logistics and overall corporate performance, including responsiveness to customers, profitability, and return on assets. Plans call for establishing a build-to-order/direct delivery system for manufacturing and transportation, and linking this electronically with Xerox management, suppliers, shippers, and customers. The company estimates that its progress toward this goal has reduced its inventory as a percent of revenue from 25 percent to 14 percent.

As a large and complex multinational firm, Xerox has shown the value of combining integrated logistics, advanced information technology, and customer-responsive management to prosper in a fast-changing global marketplace. The company appears well positioned to meet the challenges of a unified Europe.

Source: William W. Goldsborough and David L. Anderson, "The International Logistics Environment," in *The Logistics Handbook*, ed. James F. Robeson and William C. Copacino (New York: Free Press, 1994), p. 667.

We examined the financial aspects of global logistics. Since logistics management is concerned with the costs of supplying a given level of service to foreign customers, it is important to recognize the factors that influence the costs of carrying out the process.

Some global market opportunities for companies in various regions of the world—Western Europe, the former Soviet Union and Eastern Europe, and the Pacific Rim—were identified and described. In addition to identifying some of the opportunities within each of those regions, we presented the many challenges or disadvantages facing firms attempting to penetrate those markets. Finally, maquiladora operations were examined, with emphasis given to the logistics implications of U.S. firms locating assembly and manufacturing facilities in Mexico.

With the first 10 chapters as background, we are now ready to develop an overview of a firm's organizational structures in logistics. This is the topic of Chapter 12.

Suggested Readings

Anderson, David L., and Dennis Colard. "The International Logistics Environment." In *The Logistics Handbook.* James F. Robeson and William C. Copacino, eds. New York: Free Press, 1994.

Augustin, Siegfried; Peter G. Klaus; Ernst W. Krog; and Ulrich Mueller-Steinfahrt. "The Evolution of Logistics in Large Industrial Organizations in Europe." *Proceedings of the Annual Conference of the Council of Logistics Management,* Oct. 20–23, 1996, pp. 535–53.

Aurik, Jonan C., and Jan Van De Dord. "New Priorities in Logistics Services in Europe." *Transportation and Distribution* 35, no. 2 (Feb. 1995), pp. 43–48.

Bender, Paul S. "International Logistics." In *The Distribution Management Handbook.* James A. Tompkins and Dale Harmelink, eds. New York: McGraw-Hill, 1994.

Bovet, D. "Logistics Strategies for Europe in the '90s." *Planning Review* 19, no. 4 (July–Aug. 1991), pp. 12–18.

Copacino, William C., and Frank F. Britt. "Perspectives on Global Logistics." *The International Journal of Logistics Management* 2, no. 1 (1991), pp. 35–41.

Damas, Philip. "Shippers' Unfulfilled Dreams." *American Shipper* 38, no. 11 (Nov. 1996), pp. 37–46.

Dempsey, William, and Richard A. Lancioni. "How to Improve Your International Customer Service." *Management Decision* 28, no. 3 (1990), pp. 35–38.

Dittmann, Paul. "Planning for Logistics in a Global Corporation." *Proceedings of the Annual Conference of the Council of Logistics Management,* Oct. 20–23, 1996, pp. 589–95.

Fawcett, Stanley E., and Laura M. Birou. "Exploring the Logistics Interface between Global and JIT Sourcing." *International Journal of Physical Distribution and Logistics Management* 22, no. 1 (1992), pp. 3–14.

Fernie, John. "Quick Response: An International Perspective." *International Journal of Physical Distribution and Logistics Management* 24, no. 6 (1994), pp. 38–46.

Garreau, Alain; Robert Lieb; and Robert Millen. "JIT and Corporate Transport: An International Comparison." *International Journal of Physical Distribution and Logistics Management* 21, no. 1 (1991), pp. 42–47.

Gilmore, James H. "Designing a Distribution Strategy for Canada." *CCA White Paper.* Cleveland, OH: Cleveland Consulting Associates, n.d.

Goldsborough, William W., and David L. Anderson. "Import/Export Management," In *The Logistics Handbook.* James F. Robeson and William C. Copacino, eds. New York: Free Press, 1994.

Louter, Pieter J.; Cok Ouwerkerk; and Ben A. Bakker. "An Inquiry into Successful Exporting." *European Journal of Marketing* 25, no. 6 (1991), pp. 7–23.

MacDonald, Mitchell E. "Who Does What in International Shipping." *Traffic Management* 30, no. 9 (Sept. 1991), pp. 38–40.

McKeon, Joseph E. "Outsourcing Begins In-House." *Transportation and Distribution* 32, no. 9 (Sept. 1991), pp. 24–28.

Min, Hokey, and Sean B. Eom. "An Integrated Decision Support System for Global Logistics." *International Journal of Physical Distribution and Materials Management* 24, no. 1 (1994), pp. 29–39.

Mottley, Robert. "Troika of Third Parties." *American Shipper* 38, no. 11 (Nov. 1996), pp. 47–52.

Rinehart, Lloyd M. "Global Logistics Partnership Negotiation." *International Journal of Physical Distribution and Logistics Management* 22, no. 1 (1992), pp. 27–34.

Roberts, John H. "Formulating and Implementing a Global Logistics Strategy." *The International Journal of Logistics Management* 1, no. 2 (1990), pp. 53–58.

Rodnikov, Andrei N. "Logistics in Command and Mixed Economies: The Russian Experience." *International Journal of Physical Distribution and Logistics Management* 24, no. 2 (1994), pp. 4–14.

Samiee, Saeed, and Kendall Roth. "The Influence of Global Marketing Standardization on Performance." *Journal of Marketing* 56, no. 2 (Apr. 1992), pp. 1–17.

U.S. Department of Commerce. *A Basic Guide to Exporting.* Washington, DC: U.S. Government Printing Office, 1986.

Van der Ven, and A. M. A. Ribbers. "International Logistics: A Diagnostic Method for the Allocation of Production and Distribution Facilities." *The International Journal of Logistics Management* 4, no. 1 (1993), pp. 67–83.

Vantine, José G., and Claudirceu Marra. "Logistics Challenges and Opportunities within MERCOSUR." *The International Journal of Logistics Management* 8, no. 1 (1997), pp. 55–66.

Waller, David G.; Robert L. D'Avanzo; and Douglas M. Lambert. *Supply Chain Directions for a New North America.* Oak Brook, IL: Council of Logistics Management, 1995.

Whitehurst, Clinton H., Jr. "Western Australia's Place in a Global Economy: A Logistics Point of View." *The Strom Thurmond Institute Working Paper,* Series #022195, Feb. 1995.

Wiggin, Peter. "Europe, All Together." *Sky Magazine* 20, no. 6 (June 1991), pp. 10–19.

Zinn, Walter, and Robert E. Groose. "Barriers to Globalization: Is Global Distribution Possible?" *The International Journal of Logistics Management* 1, no. 1 (1990), pp. 13–18.

Questions and Problems

1. An increasing number of firms are engaging in international marketing and distribution. What factors would influence a company to enter international markets?

2. Companies that enter global markets have four main channel strategies available: (*a*) exporting, (*b*) licensing, (*c*) joint ventures, and (*d*) ownership. Briefly discuss each strategy and identify the advantages and disadvantages of each.

3. Explain the role of each of the following exporting organizations in global logistics:

   • Export distributor.

   • Customshouse broker.

   • International freight forwarder.

   • Trading company.

4. Explain why it is usually more difficult for a firm to provide the same level of customer service in its international markets that it provides in its domestic markets. Under what circumstances might an organization be able to provide better customer service to international markets than to domestic markets?

5. Identify the factors that make the packaging component of the logistics process so much more important in international systems than in domestic logistics systems.

6. Discuss the relative importance of inventories in domestic and global logistics. In your response, consider the financial impact of inventory decisions on the strategic position of the firm.

7. Discuss how "letters of credit" are used in international business transactions. Why are they important?

8. Briefly identify the opportunities and challenges facing firms seeking to market products in the following regions:

   • Western Europe
   • The Commonwealth of Independent States (CIS) and Eastern Europe
   • Pacific Rim

9. What are the logistics implications of trading blocs such as NAFTA and the EU?

THE DISTRIBUTION CHALLENGE!
PROBLEM: THE BLAME GAME

Frank Havlat is a freight forwarder and customs broker with DFM International Inc. His problem is related to shipment security, for which he sees no easy solution.

Let's say that DFM is the forwarder of a shipment of high-value computer parts headed to South America via Miami. The cartons are contained in a half-dozen shrink-wrapped pallets, and the shipper's instructions are explicit: Don't break down the pallets. As a result, DFM is able to perform only a cursory inspection of the outside.

The shipment reaches Miami where an agent receives it, sees nothing wrong, and sends it on. But when the shipment gets to its destination, several of the cartons deep inside the pallets are empty. Havlat starts to worry.

The question is one of liability. Havlat may well have signed a liability release based on the shipper's instructions not to disturb the contents of the pallet, but that doesn't mean the consignee won't try to include him in a lawsuit for damages.

Havlat says that shippers often are ignorant of the basics of international moves, including what must be done to protect their shipments. For some, the first impulse is to blame the middleman.

What advice do you have for Havlat, a relatively small forwarder, that would protect him from lawsuits while helping him to ensure the security of shipments moving under his control? And when inspections are possible, how can he monitor the hundreds, if not thousands, of individual cartons that are generated by his global customers on a daily basis? "If we had to do this for every single shipment," he says, "we wouldn't move anything."

What Is Your Solution?

Source: "Distribution: The Challenge," *Distribution* 96, no. 3 (Mar. 1997), p. 86.

Chapter Objectives

- To identify how an effective logistics organization can impact a firm's efficiency and effectiveness.
- To describe various types of logistics organizational structures.
- To explore the factors that can influence the effectiveness of a logistics organization.
- To examine an approach to developing an optimal logistics organization.
- To identify attributes that can be used to measure organizational effectiveness.

Introduction

In the decade of the 1990s, quality and customer service became the focus of top management. As we enter the 21st century, speed and supply chain management are taking hold as key competitive issues. Embracing the concepts is only the first step. A firm must be able to implement the strategies, plans, and programs to deliver acceptable levels of quality and service to its customers. Logistics and the people that are part of the logistics function play vital roles in that process.

The State of Quality in Logistics

A study by Cleveland Consulting Associates highlighted the importance of quality programs in over 200 U.S. and European businesses. *The State of Quality in Logistics* identified several barriers to instituting a high-quality program. Interestingly, the top six barriers identified were related to employees or organizational issues. In order of importance, they included:

- Changing the corporate culture.
- Establishing a common vision throughout the organization.
- Establishing employee ownership of the quality process.
- Gaining senior executive (top-down) commitment.
- Changing management processes.
- Training and educating employees.[1]

The roles of individual employees and logistics departments are especially important in strategic logistics management, and each will be explored in this chapter.

Logistics executives have seen their discipline develop over the past 30 years from infancy, when the logistics functions were dispersed throughout the organization, to a highly structured, computerized, and large-budget activity. The role of the logistics executive is far different today from what it was 30 years ago and probably quite different from what it will be 30 years hence. The next decade promises unprecedented challenges. Box 12–1 discusses the changing role of women in the logistics profession.

Environmental Factors Impacting Logistics

The logistics executive has been affected by a multitude of factors, including economic uncertainty, inflation, product and energy shortages, environmentalism, green marketing, regulatory constraints, and rising customer demands and expectations. The logistics activity is becoming increasingly more difficult to manage. In this chapter, we will examine the issues of how to organize logistics within the firm and how to measure its effectiveness. We will see how important an effective logistics organization is to firms, and the types of organizational structures that exist. Although no single "ideal" structure is appropriate for all companies, we will see how to evaluate various organizational structures and describe the approaches that can be used to develop an effective logistics organization.

---

[1]William R. Read and Mark S. Miller, *The State of Quality in Logistics* (Cleveland, OH: Cleveland Consulting Associates, 1991), pp. 12–13.

Box 12–1

No Longer in the Shadows

In 1997, *Working Women* magazine identified logistics as the 14th hottest career for women. Traditionally, men have dominated the logistics discipline, and while men still outnumber women in the profession, the gap is narrowing.

As an indicator of the growing importance of women in logistics, various professional logistics associations have evidenced an increase in the number of women members. For example, the memberships of the Warehousing Education and Research Council (WERC) and the Council of Logistics Management (CLM) are comprised of approximately 10 percent women; that number is growing.

"The corporate mind-set is replacing brawn with brains. This awakening affords women opportunities in a field that reaches beyond trucks and warehouses into such disciplines as marketing, sales, production, finance and MIS [management information systems]. Not only is the widening of the field attracting women, so are the salaries . . . Top logisticians can make, on average, more than $100,000 per year."

Logistics is a terrific opportunity, according to Rick Achan, vice president of operations, Menlo Logistics. "Our company, and our competitors, are recognizing that there is value, not only to our companies, but to our customers, to seek diversity in our organizations."

Source: Jodi E. Melbin, "No Longer in the Shadows," *Distribution* 96, no. 3 (Mar. 1997), pp. 34–39.

Logistics issues have become important components in the strategic planning and budgeting processes of many firms.

Importance of an Effective Logistics Organization

An effective and efficient logistics organization is a vital part of a firm's strategic management process. The problems and challenges that organizations face do not lie primarily with strategic decision making, but in systems, structure, mission, people, corporate culture, and reward structure.[2] In essence, each can be considered an important strategic resource and a long-term corporate asset. The way they interact to create a synergistic system is critical. Thus, many organizations have engaged in reengineering; that is, they are essentially "recreating" their organizations and systems rather than making minor changes.[3]

Many firms have not employed their strategic resources properly. Some argue that their lack of success may have been due to the lack of a competitive organizational design or structure. An example can be seen in IBM's PC division (see Box 12–2).

Many Firms Have Reengineered Their Logistics Processes

Examples of firms that have been successful in reengineering include Atlas Supply and Case Corporation. Atlas Supply, a distributor of automotive parts, was formed in 1992 to integrate the distribution and logistics of two merged companies. It developed a shared system that allowed them to reduce the number of distribution centers by over 50 percent. Transportation costs fell over 20 percent, including an estimated savings of more than $300,000 due to a reduction in empty backhauls. The savings resulted from pulling together a number of logistics-related activities under a single organizational unit, and utilizing third parties where it made sense to do so.[4]

Case Corporation, a manufacturer of agricultural equipment, is in a tough market and faces excess capacity and lower demand. Despite this, Case's profits are up. Why? Reengineering. Case has placed a new focus on satisfying the customer and is revamping its operations accordingly. One of the focal points is inefficient distribution. It has outsourced about half of its parts distribution operation to a third party. In 1993, the restructuring created approximately $50 million in annual savings. The cost reductions were achieved through modifications of the firm's organizational structure, customer service levels, warehousing operations, and inventory and ordering polices.[5]

Companies as diverse as Abbott Laboratories, Eastman Kodak, Karolinska Hospital of Sweden (see the Global box), Maremont Corporation, Mead Johnson and Company, Rohm and Haas, and Uniroyal have undergone similar changes and achieved much the same results as Atlas Supply and Case Corporation.

In traditional organizations, logistics functions were scattered throughout the firm, with no single executive, department, or division responsible for managing the entire distribution process. This type of situation is depicted in Figure 12–1.

---

[2]Tom Peters, *Tom Peters Live* (Boulder, CO: Career Track Publications, 1991).

[3]See Michael Hammer and James Champy, *Reengineering the Corporation: A Manifesto for Business Revolution* (New York: Harper Business, 1993); and James Champy, *Reengineering Management: The Mandate for New Leadership* (New York: Harper Business, 1995).

[4]Helen Richardson and Tom Andel, "Celebrate Best Practices," *Transportation and Distribution* 35, no. 10 (Oct. 1994), p. 28.

[5]Ibid., p. 30.

Box 12–2

IBM: Reorganizing to Regain Competitive Advantage

IBM presents an example of a company that did not employ its strategic resources properly. Once the leader in all types of computing, its sluggish personal computer (PC) division lost an estimated $1 billion in 1994. What happened? Much of the problem can be blamed on IBM's internal operating structure.

Previously, IBM had its major functions spread out physically across the United States in nine different locations. This created extremely long introduction cycles for new products—over two years at least. This is unacceptable in an industry with nine-month product life cycles!

Since 1994, IBM's PC division has made radical moves to restructure for strategic reasons. New product development processes have been revamped from the old, geographically spread-out functions to teams. These teams include personnel from procurement, logistics, research, design, and manufacturing, now colocated in Raleigh, North Carolina. This team approach led to the creation of the Butterfly subnotebook from lab to finished product in 18 months—a record for IBM, but still in need of improvement.

Previously, IBM's new product introductions were hurt because the product development group was sending designs to manufacturing past deadlines, and two-thirds complete! Under the new structure, logistics, procurement, and manufacturing work closely on product development. This ensures that once a part is selected (design engineering), the source, availability, and price are known (purchasing), as well as how long it will take to arrive (logistics), and how easy it will be to use the component (manufacturing).

The competition beat IBM by paying attention to the details of purchasing and logistics; building millions of PCs requires the coordination of hundreds of suppliers to deliver thousands of components. Yet IBM's old structure prevented it from doing this effectively.

Some other signs that IBM's new organizational structure is working include:

- Finished goods inventory is down 65 percent, yet factory delivery promises are met 80 percent of the time instead of 45 percent of the time, as in 1994.
- Procurement and distribution costs are down 50 percent.
- The PC division closed 13 European warehouses due to improved management of supplies.
- Inventory supply is 60 days instead of the 80 days it was in 1994.
- In July 1995, IBM's stock price hit $100 a share for the first time in three years [Note: by October 1997, the stock price was near $100 a share, after having split 2-for-1].

Restructuring has helped IBM tremendously. However, IBM realizes it still has a long way to go to regain its competitive advantage.

Source: Adapted from Ira Sager, "The Man Who's Rebooting IBM's PC Business," *Business Week,* July 24, 1995, pp. 68–72.

The Trend Is Toward Integrating Logistics Functions

The lack of an organizational structure that combines the activities of logistics under a single, high-level executive indicates a failure to adopt and implement the integrated logistics management concept (discussed in Chapter 1).

Since the 1960s, the trend has been toward the integration of many logistics functions under one top-ranking corporate executive. Table 12–1 lists the range of activities over which the logistics executive has had authority. In general, there has been an expansion of the logistics executive's span of control to include transportation, warehousing, inventories, order processing, packaging, materials handling, forecasting and planning, and purchasing.

Global

Organizing for the 21st Century

The Karolinska Hospital in Stockholm, Sweden, underwent a significant reorganization in which it redesigned its traditional structure around patient flow. In other words, the patient stay in the hospital was viewed as a process, with admitting, surgery, and so on being individual steps in the process.

The hospital had 47 separate departments and was highly decentralized. Customer service levels for patient care were unacceptable. For example, some patients spent 255 days between their first contact with the hospital and the time they received treatment. And treatment represented only 2 percent of the entire process.

The departments in the hospital were reduced in number and redesigned. Eleven departments were formed, and two new positions were created: nurse coordinator and medical chief. Nurse coordinators are responsible for ensuring that all operations within and between departments occur smoothly. Medical chiefs are responsible for maintaining high levels of medical expertise within each department. One of the unique results of the organizational restructuring is that doctors report to nurses on administrative matters.

The results have been significant. "Waiting times for surgery have been cut from six or eight months to three weeks. Three of 15 operating rooms have been closed, yet 3,000 more operations are performed annually, a 25 percent increase."

Source: Adapted from Rahul Jacob, "The Struggle to Create an Organization for the 21st Century," *Fortune,* Apr. 3, 1995, pp. 90–99.

Coordination of the various logistics activities is crucial to the well-being of a firm. James Alampi, president of Van Waters & Rogers, the largest U.S. chemicals distributor, noted, "Frankly, the cost of making a product is almost irrelevant. You have far more opportunity to get cost out of the supply chain than you do out of manufacturing. There's so much duplication and inefficiency."[6]

In the next section, we will examine the major organizational types of logistics found in business firms.

Types of Logistics Organizational Structures

To understand how various departments within a firm interact with one another, it is helpful to understand how business organizations have developed over the past 100 years. This will provide a background for understanding major types of interaction patterns, including functional silos, teams, and committees.[7]

---

[6]Ronald Henkoff, "Delivering the Goods," *Fortune,* Nov. 28, 1994, p. 66.

[7]This section draws heavily from Lisa M. Ellram and Laura M. Birou, *Purchasing for Bottom Line Impact* (Burr Ridge, IL: Irwin Professional Publishing, 1995), pp. 84–87.

FIGURE 12–1

Traditional approach to logistics management

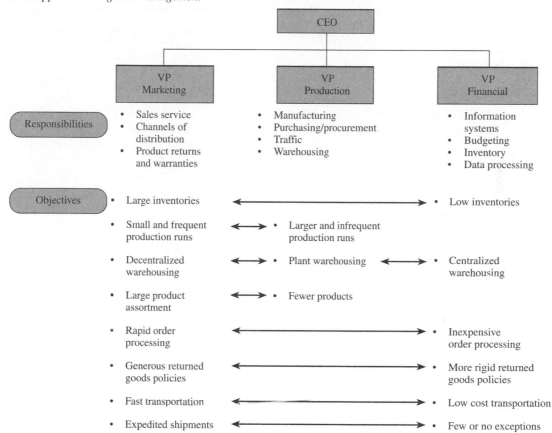

Development of Business Structures

At the time of the founding of the United States, companies tended to be "one-person" operations. Only a few people at most were needed to run the entire operation. The companies were generally small and specialized and served a local area.

Toward the middle of the 19th century, as companies began to grow, it was no longer possible for one person or a few people to manage all of the organization's operations. Companies began hiring people to specialize in working with or managing various functions, such as manufacturing, sales, distribution, and accounting. It was believed that this created efficiency and expertise.

Functional Specialization

Divisions. By the beginning of the 20th century, as companies continued to grow and diversify their product or service offerings, functional specialization by itself was no longer sufficient for effective management. Large organizations began to set up divisions organized vertically around similar product or service offerings. Employees became specialized in terms of function and product.

TABLE 12–1   **Control Exercised by the Logistics Executive over Selected Logistics Activities**

	Percent of Reporting Companies				
Activities	*1966[a]*	*1976[b]*	*1985[c]*	*1990[d]*	*1995[e]*
Transportation	89%	94%	97%	98%	95%
Warehousing	70	93	95	97	94
Inventory control	55	83	81	79	80
Order processing	43	76	67	61	59
Packaging	8	70	37	48	41
Purchasing and procurement	15	58	44	51	47
Number of reporting companies	47	180	161	216	208

Sources:

[a]John F. Spencer, "Physical Distribution Management Finds Its Level," *Handling and Shipping* 7, no. 11 (Nov. 1966), pp. 67–69.

[b]Bernard J. La Londe and James F. Robeson, "Profile of the Physical Distribution Executive," in *Proceedings of the Fourteenth Annual Conference of the National Council of Physical Distribution Management,* 1976, pp. 1–23.

[c]Data reported are for directors of logistics. From Bernard J. La Londe and Larry W. Emmelhainz, "Where Do You Fit In?" *Distribution* 8, no. 11 (Nov. 1985), p. 34.

[d]James M. Masters and Bernard J. La Londe, "The 1990 Ohio State University Survey of Career Patterns in Logistics," *Proceedings of the Annual Conference of the Council of Logistics Management* 1 (1990), pp. 33–52.

[e]James M. Masters and Bernard J. La Londe, "The 1995 Ohio State University Survey of Career Patterns in Logistics," *Proceedings of the Annual Conference of the Council of Logistics Management* (1995), pp. 195–215.

In some organizations, functions that did not directly affect the organization's product or service offering and that cut across divisional boundaries were left at a "corporate" level, supporting various divisions. This was common for human resources, accounts payable, purchasing, and treasury. There was no reporting relationship between "line" divisional employees and "staff" or corporate employees.

Matrix Organizations.   By the 1950s, some large organizations such as the Pillsbury Company realized that the divisionalized structure was not working well. It did not provide linkages between line people in various divisional and corporate positions, so that the synergies of being part of a large corporation were lost. To combat this problem, many organizations began to implement **matrix organizations.**

Matrix Management   Instead of replacing the divisional structure, a matrix structure overlays the divisional structure. In addition to divisional reporting relationships, managers in matrix organizations have reporting responsibility to another person in their function outside of the division, often at a corporate level. This structure also may be used to create reporting relationships for special projects which straddle two or more divisions.[8]

---

[8]Robert J. Kramer, *Organizing for Global Competitiveness: The Matrix Design,* Report No. 1088–94–RR (New York: The Conference Board, 1994).

Hollow Corporations.   As we approach the end of the 20th century, there has been much speculation about the prevailing form of organizations.[9] As organizations have increased their outsourcing, contracting for many activities that had been done internally, some speculate that a **"hollow corporation"** will develop.[10]

The "Hollow" Corporation

This hollow corporation, also called a **network,** will exist as a small organization of managers and "idea" people who hire external companies to perform all types of activities, including manufacturing, logistics, distribution, billing, and even sales and marketing. There are just as many experts who say that this will not happen because of loss of control, coordination issues, and a host of other concerns.

The rationale for the hollow organization is that organizations should specialize and focus on what they do best, and hire specialists to perform other activities. A variation on this concept is the **"virtual corporation,"** where a number of companies come together to develop, produce, and distribute or sell a product or service of limited scope. These organizations establish a very close working relationship which exists only as long as the product or service is viable.

Interorganizational or Interfunctional Teams.   An organization may be engaged simultaneously in a number of such relationships across a variety of products and services. These organizations focus on the product or service to be delivered to the customer, relying heavily on interorganizational and interfunctional teams. This type of organization is apparent in strategic alliances, such as the relationship between Apple Computer, IBM, and Motorola to develop a comprehensive microprocessor and operating system for future generations of computers.[11] With the evolution of various organizational forms in mind, the discussion now turns to how this affects relationships within the firm.

Functional Silos

The term **functional silos** signifies the type of organization in which each individual functional area, such as purchasing, finance, marketing, and accounting, focuses primarily on its internal operations, rather than on its obligations to the success of the corporation as a whole. While the function may have defined its goals with the overall corporate perspective in mind, it may not be sensitive to how its activities interact with the efforts of other functions within the firm in supporting overall corporate objectives.

The Difficulty of Making Cost-Service Trade-Offs with Functional Silos

To use a simple illustration, the purchasing function may have the goal of providing the organization with the lowest-priced inputs that meet specifications. The manufacturing group may be rewarded for providing high-quality products at the lowest cost per unit. The distribution/logistics group may have the goal of getting the product to the customer in a timely, cost-effective manner.

---

[9]See Ian I. Mitroff, Richard O. Mason, and Christine M. Pearson, "Radical Surgery: What Will Tomorrow's Organizations Look Like?" *Academy of Management Executive* 8, no. 2 (1994), pp. 11–21; Thomas A. Stewart, "The Search for the Organization of Tomorrow," *Fortune,* May 18, 1992, pp. 92–98; and *World Class Logistics: The Challenge of Managing Continuous Change* (Oak Brook, IL: Council of Logistics Management, 1995). This three-year study was conducted by the Global Logistics Research Team at Michigan State University.

[10]See Ellram and Birou, *Purchasing for Bottom Line Impact.*

[11]William H. Davidow and Michael S. Malone, *The Virtual Corporation* (New York: HarperCollins, 1992).

In this example, by focusing primarily on the goal of low price, purchasing chooses a supplier with a varying delivery lead time. That supplier's delivery may frequently arrive late or early. Thus, while purchasing is meeting its goal of a low price and at the same time contributing to manufacturing's cost concerns by providing low-cost materials, it is ignoring the impact of additional production setup costs on total product costs and it may inadvertently decrease customer service by creating stockouts of key products.

This may in turn create significant costs for the company as line stoppages occur, orders are expedited, and orders must be shipped to customers using expensive "overnight" methods to meet the customers' due dates. Thus, the savings accrued from using the low-price supplier may increase the company's total costs.

Therefore, while purchasing may think that the purchasing function is meeting its goals, purchasing is not really supporting the organization as a whole. By not examining the broader picture of how the purchasing function's decisions affect other functional areas and the organization's overall efficiency, higher costs may be incurred.

A functional silo mentality or culture is extremely difficult to change. Each member of a functional area tends to develop a loyalty and a commitment to his or her function, with the needs of the total organization coming second. Interactions with other functions become a zero-sum proposition. Adversarial relationships may develop among functions within the organization, as they vie for scarce resources and strive to achieve goals that may be in conflict. The advantages of specialized functions, such as focus, expertise, and scale, may be overwhelmed by myopia and poor communications.

Generic Logistics Strategies

Manufacturers, wholesaler, and retailers all perform logistics activities, but they often are organized differently. Manufacturers may use one of three organizational strategies: process-based, market-based or the channel-based strategy. Each of these approaches is described below:

Process-Based Strategies

• **Process-based strategy** is concerned with managing a broad group of logistics activities as a value-added chain. The emphasis of a process strategy is to achieve efficiency from managing purchasing, manufacturing scheduling, and physical distribution as an integrated system.

Market-Based Strategies

• **Market-based strategy** is concerned with managing a limited group of logistics activities across a multidivision business or across multiple business units. The logistics organization that follows a market-based strategy seeks (1) to make joint product shipments to customers on behalf of different business units or product groups, and (2) to facilitate sales and logistical coordination by a single order-invoice. Often the senior sales and logistics executives report to the same senior manager.

Channel-Based Strategies

• **Channel-based strategy** focuses on managing logistics activities performed jointly in combination with dealers and distributors. The channel orientation places a great deal of attention on external control.[12]

---

[12]Donald J. Bowersox et al. *Leading Edge Logistics: Competitive Positioning for the 1990s* (Oak Brook, IL: Council of Logistics Management, 1989), pp. 34–35.

Wholesalers are structured differently from manufacturers because of their position in the channel of distribution and the nature of the activities they perform. In addition to the traditional wholesaling functions such as transport and storage, wholesalers offer a number of value-added services, including light manufacturing and assembly, pricing, order processing, inventory management, logistics system design, and development of promotional materials.[13]

Retailers, because of their direct contact with final customers and the high level of competition they face, often place more emphasis on inventory, warehousing, and customer service activities than manufacturers. They tend to be more centralized than manufacturers and wholesalers. Rapid response is critical due to low margins, product substitutability at competitive retailers, and first-level contact with customers. Many retailers are requesting deliveries direct to the store from manufacturers and are purchasing many logistics services from third parties rather than performing those activities themselves.

Logistics Coordination

Coordination of the various logistics activities can be achieved in several ways. The basic systems are generally structured through a combination of the following:

1. Strategic versus operational structure.
2. Centralized versus decentralized structure.
3. Line versus staff structure.

Strategic versus Operational Organizational Structures

Strategic vs. Operational.   Strategic versus operational refers to the level at which logistics activities are positioned within the firm. Strategically, it is important to determine the position of logistics in the corporate hierarchy relative to other activities, such as marketing, manufacturing, and finance/accounting. Equally important is the operational structure of the various logistics activities—warehousing, inventory control, order processing, transportation, and other—under the senior logistics executive.

Centralized versus Decentralized Organizational Structures

Centralized vs. Decentralized.   The term *centralized distribution* can reflect a system in which logistics activities are administered at a central location, typically a corporate headquarters, or a system in which operating authority is controlled under a single department or individual. Centrally programming activities, such as order processing, traffic, or inventory control, can result in significant cost savings due to economies of scale.

On the other hand, decentralization of logistics activities can be effective for some firms. Some argue, with justification, that decentralizing logistics activities can lead to higher levels of customer service. Developments in computer technology and information systems, however, make it possible to deliver high levels of customer service with a centralized logistics activity.

Line versus Staff Organizational Structures

Line vs. Staff.   Within the three basic types of organizational structures, logistics activities can be line, staff, or some combination of both. Logistics as a line activity is comparable to

---

[13]Ibid., p. 37.

sales or production, in that employees are "doing things"; that is, performing various tasks. When this is done, one individual is made responsible for doing the distribution job.

In the staff organization, the line activities, such as order processing, traffic, and warehousing, may be housed under a logistics vice president, or under production, marketing, or finance/accounting. The various staff activities assist and coordinate the line functions. The combination of line and staff activities joins these two organizational types, thus eliminating the shortcomings inherent in systems where line and staff activities are not coordinated.

In the typical staff approach to organization, logistics finds itself primarily in an advisory role. In line organizations, logistics responsibilities are operational; that is, they deal with the management of day-to-day activities. Combinations of line and staff organizations are possible, and most companies are structured in this fashion.

Logistics as a Function

Other organizational approaches are possible.[14] Examples include logistics as a function, logistics as a program, logistics as a process, and the matrix organization approach. Figure 12–2 shows the organizational design for logistics as a *function.* An example of a company that utilizes a functional approach is the Bechtel Group, a provider of technical, management, and related services, primarily within the transportation, aerospace, power generation, and construction industries.[15]

It has been argued by some logistics experts that if a firm treats logistics as a functional area, without regard to other activities, the results will be less than optimal. Logistics is cross-functional and therefore requires a different organizational structure, not the "functional silo" approach.

Logistics as a Program

When logistics is organized as a *program* (see Figure 12–3), the distribution activity assumes the role of a program in which the total company participates. Individual functional areas are subordinate to the program.

Logistics as a Matrix Organization

It can be argued that the optimal logistics organization lies between the two extremes represented by the functional and program approaches. One approach has been termed the *matrix organization* and was explained earlier in the chapter (see Figure 12–4). Many firms utilize a matrix management approach, including Asea Brown Boveri Ltd. (European company specializing in electrical engineering and equipment), Caterpillar (earth-moving equipment), Dow Chemical, and Royal Dutch/Shell Group (petroleum, gas, and chemicals).[16]

The matrix management approach requires the coordination of activities across unit lines in the organization. Therefore, it is essential that top-level management wholeheartedly support the logistics executive. Even with high-level support, the complexities of coordination are difficult to master.

For example, any time there are multiple reporting responsibilities—common in matrix organizations—problems may arise from reporting to multiple managers who may have different goals. As a result, many organizations have adopted a team structure.

---

[14]For an examination of a variety of organizational forms, see Robert J. Kramer, *Organizing for Global Competitiveness: The Business Unit Design,* Report No. 1110–95–RR (New York: The Conference Board, 1995).

[15]Ibid., pp. 15–17.

[16]Ibid.

FIGURE 12–2

Organization design for logistics as a function

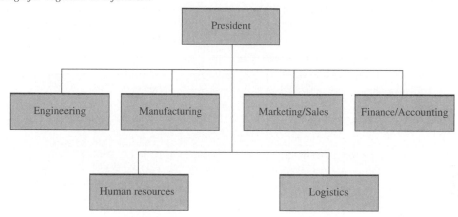

FIGURE 12–3

Organization design for logistics as a program

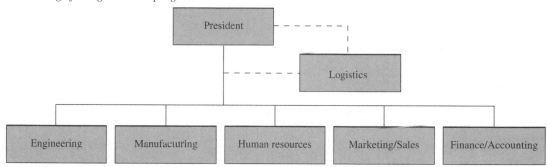

For some industries, team organizations can be very effective. High-technology firms are especially suited to organizing in a team structure because of the high incidence of task or project-oriented activities that overlap several functional areas. A team structure also supports the "flattening" of organizational layers many firms are experiencing today.[17]

A team structure involves a small group of people with complementary skills, a common goal, mutual accountability, and the resources and empowerment to achieve that goal. This differs from a work group, which is more like the traditional matrix organization, because people on the team hold themselves mutually accountable for results, rather than only individually accountable.[18] Because of the number of people involved, it is

[17]Donald J. Bowersox, Patricia J. Daugherty, Cornelia Dröge, Richard N. Germain, and Dale S. Rogers, *Logistical Excellence: It's Not Business as Usual* (Burlington, MA: Digital Equipment Corp., 1992), pp. 29–32.

[18]Jon R. Katzenback, and David K. Smith, "The Discipline of Teams," *Harvard Business Review* 71, no. 2 (Mar.–Apr. 1993), pp. 111–23.

FIGURE 12–4

Logistics in a matrix organization

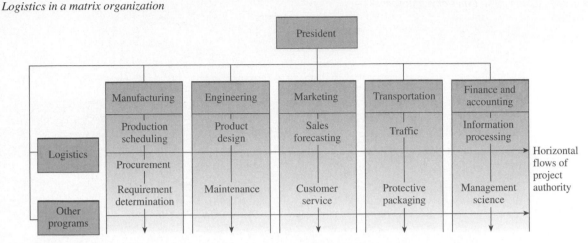

Source: Adapted from Daniel W. DeHayes, Jr., and Robert L. Taylor, "Making 'Logistics' Work in a Firm," *Business Horizons* 15, no. 3 (June 1972), p. 44.

often difficult to make decisions in matrix organizations. Thus, team structures are becoming increasingly popular.

Committees[19]

Work Groups

To counteract some of the problems of poor interfunctional communications, organizations are increasingly using work groups of which there are a wide variety in practice. The goal of a work group is to combine the skills and expertise of a number of people, generally from different functional areas, to develop a better plan, decision, or execution of some action than if each worked on the problem individually. These work groups can take on a number of forms: ad hoc committees, standing committees, task teams, and work teams. The level of time commitment and ongoing responsibility varies; ad hoc committees generally represent the lowest level while work teams represent the highest level. The differences among these various types of work groups are shown in Figure 12–5.

Ad Hoc Committees

Ad Hoc Committees.   Generally **ad hoc committees** are formed to resolve a certain, focused issue within a specified time frame. For example, a committee may be instituted to recommend improvements in the way office supplies are ordered and managed. Once the committee has made an analysis and recommendation, it will likely disband, never to exist in that form again.

Ad hoc committees vary significantly in intensity and duration, depending on the type of decision to be made and the urgency of the decision. Committee members must be dedicated to the goal they are trying to achieve or to the decision they are trying to

---

[19]This section draws heavily from Ellram and Birou, *Purchasing for Bottom Line Impact,* pp. 87–90.

FIGURE 12–5

Types of work groups

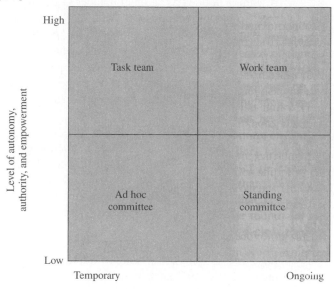

Source: Lisa M. Ellram and Laura M. Birou, *Purchasing for Bottom Line Impact* (Burr Ridge, IL: Irwin Professional Publishing, 1995), p. 87.

make. They may not need to be dedicated to the other team members or the functioning of the team, because they know it is a temporary assignment. Thus, they may not want to expend much effort on issues of group dynamics. By definition, committees are generally not all-encompassing; the employee still has other duties to maintain while serving as a member of a committee.

Standing Committees.   **Standing committees** are distinguished from ad hoc committees because their duration is indefinite. For example, there may be a committee in charge of carrier certification. As long as the organization continues to certify carriers, that committee will exist.

Because these are ongoing committees, their structure and functioning tends to take on more importance than that of ad hoc committees. Southern Pacific Lines uses a "standing committee" approach to commodity management. A committee is established for commodities that require a high level of attention, and includes representatives from all departments with a vested interest in that commodity. The committee establishes and executes the commodity management plan, which is reviewed, approved, and monitored by a steering committee of top management.[20]

---

[20]Roger Berndt, "Commodity Team Management: A Cross-Functional Approach to Procurement," *Annual Conference Proceedings,* National Association of Purchasing Management (Tempe, AZ: NAPM, 1993), pp. 45–49.

Teams

A team is defined as "a small number of people with complementary skills who are committed to a common purpose, set of performance goals and approach for which they hold themselves mutually accountable."[21] A key difference between teams and committees relates to their accountability and the manner in which they actually perform work, as expanded on below. A distinction is made between task teams and work teams. Task teams exist for a specific, identifiable purpose with a clear end, whereas **work teams** are ongoing in nature, much like a divisional structure, with specific, continuing goals.

Task Teams

Task Teams.   While both task teams and ad hoc committees focus on a discrete task, they function differently. The key distinction between a task team and an ad hoc committee is that the members of an ad hoc committee still function primarily as individuals rather than as a team. Ad hoc committees may meet to decide what has to be done, but each person individually completes his or her "piece" and is accountable for the results. In a task team, there is mutual accountability, and much of the work may even be performed with other teams' members.

Another important distinction is that the task team "owns" the project it is working on. For example, a task team to implement carrier certification would be fully empowered to design and implement the program without further approvals. An ad hoc committee would require approval from parties outside the team, generally top management, before proceeding with each step. Thus, a task team has a much higher level of task and group responsibility than an ad hoc committee.

Work Teams

Work Teams.   Returning to the definition of teams above, work teams, also known as **self-directed teams,** are distinguished from other types of organizations by their commitment to a common purpose and goals, but more importantly by their ongoing mutual accountability to achieve those goals. These cross-functional groups are often organized around a product or a service, and may be responsible for all aspects of that product or service from design and development to customer support.

The work team framework is unique in that it is not a temporary structure that overlays another organizational form. In practice, the work team is relatively rare. Its use represents a major change for most organizations. A key question is whether joint performance and extensive cross-functional interaction and participation will yield significantly better results than a more traditional approach. Only if the answer is yes should an organization implement work teams. Otherwise, committees may suffice.

One firm that has implemented a work team approach (empowered people on empowered teams) is Chrysler in its model platform teams. Each team is responsible for the design, development, logistics, engineering, and purchasing aspects of a new model, such as the Neon.[22]

---

[21]Katzenbach and Smith, "The Discipline of Teams," pp. 111–20.

[22]Thomas T. Stallkamp, "Beyond Reengineering: Developing the Extended Enterprise," *NAPM Insights,* Feb. 1995, p. 76.

Work groups, teams, and committees have become more important in the planning, implementing, and control of corporate strategies and programs. At Compaq Computer, an impromptu work group meeting often occurs right on the assembly floor.

Empowered teams should not be confused with consensus management. Team members are empowered to commit for the team on many business issues. Consensus is used for systemic issues and problem resolution. The Japanese quality circles are based more on consensus decision making.

Using Teams and Committees

Organizations are not limited to the use of one type of team or committee at a time. The organizational structure used should fit both the activity to be performed and the culture of the organization. Because the team structure is a new idea, organizations may evolve toward it slowly, using committees first, then task teams, before evolving to work teams. Conversely, an organization may decide that work teams would be of little benefit to its performance.

Because most people are educated and employed in environments where individual results and accountabilities are paramount, use of teams and committees can be threatening and even dysfunctional. To combat potential problems, most organizations train employees to function as a contributing group or team member. Training may include topics such as appreciating diversity and individual differences, team interaction, and team accountability.[23] It could involve team-building exercises or activities outside the workplace. Other issues that must be addressed in developing teams and committees are accountability, degree of responsibility and decision-making authority, and the impact of team/committee performance on individual performance appraisals.[24]

---

[23]See Lisa Harrington, "Why Managing Diversity Is So Important," *Distribution* 92, no. 11 (Nov. 1993), pp. 88–92.

[24]See Susan Caminiti, "What Team Leaders Need to Know," *Fortune,* Feb. 20, 1995, pp. 93–100.

Interfunctional Coordination Is a Key to Success

Regardless of the formal structures chosen, interfunctional relationships remain a key component of the logistics job. Good working relationships with other functions are critical to a logistics manager's effectiveness. Companies that revamp their logistics systems by decentralizing authority and implementing self-directed teams may have difficulty. The reason is that "in an age of delegation and empowerment, logistics demands centralized control."[25] Thus, logistics is often a "matrixed" team member, retaining dual reporting to both the team and a centralized logistics function, where efficient and effective strategies can be leveraged on a companywide scale.

A review of the multitude of organizational types found in companies reveals a variety of structural forms. Firms can be successful utilizing one or more organizational structures. However, the form that is best for any given company is a difficult question to answer. Instead of examining organizational structures of several companies and speculating about "ideal" organizations, we need to employ some empirical measures to correlate organizational structure and efficiency-productivity. The logistics executive must not only determine the firm's organizational structure, but evaluate its performance or effectiveness.

Decision-Making Strategies in Organizing for Logistics

In the face of higher costs of operation and increasing pressures from customers for better service, the logistics organization must adapt to meet the challenge. An understanding of the factors that make organizations effective, and a knowledge of how these factors interrelate, are the first steps toward developing the optimal system for a firm's customers.

Mission Statements

Like individuals, an organization can and should establish a mission statement to define its overall purpose for existence.

Personal Mission Statements

Personal Mission Statement. A personal mission statement sets a person's overall guidelines for living. An organization is simply a group of individuals. It cannot be more focused or effective than the individuals that make up the organization. As a result of this realization, many individuals are trying to discover their true "missions"—what they want out of work. Many are being supported in their efforts by their employers.

Organizations such as Aetna, AT&T, the U.S. Department of Energy, Hoechst Celanese, Intel, PepsiCo, and Saturn are integrating courses on introspection and personal mission clarification into their management development training. Organizations are encouraging self-mastery and personal fulfillment.[26] The reasons are not entirely selfless.

---

[25]Henkoff, "Delivering the Goods," p. 70.

[26]Stratford Sherman, "Leaders Learn to Heed the Voice Within," *Fortune,* Aug. 22, 1994, pp. 92–100; and Timothy K. Smith, "What's So Effective about Stephen Covey?" *Fortune,* Dec. 12, 1994, pp. 116–26.

How can an organization successfully empower employees who feel powerless and not in command of their own lives?

Some of the key messages stressed are the need for continuous learning, a growth in self-confidence and personal responsibility, and a tolerance for ambiguity and change.[27] These beliefs should work together to create a balance in life—as expressed in a personal mission statement. The ability to reflect and relax is becoming even more important as many people feel more pressure and conflict between inner needs/personal life, and increasingly demanding job requirements.[28]

Logistics Mission Statements

The Logistics Mission Statement.[29] On an organizational level, mission statements provide a foundation upon which a company develops strategies, plans, and tactics. The mission statement defines the basic purpose of an organization and identifies the parameters under which the firm will operate.

As corporate mission statements serve to provide the starting point for development corporate goals and objectives, so too will **logistics mission statements** provide direction for developing business strategies.

> Logistics has the potential to become the next governing element of strategy as an inventive way of creating value for customers, an immediate source of savings, an important discipline on marketing, and a critical extension of product flexibility.[30]

The components of a corporate mission statement or a logistics mission statement will be similar.[31] They will vary in their specific content because the logistics mission statement is only one element of a firm's total corporate mission, but both will contain similar components. Typically, mission statements will contain eight key components:[32]

Components of a Mission Statement

1. *Targeted customers and markets.* Who are the firm's customers? The selection of target markets and the development of marketing strategies to research those segments are vital components of a firm's activities. The following is illustrative of mission statements including such material:

> To deliver quality products to our customers and manufacturing groups in the fastest and most cost-effective mode possible. [Hospital supply company]

---

[27]Sherman, "Leaders Learn to Heed the Voice Within," pp. 96–100.

[28]See also Peter Senge, *The Fifth Discipline* (New York: Doubleday, 1990); and Stephen R. Covey, *The Seven Habits of Highly Effective People* (New York: Simon and Schuster, 1989).

[29]This material is based on James R. Stock and Cornelia Dröge, "Logistics Mission Statements: An Appraisal," *Proceedings of the Nineteenth Annual Transportation and Logistics Educators Conference,* ed. James M. Masters and Cynthia L. Coykendale (Columbus: The Ohio State University, 1990), pp. 79–91.

[30]Joseph B. Fuller, James O'Conor, and Richard Rawlinson, "Tailored Logistics: The Next Advantage," *Harvard Business Review* 72, no. 3 (May–June 1993), pp. 87–98.

[31]See Bowersox et al., *Logistical Excellence,* pp. 45–48, for a discussion of logistics mission statements.

[32]John A. Pearce II and Fred David, "Corporate Mission Statements: The Bottom Line," *Academy of Management Executive* 1, no. 2 (1987), p. 109; and Stock and Dröge, "Logistics Mission Statements," pp. 82–84.

2. *Principal products and services.* What products or services does the firm produce? Most firms mention these in the logistics mission statement. An example is:

> [To] provide timely and effective services for the storage and commercial movement of all company finished products and of materials and supplies necessary for company operations. [Tobacco company]

3. *Geographic domain.* Where are the firm's markets located. Few firms refer to competitive markets in their logistics mission statements.

4. *Core technologies.* What technologies does the firm utilize? Few firms include core technologies in their logistics mission statements, which perhaps can be attributed to the distinction between manufacturing technologies and logistics technologies.

5. *Survival, growth, and profitability.* Corporate mission statements almost universally include the issues of survival, growth, and profitability. An example is:

> [To] provide timely, cost-effective shipment and delivery; to enhance our position . . . and to provide career growth for our employees. [Metal products manufacturer]

6. *Company philosophy.* What are the basic priorities to the firm? Logistics mission statements seldom include overall company or logistics philosophy. When logistics mission statements do mention philosophy, they include the notion that logistics can create competitive advantage for the firm:

> Logistics will be active in the integration and differentiation strategies that produce competitive advantage. [Lighting manufacturer]

7. *Company self-concept.* What are the firm's strengths and weaknesses relative to its competitors? When firms include such statements, they are often stated as follows:

> [To] provide our customers the quality product they need when they desire it so that our service is better than our competitors. [Optical manufacturer]

8. *Desired public image.* What is the firm's social responsibility and what image does it wish to project? Most logistics mission statements include the firm's desired public image, if only generally stated. For example:

> To promote the firm's image, physical distribution is committed to excellence. [Pharmaceutical firm]

Firms Need a Clear Statement of Purpose   Firms need a clear statement of purpose in order to develop the best combination of activities that must be performed in the day-to-day operations of the enterprise. In sum, the logistics mission statement is an important document to guide the planning, implementation, and control of a firm's logistics activities.

Components of an Optimal Logistics Organization

Many factors can influence the effectiveness of a logistics organization. In general, the factors contributing to organizational effectiveness can be summarized as (1) organizational characteristics, (2) environment characteristics, (3) employee characteristics, and (4) managerial policies and practices.[33]

---

[33]See Kim S. Cameron and David A. Whetten, eds., *Organizational Effectiveness: A Comparison of Multiple Models* (New York: Academic Press, 1983); and Richard M. Steers, *Organizational Effectiveness: A Behavioral View* (Santa Monica, CA: Goodyear, 1977).

Structure and Technology Are the Most Important

Organizational Characteristics.   Structure and technology are the major components of a firm's organizational characteristics. *Structure* refers to the relationships that exist between various functional areas: interfunctional (marketing, finance, operations, manufacturing, logistics) or intrafunctional (warehousing, traffic, purchasing, customer service). The relationships are frequently represented by a company's organization chart. Examples of structural variables are decentralization, specialization, formalization, span of control, organization size, and work-unit size.

Technology "refers to the mechanisms used by an organization to transform raw inputs into finished outputs. Technology can take several forms, including variations in the materials used, and variations in the technical knowledge brought to bear on goal-directed activities."[34]

Organizational Climate/Corporate Culture

Environmental Characteristics.   The effectiveness of the organization is influenced by factors internal and external to the firm. Internal factors, which are more or less controllable by the logistics executive, are known as **organizational climate.**[35] Sometimes, this is referred to as **corporate culture.**

External factors, sometimes referred to as uncontrollable elements, include the political and legal, economic, cultural and social, and competitive environments.

Employee Characteristics.   The keys to effective organizations are the employees who "fill the boxes" on the organization chart. The ability of individuals to carry out their respective job responsibilities ultimately determines the overall effectiveness of any organization.

All employees possess different outlooks, goals, needs, and abilities. These human variations often cause people to behave differently, even when placed in the same work environment. Moreover, individual differences can have a direct bearing on two important organizational processes that can have a marked impact on effectiveness. These are **organizational attachment,** or the extent to which employees identify with their employer, and individual **job performance.** Without attachment and performance, organizational effectiveness becomes all but impossible.[36]

Organizational Attachment and Job Performance

Managerial Policies and Practices.   Policies at the macro (entire company) level determine the overall goal structure of the firm. Policies at the micro (departmental) level influence the individual goals of the various corporate functions, such as warehousing, traffic, order processing, and customer service. Macro and micro policies in turn affect the procedures and practices of the organization . The planning, coordinating, and facilitating of goal-directed activities—which determine organizational effectiveness—depend on the policies and practices adopted by the firm at the macro and micro levels.

---

[34]Steers, *Organizational Effectiveness,* pp. 7–8.

[35]F. T. Sepic, "Culture, Climate, and Total Quality Management: Measuring Readiness for Change," *Public Productivity & Management Review* 18, no. 4 (Summer 1995), pp. 369–80; B. Schneider, "Creating the Climate and Culture of Success," *Organizational Dynamics* 23, no. 1 (Summer 1994), pp. 17–24; and A. H. Church, "Managerial Behaviors and Work Group Climate as Predictors of Employee Outcomes," *Human Resource Development Quarterly* 6, no. 2 (Summer 1995), pp. 173–82.

[36]See Garry D. Brewer, "Assessing Outcomes and Effects," in *Organizational Effectiveness: A Comparison of Multiple Models,* Kim S. Cameron and David A. Whetten, eds. (New York: Academic Press, 1983), pp. 207–14; and Steers, *Organizational Effectiveness,* p. 9.

A number of factors can aid the logistics executive in improving the effectiveness of the organization. Six of the most important factors that have been identified are:

Ways of Improving Logistics Organizational Effectiveness

1. Strategic goal setting.
2. Resource acquisition and utilization.
3. Performance environment.
4. Communication process.
5. Leadership and decision making.
6. Organizational adaptation and innovation.[37]

Strategic Goal Setting

Strategic Goal Setting.   Strategic goal setting involves the establishment of two clearly defined sets of goals: the overall organization goal or goals and individual employee goals. Both sets must be compatible and aimed at maximizing company-employee effectiveness. For example, the company may have an overall goal to reduce order cycle time by 10 percent, but the actions of each employee attempting to improve his or her component of the order cycle are what brings about achievement of that goal.

Resource Acquisition and Utilization

Resource Acquisition and Utilization.   Resource acquisition and utilization includes the use of human and financial resources, as well as technology, to maximize the achievement of corporate goals and objectives. For example, this involves having properly trained and experienced persons operating the firm's private truck fleet, using the proper storage and retrieval systems for the company's warehouses, and having the capital necessary to take advantage of forward buying opportunities, massing of inventories, and other capital projects.

Performance Environment

Performance Environment.   The performance environment is concerned with having the proper organizational climate to motivate employees to maximize their effectiveness and, subsequently, the effectiveness of the overall logistics function. Strategies that can be utilized to develop a goal-directed performance environment include (1) proper employee selection and placement, (2) training and development programs,[38] (3) task design, and (4) performance evaluation, combined with a reward structure that promotes goal-oriented behavior.[39]

Many dysfunctional behaviors are caused by myopic reward structures. For example, IBM's policy of giving bonuses to engineers whose products got favorable reviews in technical magazines was delaying new product introduction and increasing costs because engineers added "special features" to catch the media's attention.[40]

Communication Process

Communication Process.   One of the most important factors influencing logistic effectiveness in any organization is the communication process. Without good communica-

---

[37]Ibid., p. 136.

[38]See *Competency Based Development: Giving People the Wisdom to be Effective,* Monograph No. M0024 (Raleigh, NC: Tompkins Associates, 1995).

[39]Steers, *Organizational Effectiveness,* p. 142.

[40]Sager, "The Man Who's Rebooting IBM's Business," p. 70.

tion, logistics policies and procedures cannot be effectively transmitted throughout the firm, and the feedback of information concerning the success or failure of those policies and procedures cannot take place. Communication flows within the logistics area can be downward (boss-employee), upward (employee-boss), or horizontal (boss-boss or employee-employee).[41]

Leadership and Decision-Making Expertise

Leadership and Decision Making.   Comparable to the importance of effective communication in an organization is the quality of leadership and decision-making expertise exercised by the senior logistics executive. In many companies, the logistics department or division is a mirror image of the top logistics executive. If the top executive is a highly capable and respected individual who makes thoughtful, logical, and consistent decisions, then the logistics organization that reports to him or her also is likely be highly effective. Conversely, a logistics organization led by an executive who lacks the necessary leadership and decision-making skills usually will not be as efficient.

Organizational Adaptation and Innovation

Organizational Adaptation and Innovation.   Finally, organizational adaptation and innovation is an important attribute of effective organizations. The environment that surrounds the logistics activity requires constant monitoring. As conditions change, logistics must adapt and innovate to continue to provide an optimal cost-service mix to the firm and its markets.[42] Examples of fluctuating environmental conditions include changes in transportation regulations, service requirements of customers, degree of competition in the firm's target markets, economic or financial shifts in the marketplace, and technological advances in the distribution sector. It is important that adaptation and innovation not be haphazard and unplanned.

An effective organization must exhibit stability and continuity; it must find a unique offering that it can deliver to the market and stick with it to provide customer value.[43]

An Approach to Developing an Optimal Logistics Organization[44]

Logistics organizations evolve and change; that is, there are probably a variety of good organizational designs for a firm and, over time, a company may have to modify its design to reflect environmental or corporate changes. As an executive attempts to structure

---

[41]For a summary of employee-boss communication strategies, see Helen L. Richardson, "Communicate through Listening," *Transportation and Distribution* 30, no. 8 (Aug. 1989), pp. 32–33; and J. J. Gabarro and J. P. Kotter, "Managing Your Boss," *Harvard Business Review* 71, no. 3 (May–June 1993), pp. 150–57.

[42]Les B. Artman and Robert E. Sabath, "Are YOU Ready for Change?" *American Shipper* 37, no. 2 (Feb. 1995), pp. 42–48.

[43]Micheal Treacy and Fred Wiersema, "How Market Leaders Keep Their Edge, *Fortune,* Feb. 6, 1995, pp. 88–98.

[44]Much of the material in this section has been developed and adapted from James P. Falk, "Organizing for Effective Distribution," in *Proceedings of the Eighteenth Annual Conference of the National Council of Physical Distribution Management* (Chicago: National Council of Physical Distribution Management, 1980), pp. 181–99.

a new logistics organizational unit or perhaps restructure an existing one, he or she should proceed through the following steps or stages:

Developing an Optimal Logistics Organizational Structure

1. Research corporate strategy and objectives.
2. Organize functions in a manner compatible with the corporate structure.
3. Define the functions for which the logistics executive is accountable.
4. Know his or her management style.
5. Organize for flexibility.
6. Know the available support systems.
7. Understand and plan for human resource allocation so that it complements the objectives of both the individual and organization.[45]

Corporate Objectives

Corporate Objectives.   Overall corporate strategy and objectives provide the logistics activity with long-term direction. They provide the underlying foundation and guiding light for each functional component of the firm—finance, marketing, production, and logistics. The logistics structure must support the overall corporate strategy and objectives. It is imperative that logistics executives completely understand the role their activity will play in carrying out corporate strategy. Furthermore, the logistics organizational structure must be compatible with the primary objectives of the firm.

Corporate Structure

Corporate Structure.   While the specific organizational structure of the logistics activity is affected by the overall corporate structure, logistics is increasingly being centralized.[46] In reporting relationships, logistics will typically report to the marketing group if the firm is a consumer goods company and to manufacturing/operations/administration if the firm is primarily an industrial goods producer. Logistics is often a separate organizational activity reporting directly to the CEO in firms that have a combination of consumer and industrial goods customers. This practice is growing as the strategic importance of logistics is more widely recognized.[47]

Functional Responsibilities

Functional Responsibilities.   Identifying a clear definition of the function of the logistics organization can be difficult, especially if the function has been restructured from an organizational structure having a traditional responsibility."[48] It is important to most of the logistics subfunctions housed under a single division or department. Full functional responsibility in one department allows the firm to implement the concepts of integrated logistics management and total cost trade-offs. Many of the functional responsibilities of the logistics organization are shown in Table 12–1.

An examination of more than 100 U.S. companies found that logistics typically had responsibility for outbound transportation, intracompany transportation, warehousing, inbound transportation, materials handling, and inventory management. Because these are

---

[45]Ibid., p. 195.

[46]Henkoff, "Delivering the Goods," p. 70.

[47]See Helen L. Richardson, "Get the CEO on Your Side," *Transportation and Distribution* 36, no. 9 (Sept. 1995), pp. 36–38.

[48]Falk, "Organizing for Effective Distribution," p. 188.

basic logistics functions, it is vital that these areas be administered by the senior logistics executive. Functions that are important to carrying out the logistics mission of the firm—but for which logistics often does not have responsibility—include sales forecasting and international distribution activities.[49]

Management Style

Management Style.   Almost as important as the formal structure of the organization is the **management style** of the senior logistics executive. Many firms have undergone significant changes in personnel, employee morale, and productivity as a result of a change in top management. Organizational restructuring does not necessarily have to occur. The style or personality of the senior logistics executive, and to a lesser degree his or her lower-level managers, influences the attitudes, motivation, work ethic, and productivity of employees at all levels of the organization.

Management style is one of those intangibles that can make two companies with identical organizational structures perform at significantly different levels of efficiency, productivity, and profitability. Management style is a vital ingredient to the success of a firm's logistics mission and is one of the primary reasons that many different organizational structures can be equally effective.

Flexibility

Flexibility.   Any logistics organization must be able to adapt to changes which inevitably occur. Unresponsive and unadaptable organizations typically lose their effectiveness after a period of time. While it may be difficult to anticipate future changes in the marketplace or the firm, the logistics organization must be receptive to those changes and respond to them in ways that are beneficial to the firm.

Support Systems

Support Systems.   The nature of the logistics activity makes support systems essential. The logistics organization cannot exist on its own. There must be a variety of support services as well as support specialists available to aid the logistics department or division. As we saw in Chapter 3, a good management information system (MIS) system, manual or automated, is an important facet of an effective logistics network. Other support services or systems include legal services, computer systems, administrative services, and financial/accounting services. The Technology box discusses how technology affects the way we work.

Human Resource Considerations

Human Resource Considerations.   Perhaps the most important component of an effective logistics organization is people. It is the people who ultimately determine how well the company operates. Therefore, employees' skills and abilities, pay scales, training programs, selection and retention procedures, and other employee-related policies are vital to the structuring or restructuring of a logistics organization.

Logistics managers are essential to a successful organization. Productive and efficient employees must be effectively led. Managers must possess certain important qualities or characteristics:

Qualities or Characteristics of Successful Logistics Managers

- Personal integrity and an awareness of business ethics.
- The ability to motivate.

---

[49]Bowersox et al., *Leading Edge Logistics,* pp. 74–77.

During the Annual Conference of the Council of Logistics management, practitioners, educators, and consultants discuss a broad range of logistics-related topics.

- Planning skills.
- Organization skills.
- Self-motivation.
- Managerial control.
- Effective oral communication.
- Supervisory ability.
- Problem-solving ability.
- Self-confidence.[50]

Successful organizations are those that blend the optimal combination of organizational structure, planning process, people, and style.

Organizational Structures of Successful Companies.   While there is no single best organizational form for a firm's logistics activity, benefits can be obtained by examining

---

[50]Paul R. Murphy and Richard F. Poist, "Skill Requirements of Senior-Level Logistics Executives: An Empirical Assessment," *Journal of Business Logistics* 12, no. 2 (1991), pp. 83–87; see also Jonathan L. S. Byrnes and William C. Copacino, "Develop a Powerful Learning Organization," *Transportation and Distribution,* Presidential Issue 31, no. 11 (Oct. 1990), pp. 22–25.

Technology

New Technologies Are Changing the Way We Work

To compete more effectively in today's global and fast-paced environment, intra- and interdepartmental and organizational communication and coordination are keys to survival. Technology is rapidly affecting how organizations are structured and how they can communicate and coordinate most effectively and efficiently.

One aspect of technology that will have a significant effect on how individuals and firms interrelate is "Groupware." Groupware is a software technology defined as a "computer-mediated collaboration that increases the productivity or functionality of person-to-person processes." Several categories of Groupware exist, including:

1. Electronic mail.
2. Calendaring/scheduling.
3. Group document handling.
4. Work group utilities and development tools.
5. Group decisions and meeting support.
6. Information sharing and conferencing.
7. Workflow management and business process design.

Spaulding Sports Worldwide implemented some Groupware solutions that resulted in a reduction of its product design/implementation process from one year to six months. "Spaulding implemented a document and image management system . . . to streamline the design/implementation process. 'Our initial software investment of $100,000 paid for itself overnight,' says H. Oldham Brooks in operations research. 'We were spending $85,000 a year in copying, mailing, and distributing product specifications.'"

The use of Groupware technology is not an answer to all the problems facing an organization, but it can help "find a way to improve collaboration, communication, and coordination within [an] enterprise, department, or work group."

Source: David Coleman and Ronni T. Marshak, "Changing Your Organization with Groupware," *Fortune,* special advertising supplement, Sept. 1994.

the organizational structures of successful companies. First, as a purely graphical representation, an organization chart allows a person to view how the functional areas of the firm relate and how the logistics activities are coordinated. Second, viewing several organization charts of companies in a variety of industries shows that there is no single ideal structure. Third, the commonality of the logistics activities across industry types leads to marked similarities in the various organization charts. Companies have found through experience that certain logistics functions should be structured or organized in certain ways.

Representative organizational charts from three industry groups—chemical manufacturing, consumer and industrial products manufacturing, and mass merchandising—are shown in Figures 12–6 through 12–8. Peers within their respective industries consider these companies to have good logistics organizations.

Logistics Structure at the Rohm and Haas Company

Rohm and Haas.   The Rohm and Haas Company is a manufacturer of specialty chemicals, with operations worldwide and annual sales of $4 billion. Figure 12–6 shows the logistics activity, which was reorganized in 1996 to incorporate all logistics functions under a di-

FIGURE 12–6

Rohm and Haas Company

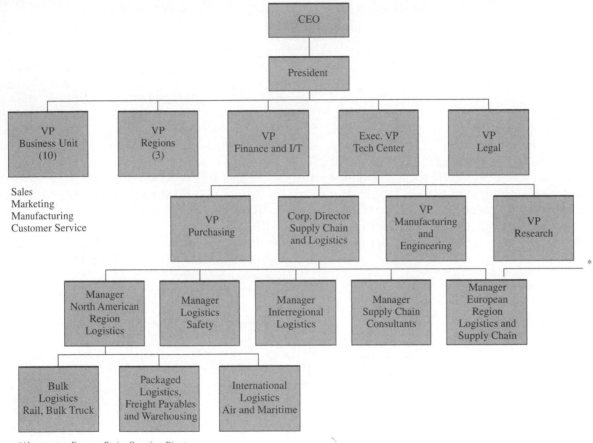

*Also reports to European Region Operations Director

Source: Rohm and Haas Company. Used with permission.

rector of supply chain and logistics. The company has 16 producing locations, 30 off-site warehouses, and 400 employees in the logistics area. With a 1997 logistics budget of $120 million, Rohm and Haas utilizes all transport modes to ship its chemical products to locations throughout the world.

Logistics Structure at the 3M Company

3M Company.   As a $14 billion manufacturer of innovative high-tech products that are produced and sold worldwide, the 3M Company utilizes the organization structure shown in Figure 12–7. With numerous divisions and products, 3M employs approximately 6,000 logistics personnel throughout the world. The company operates 8 warehouses or distribution centers in the United States and has 15 sales or order-entry locations.

Some of the functions at 3M reporting to logistics include customer service, distribution operations, transportation, supply chain management, and international logistics. Inventory control decisions are made by each warehouse. Overall inventory management decisions

FIGURE 12–7

3M Company

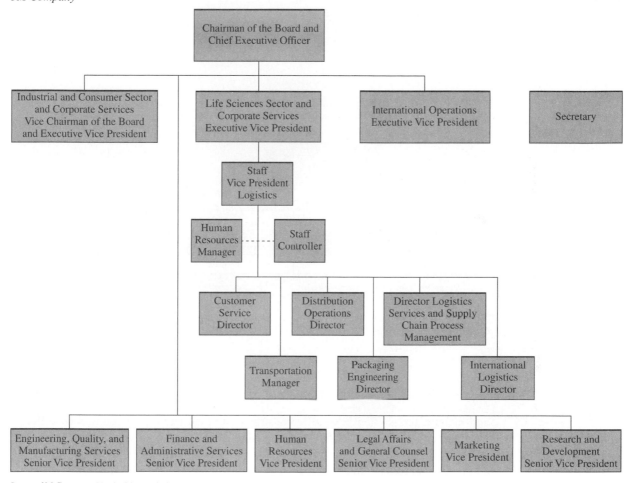

Source: 3M Company. Used with permission.

(i.e., how much product to stock where and when) are the responsibility of each product division. 3M's structure makes the firm well suited for competing in a global marketplace.

Logistics Structure at Target Stores

Target Stores.   A division of Dayton Hudson Corporation, Target Stores is an upscale discount retail store in the United States, with 752 stores located in 39 states. The company is the largest and most successful upscale discounter in the country, with 1996 sales of $17.7 billion. Target employs 8,000 logistics personnel and operates 10 regional distribution centers with a total space of more than 10.9 million square feet.

Figure 12–8 illustrates a significantly different organization chart for Target compared with those for manufacturing companies such as Rohm and Haas and 3M. Retailers

FIGURE 12–8

Target Stores Distribution

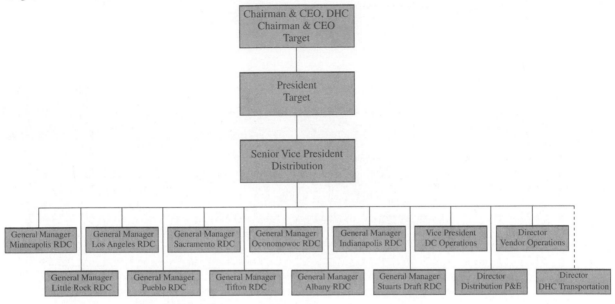

DHC = Dayton Hudson Corp.
DC = Distribution Center
RDC = Regional distribution center
P&E = Planning and Engineering

Source: Target Stores, Inc. Used with permission.

and manufacturers often have different organization structures, reflecting their different markets and customers. All of the firms illustrated here are extremely efficient in carrying out their logistics activities and in each case, the senior logistics executive is positioned at a high level in the organization.

Measuring the Effectiveness of the Logistics Organization

Organizational performance can be measured against many criteria. Box 12–3 shows one organization's approach to the measurement of individual performance effectiveness in logistics. Of course, it is not enough to merely identify the dimensions of organizational effectiveness, although this is a necessary first step.

The second step is to prioritize the various categories of effectiveness and to develop specific measuring devices to evaluate the level of effectiveness achieved by the logistics organization. It is vital that management identify the measures of organizational effectiveness it wishes to utilize, and to put them in order of priority. It is impractical in most instances to employ every effectiveness measure in the evaluation process. Time and monetary constraints impede the collection and monitoring of all the data needed for this type of evaluation.

Box 12–3

Measure It to Manage It

Employees of C. R. England, a long-haul refrigerated trucking company in Salt Lake City, Utah, have had to adapt to a structured environment. Strict centralized control is maintained by a computerized system that monitors roughly 500 procedures a week, everything from arrival times (a late shipment is anything that arrives less than 15 minutes early), to billing accuracy, to how well truckers feel they are treated by the company's repair shop. Vice president for technology Stephen Glines says: "We want to run this place like the cockpit of a jetliner, where you have hundreds of different instruments before you at all times and know exactly where you are."

Do you cringe at the idea of your annual performance review? At this family-owned company, feedback is force-fed weekly. Every trucker, manager, and back-office worker receives a grade from A to F based on computerized data linked to the individual's performance. Nothing is overlooked: from the number of minutes it takes to wash a truck, to the number of days it takes to complete a bill, to how well telephone operators treat their customers.

And how do folks out there on the open road feel about all this throttling? Says Glines: "I don't think anyone likes to be this closely monitored. But most people start using the information as a learning tool." High marks are important to C. R. England employees because the company ties

bonuses and extra vacation days to performance targets. Truckers, for instance, can earn up to $9,000 a year extra if they meet their safety and fuel-consumption goals. Surprisingly, C. R. England's employee turnover dropped when it began its strict controls—from over 100 percent a year, which is consistent with the industry, to less than 75 percent a year.

A crisis catapulted this third-generation family team into action. Says CEO Dan England, age 47: "In 1985 we were losing money. Prospects for the future did not look good." He and his family decided to pour $12 million into satellites and other computerized technology to get control of their unwieldy business. Says England: "Our view was, if we could measure it, we could manage it." Indeed. Now among the top five companies in its industry, C. R. England had revenues of $190 million last year, up from $25 million a decade ago; profit before taxes and interest was over $12 million. Says William Davidson, head of Mesa Research, a consulting firm in Redondo Beach, California: "I don't see anyone within leagues of where they are. C. R. England captures information on everything and recycles it back through the engine to improve performance."

Source: Jaclyn Fierman, "Winning Ideas from Maverick Managers," *Fortune,* Feb. 6, 1995, p. 78.

Usually, it is sufficient to examine only a portion of the available measures, because patterns or trends are often exhibited very early in the evaluation process. The selection of particular measures of logistics organizational effectiveness depends on a firm's characteristics and needs. Perhaps the most difficult process is developing the techniques or procedures needed to measure the criteria of effectiveness. In this regard, there are a number of alternatives.

Cost-to-Sales Ratios   **Cost-to-Sales Ratios.**   Businesses use **cost-to-sales ratios** extensively to evaluate organizational effectiveness. However, in isolation, these ratios are poor measures. For example, in retailing, transportation costs are often measured as a percent of sales. When buyers purchase the wrong product and big markdowns are taken, transportation is expected to reduce costs. Also, problems exist with regard to which costs to include under the logistics activity. For example: "Were net or gross sales used? What logistics functions were included in the cost total? Were management salaries included? Was inventory carrying cost included? Has there been a change in order mix or service levels?"[51] There are no simple answers to these questions. All costs that are rightfully logistics costs should be included when computing measures of cost effectiveness. If management has implemented the integrated logistics management concept, there is greater likelihood that all relevant costs will be included. Caution should be exercised when comparing these ratios across companies.

Logistics Performance Measures Must Be Evaluated against Some Standard	**Predetermined Standards.** Every measure must be evaluated against some predetermined standard. Financial measures are presented more fully in Chapter 13. Many managers believe that the firm's standards should be based on those of other firms within the same industry or of the leading firms in other industries with similar characteristics. There are many arguments in favor of this approach, but the major one is that a firm should be most concerned with its position in relation to its competition; therefore, the competition should influence the way management evaluates the firm's effectiveness. After all, customers are evaluating a firm's performance through their buying decisions.

A limitation of this approach is that each competitor has a different marketing mix and perhaps slightly different target markets. Thus, the competitive benchmark that is most valuable is "How are we doing in satisfying the customers, compared with our competitors?"

Logistics Management Personnel.   One area in which performance measurement is critical is logistics management personnel. Typically, managers are evaluated on three attributes:

How Logistics Managers Are Often Evaluated

1. *Line management ability.* This criterion considers the manager's ability to manage the department's day-to-day operations and to meet the established goals for productivity, utilization, and all aspects of performance, including budget.

2. *Problem-solving ability.* This criterion covers the ability to diagnose problems within the operation and to identify opportunities for savings, service improvement, or increased return on investment.

3. *Project management ability.* This refers to the ability to structure and manage projects designed to correct problems, improve productivity, and achieve improvement benefits.[52]

Other Measures.   Firms may employ other measures (e.g., the ability to motivate and train employees) but they are not as easily measurable.

360 Degree Evaluation

Many public and private sector firms have used an approach known as a **360 degree evaluation** to assess their managers. Decision making usually involves anonymous inputs

---

[51]A. T. Kearney, Inc., *Measuring and Improving Productivity in Physical Distribution* (Oak Brook, IL: National Council of Physical Distribution Management, 1984), pp. 307–8; see also Robert A. Novack, C. John Langley, Jr., and Lloyd M. Rinehart, *Creating Logistics Value: Themes for the Future* (Oak Brook, IL: Council of Logistics Management, 1995), pp. 116–175.

[52]Ibid., p. 305.

from the boss, workers/peers, and subordinates. While the results generated are more qualitative than quantitative, the 360 degree evaluation generates a clear picture of how the employee is perceived at all levels and identifies areas of ambiguity and conflict between participants. Once those problems are overcome, the manager becomes much more efficient and effective. Performed effectively, the bottom line is better managers.[53]

If management is to measure the firm's organizational effectiveness, it must employ a variety of factors that are measurable, and standards of performance need to be established. Finally, management should compare the firm with others in its industry. There is no single ideal organizational structure that every company should adopt. The most logical approach to organizing a firm's logistics activities is to understand the factors that contribute to effective organizational performance and to include them in the planning, implementation, and control of the organization.

Summary

What is it that makes some organizations more effective than others? Where there is no vision, the people will perish.[54] Logistics organizations with clear statements of purpose, specific and measurable objectives, strategies and plans for achieving those objectives, and a committed workforce undoubtedly will achieve higher levels of efficiency.

Logistics organizations must of necessity become more cost- and service-efficient. An understanding of the factors that affect a firm's organizational effectiveness, along with strategies to reveal weaknesses or deficiencies, can help create more efficient logistics systems. Organizational changes form the basis for procedural modifications that can reduce costs or improve service.

In this chapter, we described the importance of an effective logistics organization to a firm. Many firms have shown significant improvements in their logistics cost-service mix as a result of organizational changes. The most important ingredient in successful management is the integration of all of the logistics activities under a single individual, department, or division.

Logistics organizations are generally structured along the following lines: strategic versus operational, centralized versus decentralized, and line versus staff, in various combinations. There is no single ideal organizational structure, but there are important elements that comprise an effective organization. In general, the factors contributing to organizational effectiveness can be categorized as organizational characteristics, environmental characteristics, employee characteristics, and managerial policies and practices.

Logistics managers can use a number of approaches to measure the effectiveness of their organizations. Each approach requires management to identify the elements that impact effectiveness, and to evaluate their relative importance. Next, the elements must be measured and performance evaluated. Evaluation requires that standards of performance be established.

---

[53]Sherman, "Leaders Learn to Heed the Voice Within," p. 96.
[54]Prov. 29:18 King James Bible.

Creative Solutions

Yellow Freight Reorganizes to Improve Customer Focus and Profits

Yellow Freight System is the largest less-than-truckload (LTL) motor carrier in the United States. The company created five business units organized by geographic region, with group vice presidents who report to the company president. It also downsized by offering early retirement to 153 employees and initiating some layoffs during early 1997.

The company has three objectives in its reorganization. According to the president of Yellow Freight, "One is to get closer to customers. We're de-layering and flattening the organization . . . By forming customer focus teams, it makes it easier to do business with us. It gives accountability, responsibility, and support to those making decisions.

Second, it will improve our productivity. We're not only taking layers out, but it's allowing us to take a $3 billion profit-and-loss statement and break it into more bite-sized pieces. It will allow more customized solutions for customers.

Finally, the reorganization will allow the carrier to take better advantage of its technology."

Source: "Yellow Freight Reorganizes," *Logistics Management* 36, no. 1 (Jan. 1997), p. 27.

With this and the preceding chapters as background, the concepts and principles already learned can be applied to logistics financial management issues, which is the subject of Chapter 13.

Suggested Readings

Ayers, Allan F. "Function vs. Form: The Logistics Dilemma." *Transportation and Distribution, Presidential Issue,* 31, no. 11 (Oct. 1990), pp. 10–14.

Bartlett, Christopher A., and Sumantra Ghoshal. "Changing the Role of Top Management: Beyond Strategy to Purpose." *Harvard Business Review* 72, no. 6 (Nov.–Dec. 1994), pp. 79–88.

Bowersox, Donald J., and Cornelia Dröge. "Similarities in the Organization and Practice of Logistics Management among Manufacturers, Wholesales and Retailers." *Journal of Business Logistics* 10, no. 2 (1989), pp. 61–72.

Bowersox, Donald J.; Patricia J. Daugherty; Cornelia L. Dröge; Richard N. Germain; and Dale S. Rogers. *Logistical Excellence: It's Not Business as Usual.* Burlington, MA: Digital Press, 1992.

Carlsson, Jan, and Hans Sarv. "Mastering Logistics Change." *The International Journal of Logistics Management* 8, no. 1 (1997), pp. 45–54.

Cooke, James Aaron. "CEOs Seize Logistics Opportunities." *Traffic Management* 34, no. 3 (Mar. 1995), pp. 29–35.

Covey, Stephen R. *Principle-Centered Leadership.* New York: Simon and Schuster, 1991.

———. *The Seven Habits of Highly Effective People.* New York: Simon and Schuster, 1989.

Fishman, Shirley R., and Allon Bross. "Developing a Global Workforce." *Canadian Business Review* 23, no. 1 (Spring 1996), pp. 18–21.

Gooley, Toby B. "Logistics in the Boardroom." *Logistics Management* 35, no. 5 (May 1996), pp. 51–52.

Gunn, Thomas G. *In the Age of the Real-Time Enterprise.* Essex Junction, VT: Oliver Wight, 1994.

Henkoff, Ronald. "Delivering the Goods." *Fortune,* Nov. 28, 1994, pp. 64–78.

Jackson, Thomas L., and Constance E. Dyer. *Corporate Diagnosis: Setting the Global Standard for Excellence.* Portland, OR: Productivity Press, 1996.

Kanter, Rosabeth M.; Barry A. Stein; and Todd D. Jick. *The Challenge of Organizational Change—How Companies Experience It and Leaders Guide It.* New York: Free Press, 1992.

Mitroff, Ian I.; Richard O. Mason; and Christine M. Pearson. "Radical Surgery: What Will Tomorrow's Organizations Look Like?" *Academy of Management Executive* 8, no. 2 (1994), pp. 11–21.

Naisbitt, John, and Patricia Aburdene. *Re-inventing the Corporation.* New York: Warner Books, 1985.

Pagonis, William G. *Moving Mountains: Lessons in Leadership and Logistics from the Gulf War.* Boston: Harvard Business School Press, 1992.

Senge, Peter M. *The Fifth Discipline: The Art and Practice of the Learning Organization.* New York: Doubleday, 1990.

Sharman, Graham. "The Rediscovery of Logistics." *Harvard Business Review* 62, no. 5 (Sept.–Oct. 1984), pp. 71–79.

Stewart, Thomas A. "The Search for the Organization of Tomorrow." *Fortune,* May 18, 1992, pp. 92–98.

———. "Welcome to the Revolution." *Fortune,* Dec. 13, 1993, pp. 66–78.

Stuart, Ian. "Purchasing in an R&D Environment: Effective Teamwork in Business." *International Journal of Purchasing and Materials Management* 27, no. 4 (1991), pp. 29–34.

Totoki, Akira. "Management Style for Tomorrow's Needs." *Journal of Business Logistics* 11, no. 2 (1990), pp. 1–4.

Questions and Problems

1. Describe the relationship between a firm's organizational structure and the integrated logistics management concept.

2. Coordination of the various logistics activities can be achieved in a variety of ways. Explain each of the following within the context of logistics organizational structure.

    a. Process-based versus market-based versus channel-based strategies.

    b. Strategic versus operational.

    c. Centralized versus decentralized.

    d. Line versus staff.

3. "There is no single ideal or optimal logistics organizational structure." Do you believe this statement is accurate? Briefly present the arguments for and against such a statement.

4. How do personnel affect the degree of organizational effectiveness or productivity of a firm's logistics activity?

5. What is the major value of a personal mission statement? A logistics mission statement? A corporate mission statement?

6. What role does the communication process have in influencing logistics effectiveness? Describe several strategies that can be followed to improve communication within a firm.

7. Identify how a firm's logistics management can be evaluated on each of the following factors:

   a. Total logistics cost.

   b. Cost-specific logistics functions.

   c. Performance.

Methods to Control Logistics Performance

Chapter Outline

Chapter Objectives

- To demonstrate how to use logistics costs for decision making.
- To explain how to measure and control performance of the logistics function.
- To show how to cost justify changes in logistics structure.

Introduction

Logistics costs may exceed 25 percent of the cost of doing business at the manufacturing level. For this reason, better management of the logistics function offers the potential for large savings, which can contribute to improved corporate profitability.[1] In mature markets—in which large percentage sales increases are difficult to achieve and corporate profitability is continuously being eroded by increasing costs and competition—it is necessary to look for ways to improve productivity.

In many firms, logistics has not been managed as an integrated system. Even in firms that have accepted the concept of integrated logistics management, evidence suggests that the cost data required for successful implementation are not available.[2] The accurate measurement and control of logistics costs offers significant potential for improving cash flow and return on assets. In this chapter, we will concentrate on the financial control of logistics performance.

Importance of Accurate Cost Data

Prior to 1960, logistics was viewed as a fragmented and often uncoordinated set of activities spread throughout various organizational functions. However, many major corporations have since accepted the notion that a firm's total logistics costs can be reduced, customer service improved, and interdepartmental conflicts substantially reduced by the coordination of logistics activities. Computers, operations research techniques, and the systems approach brought high-speed processing and the logic of mathematics to the field of logistics and led not only to changes in transportation strategy, inventory control techniques, warehousing location policy, order processing systems, and logistics communication, but also to the desire to manage the costs associated with these functions in an integrated format.

Lack of Adequate Cost Data

Most of the early obstacles confronting full implementation of the concept of integrated logistics management have been overcome. The lack of adequate cost data, however, has prevented logistics management from reaching its full potential. In general, accounting has not kept pace with developments in logistics. In an attempt to solve this problem, many organizations are using **activity-based costing/activity-based management (ABC/ABM)** to analyze and manage costs.[3]

Accurate cost data are required for successful implementation of the integrated logistics management concept using total cost analysis. They also are required for the management and control of logistics operations.

---

[1]See Ron Henkoff, "Delivering the Goods," *Fortune,* Nov. 28, 1994, pp. 64–78.

[2]Douglas M. Lambert and Jay U. Sterling, "What Types of Profitability Reports Do Marketing Managers Receive?" *Industrial Marketing Management* 16, no. 4 (1987), pp. 295–303.

[3]Lisa M. Ellram et al., "Understanding the Implications of Activity-Based Costing for Logistics Management," *Proceedings of the Annual Conference of the Council of Logistics Management* (Oak Brook, IL: Council of Logistics Management, 1994), pp. 12–25.

Total Cost Analysis

The key to managing the logistics function is **total cost analysis.**[4] That is, at a given level of customer service, management should minimize total logistics costs, rather than attempt to minimize the cost of individual activities. The major shortcoming of a nonintegrative approach to logistics cost analysis is that attempts to reduce specific costs within the logistics function may be less than optimal for the system as a whole, leading to greater total costs.

Total logistics costs do not respond to cost-cutting techniques individually geared to warehouse, transportation, or inventory costs. Reductions in one cost invariably result in increases in one or more of the others. For example, aggregating all finished goods inventory into fewer distribution centers may minimize warehousing costs and increase inventory turnover, but it also may lead to increased transportation expense. Table 13–1 shows an analysis of this type of situation. Similarly, savings resulting from favorable purchase prices on large orders may be entirely offset by greater inventory carrying costs. Thus, to minimize total cost, management must understand the effect of trade-offs within the distribution function, and how various cost factors interact.

Cost Trade-Offs among Logistics Components Are Essential

Cost trade-offs among the various components of the logistics system are essential. Profit can be enhanced, for example, if the reduction in inventory carrying cost is more than the increase in the other functional costs (see Figure 13–1), or if improved customer service yields greater overall revenue. If knowledgeable trade-offs are to be made, management must be able to account for the costs of each component and to explain how changes in each cost contribute to total costs. Too often, managers are concerned only with the impact on their own functional costs or revenues.

As Logistics Costs Increase, Accurate Accounting Data Become More Critical

As the cost of logistics increases, the need for accurate accounting for the costs becomes increasingly more critical. Because the logistics function is relatively more asset- and labor-intensive than most other areas of the firm, its ratio of costs to total company costs has been increasing in many companies, although in some firms, because of TQM, JIT and other programs, logistics costs as a portion of total costs may have stabilized or actually gone down. Management cannot realize the full potential of logistics cost trade-off analysis until it can fully determine the costs related to separate functional areas and their interaction.

Types of Cost Data Needed

The quality of the accounting data influences management's ability to enter new markets, take advantage of innovative transportation systems, choose between common carriers and private trucking, increase deliveries or inventories, make changes in distribution center configuration, restructure the levels of inventories, make changes in packaging, and determine the extent of automation in the order processing system. The

---

[4]This section is adapted from Douglas M. Lambert and Howard M. Armitage, "Distribution Costs: The Challenge," *Management Accounting* 60, no. 11 (May 1979), p. 33.

TABLE 13–1   Potential Savings Due to Reduction in Number of Distribution Locations

Annual savings from reduction in number of distribution centers (operating costs)	$350,000
Savings in inventory carrying costs associated with higher turnover	$550,000
Gross savings	$900,000
Less increased expenses in transportation	
Increased distance	450,000
Premium transportation to maintain same customer service level/lead time	200,000
Total cost increase	$650,000
Net savings from DC reduction	$250,000

Note: This would still be a good decision because it results in a *net* savings of $250,000. Cost increases that result from a system change should be offset against the savings to give a true picture of the impact of the change.

FIGURE 13–1

Cost trade-offs required in marketing and logistics

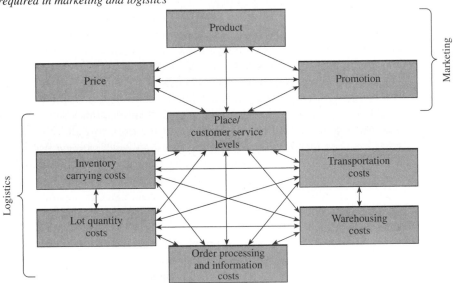

Marketing objective: Allocate resources to the marketing mix as to maximize the long-term profitability of the firm.

Logistics objective: Minimize total costs given the customer service objective where total costs = transportation costs + warehousing costs + order processsing and information costs + lot quantity costs + inventory carrying costs

Source: Adapted from Douglas M. Lambert, *The Development of an Inventory Costing Methodology: A Study of the Cost Associated with Holding Inventory* (Chicago: National Council of Physical Distribution Management, 1976), p. 7.

accounting system must be capable of providing information to answer questions such as the following:

Accounting Systems Must Provide Data to Answer Many Questions

- How do logistics costs affect contribution by product, territory, customer, and salesperson?
- What are the costs of providing additional levels of customer service? What trade-offs are necessary, and what are the incremental benefits or losses?
- What is the optimal amount of inventory? How sensitive is the inventory level to changes in warehousing patterns or customer service levels? How much does it cost to hold inventory?
- What mix of transport modes or carriers should be used?
- How many field warehouses should be used and where should they be located?
- How many production setups are required? Which plants will be used to produce each product? What are the optimum manufacturing plant capacities based on alternative product mixes and volumes?
- What product packaging alternatives should be used?
- To what extent should the order processing system be automated?
- What distribution channels should be used?

To answer these and other questions, management must know what costs and revenues will change if the logistics system changes. That is, the determination of a product's contribution should be based on how corporate revenues, expenses, and hence profitability would change if the product line were dropped. Any costs or revenues that are unaffected by this decision are irrelevant to the problem. For example, a relevant cost is the public warehouse handling charges associated with a product's sales. An irrelevant cost is the overhead associated with the firm's private trucking fleet.

Implementation of this approach to decision making is severely hampered by the nonavailability of accounting data or the inability to use the right data when they are available. The best and most sophisticated models are only as good as the accounting input. A number of studies attest to the inadequacies of logistics cost data.[5]

Controlling Logistics Activities

Performance Measurement Requires Good Accounting Data

A major reason for improving the availability of logistics cost data is to control and monitor logistics performance. Without accurate cost data, performance analysis is next to impossible. How can a firm expect to control the cost of shipping a product to a customer if it does not know what the cost should be? How can management determine if distribution center costs are high or low in the absence of performance measurements? What is "good" performance for the order processing function? Are inventory levels

---

[5]See, for example, Joseph L. Cavinato, "A Total Cost Value Model for Supply Chain Competitiveness," *Journal of Business Logistics* 13, no. 2 (1992), pp. 285–302; and Terrance L. Pohlen, *The Effect of Activity Based Costing on Logistics Management,* doctoral dissertation, The Ohio State University, 1993.

The lack of information, or its timely availability, makes it very difficult for firms to properly control their logistics activities. Many suppliers, such as Yellow Freight, provide a variety of information to their customers that allows them to make more optimal logistics decisions.

satisfactory, too high, or too low? These and similar questions illustrate the need for accurate cost data.

As the cost of logistics continues to rise, the need for management to account for the costs associated with each component becomes increasingly critical.[6] It also is necessary to know how changes in the costs of each component affect total costs and profits. Estimates of logistics costs ranging from 10 to 30 percent of total sales are not uncommon, depending on the nature of the company. At best, these are only educated guesses because they are usually based on costs incorrectly computed by management.

The Inability to Measure and Manage Logistics Costs Lead to Missed Opportunities

From a corporate standpoint, the inability to measure and manage logistics costs leads to missed opportunities and expensive mistakes. Boxes 13–1 through 13–4 provide actual case studies that highlight the problems associated with most logistics accounting systems. These are interspersed throughout the chapter as they are relevant.

---

[6]This material is adapted from Douglas M. Lambert and Howard M. Armitage, "Management Distribution Cost for Better Profit Performance," *Business* 30, no. 5 (Sept.–Oct. 1980), pp. 46–52. Reprinted by permission from *Business* magazine.

Limitations of Current Profitability Reports

Segment Profitability Reports

Full Costing

Research has shown that gross inadequacies exist in the segment profitability reports used by managers in the majority of U.S. corporations.[7] Most segment profitability reports are based on average cost allocations rather than on the direct assignment of costs at the time a transaction occurs. Period costs such as fixed plant overhead and general/administrative costs are allocated to customers and products based on direct labor hours, sales revenue, cost of sales, and other similarly arbitrary measures. Opportunity costs, to cover investments in inventories and accounts receivable, are not included.

Insufficient accounting information is a significant problem in most firms.[8] Many of the problems encountered by manufacturers result from the use of a "full costing" philosophy that allocates all indirect costs (e.g., overhead and general administrative expenses) to each product or customer group on some arbitrary basis. As a result, companies use management controls that focus on the wrong targets: direct manufacturing labor or sales volume.

Figure 13–2 shows how costs of a warehousing operation might be allocated using "full costing." Reward systems based on such controls drive behavior toward either simplistic goals that represent only a small fraction of total cost (labor) or single-minded sales efforts (volume). They ignore more effective ways to compete, such as emphasizing product quality, on-time delivery, short lead times, rapid product innovations, flexible manufacturing and distribution, and efficient deployment of scarce capital.

Unfortunately, most managers do not know the true cost of their company's products or services, how to reduce expenses most effectively, or how to allocate resources to the most profitable business segments because of the following factors:[9]

Reasons Why Companies Do Not Know Their True Costs

• Accounting systems are designed to report the aggregate effects of a firm's operations to its stockholders, creditors, and governmental agencies.

• Accounting costs are computed to provide a historical record of the company's operations. All of the firm's costs are allocated to the various business segments. Because costs common to multiple segments are allocated, the process is necessarily subjective and arbitrary.

• Accounting systems typically record marketing and logistics costs in aggregated natural accounts, and seldom attempt to attach the costs to functional responsibilities and to individual products or customers.

---

[7]Lambert and Sterling, "What Types of Profitability Reports Do Marketing Managers Receive?" pp. 295–303; Robert S. Kaplan, *Flying Blind,* Harvard Business School Videotape Series on Measuring Corporate Performance, Tape 1, Harvard Business School Press, 1995.

[8]Robin Cooper and Robert S. Kaplan, "Measure Costs Right: Make the Right Decisions," *Harvard Business Review* 66, no. 5 (Sept.–Oct. 1988), pp. 96–103; and George Foster, Mahendra Gupta and Leif Sjoblom, "Customer Profitability Analysis: Challenges and New Directions," *Journal of Cost Management* 10, no. 1 (Spring 1996), pp. 5–17.

[9]Cooper and Kaplan, "Measure Costs Right," pp. 96–103; Robert S. Kaplan, "How Cost Accounting Distorts Product Costs," *Management Accounting,* Apr. 1988, pp. 20–27; Ford S. Worthy, "Accounting Bores You? Wake Up," *Fortune,* Oct. 12, 1987, pp. 43–50; James T. Mackey and Vernon H. Hughes, "Decision Focused Costing at Kenco," *Management Accounting* 75 (May 1993), pp. 22–26; and Daniel P. Keegan and Stephen W. Portik, "Accounting Will Survive the Coming Century, Won't It?" *Management Accounting* 77 (Dec. 1995), pp. 24–30.

FIGURE 13–2

Typical full costing/traditional overhead allocation

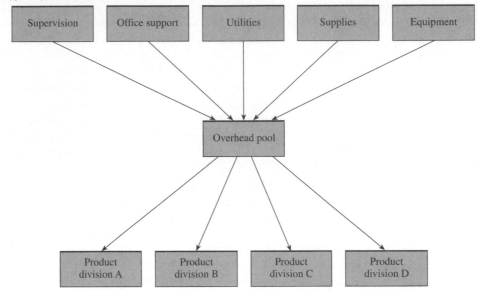

- Profitability reports do not show a segment's contribution to profitability, but include fixed costs, joint product or service costs, and corporate overhead costs. Top management often encourages this approach because it fears that knowledge of variable costs will lead to unrealistically low prices. In most cases, however, prices are set by the marketplace, not on the basis of costs.

- In most standard cost systems, fixed costs are often treated the same as variable costs, which masks the true behavior of the fixed costs.

Solving the Problem of Insufficient Cost Data

Natural Accounts   One of the difficulties in obtaining logistics costs is that they may be grouped under a series of natural accounts instead of by functions. **Natural accounts** are used to group costs for financial reporting on the firm's income statement and balance sheet. For example, all payments for salaries might be grouped into a salaries account. Whether they apply to production, marketing, logistics, or finance, they usually are lumped together and the total shown on the financial statements at the end of the reporting period. Other examples of natural accounts include rent, depreciation, selling expenses, general and administrative expenses, and interest expenses. These cost may be lumped into such diverse catchalls as overhead, selling, or general expense.

In addition, freight bills are often charged directly to an expense account as they are paid, regardless of when the associated orders are recognized as revenue. This type of situation is illustrated in Box 13–1. These conditions make it difficult to determine logistics expenditures, to control costs, or to perform trade-off analyses.

Box 13–1

The Effect of Average Freight Costs on Customer or Product Profitability

Freight costs are a major expense in most companies, yet few accounting systems track actual freight costs by customer or product. When management does try to determine these costs, it usually relies on national averages which do not indicate the actual costs of moving each product to its destination; hence, profitability calculations are erroneous.

For example, the management of Company A used a national average freight rate when calculating customer and product profitability. It determined the rate by taking the total corporate transportation bill as a percentage of total sales revenue. It applied the same cost—4 percent of sales—to products moving by common carrier from Chicago to New York and from Chicago to Los Angeles, as well as to deliveries in the Chicago area where the company used its own vehicles. It used the 4 percent figure for transportation cost regardless of the product being shipped, the size of the shipment, or the distance involved.

The fallacy of this approach is threefold. First, management was unable to determine the profitability of individual products or customers. The averaging process hid the highly unprofitable nature of delivery of small quanti-

ties to distant customers, thereby reducing the overall corporate rate of return.

Second, using the same percentage rate for all products ignored the impact of product characteristics such as weight and cube, and distance on freight rates and, consequently, on product and customer profitability.

Finally, management did not know the actual delivery costs for customers, which made it more difficult to perform a trade-off analysis between the cost of the current system and the cost of an alternative system where carload shipments would go first to a regional warehouse on the West Coast, and from there by motor carrier to customers in that market. In this company, the allocation of freight costs on a percentage of sales basis led to erroneous profitability figures for customers and products, and lower overall performance.

Source: This material is adapted from Douglas M. Lambert and Howard M. Armitage, "Management Distribution Cost for Better Profit Performance," *Business* 30, no. 5 (Sept.–Oct. 1980), pp. 46–52. Reprinted by permission from *Business* magazine.

It Is Difficult to Manage What You Do Not Measure

The challenge is not so much to create new data, since much of it already exists in one form or another, but to tailor the existing data in the accounting system to meet the needs of the logistics function. By improving the availability of logistics cost data, management is in a better position to make both operational and strategic decisions. Abnormal levels of costs can be detected and controlled only if management knows what they ought to be for various levels of activity.

As Figure 13–3 shows, logistics performance can be monitored by using standard costs, budgets, productivity standards, statistical process control, and activity-based management.[10] When using a third party, open book contracts can help improve the availability and understanding of logistics cost data. An example of this is shown in the Creative Solutions box at the end of this chapter.

[10]The following sections on standard costs, budgets, and productivity standards are adapted from Douglas M. Lambert and Howard M. Armitage, "Management Distribution Cost for Better Profit Performance," *Business* 30, no. 5 (Sept.–Oct. 1980), pp. 50–51. Reprinted by permission from *Business* magazine.

FIGURE 13–3

Controlling logistics activities

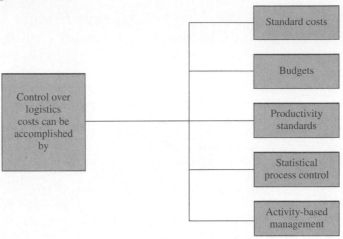

Standard Costs and Flexible Budgets

Defining Standard Costs

Control of costs through predetermined standards and flexible budgets is the most comprehensive type of control system available. A *standard* can be defined as a benchmark or "norm" for measuring performance. **Standard costs** are what the costs should be if the firm is operating as planned. Using management by exception, managers direct their attention to variances from standard. A flexible budget is geared to a range of activity. Given the level of activity that occurs, managers can determine what the costs should have been; the use of standard costs with a flexible budget represents a direct, effective approach to the logistics costing problem. No longer are future cost predictions based simply on past cost behavior.

Managers who use standard costs must systematically review logistics operations to arrive at the most effective means of achieving the desired output. Obviously, this will not work if logistics costs are pooled, and there is one "standard" number for freight regardless of weight, cube, or destination. This is how "standard costing" for logistics is performed at most companies.

Accounting, logistics, and engineering personnel must work together, using techniques such as regression analysis, time and motion studies, and efficiency studies, so that a series of flexible budgets can be drawn up for various operating levels in different logistics costs centers. Standards can and have been set for virtually all warehouse operations, in order processing, transportation, and clerical functions. However, the use of standard costs in logistics has not been widespread.

Only recently has the importance of logistics cost control been recognized. However, management accountants and industrial engineers have a wealth of experience in establishing standard costs in the production area which, with some effort, could be expanded into logistics.

Developing Standard Costs Can Be Complex

Standard costs for logistics may be more complex to develop because the output measures can be considerably more diverse than in the case of production. For example, in developing a standard for the picking function, it is possible that the eventual control measure could be stated as a standard cost per order, per order line, per unit shipped, or per shipment or even a combination of these factors. Despite the added complexities, work measurement does appear to be increasing in logistics activities.[11]

Standard Costs: An Example

For example, one firm used a computerized system with standard charges and routes for 25,000 routes and eight different methods of transportation.[12] Up to 300,000 combinations were possible, and the system was updated regularly. Clerks at any location could obtain from the computer the optimum method of shipment. A monthly computer printout listed the following information by customer:

- Destination.
- Standard freight cost to customer.
- Actual freight charges paid for shipments to customer.
- Standard freight to warehouse cost.
- Total freight cost.
- Origin of shipment.
- Sales district office.
- Method of shipment.
- Container used.
- Weight of shipment.
- Variance in excess of a given amount per hundredweight.

Another monthly report listed the deviation from standard freight cost for each customer and the amount of the variance. This system provided the firm with a measure of freight performance, but equally important, the standards provided the means for determining individual customer profitability and identifying opportunities for logistics cost trade-offs. Because this firm used standards as an integral part of its management information system, it could determine the impact of a system change (e.g. an improved, automated order processing system) on transportation costs fairly easily.

The use of standards as a management control system is depicted in Figure 13–4. As the figure indicates, standards may result from either formal investigation, philosophy/intuition, or both.

---

[11]See for example, Ernst and Whinney, *Transportation Accounting and Control: Guidelines for Distribution and Financial Management* (Chicago: National Council of Physical Distribution Management; New York: National Association of Accountants, 1985).

[12]Michael Schiff, *Accounting and Control in Physical Distribution Management* (Chicago: National Council of Physical Distribution Management, 1972), pp. 4-63 to 6-70.

FIGURE 13–4

The use of standards as a management control system

The control system

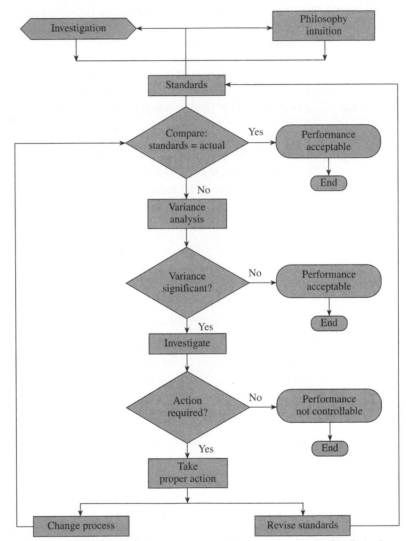

Source: Richard J. Lewis and Leo G. Erickson, "Distribution System Costing: An Overview," in *Distribution System Costing: Concepts and Procedures,* ed. John R. Grabner and William S. Sargent (Columbus, OH: Transportation and Logistics Research Foundation, 1972), p. 17A.

Variance Management.   Once standards have been set, the actual performance is compared to the standard to see if it is acceptable. If so, the system is under control and that is the end of the control process. Where performance differs from the standard, investigation may be warranted. It is most meaningful to judge variances in terms of their *practical* significance. How significant is the variance in its effects on bottom-line perfor-

How Significant Is the Variance?

mance, that is, net profit? If significant, the next question to ask is whether some action is required.

If the variance is significant but uncontrollable, no action may be indicated and the control process terminated. If action is indicated, it may be that the standard is considered wrong and must be changed, or the process itself is creating the problem and thus should be changed. The new process or standard will be judged following the same cycle.[13]

A standard tells management the expected cost of performing selected activities and allows management to make comparisons that point out any operating inefficiencies. For example, Table 13–2 illustrates a report that is useful at the operating level. It shows why the warehouse labor for the picking activity was $320 over budget. The costs of logistics activities can be (1) reported by department, division, function, product group, or total, (2) compared with their standard, and (3) included as part of regular weekly or monthly performance reports.

Table 13–3 shows a level of aggregation that would interest the firm's president. This report allows the president to see at a glance why targeted net income has not been reached. On the one hand, there is a $3 million difference due to ineffectiveness, which indicates the net income the company has forgone because of its inability to meet its budgeted level of sales.

On the other hand, there is an inefficiency factor of $1.4 million, which indicates that at the actual level of sales the segment-controllable margin should have been $18.0 million. The difference between $18.0 million and the actual outcome of $16.6 million is a $1.4 million variation due to inefficiencies within the marketing and logistics functions.

Budgetary Practices

When Should Standards Not Be Used?

Conceptually, standard costs are generally superior to budgetary practices for control purposes. Sometimes, however, the use of standards is inappropriate. This is particularly true in situations with essentially nonrepetitive tasks and for which work-unit measurements are difficult to establish. In these situations, control can be achieved through budgetary practices. However, the extent to which the budget is successful depends on whether individual cost-behavior patterns can be predicted and whether the budget can be flexed to reflect changes in operating conditions.

Most Logistics Budgets Are Static

Most logistics budgets are static; that is, they are a plan developed for a budgeted level of output. If actual activity happens to be the same as budgeted, management can make a realistic comparison of costs and establish effective control. However, this is seldom the case. Seasonality or internal factors invariably lead to different levels of activity, the efficiency of which can be determined only if the reporting system can compare the actual costs with what costs should have been at the operating level achieved. Box 13–2 illustrates this problem in more detail.

For instance, a firm's warehousing unit may have an estimated or budgeted level of activity of 10,000 line items per week. The actual level of activity may be only 7,500.

---

[13]Richard J. Lewis and Leo G. Erickson, "Distribution System Costing: An Overview," in *Distribution System Costing: Concepts and Procedures,* John R. Grabner and William S. Sargent, eds. (Columbus, OH: Transportation and Logistics Research Foundation, 1972), pp. 18–20.

TABLE 13–2   Summary of Warehouse Picking Operations Week of _____

Items picked during week	14,500
Hours accumulated on picking activities	330
Standard hours allowed for picks performed based on 50 items per hour	290
Variation in hours	40
Standard cost per labor hour	$8
Variation in cost due to inefficiencies	$320*

*The cost was $320 over budget because there were 40 picking hours in excess of the standard number of hours allowed for efficient operation, at a standard cost per labor hour of $8.

TABLE 13–3   Segmental Analysis Using a Contribution Approach ($000)

		Explanation of Variation from Budget			
	Budget	Variance Due to Ineffectiveness	Standard Allowed for Output Level Achieved	Variance Due to Inefficiency	Actual Results
Net sales	$90,000	$10,000	$80,000	—	$80,000
Cost of goods sold (variable manufacturing cost)	40,500	4,500	36,000	—	36,000
Manufacturing contribution	$49,500	$5,500	$44,000	—	$44,000
Variable marketing and logistics costs (out-of-pocket costs that vary directly with sales to the segment)*	22,500	2,500	20,000	$1,400	21,400
Segment contribution margin	$27,000	$3,000	$24,000	$1,400	$22,600
Assignable nonvariable costs (costs incurred specifically for the segment during the period)†	6,000	—	6,000	—	6,000
Segment controllable margin	$21,000	$3,000	$18,000	$1,400	$16,600

Notes: This analysis can be performed for segments such as products, customers, geographic areas, or divisions.

Assumption: Actual sales revenue decreased, a result of lower volume. The average price paid per unit sold remained the same. (If the average price per unit changes then an additional variance—the marketing variance—can be computed.)

Difference in income of $4,400 ($21,000 – 16,600) between budgeted and actual results can be explained by the following variances:

Ineffectiveness—inability to reach target sales objective	$3,000
Inefficiency at operating level achieved of $80,000	1,400
	$4,400

*These costs might include: sales commissions, transportation costs, warehouse handling costs, order processing costs, and a charge for accounts receivable.

†These costs might include: salaries, segment-related advertising, bad debts, and inventory carrying costs. The fixed costs associated with corporate-owned and operated facilities would be included if, and only if, the warehouse was solely for this segment of the business.

Box 13–2

Control Deficiencies

Control of costs and motivation of key personnel is critical in every business activity. Logistics is no exception. However, the control concepts successfully utilized by other functional areas have not been widely adopted for logistics activities. It might be argued that logistics is different from other disciplines and cannot be evaluated with the same tools. In most cases, however, the application has never been attempted. A particular case in point is the application of the **flexible budgeting** concept.

Company B maintained an annual budget for its branch warehousing costs. These costs consisted of variable and fixed expenses. Each month, the annual budget was divided by 12 and compared with the actual costs for that month. Differences from the budget were recorded as variances, and management took action on these. However, company B's sales were seasonal, with some months far more active than others. The variances were always unfavorable during peak months and favorable during slow months. Productivity ratios, on the other hand, gave different results. They were high during peak periods and dropped during slower periods.

In this type of situation, neither cost control nor employee motivation is adequately addressed. Dividing the annual budget by 12 and comparing it with actual monthly costs means that management is trying to compare costs at two different activity levels. The costs should be the same only if actual monthly activity is equal to 1/12 of the planned annual activity. A far more acceptable approach is to recognize that a portion of the costs are variable and will rise or fall with the level of output. Flexing the budget to reflect what the costs should have been at the operating activity level experienced permits a true measure of efficiency and productivity, and provides more meaningful evaluations of performance.

Source: This material is adapted from Douglas M. Lambert and Howard M. Armitage, "Management Distribution Cost for Better Profit Performance," *Business* 30, no. 5 (Sept.–Oct. 1980), pp. 46–52. Reprinted by permission from *Business* magazine.

Comparing the budgeted costs at 10,000 line items with the actual costs at 7,500 leads to the erroneous conclusion that the operation has been efficient, since items such as overtime, temporary help, packing, postage, and order processing are less than budget. A flexible budget, on the other hand, indicates what the costs should have been at the level of 7,500 line items of activity, resulting in a true dollar measure of efficiency.

Key to Successful Implementation of a Flexible Budget

Analysis of Cost Behavior Patterns.   The key to successful implementation of a flexible budget lies in the analysis of cost behavior patterns. In most firms, little of this analysis has been carried out in the logistics function. The expertise of the cost accountant and industrial engineer can be invaluable in applying tools such as scatter-diagram techniques and regression analysis to determine the fixed and variable components of costs. These techniques use previous cost data to determine a variable rate per unit of activity and a total fixed cost component. Once this is accomplished, the flexible budget for control becomes a reality.

Unlike engineered standards, the techniques are based on past cost behavior patterns, which undoubtedly contain inefficiencies. The predicted measure of cost, therefore, may not be a measure of what the activity *should* cost, but an estimate of what it *will* cost, based on the results of previous periods.

Capital Budgets Are Used to Control Capital Expenditures

Capital Budgets. **Capital budgets** are used to control capital expenditures, such as long-term investments in property, facilities, and equipment. In logistics, this would include purchases of new trucks, computer equipment, materials handling and warehouse equipment, the building of new distribution centers, and similar long-term investments. These items are controlled by limiting the dollar amount to be spent in a given year (annual capital expenditure budget), and requiring a minimum net present value or payback on productive investments. A discussion of how these items are calculated is included in any basic finance textbook.[14]

Productivity Standards

Logistics costs can be controlled by the use of productivity ratios. These ratios take the form of:

Productivity Ratios

$$\text{Productivity} = \frac{\text{Measure of output}}{\text{Measure of input}}$$

For example, a warehouse operation might make use of such productivity ratios as:

$$\frac{\text{Number of orders shipped this period}}{\text{Number of orders received this period}}$$

$$\frac{\text{Number of orders shipped this period}}{\text{Average number of orders shipped per period}}$$

$$\frac{\text{Number of orders shipped this period}}{\text{Number of direct labor hours worked this period}}$$

Productivity ratios for transportation might include:[15]

$$\frac{\text{Ton-miles transported}}{\text{Total actual transportation cost}}$$

$$\frac{\text{Stops served}}{\text{Total actual transportation cost}}$$

$$\frac{\text{Shipments transported to destination}}{\text{Total actual transportation cost}}$$

Productivity ratios can be generated for the following transportation resource inputs: labor, equipment, energy, and cost. Table 13–4 illustrates the specific relationships between these inputs and transportation activities. An X in a cell of the matrix denotes an activity-input combination that can be measured. Table 13–5 illustrates an activity-input

---

[14]See, for example, Gaylord N. Smith and Gregg K. Dimkoff, *Managerial Finance,* 3rd ed. (Cincinnati, OH: South-Western Publishing, 1996).

[15]A.T. Kearney, Inc., *Measuring and Improving Productivity in Physical Distribution* (Oak Brook, IL: National Council of Physical Distribution Management, 1984), p. 170.

TABLE 13–4   Transportation Activity-Input Matrix

Activities	Labor	Facilities	Equipment	Energy	Overall (cost)
Transportation strategy development	—	—	—	—	X
Private fleet over-the-road trucking					
Loading	X	—	—	—	X
Line-haul	X	—	—	X	X
Unloading	X	—	—	—	X
Overall	X	—	—	X	X
Private fleet pickup/delivery trucking					
Pretrip	X	—	—	—	X
Stem driving	X	—	—	X	X
One-route driving	X	—	—	X	X
At-stop	X	—	—	—	X
End-of-trip	X	—	—	—	X
Overall	X	—	X	X	X
Purchased transportation operations					
Loading	—	—	—	—	X
Line-haul	—	—	—	—	X
Unloading	—	—	—	—	X
Rail/barge fleet management	—	—	—	—	X
Transportation/traffic management	—	—	—	—	X

Source: A.T. Kearney, Inc., *Measuring and Improving Productivity in Physical Distribution* (Oak Brook, IL: National Council of Physical Distribution Management, 1984), p. 144.

matrix for warehousing. Table 13–6 illustrates how warehouse productivity ratios can be calculated, and interprets the results.

Productivity measures of this type have been developed for most logistics activities. In the absence of a standard costing system, they are particularly useful with budgetary practices, because they provide guidelines on operating efficiencies. Furthermore, such measures are easily understood by management and employees.[16] However, productivity measures are not without their shortcomings:

Limitations of Productivity Measures

1. Productivity measures are expressed in terms of physical units and actual dollar losses caused by inefficiencies, and predictions of future logistics costs cannot be made. This makes it difficult to cost-justify any system changes that will result in improved productivity.

---

[16]For more information on the development of productivity ratios refer to A.T. Kearney, Inc., *Measuring and Improving Productivity in Physical Distribution;* Howard M. Armitage, "The Use of Management Accounting Techniques to Improve Productivity Analysis in Distribution Operations," *International Journal of Physical Distribution and Materials Management* 14, no. 1 (1984), pp. 41–51.

TABLE 13–5   Warehouse Activity-Input Matrix

Activities	Labor	Facilities	Equipment	Energy	Overall (cost)
Company-operated warehousing					
Receiving	X	X	X	—	X
Put-away	X	—	X	—	X
Storage	—	X	—	—	X
Replenishment	X	—	X	—	X
Order selection	X	—	X	—	X
Checking	X	—	X	—	X
Packing and marking	X	X	X	—	X
Staging and order consideration	X	X	X	—	X
Shipping	X	—	X	—	X
Clerical and administration	X	X	X	—	X
Overall	X		X	—	X
Public warehousing					
Storage	—	—	—	—	X
Handling	—	—	—	—	X
Consolidation	—	—	—	—	X
Administration	—	—	—	—	X
Overall	—	—	—	—	X

Source: A.T. Kearney, Inc., *Measuring and Improving Productivity in Physical Distribution* (Oak Brook, IL: National Council of Physical Distribution Management, 1984), p. 195.

2. The actual productivity measure calculated is seldom compared to a productivity standard. For example, a productivity measure may compare the number of orders shipped this period to the number of direct labor-hours worked in the same period, but it does not indicate what the relationship *ought* to be. Without work measurement or some form of cost estimation, it is impossible to know what the productivity standard should be in efficient operations.

3. Changes in output levels may in some cases distort measures of productivity. This distortion occurs because the fixed and variable elements are seldom delineated. Consequently, the productivity measure computes utilization, not efficiency. For example, if 100 orders shipped represents full labor utilization and 100 orders were received this period, then productivity as measured by:

$$\frac{\text{Number of orders shipped this period}}{\text{Number of orders received this period}} \times 100\%$$

The result would be 100 percent. However, if 150 orders had been received and 100 orders were shipped, productivity would have been 66.67 percent, even though there was no real drop in either efficiency or productivity.

TABLE 13–6   The Calculation of Warehouse Productivity Ratios

---

Data:

Number of orders shipped this period	2,750
Number of orders received this period	2,800
Average numbers of orders shipped per period	2,500
Number of direct labor hours worked this period in shipping	200

Calculation of ratios:

1. $\dfrac{\text{Numbers of orders shipped this period}}{\text{Number of orders recieved this period}} = \dfrac{2{,}750}{2{,}800} = 98.2\%$

A ratio of less than 100% means the firm is building up unshipped orders, under 100% means the firm is reducing backlog.

2. $\dfrac{\text{Numbers of orders shipped this period}}{\text{Average number of orders shipped per period}} = \dfrac{2{,}750}{2{,}500} = 110\%$

The firm had a busier than usual month (ratio greater than 100%); this combined with ratio 1 shows that the firm is building up a backlog.

3. $\dfrac{\text{Numbers of orders shipped this period}}{\text{Number of direct labor hours worked this period in shipping}} = \dfrac{2{,}750}{200} = 13.75 \text{ orders per hour}$

This number is only meaningful in comparison with a standard or benchmark. It tells us the number of orders shipped per person hour.

Statistical Process Control

The Japanese demonstrate a high level of sophistication in the use of statistical methods to enhance the quality of products and services.[17] The use of such approaches is increasing in North America in the automobile industry, in high-tech firms, and among consumer products manufacturers. The output of successful logistics is the level of customer service provided. Although many firms measure the proportion of shipments that arrive on time or the average length of the order cycle from a particular supplier, further insight into these areas is seldom obtained through the use of statistical process control techniques.

The use of statistical methods offers an alternative to conventional management control processes. **Statistical process control (SPC)** requires an understanding of the variability of the process itself prior to making management decisions. To analyze delivery times from several suppliers, for example, it is necessary to know the mean, or average, time elapsed from the issuance of a purchase order to the receipt of a shipment and the likely variation in delivery times.

---

[17]This material is adapted from C. John Langley, Jr., "Information-Based Decision Making in Logistics Management," *International Journal of Physical Distribution and Materials Management* 15, no. 7 (1985), pp. 48–52; and James R. Evans and William M. Lindsay, *The Management and Control of Quality* (Minneapolis, MN: West Publishing Co., 1993), pp. 529–656.

The SPC Process.   Figure 13–5 illustrates the steps of SPC. As with classical approaches to control, the first three steps are:

Steps of Statistical Process Control

1. Design system.
2. Establish standards.
3. Perform process.

Once the first three steps are accomplished, SPC requires that the following questions be raised. First, are the measurements "in control"? That is, do all measurements fall within reasonable proximity of the mean? Second, is the process "capable"? That is, does the observed variability have a lesser magnitude than a prespecified range? Third, do the measurements meet standards? Only if the answers to these three questions are yes is the process itself said to be in control.

Control Charts

The **control chart** is perhaps the most widely used statistical approach to gain insight into these questions. The control chart permits an examination of process behavior measurements in relation to both upper and lower control limits. These limits are statistically derived and are used to identify instances where the observed behavior differs significantly from what was expected and where a problem is likely to exist. The calculation of these limits is beyond the coverage of this text, but it is generally included in a good introductory statistics or quality course.[18] The search for explanations can proceed in an organized efficient manner.

Figure 13–6 shows two control chart applications developed from actual logistics-related data. Part A resulted from an examination of transit time data (in minutes) of shipments traveling between two cities 260 miles apart. Once the three points located outside the control limits were identified and isolated, an inquiry determined their causes and assured removal of those causes.

Part B of Figure 13–6 shows the percentages of carrier freight bills which a particular shipper found to contain errors. In this example, the only error percentages of real concern are those which are excessively high as to be labeled out-of-control in a statistical sense; that is, above the upper control limit (UCL). In this instance, subsequent investigation resulted in the identification and removal of the cause of the problem at hand.

A number of other activities in logistics management could serve equally well for purposes of illustration, including warehousing, materials handling, packaging, inventory control, order processing, and customer service. Large cost savings can be captured in these areas through the appropriate use of statistical methods.

Prerequisites to Successful Statistical Process Control

Making SPC a Success.   There are a number of prerequisites to success with SPC.

1. It is important to recognize that the use of statistical methods is simply a tool that can assist in improving quality. SPC provides valuable insight into the behavior of the various processes under scrutiny.

2. Top management support is necessary for success. The effective use of SPC approaches may involve a cultural change in a firm. Successful firms have commitment from top management and require a high level of familiarity with the various approaches.

---

[18]Evans and Lindsay, *The Management and Control of Quality,* contains a comprehensive presentation of the mathematics supporting SPC.

FIGURE 13–5

Statistical process control (SPC)

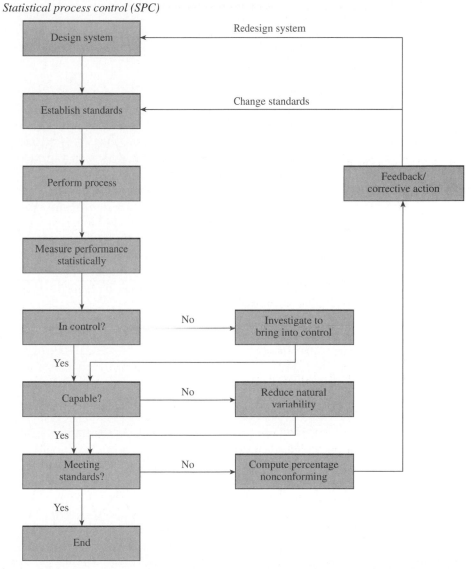

Source: C. John Langley, Jr., "Information-Based Decision Making in Logistics Management," *International Journal of Physical Distribution and Materials Management* 15, no. 7 (1985), p. 50. Copyright MCB University Press Limited.

FIGURE 13–6

Control chart examples

A. Transit time performance

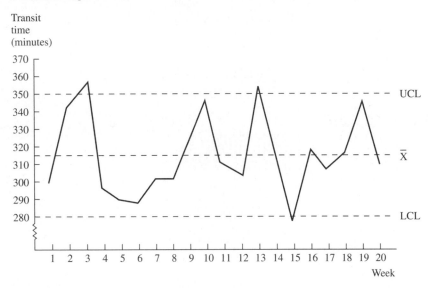

B. Freight bill accuracy

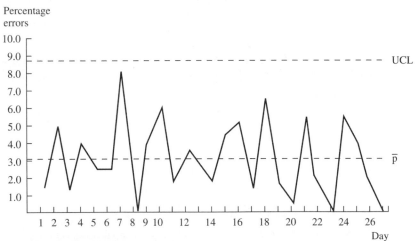

Key: UCL = Upper control limit.
LCL = Lower control limit.
$\overline{X}$ = Mean (of measurements).
$\overline{p}$ = Mean (of percentages or proportions).

Source: C. John Langley, Jr., "Information-Based Decision Making in Logistics Management," *International Journal of Physical Distribution and Materials Management* 15, no. 7 (1985), p. 51. Copyright MCB University Press Limited.

3. Finally, the use of statistical methods should be viewed as a key component of an overall total quality management program. Other elements of this program may include the establishment of quality policies, the setting of goals and objectives, supervisory training, quality awareness and programs for the removal of error causes, and performance management.[19]

The issue of quality in logistics is frequently addressed in conjunction with productivity. However, attention has focused on the identification of specific data and information needs rather than on what to do with the information once it has been acquired. Until more progress is made in this direction, the benefits of improved productivity will continue to represent a largely untapped resource.

Successful implementation of SPC approaches depends on the timely availability of appropriate information. For this reason, SPC provides an opportunity for the logistics and information systems areas to work together to enhance productivity and improve quality.

Logistics Costs and the Corporate Management Information System (MIS)

While substantial savings can be generated when management is able to compare its actual costs with a set of predetermined standards or budgets, even greater opportunities for profit improvement exist in the area of decision making. If management is to make informed decisions, it must be able to choose between alternatives such as utilizing additional common carrier transportation or enlarging the company's private fleet, increasing the number of deliveries or increasing inventories, expanding or consolidating field warehouses, and automating the order processing and information system.

The addition or deletion of sales territories, salespeople, products, or customers requires a knowledge of how well existing segments are currently performing, and how revenues and costs will change with the alternatives under consideration. For this purpose, management needs a database capable of aggregating data, so that it can obtain routine information on individual segments such as customers, salespeople, products, territories, or channels of distribution.

The system must be able to store data by fixed and variable components, so that the incremental revenues and costs linked to alternative strategies can be determined. Some problems connected to the inability to distinguish between variable and fixed costs are presented in Box 13–3.

Barriers to Effective Information Management.   Several types of transactions occur in every business, and each transaction results in the creation of source documents (e.g., customer orders, shipment bill of lading, sales invoices to customers, invoices from suppliers and vendors). In addition, companies perform a variety of internal transactions and activities that are documented (e.g., "trip reports" for private fleet activities, "call reports"

---

[19]Evans and Lindsay, *The Management and Control of Quality;* Jari Juga, "Redesigning Logistics to Improve Performance," *The International Journal of Logistics Management* 6, no. 1 (1995), pp. 75–84; and A. Ansari and Batoul Modarress, "Quality Function Deployment: The Role of Suppliers," *International Journal of Purchasing and Materials Management* 30, no. 4 (Fall 1994), pp. 27–35.

Box 13–3

Inability to Distinguish between Fixed and Variable Costs

Management of company C used a product reporting statement that deducted manufacturing, logistics, and marketing costs from sales to arrive at a net income for each product. It used the profit statement for making decisions about the acceptability of product performance, the assignment of marketing support, and the deletion of products. The allocation of logistics costs to each product was carried out using ABC analysis, in which A products were allocated a certain amount of logistics costs, B products twice as much as A, and C products three times as much as A. These allocations contained costs that varied with activity, such as warehouse labor, supplies, and freight expenses. They also included costs that remained fixed regardless of activity levels (e.g., corporate allocations, depreciation, and administrative costs of the corporate fleet).

Several of the company's products, including one that was among the "top 10" in sales performance, were showing losses and were candidates for being discontinued.

However, analysis revealed that a large proportion of the total distribution cost, along with approximately 30 percent of the manufacturing cost, was fixed and would not be saved if the products were eliminated. Indeed, by discontinuing these products, total corporate profitability would decline because all of the revenues related to these products would disappear, but all of the costs would not.

Although the variable costs and the identifiable fixed costs would be saved, the company would continue to incur the majority of fixed costs—which in this case were substantial—regardless of the product deletions under consideration. If the firm discontinued the products, the existing fixed costs would be redistributed to the remaining products, leading to the very real possibility that even more products would appear to be unprofitable.

Source: This material is adapted from Douglas M. Lambert and Howard M. Armitage, "Management Distribution Cost for Better Profit Performance," *Business* 30, no. 5 (Sept.–Oct. 1980), pp. 46–52. Reprinted by permission from *Business* magazine.

---

from salespeople, warehouse labor time cards). Other costs may be recognized by means of standard cost systems, engineering time studies, or statistical estimating (e.g., multiple regression techniques).

Source Documents Must Be Computerized

The key for success is that source documents *must* be computerized. Data need to be linked using the relational database concept (see Chapter 3), so that it can be analyzed in a variety of ways that are useful for supporting decision making. This is still rare in practice.

Why does this condition exist? Many managers mistakenly feel that the same accounting practices (i.e., the allocation of all costs) used to value inventories and report results to the Internal Revenue Service or the Securities and Exchange Commission are required to generate reports for managing the business. Managers also may feel that using only variable and direct fixed costs might encourage suboptimal pricing by salespeople.

Accountants frequently oppose a separate management accounting system while managers often fail to recognize the differences between fixed and variable costs, the distinction between direct and indirect expenses, or the usefulness and purpose of contribution reports.

Finally, management information systems personnel often discourage the development of such reports by citing the difficulties in creating the databases and operating systems required to assign direct costs to specific product and market segments. With the revolution in information technology, these reasons are no longer valid.

Importance of Good Information.   With the information from the relational database, management is in a position to evaluate the profitability of various segments. The database permits the user to simulate trade-off situations and determine the effect of proposed strategic and system changes on total cost. The Technology box provides an example of how software can aid in modeling supply chain trade-offs.

The key to measuring logistics performance is an integrated, broad-based computer data file. To track an order and its associated costs from origin to receipt by customer, for example, it is necessary to access a number of files in the logistics information system:

Important Data Files in a Logistics MIS

- Open orders (for back orders).
- Deleted orders (order history file).
- Shipping manifest (bills of lading).
- Transportation freight bills paid.

With today's information processing capabilities, it is possible to access desired information automatically from these and other necessary files (e.g., inventory, customer retail feedback data, damage reports and claims, billing and invoicing files). From these files, management can construct a condensed "logistics performance" database which can provide all of the necessary information required to measure overall as well as individual activities on a regular basis. What used to take several "person-years" of concerted programming effort and cost large sums of money, can now be developed in a matter of weeks or months, using personal computers and standard statistical packages.

A major consumer products company uses this approach to construct a series of more than 50 reports using a common "logistic performance" file, and these cover more than just logistics costs. The same data files are used to report financial, customer service, or productivity-related reports.

Activity-Based Costing

Activity-based costing has received increased attention as a method of solving the problem of insufficient cost data. Traditional accounting systems in manufacturing firms allocate factory/corporate overhead to products based on direct labor. In the past, this method of allocation may have resulted in minor distortions. However, product lines and channels have proliferated and overhead costs have increased dramatically, making traditional allocation methods dangerously inaccurate.

An activity-based system examines the demands made by particular products (or customers) on indirect resources.[20] Three rules should be followed when examining the demands made by individual products on indirect resources:

1. Focus on expensive resources.
2. Emphasize resources whose consumption varies significantly by product and product type.
3. Focus on resources whose demands are uncorrelated with traditional allocation methods such as direct labor or materials costs.[21]

---

[20]Cooper and Kaplan, "Measure Costs Right," pp. 96–103, and Foster, et al., "Customer Profitability Analysis," pp. 5–17.
[21]Ibid., p. 98.

Technology

Software Helps Manage Financial and Service Issues

Phydias is a Logistics Network Modeling optimization system created by Bender Management Consultants. The version based on Windows 95 allows users to model worldwide supply chains and logistics operations. It can handle virtually any size supply chain and perform rapid optimization analysis, including problem identification.

From a financial standpoint, it allows multicurrency input and exchange rate sensitivity analysis. It

incorporates virtual logistics and production facilities, ensuring correct modeling of the cost structure. Such advanced modeling capabilities have come a long way in supporting improved financial analysis and modeling of supply chains.

Source: "Bender Claims Phydias Optimizes Networks Best," *Mt Logistica*, Oct. 1996, p. 14.

Computer software programs, such as this one that identifies recommended warehouse site locations, help firms to reduce logistics costs and optimize customer service.

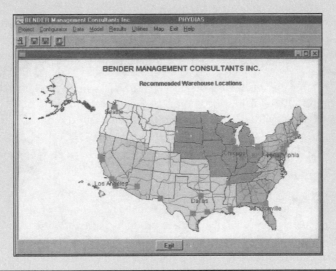

Activity-Based Costing Requires Identification of Cost Drivers

The process of tracing costs, first from resources to activities that "drive" resource usage (cost drivers) and then from activities to specific products (or customers), cannot be done with surgical precision.

Limitations of ABC. It is better to be mostly correct with activity-based costing—say, within 5 or 10 percent of the actual demands a product or customer makes on organizational resources—than to be precisely wrong (perhaps by as much as 200 percent) using outdated allocation techniques or including indirect common costs.[22]

---

[22]See Peter B. Turney, "Activity Based Management: The Comprehensive Weapons of the 90s," *U.S. Electronics Management Review,* Jan. 1993, pp. 4–8.

It should be noted that anytime costs are *allocated,* we are admitting that we cannot identify the cause of the cost—on an avoidable cost basis. If this information were available, we could *attach* (assign) the cost to the appropriate segment. Some of the potential problems of cost allocation are detailed in Box 13–4.

Using Activity-Based Costing in Warehousing

ABC in a Warehousing Example.   Figure 13–7 shows how activity-based costing may be used to apportion activity costs in a warehouse. Compare this with Figure 13–2 to understand the difference between ABC and traditional accounting systems. The major shortcoming of activity-based costing is that it is simply another method of allocation. Caution must be exercised since any method of allocation can result in charges against segment revenue that would not disappear if the revenue stream was lost.

The Fallacy of Using Average Costs

The potential problems associated with using activity-based costing for logistics were illustrated in a 1991 article in *Management Accounting.* The examples used were simply average costs where selling costs were 5 percent of sales, advertising costs were 40 cents per unit sold, warehousing costs were 10 cents per pound shipped, packing and shipping costs were 20 cents per unit sold, and general office expenses were allocated at $20 per order.[23] ABC implemented in this manner represents an average cost system and these costs are no longer useful for decision making.

For example, transportation costs need to be identified by origin and destination zip codes and by shipment size categories before they can be assigned to customers or products. It is important to identify how costs and revenues will change with a decision that is being made.

Managers responsible for product and customer business segments need to understand the financial implications of their decisions. Executives must be able to talk the language of accountants—to understand the true meaning of data used for decision making. The support and active participation by top management, including the chief executive, is necessary to improve accounting data because resistance to change is a major barrier facing manufacturers in their quest to become world class.

Using Segment Contribution Reports

Segment Contribution Reports.   Using segment contribution reports, managers can begin to accurately assess strategic options; for example, which product lines to drop or whether prices can be raised on inelastic products or reduced on high-volume products. They can place added emphasis on those segments that are most profitable, and eliminate unprofitable product lines.

Firms that have developed and implemented segment profitability reports with accurate cost assignments have been able to identify products and customers that were either unprofitable or did not meet corporate financial objectives. Ironically, many of these products or customers were previously thought to be profitable because of the way costs had been arbitrarily allocated.

The Role of the Order Processing System

Order Processing System Impacts Logistics in Two Major Ways

The order processing system can affect the performance of the logistics function in two major ways. First, the system can improve the quality of the management information

[23]Ronald J. Lewis, "Activity-Based Costing for Marketing," *Management Accounting* 73, no. 5 (Nov. 1991), pp. 33–38.

Box 13–4

The Pitfalls of Cost Allocation

Most logistics costing systems are in their infancy and rely heavily on allocations to determine the performance of segments such as product, customers, territories, division, or functions. Such allocations in company D led to erroneous decision making and a loss of corporate profits.

Company D was a multidivisional corporation that manufactured and sold high-margin pharmaceutical products and a number of lower-margin packaged goods. The company maintained a number of field warehouse locations managed by corporate staff. These climate-controlled facilities were designed for the pharmaceutical business and required security and housekeeping practices far exceeding those necessary for packaged goods.

To fully utilize the facilities, the company encouraged nonpharmaceutical divisions to store their products in these distribution centers. The costs of operating the warehouses were primarily fixed, although overtime or additional warehouse employees were necessary if throughput increased. The corporate policy was to allocate costs to user divisions on the basis of the square footage occupied. Pharmaceutical warehousing requirements made this charge relatively high. Furthermore, the corporate divisions were managed on a decentralized profit center basis.

The vice president of logistics in a division that marketed relatively bulky and low-value consumer products realized that similar services could be obtained at lower cost to his division by using a public warehouse. He with-

drew the division's products from the corporate facilities and began to use public warehouses in these locations. Although the volume of product handled and stored in the corporate distribution centers decreased significantly, the cost savings were minimal in terms of the total costs incurred by these facilities because of the high proportion of fixed costs. Consequently, approximately the same cost was allocated to fewer users, making it even more attractive for the other divisions to change to public warehouses in order to obtain lower rates. The result was higher, not lower, total company warehousing costs.

The corporate warehousing costs were primarily fixed, so whether the space was fully occupied would not significantly alter these costs. When the nonpharmaceutical divisions moved to public warehouses, the company continued to incur approximately the same total expense for the corporate-owned and operated warehouses and in addition incurred the new public warehousing charges. In effect, the costing system motivated the divisional logistics managers to act in a manner that was in the best interest for divisional profitability, but not in the best interest of the total company. Thus, costs to the total company escalated, reducing profitability.

Source: This material is adapted from Douglas M. Lambert and Howard M. Armitage, "Management Distribution Cost for Better Profit Performance," *Business* 30, no. 5 (Sept.–Oct. 1980), pp. 46–52. Reprinted by permission from *Business* magazine.

system by providing data such as customer names, customer locations, items demanded by customers, sales to customers, sales patterns (when items are ordered), order size, sales by salesperson, and sales data for the company's sales forecasting package.

Second, the customer order is the message that sets the logistics function in motion. The speed and quality of the information provided by the order processing system has a direct impact on the cost and efficiency of the entire logistics process.

Slow and erratic communication can lead to lost customers or excessive transportation, inventory, and warehousing costs. It can bring about production inefficiencies because of frequent line changes. Implementation of the latest technology in order processing and communications systems can lead to significant improvements in logistics performance.

FIGURE 13–7

Assignment of costs with an activity-based cost system

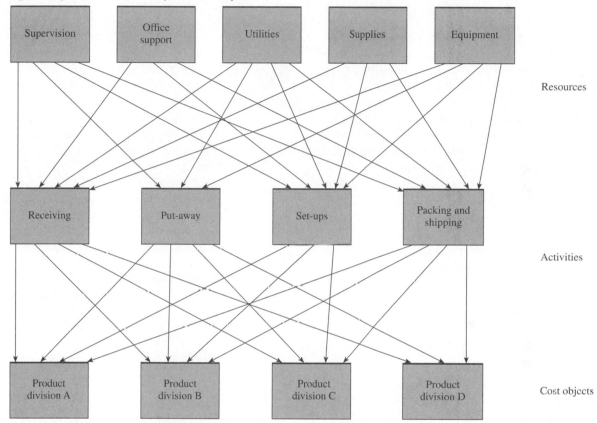

Source: Lisa M. Ellram et al., "Understanding the Implications of Activity Based Costing for Logistics Management," *Proceedings of the Annual Conference of the Council of Logistics Management* (Oak Brook, IL: Council of Logistics Management, 1994), p. 13.

Cost Justification of Logistics System Changes

In Chapter 2 we saw how an integrated approach to the management and control of the logistics function can significantly improve a firm's profitability. However, successful implementation of integrated logistics management depends on total cost analysis. That is, changes in the logistics system structure must be cost-justified by comparing total costs before and after a change. The availability of accurate cost data is critical for the cost justification of logistics system changes. The Global box illustrates the importance of understanding cost trade-offs in the supply chain.

Qualitative-Based Benefits of Integrated Logistics Systems

In addition to the financial analysis, a number of qualitative—or less easily quantified —benefits can be presented to management. These should not be relied upon to justify the system or process change, but should instead supplement the financial analysis as icing on

Global

When a Global Supply Chain Doesn't Work

A major European manufacturer of industrial components and related products had continual problems with the profitability of its North American subsidiary, which was a major supplier of industrial components to the parent company.

The parent company had significant economies of scale in engineering and manufacturing of industrial components. This should have given the subsidiary a competitive advantage in cost and quality. However, this never materialized. Why?

The North American subsidiary's major supplier (over 60 percent of finished goods) was the parent, but the parent was the subsidiary's most unreliable source. This created:

- Poor supply performance.
- Long lead times.
- Poor supply or fulfillment to its customers.
- High logistics costs for transportation and inventory.

This unreliability was compounded by local sourcing on the part of most of the subsidiary's North American competitors, providing them with lower transportation costs and shorter replenishment cycles.

In this case, being the low-cost producer was not enough for the parent company. The company needed to consider the trade-offs between price/cost, delivery cost, inventory, and customer service levels. The subsidiary's performance measurements—aggressive inventory turns and high fill rates—were impossible to achieve owing to the parent's poor performance!

While these problems showed up in the poor financial performance of the subsidiary, their roots were a lack of an understanding of the true nature and interrelatedness of supply chain companies, and a dysfunctional performance measurement and reporting system. As a result, the global company has now changed its strategy and realigned its processes to support this new strategy. The strategy includes:

- Integrating supply chain strategic planning.
- Inventory planning.
- Performance measurement.
- Interorganizational information exchange and integration.

Source: Les B. Artman and Ted Pollock, "Supply Chain Alignment," *Logistics!* (Fall 1996), pp. 21–26.

the cake. For example, the additional benefits associated with an improved order processing system could (or might) include the following:

• Customer service improvements. Customer service may be improved in two ways. First, the improved communication may allow the customer and the customer service representative to arrange for immediate substitution if a stockout occurs, or the representative can provide the customer with a realistic estimated delivery date if it is necessary to wait for the product to be manufactured. The new system may facilitate inquiries about order status after the order has been made. Second, if the improved communication reduces the variability of the order cycle time, this improvement should be documented. Suppose that the current order cycle is 10 days and ranges from 7 to 13 days—a variability of 3 days. Reducing order cycle variability by 2 days, to a range of 9 to 11 days, will enable the customers to reduce their safety stocks.

• Improved cash flow. The advanced order processing system should result in more accurate and timely invoicing of customers, thereby improving cash flow.

• Improved information. The advanced order processing should improve information in two major ways. First, sales data should be captured sooner and more reliably, leading to more timely and better information for sales forecasting and production planning. Second, the improved system can be used as a source of valuable input for the logistics management information system.

Management must have access to good cost data in order to determine the financial impact of purchasing a new forecasting model, an inventory control package, or any other logistics system change. With a well-thought-out financial analysis, the logistics executive will be able to determine the probable profit impact of any proposed system.

Summary

Accurate cost data are required to achieve least-cost logistics. Successful implementation of integrated logistics management depends on a full knowledge of the costs involved. Cost data also are required to manage logistics operations.

In this chapter, we saw how to use logistics costs for decision making and how erroneous decisions result from the use of inaccurate costs. We examined the measurement and control of logistics performance, using standard costs and flexible budgets, budgetary practices, activity based costing, and productivity standards. Finally, we described how the total cost concept can be used to cost-justify changes in logistics structure.

In the next chapter, we will explore supply chain management, for which good data are critical for decision making and supply chain design.

Suggested Readings

Armitage, Howard M. "The Use of Management Accounting Techniques to Improve Productivity Analysis in Distribution Operations." *International Journal of Physical Distribution and Materials Management* 14, no. 1 (1984), pp. 41–51.

Carter, Joseph R., and Bruce G. Ferrin. "The Impact of Transportation Costs on Supply Chain Management." *Journal of Business Logistics* 16, no. 1 (1995), pp. 189–212.

Cavinato, Joseph L. "A Total Cost/Value Model for Supply Chain Competitiveness." *Journal of Business Logistics* 13, no. 2 (1992), pp. 285–301.

Cooper, Robin. "You Need a New Cost System When . . ." *Harvard Business Review* 67, no. 1 (Jan.–Feb. 1989), pp. 77–82.

Cooper, Robin, and Robert S. Kaplan. "Measure Costs Right: Make the Right Decisions." *Harvard Business Review* 66, no. 5 (Sept.–Oct. 1988), pp. 96–103.

Ellram, Lisa M. "Activity-Based Costing and Total Cost of Ownership: A Critical Linkage." *Journal of Cost Management* 8, no. 4 (Winter 1995), pp. 14–21.

———. *Total Cost Modeling in Purchasing.* Tempe, AZ: Center for Advanced Purchasing Studies, 1994.

Creative Solutions

Open Book Contract Warehousing at Quantum Chemicals

Quantum Chemical Company completely reengineered its distribution network in 1994. In doing so, it changed its financial arrangements with its third-party service providers to one based on five-year, open book contracts.

These open book contracts require the service provider to open its accounting records to the customer (Quantum), disclosing all of the costs related to the distribution facility in question. The customer and service provider work closely to reduce and control costs. However, this can be stressful for service providers who are unaccustomed to sharing such sensitive data.

The premise of an open book arrangement is that Quantum will pay **cost-plus,** a management fee based on the service provider's books. This helps Quantum because:

- It can begin to understand the cost drivers of an operation.
- It can have increased input in the operation.

- The arrangement allows Quantum to focus on performance, not price.

Because cost-plus doesn't have built-in incentives for the service provider that **gainsharing**[24] has, Quantum is developing an incentive plan tied to exceeding expectations in:

- On-time shipments
- Order accuracy
- Inventory accuracy
- Customer complaints
- Reporting timeliness

So far, the arrangement has worked very well.

Source: "Open Book Contract Warehousing Can Be an Effective Way to Begin Outsourced Relationship, Quantum Finds," *Outsourced Logistics Report,* May 1996, pp. 7–8.

[24]Gainsharing means that productivity improvements beyond some agreed upon number are split in some pre-determined way.

Ernst and Whinney. *Transportation Accounting and Control: Guidelines for Distribution and Financial Management.* Chicago: National Council of Physical Distribution Management; New York: National Association of Accountants, 1983.

———. *Warehouse Accounting and Control: Guidelines for Distribution and Financial Managers.* Chicago: National Council of Physical Distribution Management; New York: National Association of Accountants, 1985.

"Finding the Hidden Cost of Logistics." *Traffic Management* 34, no. 3 (Mar. 1995), pp. 47–50.

Gustin, Craig; Patricia Daugherty; and Theodore P. Stank. "The Effects of Information Availability on Logistics Integration." *Journal of Business Logistics* 16, no. 1 (1995), pp. 1–22.

Kaplan, Robert S. "How Cost Accounting Distorts Product Costs." *Management Accounting* 70 (Apr. 1988), pp. 20–27.

———. "One Cost System Isn't Enough." *Harvard Business Review* 66, no. 1 (Jan.–Feb. 1988), pp. 61–66.

Kearney, A.T., Inc. *Measuring and Improving Productivity in Physical Distribution.* Oak Brook, IL: National Council of Physical Distribution Management, 1984.

Keegan, Daniel P., and Stephen W. Portik. "Accounting Will Survive the Coming Century, Won't It?" *Management Accounting* 77 (Dec. 1995), pp. 24–30.

Kelly, Kevin. "A Bean-Counter's Best Friend." *Business Week,* special issue on "The Quality Imperative," Oct. 25, 1991, pp. 42–43.

La Londe, Bernard J., and Terrance L. Pohlen. "Issues in Supply Chain Costing." *The International Journal of Logistics Management* 7, no. 1 (1996), pp. 1–12.

Lambert, Douglas M., and Jay U. Sterling. "What Types of Profitability Reports Do Marketing Managers Receive?" *Industrial Marketing Management* 16, no. 4 (1987), pp. 295–303.

Mackey, James T., and Vernon H. Hughes. "Decision Focused Costing at Kenco." *Management Accounting* 75 (May 1993), pp. 22–26.

Mentzer, John T., and Brenda Ponsford Konrad. "An Efficiency/Effectiveness Approach to Logistics Performance Analysis." *Journal of Business Logistics* 12, no. 1 (1991), pp. 33–62.

Novak, Robert A. "Quality and Control in Logistics: A Process Model." *International Journal of Physical Distribution and Materials Management* 19, no. 11 (1989), pp. 1–44.

Roth, Harold P., and A. Faye Borthick. "Are You Distorting Costs by Violating ABC Assumptions?" *Management Accounting* 73 (Nov. 1991), pp. 39–42.

Shank, John K., and Vijay Govindarajan. "Strategic Cost Management and the Value Chain." *Journal of Cost Management* 5, no. 1 (Winter 1992), pp. 5–21.

Shapiro, Jeremy. "Integrated Logistics Management, Total Cost Analysis and Optimization Modeling." *International Journal of Physical Distribution and Logistics Management* 22, no. 3 (1992), pp. 33–36.

Tyndall, Gene R., and John R. Busher. "Improving the Management of Distribution with Cost and Financial Information." *Journal of Business Logistics* 6, no. 2 (1985), pp. 1–18.

Worthy, Ford S. "Accounting Bores You? Wake Up." *Fortune,* Oct. 12, 1987, pp. 43–44, 48–50.

Questions and Problems

1. Why is it important to have accurate cost data for management of the logistics function?

2. What problems are associated with the use of average cost data for decision making?

3. How does the inability to distinguish between fixed and variable costs hamper good management practice?

4. What problems are associated with the arbitrary allocation of logistics costs?

5. How do accurate cost data contribute to the motivation of personnel?

6. Why is it difficult to obtain logistics cost data in many firms?

7. Identify and describe the methods that can be used for controlling logistics activities. What are the advantages and disadvantages of each?

8. What is activity-based costing? What are its advantages? What are its potential limitations?

9. How can the order processing system improve the quality of the logistics information system?

10. What nonfinancial measures can be used to justify logistics system changes?

11. As a logistics intern at a major company, you are given the following information to analyze potential trends and issues in transportation productivity.

    - Ton-miles transported were 25,000
    - Total actual transportation cost was $5,500
    - Stops served equals 12
    - Number of shipments transported to destination was 45
    - Average stops served per period was 45

    What can you discern from these data?

12. The marketing department has indicated that it can increase sales by 5 percent if customer service is increased from the current level of 95 to 97 percent. They believe it is a "good deal" to get a 5 percent increase in sales for only a 2 percent increase in customer service. Is this a good assumption? Why or why not? What costs might increase as a result of increasing customer service levels? List all the costs you believe might be affected and why they might be affected.

THE DISTRIBUTION CHALLENGE!
PROBLEM: ALL SKU'ED UP

The client is a leading manufacturer and assembler of agricultural and construction equipment. The third-party logistics provider is FDSI Logistics, Inc. The challenge is about as basic as you can get: knowing your true cost of transportation.

FDSI started with a company whose transportation department had little control of freight moving in any direction. On the inbound side, purchasing had minimal interaction with transportation, and many shipments were vendor routed. Outbound shipments largely conformed to routing instructions and carriers requested by the dealer. As a result, the client had neither control of its freight nor visibility of the cost and handling of shipments.

There's no particular secret to getting control of inbound and outbound movements. In this case, however, the major stumbling block was a lack of essential data, according to FDSI vice president Deidric Weller. How could its client find out what customers had been paying for freight? How could it learn what it should be paying? How could it get around the motor carriers' arcane system of rate classification?

Most of all, how could the client determine its transportation expense down to the stockkeeping unit (SKU) level? The client company had about 570 SKUs and it wanted to know the cost of moving every single one. The solution would have to take into account differences in weight, cube, route segment, and mileage.

Describe the stages that a company must undertake to reach this goal.

What Is Your Solution?

Source: "Distribution: The Challenge," *Distribution* 96, no. 1 (Jan. 1997), p. 76.

Chapter Objectives

- To show how supply chain management and distribution channels play integral roles in a firm's marketing strategy.
- To familiarize the reader with the concept of supply chain management and the types of channel structures.
- To describe the factors that influence channel design, development, and performance.
- To illustrate how to implement logistics cost trade-offs in a channel of distribution.
- To show the role of logistics in supply chain management.

Introduction

In any industrialized or nonindustrialized society, goods must be physically moved between the place they are produced and the place they are consumed. Except in very primitive cultures, in which each family meets its own household needs, the exchange process has become the cornerstone of economic activity. Exchange takes place when there is a discrepancy between the amount, type, and timing of goods available and the goods needed. If a number of individuals or organizations within a society have a surplus of goods that someone else needs, there is a basis for exchange. **Channels** develop when many exchanges take place between producers and consumers. The alignment of firms that bring products or services to market has been called the **supply chain,** the demand chain or the value chain. In this book we will use the term supply chain to represent this alignment of firms.

Supply chain management (SCM) is a term that has grown significantly in use and popularity since the late 1980s, although considerable confusion exists about what it actually means. Many people use the term as a substitute or synonym for logistics. However, the definition of supply chain management used in this book is much broader than logistics.

What Is Supply Chain Management?

Supply chain management is the integration of business processes from end user through original suppliers that provides products, services, and information that add value for customers.[1]

A number of important differences exist between this definition of supply chain management and the Council of Logistics Management's definition of logistics. Foremost, supply chain management is the management of all key business processes across members of the supply chain. While SCM represents a relatively new way of approaching business and different views exist regarding the processes involved, the key processes typically would include: customer relationship management, customer service management, demand management, order fulfillment, manufacturing flow management, procurement, and product development and commercialization. At some companies such as Xerox, the returns channel process is also included.[2] Key areas required for successful implementation of SCM are executive support, leadership, commitment to change, and empowerment. These areas will be described along with the key processes later in the chapter.

Thus, SCM is a systems approach that is highly interactive and complex, and requires simultaneous consideration of many trade-offs. As shown in Figure 14–1, SCM spans organizational boundaries, considering trade-offs both within and among organizations regarding where inventory should be held and where activities should be performed.

The dynamic nature of the business environment requires management to monitor and evaluate the performance of the supply chain regularly and frequently. When perfor-

---

[1]The International Center for Competitive Excellence, University of North Florida, 1994. In July 1996, the Center members moved with Douglas M. Lambert to The Ohio State University and the Center was renamed The Global Supply Chain Forum.

[2]John A. Clendenin, "Closing the Supply Chain Loop: Reengineering the Returns Channel Process," *The International Journal of Logistics Management* 8, no. 1 (1997), pp. 75–85.

FIGURE 14–1

Supply chain management

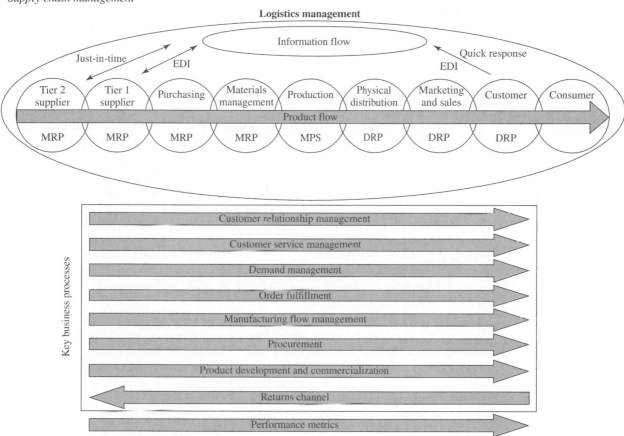

Source: *The International Center for Competitive Excellence,* University of North Florida.
MRP is materials requirements planning. DRP is distribution requirements planning.

mance goals are not met, management must evaluate possible supply chain alternatives and implement changes. SCM is particularly important in mature and declining markets and during periods of economic slowdown when market growth cannot conceal inefficient practices. SCM also is critical in new product development and market development, when the organization is making decisions related to supply chain configuration.

This chapter begins with an overview of channels of distribution and why they evolve. Next, issues related to the design and structure of the supply chain are presented. A summary of key financial and performance considerations in SCM is provided. The chapter closes with sections on integrated SCM, reengineering improvement into the supply chain, and implementing integrated SCM which draw heavily on the experience of 3M Company and the work of Gary J. Ridenhower, Director, Logistics Services and Supply Chain Process Management.

SCM is an integrative approach that considers both the inbound (upstream) and outbound (downstream) flow of materials, services and goods to the firm. Chapter 10 covered many of the upstream supply chain management concerns. This chapter focuses primarily on the downstream concerns and the integration of upstream and downstream supply chain issues.

What Is a Channel of Distribution?

A Channel of Distribution Defined

A **channel of distribution** can be defined as the collection of organizational units, institutions, or agencies within or external to the manufacturer, which perform the functions that support product marketing.[3] The marketing functions are pervasive; they include buying, selling, transporting, storing, grading, financing, bearing market risk, and providing marketing information.[4] Any organizational unit, institution, or agency that performs one or more of the marketing functions is a member of a channel of distribution.

The structure of a distribution channel[5] is determined by the marketing functions that specific organizations perform. Some channel members perform single functions—carriers transport products, and public warehousers store them. Others, such as third-party logistics providers and wholesalers, perform multiple functions. Channel structure affects (1) control over the performance of functions, (2) the speed of delivery and communication, and (3) the cost of operations.[6]

While a direct manufacturer-to-user channel usually gives management greater control over the performance of marketing functions, distribution costs normally are higher, making it necessary for the firm to have substantial sales volume or market concentration. With indirect channels, the external institutions or agencies (e.g., carriers, warehousers, wholesalers, retailers) assume much of the cost burden and risk, so the manufacturer receives less revenue per unit.

Channel Structure Is Influenced by the Target Market and the Product

Most distribution channels are loosely structured networks of vertically aligned firms. The specific structure depends to a large extent on the nature of the product and the firm's target market. There is no "best" channel structure for all firms producing similar products. Management must determine channel structure within the framework of the firm's corporate and marketing objectives, its operating philosophy, its strengths and weaknesses, and its infrastructure of manufacturing facilities and warehouses. If the firm has targeted multiple market segments, management may have to develop multiple channels to service these markets efficiently. For example, Whirlpool Corporation sells a major portion of its product through Sears under the Kenmore name, uses dealers for its Whirlpool brand line, and sells to original equipment manufacturers (OEM accounts).

---

[3]Revis Cox and Thomas F. Schutte, "A Look at Channel Management," in *Marketing Involvement in Society and the Economy,* Philip McDonald, ed. (Chicago: American Marketing Association, 1969), p. 105.

[4]Fred E. Clark, *Principles of Marketing* (New York: Macmillan, 1992), p. 11; and Robert Bartels, *Marketing Theory and Metatheory* (Burr Ridge, IL: Richard D. Irwin, 1970), pp. 166–75.

[5]Channel structure is determined by the types of middlemen the manufacturer uses.

[6]Louis W. Stern, "Channel Control and Interorganization Management," in *Marketing and Economic Development,* Peter D. Bennett, ed. (Chicago: American Marketing Association, 1965), pp. 655–65

Why Do Channels of Distribution Develop?[7]

The emergence of channels of distribution has been explained in terms of the following factors:[8]

1. Intermediaries evolve in the process of exchange because they can increase the efficiency of the process by creating time, place, and possession utility.

2. Channel intermediaries enable the adjustment of the discrepancy of assortment by performing the functions of sorting and assorting. Discrepancy of assortment will be described shortly.

3. Marketing agencies form channel arrangements to make transactions routine.

4. Channels facilitate the searching process by consumers.

The Evolution of Marketing Channels

Intermediaries Reduce Market Contacts

Marketing channels develop because intermediaries (e.g., wholesalers and retailers) make the marketing process more efficient by reducing the number of market contacts. In primitive cultures, for example, most household needs are met by family members. But many household needs can be met more efficiently by exchange. Specialization in production creates efficiency; for this reason, it has become a way of life. A household must exchange goods and services to provide for all of its needs.

Calculating the Advantage of an Intermediary

The advantage of an intermediary is greater as the number of specialized producers increases. Figure 14–2 shows that 10 customers purchasing from 4 suppliers results in 40 market contacts. If the suppliers sell to these customers through one intermediary, the number of required contacts is 14, a 65 percent reduction! This example demonstrates that a manufacturer selling to low-volume customers could reduce selling and logistics costs substantially by using an intermediary.

The Discrepancy of Assortment and Sorting

Intermediaries Provide Utility

Intermediaries provide possession, time, and place utility. They create possession utility through the process of exchange, the result of the buying and selling functions. They provide time utility by holding inventory available for sale. And they provide place utility by physically moving goods to the market. The assortment of goods and services held by a producer and the assortment demanded by the customer often differ. The primary function of channel intermediaries is to adjust this discrepancy by performing the following "sorting" processes:[9]

1. **Sorting out.** Grouping a heterogeneous supply into relatively homogeneous separate stocks. "Sorting out is typified by the grading of agricultural products or by pulling out rejects in some manufacturing operations."

---

[7]This section is adapted from Douglas M. Lambert, *The Distribution Channels Decision* (New York: National Association of Accountants; Hamilton, Ontario: Society of Management Accountants of Canada, 1978), pp. 12–19.

[8]Wroe Alderson, "Factors Governing the Development of Marketing Channels," in *Marketing Channels for Manufactured Products,* R. M. Clewett, ed. (Burr Ridge, IL: Richard D. Irwin, 1954), pp. 8–16.

[9]Ibid., pp. 12–13.

FIGURE 14–2

How intermediaries reduce the cost of market contact between supplier and customer

A. Direct selling

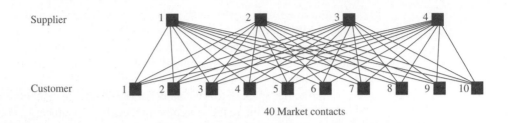

40 Market contacts

B. Selling through one intermediary

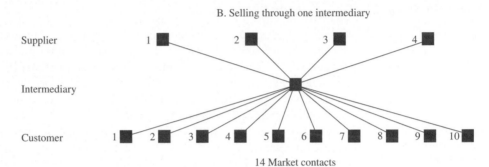

14 Market contacts

Source: Douglas M. Lambert, *The Distribution Channels Decision* (New York: National Association of Accountants; Hamilton, Ontario: Society of Management Accountants of Canada, 1978), pp. 15–16. Reprinted with permission. Copyright © 1978 by National Association of Accountants. All rights reserved.

2. **Accumulating.** Bringing similar stocks together into a larger homogeneous supply.

3. **Allocation.** Breaking down a homogeneous supply into smaller lots. Allocating at the wholesale level is referred to as "breaking bulk." Goods received in carloads are sold in case lots. A buyer in case lots in turn sells individual units.

4. **Assorting.** Building up the assortment of products for use or sale in association with each other. Wholesalers build assortment of goods for retailers, and retailers build assortment for their customers.

Sorting out and accumulating predominate in the marketing of agricultural and extractive products. Allocation and assorting predominate in the marketing of finished manufactured goods. Because customers may demand a much broader assortment of goods and services than that provided by a single manufacturer, specialization develops in the exchange process to reduce distribution costs. That is, the customer's desire for **discrepancy of assortment** drives the producer to use intermediaries to reach the customer because doing so leads to improved distribution efficiency.

Routinization of Transactions

Routinization Reduces Costs

The cost of distribution can be minimized if transactions are routine; that is, if every transaction is not subject to bargaining with its resulting loss of efficiency. Marketing agencies form channel arrangements to make routinization possible. Channel cooperation and efficiency are improved by the routine handling of transactions. Logistics operations can be made more efficient by using the same processes; they may be even more efficient if third parties are utilized.

Searching through Marketing Channels

Buyers and sellers engage in a process in which consumers try to satisfy their consumption needs and producers attempt to predict those needs. If the searching process is successful, allocation and assorting will take place, resulting in benefits to both the consumer and producer. Marketing channels facilitate the process of searching when institutions organize by separate lines of trade and provide information to their markets.

In summary, the use of an intermediary reduces some or all of the following costs:

Costs Reduced by Intermediaries

- Selling costs (because fewer market contacts are required).
- Transportation costs (because intermediaries may result in fewer but larger volume shipments).
- Inventory carrying costs (if the intermediary takes ownership).
- Storage costs.
- Order processing costs.
- Accounts receivable or bad debts (if the intermediary takes ownership).
- Customer service costs.

Channel Structure

Bucklin's Theory of Channel Structure

Channel structure may be viewed as a function of product life cycle, logistics systems, effective communication networks, product characteristics, or firm size.[10] However, the most detailed theory of channel structure was developed by Louis P. Bucklin,[11] who stated that the purpose of the channel is to provide consumers with the desired combination of its outputs (i.e., lot size, delivery time, and market decentralization) at minimal cost. Consumers determine channel structure by purchasing combinations of service outputs. The best channel forms when no other group of institutions generates more profits or more consumer satisfaction per dollar of product cost. Bucklin concluded that functions will be shifted from one channel member to another in order to achieve the most efficient and effective channel structure.

---

[10]Ronald Michman, "Channel Development and Innovation," *Marquette Business Review* (Spring 1971), pp. 45–49; Leo Aspinwall, "The Characteristics of Goods and Parallel Systems Theories," in *Marketing Management,* Eugene Kelley and William Lazer, eds. (Burr Ridge, IL: Richard D. Irwin, 1958), pp. 434–450; Robert E. Weigand, "The Marketing Organization, Channels and Firm Size," *Journal of Business* 36 (Apr. 1963), pp. 228–36.

[11]Louis P. Bucklin, *A Theory of Distribution Channel Structure* (Berkeley: University of California, Institute of Business and Economic Research, 1966).

Outsourcing of one or more logistics activities can be a viable option for some firms involved in global supply chain management.

Given a desired level of output by the consumer and competitive conditions, channel institutions will arrange their functional tasks in a way that minimizes total channel costs. This shift of specific functions may lead to the addition or deletion of channel members.

In deciding when and where to use channel intermediaries, a firm is really considering the make/buy or "outsourcing" decision. Does the organization need to develop the required skills and capabilities internally, or can it be done faster and more efficiently by a third party?

Outsourcing

Approximately $10 billion or 2.5 percent of logistics services in the United States are being outsourced and there are significant opportunities to outsource additional logistics services.[12] Examples of available outsourcing services include:

• A large pharmaceutical company will outsource its worldwide distribution, providing on-site pharmacists at some centers to dispense high-value products.

---

[12]Helen L. Richardson, "How Much Should You Outsource?" *Transportation and Distribution* 35, no. 9 (Sept. 1994), p. 61.

- A third party handles the entire finished goods inventory for a large women's clothing company. When garments are purchased by a retailer, the distributor attaches the store's private label, refreshes the garment, packs it in the store's packaging, and ships it to the retailer.
- A mail-order retailer is having Federal Express handle not only its shipments, but storage and management of the inventory in all aspects of distribution.
- In addition to handling store replenishment and delivery of product to consumers for a tool manufacturer, UPS will now manage the warehouse. If the retail store needs a product, an order that reaches the distribution center as late as 9:00 P.M. will be at the store by the next morning.[13]

Outsourcing Should Be Evaluated in Supply Chain Design

Thus, outsourcing represents an opportunity that a firm should consider in its supply chain design and evaluation of existing channels. In addition, the role and utility of the distributor is changing. In some cases, the consolidation of suppliers and customers has reduced the value and functionality of distributors.

For example, Wal-Mart uses direct distribution and may replace 10 small independent stores that used distributors with one of its stores, that uses direct distribution. Similarly, advanced technology like EDI trades information for inventory, reducing the need to hold inventory at distributors and retailers. Better information technology and increased service offerings by carriers (e.g., cross-docking) may reduce the need for a distributor's services.[14]

Postponement and Speculation

Postponement

Bucklin's theory of channel structure is based on the concepts of **postponement** and speculation.[15] Costs can be reduced by:

1. Postponing changes in the form and identity of a product to the last possible point in the marketing process.
2. Postponing inventory location to the last possible point in time since risk and uncertainty costs increase as the product becomes more differentiated.

Postponement results in savings because it moves differentiation nearer to the time of purchase, when demand is more easily forecast. This reduces costs from risk and uncertainty. Logistics costs are reduced by sorting products in large lots in relatively undifferentiated states. Third-party service providers can support postponement (see Box 14–1).

Companies can use postponement to shift the risk of owning goods from one channel member to another. A manufacturer may refuse to produce until it receives firm orders. A middleman may postpone owning inventories by purchasing from sellers who offer faster delivery, purchasing on consignment, or purchasing only when a sale has been made. Consumers may postpone ownership by buying from retail outlets that have the products in stock.

---

[13]Ibid.

[14]William C. Copacino, "The Changing Role of the Distributor," *Traffic Management* 33, no. 2 (Feb. 1994), p. 31.

[15]Louis P. Bucklin, "Postponement, Speculation and the Structure of Distribution Channels," *Journal of Marketing Research* 2, no. 1 (Feb. 1965), pp. 26–31.

Box 14–1

Third Parties Support Postponement

Management at Excel Logistics views postponement as a "micromarketing" opportunity. Customers of Excel ship full pallets of product, thereby postponing the mixing of product on pallets until orders are received. Excel helps its customers to better match local marketing requirements in order to compete more effectively at the local level. For example, Excel builds "store packages" for its customers. This allows store managers to choose from a custom mix of products, mixing items on pallets to meet a customer's needs instead of forcing the customer to take a "full pallet" or a pallet that is "premixed" by the manufacturer.

This kind of postponement can support transportation economies because products can be shipped a greater distance in bulk. For example, Excel receives bulk chemicals from the shipper and then repackages them in the language and packaging needs of different countries. Thus, third parties can play an important role in supporting postponement and improving overall supply chain efficiency and customer service goals.

Source: Adapted from Helen L. Richardson, "Cut Inventory, Postpone Finishing Touches," *Transportation and Distribution* 35, no. 2 (Feb. 1994) pp. 38–39.

An excellent example of postponement is the mixing of paint colors at the retail store. Instead of having to forecast the exact colors that consumers will want to buy, the retailer mixes paint in any color the consumer wishes at the time of purchase. Other examples include the color panels in the front of built-in kitchen appliances that enable the same unit to be in any one of a number of colors to match the kitchens; the centralization of slow-selling products in one warehouse location; and the assembly of slow-moving items only after orders have been received.

Speculation

Speculation is the opposite of postponement; that is, a channel institution assumes risk rather than shifting it. Speculation can reduce marketing costs through:

1. Economies of large-scale production.
2. Placement of large orders that reduce the costs of order processing and transportation.
3. Reduction of stockouts and their associated costs.
4. Reduction of uncertainty.

To reduce the need for speculative inventories, many firms are exploring strategies of time-based competition.[16] A 1994 survey indicated that by using time-based competition, firms could reduce their time to manufacture products significantly while reducing inventory, improving inventory turns, and reducing the cost of ownership. Customer satisfaction also has improved.[17]

---

[16]See Robert Handfield, "The Role of Materials Management in Developing Time-Based Competition," *International Journal of Purchasing and Materials Management* 29, no. 4 (Winter 1991), pp. 2–10.

[17]Thomas Hendrick, *Purchasing's Contribution to Time-Based Strategies* (Tempe, AZ: Center for Advanced Purchasing Studies, 1994).

Time to Market Pressures

**Speed as a
Competitive
Advantage**

"Speed" can be used as a source of competitive advantage. This is true in virtually all market sectors: services, manufacturing, and retailing. Retailers have been leaders in the area of time-based competition, relying heavily on advanced computer systems involving bar coding and EDI to support quick response (see Chapter 3). The use of such systems is growing among carriers. However, computer systems are not enough to create speed to market; fundamental changes in operational relationships are required, such as information sharing between suppliers, manufacturers, and retailers about lead-times, forecasts of sales, production and purchasing needs, shipping, new product plans, and payment information.

Some of the benefits of effective time-based management include:

- Improved customer service through better responsiveness.
- Reduced inventory requirements due to shorter lead times.
- Improved quality or product freshness through reduced handling and lower inventories.
- Faster throughput.
- Reduced supply chain cost.[18]

Other Issues In Channel Structure

Additional factors that might influence channel structure include:

- Technological, cultural, physical, social, and political factors.
- Physical factors—geography, size of market area, location of production centers, and concentration of population.
- Local, state, and federal laws.
- Social and behavioral variables.

For example, social, cultural, political, and economic variables may support channels that are not necessarily as efficient or effective as they should be.

Flows in the Channel of Distribution

An example of the various channels of distribution that a manufacturer of grocery products might use is shown in Figure 14–3. The manufacturer sells its products to wholesalers, chain stores, cooperatives, and the military. The wholesalers and co-ops service retail accounts. Accounts are serviced by a national sales force.

Product and Information Flows

**Information Flows
Precede Product
Flows**

Figure 14–3 illustrates the product and information flows that take place in a channel. Remember that product flows take place only after information flows are initiated. In addition to product and information flows, payments for the merchandise and promotional

---

[18]Adapted from E. J. Muller, "Faster, Faster: I Need it Now!" *Distribution* 93, no. 2 (Feb. 1994), pp. 30–36.

FIGURE 14–3

Distribution channels: Grocery products manufacturer

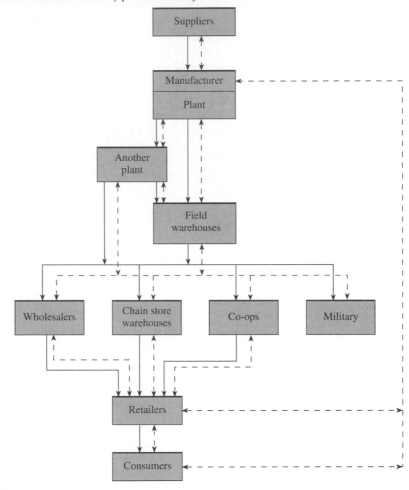

materials move through the system. The manufacturer may send salespeople to call on wholesalers and retailers, reach them by telephone using an inside sales force, or use some combination of these approaches.

Customers Are the Source of Sales and Market Research Information

Sales data and market research data also flow from customers to the manufacturer. These data help the manufacturer determine whether its products are selling, to whom they are selling, and possibly why they are selling. Other types of information continually flowing between channel members include the quantity of inventory at each point in the channel, future production runs, service requirements, and delivery schedules.

Information Flows Affect Inventory Levels

To maximize profitability, manufacturers traditionally, have encouraged wholesalers and retailers to hold large inventories. Increasingly, wholesalers and retailers want to shift inventories back in the channel. The quality and speed of the information flows determine the safety stock held at each level of the channel.

Communication Linkages

Firms Need a Communications Link with Consumers

In many cases, manufacturers need to include a direct communication link between the consumer and the firm because product problems often do not become apparent until the product is in the hands of the end user. Given no direct method of communicating with the manufacturer, the consumer may take a course of action that is costly to the manufacturer and to other users.

For instance, an unhappy consumer may tell a government agency or consumer advocate group about the problem with the product. This could prompt costly government regulation or even result in a direct reprimand, monetary or otherwise, for the firm. The consumer is likely to share his or her dissatisfaction with friends, neighbors, and family. Such unfavorable word-of-mouth advertising could hurt sales. The consumer also might write to the manufacturer, but letter writing takes time and effort and is therefore the least likely course of action. The defective product could incur serious and costly liabilities for the manufacturer significantly altering its ability to compete in the marketplace.

Communication Acts as a Buffer

If consumers have a direct and convenient way to communicate with a firm, the system can provide the firm with early warning of product defects, as well as advertising and promotion problems and product availability. A formal consumer response department can alert the manufacturer to the need to recall a product before major liabilities occur. Just as inventory acts as a buffer throughout the channel, so does communication. With the advent of lower cost and significantly improved computer networks, channel communication is improving significantly. This was the case with Advance Micro Devices (AMD) when it reconfigured its logistics operations (see Box 14–2).

Marketing Strategy

Management must coordinate a firm's logistics strategy with the other components of the marketing mix to successfully implement an overall marketing strategy. In some cases, existing channels of distribution may dictate the types of products a firm sells and how it prices and promotes them. For example, General Mills and Procter & Gamble make excellent products that are well advertised and competitively priced, but the most important factors that separate these companies from their smaller competitors is the size and effectiveness of their distribution channels. Generally, management expects new products to be compatible with current distribution channels.

Channel Separation

Both the physical flow of products (logistics channel) and the legal exchange of ownership (transaction channel) must take place for the channel of distribution to be successful. But a product may change ownership without physically moving and it may be transported from one location to another without changing ownership. One major manufacturer's distributors sell home appliances to dealers, but the manufacturer bypasses the distributors and

Box 14–2

AMD Takes Control of Its Distribution Channel

Since mid-1991, Advanced Micro Devices (AMD) has turned over about half of its Los Angeles distribution operations to Circle International. However, it has focused its internal efforts on providing reliable delivery directly to its customers from its factories in the Far East. Why is AMD doing this internally?

Improved transit time and reliability worldwide has provided the logistics capability. Yet another important factor in managing the whole process is an improved information system. Gerald Moloney, AMD's corporate manager for distribution logistics, explained that with its improved information system, AMD will "be able to take an order anywhere in the world and have it visible and processable within hours."

The direct delivery system also cuts out the middle man, making AMD the direct contact for any problems related to customer service. At first, customers were skeptical because they were accustomed to having control of the inbound logistics of AMD's products. However, actual experience and performance has "far exceeded the customers' expectations."

Source: Peter A. Buxbaum, "Coming Fullcircle," *Distribution* 93, no. 2 (Feb. 1994), pp. 47–49.

Channel Separation

ships large orders directly to the dealers. The "dealer direct" program accounted for approximately 50 percent of the firm's sales volume. Although ownership passes from the manufacturer to the distributor to the dealer, the product flows directly from the manufacturer to the dealer, resulting in greater logistics efficiency.[19] This is referred to as **channel separation.**

Successful channel separation requires:

1. A fast, reliable transportation system.
2. An on-line, interactive order processing system.
3. Swift, efficient information flows, such as inward Wide Area Telephone Service (WATS) lines or computer-to-computer transmission of orders and other information.

While both the logistics channel and transaction channel must function in order to achieve a profitable sale, a firm should use channel separation if it results in improved performance.

Channel Design

Even though leading-edge firms are doing more planning of their channels, evidence suggests that the majority of supply chains were not designed, but were developed over time.

---

[19]Douglas M. Lambert and James R. Stock, *Strategic Logistics Management,* 3rd ed. (Burr Ridge, IL: Richard D Irwin, 1993) p. 86.

For example, companies like Hewlett-Packard and Digital Equipment plan new channels or supply chains and use supply chain management strategies to modify existing channels.[20] However, these examples appear to be the exception rather than the rule.

Most Channels of Distribution Are Not Planned

Current practice reveals a lack of planning by most firms. Better management of supply chains can create significant benefits. In many cases, for example, not all channel alternatives are known when structural arrangements are initially negotiated; these decisions may later prove to be less than optimal. Identifying suboptimal channel arrangements and making structural changes will lead to increased profitability. Later in this chapter, we will provide an example of profitability analysis by channel type.

In addition, unanticipated changes in the environment may make it necessary to reconsider the channels of distribution. Environmental factors may include changes in consumer needs, markets, products and product lines, the competitive situation, the economic environment, and government regulation and incentives.

Supply chain strategy must support overall corporate and marketing objectives. Supply chain performance goals must be stated in operational terms, such as projected market coverage, sales and service support, sales volume, profitability, and return on investment. The supply chain strategy includes decisions regarding intensity of distribution, use of direct or indirect channels, the services of intermediaries in each geographic area, and implementation plans.

A firm must become involved in the channel design process when it is considering entering the market with a new product or when existing supply chains are falling short of performance objectives. The design process consists of the following steps:[21]

Steps in the Design Process

1. Establish objectives.
2. Formulate a strategy.
3. Determine structure alternatives.
4. Evaluate structure alternatives.
5. Select structure.
6. Determine alternatives for individual channel members.
7. Evaluate and select individual members.
8. Measure and evaluate channel performance.
9. Evaluate alternatives when performance objectives are not met, or attractive new options become available.

The manufacturer, wholesaler, or retailer may lead the design process, depending on the relative market power, financial strength, and availability of desired channel members. The Creative Solutions box at the end of the chapter shows how the leading U.S. textile manufacturer improved its performance through supply chain integration.

---

[20]Hau L. Lee and Corey Billington, "Managing Supply Chain Inventory: Pitfalls and Opportunities," *Sloan Management Review* 33, no. 3 (Spring 1992), pp. 65–73; Tom Davis "Effective Supply Chain Management," *Sloan Management Review* 34, no. 4 (Summer 1993), pp. 35–46; Bruce C. Arntzen, Gerald G. Brown and Linda L. Traffton, "Global Supply Chain Management at Digital Equipment Corporation," *Interfaces* 25, no. 1 (1995), pp. 69–78.

[21]Adapted from Lambert, *The Distribution Channels Decision,* pp. 44-45.

The Manufacturer's Perspective

A manufacturer has market power when customers demand its product. When consumers demand a manufacturer's brand, retailers and wholesalers are anxious to market the manufacturers old and new products because they draw customers. Increasingly, the consolidation of manufacturers, wholesalers and retailers on a national and global basis has resulted in a power shift to retailers because they have access to consumers. The consolidation of manufacturers results in a reduced set of global suppliers that produce brands which consumers increasingly view as substitutable. The store brands of retailers such as Wal-Mart become national and sometimes global brands, which further contributes to the weakening of traditionally strong manufacturer brands.

A small manufacturer of a little-known brand may find it difficult to attract supply chain members for its existing or new product offerings. Small manufacturers lack market power when entering supply chain negotiations and because financial resources determine any manufacturer's ability to perform marketing functions internally, they usually cannot afford to distribute directly to retailers or geographically dispersed industrial customers, relying instead on wholesalers. Furthermore, acceptable middlemen may not be available in every line of trade in some locations. Firms in this situation include certain manufacturers of electrical supplies and small hand tools.

Even the manufacturer of a full line of products who has geographically concentrated customers may find direct channels less profitable than indirect channels for some of its products and customers. For example, many pharmaceutical companies have increased their use of wholesalers to service small-volume customers, even in concentrated market areas, because the high levels of customer service required make them unprofitable to deal with on a direct basis.

The Wholesaler's Perspective

Wholesalers make it possible to efficiently provide possession, time, and place utility. Wholesalers are economically justified because they improve distribution efficiency by breaking bulk, building assortments of goods, and providing financing for retailers or industrial customers.

The market power of wholesalers is greatest when retailers order a small amount of each manufacturer's products or when the manufacturers have limited financial resources. The financial strength of wholesalers and distributors determines the number of marketing functions they can perform. Each function represents a profit opportunity as well as a risk and cost. The presence or absence of comparable services offered by other firms influences the market power of individual wholesalers. Traditionally, wholesalers have been regional in scope. In some industries such as pharmaceuticals, wholesaler mergers have occurred. Foremost-McKesson and Cardinal Health are large pharmaceutical wholesalers that have become national in scope. Together they control about one-half of the drugstore wholesale business in the United States.

The Retailer's Perspective

Retailers exist in the channel of distribution when they provide convenient product assortment, availability, price, and image within the geographic market served. The degree of customer preference (i.e., loyalty due to customer service and price or value performance) that a retailer enjoys in a specific area directly affects its ability to negotiate channel relationships. The retailer's financial capability and size also determine its degree of influence over other supply chain members.

Considerations of Channel Design

When establishing a channel of distribution, management must consider market coverage objectives, product characteristics, customer service objectives, and profitability.[22]

Market Coverage Objectives

To establish market coverage objectives, management must consider customer buying behavior, the type of distribution required, channel structure, and the degree of control necessary for success.

Customer Buying Behavior.   The buying motives of potential customer segments must be determined in order to select intermediaries who can perform the selling function most efficiently and effectively. This analysis enables the channel designer to determine the retail segment or segments most capable of reaching the target market or markets. Industrial marketers also must identify potential users and determine how these consumers will make the purchase decision. The industrial purchaser's decision-making process depends on whether the firm is a user, an original equipment manufacturer (OEM), or a distributor.

Type of Distribution.   Three types of distribution can be used to make product available to consumers: (1) intensive distribution, (2) selective distribution and (3) exclusive distribution. In **intensive distribution,** the product is sold to as many appropriate retailers or wholesalers as possible. Intensive distribution is appropriate for products such as chewing gum, candy bars, soft drinks, bread, film, and cigarettes where the primary factor influencing the purchase decision is convenience. Industrial products that may require intensive distribution include pencils, paper clips, transparent tape, file folders, typing paper, transparency masters, screws, and nails.

In **selective distribution,** the number of outlets that may carry a product is limited, but not to the extent of exclusive dealing. By carefully selecting wholesalers or retailers, the manufacturer can concentrate on potentially profitable accounts and develop solid working relationships to ensure that the product is properly merchandised. The producer also may restrict the number of retail outlets if the product requires specialized servicing or sales support. Selective distribution may be used for product categories such as clothing, appliances, televisions, stereo equipment, home furnishings, and sports equipment.

When a single outlet is given an exclusive franchise to sell the product in a geographic area, the arrangement is referred to as **exclusive distribution.** Products such as specialty automobiles, some major appliances, certain brands of furniture, and lines of

Intensive Distribution

Selective Distribution

Exclusive Distribution

---

[22]The material in this section is adapted from Donald J. Bowersox, M. Bixby Cooper, Douglas M. Lambert, and Donald A. Taylor, *Management in Marketing Channels* (New York: McGraw-Hill, 1980), pp. 201–209.

clothing that enjoy a high degree of brand loyalty are likely to be distributed on an exclusive basis. This is particularly true if the consumer is willing to overcome the inconvenience of traveling some distance to obtain the product. Usually, exclusive distribution is undertaken when the manufacturer desires more aggressive selling on the part of the wholesaler or retailer, or when channel control is important. Exclusive distribution may enhance the product's image and enable the firm to charge higher retail prices.

Sometimes manufacturers use multiple brands in order to offer exclusive distribution to more than one retailer or distributor. Exclusive distribution occurs more frequently at the wholesale level than at the retail level. Anheuser-Busch, for example, offers exclusive rights to distributors, who in turn use intensive distribution at the retail level (in states such as Florida where this is allowed). In general, exclusive distribution lends itself to direct channels (manufacturer to retailer). Intensive distribution is more likely to involve indirect channels with two or more intermediaries.

Channel Structure.   With customer requirements and the type of distribution determined, management must select channel institutions. The increased use of scrambled merchandising has made this task somewhat more difficult. For example, grocery stores have added nongrocery products like pots and pans, children's toys, hardware items, and in some cases television sets to improve margins and profitability.

Factors Restricting Availability of Intermediaries   Other factors may restrict the availability of intermediaries. These include (1) the financial strength of the intermediaries, (2) the need for specialized facilities, (3) market coverage provided, (4) product lines carried, (5) the degree of support given to the product, (6) logistics capabilities, and (7) an intermediary's ability to grow with the business.

Control.   In many cases, a firm may have to exercise some control over other channel members to ensure product quality or postpurchase services. The need for control stems from management's desire to protect the firm's long-term profitability.

For example, a manufacturer of premium confectionery products achieves national distribution through a chain of company-owned retail outlets and selected department stores, drug stores, and specialty outlets. The marketing manager said the company does not sell to wholesalers because it wishes to avoid the mass market, fearing a loss of control over margins and product quality. If the manufacturer sold the product to a wholesaler, it could not prevent the wholesaler from selling to a mass merchant such as Kmart. A mass merchandiser would undoubtedly discount this nationally recognized brand, thus jeopardizing the very profitable company stores and other channels of distribution that rely on the substantial margins allowed by premium prices.

Product Characteristics

In addition to market coverage objectives, product characteristics are a major consideration in channel design. Nine product characteristics should be analyzed by the channel designer:

1. Product value.
2. Technicality of the product.
3. Degree of market acceptance.

4. Degree of substitutability.
5. Product bulk.
6. Product perishability.
7. Degree of market concentration.
8. Seasonality.
9. Width and depth of the product line.

Value.   Products with a high per unit cost require a large inventory investment. Consequently, manufacturers with limited resources usually shift some of the inventory burden by using intermediaries. The requirement of large inventories limits the number of available intermediaries. In some cases, the large dollar per unit margin may cover the cost of direct sales and result in the manufacturer's selecting direct distribution. But channels tend to be indirect when the unit value is low unless the sales volume is high enough to support direct channels. In general, intensive distribution is used for low-value products.

The product's value also influences its inventory carrying cost and the desirability of premium transportation. Low-value, low-margin grocery products may be shipped by railcar and stored in a number of field warehouses. High-value component parts and products such as high-fashion merchandise may be shipped by air freight from a centralized facility to minimize in-transit inventories and reduce inventory carrying costs.

Technicality.   Highly technical products usually require demonstration by a salesperson. In addition, prepurchase and postpurchase service often require the stocking of repair parts. Technical products include items such as home computers, high-priced stereo components, expensive cameras and video equipment, imported sports cars, and a multitude of industrial products. Generally, direct channels and selective or exclusive distribution policies are used for these kinds of products.

Market Acceptance.   The degree of market acceptance determines the amount of selling effort required. If a leading manufacturer offers a new product and plans significant introductory advertising, customer acceptance will be high and intermediaries will want to carry the product. But new products with little market acceptance and low brand identification require aggressive selling at each level of the channel. If middlemen are reluctant to support the line, the manufacturer may have to employ "missionary salespeople" or "detail people" to promote the line to various channel members.

Substitutability.   Product substitutability, closely related to brand loyalty, is lowest for convenience goods and highest for specialty goods. When brand loyalty is low, product substitution is likely and intensive distribution is required. Firms place a premium on point-of-purchase displays in high-traffic areas. To gain support from wholesalers and retailers, the producer may offer higher than normal margins. Selective or exclusive distribution makes product support easier.

Bulk.   Generally, low-value, high-weight products are restricted to markets close to the point of production. These products often require special materials handling skills. With low weight and small cubes, more units can be shipped in a truck, railcar, or container, thereby reducing the per unit cost of transportation. Tank truck shipment of orange juice concentrate from Florida to northern markets for packaging is an example of moving a product closer to the point of consumption to overcome value and bulk restrictions.

Perishability.   Perishability refers to physical deterioration or to product obsolescence caused by changing customer buying patterns or technological change. Perishable products are usually sold on a direct basis to move the product through the channel more quickly and to reduce the potential for inventory loss.

Market Concentration.   When the market is concentrated in a geographic area, direct channels may be the most effective and efficient method of distribution. When markets are widely dispersed, specialized intermediaries are necessary; they can capitalize on the efficiencies linked to the movement of large quantities. Because of widely dispersed markets, many food-processing companies use brokers to market their products. Pooling agencies, such as freight forwarders and local cartage firms, which aggregate small shipments into truckload or carload units for movement to distant points, also are used.

Seasonality.   Seasonality must be considered when applicable. For some products, sales volumes peak at certain times of the year (e.g., toy sales at Christmas); in other cases, raw materials (e.g., fresh fruits and vegetables) may be available only at specific times. Both cases require out of-season storage. Manufacturers must invest in warehouses, use third parties, or provide incentives to intermediaries so they will perform the storage function. For example, manufacturers might offer a seasonal discount or consignment inventories to wholesalers or retailers who agree to take early delivery.

Width and Depth.   The width and depth of a supplier's product line influence channel design. A manufacturer of products with low per unit values may use intensive distribution with direct sales if the product line is broad enough to result in a relatively large average sales volume. Grocery manufacturers such as Kellogg and General Foods are examples. Usually, a manufacturer of a limited line of products will use indirect channels to achieve adequate market coverage at a reasonable cost.

Customer Service Objectives

Customer service represents the place component of the marketing mix. It can be used to differentiate the product or influence the market price—if customers are willing to pay more for better service. In addition, the channel of distribution selected determines the costs of providing a specified level of customer service.

Customer Service Measures

As presented in Chapter 2, customer service is a complex subject, receiving a great deal of attention. It is usually measured in terms of the (1) level of product availability, (2) speed and consistency of the customer's order cycle, and (3) communication that takes place between seller and customer. Management should establish customer service levels only after carefully studying customer needs.

Availability.   The most important measure of customer service is inventory availability within a specified order cycle time. Availability is usually expressed in terms of the

(1) number of out-of-stock items compared to the total number of items in inventory, (2) items shipped as a percentage of the number of items ordered, (3) value of items shipped as a percentage of the value of items ordered, or (4) number of orders shipped complete as a percentage of total orders received.

Measure 1 is deficient unless products are categorized according to profit contribution; otherwise a stockout on a fast-moving item would be treated the same as a stockout on a slow-moving item. The weakness of measure 2 is its failure to recognize the importance of products to the customer. Furthermore, some products have higher contribution margins than others, so losing the sale of one of these will have a greater impact on corporate profits.

Measure 3, based on the value of items ordered, is somewhat better than the first two measures, but it still does not eliminate their weaknesses. Measure 4 is most likely to reflect the customer's view of customer service. The best measure of customer service reflects the product's importance to the customer and the customer's importance to the company.

Order Cycle.   The order cycle is the time that elapses between the customer's order placement and receipt of the product. The ability to achieve the targeted order cycle time consistently influences the amount of inventory held throughout supply chain. Consequently, the speed and consistency of the order cycle are prime factors in channel design. Most customers prefer consistent service to fast service, since the former allows them to plan inventory levels to a greater extent than is possible with a fast but highly variable order cycle.

Communication.   Communication refers to the firm's ability to supply timely information to the customer about factors such as order status, order tracking, back order status, order confirmation, product substitution, product shortages, and product information requests. The use of automated information systems results in fewer errors in shipping, picking, packing, labeling, and documentation. The ability of channel members to provide good communications systems is a major factor in channel design.

Profitability

Management Must Estimate the Profitability of Alternative Channel Structures

The profitability of various channels of distribution is the major criterion in channel design. Table 14–1 illustrates the framework for judging alternative channel structures on the basis of estimated costs and revenues. Management can use market research to formulate revenue estimates for each alternative channel structure. It must estimate variable manufacturing costs for different levels of activity and variable marketing and logistics costs (e.g., sales commissions, transportation, warehousing, and order processing) along with accounts receivable.

Management should apply the corporate cost of money to accounts receivable. It also should add to each channel alternative the assignable nonvariable costs incurred for each segment, including bad debts, sales promotion, salaries, and inventory carrying costs.

Finally, management should use the corporate opportunity cost of money as a charge for all other assets required by each channel structure alternative. This information,

TABLE 14–1   Channel Cost/Revenue Analysis: Contribution Approach with a Charge for Assets Employed

	Total Company	Segment A	Segment B	Segment C
Net sales				
Cost of goods sold (variable mfg. cost)	_____	_____	_____	_____
Manufacturing contribution	_____	_____	_____	_____
Variable marketing and logistics costs				
Sales commissions				
Transportation				
Warehousing (handling in and out)				
Order processing				
Charge for investment in accounts receivable	_____	_____	_____	_____
Segment contribution margin	_____	_____	_____	_____
Assignable nonvariable costs				
Salaries				
Segment-related advertising				
Bad debts				
Inventory carrying costs	_____	_____	_____	_____
Segment controllable margin	_____	_____	_____	_____
Charge for assets used by segment	_____	_____	_____	_____
Net segment margin	_____	_____	_____	_____

Assumption: Public warehouses are used for field inventories.

combined with estimates of future growth for each structural alternative, permits the supply chain designer to select the best option. The size of the net segment margin will determine which structural alternative is the best option from the standpoint of financial performance. Management can use the cost-revenue analysis shown in Table 14–1 to measure channel structure and channel member performance.

The following example illustrates the recommended approach. Traditional accounting data showed a net profit of $2.5 million before taxes on sales of $42.5 million. While management believed that this profit was inadequate, traditional accounting gave few clues about the specific problem. However, a contribution approach to profitability analysis by type of account can be used to diagnose areas where performance is inadequate (see Table 14–2).

In this example, sales to drugstores were the largest of the four channels used by the manufacturer, but the segment controllable margin-to-sales ratio was the lowest; it was less than one-half that of the second most profitable segment, and only 37 percent of the most profitable segment. Nevertheless, at $3.1 million the segment controllable margin is substantial, so it is doubtful that the elimination of drugstores would be a wise decision. A product-channel matrix analysis showed that product mix was not the source of the problem.

TABLE 14–2   Profitability by Type of Account: A Contribution Approach ($ thousands)

	Total Company	Department Stores	Grocery Chains	Drugstores	Discount Stores
			Type of Account		
Sales	$42,500	$6,250	$10,500	$19,750	$6,000
Less discounts, returns, and allowances	2,500	250	500	1,750	--------
Net sales	40,000	6,000	10,000	18,000	6,000
Cost of goods sold (variable manufacturing costs)	20,000	2,500	4,800	9,200	3,500
Manufacturing contribution	20,000	3,500	5,200	8,800	2,500
Variable selling and distribution costs:					
Sales commissions	800	120	200	360	120
Transportation costs	2,500	310	225	1,795	170
Warehouse handling	600	150	----------	450	--------
Order processing costs	400	60	35	280	25
Charge for investment in accounts receivable	700	20	50	615	15
Contribution margin	15,000	2,840	4,690	5,300	2,170
Assignable nonvariable costs (costs incurred specifically for the segment during the period):					
Sales promotion and slotting allowances	1,250	60	620	400	170
Advertising	500	--------	----------	500	--------
Bad debts	300	--------	----------	300	--------
Display racks	200	--------	----------	200	--------
Inventory carrying costs	1,250	150	200	800	100
Segment controllable margin	$11,500	$2,630	$ 3,870	$ 3,100	$1,900
Segment controllable margin-to-sales ratio	27.1%	42.1%	36.9%	15.7%	31.7%

Note: This approach could be modified to include a charge for the assets employed by each of the segments, as well as a deduction for the change in market value of these assets. The result would be referred to as the net segment margin (residual income).

Source: Douglas M. Lambert and Jay U. Sterling, "Educators Are Contributing to Major Deficiencies in Marketing Profitability Reports," *Journal of Marketing Education* 12, no 3 (Fall 1990), pp. 43–44.

Further segmentation of the drugstore channel revealed that:

- National drugstore chains had a segment controllable margin-to-sales ratio almost as large as that of the grocery chains and somewhat better than discount stores.
- Regional drugstore chains were almost as profitable as discount stores.
- Small independent pharmacies were losing money (see Table 14–3).

With this information, management could determine the impact on corporate profitability if the independent pharmacies were served by drug wholesalers or by field warehouses supported by telemarketing and scheduled deliveries. The alternative that would lead to the greater improvement in long-term profitability should be selected.

TABLE 14-3   Profitability by Type of Account: A Contribution Approach ($ thousands)

	Type of Account			
	Drugstore Channel	National Drug Chains	Regional Drug Chains	Independent Pharmacies
Sales	$19,750	$4,250	$5,500	$10,000
Less discounts, returns, and allowances	1,750	250	500	1,000
Net sales	18,000	4,000	5,000	9,000
Cost of goods sold (variable manufacturing costs)	9,200	2,100	2,600	4,500
Manufacturing contribution	8,800	1,900	2,400	4,500
Variable selling and distribution costs:				
Sales commissions	360	80	100	180
Transportation costs	1,795	120	200	1,475
Warehouse handling	400	--------	100	350
Order processing costs	280	25	55	200
Charge for investment in accounts receivable	615	20	35	560
Contribution margin	5,300	1,655	1,910	1,735
Assignable nonvariable costs (costs incurred specifically for the segment during the period):				
Sales promotion and slotting allowances	400	90	110	200
Advertising	500	--------	--------	500
Bad debts	300	--------	--------	300
Display racks	200	--------	--------	200
Inventory carrying costs	800	80	100	620
Segment controllable margin	$ 3,100	$1,485	$1,700	($ 85)
Segment controllable margin-to-sales ratio	15.7%	34.9%	30.9%	---------

Note: This approach could be modified to include a charge for the assets employed by each of the segments, as well as a deduction for the change in market value of these assets. The result would be referred to as the net segment margin (residual income).

Source: Douglas M. Lambert and Jay U. Sterling, "Educators Are Contributing to Major Deficiencies in Marketing Profitability Reports," *Journal of Marketing Education* 12, no 3 (Fall 1990), pp. 44–45.

Instead of contribution reports, most firms use a full costing system which assigns fixed costs to individual segments.[23] As explained in Chapter 13, this system provides incorrect information because costs that are "common" to multiple segments are allocated to individual segments according to some arbitrary measure of activity. Vital information about the controllability and behavior of segment costs is lost. For example, if a segment is unprofitable under a full costing approach and is discontinued, the fixed costs will simply be reallocated to the remaining segments.

---

[23]Douglas M. Lambert and Jay U. Sterling, "What Types of Profitability Reports Do Marketing Managers Receive?" *Industrial Management* 16, no. 4 (1987), pp. 295–303.

TABLE 14–4   **Profitablitiy by Type of Account: Full-Cost Approach ($ thousands)**

	Type of Account				
	Total Company	Department Stores	Grocery Chains	Drug Stores	Discount Stores
Net sales	$40,000	$6,000	$10,000	$18,000	$6,000
Cost of goods sold (full manufacturing costs)	25,000	3,750	6,250	11,250	3,750
Manufacturing margin	15,000	2,250	3,750	6,750	2,250
Less expenses:					
Sales commissions	800	120	200	360	120
Transportation costs ($ per case)	2,500	375	625	1,125	375
Warehouse handling ($ per cu. ft.)	600	90	150	270	90
Order processing costs ($ per order)	400	30	50	300	20
Sales promotion (% of sales)	1,250	187	312	563	188
Advertising (% of sales)	500	75	125	225	75
Bad debts (% of sales)	300	45	75	135	45
General overhead and administrative expense (% of sales)	6,150	922	1,538	2,768	922
Net profit (before taxes)	$ 2,500	$ 406	$ 675	$ 1,004	$ 415
Profit-to-sales ratio	6.3%	6.8%	6.8%	5.6%	6.9%

Source: Douglas M. Lambert and Jay U. Sterling, "Educators Are Contributing to Major Deficiencies in Marketing Profitability Reports," *Journal of Marketing Education* 12, no. 3 (Fall 1990), p. 49.

Cost Allocations Can Seriously Distort Profitability

Thus, cost allocations can seriously distort a segment's profitability.

Seriously distorted product costs can lead managers to choose a losing competitive strategy by de-emphasizing and overpricing products that are highly profitable and by expanding commitments to complex, unprofitable lines. The company persists in the losing strategy because executives have no alternative sources of information to signal when product costs are distorted.[24]

Table 14–4 illustrates how the channel profitability analysis contained in Table 14–2 would change if it were calculated using average costs. Drugstores would show by far the largest dollar profit. The profit-to-sales ratio for drugstores would compare favorably with that of the other channels (82 percent of the profit-to-sales ratio for grocery chains), whereas the segment controllable margin-to-sales ratio of the drugstore channel was less than half (43 percent) of that earned by the grocery channel. The differences in the two methods of accounting would be much greater in a product profitability analysis because actual manufacturing, marketing, and logistics costs usually would vary more across products. If the costs in Table 14–4 had been allocated on the basis of a percentage of sales, as is the practice in many firms, the profit-to-sales ratios for the four channels would have been equal.

---

[24]Robert S. Kaplan, "One Cost System Isn't Enough," *Harvard Business Review* 66, no. 1 (Jan.–Feb. 1988), pp. 61–66.

Channel Performance Measurement

The logistics and marketing literature rarely focuses on measuring channel performance or supply chain performance for a number of reasons:

1. Measuring supply chain performance is difficult.
2. Some aspects of supply chain performance are hard to quantify, making it difficult to establish a common performance standard.
3. Differences in supply chains make it difficult to establish standards for comparison.

One measure of channel performance is the extent to which the company's target markets are being satisfied, given the firm's goals and objectives. This would include measures of product availability in the store, adequacy of customer service, and strength of brand image.

Measures of Channel Structure Efficiency
   Next, management must analyze channel structure to determine if the corporate channel strategy has been implemented successfully. Measures of channel structure efficiency include channel member turnover, competitive strength of the channel, and related issues. When management evaluates channel structure, it must compare the firm's ability to perform the marketing functions internally with the channel member's ability to perform these functions.

Potential Qualitative Measures

Some potential quantitative measures of channel performance include distribution cost per unit, errors in order filling, and percent of damaged merchandise. Qualitative measures that managers may use when reevaluating the channel of distribution and specific channel members include degree of channel coordination, degree of channel conflict, and availability of information as needed. Management should set objectives for the channel and measure actual performance against planned performance. Also, evaluation measures should be developed over time and used to isolate potential problem areas. Perhaps the best measure of channel performance is profitability.

Cost Trade-Off Analysis

In Chapter 1 we introduced the integrated logistics management concept and the cost trade-offs required in marketing and logistics (see Figure 14–4). Cost trade-off analysis can be performed either within a single firm or between different levels of the supply chain. For the individual firm, the goal is to find the most efficient way to offer the desired level of customer service. For the supply chain, the goal is to improve overall efficiency by reallocating functions, and therefore costs, among its members. The level of customer service offered by the manufacturer, for example, will have a significant impact on other members of the supply chain.

A manufacturer with poor product availability and inconsistent order cycle times may force wholesalers to carry more inventory as safety stock in order to offer an acceptable level of service to the retailers. In this case, lower logistics costs for the manufacturer would be achieved at the expense of the other supply chain members, possibly making the

FIGURE 14–4

Cost trade-offs required in marketing and logistics

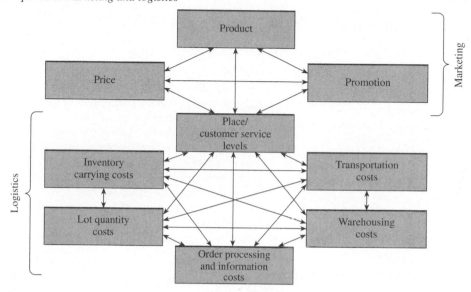

Marketing objective: Allocate resources to the marketing mix as to maximize the long-term profitability of the firm.

Logistics objective: Minimize total costs given the customer service objective where total costs = transportation costs + warehousing costs + order processsing and information costs + lot quantity costs + inventory carrying costs

Source: Adapted from Douglas M. Lambert, *The Development of an Inventory Costing Methodology: A Study of the Cost Associated with Holding Inventory* (Chicago: National Council of Physical Distribution Management, 1976), p. 7.

entire channel less efficient and effective. Box 14–3 highlights some of these problems within the context of supply chain management.

Information Technology Can Increase Channel Efficiency and Effectiveness

However, if management concentrates on systems changes that improve logistics efficiency or effectiveness, it may be possible to satisfy all of the firm's objectives. In order processing, for example, by replacing an outdated order processing and information system with advanced technology, a firm may be able to achieve some or all of the following:

1. Increased customer service levels.
2. Lower inventories.
3. Speedier collections.
4. Decreased transportation costs.
5. Lower warehousing costs.
6. Improvement in cash flow.
7. High return on assets.

Thus, all supply chain decisions are best viewed from a systems perspective, as an integrated whole.

Box 14–3

Supply Chain Management Pitfalls

Supply chain management faces the following 14 key pitfalls.

1. No supply chain strategy.
2. Inadequate definition of customer service.
3. Inaccurate delivery status data.
4. Inefficient information systems.
5. Ignoring the impact of uncertainties.
6. Simplistic inventory stocking policies.
7. Discrimination against internal customers.
8. Poor coordination.
9. Incomplete analysis of shipment methods.
10. Incorrect assessment of inventory costs.
11. Organizational barriers.
12. Product-process design without supply chain consideration.
13. Separation of supply chain design from operational decisions.
14. Incomplete supply chain strategy.

But don't despair! There are excellent ways to overcome these problems. The suggested approaches deal with design and measurement. First, the design of the product or service should give consideration to the cost and service implications for the existing or proposed supply chain.

Second, databases should be integrated throughout the supply chain to ensure operational control. Appropriate data include past performance, current inventory levels, positions and schedules, as well as forecast data. This system would support the third opportunity for improved supply chain performance: the integration of control and planning support systems. This in turn would reduce independent decision making, which ignores the systems approach. Thus, the fourth point—to expand the view of the supply chain—is critical. Supply chain members should embrace the systems approach with the realization that each member's activities have an impact on the others.

The last two issues concern internal and external measurement. The organization must redesign its incentives, so that individuals, divisions, and sites are rewarded for taking a systemwide, supply chain approach. In addition, the organization should institute supply chain performance measurement. For example, inventory measurement should be viewed across the supply chain instead of site by site.

Source: From: Hau L. Lee and Corey Billington, "Managing Supply Chain Inventory: Pitfalls and Opportunities," *Sloan Management Review* 33, no. 3 (Spring 1992), pp. 65–73.

The manufacturer has minimal additional cash invested in inventory held by the customer rather than in the manufacturer's warehouse. Furthermore, the noncost-of-money components of inventory carrying cost are shifted to the next level of the channel. However, this may not be most efficient move for the channel as a whole, as the value of inventory increases the closer it gets to the consumer due to markups by each channel member or value-added services added at various stages in the channel. The channel would be better off as a whole to have inventory held in less valuable forms. In addition, the less differentiated inventory becomes, the more likely, in general, that it can be used in a different application or for a different customer. This was explained earlier in the description of postponement.

Automation and Integration of Systems within the Supply Chain

In addition to rethinking traditional strategies for improving supply chain cash flow and return on assets, supply chain leaders may wish to consider automating and integrating the order processing and information systems within the channel. This can reduce lead time variability and create time for planning. The latest communications technology offers a unique opportunity for improving the efficiency and effectiveness of the supply chain. If communication flows throughout the supply chain are improved, all members will be able to reduce inventories while improving customer service.

In addition, the extra planning time that results due to increased communication speed will allow freight consolidations, warehousing cost savings, and lower lot quantity costs. Customer service levels can be improved and total operating costs reduced—truly a unique opportunity.

In the last section of this chapter, we will describe how leading-edge firms are implementing an integrated approach to managing the supply chain.

Processes of Integrated Supply Chain Management[25]

Successful supply chain management requires a change from managing individual functions to integrating activities into key supply chain processes. Traditionally, both upstream and downstream portions of the supply chain have interacted as disconnected entities that receive sporadic flows of information over time.

The purchasing department placed orders as requirements became necessary. Marketing, responding to customer demand, attempted to satisfy this demand by interfacing with various distributors and retailers. The firm gave orders periodically to suppliers and they gave orders to their suppliers without any clear picture of demand at the point of sale or use. Satisfying the customer often translated into demands for expedited operations throughout the supply chain as channel members reacted to unexpected changes in demand.

The Customer Is the Primary Focus in Supply Chain Management

Operating an integrated supply chain requires continuous information flows which in turn help to create the best product flows. The customer remains the primary focus of the process. However, improved linkages with suppliers are necessary because controlling uncertainty in customer demand, manufacturing processes, and supplier performance are critical to effective supply chain management (SCM). Achieving a good customer-focused system means that information must be processed with accuracy and timeliness, because quick response systems require frequent changes in response to fluctuations in customer demand.

Optimizing the product flows cannot be accomplished without an exhaustive review of the underlying processes. After considerable effort, 3M managers identified seven key processes requiring analysis which support the integrated SCM approach. These key processes are:

Key Supply Chain Processes Identified at 3M

- Customer relationship management.
- Customer service management.
- Demand management.
- Order fulfillment.

---

[25]This material is adapted from Douglas M. Lambert, Larry C. Guinipero, and Gary J. Ridenhower, "Supply Chain Management: A Key to Achieving Business Excellence in the 21st Century," unpublished manuscript. All rights reserved.

Delivering orders on time, in full, and correctly, are key elements of 3M's effort to be the preferred supplier globally. In many markets, automated 3M systems monitor usage of 3M products on site, ensuring customers receive the needed amount of product at the right time and place.

An Even Stronger 3M

Our vision is to be the most innovative enterprise and the preferred supplier by:

- Developing technologies and products that create a new basis of competition.

- Earning our customers' loyalty by helping them grow their businesses.

- Expanding internationally, where we already generate more than half our sales.

- Improving productivity and competitiveness worldwide.

- Manufacturing flow management.
- Procurement.
- Product development and commercialization.

At some companies such as Xerox, the returns channel process is also included.[26] While the specific processes identified by individual firms may vary somewhat from those above (see Figure 14–1), managers involved in SCM should consider five fundamental processes:

1. Selling.
2. Customer order fulfillment.
3. Manufacturing flow.
4. Procurement.
5. Product development.

Of course, performance metrics must be changed to reflect process performance across the supply chain, and rewards and incentives must be aligned to these metrics in order to affect change. Each of the eight processes identified in Figure 14–1 will now be described.

---

[26]Clendenin, "Closing the Supply Chain loop: Reengineering the Returns Channel Process," pp. 75–85.

Customer Relationship Management

Partnering Programs with Key Customers

The first step toward integrated SCM is to identify the key customer or customer groups which the organization has targeted as critical to its business mission. The corporate business plan is the starting point for this analysis. Customer service teams develop and implement partnering programs with key customers. Product and service agreements specifying the levels of performance are established with these key customers.

New customer interfaces lead to improved communications and better predictions of customer demand, which in turn lead to improved service for customers. Customer service teams work with customers to further identify and eliminate sources of demand variability. Performance evaluations are undertaken to analyze the levels of service provided to customers and customer profitability.

Customer Service Management

A Single Source of Customer Information

Customer service provides the single source of customer information. It becomes the key point of contact for administering the product and service agreement. Customer service provides the customer with real-time information on promised shipping dates and product availability through interfaces with the organizations' production and distribution operations.

Managing customer service in a SCM environment requires an on-line, real-time system to provide product and pricing information to support customer inquiries, facilitate order placement, and follow up with postsale service. Finally, the technical customer service group must be able to efficiently assist the customer with product applications and recommendations.

Demand Management

Hewlett-Packard's experience with SCM shows that inventory is either essential or variability driven.[27] Essential inventory includes work-in-process in factories and products in the pipeline moving from location to location. Time-based and periodic review systems lead to certain amounts of incoming inventory stock. Safety stock is present because of variance in process, supply, and demand. Customer demand in the form of irregular order patterns is by far the largest source of variability. Given this variability in customer ordering, demand management is a key to an effective SCM process.

The Demand Management Process Is Key to Success

The demand management process must balance the customer's requirements with the firm's supply capabilities. Part of managing demand involves determining what and when customers will purchase. A good demand management system uses point-of-sale and "key" customer data to reduce uncertainty and provide efficient flows throughout the supply chain.

Marketing requirements and production plans should be coordinated on an enterprisewide basis. Thus, firms should consider multiple sourcing and routing options at the time the order is received, which allows market requirements and production plans to be

---

[27]T. Davis, "Effective Supply Chain Management," *Sloan Management Review* 34, no. 4 (Summer 1993), pp. 35–46.

Technology

The Value Chain Initiative

The goal in supply chain management is to link the ultimate consumer, the supplier of original materials, and all trading partners in between with a seamless information flow. The charter of the **Value Chain Initiative (VCI)** calls for moving a high-level uninterrupted data stream from raw materials to the consumer's hands using the Internet, a communications medium that promises to revolutionize business protocols worldwide. The goal is to extend the powerful Microsoft Windows NT client-server technology to all facets of the supply chain and to make these data accessible, in real time!

Today's supply chain data stream is largely paper based and event driven; hence, it is essentially a static or EDI-like data stream. After an event has occurred, the opportunity to make or save money has elapsed.

The goal of the VCI data stream is to give decision makers access to and control over data prior to an event, so that the ability to dynamically model or reallocate these resources is continuously available. Most retailers and manufacturers know that by saving nickels and dimes at the lower reaches of the supply chain, they can move these incremental savings all the way up to the highest levels. Eventually, the savings will amount to millions in new or "rediscovered" savings and profits.

Why is this the "value chain"? Because providing the power to control these far-flung resources makes them assets rather than liabilities. Making this value available by leveraging existing internal information technology (IT) investment is truly a sound business reason to embrace the VCI.

Source: Mark Waller, Microsoft Corporation, based on a presentation at The Global Supply Chain Forum, The Ohio State University, Feb. 12, 1997.

coordinated on an organizationwide basis. In advanced SCM systems, customer demand and production rates are synchronized to manage inventories globally. The Technology box discusses how the value chain initiative can revolutionize supply chain management.

Customer Order Fulfillment

The Objective Is to Provide a Seamless Process

The key to effective SCM is meeting or exceeding customer need dates. It is important to achieve high order fill rates either on a line-item or order basis. Performing the order fulfillment process effectively requires integration of the firm's manufacturing, distribution, and transportation plans. As previously discussed, partnerships should be developed with key channel members in order to meet customer requirements and reduce total delivered cost to customer. The objective is to develop a seamless process from the supplier to the organization and then on to the various customer constituencies.

Manufacturing Flow Management

In a make-to-stock environment, manufacturers produced and supplied product to the distribution channel based on historical forecasts. Products were pushed through the plant to meet a schedule. Often the wrong mix of products was produced, resulting in unneeded inventories, excessive inventory carrying costs, and markdowns and transshipments of product.

Matching Demand and Production Capability	With SCM, product is pulled through the plant according to customer needs. Manufacturing processes must be flexible to respond to market changes. This requires the flexibility to perform rapid changeover to accommodate mass customization. Orders are processed on a just-in-time basis in minimum lot sizes. Production priorities are driven by required delivery dates.

At 3M, manufacturing planners work with customer planners to develop strategies for each customer segment. Changes in the manufacturing flow lead to shorter cycle times, meaning improved responsiveness to customers. |

Procurement

	Strategic plans are developed with suppliers to support the manufacturing flow management process and the development of new products. Suppliers are categorized strategically based on several dimensions, such as their contribution and criticality to the organization. In companies with worldwide operations, sourcing should be managed from corporate headquarters on a global basis.
Supplier Development	Long-term partnerships are developed with a core group of suppliers. The desired outcome is a win-win relationship for both parties. This is a change from the traditional bid-and-buy system to one that includes key suppliers early on in the design cycle, which can lead to dramatic reduction in product development cycle times. Early supplier input reduces time by getting the required coordination between engineering, purchasing, and the supplier prior to determining the final design.

To quickly transfer requirements, the purchasing function develops rapid communication mechanisms such as EDI and Internet linkages. These rapid communication tools provide a means to reduce the time and cost spent on the transaction portion of the purchase. Purchasers can focus their efforts on managing suppliers instead of on placing and expediting orders. |

Product Development and Commercialization

Customers and Suppliers Must Be Integrated Into the Product Development Process	If new products are the lifeblood of a company, then product development is the lifeblood of a company's new products. Customers and suppliers must be integrated into the product development process to reduce time to market. As product life cycles shorten, the right products must be developed and successfully launched in ever shorter time frames for the firm to remain competitive. The Global box covers Hewlett-Packard's wrestling with the matter of a generic printer for use in the worldwide market.

Returns Channel

	Managing the returns channel as a business process offers the same opportunity to achieve a sustainable competitive advantage as managing the supply chain from an outbound perspective.[28] Effective process management of the returns channel enables the identification of productivity improvement opportunities and breakthrough projects.

---

[28]Clendenin, "Closing the Supply Chain Loop: Reengineering the Returns Channel Process," p. 84.

Global

Localizing Generic Products at Hewlett-Packard

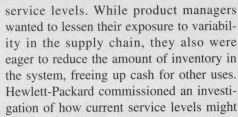

In an industry characterized by punishingly short product life cycles and extreme unpredictability, getting the right products to the right market on time is an absolute imperative. For computer equipment manufacturer Hewlett-Packard, the need to manufacture and deliver its products quickly, reliably, and ever more cost effectively has led to the development of capabilities that put it at the forefront of global supply chain management.

Tailoring Products to Local Specifications

Product complexity was a hidden enemy for Hewlett-Packard. While the company served a global marketplace with seemingly global products, these products almost always were tailored to meet local specifications. They had to be delivered with power cords and transformers to meet the local voltage and supplied with keyboards, manuals, and operating software in the local language. Instead of dealing with a single product line, produced and distributed to meet an overall global forecast, Hewlett-Packard was producing differently configured machines to meet estimated demand in each of a number of relatively small markets. The smaller the market, the more erratic the order patterns were likely to be, and the more difficult it was to predict demand accurately.

This uncertainty reverberated through every stage of the supply chain, leading to exaggerated safety stocks and increased risk from obsolete stock or of expensive reworking for internal and external suppliers alike. There were, for example, five physically separate Hewlett-Packard facilities contributing to the manufacture and distribution of its best-selling family of low-cost DeskJet printers, resulting in a pipeline that was nearly six months long.

Supplying the European market with its tightly packed cluster of nations and linguistic differences was particularly troublesome, requiring huge safety stocks to meet Hewlett-Packard's goal of 98 percent service levels. While product managers wanted to lessen their exposure to variability in the supply chain, they also were eager to reduce the amount of inventory in the system, freeing up cash for other uses. Hewlett-Packard commissioned an investigation of how current service levels might be maintained at lower cost.

Under the system at that time, the printers were "localized" and packaged at the central factory and sent ready for sale to the country of destination. Stockpiles of each of the different language variants were held at regional distribution centers, ready to meet sudden fluctuations in demand. The question quickly arose of what the value would be to switch production over to a single form of generic printer, postponing localization until the distribution center stage, thereby delaying the point of commitment until a firm order had been received.

Introducing a Generic Printer

Hewlett-Packard had been honing its inventory network modeling skills for some time, and was able to apply these skills to modeling the DeskJet supply chain. The result indicated that the costs of safety stocks could be significantly reduced if a generic printer was introduced.

- First, safety stocks could be lowered from seven weeks of finished goods to around five weeks of the generic version, because fewer generic printers would be required to maintain service levels.
- Second, the cost of each unit stockpiled would be reduced because less value had been added by this point. Anticipated savings were in excess of $30 million per year.

The costs of performing the localization process at the distribution centers were slightly higher than if they were performed at the factory because higher

---

Global box concluded

overall inventories of local materials would be required with the dispersal of this activity. However, these costs were dwarfed by the overall savings on product inventory. Also, Hewlett-Packard identified savings of several million dollars a year from reduced shipping costs. The generic printers could be packed more densely and transported more cheaply.

The Logic of the Product Switch

The logic of switching to a generic printer for the European market was unimpeachable. The U.S. market already had its own factory-produced version of the generic printer in the works. An extension of the DeskJet study evaluated a proposal to produce two versions of the printer at the factory: an ultra low-cost U.S. version and a generic one to serve the rest of the world. This proposal was rejected, however, because of the potential strategic time advantage offered by the single generic printer. The critical factor was the increased unpredictability of regional forecasts (e.g., the Americas, Asia, and Europe) compared with a forecast for overall global demand. If, contrary to all earlier indications, demand for a new product failed to materialize in, say, the United States while sales in the rest of the world took off at an unprecedented rate, pipelines would already be filled to meet predicted demand. A generic printer strategy would allow the immediate diversion of stocks to wherever they were required, at minimal cost, and with minimal delay and loss of service. Contrast this with the prospect of reworking unneeded stocks before redirection, or waiting until forecasted output could meet demand. In a market with narrowing windows of opportunity, the risk of the latter was deemed to be too great. Hewlett-Packard introduced its global generic printer.

Source: Adapted from material in Martin Christopher, *Marketing Logistics* (Oxford, England: Butterworth Heinemann, 1997), pp. 128–30; and T. Davis, "Effective Supply Chain Management," *Sloan Management Review* 34, no. 4 (Summer 1993), pp. 35–46.

At Xerox, returns are managed in four categories: equipment, parts, supplies, and competitive trade-ins. "Return to available" is a velocity measure of the cycle time required to return an asset to a useful status. This metric is particularly important for those products where customers are given an immediate replacement in the case of product failure. Also, equipment destined for scrap and waste from manufacturing plants are measured in terms of the time until cash is received.

Goals of Managing the Supply Chain Processes

Focusing efforts on the key business processes, which extend from the end users to the original suppliers, provides the foundation for a philosophy of supply chain management. The goals or outcomes of these processes are to:

- Develop customer-focused teams that provide mutually beneficial product and service agreements to strategically significant customers.
- Provide a point of contact for all customers which efficiently handles their inquiries.

- Continually gather, compile, and update customer demand to match requirements with supply.
- Develop flexible manufacturing systems that respond quickly to changing market conditions.
- Manage supplier partnerships that allow for quick response and continuous improvement.
- Fill 100 percent of customer orders accurately and on time.
- Enhance profitability by managing the returns channel (reverse logistics).

A responsive, flexible, integrated supply chain can accomplish these objectives. Because these processes cut across business functions, it is important to reengineer each key process using a systematic approach.

Reengineering Improvement into the Supply Chain

A critical part of streamlining supply chains involves reengineering the key processes to meet customer needs. Reengineering is a process aimed at producing dramatic changes quickly. It has been defined as the fundamental rethinking and radical redesign of business processes to achieve dramatic improvements in critical contemporary measures of performance such as cost, quality service, and speed.[29] Improvement through reengineering cannot be accomplished in a haphazard manner. These changes must be supported at the top and driven by an overall management plan.

Three Stages in the Reengineering Process

A typical reengineering process proceeds through three stages:

1. Fact finding.
2. Identifying areas for improvement to business process redesign.
3. Creative improvements.

The fact-finding stage is a very detailed examination of the current systems, procedures, and work flows. The key focus is placed on separating facts from opinions.

Armed with the facts collected in the first stage, reengineering teams identify areas for improvement. They analyze where value was added for the final customer, with particular emphasis on currently ineffective or inefficient customer contact points and product information transfers. After identifying improvement points, the creative phase of redesigning business process and information flow begins. The outcomes of the creative phase will fundamentally change the nature of the work and how it is performed.

Figure 14–5 illustrates a general plan for undertaking business process reengineering. Organizational energy needs to focus on the firm's mission statement. The mission statement drives the business requirements in the organization. A complete assessment is made of the firm's culture, strategies, business practices, and processes.

If this analysis proves acceptable, management implements its business solution across the supply chain. Typically improvements are required in one of the areas to en-

---

[29]Michael Hammer and James Champy, *Reengineering the Corporation: A Manifesto for Business Revolution* (New York: HarperCollins, 1993).

FIGURE 14–5

Reengineering SCM process flow chart

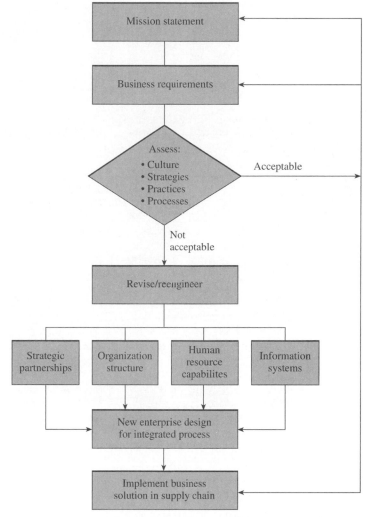

hance supply chain performance. An example of this reengineering is the new Mercedes-Benz microcar which is based on the principle of systems supply.[30] Reengineering of the process resulted in Mercedes-Benz delegating more design activities to suppliers, and reducing the amount of engineering and labor at their facilities. The savings from these efficiencies are passed along to the customer in the form of increased value.

---

[30]J. L. Coleman, A. K. Bhattacharya, and G. Brace, "Supply Chain Reengineering: A Supplier's Perspective," *The International Journal of Logistics Management* 6, no. 1 (1995), pp. 85–92.

FIGURE 14–6

Implementation of supply chain management

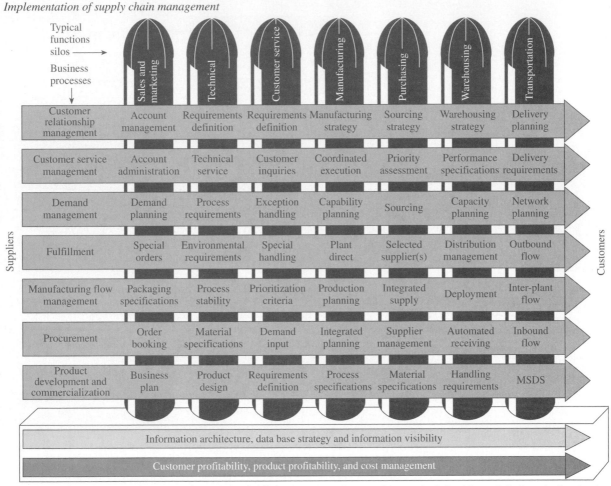

Note: Process sponsorship and ownership must be established to drive the attainment of the supply chain vision and eliminate the functional barriers that artificially separate the process flows.

Implementing Integrated Supply Chain Management

Implementing SCM requires making the transition from a functional organization to a focus on process. Figure 14–6 illustrates one way of viewing how each function in the organization relates to the seven key processes.

In the customer relationship management process, marketing provides the account management expertise, engineering provides the specifications that define the requirements, and customer service provides knowledge about customer requirements. These requirements must be used as input to manufacturing, sourcing, and warehousing strategies.

A Baxter employee delivers supplies directly to the floors of a hospital. Baxter is sharing risk with customers to lower their costs and increase its profits.

If the proper coordination mechanisms are not in place across the various functions, the process will be neither effective nor efficient. The adoption of a process focus means that all functions touching the product or providing information must work together. For example, purchasing depends on sales or marketing data fed through a production schedule to assess specific order levels and the timing of requirements. These orders drive production requirements which in turn are transmitted upstream to suppliers.

The increasing use of outsourcing has accelerated the need to coordinate supply chain processes since the organization becomes more dependent on outside contractors and suppliers. Consequently, coordination mechanisms must be in place within the organization. The critical decisions are where to place these coordination mechanisms and which team and functions are responsible for them.

Several process redesign and reengineering techniques can be applied to the seven key processes. Chrysler Corporation's development of the Neon automobile was accomplished through the efforts of 150 internal employees. This core group leveraged their efforts to 600 engineers, 289 suppliers, and line employees. Concurrent engineering techniques required personnel from all key functional areas to work with suppliers to develop the vehicle in 42 months. The use of concurrent engineering resulted in the avoidance of later disagreements, misunderstandings, and delays.

To successfully implement SCM, all firms within the supply chain must overcome their own functional silos and accept a process approach. The requirements for successful implementation of SCM include:

Requirements for Successful Supply Chain Management

- Executive support, leadership, and commitment to change.
- An understanding of the degree of change necessary.
- Agreement on the SCM vision and the key processes.
- The necessary commitment of resources and empowerment to achieve the stated goals.

Creative Solutions

How Milliken Drives Supply Chain Integration

In 1981, U.S. textile and apparel producers enjoyed an 80 percent share of their domestic market. Six years later, their share was 60 percent. Protectionist legislation slowed this decline, but profits went into free fall, plunging from $1.9 billion in 1987 to $600 million in 1991.[1]

In 1986, the industry commissioned consultants Kurt Salmon Associates to study supply chains in the U.S. apparel industry. The results were alarming. The supply chains were too long and too poorly coordinated to respond effectively to marketplace demands. Time to market averaged one and one-quarter years from textile loom to store rack. Industrywide, the cost of this inefficiency was estimated to be $25 billion a year, or about 20 percent of the industry's total sales.[2] The supply chain could not absorb these costs, so they were passed on to the customer—until imports became a threat.

The U.S. industry had to find new ways of working if it was to survive. Several pilot studies were commissioned to determine whether pipelines could be shortened by collaboration between retailers, apparel manufacturers, and textile producers. Among the first to participate in the pilot studies was Milliken & Company, the country's largest textile producer.

Before embarking on the experiment, Milliken's performance was as follows:

- Milliken received incoming orders slowly, by mail.
- Weaving would normally be completed eight weeks after the yarn became available.
- Dyeing and finishing took a further four to five weeks.
- The stock would be forwarded to the central warehouse until required by the customer.
- Throughput times were 18 to 20 weeks from receipt of order.
- Keeping the factory operating at maximum capacity was the overriding priority.

After receiving the finished cloth from Milliken, an apparel manufacturer might require from 18 to 20 weeks to get the clothing to a retailer.[3] Retailers, fearing stockouts, regularly ordered more than they needed, increasing their inventory carrying costs and resulting in markdowns of excess stock. If the retailers' inventories got too high, they would cut back on purchasing, leaving the apparel manufacturers with excess stock. They in turn would cancel fabric orders, leaving Milliken holding unwanted inventory.

In the pilot study, Milliken partnered with Seminol, the apparel manufacturer, and Wal-Mart. Consultants monitored a single product line (basic slacks), measuring the sales and profit improvement achieved by the implementation of quick response. The results showed increased sales of 31 percent and a 30 percent improvement in inventory turns.[4]

This exercise taught Milliken to look beyond its immediate customer—the apparel producer who paid the fabric invoice—and to be responsive to the requirements of the end consumers. If point-of-sale information could be shared between the members, long-range forecasting, overstocking, and order cancellations would no longer be necessary. Milliken began seeking out like-minded supply-chain members who were willing to set aside short-term self-interest to create integrated supply chains.

The lessons learned in the apparel industry were used to improve other areas of Milliken's textile business. For example, the company approached one of its customers, a retailer of oriental-style rugs with an offer to manufacture the rugs to order by quick response, and ship them by UPS direct to the customer's home. The retailer would have to forward its customer orders to Milliken on a daily basis and keep it fully informed of planned promotional activity. At first the retailer hesitated, but then agreed to accept Milliken's plan. The move allowed the retailer not only to eliminate its entire product inventory, keeping only display items, but also to cut delivery times and costs since the rugs no longer passed through its distribution center.

Source: Adapted from Martin Christopher, *Marketing Logistics* (Oxford, England: Butterworth Heinemann, 1997), pp. 81–84.

[1]Walecia Konrad, "Why Leslie Wexner Shops Overseas," *Business Week,* Feb. 3, 1992, p. 33.

[2]George Stalk, Jr., and Thomas M. Hout, *Competing against Time* (New York: Free Press, 1990), p. 249.

[3]Harvard Business School, "Time-Based Competition," Program 2, *Harvard Business School Management Programmes,* 1993, videocassette.

[4]Stalk and Hout, *Competing against Time,* p. 252.

Summary

In this chapter, we saw that (1) the channel of distribution plays an integral part in a firm's marketing strategy, (2) various types of supply chain structures are used, (3) a number of factors influence supply chain and channel design, evolution, and performance, and (4) supply chain management is a process-oriented approach to manage relationships in the channel. Leading-edge firms such as 3M and Xerox are implementing SCM. With this material established as necessary background, we are ready to present the role of logistics in corporate strategy in Chapter 15.

Suggested Readings

Andraski, Joseph C. "Foundations for Successful Continuous Replenishment Programs." *The International Journal of Logistics Management* 5, no. 1 (1994), pp. 1–8.

Bechtel, Christian, and Jayanth Jayaram. "Supply Chain Management: A Strategic Perspective." *The International Journal of Logistics Management* 8, no. 1 (1997), pp. 15–34.

Bhattacharya, Arindam K.; Julian L. Coleman; Gordon Brace; and Paul J. Kelly. "The Structure Conundrum in Supply Chain Management." *The International Journal of Logistics Management* 7, no. 1 (1996), pp. 39–48.

Blaser, J., and B. Scott Westbrook. "The Supply Chain Revolution." *APICS The Performance Advantage* 5, no. 1 (Jan. 1995), pp. 43–49.

Bowersox, Donald J.; M. Bixby Cooper; Douglas M. Lambert; and Donald A. Taylor. *Management in Marketing Channels.* New York: McGraw-Hill, 1980.

Carty, A.G.; M.W. Peters; and M.G. Rocke. "A Logistics Outsourcing Experience: SunExpress Joins Forces with CLS in a Partnership for Growth." *Proceedings of the Annual Conference of the Council of Logistics Management.* Oak Brook, IL: Council of Logistics Management, 1993.

Cavinato, Joseph L. "Identifying Interfirm Total Cost Advantages for Supply Chain Competitiveness." *International Journal of Purchasing and Materials Management* 27 no. 4 (Fall 1991), pp. 10–15.

Christopher, Martin. *Logistics and Supply Chain Management.* London: Pitman, 1992.

Clendenin, John A. "Closing the Supply Chain Loop: Reengineering the Returns Channel Process." *The International Journal of Logistics Management* 8, no. 1 (1997), pp. 75–85.

Coleman, Julian L.; Arindam K. Bhattacharya; and Gordon Brace. "Supply Chain Reengineering: A Suppliers Perspective." *The International Journal of Logistics Management* 5, no. 2 (1994), pp. 1–10.

Cooper, Martha C., and Lisa M. Ellram. "Characteristics of Supply Chain Management and the Implications for Purchasing and Logistics Strategy." *The International Journal of Logistics Management* 4, no. 2 (1993), pp. 13–24.

Cooper, Martha, Douglas M. Lambert, and Janus D. Pagh. "Supply Chain Management: More Than a New Name for Logistics." *The International Journal of Logistics Management* 8, no. 1 (1997), pp. 1–14.

Ellram, Lisa M., and Martha C. Cooper. "The Relationship Between Supply Chain Management and Keiretsu." *The International Journal of Logistics Management* 4, no. 1 (1993), pp. 1–12.

Fernie, John, and Clive Rees. "Supply Chain Management in the National Health Service." *The International Journal of Logistics Management* 6, no. 2 (1995), pp. 83–92.

Giunipero, Larry C., and Richard R. Brand. "Purchasing's Role in Supply Chain Management." *The International Journal of Logistics Management* 7, no. 1 (1996), pp. 29–38.

Gunn, T. G. *In the Age of the Real-time Enterprise.* Essex, VT: Omneo, 1994.

Hendrick, Thomas, and Lisa M. Ellram. *Strategic Supplier Partnering: An International Study.* Tempe, AZ: Center for Advanced Purchasing Studies, 1993.

Hewitt, Fred. "Supply Chain Redesign." *The International Journal of Logistics Management* 5, no. 2 (1994), pp. 1–10.

Hines, Peter. "Integrated Materials Management: The Value Chain Redefined." *The International Journal of Logistics Management* 4, no. 1 (1993), pp. 13–22.

Horscroft, Peter, and Alan Braithwaite. "Enhancing Supply Chain Efficiency: The Strategic Lead Time Approach." *The International Journal of Logistics Management* 1, no. 2 (1990), pp. 47–52.

Houlihan, John B. "International Supply Chains: A New Approach." *Management Decision* 26, no. 3 (1988), pp. 13–19.

Johnson, D.T., and A. Simpson. "International Service Parts Management." *Proceedings of the Annual Conference of the Council of Logistics Management,* vol. 2. Oak Brook, IL: Council of Logistics Management, 1993.

Johnston, Russell, and Paul R. Lawrence. "Beyond Vertical Integration—The Rise of the Value-Adding Partnership." *Harvard Business Review* 66, no. 4 (July–Aug. 1988), pp. 94–101.

La Londe, Bernard J., and Terrance L. Pohlen. "Issues in Supply Chain Costing." *The International Journal of Logistics Management* 7, no. 1 (1991), pp. 1–12.

Lamming, Richard. *Beyond Partnerships.* Englewood Cliffs, NJ: Prentice Hall, 1993.

Pano, Robin. "Pull Out the Stops in Your Network." *Transportation and Distribution* 35, no. 8 (Aug. 1994), pp. 38–40.

Stern, Louis W.; Adel I. El-Ansary; and Anne T. Coughlan. *Marketing Channels,* 5th ed. Englewood Cliffs, NJ: Prentice Hall, 1996.

Trafton, L., and M. McElroy. "Logistics Network Design and Pipeline Optimization: 'The Optimizer.'" *Proceedings of the Annual Conference of the Council of Logistics Management,* vol. 2. Oak Brook, IL: Council of Logistics Management, 1991.

Treacy, M., and F. Wiersma. "Customer Intimacy and Other Value Disciplines." *Harvard Business Review* 71, no. 1 (Jan.–Feb. 1993), pp. 84–93.

Questions and Problems

1. Define supply chain management, including an identification of upstream and downstream supply chain elements.

2. Why do channels of distribution develop?

3. How do you believe the development of supply chain structure will change in the future?

4. Give an example of:
   (a) A firm that uses postponement.
   (b) A firm that uses speculation in the channel of distribution.

5. Explain the concept of structural separation and its implications for channel design.

6. What is meant by intensive, exclusive, and selective distribution? Give examples illustrating when each would be an acceptable strategy.

7. Explain how product characteristics influence channel design.

8. How can communications technology be used to improve channel efficiency and effectiveness?

9. Compare and contrast the advantages and disadvantages of a process approach and the more traditional approach to managing the supply chain.

10. What are the major obstacles to successful implementation of supply chain management?

THE DISTRIBUTION CHALLENGE!
PROBLEM: QUALITY ON THE RUN

It's one thing to overhaul a supply chain, but how do you know whether you've succeeded? And how do you monitor performance on an ongoing basis without drowning in a sea of meaningless data? One company found an answer.

Imagine a freight train tearing down the tracks at 100 miles an hour and going faster by the minute. All activity is geared toward coaxing even more speed out of the hurtling machine. In the midst of the commotion, the engineer turns to his assistant and calmly asks, "How are we doing?"

That must be something like the way Resource Net International, based in Covington, Kentucky, felt when it decided to adopt a series of strict performance measurements during a time of massive expansion. This wholesale distributor of printing paper, industrial products, and graphic supplies and equipment has seen its revenues grow by a whopping $1 billion to $2 billion a year.

The growth has come mostly through acquisitions, according to Joel Sutherland, vice president of logistics. For a company trying to get a handle on quality, that posed a special set of problems.

How, for example, do you communicate a fixed set of standards and performance measures to a workforce with origins in vastly different corporate cultures? At one point, Resource Net found itself with 20 different information systems. Recalls Sutherland: "It created a hodgepodge of systems, with a lot of people protecting their turf."

The sprawling nature of Resource Net's distribution network made matters even worse. The company had some 130 warehouses in 100 cities as well as 150 retail stores. Standardizing the criteria for quality across that entire system wasn't going to be easy.

Sutherland started out by involving the entire organization in the development of common standards. He got back 150 distinct measurements.

Sutherland knew the standardization project was vital to keeping the company competitive and profitable. But he was faced with a problem that turned out to be nearly virgin territory: How do you measure the cost of quality?

For years, companies have installed expensive and often disruptive quality programs without any clear idea of their impact on the bottom line. And they frequently fail to quantify the cost of failure properly. To Sutherland, that meant more than the cost of bringing back a defective or unwanted part and then redelivering the right one. It also meant the possible loss of a sale—and that customer's future business.

Sutherland's team managed to boil down the original 150 measurements to 15. Their goal was to end up with no more than 10–four or five in the areas of quality and customer satisfaction and an equal number related to productivity and cost reduction.

Sutherland was determined to create a small number of high-level measurements that would have a "cascading effect" on activities throughout the organization. The trick was to come up with standards that were general enough to encompass everyone, but not so general as to be meaningless.

The challenge is this: What is the least number of measurements that addresses all of the major issues with respect to customer satisfaction, quality, and operating performance? And how should these measurements be scored?

What Is Your Solution?

Source: "Distribution: The Challenge," *Distribution* 95, no. 2 (Feb. 1996), p. 68.

Chapter Outline

Chapter Objectives

- To develop an understanding of the concept of strategy and strategic planning.
- To illustrate how logistics can contribute specifically to the strategic success of an organization, and the importance of logistics participation in the strategic planning process.
- To show the key steps and issues in developing a logistics strategic plan.
- To discuss trends and issues that will present challenges for logistics professionals in the future.

Introduction

Logistics is positioned well to be a full participant and valuable contributor to an organization's strategy and strategic planning process. The chapter opens with an introduction to the concepts of mission, strategy, and the hierarchical nature of planning. This is followed by a presentation of the key elements of the strategic planning process and, more specifically, how to develop a logistics strategic plan. Critical issues to consider in the strategic planning process are developed. These issues are based on the key challenges facing logistics professionals now and in the future.

The chapter closes with a description of the many opportunities and challenges that logistics professionals will face in the 21st century.

What Are Strategy and Strategic Planning?

Strategy Defined

Because the strategic planning process exists to support an organization's strategy, it is important to develop an understanding of the overall concept of organizational strategy before discussing logistics strategy. *The Random House College Dictionary* defines **strategy** as "a plan, method, or series of maneuvers or stratagems for obtaining a specific goal or result." Strategy also has been defined as "a set of dynamic, integrated decisions you absolutely must make in order to position your business in its complex environment."[1] Thus, strategy represents the overall actions or approach to be taken to achieve the firm's goals and objectives.

Mission Statements

Corporate and Functional Area Mission Statements

The corporate mission statement is the overriding objective of the organization which serves to guide the organization's strategy, activities, and goals. It describes the organization's business. The mission concept was presented in Chapter 12, so it will be only briefly reviewed here.

Every organization should have a mission to guide management's strategy development and implementation. These should be communicated clearly to all employees, so that they understand and can support the organization's overall direction. It is critical that all functional areas understand the general and specific strategies that an organization is pursuing, so that they can properly support those strategies and formulate strategies of their own. Therefore, each functional area should have a mission to guide its actions in supporting the corporate mission.

Why Strategy Is Important to Logistics

If logistics managers do not understand corporate strategy, they will not be able to make decisions that are in the best interest of the organization. Even if logistics managers use the systems approach to make decisions and analyze trade-offs, they will still not be able

---

[1]Dan R. E. Thomas, *Business Sense: Exercising Management's Five Freedoms* (New York: Free Press, 1993), quoted in Audio-Tech Business Book Summaries 3, no. 7 (1994), p. 11 (sound cassette).

to make the best decisions without a good understanding of the corporate strategy and the corresponding logistics strategy. Without this knowledge, logistics personnel will not know how to value various alternatives in making trade-offs.

For example, if the goal is to achieve differentiation by offering fast, reliable deliveries (i.e., it is making the trade-off of cost versus delivery reliability), management would choose trucking over rail. If low cost is the primary objective, management might choose rail to deliver products to customers.

It is clear that if logistics managers do not understand corporate strategy, they will be unable to make decisions that are consistently in the best interests of the company as a whole. Thus, a plan should be developed in order to execute strategy and monitor progress.

Why Plan?

There are many reasons to plan. As one popular expression states: "If you don't know where you're going, how can you expect to get there?"[2] When planning, management should consider the overall mission of the organization and develop specific action plans and activities to move the organization in the desired direction. In today's rapidly changing business environment, it is essential for managers to anticipate changes and prepare their organizations to best incorporate, respond to, and take advantage of such change. Without taking a proactive approach, managers will be constantly reacting in a crisis mode, and they will not be able to move forward in achieving their firm's mission.

The Hierarchy of Planning

Planning Is a Continuous, Ongoing Process

Planning within an organization exists at many levels, as well as in many functional areas. At a minimum, most organizations *formally* update their plans on a yearly basis. However, planning is ideally an ongoing process. In addition, it is important to tie all of the functional plans together to ensure that they mesh and support the overall corporate plan and objectives. It also is important to have plans for different time frames, and that these time-phased plans fit together to support the long-range plan. The various types of planning are shown in Table 15–1 and are described in the following sections.

Strategic Plan

Strategic Plan

Organizations use a variety of terms to explain the various planning levels. At the highest level, which extends the furthest in time, is the **strategic plan.** Most U.S.-based organizations tend to extend their planning horizon about 5 to 10 years. The strategic plan for Japanese firms may look forward 50 or more years. The further into the future a plan extends, the less detail it will need. This is true because it is extremely difficult to anticipate the changes that may occur in the environment and the organization that will affect the organization's mission and its strategy.

---

[2]This has been credited to the Cheshire Cat in *Alice in Wonderland,* by Lewis Carroll.

TABLE 15–1 **Characteristics of Planning Types**

Type	Time Frame	Focus	Level of Detail	Level of Integration
Operational	Day to day < 1 year	Efficiency	Heavy financial orientation	Functional
Tactical	> 1 to 5 years	Event	Somewhat financially oriented	Integrated-functional
Strategic	5 to 10 years or more	Competition, resources, stakeholders	Few financials, more goal oriented	Integrated-corporate and supply chain

Source: Adapted from Martha C. Cooper, Daniel E. Innis, and Peter R. Dickson, *Strategic Planning for Logistics* (Oak Brook, IL: Council of Logistics Management, 1992), p. 28.

Components of a Strategic Plan

The strategic plan considers an organization's objectives, overall service requirements, and how management intends to achieve the corporate vision. The plans are very general and usually include projected revenues and expenses, lines of business, anticipated relative share of business within the market, and sales and profits from existing business lines compared with new lines of business.

Tactical Plan

Tactical Plan

At an intermediate level, generally one to five years into the future, an organization may have a medium-range plan, often called a **tactical plan.** Tactical plans are often more specific than strategic plans in terms of product lines, and may be broken down into detailed quarterly revenues and expenses. Nevertheless, such plans tend to show only a "top" line, without much detail about sales by stockkeeping unit (SKU).

Tactical plans usually include a capital expenditure plan that indicates how much the organization will invest each year in new plant, equipment, and other capital expenditure items. Issues like building warehouses, purchasing transportation or materials handling equipment, and other major expenditures to support the logistics infrastructure should be addressed as part of the capital expenditure plan.

Operating Plan

Operating Plan

The most detailed level of plan is called the **operating plan** or the annual plan. It breaks out revenues, expenses, and associated cash flows and activity by month for a one-year period. The detailed operating plan is prepared to guide the activities for the following year. Actual performance is monitored and compared to planned performance in order to anticipate problems and respond accordingly, and to communicate results.

Production scheduling and materials purchases may be based on the operating plan. A firm can use this plan to anticipate its logistics needs from warehouse space to shipping. This allows logistics to anticipate its labor needs and to negotiate contracts with third-party providers. As the year unfolds and actual results occur, the plan may be adjusted for actual activity levels and revised to reflect expected performance.

Linking Logistics Strategy with Corporate Strategy

Logistics strategic planning can be defined as:

Logistics Strategic Planning Defined

A unified, comprehensive, and integrated planning process to achieve competitive advantage through increased value and customer service, which results in superior customer satisfaction (where we want to be), by anticipating future demand for logistics services and managing the resources of the entire supply chain (how to get there). This planning is done within the context of the overall corporate goals and plan.[3]

Logistics strategic planning is a complex process that requires an understanding of how the different elements and activities of logistics interact in terms of trade-offs and the total cost to the organization. Only by understanding the corporate strategy can logistics best formulate its own strategy.

A study sponsored by the Council of Logistics Management reported that only 55 percent of the logistics professionals surveyed indicated that their company's executives believed that the logistics plan was critical to the corporation's strategic plan, while 16 percent were neutral and 29 percent disagreed.[4]

Strategic Planning in Logistics Is Less Common Than in Marketing or Manufacturing

Another finding was that strategic planning in logistics is less common than strategic planning in marketing or manufacturing. However, some logistics organizations such as the one in Levi Strauss and Company have taken a proactive role in the strategic planning process in their companies (see Box 15–1).

Logistics can contribute to and support an organization's strategic planning process in a number of ways. Intel has identified six specific ways that show how logistics supports corporate strategy (see Table 15–2). The benefits of this participation in strategic planning include operating improvements (e.g., lower inventory and shorter lead times) which can lead to strategic advantages (e.g., lower total cost and improved customer service). Before discussing the logistics planning process, we present an overview of the organizational planning process.

The Organizational Planning Process

The logistics plan is dependent upon and takes direction from corporate strategic planning, which requires that consideration be given to the following environments:

Strategic Plans Must Consider the External Environments

- Legal and political environment.
- Technological environment.
- Economic and social environment.
- Overall competitive environment.

---

[3]Martha C. Cooper, Daniel E. Innis, and Peter R. Dickson, *Strategic Planning for Logistics* (Oak Brook, IL: Council of Logistics Management, 1992), pp. 4–5.

[4]Ibid., p. 43.

Box 15–1

Levi's Moves Logistics in a Strategic Direction

Levi Strauss and Company is the world's largest manufacturer of apparel. It has been in the clothing business for over 140 years. It designs, manufactures, and markets a broad line of casual apparel for all ages. Major brands include Levi's, Britannia, and Dockers.

Distribution and Transportation, which is Levi Strauss's logistics operation, has direct responsibility for inbound, outbound, and intracompany transportation, and for the customer service centers for finished goods. To give it a strong customer focus, logistics reports to marketing.

Distribution and Transportation began formal strategic planning in 1990 with a profile of its operating environment and expected services for the 1990s. Distribution and Transportation uses the same approach and covers the same issues as other functions within the organization, but does so from a logistics perspective. It uses the term *key objectives* rather than *strategies* in identifying the issues to pursue. See below the "Key Objectives Outline," which guides the process for Levi Strauss. Key objectives are identified through a series of meetings, involving a variety of Distribution and Transportation personnel at a number of different locations.

Distribution and Transportation has taken a proactive approach in educating its personnel about strategic planning. In addition, it involves them in the planning process itself, which helps to create buy-in. To further encourage support for strategic thinking, Distribution and Transportation has developed a new performance evaluation system. Fifty percent of the rating is based on strategic planning and execution, such as activities that support the operation's strategic mission. Fifteen percent is tied to operational objectives and 35 percent to management practices.

Logistics managers view the strategic planning process as ongoing, and they refer to it throughout the year and assess its progress. Strategic issues and the strategic planning process for Levi's Distribution and Transportation receive a great deal of attention and visibility. Distribution and Transportation took the initiative in developing their strategic plan and continues to focus on strategic initiatives.

Key Objectives Outline

Key Objective Statement: This should reflect the final recommended wording as well as quantified objective(s) through year 3. Where appropriate, objectives may be staged in annual increments.

Environment: Review and update internal and external environment of the key objectives if appropriate.

Critical Issues: Review and update critical issues for success in attaining the objective if appropriate.

Benefits and Risks: Why should we pursue this objective and what exposures might we face?

Action Plans—Year 1: Detailed action plans for the balance of year 1. These will serve as the basis for quarterly reporting and measurement.

Action Plans—Years 2 and 3: Broad outline action plans for years 2 and 3. These will serve as the basis for development of each year's detailed plan as a particular year approaches.

Resources and Organization: What human, monetary, and other resources are needed and when?

Measurement: How the success of the action will be measured and reported quarterly per year 1 objectives. Include timeline for accomplishments through year 3.

The account management program designed using the planning process resulted in reduced customer returns and handling charges, and improved relationships with customers.

Source: Adapted from Martha C. Cooper, Daniel E. Innis, and Peter R. Dickson, *Strategic Planning for Logistics* (Oak Brook, IL: Council of Logistics Management, 1992), pp. 172–73.

TABLE 15–2   The Value Logistics Adds to the Corporation

- Increased planning capability and reduced inventory as a result of reliable delivery time
- Increased margin and improved customer service
- Reduced inventory levels through shorter cycle times
- Increased marketing advantage from consistent, shorter order cycles
- Uninterrupted supply of inbound material
- Reduced total cost by incorporating logistics into the corporate planning process

Source: Adapted from Lisa Ellram and L. Wayne Riley, "Purchasing/Logistics Strategic Planning: Value to the Corporation," *Proceedings of the Annual Conference of the Council of Logistics Management* (Oak Brook, IL: Council of Logistics Management, 1993), p. 461.

Some of the key issues to consider in each environment are illustrated in Figure 15–1, which shows how these four environments interact with one another. The effects of each environment upon the others greatly complicates the environmental assessment process. It is not unusual for an organization to have economists on staff to help forecast trends and identify external data sources to use as a basis for plan assumptions. Government forecast data of projected inflation and economic growth rates are frequently used as a starting point. Major steps in the corporate strategic planning process are shown in Figure 15–2.

The decisions made to support the steps in corporate strategic planning have a strong influence on the cost trade-offs required in marketing and logistics. For example, the decisions related to the evaluation of the potential consumers and the identification, evaluation, and selection of the target markets will have a profound impact on the type or types of logistics channels, intermediaries, facility locations, and so on. Thus, the "place" decision is highly dependent on the target customer. Steps 1–4 in Figure 15–2 were presented in more detail in Chapter 2, "Customer Service," and Chapter 14, "Supply Chain Management." Steps 5–7 are described in greater detail below.

Target Customers and Markets Must Be Selected

Formulation of Channel Objectives and Strategy.   Formulation of the channel objectives and strategy can begin only after target customers and target markets have been selected. It is critical that the logistics function participate in the strategic planning process from this point forward.

The logistics function plays a major role in the channel of distribution as both a performer of many activities and an interface with channel members who support the organization's channel of distribution. Most logistics executives agree that the logistics plan needs to mesh well with the plans of other departments.[5] With the channel strategy determined, the next step is to identify channel alternatives.

---

[5]Ibid., p. 45.

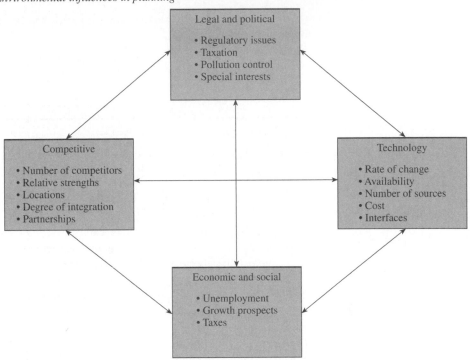

FIGURE 15–1

Environmental influences in planning

Identifying Channel Alternatives.   With greater interest and participation in partnering, outsourcing, and supply chain management, the complexity of identifying channel alternatives has increased. By limiting itself only to traditional options and structures, management may weaken their organization's competitiveness.

Issues to consider in formulating channel alternatives include the desired consistency and speed of delivery, information flows, the degree of control desired, and the cost of service. Activities may be performed internally or externally (outsourced). External service suppliers may provide full or limited service. If the current channel structure is meeting the organization's objectives, a less comprehensive review of channel alternatives may be sufficient.

Even if current objectives are being met, it is good policy to review the channel structure to identify opportunities for meeting objectives more effectively and efficiently, and to remain aware of new opportunities in channel design. The Creative Solutions box at the end of this chapter presents how U.S. West changed the way it viewed carriers in order to improve its performance.

Selection of the Channel Structure.   The channel structures that appear to hold the most promise in terms of meeting organizational objectives should be analyzed in depth. Factors to consider are operating costs, investment required, degree of control, flexibility,

Factors in Formulating Channel Alternatives

FIGURE 15–2

Major steps in the corporate strategic planning process

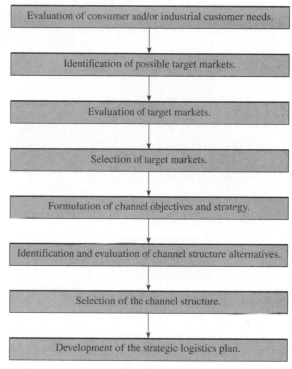

and the ability to meet channel objectives. It is not unusual for an organization to use multiple channels to meet the needs of different customers.[6]

Some Firms Use Multiple Channels

For example, a paint manufacturer may sell directly to contractors, own some retail stores to sell directly to consumers, and have a dealer network to sell to other retail stores. The channel must be matched with the firm's objectives. Once the channel structure has been determined, the strategic logistics plan can be formulated.

The Strategic Logistics Plan

The strategic logistics plan is not developed in isolation. It depends on a number of inputs from various functional areas, each of which will be described.

Marketing's Input into the Strategic Logistics Plan

1. **Marketing** provides the key inputs to the logistics plan because of the close interrelation between marketing and logistics discussed throughout this text, and illustrated in Figure 15–3. Marketing provides information about product or service offerings, pricing,

---

[6]Louis W. Stern and Fredrick D. Sturdivant, "Customer-Driven Distribution Systems," *Harvard Business Review* 64, no. 4 (July–Aug. 1986), pp. 34–41.

FIGURE 15–3

Cost trade-offs required in marketing and logistics

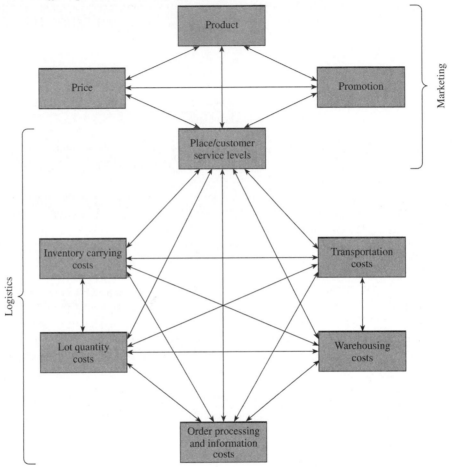

Marketing objective: Allocate resources to the marketing mix to maximize the long-run profitability of the firm. Logistics objective: Minimize total costs given the customer service objective share: Total costs = transportation costs + warehousing costs + order processing and information costs + lot quantity costs + inventory carrying costs.

Source: Adapted from Douglas M. Lambert, *The Development of an Inventory Costing Methodology: A Study of the Cost Associated with Holding Inventory* (Chicago: National Council of Physical Distribution Management, 1976), p. 7.

and promotion for each channel. This includes planned sales volume by month, type of customer, and regional area; product introductions and deletions; and customer service policies for various types of customers and geographical areas. In certain instances, there may be specific policies related to key customers which the logistics function must be aware of and be able to support.

Customer service policies are very important to logistics strategy. Logistics should be involved in setting such policies to make sure that they are feasible and economical. In addition, participation and input by logistics increases its understanding of and commitment to those policies. Customer service policies should include information by type of customer and region, covering issues such as:

- Order placement methods.
- Order entry.
- Target cycle time.
- Order cycle variability.
- Desired fill-rate or in-stock levels.

Customer service policies also should relate to product substitution, expediting, transshipment and customer pickup.

Logistics Strategy at Sara Lee Hosiery

Sara Lee Hosiery relies heavily on its logistics organization to support its changing customer service needs (see the Technology box). This example shows some of the operational, day-to-day elements of the role of logistics in supporting corporate strategy.

Manufacturing Input into the Strategic Logistics Plan

2. **Manufacturing** provides information important to the logistics strategic plan, such as locations of current and planned production facilities, and planned volume and product mix for each site. When the same product is produced at multiple locations, logistics can determine how to serve each market most efficiently.

Finance and Accounting's Input into the Strategic Logistics Plan

3. **Finance/Accounting** provides cost forecasts related to inflation rates and growth assumptions that need to be built into the planning process to project future costs. Finance/Accounting provides the cost data required to perform the cost trade-off analysis. It also is responsible for capital budgeting, which determines the availability of capital to finance expenditures to improve logistics equipment and infrastructure.

Logistics Provides Data and Analysis to Other Functions

4. **Logistics** provides data and analysis related to the existing logistics network to the other functions, including current storage and distribution facilities owned and rented, both at manufacturing locations and in the field; equipment capacity and capabilities at each location; and current transportation arrangements between various channel members. Logistics must identify the costs associated with these activities and the various channels used and proposed. Evaluation and selection of channel members are a critical aspect of this process.

Evaluation and Selection of Channel Members

Management needs to put the logistics plan into operation through the channel members it chooses. Thus, alternatives related to the choice of carriers, warehousers, and other logistics service providers need to be developed. Channel members should be judged and selected according to predetermined criteria designed to meet logistics objectives, such as reliability, consistency, geographical coverage, variety of service offerings, use of information technology, and cost. An example of this is presented in the Creative Solutions box at the end of this chapter.

Technology

Sara Lee Hosiery Uses Information Technology to Support Its Logistics Strategy

Sara Lee Hosiery, manufacturer of Hanes and L'Eggs hosiery, finds itself in a tough position because the worldwide hosiery market has been declining. Sara Lee, the world's largest hosiery manufacturer, has faced that challenge by restructuring its operations to be more efficient and to better meet the shifting demands of retailers and consumers. The shifting demands focus heavily on logistics issues:

- Demands for smaller quantities of a greater variety of products.
- More value-added services, especially information support such as electronic ordering, quick response, electronic advance shipping notices, and simplified returns.

The key to meeting these needs is electronic data interchange (EDI) with its customers. Retailers benefit by being able to better plan inventories because they get smaller, more frequent shipments using quick response. Sara Lee responds by transmitting EDI advance shipping notices. Both Sara Lee and its customers share information on a near real-time basis, which allows them to reduce inventories and plan more effectively.

Sara Lee has increased its use of small-package delivery service for shipping orders to customers. Its small-package carriers use information technology to improve service levels and provide value-added services. For example, RPS, a subsidiary of Roadway Services, provides Sara Lee with:

- A call tag service for returns from retailers in order to salvage products that may otherwise have gone to liquidators.
- Instant tracing of shipments.
- Proof of delivery through a telephone tracing system.
- Full support of Sara Lee's bar-coding system.

The use of information technology in logistics has been instrumental in supporting Sara Lee's customer service objectives. It has allowed Sara Lee to remain the leader in a changing competitive environment.

Source: Lisa Harrington, "Delivering True Value-Added to Customers," *Transportation and Distribution* 36, no. 3 (Mar. 1995), pp. A2–A8.

Ongoing Channel Evaluation and Improvement

Measures of Performance

Keeping performance on track requires regular monitoring and reporting of actual performance results. It is important to report expected levels of performance as a basis for comparison. Some of the relevant measures of performance of both the logistics function and external channel members were described in previous chapters. These include, but are not limited to, on-time delivery, response speed for emergencies, delivery time variability, and response to customer inquiries.

Additional examples of such measures are given in the Creative Solutions box. If management determines that channel performance is unsatisfactory, it must decide whether to continue to work with existing channel members toward improvement, replace the intermediary with one providing similar services, or restructure the channel.

Developing a Strategic Logistics Plan

The development of a strategic logistics plan requires the following:

Requirements of a Strategic Logistics Plan

- A thorough grasp and support of corporate strategy and supporting marketing plans in order to optimize cost-service trade-offs.
- A thorough understanding of how customers view the importance of various customer service elements, and the performance of the firm compared with its competitors.
- A knowledge of the cost and profitability of channel alternatives.[7]

It is clear that the strategic planning process as it relates to logistics should focus on determining required customer service levels. Information can be obtained utilizing internal and external market research (see Chapter 2). Firms often obtain this information as part of a logistics audit.

Logistics Audit. The logistics audit should be conducted routinely and is a review of how logistics is performing versus its objectives (see Figure 15–4). The audit complements and supports the strategic planning process by:

Ways the Logistics Audit Complements the Strategic Planning Process

- Linking logistics strategies and objectives to corporate strategies and objectives.
- Identifying key measures of logistics performance.
- Comparing customer perceptions of logistics performance with key measurements and objectives.
- Analyzing "gaps" in actual performance and comparing them with desired performance.
- Analyzing trade-offs among desired performance levels on key results areas.
- Designing systems to reflect key goals and objectives.
- Identifying expected performance and continuously monitoring results.

A formal logistics audit may be an annual event to help align the efforts of the logistics function and to focus the strategic planning process.

The First Step in a Logistics Audit Is the Selection of an Audit Team

A logistics audit is performed most effectively by a team of representatives that includes logistics personnel, and other company personnel. Customer input to this group is important. A mix of people is required to provide a balanced view of logistics performance and critical issues. Each of the elements of a logistics audit will be described. The logistics audit process begins with the formulation of a logistics audit team.

Logistics Audit Team. The logistics audit team should include those involved in managing or performing logistics activities, such as warehousing, customer service, and traf-

---

[7]Ibid., pp. 34–41.

FIGURE 15–4

The logistics audit: a conceptual model

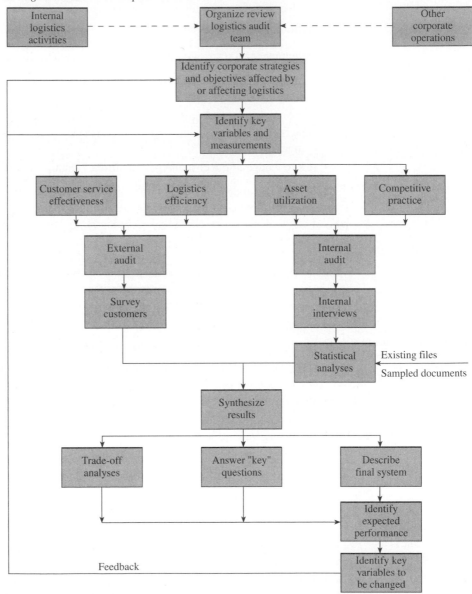

Source: Jay U. Sterling and Douglas M. Lambert, "A Methodology for Assessing Logistics Operating Systems," *International Journal of Physical Distribution and Materials Management* 15, no. 6 (1985), p. 13.

fic, and those who use logistics services, such as other corporate functions, particularly MIS and finance/accounting, and even external customers. The team may include representatives from sales, manufacturing, and key customers.

Inviting participation from multiple functions helps to improve cooperation, support and gives logistics more visibility and a broader organizational perspective. This should ease the acceptance and implementation of the team's recommendations. The logistics audit team begins with a review of the organization's strategy.

Review of Organizational Strategy.   The corporate mission, goals, and strategies must be reviewed early in the logistics audit to provide an overall direction and perspective. In addition, the strategies of both marketing and production/operations must be reviewed to ensure that logistics objectives and activities are supporting those key business functions. In more advanced organizations, management solicits logistics input when it develops corporate strategy and strategies for other functional areas. This review process helps to identify:

The Review Process Helps to Identify Important Factors

- Critical areas for review and focus during the logistics audit.
- Important logistics performance measures in the eyes of the customers.
- Alternative strategies to achieve desired objectives.

A review of corporate strategies helps the logistics audit team focus on the areas and issues to be investigated in the audit process.

Development of Key Issues to Investigate.   To develop a comprehensive assessment of logistics performance on key activities, the logistics audit team needs to develop a list of questions to ask customers as well as key operating personnel within the company. The questions should be broad enough to identify potential opportunities and barriers to logistics contributing to a competitive advantage for the organization. Examples of possible questions include:

What Questions Should the Logistics Audit Team Ask Customers?

- What is the organization's overall customer service strategy and what should it be?
- How should the overall customer service strategy differ by market or customer segment?
- What approaches to logistics are the competition using, and what are their strengths and weaknesses?
- What are the best opportunities for cost reduction in the organization's logistics system?
- Are there benefits to outsourcing all or part of our logistics activities?
- Are there any opportunities for consolidating any logistics facilities and efforts, either within or between strategic business units?
- What type of order processing flexibility and response time must the organization meet to be the industry leader in customers' minds?
- How can the organization improve logistics productivity?

Identifying Critical Measures and Variables.   Once key questions have been identified, the logistics audit team can determine *how* it will judge whether logistics is meeting

Four Categories of Variables Must Be Identified

the organization's objectives. This requires identification of specific variables and measurements in each of four broad categories: customer service effectiveness, logistics efficiency, asset utilization, and analysis of competitor performance.

Customer Service Effectiveness.   This category addresses issues such as order cycle time and order cycle consistency, fill rate, response times to customer inquiries, and flexibility to adapt to changes in order quantities, delivery dates, production schedules, and product substitutions.

Logistics Efficiency.   This category focuses on the costs of meeting customer service objectives, such as the cost of transportation, warehousing, inventory management, purchasing, order entry, and the scheduling of shipments.

Asset Utilization.   This category considers the efficiency and effectiveness of asset use, focusing on inventory, storage facilities, and transportation equipment.

Analysis of Competitor Performance.   It is imortant to measure how the organization's performance of logistics activities compares with that of other organizations. This activity is often termed **benchmarking,** and may consider the performance of both competing and noncompeting organizations concerning important customer service activities and asset utilization. Proper investigation of these four categories means that both an external and an internal audit must be conducted.

External Audit.   An external audit of customers may involve a survey, interviews, or focus groups with various customer constituencies (see Chapter 2). It is important to reach a representative mix of the firm's customers in terms of their size, rate of growth, and product demand. The external audit considers:

The External Audit Examines a Variety of Issues

1. How are current logistics systems performing in the customers' eyes? How would the customers like the system to perform?
2. How do these perceptions compare with the customers' perceptions of the performance of the competitions' logistics systems? Does the firm's performance meet the customers' requirements?
3. What changes in customer requirements are anticipated in the future?
4. What changes in logistics customer service might the competition offer in the future?

Management will often employ outside organizations to conduct the logistics audit in order to encourage unbiased feedback from their customers and the customers of competitors. In addition, outside researchers often have specialized training and experience that allow them to conduct such studies more effectively.

Internal Audit.   The internal audit involves collecting data from the firm's own operations and examining external documentation and flows within the organization's logistics processes. To properly and consistently address the relevant logistics interfaces with

Data used in logistics decision making are often obtained utilizing the latest computer and information technology, such as is the case in this information center located at a SuperValu facility.

other functions, a formal interview guide should be prepared. A sample of a guide appears in Appendix A to this chapter. An interview guide should cover areas such as:

Information Should Be Obtained from Company Personnel (or Employees) on a Number of Issues

- What is the activity level in the area?
- What are the key performance parameters?
- How is actual performance measured? How often is it measured? How are the results reported?
- Who is empowered to make decisions?
- How does that area interface with other functions?

A copy of the interview guide should be provided in advance, so that individuals can be prepared and have the data readily available.

For the more quantitative phase of the logistics audit, many internal documents and data sources can be relied upon, including:

Possible Data Sources for the Internal Audit

- Order history.
- Bills of lading.
- Freight bills.

- Private fleet trip logs.
- Warehouse time cards.
- Inbound and outbound shipment contents.
- Destination and trailer utilization.
- Warehouse labor hours for various activities.
- Order cycle and fill rate information.

Most of this information will include a great deal of detail related to customers, locations, items ordered, and so on. This detail makes it possible to perform a wide range of analysis. If the organization does not have a user-friendly decision support system to allow easy analyses and interface with the organization's database, the data sources listed previously can be "coded" or put into a standard format, and input into a file for manipulation and analysis with a standard statistical package. Many reports can be developed.

Analysis of Results.   Upon completion of the internal and external audits, the logistics audit team is ready to analyze the identified trade-off opportunities and to review the key questions originally developed to ensure that they have been addressed. Based on this analysis, the team should be able to develop and recommend a strategy and the supporting measurements needed to monitor the progress made in pursuing that strategy.

The team should be able to use the data gathered to analyze the historical performance of the firm and to predict how changes in service levels will affect costs. It is desirable to analyze the impact of proposed strategy on order cycle times, fill rates, various customer segments, product segments, and channel segments. This will help to ensure that there are few unforeseen consequences.

The Logistics Plan

Logistics Decisions Are Made in a Hierarchical Manner

Now that a logistics strategy has been formulated, a logistics plan needs to be developed to support that strategy. The plan includes the specific activities that the logistics function will undertake to achieve its objectives. Thus, logistics decisions are made in a hierarchical manner.

The highest level is the strategic level, which considers issues such as business objectives and customer service requirements. The next level is the tactical level, which considers decisions such as the number, size, and location of distribution centers; transportation modes preferred; and the type of inventory control system. Finally, the operating level focuses on day-to-day decisions, such as expediting policies, vehicle routing, and scheduling. Because all of these decisions are related, they must be made in an iterative fashion (see Figure 15–5).

The logistics plan itself covers a variety of issues and requires inputs from representatives who participate in each of the logistics activities. A sample outline of a logistics strategic plan is shown in Table 15–3. This outline illustrates that the plan moves from the general to the specific. It begins with the mission because all of logistics actions and activities should be driven by the logistics mission.

The key issues and objectives, review of past performance, and internal and external analysis are all completed as part of the logistics audit. The five-year vision represents

FIGURE 15–5

Making logistics decisions

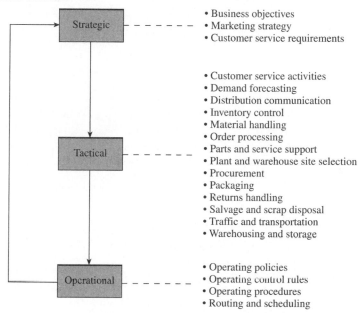

- Business objectives
- Marketing strategy
- Customer service requirements

- Customer service activities
- Demand forecasting
- Distribution communication
- Inventory control
- Material handling
- Order processing
- Parts and service support
- Plant and warehouse site selection
- Procurement
- Packaging
- Returns handling
- Salvage and scrap disposal
- Traffic and transportation
- Warehousing and storage

- Operating policies
- Operating control rules
- Operating procedures
- Routing and scheduling

Logistics decisions tend to be made hierarchically, but in an iterative manner.

Source: Adapted from William C. Copacino, Andersen Consulting, from a presentation at the International Logistics Management and Strategy Seminar, University of North Florida, March 9–11, 1992. All rights reserved by the author.

the performance level that logistics would like to be moving toward over the next five years, based on the logistics audit results. The next step is the development of specific action plans to meet those goals, as well as how progress toward the vision will be measured. This part of the plan needs to be broken down into detailed activity on a year-by-year basis, with the greatest detail shown for the next year. Implementation issues, such as funds needed, personnel to be hired or redeployed, and other potential resource requirements need to be identified and addressed along with other critical issues.

Future Challenges and Critical Issues in the Strategic Planning Process

Several major issues are emerging in logistics. These issues should be described, since many of them are critical considerations.[8] The focus of this section is on supply chain management and integrated channel management, including quick response and efficient consumer response, total quality management, just-in-time, information systems, reengineering,

---

[8]Some of these issues have not been dealt with in earlier chapters of the book.

TABLE 15–3   Example Outline of Logistics Plan

Logistics mission

Key issues and objectives
- Customer service performance
- Information systems
- Human resource management
- Supplier relationships
- Outsourcing

Comparison with previous plan performance

Internal analysis (Current position)
- Organization
- Human resources
- Transportation
- Relations with internal customers
- Quality
- Service

External/situational analysis
- Competitor logistics performance
- Trends
- Public, private and contract warehouses
- Public, private and contract carriage

Five-year vision

Action plans to achieve vision

Implementation issues

Other critical issues

Source: Adapted from Martha C. Cooper, Daniel E. Innis, and Peter R. Dickson, *Strategic Planning for Logistics* (Oak Brook, IL: Council of Logistics Management, 1992), pp. 72–79.

time-based competition, environmental issues, and reverse logistics. Management should integrate these issues into the strategic planning process and consider them in terms of how logistics can be used to gain a sustainable competitive advantage.

Supply Chain Management

Supply chain management, described in detail in Chapter 14, reflects the notion that the channel should be viewed and analyzed as a whole, from a systems perspective. Whichever party within the channel can most efficiently and effectively perform a task—from holding inventory to adding value through product differentiation—should perform that task. Thus, an organization should consider supply chain management during the strategic planning process when management is deciding to what extent it should manage the firm's supply chain, and what activities should be performed, where, and by whom, within the supply chain. The Global box describes how one firm used a global supply chain approach to improve its buying strategy.

Global

Create a Global Buying Strategy

A major international pharmaceutical firm with $14.5 billion in annual procurement spending, had its purchasing activity spread out among 14 distinct and separate locations, with over 100,000 suppliers. As a result, it was virtually impossible to generate and analyze timely data by supplier or commodity. To overcome this, management created a global sourcing team to focus its understanding and leverage on a worldwide scale.

As a first step, it extracted all of its procurement spending information. Next, it developed a common commodity coding structure for item numbers and it classified purchases by strategic areas. Next, it identified supplier affiliations/ownership/certification to better understand supplier capabilities and their potential for supplier leverage.

Working with its business units, management identified 50 potential sourcing and renegotiating opportunities within six weeks of the project start date. It is currently expanding the project.

Source: James M. Holer, Jr., Jon H. Bentley, and Robert B. Earle, "Full-Value Procurement," *Price Waterhouse* (1996), p. 10.

The supply chain management concept does not dictate a particular channel arrangement. It may involve forming partnerships with a few channel members in an effort to integrate most of the channel's activities, or making a conscious decision to let other channel members manage as they have been, perhaps because they have been doing an excellent job.

A supply chain management approach focuses on making a conscious, coordinated effort to improve channel management and channel efficiency through increased information sharing, efficient inventory placement, and coordinated decision-making across all key business processes. Some persons have referred to supply chain management as integrated channel management.

Benetton Creates an Integrated Channel

Integrated Channel Management.   This is the concept of integrating all channel members' programs and activities in order to achieve a higher level of customer satisfaction. Benetton, an Italian clothing manufacturer and retailer, has focused its efforts on this. Benetton's channel structure is discussed in Box 15–2. The company is at the center of this channel structure and exercises a great deal of control over all aspects of it.

How to Carry Out Integrated Channel Management.   One of the challenges of the integrated channel management philosophy is how to execute the strategy. Four major options are identified: implement channel integration strategies, assume channel leadership, form alliances with the channel leader, and improving selected, high leverage activities. Each of these approaches will be described.

Implement Channel Integration Strategies.   This approach involves utilizing some or all of the following activities:

Channel Integration Strategies

• Joint inventory management by means of channelwide distribution resources planning.

Box 15–2

Benetton: A Supply Chain Leader

Benetton is a global fashion manufacturer and retailer with headquarters near Venice, Italy. The company was founded in 1965 by the three Benetton brothers and a sister. It began as a manufacturer before opening three retail stores of its own in 1968. Benetton experienced rapid growth throughout the 1980s. It experienced difficulty when it attempted to diversify into financial services, but it has since refocused its efforts and left that arena.

Benetton follows a global strategy of selling the same garments throughout the world in similar small specialty shops. This creates a uniform look which is supported by strict corporate merchandising guidelines and media support.

Because Benetton is in the fashion industry, it must deal with a highly competitive, time-sensitive market with extremely short product life cycles. The short product life cycles—often a complete change of product lines 10 times a year—help hold consumer interest. With a rapid changeover in products and the need to get the merchandise to market quickly to meet the immediate demand of consumers, Benetton needs a highly responsive logistics

system. To remain competitive, Benetton's system also must be fast and flexible, yet efficient.

To fully leverage its marketing and logistics prowess, Benetton has taken a clear leadership role in its supply chain (see the figure in this box). Benetton uses a network of subcontractors, most of whom are exclusive manufacturers for Benetton, to produce its product. Benetton has established relationships with raw materials suppliers and provides the subcontractors with schedule data, raw materials, technical assistance, and financial assistance to buy or lease production equipment.

Benetton has agents that coordinate stores' demand information, ordering and marketing, product mix, and financial managements. These agents use EDI to transmit orders directly to Benetton. Benetton also receives other demand information, which it uses to determine its production. It does all the cutting and dyeing of garments based on actual demand patterns. Relevant demand data are forwarded to subcontractors. Undyed pieces are sent to subcontractors who sew them and return them to Benetton. These "gray goods" are held undyed until the

Benetton's central supply chain position

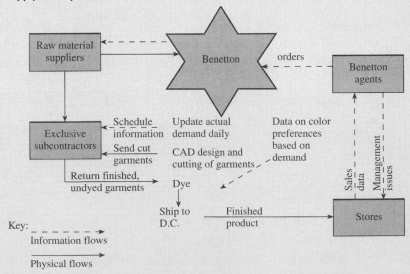

Box 15–2 concluded

consumer's preferred colors are determined based on actual sales. At that time, Benetton dyes the product and sends it to its $50 million, highly automated distribution center located in Treviso, 20 km north of Venice. This operation supplies all garments to more than 4,000 Benetton stores in 83 countries, using only six operators per shift for three shifts.

Thus, Benetton has taken control of all aspects of its logistics operations, and has chosen to play the role of channel leader. By doing this, the firm is able to leverage economies of scale with in-house and outsourced expertise. It relies heavily on information technology, such as

CAD/CAM [Computer Aided Design/Computer Aided Manufacturing] in cutting and dyeing materials, and EDI and bar coding for gathering point-of-sale data. It leverages its volume by performing centralized strategic and capital-intensive activities. Benetton takes advantage of the flexibility and relatively low cost of small subcontractors in its assembly operations.

Sources: Adapted from Joseph R. D'Cruz and Alan M. Rugman, "Developing the Five Partners Model," *Business Quarterly,* Winter 1993, pp. 60–71; and Peter Dapiran, "Benetton—Global Logistics in Action," *International Journal of Physical Distribution and Logistics Management* 22, no. 6 (1992), pp. 7–11.

- Joint management of transportation activities.
- Coordination of promotional effort.
- Channelwide electronic data interchange (EDI).
- Advance information sharing (POS data, inventory levels and positions, promotion response).
- Automatic replenishment of inventory.
- Colocation of suppliers at manufacturer's site to place orders, manage inventory, and solve problems.
- Channelwide performance measurement.[9]

Channel integration strategies are most likely to be appropriate when large firms, such as distributors, retailers, or manufacturers, deal with other large firms, although firms of unequal size can work together. The keys to success are mutual dependence and not having one firm dominate the other. These strategies can be maintained by firms of varying size, but more typically occur with firms who are comparable in size or power.

Assume Channel Leadership.   Assumption of channel leadership is appropriate when a large firm is dealing with smaller trading partners, as in the Benetton example (see Box 15–2). Such an approach allows the channel leader and its trading partners to improve their efficiency and to lower costs by sharing information and focusing on channel productivity improvements. The central role assumed by the channel leader further reinforces and enhances its leadership role.

---

[9]This material is adapted from William C. Copacino and Douglas M. Lambert, "Integrated Channel Management," unpublished manuscript, 1992. All rights reserved by the authors.

Form Alliance with Channel Leader.   This is a strategy for smaller or less powerful firms to pursue. The goal is to maintain good relations with the channel leader in order to influence the actions taken in the channel and to ensure that the interests of smaller firms are considered when the leader sets channel policy.

Focus on Selected, High Leverage Activities.   When small- or medium-sized organizations deal with other organizations of similar size, they often have limited resources and find themselves competing against much larger firms. They may need to focus their improvement efforts on a few key areas instead of on the whole channel by implementing automated ordering, sharing long-term plans, and focusing on time compression to speed up the time to market and to reduce channel investment in inventory and associated assets.

Partnerships within Supply Chains

Formation of Partnerships.   As described in Chapter 10, one of the issues management must consider is the **formation of partnerships.** "A partnership is a tailored business relationship based on mutual trust, openness, shared risk and shared rewards that yields a competitive advantage, resulting in business performance greater than would be achieved by the firms individually."[10] This type of arrangement can work well in supporting logistics objectives such as improved order cycle consistency or reduced lead time by working closely with key suppliers. Partnerships are not appropriate with all customers and suppliers because of the time and effort to successfully implement them. Therefore, they should be reserved for those key firms where the outcomes justify the effort.[11]

P&G and Wal-Mart Develop a Quick Response Program

Retail Quick Response Programs.   As described throughout this text, *quick response (QR)* programs are ways for retailers and manufacturers to integrate their information systems, giving them the ability to better coordinate production and inventory levels, reordering, and product stocking. An example of this is the relationship between Procter & Gamble (P&G) and Wal-Mart. P&G has over 90 people located at Wal-Mart's Bentonville, Arkansas, headquarters, working on joint strategy and coordination issues. This has given Wal-Mart better service and allowed P&G to significantly increase its business with Wal-Mart.[12] These same principles are applied in the grocery sector under the name **efficient consumer response (ECR).**

Total Quality Management

Total quality management (TQM) needs to be kept in the forefront of decision making throughout the strategic planning process and in the implementation of the strategies chosen. Quality is one performance issue that could be "traded off" as the organization attempts to reduce costs or cycle time to market. Yet, quality remains a key aspect of customer service, so any reduction in the quality of service might spur an increase in

---

[10]Douglas M. Lambert, Margaret A. Emmelhainz, and John T. Gardner, "Developing and Implementing Supply Chain Partnerships," *The International Journal of Logistics Management* 7, no. 2 (1996), p. 2.

[11]Ibid., pp. 1–12.

[12]Zachary Schiller, "Stalking the New Customer," *Business Week,* Aug. 28, 1989, p. 62.

Wal-Mart monitors and controls its worldwide marketing and logistics operations with the aid of state-of-the-art satellite communication systems.

Quality Is a Key Aspect of Customer Service

complaints and/or fewer sales that could more than offset any cost savings. Customers expect quality in service.

The impact of any changes in the level of quality must be explicitly evaluated. TQM must focus on the customer's view of quality, and what changes in performance quality mean to the customer.[13] This should be explicitly investigated as part of the logistics external audit.

Just-in-Time

JIT Eliminates Waste and Redundancies in the Supply Chain

The use of a just-in-time (JIT) inventory philosophy has a profound affect on logistics activity at all levels. JIT is a philosophy aimed at reduction of waste, redundancy, and inefficiency throughout the entire production system. JIT has been extended to the supply chain to eliminate waste and redundancy among trading partners beyond the immediate organization.[14]

---

[13]Rahul Jacob, "TQM: More Than a Dying Fad?" *Fortune,* Oct. 18, 1993, pp. 66–72.

[14]Bruce Ferrin, "Planning J.I.T. Supply Operations: A Multiple Case Analysis," *Journal of Business Logistics* 15, no. 1 (1994), pp. 53–69; and Steven Demmy and Arthur B. Petrini, "MRP + JIT + TQM + TOC: A Path to World Class Management," *Logistics Spectrum* 26, no. 3 (Fall 1992), pp. 8–13.

For organizations using or considering the use of JIT, the implications should be considered throughout the processes of corporate strategic planning and annual logistics planning. For example, management should consider:

- Which parts of the organization will implement JIT?
- Since the number of carriers and suppliers are generally reduced in JIT systems, how many should be utilized and how should they be selected?
- What kind of information system linkages are required to ensure visibility of production schedules and inventory levels?
- How will logistics interface with manufacturing to coordinate shipments?

These are only a few of the many issues to be considered in planning for JIT.[15]

Information Systems

Logistics activities are transaction intensive: Transactions, such as receiving, stocking, order filling, and shipment, generate large quantities of data. The data can be useful in assessing not only actual logistics performance but in identifying attractive areas for improving performance.[16] As shown in Chapter 3, the sheer volume of data makes it virtually impossible to manage without an adequate information system.

Information systems are much more than receptacles for storing data. The manner in which the data are stored and the types of database management systems available within an organization play a large role in whether that data can be readily utilized for analysis of logistics performance. These data are valuable in the strategic planning process.

Examples of Information Systems Technology

Information systems enable logistics to communicate and interface with customers and others within the organization. Information technology makes QR and ECR possible. Examples of key information systems technology for sharing information include EDI, point-of-sale (POS) information gathering, electronic funds transfer, access to DRP/MRP files through information linkages, and bar coding. Without such technologies, vendor-managed inventories and QR systems would be extremely difficult, if not impossible, to manage. Logistics executives must ensure that these technologies are getting the proper visibility and funding commitment as part of the information systems plan and capital budgeting process of the strategic planning process.

Reengineering

Reengineering Creates Breakthroughs

Reengineering focuses on an important means of improving an organization's efficiency and effectiveness. The term reengineering is used to describe the elimination of old methods of operation and the creation of new, better approaches from scratch. More than simply modifying existing systems, reengineering challenges the organization to reinvent its

---

[15]"JIT Transportation: Saturn and Ryder: Linking Logistics with Production," *Purchasing* 115, no. 3 (Sept. 9, 1993), p. 49.

[16]Cornelia Dröge and Richard Germain, "Evaluating Logistics Management Information Systems," *International Journal of Physical Distribution and Logistics Management* 21, no. 7 (1991), pp. 22–27.

operations without considering the way it currently does business. This creates the potential for major breakthroughs instead of only small incremental improvements.

The strategic planning process represents an excellent opportunity to evaluate making such bold moves. Reengineering works particularly well in people-intensive, transaction-intensive processes such as accounts payable or order processing. It can be used to identify ways to eliminate unnecessary or redundant activities and to automate routine, mundane activities. This frees up the productive resources of the organization to provide greater value added.[17] In describing reengineering, the following analogy has been used:

- The optimist says the glass is half full.
- The pessimist says the glass is half empty.
- The reengineer says the glass is twice as large as is needed.[18]

Time-Based Competition

Time-based competition refers to ways of "taking time out" of operations. It could entail reducing the order cycle time, speeding up order placement, or introducing new products to market more quickly. Time-based competition is receiving a great deal of attention as organizations have discovered that time really is money. Longer processes can create inefficiencies; require higher inventory levels, greater handling, and more monitoring; incur a greater possibility for error and obsolescence; and decrease the efficiency of the whole supply chain.[19]

Logistics is in an excellent position to help reduce the organization's cycle time by working with carriers, suppliers, and customers to share more real-time information, improve information accuracy, and identify current inefficiencies. This represents a significant opportunity for logistics to provide a competitive advantage for the organization.

Lead-Time Reduction

The importance of lead-time reduction to customers should be investigated as part of the logistics audit. Lead-time reduction must be linked to customer requirements and the firm's marketing efforts to have a positive impact on the organization's competitiveness.[20] Shorter lead-times may result in lower inventories for the customer, depending on the volatility of sales and the degree of difficulty in forecasting.

Environmental Issues/Reverse Logistics

Environmental issues have received a great deal of attention in recent years. Not only has there been an increase in legislation on a domestic and global scale, but there has been an increasing demand by consumers for "green" or environmentally friendly

---

[17]For an in-depth discussion of the concept of reengineering, see Michael Hammer and James Champy, *Reengineering the Corporation* (New York: HarperCollins, 1993).

[18]Thomas A. Stewart, " Evidence That Reengineering Has Lost its Buzz," *Fortune,* Nov. 13, 1995, p. 60.

[19]Thomas E. Hendrick, *Time Based Competition* (Tempe, AZ: Center for Advanced Purchasing Studies, 1994), p. 4.

[20]George Stalk, Jr., and Alan M. Weber, "Japan's Dark Side of Time," *Harvard Business Review* 71, no. 4 (July–Aug. 1993), pp. 93–102.

products and practices. Recycling, proper management and disposal of hazardous waste, reusable packaging materials, use of renewable resources, and energy conservation have become visible political and emotional issues. As such, consideration of environmental factors should be ongoing throughout the strategic planning process and during its implementation.

Reverse Logistics Described

Reverse Logistics.   *Reverse logistics* is concerned with issues such as reducing the amount of raw materials or energy used, recycling, substitution, reusable packaging, and disposal. However, logistics cannot deal effectively with these issues in isolation. It must interface with manufacturing, marketing, purchasing, and packaging engineering. Decisions made in each of these areas have an impact on the ability of logistics to conserve resources and achieve green goals.[21]

Hazardous Materials

Hazardous Materials.   Specific legislation covers the movement and disposal of hazardous materials. Personal liability can be created if materials are knowingly mishandled or mishandled through negligence. It is important for logistics professionals to become familiar with the laws governing any hazardous materials that their organization uses, and to ensure proper handling, transportation, storage, and disposal. Hazardous materials are generally disposed of in approved dump sites, incinerated, or otherwise destroyed. The best approach is to avoid the creation of waste through careful selection of materials and recycling, reclamation, and revision of materials on-site.[22]

Life Cycle Analysis

Life Cycle Analysis.   Implied in the process of reverse logistics is that organizations use **life cycle analysis** in evaluating product or packaging decisions. Life cycle analysis involves viewing the purchased item from cradle to grave to determine its impact on the environment and on the total cost of doing business. Looking at it from an environmental perspective, this approach is useful because it examines the impact of the item on the environment at all stages of its life cycle, from product development up to and including ultimate disposal. Life cycle analysis should consider all available methods for waste reduction and management, including source reduction, recycling, substitution, and disposal.

Legislation.   Italy, Denmark, Norway, and Germany have led the way in environmental and recycling legislation in Europe. There are a number of bans on plastic foam, polyethylene, corrugated containers, and similar materials from landfills and incineration.[23] Logistics and packaging engineering need to work on reducing and reusing packaging, and developing more creative packaging materials, such as the foam "peanuts" that melt in water and actual "popcorn," which is biodegradable.

---

[21]Terrence L. Pohlen and M. Theordore Farris II, "Reverse Logistics in Plastics Recycling," *International Journal of Physical Distribution and Logistics Management* 22, no. 7 (1992), p. 35.

[22]James R. Stock, *Reverse Logistics* (Oak Brook, IL: Council of Logistics Management, 1992).

[23]Corey Billington, "Strategic Supply Chain Management," *OR/MS Today* 21, no. 2 (Apr. 1994), pp. 26–27.

Hewlett-Packard Reduces Packaging in Europe

In Europe, Hewlett-Packard switched from shipping printers in individual units to packaging them in bulk. This not only significantly reduced the amount of packaging materials, but reduced the shipping weight and allowed more efficient space utilization during shipment.[24]

Many countries have tried to minimize the creation of waste through the use of tax incentives and the provision of public information and technical assistance. Waste minimization policies tend to be favored as the most efficient strategy. As the trend toward greater environmental awareness continues, logistics professionals must remain attuned to legislation and public sentiment, and be ready to suggest and support green strategies.

Such strategies represent a potentially attractive marketing opportunity because they create a favorable public image. The correct corporate response could create a distinct advantage for an organization, allowing it to command higher prices for its products and services. As you have read throughout these chapters, many other opportunities exist for logistics to contribute to an organization's competitive advantage.

Logistics as a Source of Distinctive Competitive Advantage

How can logistics provide the firm with a distinct competitive advantage? This should be one of the key focuses of logistics during the strategic planning process and the implementation of strategy. There are many opportunities for logistics' services and activities to give the firm an important advantage: supply chain management, quality of service, outstanding information systems, and effective time-based competition. Organizations such as Wal-Mart and McKesson Drug have effectively used information technology to give them a distinct advantage in terms of improved customer service and in-stock availability while lowering inventory.[25]

Coca-Cola's Logistics Operations in Japan

An example of the strategic use of logistics is Coca-Cola's operation in Japan. Coke has a variety of types of customers in Japan, all of which demand different types of service. Coca-Cola's major Japanese customers—supermarkets and convenience store chains—want predictable deliveries and to have displays set up for them. Operators of vending machines want assurance that their machines are full to avoid lost sales. Coca-Cola has adapted its logistics services to meet the needs of each customer segment or channel.

Coca-Cola focuses on delivery, timing, frequency, in-store display, and merchandising for supermarkets and retailers because that is what these customers want. In the small, family-owned stores, Coca-Cola focuses on helping with paperwork, setting up displays, and cleaning the storeroom.

On the other hand, vending-machine owners do not care about such services; they want a fully stocked machine. To meet their needs, Coca-Cola has installed sophisticated information systems in the vending machine to monitor inventory levels. This allows the delivery vehicle to stock the right mix and level of products and to deliver in a timely

---

[24]Frances Cairncross, "How Europe's Companies Reposition to Recycle," *Harvard Business Review* 70, no. 2 (Mar.–Apr. 1992), pp. 35–45.

[25]Russell Jonston and Paul R. Lawrence, "Beyond Vertical Integration—The Rise of the Value Adding Partnership," *Harvard Business Review* 66, no. 4 (July–Aug. 1988), pp. 94–104.

manner before the inventory is depleted. As a result, Coca-Cola does not dispatch trucks when machines do not need replenishment and it has the correct mix of product which reduces costs.

By monitoring demand, Coca-Cola avoids carrying products that do not sell.[26] Coca-Cola in Japan uses logistics strategically, differentiating its service offerings to provide it with a competitive advantage. This has been a successful strategy for Coke, which holds a 34 percent market share in Japan, compared with Pepsi's 5 percent.[27]

Tailored Logistics

On the other hand, "traditional services" that logistics has provided should not be overlooked. Tailoring the logistics system to meet customers needs better than the competition can be an important source of competitive advantage.[28] If logistics is to continue to grow in stature and be recognized as an important player in corporate strategy, it is incumbent upon logistics professionals to recognize and seize the opportunities to contribute to the overall success and distinctive competence of the organization.

Summary

While logistics has been recognized as an important business function worthy of study only in the past 40 years, much has been gained during that time. Logistics has grown from a transaction-oriented, tactical function to a process-oriented, strategic function. The challenges and opportunities for logistics professionals to participate actively in setting strategy and to contribute to the success of the organization have never been greater. The rewards for recognizing and accepting these challenges in a creative and proactive manner should prove to be substantial. It is the hope and sincere desire of the authors that we have presented the material in such a way as to encourage bright, ambitious young men and women to seek careers within the logistics profession.

Suggested Readings

Bowersox, Donald J. "The Strategic Benefits of Logistics Alliances." *Harvard Business Review* 68, no. 4 (July–Aug. 1990), pp. 36–45.

Bowersox, Donald J.; Patricia J. Daugherty; Cornelia L. Dröge; Richard N. Germain; and Dale S. Rogers. *Logistical Excellence: It's Not Business as Usual.* Burlington, MA: Digital Press, 1992.

Camp, Robert C. *Benchmarking: The Search for Industry Best Practices That Lead to Superior Performance.* Milwaukee, WI: ASQC Quality Press, 1989.

Cooper, Martha C.; Daniel E. Innis; and Peter R. Dickson. *Strategic Planning for Logistics.* Oak Brook, IL: Council of Logistics Management, 1992.

---

[26]Joseph B. Fuller, James O'Conor, and Richard Rawlinson, "Tailored Logistics: The Next Advantage," *Harvard Business Review* 93, no. 3 (May–June 1993), pp. 87–98.

[27]Patricia Sellers, "How Coke Is Kicking Pepsi's Can," *Fortune,* Oct. 28, 1996, p. 78.

[28]Fuller, O'Conor, and Rawlinson, "Tailored Logistics"; and Donald J. Bowersox, et al., *Logistical Excellence: It's Not Business as Usual* (Burlington, MA: Digital Press, 1992).

Creative Solutions

U.S. West Understands Strategic Importance of Logistics

US West Communications is a regional telephone operating company covering 14 states west of the Mississippi River. It saw an opportunity to reengineer its transportation and logistics to better support its overall strategy. In doing this, U.S. West specifically looked for companies who would:

- Focus on the total cost of the relationship, rather than simply providing a low price.
- Provide excellent reporting and service by means of EDI, advanced information systems, and the development of integrated logistics strategies.
- Embrace a quality focus, and determine who could add value to the process.

U.S. West chose CF MotorFreight as its less-than-truckload (LTL) carrier, and they have built a partnership which they hope will last at least seven to eight years. Both firms have committed themselves to the relationship by focusing on continuous improvement, investing in information technology and EDI, sharing of resources and people, and focusing on value added. CF has an employee on-site at U.S.

West, and is involved in managing the supply chain where it seeks opportunities to take time and costs out of the system.

CF is focused on helping U.S. West better serve its customers. It has been part of the decision-making process in many of U.S. West's supply chain decisions. The real test is in the results. In the first 16 months of this relationship, U.S. West enjoyed the following performance gains:

	Initial	*After 16 Months*
On-time delivery	94%	+98%
Claims ratio	1.5%	.41%
Claims processing	47 days	7 days
Billing errors	.40%	.11%

U.S. West's base transportation rate also went down 15 percent. CF benefited too; its revenues from U.S. West went up by 17 percent and its bill-to-pay cycle time decreased by 9 percent.

Source: Peter A. Buxbaum, "Winning Together," *Transportation and Distribution* 36, no. 4 (Apr. 1995), pp. 47–50.

Fuller, Joseph B.; James O'Conor; and Richard Rawlinson. "Tailored Logistics: The Next Advantage." *Harvard Business Review* 71, no. 3 (May–June 1993), pp. 87–98.

Hamel, Gary, and C. K. Prahalad. *Competing for the Future.* Cambridge: Harvard Business School Press, 1994.

Hammer, Michael, and James Champy. *Reengineering the Corporation.* New York: HarperCollins, 1993.

Heskett, James L. "Logistics—Essential to Strategy." *Harvard Business Review* 51, no. 6 (Nov.–Dec. 1973), pp. 85–96.

Lambert, Douglas M.; Margaret A. Emmelhainz; and John T. Gardner. "Developing and Implementing Supply Chain Partnerships." *The International Journal of Logistics Management* 7, no. 2 (1996), pp. 1–12.

McGinnis, Michael A., and Jonathan Kohn. "A Factor Analytic Study of Logistics Strategy." *Journal of Business Logistics* 11, no. 2 (1990), pp. 41–63.

———. "Logistics Strategy, Organizational Environment and Time Competitiveness." *Journal of Business Logistics* 14, no. 2 (1993), pp. 1–24.

Porter, Michael E. *Competitive Strategy.* New York: Free Press, 1980.

Scott, Charles, and Roy Westbrook. "New Strategic Tools for Supply Chain Management." *International Journal of Physical Distribution and Logistics Management* 21, no. 1 (1991), pp. 23–33.

Sterling, Jay U., and Douglas M. Lambert. "A Methodology for Assessing Logistics Operating Systems." *International Journal of Physical Distribution and Materials Management* 15, no. 6 (1985), pp. 3–44.

Stock, James R. *Reverse Logistics.* Oak Brook, IL: Council of Logistics Management, 1992.

Questions and Problems

1. Why is planning likely to become an increasingly important activity for logistics managers?

2. How does the logistics strategic planning process interface with the marketing strategic planning process?

3. What are the various approaches to integrated channel management? How should managers choose the appropriate channel management strategy?

4. Why is it important to perform both an internal and an external analysis in developing the logistics strategic plan?

5. What are the critical elements of the internal and external logistics audit?

6. Why is it advisable to use a team in performing a logistics audit? What functional areas should be represented on the team for a retailer? For a manufacturer?

7. Which of the many challenges facing the logistics profession in the years ahead do you believe is the most significant? Discuss why.

8. Give some examples of how increased environmental concern has affected logistics.

9. How are new operating techniques such as JIT, ECR, and QR affecting logistics operations?

APPENDIX A

CUSTOMER SERVICE/ORDER ADMINISTRATION AUDIT

1. Do you have a written customer service policy?
2. Do customers receive a copy of this policy?
3. Can you provide us with a definition of customer service as viewed by your company?
4. Do you provide different levels of customer service by product or customer?
5. Do your customer service standards change?
6. If your company designates a particular area as customer service (or customer relations, distribution services, and so on):
   a. How many people are assigned to the area?
   b. Describe the major responsibilities of these individuals.
   c. To what department does this area report?
   d. If possible, please provide all job descriptions that include customer service/customer relations in the title.
7. Relative to your company's order cycle time, how frequently do you monitor the order cycle?
8. Circle the appropriate letters from the choices below to indicate which of the following dates are part of your measurement:
   a. Order prepared by customer.
   b. Order received by you.
   c. Order processed and released by customer service.
   d. Order received at DC.
   e. Order picked and/or packed.
   f. Order shipped by DC.
   g. Order received by customer.
9. Is order processing centralized in one location or decentralized?
10. On average, how many orders do you process each day, week, and month?
11. What is the dollar value of a typical order? Number of line items?
12. What percentage of customer orders are placed by company field salespeople?
13. What percentage of total customer orders are placed by inside sales people or order clerks who call the customer to get the order?
14. What percentage of total customer orders are placed by customers unaided by either company field or inside salespeople?
15. In terms of methods of order entry: How does each customer group above enter orders? If they use multiple methods, please indicate the percentage of their total entered by each method.
16. How many order entry locations exist in the company?
17. Once received by the firm, does the order taker:
    _____ Fix out a preprinted order form? If yes, ask for a copy.
    _____ Enter the order into the computer by means of a data terminal off-line?
    _____ Enter the order into the computer by means of a data terminal on-line?

Note: This is an example of an audit for only one function. Additional examples can be found in the sources for inbound and outbound transportation, warehouse operations, inventory management and forecasting, production planning and scheduling, marketing/sales, and financial control/accounting.

Sources: From Jay U. Sterling and Douglas M. Lambert, "A Methodology for Assessing Logistics Operating Systems," *International Journal of Physical Distribution and Materials Management* 15, no. 6 (1985), p. 29; Douglas M. Lambert and M. Christine Lewis, "Meaning, Measurement and Implementation of Customer Service," *Proceedings of the Annual Conference of the National Council of Physical Distribution Management* (Chicago: NCPDM, 1981), pp. 569–95. Also see Douglas M. Lambert and James R. Stock, *Strategic Logistics Management,* 3rd ed. (Burr Ridge, IL: Richard D. Irwin, 1993), pp. 753–55.

THE DISTRIBUTION CHALLENGE!
PROBLEM: POWER TO SPARE

Phil R. Sheerer of Anderson Consulting was faced with this challenge involving recent changes at a utility company.

The company provides gas and electricity to customers in two states, one of which accounts for 90 percent of its business. Eager to reallocate resources and slash vehicle miles, the client asked Anderson to undertake a sweeping review of its service operations. The utility was willing to consolidate facilities and move personnel around, even though union restrictions would slow the process.

At the time of the review, the company had most of its personnel and vehicles stationed at distribution centers (DCs), with about 10 percent of employees working from home. It maintained more than 25 personnel classifications and more than 35 types of vehicles.

Unfortunately, the client had little historical data on hand. DCs were making their own decisions on allocating personnel and vehicles. Many origins and destinations were unknown, and mergers had created a web of overlapping networks and service areas.

Anderson had a choice of methodologies and tools. Possibilities included:

- Network flow-optimization programs to evaluate consolidation of facilities. (These programs are difficult to customize and don't give accurate mileage results.)
- Vehicle-routing tools (which produce a high degree of detail, but can end up running slowly when evaluating large networks).
- Spreadsheets (which were quick to execute and easily customized, although they lack sophisticated tools and visual interface, and don't easily lend themselves to multiple scenarios with big changes).

You're the consultant. How would you face this challenge?

What Is Your Solution?

Source: "Distribution: The Challenge," *Distribution* 96, no. 5 (May 1997), p. 68.

Credits

Figure 1–4   Cost Trade-Offs Required in Marketing and Logistics
Source: Adapted from Douglas M. Lambert, *The Development of an Inventory Costing Methodology: A Study of the Costs Associated with Holding Inventory* (Chicago: National Council of Physical Distribution Management, 1976), p. 7. © 1976. Used by permission of the Council of Logistics Management.

Figure 1–5   How Logistics Activities Drive Total Logistics Costs
Source: Adapted from Douglas M. Lambert, *The Development of an Inventory Costing Methodology: A Study of the Costs Associated with Holding Inventory* (Chicago: National Council of Physical Distribution Management, 1976), p. 7. © 1976. Used by permission of the Council of Logistics Management.

Figure 1–6   Logistics Responsibilities: Allocation of Time and Effort
Source: James M. Masters and Bernard J. La Londe, "1996 Ohio State University Survey of Career Patterns in Logistics" (Columbus, OH: The Ohio State University, 1996). © 1996. Used by permission of James M. Masters.

Table 1–2   Strategic Planning by Departments
Source: Martha C. Cooper, Daniel E. Innis, and Peter R. Dickson, *Strategic Planning for Logistics* (Oak Brook, IL: Council of Logistics Management , 1992), p. 10. © 1992. Used by permission of the Council of Logistics Management.

Chapter 2 Box Feature   Creative Solutions: Quality in Logistics
Source: Dennis M. Whan, "Quality in Logistics," *Transportation and Distribution* 34, no. 7 (July 1993), p. 33. © 1993. Used by permission of Penton Publishing Company.

Figure 2–1   Elements of Customer Service
Source: Bernard J. La Londe and Paul H. Zinszer, *Customer Service: Meaning and Measurement* (Chicago: National Council of Physical Distribution Management, 1976), p. 281. © 1976. Used by permission of the Council of Logistics Management.

Figure 2–3   Cost Trade-Offs Required in a Logistics System
Source: Adapted from Douglas M. Lambert, *The Development of an Inventory Costing Methodology: A Study of the Costs Associated with Holding Inventory* (Chicago: National Council of Physical Distribution Management, 1976), p. 7. © 1976. Used by permission of the Council of Logistics Management.

Table 2–1   A Customer-Product Contribution Matrix
Source: Adapted from Bernard J. La Londe and Paul H. Zinszer, *Customer Service: Meaning and Measurement* (Chicago: National Council of Physical Distribution Management, 1976), p. 181. © 1976. Used by permission of the Council of Logistics Management.

Table 2–2   Making the Customer-Product Contribution Matrix Operational
Source: Adapted from Bernard J. La Londe and Paul H. Zinszer, *Customer Service: Meaning and Measurement* (Chicago: National Council of Physical Distribution Management, 1976), p. 182. © 1976. Used by permission of the Council of Logistics Management.

Table 2–3   Importance and Performance of Office Furniture Manufacturers on Selected Customers Service Attributes
Source: Adapted from Jay U. Sterling and Douglas M. Lambert, "Customer Service Research: Past, Present, and Future," *International Journal of Physical Distribution and Materials Management* 19, no. 2 (1989), p. 19. © 1989. Used by permission of MCB University Press Limited.

Figure 3–4   Typical EDI Configurations
Source: GE Information Service, as reported in Lisa H. Harrington, "The ABCs of EDI," *Traffic Management* 29, no. 8 (August 1990), p. 51. © 1990. Reprinted by permission from *Logistics Management.*

Figure 3–6   Decision Support System
Source: Allan F. Ayers, "Decision Support Systems: A Useful Tool for Manufacturing Management," a paper published by K. W. Tunnell Company, Inc. (1985), p. 2. Used by permission of Allan F. Ayers.

Table 4B–6   Inventory Safety Stock Factors
Source: Professor Jay U. Sterling, University of Alabama; adapted from Robert G. Brown, *Materials Management Systems* (New York: John Wiley & Sons, 1977), p. 429. Copyright © 1977. Reprinted by permission of John Wiley & Sons, Inc.

Figure 5–1   Cost Trade-Offs Required in a Logistics System
Source: Adapted from Douglas M. Lambert, *The Development of an Inventory Costing Methodology: A Study of the Costs Associated with Holding Inventory* (Chicago: National Council of Physical Distribution Management, 1976), p. 7. © 1976. Used by permission of the Council of Logistics Management.

Figure 5–2   Normative Model of Inventory Carrying Cost Methodology
Source: Douglas M. Lambert, *The Development of an Inventory Costing Methodology: A Study of the Costs Associated with Holding Inventory* (Chicago: National Council of Physical Distribution Management, 1976), p. 68. © 1976. Used by permission of the Council of Logistics Management.

Figure 5–4   Relationship between Inventory Turns and Inventory Carrying Costs
Source: Douglas M. Lambert and Robert H. Quinn, "Profit Oriented Inventory Policies Require a Documented Inventory Carrying Cost," *Business Quarterly* 46, no. 3 (Autumn 1981), p. 65. Reprinted with permission of *Business Quarterly,* published by Ivey Management Services Inc., The University of Western Ontario, London, Canada.

Figure 5–5   Annual Inventory Carrying Costs Compared to Inventory Turnovers
Source: Jay U. Sterling and Douglas M. Lambert, "Segment Profitability Reports: You Can't Manage Your Business Without Them," unpublished manuscript, 1992. Used by permission of Douglas M. Lambert.

Figure 5–6   ABC Parts Classification
Source: Lynn E. Gill, "Inventory and Physical Distribution Management," in *The Distribution Handbook,* James F. Robeson, Editor-in-Chief, and Robert G. House, Associate Editor, p. 665.

Table 5–4 Summary of Data Collection Procedure
Source: Douglas M. Lambert and Robert H. Quinn, "Profit Oriented Inventory Policies Require a Documented Inventory Carrying Cost," *Business Quarterly* 46, no. 3 (Autumn 1981), p. 71. Reprinted with permission of *Business Quarterly,* published by Ivey Management Services Inc., The University of Western Ontario, London, Canada.

Table 5–5 The Impact of Inventory Turns on Inventory Carrying Costs
Source: Douglas M. Lambert and Robert H. Quinn, "Profit Oriented Inventory Policies Require a Documented Inventory Carrying Cost," *Business Quarterly* 46, no. 3 (Autumn 1981), p. 65. Reprinted with permission of *Business Quarterly,* published by Ivey Management Services Inc., The University of Western Ontario, London, Canada.

Box 6–2 Kanban Card Procedure
Source: "Why Everybody Is Talking About 'Just in Time,' " *Warehousing Review* 1, no. 1 (October 1984), p. 27. Reprinted with permission from *Warehousing Review,* 1984 Charter Issue, The American Warehouse Association (publisher), 1300 West Higgins Road, Suite 111, Park Ridge, IL 60068.

Box 6–3 How DRPII Forecasts Demand: A Case History
Source: "How DRP Helps Warehouses Smooth Distribution," *Modern Materials Handling* 39, no. 6 (April 9, 1984), p. 57. *Modern Materials Handling,* Copyright © 1984 by Cahners Publishing Company. Used by permission of Cahners Publishing Company, a division of Reed Elsevier Inc.

Figure 6–1 The Objectives of Integrated Materials Management
Source: Yunus Kathawala, and Heino H. Nauo, "Integrated Materials Management: A Conceptual Approach," *International Journal of Physical Distribution and Materials Management* 19, no. 8 (1989), p. 10. © 1989. Used by permission of MCB University Press Limited.

Figure 6–2 Alternative to Traditional Excess Inventory Disposal
Source: Used by permission of Educational Assistance Limited, a nonprofit organization.

Figure 6–3A Elements of an MRPI System
Source: Amrik Sohal, and Keith Howard, "Trends in Materials Management," *International Journal of Physical Distribution and Materials Management* 17, no. 5 (1987), p. 11. © 1987. Used by permission of MCB University Press Limited.

Figure 6–4 Distribution Resource Planning
Source: "How DRP Helps Warehouses Smooth Distribution," *Modern Materials Handling* 39, no. 6 (April 9, 1984), p. 53. *Modern Materials Handling,* Copyright © 1984 by Cahners Publishing Company. Used by permission of Cahners Publishing Company, a division of Reed Elsevier Inc.

Figure 6–6 MRPII System
Source: Karl A. Hatt, "What's the Big Deal About MRPII?" *Winning Manufacturing* 5, no. 2 (1994), p. 2. © 1994. Used by permission of Tompkins Associates, Inc., Raleigh NC.

Table 6–1 Materials Management: Old and New Thinking
Source: Hans F. Busch, "Integrated Materials Management," *International Journal of Physical Distribution and Materials Management* 18, no. 7 (1988), p. 28. © 1988. Used by permission of MCB University Press Limited.

Table 6–2 Traditional Management and TQM Comparison
Source: James H. Saylor, "What Total Quality Management Means to the Logistician," *Logistics Spectrum* 24, no. 4 (Winter 1990), p. 20. © 1990. Used by permission of The International Society of Logistics.

Table 6–3 Direct Relationship between TQM and Logistics
Source: James H. Saylor, "What Total Quality Management Means to the Logistician," *Logistics Spectrum* 24, no. 4 (Winter 1990), p. 22. © 1990. Used by permission of The International Society of Logistics.

Figure 7–1 Freight Transportation Outlays versus GDP
Source: Robert V. Delaney, "8th Annual State of Logistics Report," remarks by Robert V. Delaney of Cass Information Systems and Security Capital Industrial Trust to the National Press Club, Washington, DC (June 2, 1997), Figure 15. © 1997. Used by permission of Cass Information Systems and Security Capital Industrial Trust.

Figure 7–2 Freight Shift to Intermodal Transportation
Source: Adapted from Martha Spizziri, "Intermodel Overcomes the Obstacles," *Traffic Management* 33, no. 2 (April 1994), p. 39. © 1994. Reprinted by permission from *Logistics Management.*

Figure 7–4 International Distribution Shipping Options
Source: David L. Anderson, "International Logistics Strategies for the Eighties," *Proceedings of the Twenty-Second Annual Conference of the National Council of Physical Distribution Management,* 1984, p. 363. © 1984. Used by permission of the Council of Logistics Management.

Figure 7–5 Terms of Sale and Corresponding Buyer and Seller Responsibilities
Source: National Association of Purchasing Management, *The Purchasing Handbook.* Reproduced with permission of The McGraw-Hill Companies.

Table 7–2 European Freight Movements (in Billion Ton-Kilometers)
Source: Kevin A. O'Laughlin, James Cooper, and Eric Cabocel, *Reconfiguring European Logistics Systems* (Oak Brook, IL: Council of Logistics Management, 1993), p. 72. © 1993. Used by permission of the Council of Logistics Management.

Table 7–4 The Most Important Attributes Considered in the Selection and Evaluation of LTL Motor Carriers
Source: Adapted from Douglas M. Lambert, M. Christine Lewis, and James R. Stock, "How Shippers Select and Evaluate General Commodities LTL Motor Carriers," *Journal of Business Logistics* 14, no. 1 (1993), p. 135. © 1993. Used by permission of the Council of Logistics Management.

Figure 8–1 Cost Trade-Offs Required in a Logistics System
Source: Adapted from Douglas M. Lambert, *The Development of an Inventory Costing Methodology: A Study of the Costs Associated with Holding Inventory* (Chicago: National Council of Physical Distribution Management, 1976), p. 7. © 1976. Used by permission of the Council of Logistics Management.

Figure 8–3 Typical Warehouse Functions and Flows
Source: James A. Tompkins, John A. White, Yavuz A. Bozer, Edward H. Frazelle, J. M. A. Tanchoco, and Jaime Trevino, *Facilities Planning,* 2nd ed. (New York: John Wiley & Sons, 1996), p. 392. Copyright © 1996. Reprinted by permission of John Wiley & Sons, Inc.

Figure 8–4 How Cross-Docking Works
Source: James Aaron Cooke, "Cross-Docking Rediscovered," *Traffic Management* 33, no. 11 (November 1994), p. 51. © 1994. Reprinted by permission from *Logistics Management.*

Figure 8–5 Narrow-Aisle Trucks Can Reduce Floor Space
Source: James Aaron Cooke, "When to Choose a Narrow-Aisle Lift Truck," *Traffic Management* 28, no. 12 (December 1989), p. 55. © 1989. Reprinted by permission from *Logistics Management.*

Figure 8–8 A Comparison of Traditional Costing versus Activity Based Costing
Source: Terrance L. Pohlen, "Activity-Based Costing for Warehouse Managers," *Warehousing Forum* 9, no. 5 (May 1994), p. 1. © 1994. Used by permission of The Ackerman Co. (614) 488-3165.

Table 8–1   10 Best Warehouse Networks for 1997
Source: Chicago Consulting, 8 South Michigan Avenue, Chicago, IL 60603. (312) 346-5080. Used by permission.

Figures 9–1A and 9–1B   Nonautomated Storage Units—Storage Racks
Source: "The Trends Keep Coming to Industrial Storage Racks," *Modern Materials Handling* 40, no. 4 (August 1985), pp. 54–55. *Modern Materials Handling,* Copyright © 1985 by Cahners Publishing Company. Used by permission of Cahners Publishing Company, a division of Reed Elsevier Inc.

Figure 9–2   Gravity Flow Rack
Source: Department of the Navy, Naval Supply Systems Command, Publication 529. From Edward H. Frazelle, *Small Parts Order Picking: Equipment and Strategy* (Oak Brook, IL: Warehousing Education and Research Council, 1988), p. 3. Reprinted by permission of Naval Supply Systems Command Code 426.

Figure 9–3   Bin Shelving Systems
Source: From Edward H. Frazelle, *Small Parts Order Picking: Equipment and Strategy* (Oak Brook, IL: Warehousing Education and Research Council, 1988), p. 1. Reprinted with permission of Stanley Storage Systems.

Figure 9–4   Modular Storage Drawers and Cabinets
Source: Department of the Navy, Naval Supply Systems Command, Publication 529. From Edward H. Frazelle, *Small Parts Order Picking: Equipment and Strategy* (Oak Brook, IL: Warehousing Education and Research Council, 1988), p. 2. Reprinted by permission of Naval Supply Systems Command Code 426.

Figure 9–5   Bin Shelving Mezzanine
Source: From Edward H. Frazelle, *Small Parts Order Picking: Equipment and Strategy* (Oak Brook, IL: Warehousing Education and Research Council, 1988), p. 8. Reprinted courtesy of White Systems, Inc.

Figure 9–6   The Modern Shipping and Receiving Dock
Source: "Docks and Receiving—Where It All Begins," *Modern Materials Handling, 1985 Warehouse Guidebook* 40, no. 4 (Spring 1985), p. 36. *Modern Materials Handling,* Copyright © 1985 by Cahners Publishing Company. Used by permission of Cahners Publishing Company, a division of Reed Elsevier Inc.

Figure 9–7   Mini-load AS/RS
Source: Department of the Navy, Naval Supply Systems Command, Publication 529. From Edward H. Frazelle, *Small Parts Order Picking: Equipment and Strategy* (Oak Brook, IL: Warehousing Education and Research Council, 1988), p. 6. Reprinted by permission of Naval Supply Systems Command Code 426.

Figure 9–8   Minimizing Inventory at Apple Computer with a Flexible Mini-Load AS/RS
Source: "Mini-Load AS/RS Trims Inventory, Speeds Assembly," *Modern Materials Handling* 39, no. 13 (September 21, 1984), pp. 48–49. *Modern Materials Handling,* Copyright © 1984 by Cahners Publishing Company. Used by permission of Cahners Publishing Company, a division of Reed Elsevier Inc.

Figure 9–9   Horizontal Carousels
Source: From Edward H. Frazelle, *Small Parts Order Picking: Equipment and Strategy* (Oak Brook, IL: Warehousing Education and Research Council, 1988), p. 4. G. I. Handling Systems.

Figure 9–10   Vertical Carousel
Source: From Edward H. Frazelle, *Small Parts Order Picking: Equipment and Strategy* (Oak Brook, IL: Warehousing Education and Research Council, 1988), p. 5. Reprinted by permission of Kardex Systems, Inc.

Figure 9–11 Utilizing an AS/RS and AGVSs at Maybelline
Source: Gary Forger, "How Maybelline Ships Smaller, More Frequent Orders," *Modern Materials Handling* 50, no. 7 (June 1995) p. 49. *Modern Materials Handling,* Copyright © 1995 by Cahners Publishing Company. Used by permission of Cahners Publishing Company, a division of Reed Elsevier Inc.

Figure 9–12 Robots in the Warehouse
Source: "Warehousing Flexibility Aided by Robots," *Material Handling Engineering* 40, no. 9 (September 1985), p. 103. Reproduced by permission of The St. Onge Company, York, PA.

Figure 9–13 A Layout Designed for Quick Handling, High Throughput
Source: Karen A. Auguston, "A Focus on Throughput Scores a JIT Success," *Modern Material Handling* 50, no. 6 (May 1995), p. 37. *Modern Materials Handling,* Copyright © 1995 by Cahners Publishing Company. Used by permission of Cahners Publishing Company, a division of Reed Elsevier Inc.

Figure 9–14 Computers Throughout the Warehouse
Source: "Increase Productivity with Computers and Software," *Modern Materials Handling—1986 Warehousing Guidebook* 41, no. 4 (Spring 1986), p. 68. *Modern Materials Handling,* Copyright © 1986 by Cahners Publishing Company. Used by permission of Cahners Publishing Company, a division of Reed Elsevier Inc.

Figure 9–15 A Local Area Network (LAN) Example
Source: "Local Area Networks—The Crucial Element in Factory Automation," *Modern Materials Handling* 39, no. 7 (May 7, 1984), p. 51. *Modern Materials Handling,* Copyright © 1986 by Cahners Publishing Company, a division of Reed Elsevier Inc.

Table 9–1 Storage Guidelines for the Warehouse
Source: "Storage Equipment for the Warehouse," *Modern Materials Handling, 1985 Warehousing Guidebook* 40, no. 4 (Spring 1985), p. 53. *Modern Materials Handling,* Copyright © 1985 by Cahners Publishing Company. Used by permission of Cahners Publishing Company, a division of Reed Elsevier Inc.

Table 9–3 Packaging Cost Trade-Offs with Other Logistics Functions
Source: Prof. Robert L. Cook, Department of Marketing and Hospitality Services Administration, Central Michigan University, Mt. Pleasant, MI, 1991. Used with his permission.

Box 10–2 Steps in JIT II Information Flow
Source: *Purchasing,* May 6, 1993, p. 17. © 1993. Used by permission of *Purchasing* Magazine.

Figure 10–1 Supply Chain Management
Source: The International Center for Competitive Excellence, University of North Florida. Used by permission of Douglas M. Lambert.

Figure 10–2 Total Customer Satisfaction Depends on Supplier Performance
Source: Michiel Leenders and Anna Flynn, *Value Driven Purchasing: Managing the Key Steps in the Acquisition Process* (Burr Ridge, IL: Irwin Professional Publishing, 1994), p. 3. © 1994. Reproduced with permission of The McGraw-Hill Companies.

Figure 10–3 Overview of Internal Information Flows from Purchasing
Source: Adapted from Lisa M. Ellram and Laura M. Birou, *Purchasing for Bottom Line Impact* (Burr Ridge, IL: Irwin Professional Publishing, 1995), p. 74. © 1995. Reproduced with permission of The McGraw-Hill Companies.

Figure 10–4 Five Phases in the Selection Development and Management of Purchasing Relationships
Source: Lisa M. Ellram, "A Managerial Guideline for the Development and Implementation of Purchasing Partnerships," *International Journal of Purchasing and Materials Management* 31, no. 2 (1995), p. 12. © 1995. Used by permission of MCB University Press Limited.

Table 10–2 Differences between the Traditional Approach and the JIT Approach in Purchasing
Source: David Farmer and Arjan J. van Weele, *Gower Handbook of Purchasing Management,* 2nd ed. (London: Gower), p. 298. Used by permission of Gower Publishing Limited.

Table 10–3 Supply Strategy Questions
Source: Michiel Leenders and Harold E. Fearon, *Purchasing and Materials Management,* 10th ed. (Burr Ridge, IL: Richard D. Irwin, 1993), p. 643. © 1993. Reproduced with permission of The McGraw-Hill Companies.

Figure 11–2 How Duty Drawback Works
Source: Lisa H. Harrington, "How to Take Advantage of Duty Drawback," *Traffic Management,* 28, no. 6 (June 1989), p. 121A. © 1989. Reprinted by permission from *Logistics Management.*

Figure 11–3 The Global Logistics Management Process
Source: Adapted from Warren J. Keegan, *Global Marketing Management,* 5th ed., p. 37. © 1995. Reprinted by permission of Prentice Hall, Inc., Upper Saddle River, NJ.

Figure 11–4 How a Letter of Credit Works
Source: Adapted from James Aaron Cooke, "What You Should Know about Letters of Credit," *Traffic Management* 29, no. 9 (September 1990), pp. 44–45. © 1990. Reprinted with permission from *Logistics Management.*

Figure 11–6 How NVOCCs Work
Source: Toby B. Estis, "NVOCCs: A Low-Cost Alternative for LCL Shippers," *Traffic Management* 27, no. 6 (June 1988), p. 87. © 1988. Reprinted with permission from *Logistics Management.*

Table 11–2 Comparison of Domestic and International Logistics
Source: William W. Goldsborough and David I. Anderson, "The International Logistics Environment," in *The Logistics Handbook,* James F. Robeson and William C. Copacino, Editors-in-Chief (New York: The Free Press, 1994), p. 677. Copyright © 1994 by The Free Press. Reprinted with the permission of The Free Press, a Division of Simon & Schuster.

Table 11–3 Who's Responsible for Costs under Various Terms?
Source: Philip R. Cateora, *International Marketing,* 9th ed. (Burr Ridge, IL: Richard D. Irwin, 1996), p. 367. © 1996. Reproduced with permission of The McGraw-Hill Companies.

Figure 12–5 Types of Work Groups
Source: Lisa M. Ellram and Laura M. Birou, *Purchasing for Bottom Line Impact* (Burr Ridge, IL: Irwin Professional Publishing, 1995), p. 87. © 1995. Reproduced with permission of The McGraw-Hill Companies.

Figure 12–6 Organization Chart: Rohm and Haas Company
Source: Rohm and Haas Company. Used with permission.

Figure 12–7 Organization Chart: 3M Company
Source: 3M Company. Used with permission.

Figure 12–8 Organization Chart: Target Stores
Source: Target Stores, Inc. Used with permission.

Figure 13–1 Cost Trade-Offs Required in Marketing and Logistics
Source: Adapted from Douglas M. Lambert, *The Development of an Inventory Costing Methodology: A Study of the Costs Associated with Holding Inventory* (Chicago: National Council of Physical Distribution Management, 1976), p. 7. © 1976. Used by permission of the Council of Logistics Management.

Figure 13–4 The Use of Standards as a Management Control System
Source: Richard J. Lewis and Leo G. Erickson, "Distribution System Costing: An Overview," in *Distribution System Costing: Concepts and Procedures,* ed. John R. Grabner and William S. Sargent (Columbus, OH: Transportation and Logistics Research Foundation, 1972), p. 17A. © 1972. Used by permission of Richard J. Lewis.

Figure 13–5 Statistical Process Control (SPC)
Source: C. John Langley, Jr., "Information-Based Decision Making in Logistics Management," *International Journal of Physical Distribution and Materials Management* 15, no. 7 (1985), p. 50. © 1985. Used by permission of MCB University Press Limited.

Figure 13–6 Control Chart Examples
Source: C. John Langley, Jr., "Information-Based Decision Making in Logistics Management," *International Journal of Physical Distribution and Materials Management* 15, no. 7 (1985), p. 51. © 1985. Used by permission of MCB University Press Limited.

Figure 13–7 Assignment of Costs with an Activity-Based Cost System
Source: Lisa M. Ellram, Marsha J. Kwolek, Bernard J. La Londe, Sue P. Siferd, Terrance L. Pohlen, David G. Waller, and Wallace R. Wood, "Understanding the Implications of Activity-Based Costing for Logistics Management," *Proceedings of the Annual Conference of the Council of Logistics Management* (Oak Brook, IL: Council of Logistics Management, 1994), p. 13. © 1994. Used by permission of the Council of Logistics Management.

Table 13–4 Transportation Activity-Input Matrix
Source: A. T. Kearney, Inc., *Measuring and Improving Productivity in Physical Distribution* (Oak Brook, IL: National Council of Physical Distribution Management, 1984), p. 144. © 1984. Used by permission of the Council of Logistics Management.

Table 13–5 Warehouse Activity-Input Matrix
Source: A. T. Kearney, Inc., *Measuring and Improving Productivity in Physical Distribution* (Oak Brook, IL: National Council of Physical Distribution Management, 1984), p. 195. © 1984. Used by permission of the Council of Logistics Management.

Figure 14–1 Supply Chain Management
Source: The International Center for Competitive Excellence, University of North Florida. Used by permission of Douglas M. Lambert.

Figure 14–2 How Intermediaries Reduce the Cost of Market Contact between Supplier and Customer
Source: Douglas M. Lambert, *The Distribution Channels Decision* (New York: National Association of Accountants; and Hamilton, Ontario: The Society of Management Accountants of Canada, 1978), pp. 15–16. Reprinted with permission. Copyright © 1978 by National Association of Accountants. All rights reserved.

Figure 14–3 Distribution Channels: Grocery Products Manufacturer
Source: *The Distribution Channels Decision* (New York: National Association of Accountants; and Hamilton, Ontario: The Society of Management Accountants of Canada, 1978), p. 151. Reprinted with permission. Copyright © 1978 by National Association of Accountants. All rights reserved.

Figure 14–4 Cost Trade-Offs Required in Marketing and Logistics
Source: Adapted from Douglas M. Lambert, *The Development of an Inventory Costing Methodology: A Study of the Costs Associated with Holding Inventory* (Chicago: National Council of Physical Distribution Management, 1976), p. 7. © 1976. Used by permission of the Council of Logistics Management.

Figure 14–5 Reengineering SCM Process Flow Chart
Source: From Douglas M. Lambert, Larry C. Guinipero, and Gary J. Ridenhower, "Supply Chain Management: A Key to Achieving Business Excellence in the 21st Century," unpublished manuscript. All rights reserved. Used by permission of Douglas M. Lambert.

Figure 14–6 Implementation of Supply Chain Management
Source: From Douglas M. Lambert, Larry C. Guinipero, and Gary J. Ridenhower, "Supply Chain Management: The Key to Achieving Business Excellence in the 21st Century," unpublished manuscript. All rights reserved. Used by permission of Douglas M. Lambert.

Table 14–2 Profitability by Type of Account: A Contribution Approach ($ thousands)
Source: Douglas M. Lambert and Jay U. Sterling, "Educators Are Contributing to Major Deficiencies in Marketing Profitability Reports," *Journal of Marketing Education* 12, no. 3 (Fall 1990), pp. 43–44. © 1990. Used by permission of University of Colorado, Business Research Division.

Table 14–3 Profitability by Type of Account: A Contribution Approach ($ thousands)
Source: Douglas M. Lambert and Jay U. Sterling, "Educators Are Contributing to Major Deficiencies in Marketing Profitability Reports," *Journal of Marketing Education* 12, no. 3 (Fall 1990), pp. 43–44. © 1990. Used by permission of University of Colorado, Business Research Division.

Table 14–4 Profitability by Type of Account: Full-Cost Approach ($ thousands)
Source: Douglas M. Lambert and Jay U. Sterling, "Educators Are Contributing to Major Deficiencies in Marketing Profitability Reports," *Journal of Marketing Education* 12, no. 3 (Fall 1990), p. 49. © 1990. Used by permission of University of Colorado, Business Research Division.

Figure 15–3 Cost Trade-Offs Required in Marketing and Logistics
Source: Adapted from Douglas M. Lambert, *The Development of an Inventory Costing Methodology: A Study of the Costs Associated with Holding Inventory* (Chicago: National Council of Physical Distribution Management, 1976), p. 7. © 1976. Used by permission of the Council of Logistics Management.

Figure 15–4 The Logistics Audit: A Conceptual Model
Source: Jay U. Sterling and Douglas M. Lambert, "A Methodology for Assessing Logistics Operating Systems," *International Journal of Physical Distribution and Materials Management* 15, no. 6 (1985), p. 13. © 1985. Used by permission of MCB University Press Limited.

Table 15–2 The Value Logistics Adds to the Corporation
Source: Adapted from Lisa Ellram and L. Wayne Riley, "Purchasing/Logistics Strategic Planning: Value to the Corporation," *Council of Logistics Management Annual Conference Proceedings,* October 3–6, 1993, Washington, DC, pp. 455–62. © 1993. Used by permission of MCB University Press Limited.

Table 15–3 Example Outline of Logistics Plan
Source: Adapted from Martha C. Cooper, Daniel E. Innis, and Peter R. Dickson, *Strategic Planning for Logistics* (Oak Brook, IL: Council of Logistics Management, 1992). © 1992. Used by permission of the Council of Logistics Management.

Appendix 15–A Customer Service/Order Administration Audit
Source: From Jay U. Sterling and Douglas M. Lambert, "A Methodology for Assessing Logistics Operating Systems," *International Journal of Physical Distribution and Materials Management* 15, no. 6 (1985), pp. 29–55. Adapted and expanded by the author from Douglas M. Lambert and M. Christine Lewis, "Meaning, Measurement and Implementation of Customer Service," *Proceedings of the Nineteenth Annual Conference of the National Council of Physical Distribution Management,* 1981 (Chicago: National Council of Physical Distribution Management, 1981), pp. 569–95. Used by permission of the Council of Logistics Management.

Name Index

Corporate Index

Subject Index